VIDEO DUNGEON
THE COLLECTED REVIEWS

KIM NEWMAN'S VIDEO DUNGEON
print ISBN: 9781783299393
ebook ISBN: 9781785657474

Published by
Titan Books
A division of Titan Publishing Group Ltd
144 Southwark Street
London
SE1 0UP

www.titanbooks.com

First edition: September 2017
2 4 6 8 10 9 7 5 3 1

To receive advance information, news, competitions, and exclusive offers online,
please sign up for the Titan newsletter on our website:
www.titanbooks.com

A CIP catalogue record for this title is available from the British Library.

Printed and bound in the UK by CPI Group (UK) Ltd, Croydon CR0 4YY

Did you enjoy this book?
We love to hear from our readers.
Please e-mail us at: readerfeedback@titanemail.com
or write to Reader Feedback at the above address.

KIM NEWMAN's VIDEO DUNGEON

THE COLLECTED REVIEWS

TITANBOOKS

ABOUT THE AUTHOR

Kim Newman is a movie critic, author and broadcaster. He is a contributing editor to *Sight & Sound* and *Empire* magazines. His 'Video Dungeon' column has been a popular feature of *Empire* since 2000. His books about film include *Nightmare Movies*, *Millennium Movies* and BFI Classics studies of *Cat People* and *Quatermass and the Pit*. His fiction includes the *Anno Dracula* series, *Life's Lottery*, *Professor Moriarty: The Hound of the D'Urbervilles*, *An English Ghost Story*, *The Secrets of Drearcliff Grange School* and *Angels of Music*. He has written for comics, television, radio and the theatre, and directed a tiny film, *Missing Girl*. His official website is www.johnnyalucard.com. He is on Twitter as @AnnoDracula.

FOR BAZ

CONTENTS

CONFINEMENTS AND DANGEROUS GAMES

Tied Up in the Basement or Hunted Through the Woods

AFTERDEATH (2015)

'IF YOU SEE GOD, TELL HIM TO GO FUCK HIMSELF.'

In the long line of descent from *Outward Bound* (1930), most limbo-set movies try to mystify for much of the running time before admitting their characters are – gasp! – dead. *AfterDeath* gets that bombshell out of the way in the title, then gets on with post-mortem puzzles as recently deceased folk try to suss the rules of their afterlife and face what comes next.

Robyn (Miranda Raison) wakes on a drab beach after dying in the collapse of an overcrowded nightclub. Drawn to a house which resembles her childhood holiday home, she finds jack-the-lad Seb (Sam Keeley) having an impromptu threesome with just-dead clubbers Patricia (Elarica Gallacher) and Livvy (Lorna Nickson Brown). Onie (Daniella Kertesz) has the disorienting habit of *phmmphhing* in and out of the place – hovering between life and death. When Robyn tries to take charge, Seb diagnoses that she must be 'in management', but the others fall in with her efforts to explore their limited limbo, periodically tormented by painful beams from a lighthouse. This pocket universe contracts and attempts to leave only result in being zapped to the other side of the bubble ('like PacMan').

Andrew Ellard's script wittily explains the cast's good looks in that these phantoms are idealised versions of the people they were when alive – promiscuous and gorgeous Patricia turns out to have been a chubby Christian – while developing a fresh, surprisingly radical vision of merciless judgement. Since the beginning of mankind, *nobody* has been adjudged sin-free enough to get into Heaven, but if one sinner makes it through the whole system will reset. Seb is hauled over the coals when Robyn remembers he was once accused of rape; the women laugh when he is violated by a smoke demon.

There are secrets and mysteries (not all solved) for each character, including a sub-plot about what exactly happened at the club to land these people in a house where each room is plucked from an inmate's memory with significant additions like a painting of the suffering damned replacing a *Predator* poster from Seb's student flat. Co-directors Gez Medinger and Robin Schmidt balance ensemble drama – everyone here is good, with Gallacher and Keeley standouts – with ominous, creepily surreal use of a desolate beach as a shore of the afterlife.

ALREADY DEAD (2007)

This 'bottle show' follows the *Reservoir Dogs/Cube/Saw* template for high-impact low-budget cinema: set mostly inside a single location (a derelict industrial building), with story twists, shifting loyalties and shocks (including the popular tied-to-a-chair-and-tortured bit).

Banker Thomas Archer (Ron Eldard), a hollow man since the murder of his son by a home invader, is referred to psychiatrist Dr Heller (Christopher Plummer) by The Detective (Patrick Kilpatrick) who has been taken off the dead-end case. Heller introduces Archer to a shadowy, high-priced organisation (cf: *Seconds*, *The Game*) which claims to be able to get justice. After handing over a bundle of cash, Archer is ushered into a room where a man (Til Schweiger) is bound and gagged. A *Hostel*-like array of cutting tools are available. Archer is told The Man is his son's killer and he can do what he wants to him. No sooner has he started on torture than he remembers an identifying detail (a tattoo) never mentioned to the police which strongly suggests that the Man *isn't* the guilty party. When the gag comes off, The Man is persuasive, but also hints he's not exactly innocent. Is the organisation offering Archer a chance to purge his need for vengeance while offing *another* criminal or is this all a scam to get the money? Archer and The Man wind up fighting the conspiracy's hooded minions, squirreling through the usual ventilation ducts and skirmishing in stockrooms.

Script – by director Joe Chappelle (*Halloween The Curse of Michael Myers*), from a story by Robert Lynn and David Alford – and performances carry the movie. The resolution is neat, but several of the other available endings would have been stronger.

AQUARIUM (2004)

Six people wake in a small, white-walled room with no visible doors or windows. A piped-in voice (Pierre-Luc Scotto) explains rule infractions are punishable by 'execution and removal'. Middle-aged lawyer Georges (Michel Robin) tries to mediate between younger guys – naturally angry Vincent (Julien Masdoua) and arrogant journalist Alex (Abel Divol) – but cracks up and smashes a camera. Knockout gas floods the room and Georges wakes to find his forefinger amputated. Then, the game begins in earnest, with – it is implied – only one live winner possible. The sextet play 'Simon Says' (*Jacques Dit* in French), raising an arm and a leg, holding the pose for too long, failing. Director/co-writer Frédéric Grousset tries for economical, claustrophobic mystery-horror *a la Cube*. The first act works, but the film loses patience, too-quickly removing half the cast and giving the women (Karen Bruere, Capucine Mandeau, Sophie Talon) too little to do.

At the 55-minute mark, a game of Russian roulette resolves the storyline. Then, a survivor blunders onto a Paris rooftop for twelve minutes of tacked-on befuddlement. The explanation is oddly beside the point, but this isn't a social experiment or a gameshow but an act of anti-corporate art-terrorism (the apparently unconnected strangers work for branches of one company). Given the enclosed setting and limited cast, we get to know the victims too little – they don't work out their connection, which the survivor has to be told ('You mean this is because of my *job*?'). The games are familiar (even Russian roulette) in comparison with other essays in the tiny but aptly crowded trapped-in-a-room-with-sadistic-puzzles sub-genre (*Saw*, *The Experiment*, *Exam*, etc.). The subsequent *Breathing Room* feels like a larger-scale *Aquarium*, with more contestants and a bigger room. Co-written by Jean Mach.

AS GOOD AS DEAD (2010)

This thriller offers two possible outcomes. Since the one we're nudged towards is far less interesting/cool than the other, the twist is predictable.

In a prologue, Reverend James Kalahan (Brian Cox) inspires a follower to massacre a bus full of ethnic people; in reprisal, masked liberal terrorists(?) assassinate the hate-preacher. In the present, nice-guy divorced dad photojourno Ethan Belfrage (Cary Elwes) lives like a slacker, seemingly less mature than his kid Sarah (Emma Kantor). Psycho Aaron (Frank Whaley) and Kalahan's son Jake (Matt Dallas) invade Ethan's home and hang him up for torture under the supervision of the rev's scarred widow Helen (Andie MacDowell). Someone has fingered Ethan as a shooter in the Kalahan killing, and the rev's followers – notionally bossed by Helen – want him to name the other person. Snake-like, not unintelligent Aaron is willing to murder kids, drugs an innocent neighbour (Jess Weixler of *Teeth*, uncredited), won't touch an East Indian shopkeeper's hand getting change, and is pretty much a complete heavy, while Helen is less convinced of the hatred part of her husband's teachings and needs to be completely sure of Ethan's guilt before killing him. Elwes, as in *Saw*, spends much of the film tied and squirming, grasping for broken glass with bare feet, etc., while trying to talk up rifts among his tormentors.

Well written (Erez Mossek, Eve Pomerance), with an interesting theme in the rift between conservative and liberal America (more sensitively handled than in *Red State*), strongly acted and decently directed (Jonathan Mossek), this still feels cramped. Like Ethan, it keeps riffing and spinning to distract us from the inevitable.

ATM (2012)

This ordinary, contrived shocker shows the influence of Larry Cohen's high concept scripts (*Phone Booth*, *Cellular*), but writer Chris Sparling (*Buried*) cheats to keep suspense going. At an office party, stockbroker David (Brian Geraghty), who feels plot-significant guilt about losing clients' savings, finally nerves up to talk to colleague Emily Brandt (Alice Eve), who is leaving for another job and thus exiting his life. She accepts his offer of a lift home... only David's infuriatingly cock-blocking pal Corey (Josh Peck), who doesn't give a shit about ruining anyone's life or evening, insists David first drive him to an ATM in a near-deserted parking lot. A hulking, menacing dude in a parka (Mike O'Brian) murders a passing dog-walker to show how dangerous he is, and besieges the trio in the little hut. They make dashes for the car or a cellphone, turn on each other, speculate pointlessly about the villain's motive, try for moments of poignance, desperately kill a parka-clad unfortunate who happens along at the worst moment and generally squirm. The gimmick, illustrated by a montage of diagrams, is that the villain attacks isolated locales after working out the sightlines of security cameras so evidence (glimpses of ATM-cam footage) suggests victims have killed each other. Fair enough, but the trio are so unlikeable (though all three actors are good) it's hard to care whether they die or not. Directed by David Brooks.

AWAITING (2014)

A small-scale British exercise in the held-in-captivity sub-genre, typified by *Misery* but with roots as deep as *Fanatic* or *The Strange Vengeance of Rosalie*. Like most of these, a slow-burn story has an initially trusting protagonist frustrated by a seemingly reasonable, actually demented host.

Single father Morris (Tony Curran) lives on an isolated farm with his homeschooled, naïve but not stupid daughter Lauren (Diana Vickers). Arbitrarily, they have Christmas in September, complete with fairy lights, a big meal (of 'pork') and presents. Morris brings home Jake (Rupert Hill), a lawyer who has crashed his car in the woods, and treats him as a guest. When Jake wakes, he wants to leave (to propose to his girlfriend), but Morris insists he stay for the holiday. All the usual omens are noted – no mobile phone signal, no landline, no urgency about driving into town – but Jake strikes up a friendship with Lauren. Trying to walk away, he steps into a man-trap and is confined with a *Misery*-type leg injury which kicks up the horrors as we see just how delusional Morris is, get an idea of his side-business selling stolen cars, and wonder just what happened to Lauren's mother.

The claustrophobic three-way occasionally lets up as a local cop (Peter Woodward) and Jake's girlfriend (Sophie Lovell Anderson) investigate the disappearances, but the film mostly sticks to the farm. Not-unexpected Grand Guignol revelations involve the pork and what's in a basement under Morris's special shed. Scots character actor Curran – whose varied credits include *Red Road*, *The League of Extraordinary Gentlemen* (as the Invisible Man) and *Doctor Who* (as van Gogh) – does a softly evil Yorkshire accent, playing the mad farmer as quietly wrong rather than all-out insane. Morris even becomes slightly sympathetic as he clashes with his not-very-likeable forced guest, who starts using lawyer skills to drive a wedge between father and daughter. After a gory ending, a coda delivers 1970s-style cynicism as a new generation of insanity replaces the just-splattered old one. Written and directed by Mark Murphy (*The Crypt*).

BANE (2009)

Writer-director James Eaves' low-budget British film is an overlong (120 minutes) if absorbing entry in the 'confined space' horror cycle. Four contrasting women – whiny Elaine (Sylvia Robson), thoughtful Jane (Lisa Devlin), aggressive Natasha (Tina Barnes) and reticent-yet-obviously-the-lead Katherine (Sophia Dawnay) – suffer from drug-induced amnesia in a makeshift medical torture camp. Tested by sadistic whitecoats, they are also stalked and slaughtered by a bogeyman in bloody medical gear. They struggle to remember past lives and the events which have brought them to this pretty pass, which involve an alien invasion (the one visible monster is good for this budget level) and a desperate scheme to repel bug overlords. Many answers come too late to be a comfort – Natasha only realises Jane, whom she bullied, was her sister after the other woman has been killed, while Katherine has to cope with learning she's the scientist who came up with this program and volunteered for it.

BASEMENT (2010)

'NO ONE KICKS ME IN THE BOLLOCKS AND GETS AWAY WITH IT, EH!'

Another few-people-trapped-somewhere effort. An opening montage of anti-war protests and a lecture on media manipulation suggest director Asham Kamboj and writer Ewen Glass had aspirations not fulfilled by murky wandering around in the gloom. Folks driving home from a demo stop so Gary (Danny Dyer, subtler than usual) can take a leak. Unwisely venturing down a *Lost*-style hatch, they get trapped in a catacomb and find a maddened girl (Soraya Radford). After too much poorly written soap arguing, characters start getting killed. At mid-point, we learn Gary has lured the others – Jimi Mistry (trapped also in *Exam*), Emily Beecham, Kierston Wareing, Lois Winstone – here, though he's also on the victim list. The bonkers explanation involves clones trained in ruthlessness by a military annoyed that civvy slackers won't support their wars. Not long, but not good either.

BEREAVEMENT (2010)

In writer-director Stevan Mena's straight slasher *Malevolence*, fleeing crooks take refuge in a rambling abattoir and are offed by a persistent psycho. *Bereavement* doesn't make a fuss about being a prequel – after all, *Malevolence* wasn't exactly a breakout hit – but fills in the backstory of mad killer Martin Bristol. Its premise prefigures Jennifer Lynch's *Chained*.

In 1989, six-year-old Martin (Chase Pechacek) is snatched by serial killer/ butcher Graham Sutter (Brett Rickaby), who abuses him (though he suffers from a rare condition and can't feel pain) while systematically raising him to become the stock monster we met earlier. Cutting away from the farm, Mena introduces Allison (Alexandra Daddario, of *Texas Chainsaw 3D* and *Burying the Ex*), lately orphaned and living with kindly uncle Jonathan Miller (Michael Biehn, working hard). Of course, Allison is nabbed and hung up in the barn. Inevitably, Martin (Spencer List) ascends to post-credits mania.

Full of dumb stuff (the heroine telling a child to stay put in a burning house is a highlight), it squirms to set up *Malevolence* by putting a bunch of suspicious deaths down to the fire. Overlong (103 minutes) and crude (a lecture hammers on nature versus nurture), it's well acted – though the abducted, tortured and killed thing really didn't need another run round the yard. Yet again, someone shrieks, 'Why are you doing this to me?' and gets no real answer ('How frightening when it's your own flesh!' – huh). With guest crackpot John Savage.

BLACKOUT (2008)

Best of the tiny suspense sub-genre of stuck-in-a-lift films is still Louis Malle's *Ascenseur pour l'échafaud* (*Elevator to the Gallows*), but other decent examples include *The Elevator* (1974), *Abwärts* (*Out of Order*) and *Devil*. This Spanish-shot picture owes much to these precedents – specifically, the convention that one passenger is fleeing a crime scene in the building and that attempts to climb to safety only make things worse – but its basic pitch is *Lost*-in-a-lift.

Three apartment dwellers are trapped over the Fourth of July weekend in 'the Bifrost Bridge building', while fragmentary flashbacks explain how they got in this pickle. Widowed doctor Karl (Aidan Gillen) turns out to be a sexual sadist and incipient fascist; workaholic asthmatic Claudia (Amber Tamblyn) wants to be at the death-bed of her beloved Grandmother (Mabel Rivera); and sullen, short-fused Tommy (Armie Hammer) is helping his girlfriend (Katie Stuart) escape her violent drunk gambling addict father (Mark Boone Junior). All these people need to get out – Karl to dispose of a corpse from his flat before his daughter comes to stay, Claudia and Tommy to take care of loved ones. They credibly squabble and fail to escape or attract attention before the melodrama goes into screeching overdrive. Karl becomes outwardly monstrous ('If I don't get out of here soon, I'm going to cut your fucking throat and I'm going to rape the shit out of that cunt.'). He takes

Claudia's inhaler and kicks Tommy's broken leg to gain control over the situation – then comes out as a serial killer, and goes into full-on ranting hatred mode with added stabbing.

Directed by Rigoberto Castañeda, reprising the intense, music-driven approach of his Mexican horror film *KM31*. Scripted by Ed Dougherty

BLOODED (2011)

Bracketed with newsreel footage about the 2005 legislation which outlawed fox hunting in the United Kingdom, this archly constructed *Most Dangerous Game* variant is a sketchy addition to the 'hunter hunted' sub-genre. In a gambit reused by the 'My Roanoke Nightmare' season of *American Horror Story*, interviews with survivors of a (fictional) nasty experience are intercut with 'dramatic recreations' of their ordeal. Each character is played by two different actors and there's a contrast between grainy 'found footage' snippets of an uploaded-to-YouTube chronicle and coolly shot 're-enactments' which are, of course, plain old moviemaking (relying heavily on beautiful Isle of Mull locations).

After the ban is enforced, obsessed aristo Lucas Bell (Neil McDermott, Nick Clark Windo) becomes a controversial figurehead of the pro-hunting lobby. Lucas invites a group – his photojourno brother Charlie (Mark Dexter, Oliver Boot), Charlie's black American girlfriend Eve (Sharon Duncan-Brewster, Tracy Ifeachor), long-time best friend/sidekick Ben (Adam Best, Joseph Kloska) and ex-girlfriend Liv (Isabella Calthorpe, Cicely Tennant) – to his estate to hunt stag (still legal, as Ben insists). Feints about Lucas's strained relationships with Charlie and Liv hint he might be an incipient Count Zaroff, so he is the prime suspect when the guests wake up stranded in the wilds in their underwear, stalked by an expert rifle-shot. Actually, as is heavily signposted, the party are targeted by radical animal rights activists who want them to read anti-hunting statements on camera.

There are a few tiny felicities – as the women hide in a barn, a masked sinister figure stalks them in a slasher movie setup, only for the seeming psycho to be distracted by a stag's severed head and mutter that people who could do this are sick – and a clever suspense mechanism involves the major player who *isn't* interviewed. In trying for balance – none of the 'victims' are the sort of posh thugs the anti-hunting lobby really hates – it fumbles the mix of editorial and character story, and repeated cuts between actors in peril in their skivvies and other actors earnestly musing about what they've learned tends to expose the shallowness of the concept. Scripted by James Walker, from a story by Walker, producer/actor Windo and director Edward Boase (*The Mirror*).

BLOODLUST! (1961)

The Most Dangerous Game redone as shoddy exploitation in the style of *Teenage Zombies* or *She Demons*: unmemorable juveniles and a few older hams wander pointlessly around a cramped island, with tedium relieved only by a couple of for-the-time gross horror moments. Chubby, goateed Zaroff substitute Albert Balleau (Wilton Graff) – who developed a lust for killing as a sniper during 'the war' (no mention which side he was on) – expostulates pompously about fair play while wearing a smoking jacket. His victims are a bunch of alleged teenagers – notably June Kenney as a blonde judo expert and sitcom star Robert Reed. Lilyan Chauvin (*Silent Night, Deadly Night*) scores second billing as Balleau's unfaithful, soon-killed wife.

Grue extends to a cave full of stuffed and mounted human trophies, a woman drowned in an illuminated fishtank, a severed foot and the flesh of a head and torso (all rubbery) manhandled by a taxidermist, a minion tossed into an acid vat, another goon sinking into a swamp and bobbing up covered with leeches, gory crossbow bolt hits and a skeleton crawling with rats. The heroes are so bland and Graff such a ridiculous baddie that it never threatens to get exciting. Photographed by Richard E. Cunha (whose similarly rubbish directorial credits are much more fun); written and directed by Ralph Brooke.

BLOOD TRAILS (2006)

It's never a good sign when an early line of dialogue is, 'We can spend the weekend at the cabin.' Shot in Germany but set in the United States, this survival horror benefits from the physical performance of Rebecca Palmer as a toned cycle-messenger, but keeps having the heroine do stupid things to stay in danger. It has the hyper-kinetic editing, sickly-greenish DV look, gurning close-ups and posturing psycho philosophising common in its sub-genre.

After an uncomfortable night of handcuffed rough sex with supposed cop Chris

(Ben Price), guilt-ridden Anne (Palmer) heads off to the countryside with disposable, mild-mannered boyfriend Mike (Tom Frederic). Chris – in studly leathers and crash-helmet, but on a push-bike – stalks the couple, insistent that Anne is his alone. When she explains, Mike is credibly more pissed off that she's had a one-night stand than worried about the psycho – though he gets his throat cut (by a sharpened tire?) when Chris does a cycle leap across the track. Half-masked with blood, Anne proceeds to do everything wrong. A kindly Ranger (J.J. Straub) has nearly driven her to the hospital when she insists he go back and look for the dead boy, which gets him gutted. She climbs a peak to find a signal on a mobile phone and reaches the emergency services, only to flee when she finds Mike crucified on a giant cross she unaccountably doesn't cite as a landmark to putative rescuers (they have to triangulate on her phone). She bumps into a pair of creepy loggers (Kurt Rauscher, Johann Daiminger) who refuse to speak (probably because the supply of Anglophone actors has run out) but are helpful until Chris arrives and kills them – cue nasty moment as Anne has to filch the truck keys from a chainsaw-bisected corpse. She fails to run Chris down in the often-stalled truck, then fails to see him off with a thrown axe-head and winds up, as often in these films, duct-taped to a chair by the soft-spoken, it's-all-for-your-own-good villain.

The best moments come late, in a variant on that old he's-not-yet-dead trick as the heroine straddles the prone villain with a shard of mirror, waiting for his eyes to open so she can give him a killing thrust. An issue with this sub-genre is a tendency to make torture-happy lunatics into cool characters and make victims look like silly twits who deserve to suffer. Chris blathers about Anne's will to survive, but his kill-crazy thoughtlessness – murdering everyone who wanders into the film, while calmly ambling along and letting the heroine have chance after chance to escape (not to mention hauling a corpse up a mountain and nailing it up in the one place where it's sure to be found) – is just hackneyed hokum. Written and directed by Robert Krause.

BONE DRY (2007)

> 'BEING BURIED UP TO YOUR NECK IN THE DESERT WILL SURE GIVE YOU SOME ISSUES ALL RIGHT, BRO.'

Bald, sharp-suited Eddie (Luke Goss) drives across the Mojave Desert and Death Valley, spectacular scenery with a cinema history dating back to *Greed* (1924). Waylaid by Jimmy (Lance Henriksen), Eddie is forced to head north on foot, with time-outs to be buried up to his neck, pissed on, fed salt water, given instructions on how to make a compass out of everyday items, shot at and (in a *Saw*-like sequence) handcuffed naked to a giant cactus. The persecutor (cf: *Duel, Joy Ride* and the somewhat-similar *Lost* [2004]) mostly manifests as a gravelly voice on a walkie-talkie or close-ups of hat, boots and gun. Eddie is deliberately such a cipher that his sufferings don't quite make him sympathetic – obviously intentional since a cluttered last act (three extra characters are brought in and killed off rapid-time without affecting the main storyline) reveals the seeming innocent is actually a bastard hit man who once slaughtered Jimmy's wife and child and left him for dead in this very desert. Goss feels like a second- or third-choice casting: he has physical presence, isn't a bad actor, and manfully takes a lot of punishment, but can't carry a whole movie by himself. The busy Henriksen makes limited screen time tell as the calm, hollow, nagging avenger. Billed as 'A Brett A. Hart Vision', which is enough to make anyone want to throw rocks. Director Hart co-wrote with Jeff O'Brien.

BREATHING ROOM (2008)

Fragile blonde Tonya (Ailsa Marshall) is deposited in a large, windowless room, joining thirteen others of assorted ages, races and backgrounds. A camp Host (Keith Foster) appears on television and explains strict rules. Two players are already dead, punished for rule-violations (not washing hands). Another is soon despatched for trying to escape. Dynamics shift within the group, murders take place during blackouts, and it is announced that the room contains 'a rapist, a paedophile and a murderer'. Hero-type Lee (Michael McLafferty) tries to solve the mystery, protect fellow contestants and see a way of surviving within the rules. Others are unhelpful, dangerous or unpredictable – leading to further deaths, either from outright conflict, a possible 'plant' within the group or intervention by the controllers.

This low-budget suspense picture is closest to *Aquarium* and *House of 9*, but riffs on many similar movies: the abducted test subjects/gamers and limited setting of *Cube*, the sadistic challenges designed to prompt realisations and revelations from the *Saw* series (especially the housebound *Saw II*), the killer collars and *Ten Little Indians* body countdown from *Battle Royale*, the trapped blank slate characters trying to sort out who is who and how they relate to each other from *Unknown*. Is this a sadistic social experiment, a game show for rich sickos or some other charade? Explanations matter less than what happens in the room.

Writer-directors John Suits (*Pandemic*) and Gabriel Cowan (*Growth*) win few points for originality, but the film works. McLafferty is good as the guy who thinks he's the hero and Marshall interesting as the apparently vulnerable, reticent protagonist. Otherwise, characters hold back: the taciturn, tough 'Number One' (Jeff Atik) claims to be a Jesuit but has nothing else to say, prompting the others to assume he's the culprit and tie him up so he can be stabbed with mirror shards; a hysterical, middle-aged schoolteacher (Terri Marsteiner) is outed as the paedophile but never explains herself; a middle-aged, hardboiled black guy (Kim Estes) is a recovering alcoholic tempted by a bottle of hooch in the room as part of the ingredients for an explosive; the hostile young black guy (Stevens Gaston); the rebel (Brad Culver) who only identifies himself McGoohan-style as 'Number Six' comes on like a criminal but is, we find out from a glimpsed file, a police officer; and nerdy, compulsive talker Harry (David Higlen) gets on everyone's nerves before showing nasty steel as he surprisingly makes 'the final three'.

The *Prisoner* reference suggests a grandaddy for the genre of enclosed, playful torment; the TV show invented the recurrent trope whereby folks dosed with mysterious soporific wake up in an unusual prison which evokes a game show set and a torture chamber.

THE BREEDER (2011)

If you combine everything I never want to see in a horror movie again you get this Swiss-German dud. Indebted to *And Soon the Darkness* (1970), role model for many xenophobic rape-abduction-torture pictures in the early 2000s, it also slots into the 'dirty deeds in an abandoned totalitarian super-soldier factory' craze of the *Outpost* series.

Backpacking in the Caucasus, outgoing (i.e. slutty) Sophie (Julie LeGal) and mousier Amy (Theresa Joy) bicker over the lack of fun to be had in the vicinity and are spied on from the bushes by an ominous heavy-breather. Skinny-dipping Sophie is dragged underground by the breather/breeder and strapped to an operating table for a vaginal exam overlaid with a nonsense philosophy monologue about lost innocence. Kidnapped as part of a breeding program, Sophie wanders underground tunnels, occasionally with an evil hand reaching out to touch or grope her. At one point, she records a help-me message on her cameraphone and ties it to a pigeon. Meanwhile, drunk on vodka, Amy runs into two alternately sinister and helpful guys. Which is behind the breeding project? At a crucial point, Amy has a gun and has to make a guess.

Piling on weird angles and colour filters doesn't disguise director Till Hastreiter's threadbare script and cheap tricks like ogling close-ups of female body parts and strapped-down-and-cut-up sequences. Joy, a real-life former cheerleader, does gratuitous flexible high kicks. The revelation that the baddie is American (overlaid with a voice-over about Vietnam and family history) takes some of the edge off the depiction of gurning evil foreigners, but cliché is reaffirmed as he is hung up by Georgian vigilantes and bled into a bucket.

BROKEN (2006)

With *Broken*, writer-director Adam Mason progressed from wretched drivel (*The 13th Sign, Dust*) to competent drivel.

After an instantly irritating 'based on a true story' caption, this opens with a *Saw*-derivative stunt. A young woman is forced to dig out a razorblade sewn into her intestines to cut the ropes tying her to a tree. A shadowy tormentor asks the now literally gutless woman if she wants to continue, then lets her work the trigger on his rifle to end her ordeal. Hope (Nadja Brand) comes home from a blind date where she has met a nice guy who isn't put off that she's a single mother, cuddles her cute daughter, and goes to sleep… only to wake up in a wooden coffin. She survives the chained-to-a-tree, razor-in-the-stomach bit successfully and refuses the suicide option, presumably because having a child (whom she guesses is also at a psycho's mercy) gives her something to fight for. In woods miraculously free of passing birdwatchers or ramblers, Hope is trained as a slave by The Man (Eric Colvin), who dresses like director Richard Stanley.

After attempts at compliance (tending a feeble vegetable garden), escape, survival (seducing her captor) and defiance, Hope is hobbled *Misery*-style. A girl (Abbey Stirling) in school uniform (she looks in her mid-twenties) is brought on. She screams for days – until The Man cuts out her tongue and throws it on the fire. We're supposed to be as irritated by her noisemaking as the villain is and laugh with relief when she's finally shut up – think on that for a moment. For all its grimness, *Broken* deploys cheap gimmicks like the victims' plot-mandated refusal to finish off the villain when they have the chance. Existing to show the protracted torture of women, this has nothing to say about slavery as a sexual or societal aberration. Characterisation is feeble and arty touches pathetic (Hope cultivates a pretty flower, which The Man pulls because you can't eat it). The sort of film it's hard to condemn *enough* (an honest quote from a genre-savvy critic sounds like a twisted recommendation… 'so depraved it sickened even Billy Chainsaw').

BURNING BRIGHT (2010)

A simple, effective suspense picture. During a hurricane, teenager Kelly (Briana Evigan) and her autistic brother Tom (Charlie Tahan) are trapped inside a house with a Bengal tiger. The setup involves wicked stepfather Johnny Gaveneau (Garret Dillahunt), a suspect suicide and an insurance policy – so Kelly plays detective even as she tries to avoid the big cat's claws and get her recalcitrant brother to break his set ways to avoid being eaten. Director Carlos Brooks plays up claustrophobia: we get a sense of the big weather event, but are too concerned with the prowling tiger (who has a reputation for going after 'the pretty one') to think about it… until Kelly briefly gets outside and is instantly soaked. She then has to decide whether to go for help or return to rescue a kid incapable of gratitude whom she pretty much has a motive for murdering. Evigan (*Sorority Row*) is a gutsy heroine, squirming up a laundry chute, and Dillahunt (one of the best villains of his generation) subtly underplays the desperate, avaricious redneck who sits nervously drinking in a bar while he hopes his new pet does his dirty work for him. Meat Loaf *doesn't* underplay as the circus salesman who sells Gaveneau the cat, gurning as he explains that the beast is 'Evil'. The trick is to use a real cat with edible actors, even if a few perspective ruses are transparent safety measures. Kelly, fighting for her life and kin, earns the beast's respect, but this being a horror film someone's got to get eaten… and there's only one really satisfying prospect for the finale. Written by producer David W. Higgins, Christine Coyle Johnson and Julie Prendiville Roux.

CAPTIFS (CAGED) (2010)

In the former Yugoslavia *yadda yadda* foreigners take an unwise detour *blah blah* scumbag psycho local abductors *yawn yawn* captivity and chains and cages *not this again* organ harvesting *oh god please no* resourceful survivor girl makes a desperate break *here we go again* turn the tables escape and chase and brutal confrontation and it's all over. A prologue establishes doctor heroine Carole (Zoé Félix) has a phobia of attack dogs, which means the arm-wrestling champ will freeze up but find inner fortitude to get past killer dogs during her escape. Being in subtitled French doesn't make writer-director Yann Gozlan's film fresher, though he manages one good Fabrice du Welz-style overhead shot in a cornfield, as Carole and another girl lie in one row while the last of the abductors searches in the next.

The villains are the usual characterless Eastern European thugs, foolishly picking on foreigners who are more likely to be missed than the refugees and displaced people they usually snatch (which is why they set up in this region in the first place). Félix represents a 2000s action-horror tradition of gutsy French chicks – desperately drowning the baddies' housekeeper in her own stew. The most distinctive villain is a non-speaking, sallow doctor (Philippe Krhajac) who doesn't clean the blood from his operating table before strapping Carole down to harvest her eye. This gruesome touch is his undoing: the slick gore serves as a lubricant to allow the heroine to free a hand and reach for a scalpel to shove in the bastard's neck. Little is made of the fact that the victims are altruistic medics (rather than the ghastly tourists of *Train* or *Turistas*) pitted against capitalist doctors who have turned their training to non-humanitarian evil.

CAPTURED (1959)

This tough army information film from writer-director John Krish (*Unearthly Stranger*) would be acknowledged as a British classic if it hadn't been withheld from non-military audiences for decades. Ex-POW Anthony Farrar-Hockley introduces, but the bulk of the film simply illustrates interrogation techniques servicemen could expect if captured in a Korean-type conflict by an enemy who doesn't observe the Geneva Convention. An old soldier (Wilfrid Brambell) who was in a German POW camp says he knows what to expect, only to be found later in a coffin-like box. Chinese experts who guided the North Korean army refused (or professed to refuse) to recognise enemy combatants as soldiers rather than criminals and classified them not as prisoners but pupils, to be educated in the virtues of communism. This means medical care, provisions, letters from home, etc., could be withheld as part of brainwashing strategy.

The film's two acts illustrate different methods. First, a group of prisoners are nagged into turning on each other, ostracising one of their number as a collaborator to such an extent he does passively co-operate… then Daniels (Alan Dobie), an intelligence officer, is caught and subjected to now hideously familiar tortures (stress positions and water-boarding). It has a stark, noirish look – making a miserable stretch of Britain into a believable North Korea – and edgy performances from a pro cast. Made outside the conventional film industry, it's more horrific than comparable efforts – Hammer's *The Camp on Blood Island* came out the same year – and has tougher language ('effing' and 'harpic' are two terms you wouldn't have heard in a feature film then).

There is, of course, an irony in making a propaganda film about *resisting* propaganda, though the grimness of *Captured* was a problem for the folks who commissioned it: rather than instruct troops not to cooperate with the enemy, soldiers in the audience must have felt anyone would crack under these circumstances and despaired. It might have motivated them not to get captured, though. A cast of familiar British character faces includes Ray Brooks, Gerald Flood, Brian Murray, Bernard Fox and Mark Eden.

THE CELLAR DOOR (2007)

A battered, bloodied woman escapes from a cellar in which an average-looking schlub has kept her prisoner, stumbles around, fails to get a jogger's attention and is run down by her captor's car, then wrapped in plastic and buried in the garden. Herman (James DuMont) starts ogling Rudy (Michelle Tomlinson) as she is clubbing with her best friend. He creeps into the girls' house, steps over the best friend (passed out on the toilet) and drugs Rudy, who wakes up in a wooden cage as his next trophy/ pet/victim. The world scarcely needed another film about a loser who kidnaps and abuses women – but director Matt Zettell (*Axe to Grind*) and writer Christopher Nelson forged ahead anyway.

Less annoying than *Broken* or *The Girl Next Door* (2007), it's still notches below *Captivity*, which scarcely rates as a masterpiece. All it brings to the table is hypocritical relish in suffering, with a supposed uplift in the finish as the maniac gets just desserts at the hands (and edged weapons) of his victim. Blaming Rudy for things she 'makes' him do, Herman tries to be smarmily affable when cajoling her to get undressed so he can wash her soiled clothes (then shrieks, 'Show me your tits,' when she resists). On the surface, it indicts inadequate male attitudes, but the heroine is depicted as a loose-living slut who has invited punishment. Rudy's behaviour (making a fuss, trying to get round her captor, sulking when thwarted) infantilises her and irritates viewers (even if she's acting reasonably in plot context). Herman freaks out from time to time and bludgeons a co-worker at a supermarket and a pair of missionaries who show up at his house – mostly to get more murders into the film. *The Cellar Door 2: Preymates* is still threatened.

CHEAP THRILLS (2013)

A shaggy dog story ('A guy walks into a bar…') which turns into a *conte cruel, Cheap Thrills* has an *Alfred Hitchcock Presents* premise but a contemporary context as horrors rise from the widening gap between rich and poor in America.

Just laid off, mechanic Craig (Pat Healy) needs a stiff drink before he tells his wife (Amanda Fuller) the bad news. In a bar, he runs into Vince (Ethan Embry), a high school skateboarding buddy who is now a bruised-knuckles debt collector. Vince corrals Craig into a reunion bender, and they are picked up by Colin (David Koechner), a coke-snorting, glad-handing rich guy with a calculating tease of a wife, Violet (Sara Paxton). Colin lays out cash for pranks – offering the hard-up guys hundreds of dollars for slapping a stripper's ass or punching a bouncer. Back at Colin's apartment, Vince persuades Craig to attempt a heist which fails because their flabby-seeming host is a martial arts expert. Rather than call the cops, Colin ups the stakes and suggests grosser, self-harming, dangerous or odd stunts with bigger and bigger cash prizes. When Vince sucker-punches Craig to win a hold-your-breath contest, hostility escalates… and goes into overdrive when Craig gets paid to have sex with the detached, creepy Violet.

Underlying it is the fact that the guys have unfairly ended up in the same boat – trying hard at school and having ambitions didn't earn Craig a better life than loser-from-the-off Vince – and will tear each other apart for cast-off cash (much literally bloody). Some stunts are comically sick (aptly paying back a neighbour whose dog fouls Colin's garden), but others just cruel (when Colin offers Vince $25,000 to cut off his own finger, Craig underbids him). The ultimate contest – which is perhaps guessable – is capped with a subtle punch line as Colin, having spent hundreds of thousands of dollars, peels off a fifty to settle a side-bet. Trent Haaga and David Chirchirillo's script links a brand of exploitative abasement typified by reality TV/YouTube Jackassery to the desperate state of anyone in America who isn't rich. Koechner, usually a comic boob, is a genial modern incarnation of Roald Dahl's Man from South America. Healy and Embry don't descend into caricature as the good guy who goes bad and the bad guy who goes worse. Directed by E.L. Katz.

5150, RUE DES ORMES (5150 ELMS WAY) (2009)

'EVEN IF YOU GET AWAY AND I DIE, IT WON'T PROVE I'M WRONG.'

Scripted by Canadian novelist Patrick Senécal (*7 Days*), this abduction-and-torture item has more in its head than gross-out and ranks among the best of its cycle. Film student Yannick Bérubé (Marc-André Grondin) has a minor bicycle accident on rue des Ormes and asks for help at 5150, home of the Beaulieu family. After happening on a room where a wounded young man is chained, Yannick is imprisoned by patriarch Jacques (Normand D'Amour). The taxi driver/chess master serves God by murdering the 'unrighteous' (drug dealers, paedophiles, etc.) and hopes his sulky teen daughter Michelle (Mylène St-Sauveur) will take over the crusade. Maude (Sonia Vachon), Jacques' simple (but not as simple as she seems) wife, fearfully supports her husband and tries not to know what he is doing, while caring for their backward younger daughter Anne (Élodie Larivière). Because Yannick impulsively helped Anne when bullies tried to take her sweets, Maude – who is attracted to the handsome lad – insists he's not unrighteous. The plot motor is that arch-psycho Jacques has painted himself into a corner with bogus morality, which means he has to keep Yannick rather than just kill him the way he does other victims. Yannick, who has issues with his own parents, plays chess with Jacques, who has never been beaten, and begins strange relationships with all his captors – eventually persuading Maude to let him go, but choosing to stay to finish the game and prove his point.

The leads are understated, as Senécal lets crazinesses emerge slowly rather than default at once to shrill melodrama. That Jacques uses the corpses of his victims to make a human-size chess-set allows for a grotesque yet not simplistic finish. The game is finally abandoned, but neither player gets a clear loss – which will probably torture them more in the long run. Director Éric Tessier stages obligatory failed escape attempts and punitive measures powerfully – Yannick gets a *Misery*-like broken leg and spends much of the film in plaster as well as shackles – and gives some subjective fantasies a white shimmer which get us out of the claustrophobic home-prison.

CLAUSTROFOBIA (2011)

This Dutch horror film has a trauma-which-will-make-a-kid-grow-up-psycho prologue. A girl lures a naïve lad into a derelict morgue, coaxing him into a body drawer with the promise of a kiss and a feel… Naturally, she locks him in and walks off.

Years later, Eva (Carolien Spoor), a diabetic veterinary student who can't bring herself to hurt a rat and is also a struggling actress, rents a flat mysteriously vacated by a previous tenant who left her books behind. An uneasy atmosphere builds until she wakes handcuffed to a bed in a hidden room under the flat, collected by the grownup loon, Alex (Dragan Bakema). *Claustrofobia* falls into a rut of thwarted escape attempts, ironies (the staring guy across the road Eva signals to is blind), interlopers (sleazy landlord Rogier Philipoom, handsome cop Thijs Römer) who nearly rescue the heroine but get killed, and mind-games between captor and captive.

It comes up with a fresh rationale, albeit a variant on the revenge and organ-napping premises. Alex tells Eva he wants to transplant her kidney into his comatose wife, only it turns out Lisa (Nienke Römer), the woman upstairs, is the prank-playing little girl grown up. Alex has been exerting long, slow revenge by drugging Lisa so she is immobile but fully aware, and needs to harvest spare parts since the drugs inflict long-term organ damage. Of course, Eva breaks free and turns the tables. Well made and acted, but old news. Written by Robert Arthur Jansen; directed by Bobby Boermans.

THE CLINIC (2011)

An Australian strangers-wake-up-trapped movie. After a brush with a sinister road-hog ambulance, pregnant Beth (Tabrett Bethell) and boyfriend Cameron (Andy Whitfield) are sidelined at a creepy motel. In a *Vanishing* bit, Beth is spirited away while Cameron looks for food in a deserted town. The apparent plot of the hero accusing the creepy motelier (Boris Brkic) and getting no help from the local corrupt cop (Marshall Napier) fades down, though it returns intermittently. Beth wakes (no longer pregnant) in a tub full of ice, with suture marks on her stomach. Five other women in a similar state are trapped in the eponymous clinic, which looks more like a derelict factory: one dying with her suture ripped open, a helpful doctor (Freya Stafford), a relieved blonde party girl (Clare Bowen), a mute catatonic (Sophie Lowe) and a murderess (Adrienne Pickering) intent on ripping the women open to find implanted colour-coded tags so, by a process of elimination, she can determine which of the caged babies is hers.

A Pete Walker-style array of villains includes directress Ms Shepard (Elizabeth Alexander), a weird Russian couple (Slava Orel, Inga Romanostova) and a Lennie-like hulking manchild (Marcel Bracks). The absurd reveal is that they run an illicit adoption agency where prospective parents get the baby of the mother who puts up the hardest fight and is therefore blessed with the fittest-to-survive genes. Furthermore, Beth is a grown-up survivor of one of these contests (it's not said what happens to the surplus babies – nothing good, we assume). Performances and suspense mechanics are fine – but the plot is so contrived (depending on idiot Cameron getting the munchies in the middle of the night) that it's hard to take seriously. Written and directed by James Rabbitts.

COFFIN (2011)

> *WELL, MONEY IS A DRIVING FACTOR, YES, BUT – YOU KNOW WHAT – I JUST KIND OF LIKE WATCHING PEOPLE LIKE YOU SQUIRM. IT'S FUN.*

This starts as if it's going to be a coattail-rider on *Buried*, but plays a trickier, twistier game. Rona Samms (Sunny Doench) and her lover Sean (Kevin Sorbo) wake up in a coffin with matches, limited air supply and an inbuilt video feed. Wealthy, bald Jack (Patrick Barnitt), Rona's husband, is visited by a masked, cackling trickster (Johnny Alonso) who claims to have set this all up and runs Jack around town all night as he desperately tries to raise ransom money. In cutaways, the couple try to escape – eventually triggering an extra peril as water pours in – and cops (Kipp Tribble and Derik Wingo, who also wrote and directed) catch on that something is amiss. Bruce Davison plays Jack's banker, who gets suspicious about the huge late-night withdrawal. The last reel springs satisfying twists. Performances are okay, given that several characters are dissembling throughout. Weird, Lex Luthor-looking Barnitt goes through several arcs, from guilt-ridden to sadistic.

THE CONDEMNED (2007)

Another dystopian-gameshow action movie. Like the *Rollerball* remake, this purports not to take place in the future and stages death matches for dark net pay-per-view. Unethical media mogul Breckel (Robert Mammone) – and how many *ethical* media moguls are there in films? – buys condemned prisoners from tinpot Latin American countries and former Soviet Republics (but not Texas, which would have been funnier). Fitted with exploding ankle bracelets, they are cast away on an island and must fight until only one hard man (or woman) survives. When a promising Arab maniac is assassinated before he gets in the game, replacement Jack Conrad (Steve Austin) is found rotting in a Mexican jail; Breckel reasons Americans are so hated the worldwide audience will love seeing him killed. Jack is plainly a hero-type undercover operative with a nice family waiting back home. Quandaries are established: How will husband-and-wife murderers cope with the condition that only one survives? Will the alliance between British bastard (Vinnie Jones) and Japanese killer (Masa Yamaguchi) hold? Is the lethal foxy African (Emelia Burns) really sweet on the African-American (Marcus Johnson) or planning to get close enough to pull his ankle-bomb tab?

Produced without irony by World Wrestling Entertainment, *The Condemned* can't even compete with *Turkey Shoot* or *Death Race* as a hypocritical science fiction gladiator movie. Problem one is Steve Austin aka 'Stone Cold' Steve Austin – who doesn't register as a screen hero. He handles stunts and reads his (few) lines, but has the presence of a ton of walnuts shoved into a blow-up doll. Jones, barely breaking sweat, out-acts Austin in every confrontation. Building a film around Austin probably forced the casting of bland Mammone in a nefarious role which requires a standout ham like Lance Henriksen or Powers Boothe. A heavy handed

CONFINEMENTS AND DANGEROUS GAMES

message that watching spectacles of violence is wrong prompts cutaways to folks in bars looking guilty after they've clicked on the pay-site. However, this doesn't actually deliver carnage intense enough to force any audience to reassess the wicked predilection for non-stop thumping cut to classic rock. Director Scott Wiper stages a lot of fights; none particularly outstanding. Written by Wiper, Rob Hedden (*Friday the 13th Part VIII Jason Takes Manhattan*) and Andy Hedden (*Clockstoppers*). Roel Reiné of the *Death Race* sequels directed *The Condemned 2*, with Randy Orton and Eric Roberts.

CORD (HIDE AND SEEK) (2000)

Another Psycho Bitch movie – amusingly, the exact phrase the villainess uses to castigate the heroine when she tries to fight back.

In one of the most contrived premises in an already far-fetched genre, pregnant yuppie Anne (Daryl Hannah) is abducted by a white trash couple who keep her in an isolated *Misery*-style house. Anne is told ransom is demanded of her husband Jack (Bruce Greenwood, woolly as ever), but fertility lab tech Frank (Vincent Gallo) and his loopy baby-doll wife Helen (Jennifer Tilly) are really after her unborn child. Helen can't have children after Frank aborted their own baby when amniocentesis showed a deformity which runs in Frank's family. Frank has told Helen her egg is gestating inside Anne, though Frank – an extremely unlikely character, who attempts to molest Anne because Helen refuses to have sex during 'her' pregnancy – eventually admits he has used his own semen and Anne's egg, prompting an enraged Helen to baseball bat him to death.

Cutaways show Jack failing to believe his wife is dead (a burned corpse is found in a crashed car) as seasons pass, while the familiar escape and recapture gambits are trotted out. As often, the normal couple are stiffs (Hannah, supposed heroine, is utterly bland) so the villains make all the running. A surprisingly restrained Gallo takes an early bath, but value-for-money Tilly goes overboard with the breathy mannerisms which made someone murder her in *Bullets Over Broadway*. Directed by veteran Sidney J. Furie (*The Ipcress File*).

CURVE (2015)

Mallory (Julianne Hough), en route to her own wedding, has doubts about fiancé Brad. Driving his car through the Colorado desert, she shifts the seat and finds fliers for escort services. When the car stalls in the middle of nowhere – presumably because Brad didn't have it properly maintained – handsome stranger Christian (Teddy Sears) hikes by and helps out. With understandable hesitation, she offers the courtly, charming fellow a lift but light flirtation turns sinister when he comes on strong and pulls a knife, insisting she drive to an out-of-the-way motel in a ghost town. Realising how this scenario plays out in the movies, Mallory drives the car into a culvert… and is trapped in the upturned vehicle while Christian is thrown clear. Though a roving serial killer with a creepily moralistic bent, Christian opts not to murder Mallory outright but leave her stuck, returning occasionally to gloat.

The film mashes *The Hitcher* and *127 Hours* with the upside-down heroine fending off rats, ants and flood, making use of what comes to hand (including her trousseau) to survive. A third act gets into a different type of peril, with Mallory in a position to hobble away relatively unscathed but compelled to do the right thing to help her tormentor's next chosen victim. A tight script by Kimberly Lofstrom Johnson and Lee Patterson finds room for character growth as the ordeal helps Mallory think through pre-marital jitters when her world is literally upended. Hough, physically confined for much of the film (inevitably, she has to ponder cutting off her own leg – though not before she's eaten a rat and sipped her own urine), gives a gutsy performance, and there are plenty of verbal barbs in her exchanges with the curiously detached yet malign Christian (his full character name is Christian Laughton, suggesting a *Mutiny on the Bounty* fixation).

In *The Skeleton Key*, an update of 1970s TV movie woman-in-peril dramas, British Iain Softley showed he could handle female-skewing horror. Here, he again invests material which would once have been a B picture or a 73-minute movie-of-the-week with grit and character. This high-concept/low-cost, unpretentious psycho-thriller sneaks up and bites harder than expected – including very good use of the cliché mantrap left where it'll do the most damage.

DEATH RACE (2008)

Nominally a remake of *Death Race 2000* – though only producer Roger Corman gets credit for the 1975 film (that's a big fuck you to writers Ib Melchior, Charles Griffith and Robert Thom and director Paul Bartel). In the event, director/writer Paul W.S. Anderson junks all but a few character names in favour of a car-action makeover of twice-remade *The Longest Yard* (aka *Mean Machine*). *Death Race 2000* is satire – so is *The Longest Yard*, for that matter – but *Death Race* plays straight even as Joan Allen as a camp warden and the script advances lunatic notions like a racetrack with *optional short cuts*.

The original features a transcontinental road race with points awarded for running over pedestrians; champion Frankenstein (David Carradine) rebels to overthrow a corrupt dystopia. Here, the race is held within the bounds of Terminal Island prison though the presence of a causeway to the mainland hints at what'll happen in the climax. Convict racers are expected to kill other drivers or their navigators – that drivers *have* navigators is a hold-over from *Death Race 2000*, though even thickos ought to know how to go round a circle without instructions. Popular masked racer Frankenstein (nostalgically voiced by Carradine) is killed in a crash, but warden Hennessey (Allen) wants to replace him. Disgraced racing champ/laid-off steelworker Jensen Garner Ames (Jason Statham) is framed for murder and sentenced to Terminal Island. Hennessey bullies him into becoming the new Frankenstein, with a backup team including mechanical genius Coach (Ian McShane, taking the cheque) and navigator Case (Natalie Martinez), bussed in from a women's prison to up the ratings. Frankenstein's arch-rival is Machine Gun Joe (Tyrese Gibson), a gay badass with a knack of getting his navigators killed. He starts out as a hissable baddie like Sylvester Stallone's like-named character, but turns into a staunch ally and sidekick – we're expected to overlook the murders, I suppose. The rest (Max Ryan, Robin Shou, Justin Mader, Robert LaSardo) are barely characterised kooks we don't mind getting splatted and burned in the many many car-crunching pile-ups.

Death Race 2000 was the first film to inspire a computer game; Anderson (*Mortal Kombat*, *Resident Evil*) defaults to game-esque business like symbols on the course which activate weapons in the cars when drivers pass over them. Statham, well cast as the muscles behind another man's mask, doesn't get a showcase to match the *Transporter* films or (especially) *Crank*. As a noisy, well-choreographed demolition derby with speech balloon dialogue it's watchable, but it shows how much less vital exploitation cinema has become since the Corman era. In 1975, Frankenstein wanted to overthrow an unjust society; in 2008, society is still hideous (riot cops show up at the steelyard layoff to start the trouble they're paid to suppress), but all the hero wants is to escape to Mexico and run an auto junkyard with his gal pal, gay pal and baby daughter. South African sequel specialist Roel Reiné replaced Statham with Luke Goss as another Frankenstein in *Death Race 2* (2010) and *Death Race: Inferno* (2012).

DESYAT NEGRITYAT (TEN LITTLE NIGGERS) (1987)

Ten strangers are invited to a house party on an island, only to be accused by a recording of getting away with murders… then picked off, one by one, in manners relating to a cheerfully homicidal nursery rhyme. This Soviet production is unusual among adaptations of Agatha Christie's influential, brilliantly contrived story. It's based on the 1939 novel (*Ten Little Niggers*) rather than the subsequent play Christie was persuaded to retitle *And Then There Were None*. On stage and in other film adaptations, the finale reveals two among the party of ten murderers are innocent; the coup in which the apparent heroine shoots dead the leading man is a ruse to expose the culprit, whose scheme for ironic vigilante justice is thwarted. The novel, and this film, carry the premise to a ruthless, genuinely shocking conclusion.

The best film take remains Rene Clair's waspish black comedy *And Then There Were None* (1945), but this grimmer, more intense adaptation works. Characters are tormented by guilts which prompt black and white flashbacks or even phantasms of murdered folk, and a febrile, brutal neurosis washes around as murderers turn up dead and survivors suspect each other. Even a newly-written-in sex scene is desperate rather than titillating, showing how locked into their own heads the killers are while persecuted by the mysterious, mocking A.N. Owen (Anon – which works better in Russian than Christie's U.N. Owen/Unknown). The film gradually shifts from inside the luxurious house to the bare, desolate chunk of seabound rock, stressing the story's increasing harshness. It has meticulous 1930s costumes, music, décor and cars, but it's of course odd that characters with names like 'Justice Lawrence Wargrave' (Vladimir Zeldin) and 'Miss Vera Claythorne' (Tatyana Drubich) speak Russian. The arch, affected performances caricature stereotypical British repression: from a Soviet viewpoint, Christie's book can be read as an indictment of privileged, monied, classbound folk. Servants are bullied to keep breakfast coming even as corpses pile up, and the most loathsome victims are dashing Anthony Marston (Aleksandr Abdulov), who cheerily admits to squashing a couple of kids in a hit-and-run drive-by, and puritanical old spinster Emily Brent (Lyudmila Maksakova), who fired a pregnant servant girl and feels no guilt at all for her death. In the light of the implied racism of the title, it's intriguing that Philip Lombard (Aleksandr Kaydanovsky) – positioned as an affable, adventurous hero – is a colonial officer who left twenty East African tribesmen to die by walking out of a trouble spot.

The novel became the template for many *gialli*, and director Stanislav Govorukhin evokes an Italianate mood as black gloves intrude into the frame to wield a hypodermic… but, with its surreal viciousness and sense of entrapment, it could as easily be double-billed with *The Exterminating Angel* as *5 Dolls for an August Moon*. Subtitles render the setting as Negro Island and the rhyme is 'Ten Little Negro Kids'. For the stage, Christie changed her Nigger Island and 'Ten Little Niggers' to the marginally less offensive Indian Island and 'Ten Little Indians'. In 2015, the BBC mounted an *And Then There Were None* miniseries (which borrows heavily from Govorukhin's film) and ducked controversy with Soldier Island and 'Ten Little Soldier Boys'.

DOLAN'S CADILLAC (2009)

A direct-to-DVD feature based on Stephen King's hardboiled 'The Cask of Amontillado' homage. A little padded, it has mechanical, one-contrivance-on-another plotting and lopsided casting, with Christian Slater having fun as an odious gangster spitting out venomous King speeches and Wes Bentley wooden as the ordinary Joe turned fanatic avenger.

In the Nevada desert – played by Canada with colour-processing to leach the green from the grass – schoolteacher Elizabeth (Emmanuelle Vaugier) witnesses Joe Dolan (Slater) and his two-man krewe (the budget shows) committing murder. Though a dead hooker is dumped in her bedroom with a finger sewn to her mouth in a shush gesture, Elizabeth agrees to testify and – leaving her hotel hideout to buy a pregnancy test – is blown up. Shattered husband Robinson (Bentley) loses faith in society, but becomes obsessed. An attempted ambush is thwarted when Dolan's other enemies spring an attack which gets nowhere thanks to his bulletproof custom

Cadillac SUV. In a sequence a montage doesn't make credible, Robinson gets a summer job on the highways, betting his precious watch heirloom that he can stay the course, simply to rig a detour on a holiday weekend and trick Dolan into driving into a custom-dug grave so he can bury him alive. Dolan tries to talk his way out of it ('For the love of God, Robinson...').

Director Jeff Beesley manages neat moments. Having bought a bigger gun than Dirty Harry's, Robinson goes into the desert to practice and fires off a single shot which misses the target but brings down a huge rockslide. Slater is creepily funny: in one look, he shows even he is appalled by a subordinate's suggestion there's more profit in smuggling child-sized sex slaves but will still go with it. However, there's a lot of repetition and the paragraphs of talk King likes to write break the momentum. Bentley is never remotely credible and we get the point about how evil Dolan is well before the opening speech about his demonic rottenness is reprised word for word.

DREAD (2009)

'I WANT YOUR SOUL TO OPEN UP FOR ME, SPREAD-EAGLED LIKE A SPLIT BEAVER SO I CAN GAZE INTO ITS SECRETS...

'Dread' is odd story out in Clive Barker's *Books of Blood* (1984) – a non-supernatural *conte cruel* with a philosophical bent. A generation on, it seemed a torture porn forerunner and Anthony DiBlasi's adaptation aptly epitomises grungy, mean 2000s horror. Lank-haired film student Grace (Jackson Rathbone) and confident psycho Quaid (Shaun Evans) interview folk about their greatest fears for a documentary. Grace is hung up on an older brother who died in a drunk driving crash, but Quaid trumps that with his own childhood trauma – an axe-wielding madman killed his parents in front of him. Drawn into the unhealthy relationship are Cheryl (Hanne Steen), an editor abused by her butcher father, and Abby (Laura Donnelly), who has a disfiguring birthmark on her face (and, as it turns out, a third of her body).

Quaid is so plainly bad news it's hard to see why anyone trusts him enough to open up, and Evans plays him as more annoying than charismatic. It's no surprise when he takes to tormenting subjects, purportedly for their own good ('Face the beast.'), but actually from pure sadism. The torments aren't as clever as *Saw* traps, but are memorably cruel: editing a tape of Abby failing to seduce Grace into mocking footage of a portrait being defaced and broadcasting it to 'every television on campus', whereupon she gets in a bath with wire wool and bleach and tries to scrub away her marks... locking vegetarian Cheryl up with only a large steak to eat, filming her over many days until she is driven to chew the maggoty meat. It closes with a creep-around in Quaid's dark house, with a vengeance-seeker accidentally killing the wrong man, and Quaid dumping a corpse in Abby's cell while wondering 'how hungry you'll have to be to get through all that meat.'

It's beside the point that Quaid's philosophy is hypocritical/nonsensical, since he's the movie's villain – but Barker the director would have made him more than a detestable creep who gives people an unjustifiable hard time.

ELEVATOR (2011)

Trapped-in-a-lift films (*Elevator to the Gallows, The Elevator, Out of Order*) usually feature someone who's committed a crime in the building and is stuck while making a getaway. *Elevator* has a different suspense situation and a unique lift design (no hatches – ruling out usually obligatory shaft-dangling). The trapees do, however, include a regulation claustrophobic – wiseass comic George Axelrod (Joey Slotnick) whines about too many people getting on and keeps up a chatter which irritates everyone, including the brat (twins Amanda and Rachel Pace) who maliciously stabs the stop button to shut him up, only for the elevator to get stuck.

Soap opera complications roll out: Tycoon Henry Barton (John Getz), whose name is on the New York building, is upbraided for financial shady dealing. Pregnant Celine (Anita Briem) confesses workmate Don (Christopher Backus) is the father of her child, which is news to his TV reporter fiancée (Tehmina Sunny). Widow Jane Redding (Shirley Knight) reveals her husband shot himself after losing his savings on Barton's junk bonds, and admits she is carrying a bomb – then dies of a heart attack, with the bomb still attached.

Things get gory when an arm is severed during an escape attempt (thanks *again* to the little girl stabbing buttons) and a tactful black comic atrocity has the trapped folk try to cut the dead woman's corpse with a tiny knife so the part of her the bomb is wired to can be dropped. Veterans Knight (always good as crazies) and Getz (a classic sleaze) are excellent. Written by Marc Rosenberg (*Incident at Raven's Gate*); directed by Stig Svendsen.

THE ELEVATOR (1974)

A sharp little TV movie with a good gimmick premise and a fabulous if frayed cast of soap stereotypes. Alfred Hitchcock often said he'd like to follow up *Lifeboat* with a film set entirely in a stalled lift – and Carl Schenkel made that picture in the 1980s (*Abwärts* aka *Out of Order*); *The Elevator* has a bit too much going on outside the elevator for Hitch's taste, but does well by the high concept of eight randomly assembled souls in a stuck elevator in a half-built Los Angeles office building.

Sweaty claustrophobic thief Eddie Holcomb (James Farentino) clutches a briefcase full of stolen money which has the usual faulty catch so it spills out at the worst time. While Holcomb waves his gun in panic, his psycho partner Howarth (Don Stroud), who couldn't get into the crowded elevator, and sceptical girlfriend Irene (Carol Lynley), who was dubious about the whole enterprise, run about the building failing to be helpful. Also crammed in: Myrna Loy as a garrulous old lady who has a third-act Edward Albee revelation about the wonderful family she keeps going on about; Roddy McDowall as the smoothly duplicitous building manager who cracks and makes a speech about how the whole place is built on lies (he reaches for the emergency phone to find it hasn't been installed yet); a triangular ménage between competent doctor (Craig Stevens), dowdy wife (Teresa Wright) and glamorous nurse (Arlene Golonka); and the petulant young man (Barry Livingston) annoyed his mother (Jean Allison) keeps his trust fund locked away.

One surprise of the tight teleplay by David Ketchum and Bruce Sheeley is that not all the soap strands are unravelled – the doctor clearly ends his affair and gets back with his wife during the crisis, but they don't talk about it. Expected cutaways show loose bolts, sparking circuit-boards, screaming wires and falling dust, and everyone looks suitably nervous and harassed in close-ups (scored to fever pitch by John Cacavas). Directed by Jerry Jameson (*The Bat People*), who specialised in TV disaster (*Heatwave!*, *Hurricane*, *Terror on the 40th Floor*) before hitting the 'big time' with *Airport '77* and *Raise the Titanic*.

THE ENTRANCE (2006)

Despite good ideas and an interesting lead performance, *The Entrance* is maddeningly vague. It features *Saw*-style 'justifiable torture traps', but takes a metaphysical approach to a horrific elimination game as a dead-inside heroine is ensnared by a demon with an ill-defined agenda. Detective Jennifer Pornhowski (Sarah-Jane Redmond), careworn and no-longer-young, grills drug dealer Ryan James (Michael Eklund), who claims to have escaped from a mysterious kidnapper who snatches random citizens (all guilty of major crimes) and pens them in an anonymous underground parking garage. The abductees are forced to play games to decide who gets to leave and shown films of their greatest sins, which generally makes even the other sleazes in the room sick to look at them. Rather than the contraptions of *Saw* or the self-destructive tests of *Intacto*, this slightly pantomime-ish Devil (Frank Cassini) sticks to familiar party games – musical chairs, bingo and a few hands of cards. The cop eventually winds up in the car park, reluctantly involved in the games, and discovers one of the remaining players is the anonymous businessman (familiar pockmarked character actor Jerry Wasserman) who raped her as a teenager. Will she save him or get revenge, and will the script get a grip if she makes a choice? The supernatural element is unusual and brings humour to otherwise grim proceedings. Written and directed by Damon Vignale.

EXAM (2009)

Eight candidates – balanced by sex and ethnicity, though mostly ambitious, besuited twenty-somethings – sit in a room to take an examination. An Invigilator (Colin Salmon) explains they are candidates for a life-changing, rewarding position and that inside this room the only law is the company's law. He sets rules – no one is to attempt to communicate with him and no one is to spoil their paper – and tells them they have eighty minutes to answer the question, then sets a timer going and leaves. The candidates turn over their papers – which are blank. A woman (Gemma Chan) starts to write on the paper and is mercilessly expelled. The seven remaining applicants start talking to each other. An alpha male self-described as White (Luke Mably) sticks labels on the others – Black (Chukwudi Iwuji), Brown (Jimi Mistry), Blonde (Nathalie Cox), Dark (Adar Beck), Brunette (Pollyanna McIntosh) and, for a jittery Frenchman who seems out of it, Deaf (John Lloyd Fillingham). They bicker as they try to find out what the question is, waver between co-operation and vicious competition, and reveal dollops of their own (and this world's) backstory. An AIDS-like deadly condition, kept at bay by a drug devised by the company they all want to work for, has affected the lives of everyone in the room (and, presumably, on the planet).

Written and directed by Stuart Hazeldine, from a story devised with Simon Garrity, *Exam* is an ensemble-in-a-mystery-room movie (cf: *Cube*, *Unknown*, *Breathing Room*). The pressure-cooker drama means everyone gets to step up and dominate for a spell – though, significantly, the character who seems not to be in the game knows more than he's letting on. It seems from the opening statement that any extremes, including torture (by paper-cut) and murder, are tolerated or even encouraged by the presiding company, though this is not quite the case. The scenario is obviously a major contrivance: the question which has to be found and answered is snuck in early so that winning the game is just a matter of seeing through a trick rather than, as the drama suggests, demonstrating a particular set of character traits. Projects of this scale tend to look cheap, but this has a relatively lush finish – which ups the glamour content (everyone looks their best, perhaps because they're trying to impress a prospective employer) and the room itself is odd enough to suggest a stranger world outside.

THE EXPERIMENT (2010)

> 'YOU KNOW I ONLY GOT THREE RULES... EAT TWAT, SMOKE POT... AND SMILE A LOT.'

An American remake of *Das Experiment* (2001), adapted from a novel by Mario Giordano based on the 1971 Stanford experiment in which student volunteers were arbitrarily assigned roles as guards and prisoners. Though it features two Best Actor ©Oscar* winners and a solid supporting cast, it's another make-it-again project which screws up almost everything that worked in the original. Director Oliver Hirschbiegel started his German-language film with the division process and allowed only the main character an outside life. Writer-director Paul Scheuring (creator of *Prison Break*) spends a reel or so on slacker Travis (Adrien Brody) losing a job, getting in a scuffle at a peace demo and talking with his dippy girlfriend (Maggie Grace). Meanwhile, conservative-suited, supposedly religious Barris (Forest Whitaker) quivers under the lash of a bedridden tyrannical mother. Interviews load other characters with backstory: Chase (Cam Gigandet) is a sex addict, Benjy (Ethan Cohn) a chubby fantasist who wants to be a graphic novelist and is lying about his diabetes (he's pretty much Piggy in this *Lord of the Flies*), Oscar (Jason Lew) is a bit gay and Nix (Clifton Collins Jr) doesn't admit he's a real convict.

After roles have finally been assigned, mad scientist Dr Archaleta (Fisher Stevens) withdraws to be represented only by swivelling cameras and a red light on the wall which will go on if the 'rules' are violated, voiding the experiment. Guard leader Barris, played with atypical twitchy ham by Whitaker, finds hidden reservoirs of cool and cruelty as he enforces discipline, institutes a regime of excessive punishment (the guards mass-pee on the ringleader), plays obnoxious music and pushes the edges of the rules (deducing that violence is actually allowed). Travis becomes the cons' leader and suffers most (a haircut, that piss-drenching, 'solitary confinement' in what looks like a gingerbread oven complete with spy-cam) until the revolution. When fights break out, everyone gurns like Kubrickian apemen (complete with low angles and grunting) and Scheuring indulges in rants about people being animals. Full of silly stuff (Nix rapes Oscar because he can't jerk off to *Club International* in his dorm bunk) and 'significant' speeches which convey less meaning than tiny moments in *Das Experiment*.

A conspiracy movie-paranoid-dystopian-science fiction tone undermines the premise. A strength of *Das Experiment* and the thematically similar *Die Welle* (based on another American social science experiment) is that *neutral* projects expose uncomfortable truths; instead, *The Experiment* offers an *evil* experiment which seems designed to drive subjects to melodramatic excesses.

THE FACILITY (GUINEA PIGS) (2012)

Inspired by the Northwick Park clinical trial of 2006, which collapsed when unexpected side-effects of a new drug caused scarily extreme physical symptoms. Here, seven volunteers – ranging from hard-up students to professional lab rats (or 'pharma's daughters') – pitch up at a clinic in the middle of nowhere and are given shots of an experimental drug. Jed (Oliver Coleman), an obnoxious alpha male audiences hate because a caption identifies him as an estate agent, ignores medical advice and does push-ups, which means the drug affects him faster. His face goes red, he suffers extreme pains and paranoia, then becomes violent. On an hourly schedule, the others – perky blonde Carmen (Skye Lourie), desperate student Arif (Amit Shah), lab rat Joni (Alex Reid) and cynical Morty (Steve Evets) – go the same route, though journo Katie (Nia Roberts) and student Adam (Aneurin Barnard), the controls of the experiment, have been dosed with a placebo and stay sane. Some folk die and the dwindling number of unaffected alternately work alongside or try to get away from the others. To ramp up the horror angle, the clinic is locked up, cut off from the outside world and unnaturally dark, and an unseen overseer refuses to intervene until the experimental course is run, no matter how many have to die. Director-writer Ian Clark has a decent cast, but gives them a few too many awkward lines. The premise is strong enough to carry the film through shaky patches, though it devolves into familiar epidemic horror movie territory.

FAULTS (2014)

Once a celebrity cult deprogrammer and author, Ansel Roth (Leland Orser) is reduced to low-paying hotel lounge talk gigs. In a telling vignette, he tries to scam a free meal by recycling an expired voucher. Hawking the second book nobody needs to read (rights to his bestseller are held by his ex-wife), Ansel is in debt to an agent (Jon Gries) who sends a professional threatener (Lance Reddick) after him. Approached by a couple (Chris Ellis, Beth Grant) who ask him to rescue their daughter Claire (Mary Elizabeth Winstead) from a sect called Faults, he is so needy that he signs on without doing a background check. Claire is duly snatched from a parking lot and taken to a motel where Ansel schedules sessions to talk through her cult affiliation and encourage her to return to her family… However, the parents' odd behaviour, insistent visits from the enforcer and Claire's unusual reactions suggest this isn't as simple as it seems.

Writer/director Riley Stearns sets up a one-act-play situation whereby two interesting characters have a long conversation in a motel room. The balance of power shifts between them as Claire – who could be the victim of parental abuse or mistress of her own one-person cult – challenges Ansel's assumptions, probes his guilt over a previous rescuee who killed herself and generally messes with his head. In mainstream movies, Orser and Winstead tend to get pigeon-holed as one-note shifty or cute players; rising to the material Stearns gives them, they deliver compelling, layered performances. The ending is creepily ambiguous.

FEMINA RIDENS (THE FRIGHTENED WOMAN) (1969)

> 'IT'S TOO SOON YET TO KILL ME, ISN'T IT. THERE'S LOTS MORE FUN TO BE SQUEEZED OUT OF ME. IT'D BE A PITY TO WASTE IT. YOU FIEND!'

A strain of Italian cinema inhabits a limbo between colour supplement art and sado-sexploitation (cf: Liliana Cavani's *The Night Porter*, Marco Ferreri's *The Future Is Woman*, Lina Wertmüller's *Swept Away*, even Fellini's *City of Women*). This offering from the mostly unknown Piero Schivazappa could equally happily be double-billed with Fellini's *Juliet of the Spirits* or Radley Metzger's *The Lickerish Quartet*. After playing fetish and bondage games in the manner of contemporary versions of *Venus in Furs* from Jesús Franco and Massimo Dallamano (or even William Wyler's *The Collector*) it defaults to *giallo* plotting.

Slightly dowdy Maria (Dagmar Lassander), a journalist whose commitment to feminism extends to working at weekends(!), ventures into the fantasy world of wealthy Dr Sayer (Philippe Leroy), who is at once sophisticated and timid, genteel and a sexual sadist ('You can not imagine the pleasure it gives me to watch a woman in the grip of fear.'). After an interview in which Sayer rants that men will become obsolete if birth control catches on, Maria is overpowered and subjected to sado-masochistic games in the doctor's private playrooms (he is alone on a vast estate decorated with fetishist works of art), including old favourites like having a firehose aimed at her and a forcible haircut. Evidence suggests Sayer has done this before with other women, and these abductions always end with murder – but Maria doesn't completely bend to his will.

Schivazappa plays against expectations: the sounds of a beating are heard while the camera focuses on an artfully arranged tulip, but a cut to the action reveals Maria battering Sayer rather than the other way round. The first twist comes when Sayer can't go through with the murder and admits all his previous encounters have been with paid prostitutes who posed for death scene photos. He claims he's genuinely smitten with Maria, who arrived by chance in place of a girl (Lorenza Guerrieri) who would have known the goings-on were just extreme roleplay. In a syrupy phase unbelievable on first viewing (it makes sense later), Maria responds to the pathetic Sayer and enters into a seemingly redemptive relationship ('You must free yourself from these complexes and fears… Have faith in your own virility!'). When they finally make love (in the swimming pool), Sayer has a fatal heart attack and sinks – and it turns out that Maria is a vigilante serial killer who ensnares and disposes of male authority figures (a priest, a politician).

The film is littered with pop art porn (a suspended and gimp-suited female mannequin, a giant female form with splayed legs and a vagina dentata door) in have-your-cake-and-eat-it manner: all this is trotted out to titillate while script and performances critique male inadequacy, even if the final twist suggests Sayer's paranoid fantasies about scorpion ladies are justified. An hour of tying women up followed by a dissection of the infantile uselessness of the Italian male might be a slim addition to the debate on the sex war, but *Femina Ridens* is a well-acted, quirky thriller.

FINAL GIRL (2013)

The pitch for this is *La Femme Nikita* plays *The Most Dangerous Game*. It could work as a series pilot, since the 'mythology' of the heroine and her world is interesting. In an America where the sort of thing seen in slasher movies happens regularly, a well-funded group take countermeasures. Traumatised child Veronica (Gracyn Shinyei), survivor of a massacre, is given aptitude tests by the similarly bereaved William (Wes Bentley). Years later, teenage Veronica (Abigail Breslin) completes a well-resourced training program. Her graduation exercise involves turning the tables on four preppies who hunt girls in forests near a Lynchian community of '50s-style diners and the mansions of wealthy maniacs. Dressing to attract prime mover Jameson (Alexander Ludwig), Veronica goes on a Saturday night date with him and his stooges – uxorious Shane (Cameron Bright – like Breslin, a grown-up child actor), goofily grinning Danny (Logan Huffman) and mama's boy Nelson (Reece Thompson) – which involves 'truth or dare' in the woods and then a Zaroff-style chase. Thanks to a flask of truth/terror drug and her training, Veronica easily bests three of her foes, with a nice feint involving a sustained realistic hallucination after two goofily surreal sequences. However, Jameson is a (slightly) tougher nut to crack.

Scripted by Adam Prince (from a story by Stephen Scarlata, Alejandro Seri and Johnny Silver), it's given a distinctive look and tone by debuting director Tyler Shields.

Everyone is soft-spoken and reasonable under extreme circumstances (though Veronica fakes traditional lady-in-peril panic), the social range of the film is deliberately limited (no cops, almost no sense of community) and characters go through fight-by-night in-the-wilderness business while immaculately dressed in tuxes and bowties and (in Veronica's case) a Riding Hood-red formal dress (she ditches high heels and steals flats from her first victim). The psychos are characterised in broad, effective strokes: Danny struts with an axe while dancing to Who the Bossman's catchy rockabilly 'The Devil and the Duke Ride Out Tonight', Shane has a girlfriend (Emma Paetz) who's in the dark about his guy-time activities but knows something's wrong, Nelson has ice cream with his Mom and wears black gloves. Cheap, but stylish.

GAKKÔ URA SAITO (TOKYO GORE SCHOOL) (2009)

'HOW CAN YOU CARRY ON WITHOUT BEING INSANE IN THESE TIMES?'

In the near future, a Japanese law makes available a database of details about every student. This somehow mutates into an after-school activity whereby teenagers are divided into hunters and quarry and battle each other around a depopulated, adult-free city. Winners claim losers' mobile phones, racking up points which can be spent on expunging personal details and learning the loser's greatest secret ('What, you're a man?').

Hayato (Yusuke Yamada), a cool teen with a scarf and chiselled cheekbones, looks down on the game but is eventually set on by parkour teens and catches up with what's going on. A more conventional film might have Hayato learn responsibility in kicking against the system, but here he becomes a more calculating bastard to protect his own secret (he raped a girl who committed suicide) and even manipulates a seemingly nice girl to win the game, using her to draw off the villain's minions. He's on the point of snatching her phone for an easy win when she stabs him in the hand and reveals she knows his shame anyway (her secret is that she's the dead girl's sister). In the end, the protagonist becomes another pathetic suicide, joining the legion of the losers – learning as he dies that the secret on the site isn't the one he was worried about but that he shat his pants in elementary school. In a sub-plot, an earnest fellow forms a self-protective coalition of victims only for them to turn on him and wind up enslaved by the bully gang.

Director Yôhei Fukuda (who co-wrote with Kiyoshi Yamamoto) also tackled a twisted Japanese game in *Satsujin Douga Site* (*Death Tube*). The premise is nicely sketched and Hayato's mix of cool and rottenness is interesting… but other characters are cartoonish, and a few well-staged jumping-over-things stunts don't make up for the first rehearsal feel of most of the many fight scenes.

A GAME OF DEATH (1946)

This version of Richard Connell's much-filmed 'The Most Dangerous Game' uses most of the script of the 1932 version, with a reel or so of needless complication to pad the running time. The film recycles much of the spectacular jungle chase footage from the older movie, which means actor Noble Johnson plays two different minion roles and Leslie Banks's beard is sometimes visible on the clean-shaven villain. Directed by Robert Wise with a few Lewton technicians aboard (including actor Russell Wade), this is old-school melodrama rather than the brand of subtle chills Wise managed in *The Body Snatcher*, but lively enough.

In keeping with the decade, the villain is now German and his black hunting outfit has an SS look. Erich Kreiger (Edgar Barrier) fingers the scar on his forehead (he also has a white streak in his obvious wig) and talks of blinding headaches. 'Only Pleshke can give me relief,' he states, puzzlingly since he is referring to a male servant (Gene Stutenroth) who spends much of the film irritated by the heroine (Audrey Long) and her breakfast requests. The suggestion that an injury has driven Kreiger mad rather than that he is pursuing his decadent hobby to logical ends is a cop-out which lets big game hunter hero Rainsford (John Loder) off the hook.

The point of the story was once to teach Rainsford, who claims a jaguar probably enjoys being hunted as much as he enjoys hunting it, a harsh lesson, but here he never gets to take the statement back. There's still a severed head or two about, but the pre-code lascivious dialogue is toned down (Kreiger seems too preoccupied to rape the girl, though he has the speech about 'the hunt, the kill, the woman'). The climactic chase is a bit rushed, followed by a serial-style sped-up fistfight between middle-aged leading men.

GUSHA NO BINDUME (HELLEVATOR) (2004)

A Japanese weirdie set largely in one of many elevators which go up and down on a vertical surface in a world (the future?) where all humanity is gathered in a vast, multi-levelled building – though the finale, which echoes *THX 1138*, has a rebel figure expelled or escaping to a surface which might be contemporary downtown Tokyo (a fillip reprised in *We Are the Flesh*). A frame story has a cop grilling a sullen teen who wears dark glasses and earphones about a series of incidents in a stuck lift which contains a mix of volatile personalities.

The opening stretch introduces the enclosed world, with an oddly garbed elevator hostess unemotionally calling off floors and commuters (a troop of salarymen with old-fashioned phone receivers plugged into their jackets) coming and going. Trouble starts when two shaven-headed, orange-jumpsuited prisoners (a rapist and a terrorist) are brought aboard by gestapo-look brutal cops who abuse them. An explosion, perhaps caused by an illegal cigarette dropped by schoolgirl Luchino (Luchino Fujisaki), stalls the lift and the prisoners overcome the guards. They terrorise everyone in predictable manner until the girl, apparently the *really* dangerous passenger, grabs a fallen cop's gun and executes the terrorist, flashing back to her apparent murder of her inappropriately amorous father. In the bloody aftermath, an apparently meek professor with a caseful of unexplained cash (a familiar character in 'lift' movies) kills the rapist, but is overcome with worry this will get him into trouble with the authorities and tries browbeating, cajoling or bribing the others to cover it up even as he further sabotages escape attempts. There are more revelations – a greedy woman pushing a pram turns out to be smuggling food and hasn't got a baby, the teenager seems telepathically to tell the girl he's a secret agent and the professor might be a terrorist carrying funds for the underground. More people get killed in mêlées, and finally an orange-suited Luchino is escorted to the surface to be let loose.

Director-writer Hiroki Yamaguchi has an eye for disorienting detail, but performances are all over the place and the violence is ramped up too early for sustained suspense or horror. The script is so concerned with delivering surprises or copping cool, cruel attitudes that the people in the lift seem like bugs on a microscope slide and the incident-packed story becomes dramatically inert. It has a definite look, blurry and nightmarish but with sharp details and only the odd poor CGI explosion to reveal its cheapness.

LA HABITACIÓN DE FERMAT
(FERMAT'S ROOM) (2007)

Responding to an invitation in the form of a puzzle, ingenious folks – Pascal (Santi Milán), Galois (Alejo Sauras), Oliva (Elena Ballesteros) and Hilbert (Luís Homar) – convene in an isolated location and are greeted by Fermat (Federico Luppi), who they take for their mysterious host. Receiving a phone call about his hospitalised daughter, Fermat leaves. The walls, powered by hydraulic presses which Galois invented, start to close in… and can only be held back if the group huddle together to solve a series of problems.

Written and directed by Luis Piedrahita and Rodrigo Sopeña, this small-scale, cerebral thriller isn't exactly a *Cube* knock-off – but similarly features a well-designed death-trap location and a bunch of supposed strangers who must think mathematically to avoid being mangled. There's an Agatha Christie feel in the strangers-with-secrets-invited-to-a-remote-locale-suitable-for-murder business as interlocking backstories emerge, tying together the characters and explaining why they come to be in this position. The script has clever misdirection (Fermat, it turns out, *isn't* the host, but another victim – the real mastermind is in the room, calculating chances of escape) and a neat segue from personal motivation (revenge for the crippling of Fermat's daughter in a car accident) to an intellectual feud between the young turk on the point of solving a long-standing problem and an envious genius who has devoted his life to it. The problems are mostly of the old-fashioned 'How many apples has Johnny got?' type, and probably oughtn't trouble these geniuses much.

The room itself, revealed from overhead as a shrinking square, is a well-used central locale – but the film does follow Fermat's wanderings in the outside world. He is ironically disposed of in a stunning overhead shot when a well-intentioned policeman nags him into putting on a seatbelt which activates a death trap which should have taken him off the board earlier in the game. Contrivance is inherent in the premise, so the way these people hold off admitting if and how they know each other is acceptable, allowing for a pleasing succession of revelations as attempts to halt the Poe-like crushing walls are thwarted.

HOFFMAN (1970)

An odd cross between *There's a Girl in My Soup* and *The Collector*, *Hoffman* is one of the few film projects Peter Sellers took seriously enough to work hard on rather than breeze through on a talent for funny voices and unleashed chaos.

Secretary Miss Smith (Sinéad Cusack) is blackmailed by meek, middle-aged Mr Hoffman (Sellers) into spending a week of domesticity in his flat, while she tells her fiancé (Jeremy Bulloch) she's with her gran in Scarborough. At first, the tone is creepy as Miss Smith dreads the terrors of sharing a bed with Hoffman and he mutters darkly about an absent wife in terms which recall Crippen and the brides-in-the-bath murderer. It then switches to poignance. The worst Hoffman does in bed is snore loudly, while the unattainably glamorous woman suffers minor ailments like a bruised heel and night-time constipation, and the relationship between them deepens as the girl comes to understand the half-life Hoffman has been leading.

The script, by Ernest Gébler from his own novel, gives Sellers a lot of funny business, acid lines and whimsical turns, but he plays Hoffman as a repressed soul half-ashamed of his attempts to be funny, telling genuinely good jokes as if he expects no one will laugh. Cusack, more interesting than the expected dolly bird, almost makes the strangely upbeat last reel believable. Directed by Alvin Rakoff.

HOMECOMING (2009)

Small-town girl Shelby (Mischa Barton) still thinks she's with jock Mike (Matt Long), who broke up with her when he left for a college football career. She has other problems – a bar/bowling alley which is going bankrupt, a bank manager out to take her home, a recently dead mother she nursed through a long final illness (and probably murdered) and a house out in the sticks with the usual stigmata of psychosis (faded old-person décor, with a room-sized shrine to her fantasy relationship). When Mike comes home with new girlfriend Elizabeth (Jessica Stroup), Shelby tries to be smarmily manipulative and break them up by getting her drunk. Contrivances lead to her knocking her rival down on the road and hauling her back to the house to be doped, drip-fed and locked up.

As in *Misery*, the nurse blows hot and cold with the patient, needlessly 'setting' her broken ankle and taking out frustrations on the captive. As in *Misery* and every other entry in this cycle, the prisoner tries to get notes out, attract the attention of outsiders, overpower the captor and make slow, painful, awkward breaks for freedom. Suspense is defused by getting away from the house and the two girls too often, spending time with the dimwitted object of their desire, who witters about Elizabeth's disappearance and foolishly gets close to reuniting with the obvious nutjob. When the friendly cop (Michael Landes) comes calling and hears the muffled cries of the girl in the basement, he gets an axe in the gut and shot in the head ('Now look what you made me do.'). When Mike shows up and finds out what's going on, he says more stupid things ('It doesn't have to be this way.') and thumps Shelby so feebly she is obliged to come out of the cellar with an axe for another row/fight ('You said forever.'). He tries to talk Elizabeth out of revenge, but the heroine batters the loon to a not-very-bloody pulp with a football helmet – only to open her starey eyes in a feeble punch line.

A cut-and-dried melodrama, with obvious performances (token sympathy for the madwoman goes nowhere) and little suspense. Directed by Morgan J. Freeman (*American Psycho 2, Piggy Banks*). Scripted by Katie L. Fetting.

HOSTEL PART III (2011)

'THE HONEYMOON ISN'T QUITE OVER YET, ELITE HUNTING CLUB MEMBERS. NOW WHO WANTS TO BID ON KILLING THE GROOM?'

Yes, there's a *Hostel Part III*. Eli Roth scores a 'based on characters created by' credit, but makes way for director Scott Spiegel (*From Dusk Till Dawn 2: Texas Blood Money*) and sequel specialist screenwriter Michael Weiss (*The Butterfly Effect 2, I'll Always Know What You Did Last Summer*). Gone are the Euro locations – indeed, though set in Las Vegas, this was mostly made in Michigan – and the only half-recognisable face is guest star Thomas Kretschmann.

In a switcheroo, touristy looking Travis (Chris Coy) checks into a hostel room to find a bald, threateny Ukrainian guy (Nickola Shreli) and his tempting babe girlfriend (Evelina Oboza) exuding sinister vibes… but the Yank is the Elite Hunting operative and the foreigners get to be victims. Then, it becomes a gruesome riff on *The Hangover* – which would be awesome if the cast of the *Hangover* films had signed on to play the same characters – as Carter (Kip Pardue) arranges a Vegas bachelor party for his pal Scott (Brian Hallisay). After exposition with doomed characters – obnoxious party animal Mike (Skyler Stone), sensitive cripple Justin (John Hensley), nice hooker Kendra (Sarah Habel), meaner hooker Nikki (Zulay Henao) – folks are dragged out to a torture facility in the desert.

The format is a bit different, with maimings performed for an audience of high-rollers who play a sick bingo, betting on which pleas victims will make or how long they'll survive. Turns are slightly more elaborate, yet stupid: Mike has his face peeled off, Nikki is choked with cockroaches while dressed as a cheerleader, Justin is shot full of crossbow bolts by a dominatrix in a 'Japanese cyberpunk mask'. Woodenly written and flatly played – only Hensley has worthwhile moments, including telling his murderess, 'It's all right,' as he dies – this maintains the series' contempt for people and devotion to thin female characters and cartoonish villains.

HOUSE OF 9 (2005)

A strangers-wake-up-in-a-confined-space-and-turn-on-each-other horror/suspense/mystery – coming along late enough to be as influenced by *Big Brother* as *And Then There Were None*, *Cube*, *Saw* or *My Little Eye*.

A disparate group of abducted folk wake in a well-appointed, entirely sealed complex. An unseen voice (Jim Carter) reveals that the sole survivor will win five million dollars. A semi-accidental death gets the ball rolling, and soon the cross-section of averagely nasty folks are bludgeoning, stabbing, electrocuting and shooting each other. The roll call: Father Duffy (Dennis Hopper), a priest with a dodgy Irish accent; Lea (Kelly Brook), a chorus dancer who is a) hot and b) not bitchy – so plainly has a good shot at making it; Francis (Hippolyte Girardot), a washed-up French composer on the outs with his once-wealthy wife Cynthia (Julienne Davis); Max Roy (Peter Capaldi), a gay fashion designer who worries about only having one outfit ('My jacket's in there,' he complains when the others lock a loose cannon in one of the rooms); Jay (Raffaello Degruttola), a gun-toting American cop; Claire (Susie Amy), a supposed tennis player who comes on as a doesn't-give-a-shit party slut; Al B (Asher D/Ashley Walters), a mouthy, defensive rapper who is first to kill (no black stereotype there, then); and Shona (Morven Christie), a junkie waif on probation with a security anklet. In a neatly grim punch line, the survivor is let out, hugging a big bag of cash, only to face several battered strangers who are clutching their big wins and realise the game now moves up to a champions' league level.

Only Hopper is poor (and that's down to trying to do an accent): it might count as misdirection to cast him as a priest then *not* have him turn out to be shamming decency to cover craziness, but it's also a waste to employ a great screen maniac and not let him be a villain. Even players who come across as irritating (Amy, D) are plainly supposed to, and Girardot, Capaldi and Christie manage to be subtly creepy as they react in slightly off fashion to the situation (Max becomes obsessed with the food – delivered in bigger portions after each kill). The mausoleum-like lair – all marble, concrete, lush drapes over bricked-up windows and upscale hotel light-fittings and bathrooms – is well used. Written by Philippe Vidal; directed by Steven R. Monroe, who progressed to cut-above-average Syfy schlock (*Ogre*, *It Waits*) before doing humanity the dubious favour of reviving the *I Spit On Your Grave* franchise.

THE HUMAN RACE (2013)

This intense, gloomy, hyperactive science fiction film seems at first like a riff on *Battle Royale*… a selection of random folks from around the globe are snatched from ordinary lives and wake up near a derelict factory where they are told they must race around a course. They must not step on the grass or allow themselves to be lapped twice… on penalty of their heads CGI exploding. There are more exploding heads here than in the entire *Scanners* series, with the first suffered by the nice woman (Brianna Lauren Jackson) who seemed to be the protagonist. To up the brutality quotient, peculiarly shaped scimitars are available for contestants to use on each other. Many runners have handicaps, some miraculously removed – a pair of deaf joggers (Trista Robinson, T. Arthur Cottam) find they can hear, but Eddie (Eddie McGee) and Justin (Paul McCarthy-Boyington), the one-legged war veterans who emerge as lead characters, don't get their limbs back.

A variant on the wake-up-in-a-room horror contest story, but outdoors and with 75 players. Some characters try to help others, but a French cyclist (Fred Coury) is determined to win by running according to the rules – even if it means twice-lapping a pregnant woman (who dies when her unborn baby's head explodes!) – while some goons reckon they just need to lie in wait and toss folk onto the grass. Eddie and Justin try to get out of the game by not running and not letting others pass – which means they'll starve, if without the guilt of offing others – but are dragged into it. The deaf folk fall out when the guy makes the moves on the flirty girl and is rebuffed – he can't bring himself to rape her, but she *can* bring herself to kill him and becomes the most ruthless antagonist.

The survivor learns that this is an *Outer Limits* premise – the winner of the elimination heat will now represent humanity in single combat with a winged alien who has won his own contest by crucifying others of his species. Obviously misanthropic, but writer-director Paul Hough (son of John) deserves credit for non-stereotype depiction of otherly-abled characters.

HUNGER (2009)

> 'NOT TO BE NEGATIVE, BUT HOW ARE YOU GOING TO GET THROUGH A BRICK WALL WITH A TIN CUP.'

Another set of seemingly randomly assembled folk wake in a cellar, forced to participate in an experiment to test the limits of humanity. The subjects – all implicated in the deaths of others (self-defence, mercy killing, etc.) – are walled in a basement dungeon with a clock that ticks off days (suggesting a thirty-day frame for the experiment) and enough water to keep them going for a month while a bearded 'scientist' (Bjorn Johnson) listens to classical music and waits for them to resort to cannibalism.

Everyone goes mad in a different way – humane doctor Jordan (Lori Heuring) sticks up for decency despite everything, but crazy chick Anna (Lea Kohl) eventually manipulates psycho teen Luke (Joe Egender) into killing okay alpha guy Grant (Linden Ashby) for food shared with ranting nutcase Alex (Julian Rojas), triggering a body count which goes into overdrive when the thirty days are up and it becomes clear (in a muddy sort of way) they're still not getting out. The motive, established in flashbacks to 8-track tape days, is that the scientist was trapped in a car with his mother and ate bits of her. He can't bear to think this *isn't* a universal human survival impulse, making for *WAZ*-type conflict with a heroine who is prepared to die for her principles (Heuring is quite good). A happy outcome (heroic music, sunlight, newborn imagery) is more bathetic than uplifting, especially since redemption comes after 101 minutes of misery on the cheap. Written by L.D. Goffigan; directed by Steven Hentges.

THE HUNTERS (2011)

This variant on 'The Most Dangerous Game' (urtext of torture/abduction/survival horror) has a gutsy style, a great central location and surprisingly nuanced, unstereotyped characters. Though one big reveal is guessable.

In an overworked trope, a prologue shows bloodied characters screaming in extremis, followed by a 'one week earlier' caption and a loop back to calmer times. Teacher Ronny (Steven Waddington), IT drone Oliver (Tony Becker), busboy-boxer Stephen (Jay Brown) and exchange student William (Xavier Delambre) live unappreciated, put-upon lives, but spend their weekends hunting people. Ex-military cop Le Saint (Chris Briant, who also directed – and does a surprisingly good double job) is barked at by the police chief (Terence Knox) when he talks about investigating the rash of missing persons cases. Le Saint, who has PTSD, meets cute while jogging with Alice (Dianna Agron), a nice girl who figures in the climax, but not as the expected victim/trophy.

Obviously, all the characters collide one weekend at decommissioned Fort Gopin, a wooded area enclosed by a moat, concrete walls and tripwire bombs, with decommissioned bunkers suitable for torture games and a Zaroff-like museum of severed heads. Le Saint arranges to meet a snitch at the fort and, after encountering the hunters, has to go on the run, hindered by a drug-tipped blowdart wound. Alice drifts in, with a doomed boyfriend, just as the hunters are learning the resourceful Le Saint isn't an easy kill.

The array of killers is interesting, suggesting a crisis of masculinity. Mostly men in undervalued professions who take daily shit from suits and troublemakers, they are ground down, resentful and backed into a corner in daily life, but monstrous when let off the leash. The boxing busboy also has a semi-erotic relationship with the mute stone psycho William, who juggles with a severed head and plays with his prey. While the nastiest of the crew is despised by his comrades for being more interested in raping than hunting his prey. It looks good, and has decent dialogue – some in subtitled French, since this is less ashamed of its Canadian identity than most Canucksploitationers. Scripted by Michael Lehman.

I-LIVED (2015)

Vlogger Josh (Jeremiah Watkins) posts reviews of apps. i-LIVED, a smartphone life-coaching app, promises to help him attain goals with a series of challenges and rewards: a six-pack stomach, many more followers, a hot girlfriend, getting his nagging landlady of his back, remission for his mother's terminal illness. Of course, as the app's reverse-writing name suggests, there's a sinister downside to self-improvement. The wittiest element of this smart, up-to-the-moment Faust variant is that the soul-selling contract with the Devil is in the 'terms and conditions' screed Josh scrolls through to click 'accept' without even reading.

In the early 2000s, a cluster of films (the Thai *13 Game of Death* and the French *13 Tzameti* and their US remakes) had hapless protagonists play games which require they commit an escalating series of crimes to gain an ultimate reward while losing dignity, mind and soul. *i-Lived* is the Pokémon Go era version of that storyline, with YouTube clips, skype calls, phone alert pings, remote-access security cams and tech frills deployed for horrors. Director-writer Franck Khalfoun (*P2*, the *Maniac* remake) and beaky lead actor Watkins (carrying the film with nervous energy) start out light with a zeitgeisty indie comedy about relationships in the age of social media. The app's first advice is mild and positive (do six good things, be more assertive) and the credibly flawed but likeable protagonist can believe that the change in his fortunes is mostly a coincidence as he hooks up with the slinky, only slightly creepy Greta (Sarah Power) and is offered a corporate sponsor. However, when he impulsively cancels i-LIVED, it all falls apart and eventually he crawls back, even admitting that he's made a diabolic bargain, and strays well away from comedy territory into darker, torture-porn realms as the missions he's set ('Kidnap somebody.') become crueller and more dangerous. And a mystery man with a black umbrella dogs his digital footprint – a nicely enigmatic touch.

Khalfoun throws in references to earlier generations of devils, with a descending lift from *Angel Heart* and a smooth Satan (Brian Breiter) posing before strategic antlers in his *Devil's Advocate*-look den. The Faust story has been told and retold since the

15th century for very good reasons, as each age finds fresh meaning in it – *i-Lived* pertinently skewers new digital-age sins alongside age-old cruelties.

THE INCIDENT (1967)

A telling aspect of this suspenseful drama is that its villains display a fiendish sadism which prefigures 1970s exploitation horrors like *The Last House on the Left* but commit crimes which barely count as misdemeanours. As creeps hassle passengers on a New York elevated train, name-calling, intimidation and jostling seem more upsetting than many a movie killing. Screenwriter Nicholas E. Baehr wrote this first as a 1963 TV drama bluntly called *Ride with Terror*; the confined setting and the way each character gets grilled in turn evoke the stage-like construction of 1950s live-TV dramas like *Twelve Angry Men* (1954). It opens with noirish black-and-white intensity as Joe (Tony Musante) and Artie (Martin Sheen) bully the owner of a pool parlour. In a creepy chat, Joe needles Artie – 'Has anybody ever told you you're a little nuts?… They're wrong, you're a *lot* nuts.' – about the fact he has equal enthusiasm for 'pigeons' (mugging victims) and 'broads', establishing a homoerotic undercurrent to their violent double act. Joe, with vast sideburns and an open shirt, shows off his ratty, feral grin (he's a talker, using words more cruelly than his switchblade) while Artie mostly chuckles, though he has a nastily intelligent streak, coaxing a victim into accepting a roughing-up by saying he has to put on a show for his crazy friend.

Vignettes introduce other folk going home late on Sunday night, mostly after bad evenings… though hometown soldier Carmatti (Robert Bannard) has introduced Oklahoma pal Felix (Beau Bridges), who has a broken arm, to his lively ethnic family. Ex-alcoholic Douglas (Gary Merrill) brushes off a men's room pick-up by nervy, unflamboyant gay Kenneth (Robert Fields). Beckerman (Jack Gilford) complains about his ungrateful son while his wife (Thelma Ritter) wishes he'd keep quiet about his resentment of the young. Veiled Muriel (Jan Sterling) rounds on her bespectacled failure husband Harry (Mike Kellin) after a cocktail party. Stud Tony (Victor Arnold) freezes out shy blonde date Alice (Donna Mills), manipulating her into putting out. Militant (or just plain angry) black Arnold (Brock Peters) fumes against his social worker wife Joan (Ruby Dee). Cheapskate Wilks (Ed McMahon) persuades wife (Diana van der Vlis) not to spring for a cab, so they have to cart their four-year-old home on the el. All these people get into the horribly grubby train. Joe and Artie get boisterous, which makes everyone else look away, then start abusing a hapless, insensible wino. Former-boozer Douglas tells the hoods to leave the drunk alone. When no one backs him up, the rules change. Joe enforces the reasoning that if someone isn't your friend why should you care what happens to them. Joe shows near-demonic insight into his victims. Rather than accept support from passengers who enjoy watching him make people they dislike squirm, he attacks them too. Arnold enjoys the spectacle of whiteys at each others' throats, but fumes when Joe lets loose a stream of racial abuse. Arnold seems set to fight back, but he humiliatingly reins in his anger – an explanation comes at the end, when the cops barge into the carriage and instantly cuff the lone black guy on the assumption he caused all the trouble.

It's terrifically cast. Musante and Sheen – then unfamiliar, dynamic newcomers – have charisma to burn, while all the familiar faces do exceptional work (Merrill and Sterling, especially). Directed by Larry Peerce.

INSHITE MIRU: 7-KAKAN NO DESU GÊMU (DEATH GAME; THE INCITE MILL) (2010)

> 'YOU MAY ENCOUNTER IMMORAL AND IRRATIONAL SITUATIONS BEYOND THIS POINT. PROCEED ONLY IF YOU CAN ACCEPT THIS.'

In a canny mix of *And Then There Were None* with *My Little Eye*, ten random folk sign up for a suspiciously well-paid experiment. Locked in a customised subterranean facility (Paranoia House or The Incite Mill) with a ceiling-mounted enforcer robot called Guard, they have the rules explained by a talking Ten Little Indians table-piece. There's a *The Last of Sheila* element too: each participant has a card key for a lockbox containing a murder weapon from a famous fictional mystery. John Dickson Carr, Arthur Conan Doyle, Wilkie Collins, Agatha Christie and SS Van Dine are namechecked (though the fireplace poker from 'The Adventure of the Speckled Band' was a prop in a contest of strength, not a weapon). Jittery Nishino (Masanori Ishii), who starts the week throwing accusations around, is found shot dead. Since there are bonuses for being a victim, a murderer or a detective, wiseass med student Yudai (Tsuyoshi Abe) steps up and accuses Iwai (Shinji Takeda), who is confined in a jail area after a vote is taken on his guilt... but the murders continue.

With the second killing, self-harming young Wakana (Aya Hirayama) is shown using a nailgun on older mystery fan Fuchi (Nagisa Katahira) – but that doesn't tie up the whodunit since *everyone* (including the robot!) has a secret. Older drunken guy Ando (Kin'ya Kitaôji) signed up because his slacker son was killed during an earlier game, and seemingly nice girl Shoko (Haruka Ayase) is a plant by the organisers. The lead is Yuki (Tatsuya Fujiwara – from the *Battle Royale* and *Death Note* films), a spiky haircut nice guy who doesn't try to be killer, corpse or detective. A brief cutaway shows the netcast game being followed by the usual rich sicko subscribers found in these films. It takes a lot from Christie, with ten easily identifiable, contrasted characters whose interplay ups the tension and a confined setting which is eerie enough even without the deaths. The ceiling-rail-mounted robot is especially cool. Directed by Hideo Nakata (*Ringu*) and scripted by Satoshi Suzuki from a novel by Honobu Yonezawa.

IRON DOORS (2010)

Another essay in confinement, though the concrete vault – with bank-style huge circular iron doors – in which the unnamed protagonist (Axel Wedekind) is trapped affords more space than the coffin of *Buried* and is equipped with handier items (cutting and battering tools, a hidden key, edible dead vermin) than the structure of *Cube*. The lead, a slick businessman who first assumes it's a gag, rails and debases himself – recycling his urine, eating dead flies ('At least they're organic.') – before working on escape. He breaks into a near-identical chamber where he finds a French-speaking African woman (Rungano Nyoni) in a coffin. They find it hard to communicate, but eventually work together on the wall, sing songs (he favours Bert Lahr's 'If I Were King of the Forest', from *The Wizard of Oz* – which might be a clue) and even make love. An American movie might have them torture each other, but this German film doesn't go there... the only menace is imprisonment, which remains mysterious up to and beyond the end (spoiler warning!), when the doors arbitrarily open to disclose an alien (or heavenly) landscape into which this new Adam and Eve wander. The enigmatic punch line raises questions beyond the usual who-is-doing-this-and-why-is-it-happening business. The performers are good and surprisingly subtle, but Peter Arneson's script has too much what-I'm-doing-now commentary. Directed by Stephen Manuel.

JUE MING PAI DUI (INVITATION ONLY) (2009)

A basic but interesting Taiwanese torture/game-themed horror movie. Minion Wade (Bryant Chang) is among a select group of regular people offered access to an exclusive, rich folks' party. In addition to any hard-to-get item they ask for, like a grand piano or a sports car (one girl asks for her childhood teddy bear), they are given a taste of the high-life from fabulous roulette winnings to sex with a supermodel (Maria Ozawa). However, the special guest imposters (they lie to each other, too) are sneered at by the real rich folks, then hunted and tortured by masked plutocrats. There's a nice contrast between the main villain, Yang (Jerry Huang) – who suffered a traumatic kidnap in childhood and thus at least has a reason for insane hatred of the underclass – and the woman who backs this horrible game-of-death because she thinks her manicurist gossips behind her back. The stalking/torture scenes run from cabaret-style performances observed by well-dressed, jaded audiences – with the heroine Hitomi (Julianne Chu) trying to blend in wearing a formal gown whipped up from curtains – to a car chase involving the prize Ferrari. Written by Chang Chia-Cheng, Carolyn Lin; directed and edited by Kevin Ko.

THE KEEPER (2004)

That *Collector-Misery* premise again.

Pole-dancer Gina (Asia Argento) survives a brush with a murderous rapist then wakes in a basement cell under the home of sheriff-cum-puppeteer Krebs (Dennis Hopper), who believes in 'the points system' whereby the prisoner earns privileges by being 'good'. A sub-plot has an ambitious agent (Helen Shaver) trying to promote Krebs' hand-puppet character into a TV franchise and making romantic advances to the cop, who lives alone in a house in the middle of the woods (cue 'You can scream all you want...' speech) so he can pursue his hobby. Persistent deputy Burns (Lochlyn Munro) tries to trace the supposedly disappeared witness so she can identify her original attacker, and confusingly comes across earlier victims who may have fallen prey to the rapist-killer *or* the mad sheriff. Krebs' mania has a psychological 'explanation' (illustrated with puppets!): his tough cop father killed his stripper mother then himself. Gina freaks out, works out, plays nice, makes the usual botched escape attempts and survives. Argento doesn't make any acting connection with Hopper, making this a disappointing teaming of two cult players.

Not very suspenseful, it's directed in the plodding style Paul Lynch perfected on '80s schlock like *Prom Night* and *Humongous*. Written by TV journeyman Gerald Sanford, who's been around since *The Virginian* and *Night Gallery*. Smallness of scale means having to take some things on trust – there's little sense of the mushrooming popularity of Hopper's drug-bashing puppet, Deputy Rock. The subsequent, mealier-mouthed *Black Snake Moan* borrows a lot from this exploitation item.

THE KILLING ROOM (2009)

> 'THESE TAPES DO NOT EXIST. THIS ROOM DOES NOT EXIST.'

Another single-setting, sadistic social experiment (cf: *Cube*, *Exam*, *Breathing Room*), inspired by urban legends of the CIA's MK-ULTRA program.

Dr Phillips (Peter Stormare) works with potential candidate Reilly (Chloë Sevigny) to supervise one among many focus groups. Four folks – 'veteran lab rat' Crawford (Timothy Hutton), down-and-out Paul (Nick Cannon), wiseass Tony (Shea Whigham) and jittery Kerry (Clea DuVall) – fill in forms and hope to earn a few hundred dollars for a day of unknown tests. Phillips shoots Kerry dead in the room, and withdraws, leaving the other three to get through several more phases of testing built around simple questions like, 'If asked to pick a number between one and thirty-three which do most Americans choose?' and, 'How does America rank in the table of IQ?' Also involved is knock-out gas, a gun with a single bullet, possible interventions, mind games and thwarted escapes. The upshot is an attempt to identify traits which would persuade someone to become 'a civilian weapon' (i.e. American suicide bomber).

It's a decent enough premise, though the film loses tension by switching too often from the room to the observers. A better-than-expected cast deliver good performances, but the Gus Krieger-Ann Peacock script has a we've-been-here-before problem. Director Jonathan Liebesman was between early horror assignments (*Darkness Falls*, *The Texas Chainsaw Massacre: The Beginning*) and bigger budget hackwork (*Battle Los Angeles*, *Wrath of the Titans*, *Teenage Mutant Ninja Turtles*); at that, this may be his best film.

LIVE FEED (2006)

An instance of the 'premake' phenomenon, whereby something which looks like a ripoff turns out to have been made *before* the film it seems to imitate. Examples are *The Last Broadcast*, overshadowed by *The Blair Witch Project*, and *Return of the Secaucus Seven*, forerunner of *The Big Chill*. A particularly hateful torture-a-thon, *Live Feed* could easily pass as a cheapskate *Hostel*... but was made first.

Five know-nothing Yanks on a 'cocaine and porn' holiday in China wander into a Triad sex club where sordid private rooms are bugged. Their torture by a masked giant (Mike Bennett), who evokes a character in the worthless *8MM*, is videotaped and viewed by the usual nebulous rich sickos. Stressing the title's double meaning, the corpses are recycled for a cannibal buffet. Japanese dude Miles (Kevan Ohtsji), brother of a murdered undercover cop, intervenes to save the nicest of the crowd (Taayla Markell) and gets vengeance by doing away with the ring of baddies. That's about it for plot – the rest is party-hearty footage with the usual disgust at dog-eating Eastern degenerates and endless 'Why are you doing this?' torture sessions conducted by cackling baddies out of H.G. Lewis or (considering the 'Yellow Peril' angle) Fu Manchu.

Stephen Chang beats stiff competition (notably from Hawaiian-shirted Ted Friend as the pretend-innocent) to give the worst performance as the baddie boss whose evil girlfriend insists on eating white man's genitals as a delicacy (and not in a good way). Directed choppily by Ryan Nicholson, from a script co-written with Roy Nicholson; they have a makeup effects background, so the splatter is more convincing that most ketchup-sloshing cheapies. The hysterical non-performances and written-on-an-old-envelope dialogue are typical though.

THE LOVED ONES (2009)

Though at heart another tied-to-a-chair-and-tortured film, this Australian debut from writer-director Sean Byrne rings the changes on an overworked form, owing more to Stephan Elliott (in *Frauds* or *Welcome to Woop Woop* mode) than Eli Roth. Material which is usually filler – comic relief teen hijinx, the police investigation, secondary characters catching on to what's wrong, angsty family tragedy – is all tied intimately to the central situation, and considerably deepens the black comic ordeal.

In a prologue, long haired teenager Brent (Xavier Samuel) is bantering with his dad while driving home when a bloody figure shows up in the middle of the road. Brent loses control of the car and his father dies in the crash. Months later, Brent has taken to cutting himself and can't connect with his girlfriend Holly (Victoria Thaine). When wallflower Lola (Robin McLeavy) asks him to take her to the dance, he is more disturbed than touched. Later, while climbing – he seeks out dangerous situations from guilt over his father's death – he is bagged and snatched by Eric (John Brumpton), Lola's loving, disturbed father. Brent is tied to a chair (of course) in the isolated Stone house, which is festooned with balloons and party lights. Lola appears in a pink dress, expressing manic glee that shows she's gone beyond playing with Barbie dolls and dreaming of perfect romance to persuading her father to kidnap hot guys so they can be transformed into her dates by power-drill lobotomy (a prelude to the real brain-boiling process, which involves a kettle of hot water). Eric has already turned Lola's mother (Anne Scott-Pendlebury) into 'Bright Eyes', a lolling zombie, and the cellar is stocked with other failed attempts at 'loved ones' (Lola has a scrapbook about them, and chatters callously about their fates). Brent is pinned to the floor by knives through his feet, drugged and dressed up formally, and has a love-heart carved on his chest with a fork, but wisely keeps quiet through the long night as the psychos do all the spieling.

BTK horror has thrown up too many similar restraint situations, but Byrne does more with the familiar material than many an exploitative hack: we get mad tea parties, sawn-through ropes (Brent has his cutting razorblade as a necklet), gruesomely permanent assaults (the drilling is especially painful – a first try skitters off Brent's forehead because the girl doesn't put her weight behind it), casual humiliations (Brent has to pee in a glass) and a captive-overcomes-captors finale (Eric's fate goes back to Dr Moreau's). It's not a complete downer and the last-reel heroics hinge affectingly on the way Brent's ordeal opens him up emotionally (he really values the loyal Holly, who Lola is out to get). A wide-open-spaces climactic face-off (all great Aussie exploitation films take to the road eventually) ends with a satisfying punch line splat.

THE MAZE RUNNER (2014)

YA trilogies/series are almost as desirable to studios as comic book properties: an inbuilt audience of the books' fans, casts of youngish characters suitable for just-starting-out (i.e., more affordable than Tom Cruise) performers (*especially* young Brits who can do Yank accents, for some reason), simplistic yet drawn-out plots with sequel hooks, and premises reminiscent of previous successes. Yet, for each *Harry Potter*, *Twilight* or *The Hunger Games*, there's a *The Mortal Instruments*, *Beautiful Creatures* or *Golden Compass*. *The Maze Runner* falls in the middle of the pack – like *Divergent*, it did well enough not to have the sequels cancelled, but still feels makeshift and derivative. The most expensive cross-section-of-people-wake-in-a-weird-environment-not-remembering-how-they-got-there film, it's also among the least interesting.

Almost all the characters are teenage boys, with a basic conflict between innovative newcomer ('greenie') Thomas (Dylan O'Brien) and conservative semi-bully Gally (Will Poulter) over what to do rather than an all-out *Lord of the Flies* brutal pecking order. Even throwing a girl (underused Kaya Scodelario) in the mix doesn't stir things up – though Gally tries human sacrifice to appease the 'grievers', giant biomechanical spider-scorpions who police the ever-changing maze which surrounds the glade where the boys are trapped. It turns out to be a science experiment and a recorded sinister matriarch/researcher (Patricia Clarkson) yadda-yaddas about sunspots, billions of deaths, doomed humanity, a plague and essence of young brains being the answer to it all. That comes too late to satisfy as a solution to a setup which always seems more arbitrary than mysterious.

Even the title is weird – why stress running when the main job of maze runners is exploration and mapping? Of course, most of the running is because monsters no one has seen and lived to tell of before the film starts are suddenly all over the place, though ineffective in killing named characters when there are virtual extras to be grabbed and tossed away. Written by Noah Oppenheim, Grant Pierce Myers and T.S. Nowlin, from the novel by James Dashner; directed by Wes Ball.

NERVE (2016)

Like *i-Lived*, *Nerve* retools the escalating dare game scenarios of *13 Tzameti* and *13: Game of Death* for the era of Pokémon Go and brushfire social media crazes. Scripted by Jessica Sharzer (*American Horror Story*) from Jeanne Ryan's young adult novel, it benefits from the zeitgeist-surfing enthusiasm of directors Henry Joost and Ariel Schulman, who segued from trend-naming documentary *Catfish* to a couple of *Paranormal Activity* sequels.

Smart, shy Staten Island teen Vee (Emma Roberts) has a momentary spat with her more daring best friend Sydney (Emily Meade) and impulsively signs up for Nerve, a smartphone game in which players accept crowdsourced dares for money. The game hooks Vee up with Ian (Dave Franco), a veteran player with a dark past. After she kisses him in a diner and he performs an impromptu song and dance, they go on a wild ride in New York – escaping from a posh store in their underwear, Vee getting a tattoo (a lighthouse in honour of her favourite book, Virginia Woolf's *To the Lighthouse*), Ian riding a motorcycle blindfolded at 60 m.p.h. in city traffic, etc. Vee's nurse mom (Juliette Lewis) is out of the loop, but a crush-nurturing male best friend (Miles Heizer) keeps track of her course. Sydney is annoyed to be outdone by her former sidekick – which leads to an info dump exchange of cruel truth-telling – while Ian is marked by an even more out-there reckless player, Ty (Machine Gun Kelly). Most takes on this theme go dark early, but *Nerve* lightly skims the surface, playing as a teen meet-cute hijinx comedy with sinister undertones and, unusually, some depth for peripheral characters as Vee's emerging wild, fun side estranges her from longtime friends.

In the last act, horrors come to the fore as Vee learns there are three categories in the game – player, watcher and prisoner. Snitching to the cops means being reassigned to the latter role, where challenges can't be refused or a hacker collective will destroy your life. It winds up at an arena where masked anonymous watchers egg a trio of players to murder – and a moral lecture is delivered between plot twists. Roberts and Franco (slightly overage for their roles) have goofy charm to spare and Joost-Schulman frame them with a fast, restless, click-through style which puts this in a league with *Unfriended* and *Open Windows* in matching form to trending subject matter. A risk of this sort of thing, of course, is that it's dated by the time the review embargo expires – it arrived just after Pokémon Go peaked – but a nugget of universal character stuff remains meaningful. Without a *Fast & Furious* budget for action, it stretches to good suspense sequences involving dangling from high places.

NIGHT DRIVE (2010)

'IF IT'S ANY CONSOLATION, YOUR SON DIED SCREAMING LIKE A FUCKING BUSH-PIG.'

This South African production plays the survival horror game with a specific local angle. Instead of recycling American/European tropes (inbred backwoodsmen, torture porn, organ snatching), this is about poachers in a nature reserve. In addition to slaughtering rhinos for horn, they hunt refugees for body parts used in magic rituals ('muti'). The villains, unseen for most of the film, are associated with jackals, and the script spins fresh mythology about them (a witch doctor who dresses in jackal skins has a boogeyman rep)... though the storyline is standard. Sean Darwin (Christopher Beasley), an undercover cop kicked off the force after a mission gone wrong, takes a wilderness tour guided by his father, Jack (Greg Melvill-Smith), who would rather be fighting poachers, to scatter his mother's ashes (the family has too much backstory for its own good).

Vignettes establish other tourists... a young, sexy, urban black couple (Antonio David Lyons, Matshepo Maleme)... an embittered middle-aged Afrikaans cokehead and his wife (Brandon Auret, Corine Du Toit)... and a pair of British OAPs (David Sherwood, Clare Marshall) on a fiftieth anniversary trip. In the bush, the tour runs across a woman who has been dissected alive and are harried by the poachers – though the unstable, gun-toting member of the group is as much trouble until he gets killed, and an elderly Brit has a heart attack at a bad time. It picks up on the worst aspects of South Africa and exploits them for horror, but no more than American films caricature poor backwoods folks or misrepresent Eastern Europe or South America. There is some discussion of the state of crime in post-apartheid Africa, with all of the characters having been victims or perpetrators in the past, and the difficulty of shucking off the 'Dark Continent' stereotypes. Scripted by Justin Head and C.A. van Aswegen; directed by Head.

NOTHING (2003)

Admittedly, this title just begs for a put-down review. Following his influential debut *Cube*, Vincenzo Natali specialised in minimalist settings – this stab at nerd-comedy Beckett winds up in a surreally shrinking limbo.

A hectic reel establishes lifelong friends Dave (David Hewlett) and Andrew (Andrew Miller) as losers: Dave is on the point of moving out of the house under a freeway he shares with Andrew to shack up with his girlfriend, but finds she has used him to embezzle from his workplace (where everyone picks on him) and framed him; Andrew is an agoraphobic shut-in whose argument with a girl scout has escalated into molestation accusations. The pair, who argue all the time, are besieged by cops and city officials who want to knock down the house. They manage to 'hate away the world', stranding the house in a white, rubbery void where the duo find they can hate away their few remaining objects (including mental or physical aspects of themselves), but, crucially, not create anything. After wandering about, turning on each other and a final duel of hating, they are reduced to bouncing severed heads racing for an indefinite point, followed by their only friend and companion, a tortoise.

Hewlett and Miller, holdovers from *Cube*, carry the whole film, as unappealing characters who never quite reveal the depths of pathos or feeling which might make their situation involving. The void is a daring effect, reminiscent of 1960s *Doctor Who*, and the film brief enough not to get too repetitive, but it feels like a protracted short rather than, as with *Cube*, a simple idea thoroughly explored. There are, however, funny ideas: when Andrew hates away neuroses which have inhibited his creativity, Dave follows suit without improving as a drummer, then simply hates away the fact that he cares about being useless.

OCTOBER MOTH (1960)

The sole film directed by John Kruse (screenwriter of *Hell Drivers*, *Revenge* and *Assault*), this stark, pared-down British B could have been made as a silent, but also prefigures the abduction horrors of later years (a key thread is reminiscent of *The Living and the Dead*).

On an isolated farm, Finlay (Lee Patterson) – a childlike grownup given to tantrums and whims – is cared for by his sister Molly (Lana Morris, so good you wonder why she didn't go further) and haunted by memories of his evil drunkard father and saintly mother. One night, while attracting moths to a lantern, Finlay makes a car swerve off the road and brings home an unconscious woman (Sheila Raynor) he claims is his mother and won't be persuaded to take to hospital. Molly, leery of having doctors or police around for fear Finlay will be institutionalised, asks a passing telephone lineman (Peter Dyneley, doing a good Yorkshire accent) for help, though Finlay assumes he is Pa come back to torment him and reaches for a shotgun.

Kruse writes well, with the scenes between the siblings credibly on edge, and Finlay is an interesting menace. Not stupid, he argues like a clever, annoying child, pulling facts out of the sky and blankly refusing to be swayed. His mental impairment is not sentimentalised, and he becomes frightening when on the rampage, while co-dependent Molly is credibly trapped by a need to feel needed. It doesn't spell everything out – rare in A pictures of the era, let alone a 55-minute quickie. Though mostly shot in cramped interiors, a few night scenes make good use of the desolate moors.

100 FEET (2008)

> 'MIKE DID THIS TO ME.'
> 'MARNIE, MIKE'S DEAD.'
> 'YEAH? WELL, HE'S TAKING
> THE NEWS BADLY.'

Though *100 Feet* has a more interesting 'house arrest' premise than *Disturbia*, it similarly defaults to business as usual by the finale. Marnie Watson (Famke Janssen) is just out of prison after serving a brief term for killing her abusive husband Mike (Michael Paré), a cop whose angry partner Shanks (Bobby Cannavale) is responsible for supervising her house arrest. She has to wear an ankle-alarm and stay inside her large-ish New York apartment, which is haunted by the seriously pissed-off, still-violent Mike ('You know that line "till death do us part"? Well, it's a crock of shit.'). The haunting starts with glimpses, flying crockery and reappearing bloodstains, but soon becomes gruesomely physical. Marnie's delivery boy lover (Ed Westwick) is battered to death by an invisible presence, outlined *Hollow Man*-style when splattered with the victim's blood.

The 'rules' are that the ghost lingers because things he owned are still on site, giving Marnie the problem of throwing away her husband's clothes when she's not allowed to cross the street to hassle the garbage man. Janssen, onscreen throughout, is good as a tough woman in an extreme situation, as angry as she is terrified. Director/writer Eric Red (*The Hitcher*, *Near Dark*) keeps inventing ways for the ghost to force her to set off her alarm so she looks guilty when the cops come round. As in many non-supernatural stalker movies, the build-up – an innocent pushed further into a corner by an enemy who can't be touched – is more effective than the third act when the monster drops all pretence of subtlety and goes into monster mode by flinging Shanks around and starting a flaming holocaust in the building.

Red, who stayed out of prison on medical grounds after a conviction for vehicular homicide, pretties up his own record by making his heroine entirely not culpable; it might have been better drama if the original murder weren't so justifiable. Mostly manifesting as a white-faced lurker with black eyeholes, Paré – the werewolf uncle in Red's *Bad Moon* – makes a decently scary spectre.

OPEN HOUSE (2010)

Another chained-up-in-the-cellar film, with a slightly different (if implausible) angle. Alice (Rachel Blanchard) puts her minimalist home on the market. During an open house viewing session, David (Brian Geraghty) slips downstairs and hides, emerging to murder a dinner guest (Anna Paquin, sister of writer/director Andrew Paquin) and collect Alice. Lila (Tricia Helfer), David's elegant partner in crime, shows up and they settle in, murdering cleaners, estate agents and Alice's estranged husband (Stephen Moyer, husband of Anna Paquin), then stashing dismembered bits in boxes in the garage. The couple's MO involves repeatedly usurping a home, holding a dinner party which ends in an orgy of violence, then moving on... The glitch is that David wavers in his commitment to Lila and keeps Alice alive (albeit chained and occasionally whipped) as a potential replacement psycho sweetie. Naturally, it doesn't end well. Paquin tries for a low-key style to match the décor, with Geraghty playing buttoned-down and Helfer going all-out for femme fatale, but the pile of never-questioned corpses (doesn't anyone miss any of these folks?) and lack of interest in supposed normality-figure Alice make the plotting implausible and defuse attempts at will-she-make-it-and-what-will-be-left-of-her? suspense.

OTIS (2008)

The *Abbott and Costello Meet…* dictum states any given sub-genre becomes obsolete when parodied. This comedy take on the survival/abduction/torture cycle is also nasty enough to pass as just another hateful, unlovely film about captive women abused by a slobbering maniac. Despite a talented cast, the would-be comic tone means the extreme knockabout sequences fall into the Troma do-they-really-think-*this*-is-funny? category rather than the Takashi Miike/John Waters I-can't-believe-they-just-did-*that*! approach.

Blubbery forty-year-old Otis Broth (Bostin Christopher) chains abducted girls in a basement, and batters and shocks them into playing along with his high school fantasies in which they are called Kim (after a sister-in-law we never meet) and he's the football hero who has sex with her in the car on the way home from the prom. When the girls disappoint, they wind up dead, dismembered and dumped. Otis, a pizza delivery man, snatches Riley Lawson (Ashley Johnson) and puts her into his scenario. The kitsch décor and teen movie roleplay signals black comedy (prefiguring the more successful *The Loved Ones*), but the bruises Riley sustains whenever Otis knocks her out to deal with his bullying brother Elmo (Kevin Pollak) are in no way funny. Scenes in which Otis punishes Riley until she answers to 'Kim' or telephones her parents with tormenting details of what he'll do to her after the prom are authentically upsetting, and farcical treatment suggests want of feeling on the part of the writers (Erik Jendresen, Thomas Schnauz) and director (Tony Krantz of *Sublime*) rather than an attitude. As Riley suffers, her absurd family – dad (Daniel Stern), mom (Illeana Douglas) and trouble-making kid brother (Jared Kusnitz) – fret through the crisis, which is mishandled by a comedy idiot FBI agent (Jere Burns) whose *Get Smart* antics unbalance the movie. When Riley escapes, Mom insists she not identify Otis to the FBI so they can take *The Last House on the Left* revenge, which they screw up by catching the wrong Broth Brother and torturing Elmo to death in a slapstick manner (involving electric wires shoved up the ass and a too-short flex, with the possibility of a fingers-and-toes smoothie). The Lawsons realise their mistake too late and the film dawdles without any resolution.

Christopher is an inflated version of the psychos Pruitt Taylor Vince plays in *Captivity* and *Identity*; he has presence and menace, but it's too much of an ask to sympathise with Otis as a bullying victim when he's such a nasty piece of work. Stern and Douglas are broad but effective as self-involved liberals who become squabbling torturers, while Johnson is excellent in unworthy surroundings.

PAINTBALL (2009)

A hardcore paintball krewe are dropped in a forest somewhere in Eastern Europe – which should warn them something's wrong – to battle another team for a mystery championship. Assigned ranks and specialties, they are ordered to capture flags and open boxes containing useful gadgets. When the first box has a flak jacket, even more alarm bells should ring.

Yes, it's a game of death and someone is firing real bullets. It takes the green-team folks too long to catch on, even when they find an electrified fence and a fried orange-team member clutching the wire. The fully armed Hunter (Felix Pring), who uses night-sight heat-seeking goggles even in daylight, works for 'the Organisation' – who observe the kills from an underground bunker. The anonymous psycho refrains from taking easy shots early to string out the game, but soon goes off the books. The paintballers are thinly characterised: the 'final girl' (Jennifer Matter) accidentally kills an opposing team member with a machete, and needs to redeem herself; the team leader (Brendan Mackey) is a selfish baddie happy to off his own mates for reasons which remain vague.

Director Daniel Benmayor (*Tracers*) favours long shots of people squabbling or running in camo gear, which makes it hard to tell characters apart. Gamers cling to their useless paintball guns, pointing them as if they were real long after it's clear that the rules have changed. An odd, *Sin City*-ish frill is that the most gruesome moments are seen through goggles, rendering splats of blood as pure white paint. The rationale – social experiment? internet snuff? mercenary training? – is vague, the action not up to much and the no-name cast uniformly shrill. Written by Mario Schoendorff.

PERFECT STRANGERS (2003)

This starts out as a *Misery*-style captivity picture, then takes another, odd direction. Melanie (Rachael Blake), a fish and chip server in a New Zealand coastal town, is ragged on the one-night-stand scene. A handsome stranger (Sam Neill) picks her up in his boat, but the evening takes a strange course as she slumps asleep and wakes in a shack on an island with the nameless obsessive who has been stalking her. The abductor alternates fairy-tale metaphors and mild violence, then Melanie stabs him in the gut and they form a relationship as she nurses him… partly because she needs his instructions to get the boat back to the mainland, but also because she becomes strange and cracked too. The attempted escape goes wrong when The Man dies and the boat founders, leaving Melanie alone on the island with a corpse in the freezer. Former suitor Bill (Joel Tobeck) shows up late in the day, and the film again seesaws from menace to romance, as Melanie batters him with a spade and locks him up then marries him, though she's pregnant with The Man's baby and haunted by his imaginary presence. The leads are fine, even if director Gaylene Preston's script is reticent about where Neill's character is coming from. Preston (*Mr. Wrong*) is very good with actors: Blake, less familiar than Neill, is excellent, credibly appealing to a stalker but also looking like she's had more than a few rough years. Unusually, it suggests a creepy psycho lover ought to get some points for the genuine devotion that's part of the madness.

PET (2016)

On his regular bus to work at an animal shelter, lonely schmoe Seth (Dominic Monaghan) makes clumsy attempts to woo Holly (Ksenia Solo), a pretty blonde who was at high school with him. He researches her tastes (roses, seafood) on social media and rehearses pick-up lines, but his stratagems rebound because Holly, a would-be writer working as a waitress, is too fixed on her own complicated life even to notice him stalking her. After a bruising encounter with Holly's bartender ex (Nathan Parsons), Seth devises a fresh plan. He drugs Holly and cages her in a disused basement at work, intent on 'saving her'.

The first reel seems set on being another derivative of John Fowles' *The Collector* – often imitated since the 1965 William Wyler film but oddly never remade – but screenwriter Jeremy Slater (*The Lazarus Effect*, the ill-fated 2015 *Fantastic 4*) shifts tack as the balance of power in the basement changes. It turns out that the prickly Holly is by no means as ordinary as she seems, with a possible multiple personality – she has imaginary conversations with a best friend (Jeannette McCurdy) as she works angles to get out of the cage – and a maniacal streak which suggests the mild-mannered kidnapper may not be the most dangerous person in the room.

Pet depends on complex performances in initially standard-seeming roles from the leads – who are alone onscreen for much of the film. Monaghan manages a balance between creepy and pathetic, as a weak antagonist fated to become as much a captive of the situation as the girl in the cage, while Solo sells a series of far-fetched twists as a strange heroine with dark secrets and a long-term escape plan which sets up an ending that goes beyond the expected table-turning to deliver a *Tales From the Crypt*-ish nasty chuckle. Directed by Carles Torrens (*Apartment 143*).

PRESERVATION (2014)

Though basically a *The Most Dangerous Game* riff, complete with the obligatory moment where someone steps in a man-trap, writer-director Christopher Denham's neat, sharp little film has an interesting dynamic.

Wit Neary (Wrenn Schmidt), a citified vegetarian but not a dolt, is taken to a wildlife preserve by her yuppie husband Mike (Aaron Staton) and his PTS-suffering veteran brother Sean (Pablo Schreiber). The brothers, survivors of a tough childhood and uncomfortable with each other, want to return to a woodland where they once played… though the area is chained off, its tourist centre abandoned and vandalised. Aimless, simmering Sean envies the cell phone-addicted Mike's career and beautiful (just pregnant) wife. He also doesn't want to talk about why he was discharged from the services. After a night camping, the trio wake to find their shoes and supplies stolen and an unknown enemy stalking them… but Mike half-thinks his brother has staged this to show off survival skills.

The interesting drama is among the central trio, but masked hunters are in the game, tormenting prey with torture-by-hope stunts like water bottles hung over concealed traps. In *Deliverance-Southern Comfort* style, the most capable is killed and the others have to find the resources to survive. When, in a talk about hunting, Wit says she doesn't think she could ever kill anything, it's a tipoff that she'll eventually be put in a situation where she has to. The second half is more familiar as the heroine fights off the silent, masked Zaroffs – who text each other (and their victims) and turn out (when one takes a phone call from his mom) to be regular-seeming, preppie teens slightly older than the kids from *El Rey de la Montaña* but just as hung up on realising fantasy kill-games. There have perhaps been too many of these scarcely plausible bad seeds (cf: *The Strangers*), but *Preservation* makes more of its credible, complicated prey than the cliché hunters.

RAZE (2013)

A blunt, contrived entry in the cycle of films about folk abducted by rich sickos and forced to murder each other for entertainment. Films on this model (even *Gladiator*) share a problem: the scripts condemn villains who stage such spectacles (here, unarmed women fight each other to the death) and despise jaded audiences who get off on them... but the films pander to roughly the same base instincts. Snatched from her home, Jamie (exec producer Rachel Nichols) wakes up in a well-like stone walled room with Sabrina (Zoë Bell), only for the apparent viewpoint character to be killed in the first bout (an onscreen 'Jamie vs Sabrina' caption sets a convention not always followed). The tournament of 'maenads' is run by grotesque baddies: stick-thin Joseph (Doug Jones, looking like Evil John Waters), plump but glam Elizabeth (Sherilyn Fenn) and brutal guard Kurtz (Bruce Thomas). Fifty women have been snatched (with replacements for wastage, fifty-two are used – though we don't see all of them) and motivated by threats to assassinate loved ones.

Writer Robert Beaucage (who devised the story with Kenny Gage and director Josh C. Waller) finds variations on the woman versus woman scenario, with friends and enemies alike pitted against each other, some given full backgrounds, others just anonymous. Tracie Thoms, Bell's sidekick from *Death Proof*, and Bailey Anne Borders are the most sympathetic victims, while Rebecca Marshall goes over the top as a gangling, snarling sociopath who enjoys this whole game and is set up to take on Sabrina in a final bout that turns out, in a film with too much repetition, to be just a preliminary for a *final* final bout and a payback coda (Sabrina vs Everyone) capped with a '70s-style cut-down-from-afar depressing punch line. Bell is impressively physical in the repetitive fights – how many face-punches or headlocks does a film really need? – but doesn't sell Sabrina's cardboard character (an ex-POW fighting to save a daughter she gave up for adoption) or show the appealing personality displayed in *Death Proof*. Rosario Dawson, another *Death Proof* alumna, rather surprisingly pops in as one of the many brought-on-and-killed-off women. It offers sparse sets, uniform costumes, little humour (one gag about an Aussie guard happy that 'the Kiwi bitch' lost a fight is thrown away), drab visuals and unlimited misanthropy.

REDD INC. (INHUMAN RESOURCES) (2012)

'LET'S GET THIS CLEAR. I AM NOT A MURDERER – I AM A REGIONAL MANAGER!'

An inventive bunch-of-people-trapped-in-a-room movie, with several twists and an unusual degree of thematic consistency.

Caught literally red-handed in an office building lift, standing bloodied with an axe over the decapitated corpse of a CEO, Thomas Reddmann (Nicholas Hope) is convicted of being 'the head hunter', a serial murderer specialising in high-end execs. After a spell under the care of the unethical 'Dr Lansdale', he escapes – his scheme involves cutting off his own arm, which is then replaced with a scratchy hook – and kidnaps various parties (judge, cop, witnesses, psychic, lawyer) he blames for his conviction. Chaining them to a row of desks with terminals, he play-acts as strict boss, slicing marks on foreheads for infractions, supervising their meaningless tasks before revealing that their job is to go over the evidence again and find the real killer. Annabelle (Kelly Paterniti), a stripper who thought she already had the boss from hell, shows most gumption in seeking escape opportunities, but also gets enthusiastic about sleuthing when she realises the maniac was indeed innocent of the head hunter killings… Of course, a telltale wheeze reveals that one of the other abductees is the serial murderer and she finds herself trapped between the two maniacs.

A vein of office drone paranoia figures often in 2010s horror, though most economic desperation pictures focus on downsizing (*Axed*, *The Glass Man*) rather than doing anything, no matter how painful, to stay chained to the desk. Shot in Australia but set in America, it has slightly wobbly accents and an unfamiliar cast, but Brit Hope is solid as the mad boss (wearing a Patrick Troughton wig to cover the lobotomy scars), bringing conviction (even pathos) to the comic monster. Paterniti is an interesting, unconventional heroine who prospers in adversity, as shown by an extended coda when the killers show up again on the day her book about her ordeal is launched; the punch line has her stagger bloodied up to the podium at the book party to ask, 'Questions?' It has a *Saw*-ish vibe, especially when picking on the culpable – a bogus psychic (Hayley McElhinney), a shortcut-taking cop (Alan Dukes). Tom Savini has a bit-part probably shot on another continent. Scripted by Jonathon Green and Anthony O'Connor; directed by Daniel Krige.

EL REY DE LA MONTAÑA
(KING OF THE HILL) (2007)

A spare Spanish *The Most Dangerous Game* variant. Quim (Leonardo Sbaraglia), an everyman motorist (cf: Dennis Weaver in *Duel*), meets hot in a gas station rest room with Bea (María Valverde), a mystery woman he glimpses shoplifting. They have a passionate quickie – after which she takes off with his wallet and cigarette lighter, but considerately pays for his petrol so he isn't stranded in the middle of nowhere. When he spies her car on a road off the main highway, Quim takes the turn (always an ominous moment) and drives up a desolate track into unpopulated nowhere, only to become the target of a sniper. Quim and Bea, who has had a tire shot out, get together, run down a gunman (but don't look too closely at the corpse) and call the cops from an abandoned restaurant, summoning unhelpful, suspicious Guardia who arrest Quim for breaking and entering. Then the cops also become targets.

The bulk of the film is wilderness survival, with Quim becoming viciously competent as he fights a mostly unseen enemy, rugged terrain and his ambiguous fellow prey. When Quim breaks a genre rule, leaving an injured companion behind to be killed while making a run for it, the film pulls a viewpoint shift – the survivor becomes the shadowy presence and we meet the trackers, a pair of casually rifle-toting teenagers (Thomas Riordan, Andrés Juste) out with their yappy hunting dog. As the title suggests, they are playing a game (their dead friend lost), bickering over how many points deer rack up as opposed to people. For most of the film, we get the occasional sniper-view-through-telescopic sights, but once it's revealed that the killers are kids, the camera adopts the first person shooter perspective (jogging along with the gun in the frame) of computer games (subliminally suggesting, perhaps, how the little monsters got desensitised).

Of several 2000s films (*Ils*, *Eden Lake*, *The Strangers*) about homicidal young 'uns, this is the most convincing (if not necessarily scary). When the film is with the victims, the persecutors seem ruthless, efficient and sadistic (wounding, harrying and tormenting to draw out the hunt); when the chillingly amoral hunters are onscreen, they are credibly inept and bickering. The climax, in an abandoned village which suggests a local breakdown, hinges on the believable turn that a child who can kill from a distance hesitates when a prospective victim is up close and personal, while the embittered, surviving adult has no qualms about despatching underage tormentors with bare hands. Sbaraglia and Valverde (especially) are good, projecting a lot without much dialogue. Director/co-writer Gonzalo López-Gallego (*Open Grave*) delivers suspense and action, but also some depth and thought. Co-written by Javier Gullón (*Hierro*).

RIARU ONIGOKKO (TAG) (2015)

A standing joke among SF magazine editors was that they'd regularly receive amateur submissions about the last survivors of an apocalypse or two astronauts landing on a new world with the punch line being that their names are Adam and Eve (Rod Serling even seriously put this on as a *Twilight Zone* episode). Since the 1980s, this scenario has been eclipsed by stories in which protagonists fight through enormous odds – say, a space fleet battling ground defences – only to come up short at the end with a huge sign in the sky reading 'Game Over'. Sion Sono's *Tag*, based loosely on a previously filmed novel by Yûsuke Yamada, is essentially this story. After an exciting, inventive sprint through the first three acts, it gets awkward when it comes to explaining this has all been taking place in a future where a mad genius has brought his favourite classic game to life and is playing it with a body-switching heroine across parallel worlds.

Sono one-ups the mass schoolgirl death scenes of his *Suicide Club* with a bravura opening in which an entire busload of uniformed girls is sliced in half by an evil wind which bisects everyone at the midriff... except Mitsuko (Reina Triendl), who has been bending down to pick up a pen. Mitsuko flees the invisible killer, which scythes down cyclists and passing hikers (all teenage girls). She changes her bloody sailor suit for a different uniform (with an unfeasibly short skirt) and walks to a school. A complex set of friendships and enmities go out the window when the teachers (all women) turn into maniacs with machine guns. Running from this fresh massacre, Mitsuko transforms into Keiko (Mariko Shinoda), a bride in full gown who appears at a church with an all-female congregation and finds herself fleeing a howling mob and her literally pig-headed monster bridegroom (the first man sighted in the movie). Showing off martial arts moves, she shifts again and becomes Izumi (Erina Mano), a runner with a team of deftly sketched (and doomed) mates. She is pursued again by another killer team, before morphing back into Mitsuko and shuffling through several more universes – one a cave populated by what look like the spectre from *Ring* and one an all-male world that contrasts the all-female ones hitherto seen – eventually appearing before her maker, who has two bodies (a venerable one and a sleekly muscled stud literally created to have sex with her), then hitting on a way out of this cycle of chase, escape and survival, even as all around her are casually mass-murdered.

Yuki Sakurai is interesting as the heroine's perennially in-the-know best friend, who manages to get out enough of an explanation to keep her running but is also a doomed NPC in every universe. The trio of lead actresses (the player can switch protagonists at the touch of a button) manage the trick of being the same person in three different forms mostly by keeping on the move. Colourful, often funny, often imaginative, and less exploitative and grue-heavy than most Japanese schoolgirl mutant pictures (cf: *The Machine Girl, Vampire Girl vs. Frankenstein Girl, Tokyo Gore Police*). The short skirts, leering visuals and all-babe cast are explained by the fact that this woman's world has been created by men; Sono (and presumably Yamada) seem willing to take the blame shouldered by the film's sort-of pathetic creator character.

ROOM (2015)

Angel-faced five-year-old Jack (Jacob Tremblay), who has never had his hair cut, lives a rich, varied, seemingly unlimited life with his mother Ma (Brie Larson), who used to be called Joy, in Room – a fortified shed sometimes visited by Old Nick (Sean Bridgers), who abducted Joy as a teenager and keeps her imprisoned as a sex slave. Inspired by appalling true crimes, this unusual riff on the captivity narrative tells its story from the viewpoint of a child who has never known freedom and doesn't even understand the concept of imprisonment.

The first half of the film is a miracle of suggestion, with astonishing performances from young Tremblay and Larson as the loving, battling son and mother who are (obviously) never out of each other's company. Art direction is used for storytelling: repurposed bits of packaging used to decorate the soundproofed walls, the open toilet tank (because Joy once tried to bludgeon Old Nick with the lid) in which homemade toy boats float, the ill-tuned TV set and discussions of what's real and what's just on TV ('Dora's only a drawing.'), the skylight that shows the weather. The dull ritual abuse takes place out of Jack's sight but not earshot, and the abductor is banal evil personified, whining about the cost of keeping the power on and his captives fed now he's been laid off. Old Nick's capricious, barbed generosity extends to giving the boy a remote-controlled toy car which makes a noise designed to irritate any adult within earshot. Ma tells stories to Jack as a way of teaching and entertaining him. Now he's five, she changes what she's told him about their situation as part of a long-term escape plan – early on, she recounts the story of the Count of Monte Cristo, and her grand scheme is a modification of Edmond Dantès' break from the Château d'If.

After a brilliantly staged escape, which requires Jack to act intelligently while overwhelmed by the unimaginable largeness of the world (an ordinary Ohio suburb), a second act has Jack adjusting to new circumstances. In an effective what-happens-after-the-happy-ending drama, Joy is taken aback to find her parents divorced and her father (William H. Macy) unable to see her son as anything other than the child of a monster rapist. She is also latently furious that her mother (Joan Allen) raised her to be so nice she fell into Old Nick's trap when he asked her to help with his sick dog (Jack later also has an imaginary dog) – a negative inspiration to the way she has of-necessity raised her own son to escape from her as much as from Old Nick. Tremblay, after a scattering of kid actor credits in the likes of *The Smurfs 2*, is astonishingly good in a taxing role. Like any five-year-old, Jack can be dogmatic, fanatical, tantrum-prone and foolish. He doesn't even know he lives in a world where all these traits are dangerous for him and his mother... but his sense of wonder has made Room bearable for Joy by seeing it as a magical place where each fitting has character and purpose ('Toilet's the best at taking away poo.'). Scripted by Emma Donoghue from her own novel; directed by Lenny Abrahamson (*What Richard Did, Frank*).

ROVDYR (MANHUNT) (2008)

This elementary, short Norwegian backwoods horror is among the first pictures influenced by 21st century movies which were in turn influenced by 1970s classics: an early plot thread about a desperate girl who hitches a ride with a busload of kids (and gets killed as soon as her point has been made) is lifted from the *remake* of *The Texas Chain Saw Massacre* (also recalled by the use of the '70s as a period setting) and the use of a David Hess song on the soundtrack evokes Eli Roth rather than *The Last House on the Left*. A xerox of a copy, and stuck with thin, one-note victim characters, and even more insubstantial villains, it might still have been reasonably effective if it weren't hobbled by overfamiliar suspense sequences and the tactical error of killing the most engaging character too early in the ordeal. The short-term shock doesn't make up for the fact we're thereafter stuck with folks we can't care about.

The villains are apparently ordinary huntsmen, who signal each other with eerie horns as they track their young prey. Seen too often and too close to be as menacing as, say, the barely-glimpsed trucker in *Duel*, they aren't allowed to reveal *why* they pursue this sadistic pastime like the hunters in *The Most Dangerous Game* or *Open Season*. If there's a constant supply of prey (two lots are shown here), how do they evade the authorities? If there isn't, what would they have done this weekend if no vanload of kids showed up? Directed by Patrik Syversen, who co-wrote with Nini Bull Robsahm and went on to make the interesting minor vampire film *Prowl*. The widescreen Norwegian woods are ominous and a couple of sequences play the riffs adequately, but it lacks the extra value of the equally formulaic but just plain better *Cold Prey*.

RPG (REAL PLAYING GAME) (2013)

An awkward Portuguese science fiction film which crossbreeds *The Sorcerers* with *The Hunger Games*, this is also a group-wake-in-a-remote-area-with-amnesia-and-have-to-sort-out-who-they-are drama. In the future, billionaire Steve Battier (Rutger Hauer) cruises up to a chic science facility in a sleek car with cool lights and is greeted by sinister Mr Chan (Chris Tashima), who has gathered ten wealthy old folks and promised they can inhabit the brains of hot young types for a limited time. Part of the deal is an elimination game: Steve wakes up as a young guy (Cian Barry) in a derelict Portuguese estate with a group of model-look types who struggle with dialogue. Complex rules mean that not only does someone have to be killed every hour, but that afterwards the killer has to touch the hologram of the oldie they guess to be the alter ego of their victim… If they guess wrong, they combust. It's so complicated even the grasping characters have to sit down and puzzle out the premise, let alone who is who (a cross-sex incarnation is in the mix). The character types sound interesting – a Catholic dictator, a screen star, a Russian superspy/killing machine, a new-age singer and a rebel princess – but the pretty people turn out to be interchangeable. It hasn't got much action, though is nice to look at. A flurry of twists at the end doesn't quite make clear the nature of the scam. Written by Tino Navarro, who co-directed with David Rebordão.

SATSUJIN DOUGA SITE (DEATH TUBE; MURDER SITE) (2010)

Various people log onto a rarely active website and witness real murders, then black out and wake in rooms where a computer avatar of Pon-Kichi – a cute toy bear with a sugar-plum fairy theme tune – forces them to play life-or-death party games. After a round or two, longer-lasting contestants are let into a corridor where gun-wielding goons in plush bear costumes bully them to play more games. The tasks aren't especially ingenious: an *It's a Knockout* obstacle course involves eating doughnuts dangling on strings, blundering through a slippery patch (which doesn't look that slippery, prompting displays of strained falling-over) and carrying blocks to the finish line. Festooning the set are banners with contradictory instructions, asking unwilling contestants to co-operate in one game and compete in the next, adding to the sadistic thrills for the unknown organisers and their internet audience.

Protagonist Inouye (Shôichi Matsuda) contacts his fiancée to ask for help and she's assaulted by a bear-headed thug. Then he has to answer a yes or no question about whether he loves her the same way now she's been raped, with the lives of all the players forfeit if he answers wrongly. Other intrigues involve a wheedling guy who convinces Inouye that another contestant is a manipulative serial killer – a thread with a predictable punch line. The amateurish script overemphasises some elements – one victim signals his doomedness by mentioning his pregnant wife, and after he's dead everyone laboriously remembers this detail – and it runs tiresomely to nearly two hours. A new touch is onscreen comments from crass, evil, bloodthirsty internet fans ('This game sucks, no one's going to die, might as well go for a pee.'). The bears are horrible cheery villains – but their outfits are so hampering that, guns or no, contestants ought to be able to rush the bastards and overwhelm them.

It's obviously cheap, shot on video on very few sets, and – to set up the late-in-the-day who's-the-killer bit – the contestants show little individuality. While *My Little Eye*, *Saw* and *Cube* are obvious precedents, it owes as much to those cruel Japanese elimination/ordeal quiz shows which had an odd vogue when glimpsed in '80s joke documentaries about weird foreign TV. Directed by Yôhei Fukuda, cinematographer of the controversial but banal *Grotesque*, who ran this horse into the ground with *Satsujin Douga Site 2* and the similar *X Gêmu* which, confusingly, was also released as *Death Tube*.

SEASON OF THE HUNTED (2003)

Though it toplines Muse Watson, a minor icon thanks to the *I Know What You Did Last Summer* films, this crossbreed of *Deliverance* and *The Most Dangerous Game* feels like an amateur film. Note: repeated fades between scenes, the brutal truncation of (terrible) heavy metal underscore tracks (as if the needle were lifted off the record), clumsily staged gore and action, murky exterior photography and hilarious 'Vietnam flashbacks'. Moustached Viet vet Frank (Watson), sensitive buddy Steve (Timothy Gibbs), a couple of quickly killed stooges (Lou Martini Jr, Wass M. Stevens) and annoying asshole Charlie (Tony Travis) drive into the woods to a lodge run by a pack of whiskery, moonshine-drinking, cackling hillbillies. The two groups uneasily spend a night with no bathroom facilities, and split up to go bow-hunting the next morning. As has been obvious, the whole thing is a scam – the locals turn the city slickers loose to hunt for sport (there is even a speech about 'the most dangerous game') then cut up for food. Of course, Frank uses his jungle fighting skills to fight back. In several scenes, folks pull arrows out of their bodies; it may signify something that city characters remember to unscrew the arrowheads first but the rednecks don't. Written by Phil Faicco, directed by Ron Sperling. NB: anyone with a working bear trap mounted on their kitchen wall isn't to be trusted.

SENSELESS (2008)

Clean-cut businessman Eliott Gast (Jason Behr), snatched on a trip to Europe, wakes in an antiseptic white suite, with ever-present cameras. Masked, aggressive-jovial Blackbeard (Joe Ferrara) tells him he's being punished as a representative American imperialist, while veiled Nim (Emma Catherwood) seems to empathise with his suffering. After a reel of menace with political footnotes, torture begins in earnest.

Not in the *Hostel* grue league (mostly cutting away when the screaming starts), it does involve an electric iron applied to the tongue, ruptured eardrums (torturers play a message of support from the victim's wife just as they deafen him) and possible eye-gouging with a coffee spoon. Almost everything Gast is told is provisional – Blackbeard harps on about ratings and the outside world controversy about his sufferings, but it's not even clear that the charade really is being live-streamed. Though a staunch, hero-type guy, Gast has lingering guilts from his childhood which set up slightly needless flashbacks. He admits his business (expediting debts to underfinanced third world countries to force them to cooperate with American foreign policy) is basically 'like giving college kids credit cards'. Roping politics to torture porn, this also avoids getting too specific about the perpetrators. The ending has a 1960s spy-fi TV feel as Gast discovers his prison is a big set inside a warehouse and his persecutors have just wandered off. Behr is solid, though Gast is a flatly conceived everyman imperialist; Ferrara and Catherwood underplay, which makes a change from cackling and ranting. Written and directed by Simon Hynd, from a novel by Stona Fitch.

THE 7TH HUNT (2009)

A cheap Australian hunting humans/torture porn quickie. Elite sickos stage nasty games whereby they abduct, stalk, torture and kill random folks. The Mastermind (Chris Galletti) seems to be conducting a social science experiment, but his associates have other motives: The Inquisitor (Sarah Mawbey), his daughter, punishes arrogant men; The Hacker (Darren K. Hawkins) gets jollies cutting off the fingers of victims trying to get round his firewalls; and The Knife (Malcolm Frawley), a serial killer, hates pretty young girls. In a relative novelty that might draw on a twist from *Hostel Part II*, The Hand (Tasneem Roc) and The Sniper (Jason Stojanovski) are survivors of former hunts who have joined the killing circle. The victims are a goth chick (Cassady Maddox) who winds up being tortured by The Hand, her deaf athlete sister (Imogen Bailey) who is stalked by The Sniper, a princess (Olivia Solomons) who gets cut up by The Knife, a misogynist creep (Matthew Charleston) battered by The Inquisitor and a hacker (Kain O'Keeffe) who gets finger-snipped. As usual, indictment of horrible things people do to other people is couched as a gloating celebration of the same – slightly complicated by a range of attitudes among the killers, from semi-vigilante to outright sado-bastardy. Shot in one disused, semi-institutional, not-very-interesting building. Awkwardly directed and bluntly written by Jon Cohen, with overly insistent performances.

SHUTTLE (2008)

If *Speed* was *Die Hard* on a bus, *Shuttle* is *Hostel* on a bus. A well made urban nightmare, it straggles a little before getting to its cruel payoff. Just back from a weekend in Mexico, gal pals Mel (Peyton List) and Jules (Cameron Goodman) are tempted by a cheap airport shuttle. The Driver (Tony Curran) reluctantly also picks up horndog Seth (James Snyder) and his sensitive friend Matt (Dave Power), along with wound-too-tight family man Andy (Cullen Douglas). Leaving the freeway for dubious reasons, the shuttle tours a bad, depopulated part of town. Things get worse: a dark car buzzes the bus, a burst tire needs changing, Matt loses his fingers when the jack slips. A suggested trip to the hospital stalls when the Driver reaches for a street guide (always discomforting) and pulls a gun out of the book (worse). As escapes are thwarted, it becomes clear this is about more than jacking credit cards and luggage. Mel is forced to dash round a supermarket picking up odd items (kitty litter, water, torch) and one of the passengers turns out to be a sadist in on the scam.

Taking a break from rich sickos into torture (*The Most Dangerous Game*, *Hostel*) or organ harvesting (*Turistas*, *Train*), this is about human trafficking, as revealed when the girls realise the driver, though careless with male lives, sees they come through physically unscathed because they're worthless with injuries ('...even your ass, he bandaged it, right? He wanted it to heal.'). Like *Taken*, *Shuttle* features sex slaves stolen from affluent white American families, which – in terms of realism – puts it on a level with the racket in *Thoroughly Modern Millie*. Written and directed by Edward Anderson (*Flawless*), it has good performances (List, especially) and infallible queasy suspense – though there are two or three too many failed escape attempts or moments when heroines have guns or knives and *don't* kill or cripple their remorseless persecutor. A similar story is told from a different viewpoint in the British movie *Hush*.

SIL JONG (MISSING) (2009)

'I WASN'T MYSELF WHEN I SHOT HIM, BUT I WAS DEFINITELY MYSELF WHEN I FED HIM TO THE GRINDER.'

A Korean tied-up-in-the-cellar movie, loosely based on a true crime. Farmer Jang Pan-gon (Moon Seong-geun) adds ground-up people to his chicken feed, so his hens lay excellent eggs. After murdering a sleek film director who has taken a starlet Hyun-ah (Jeon Se-hong) out into the country in the hopes of copping off – the cheesewire garrotte breaks, and he has to finish the job with his chicken-beheading axe – Pan-gon keeps the girl in a dog-cage, hoses her down, throws her a party where the cake has three candles because she's his third 'guest', rapes her (using the cake icing as lubricant), reacts to her biting his dick by taking pliers to her teeth and eventually turns her into feed. Then, Hyun-jun (Chu Ja-hyeon) – Hyun-ah's Vera Miles-type older sister – shows up, annoys the uncaring local cops and investigates. Tough enough to shove a nail through the killer's hand, she also winds up in the cellar but endures and finally gets hold of a gun. Moon is good as a misogynist killer who treats women like animals. Quietly hateful rather than demented (he gets into a flowery shirt and performs a self-penned song to his victim), he becomes more fiendlike in the climax as he nags the heroine into killing him ('One more thing: she was still alive when she went through.'). It's a moot point as to whether another analysis of male rottenness is required, with the camera ogling the trim, citified victims just as the sullen doltish villain does. The real case involved a fisherman, and a tasteless-in-context coda has two leggy girls hitching a ride on the boat of a wary, hungry looking old fisherman... with a cackle over a fade to black. Directed by Kim Sung-hong.

STEEL TRAP (2007)

'YOU GUYS ARE INSANE. ANY GAME THAT STARTS WITH A ROTTING PIG'S HEAD IS NOT GOING TO END WITH A GIANT TEDDY BEAR!'

A German-made slasher mystery, directed and co-written by Luis Cámara with a mostly British cast putting on reasonable American accents.

During a New Year's party on the top floor of an empty skyscraper ('Isn't this a scream? A party on top of an abandoned building. It's sort of post-apocalyptic... Let's hope no one decides to blow it up.'), a group of minor celebs – agony auntie Nicole (Julia Ballard), rocker Wade (Mark Wilson), venal exec Pamela (Joanna Bobin), TV chef Kathy Kane (Georgia Mackenzie), crass stud Adam (Adam Rayner), groupie Melanie (Annabelle Wallis) and pissed-off boyfriend Robert

(Pascal Langdale) – get texts summoning them to a more exclusive party on a lower floor. Fun turns sour as invitees find insulting labels ('two-faced', 'heartless', 'loser', etc.) on place settings in a balloon- and tinsel-strewn room and are stalked (and slashed) by a tall guy (Frank Maier) in a sinister mask which gets even creepier when splashed with luminescent fluid.

In a cross between *And Then There Were None* and *The Last of Sheila*, horrible people are punished for sins they can barely remember by being forced to solve riddles, play party games, die appropriately (the two-faced woman has her head bisected with an axe, the heartless one gets her heart ripped out) and clamber down lift shafts. The cast bring appropriate venom and the dialogue is full of tough, cynical, unrealistic-but-entertaining backbiting; Mackenzie is especially enjoyable in the home stretch when she becomes simultaneously final girl and psycho diva ('Living well's pretty good, but I'd say killing people is the best revenge.'). Co-written by Gabrielle Galanter.

THE STRANGE VENGEANCE OF ROSALIE (1972)

This has an odd art-exploitation pedigree, with director Jack Starrett (*Cleopatra Jones, Race with the Devil*) working from a script by Anthony Greville-Bell (*Theater of Blood, Perfect Friday*) and producer John Kohn (*Goldengirl, Shanghai Surprise*) based on a novel (*The Chicken*) by English author Miles Tripp. An abduction narrative in which a woman keeps a man in her power by breaking his leg, it is occasionally footnoted as a precursor to *Misery* – though Stephen King acknowledged John Fowles' *The Collector* (which Kohn also adapted) as his specific model.

Virgil (Ken Howard), a clean-cut travelling salesman, picks up hitchhiking Rosalie (Bonnie Bedelia), a half-Indian/half-white trash teenager raised by her just-dead grandfather in a shack in the middle of nowhere. She has set out to trap a man to replace her grandfather, which she does first by sabotaging Virgil's car and locking him in a shed, then by hobbling him. Much of the film is back-and-forth between the leads, with Rosalie alternately monstrous and possessive and Virgil trying everything from abuse to cajolement to get her to free him. Things are complicated by larcenous/lecherous biker Fry (Anthony Zerbe), who comes by and makes things much worse, turning the drama into a three way battle of wits. For Starrett, it's oddly unexploitative: Bedelia is remarkable as the dirty faced, surprisingly inventive urchin (as much waiflike as monstrous), but Virgil is disturbed when the underage girl snuggles against him for warmth (he smells better than her granddaddy) – a refreshingly credible response in an era when too many films took human baseness for granted (though Zerbe's flamboyant villain has all the expected vices).

For all its desert vistas (it was shot in Spain) and physical grime, it has a theatrical feel, privileging dialogue and performance over action.

TERRITORIES (CHECKPOINT) (2010)

So many confinement/torture movies allegorically touch on Guantanamo Bay, it seems redundant to go head-on at the subject… but director-co-writer Olivier Abbou takes a shot anyway. A few stretches – long interrogations with damned-if-you-do-damned-if-you-don't questions – are relatively unfamiliar, but it's mostly overfamiliar chained-in-cages material.

A car-load of thinly characterised young-ish folks (in their thirties, mostly, which makes a change) drive back to the US from a wedding in Canada. On a lonely road, they are pulled over by aggressive customs officers Torrance (Roc LaFortune) and Sotos (Sean Devine). After a small bag of weed is found, the detainees are hooded, rectally probed, caged in the open, starved, stripped, branded with code-numbers, put in a soundproof shed and bombarded with light and noise. Under harsh questioning, they begin to doubt each other and themselves (a strong idea, not pursued). It becomes clear that the imposters are running the checkpoint as a sadistic hobby – with a profitable sideline of putting stolen goods on ebay.

Odd scenes try for sympathy with the abductors, traumatised Iraq veterans who were once Guantanamo guards. Mostly dour, it has one out-of-place gross silliness: a girl with an infected tooth gets a swollen head as if she were in a Troma movie and is treated with pliers. The initial story runs out after an hour, so a third-act development involves grizzled hippie private eye Rick Brautigan (Stephen Shellen) – an interesting character, but a feint blatantly modelled on the Martin Balsam subplot in *Psycho*. The notion of bogus border officials is potent, but LaFortune mostly riffs on R. Lee Ermey's mad sheriff in the *Texas Chainsaw* remake. Co-written by Thibault Lang Willar.

TERROR TRAP (2010)

Though about good old-fashioned live snuff theatre rather than new-fangled video or internet nonsense, this is a pretty slavish clone of the by-no-means-original *Vacancy*.

Squabbling city folks Don (David James Elliott) and Nancy (Heather Marie Marsden), driving through the middle of nowhere at dead of night, are sideswiped and run off the road. A slob sheriff (Jeff Fahey) gives them a lift to the nearest motel, run by an obviously creepy night man (Andrew Sensenig). Despite blood on the walls, the couple settle in. Nancy nags Don into telling the couple in the next room to keep the noise down, misinterpreting the sounds of torture for rough sex. A group of scumbags – an upscale businessman, some trucker types, a scary chick – pay to peep through one-way mirrors, augmented by spy-cams, as guests are taunted and then killed by a gang of masked killers… Only Don happens to be an ex-Marine and not as sissified as city folk usually are.

The basic setup is confused by a dangling plot-thread about a vanload of Eastern European sex slaves whose abductors are killed by their ostensible customers. We keep going back to the motel, as the heroes are tempted to leave the relative safety of the room to be menaced. Fahey and Michael Madsen are value-for-money guest star villains, but their freeform eccentric patter wears thin. It takes writer-director Dan Garcia reels of contrived argument to establish the rottenness of Don and Nancy's marriage, which they heal via the shared experience of fighting off a horde of silly-masked, frankly inept killers.

THAT COLD DAY IN THE PARK (1969)

This obscurity is an early Robert Altman directorial credit, but the writing pedigree is also interesting. The script is by Gillian Freeman – who wrote the novel *The Leather Boys* and worked on the screenplays of *Girl on a Motorcycle* and *I Want What I Want* – from a book by Peter Miles, who scripted *They Saved Hitler's Brain*(!) and (as Gerald Perreau) was a child actor in *Who Killed Doc Robbin?* and *The Red Pony*.

Wealthy Frances Austen (Sandy Dennis), who seems to have become a middle-aged spinster in her early thirties, lives alone in an inherited Vancouver flat, socialising only with her late parents' aged circle of friends. One day, as it's pouring, she spies a youth (Michael Burns) on his own in the park and impulsively invites him in to dry off. He's mute and oddly unresponsive, but does a Russian dance while naked behind a blanket. Frances cautiously adopts him, feeding him breakfast, buying clothes, chattering at him about the details of her empty life and showing signs of possessive neurosis by occasionally locking his bedroom door. As it happens, The Boy *isn't* a mute – 'not speaking for days' is 'his thing', as his semi-incest-minded sister (Susanne Benton, of *A Boy and His Dog*) observes – and even has crash-space in a hippie-filled house across town. A *Collector*-style captivity drama develops as Frances becomes increasingly unhinged – as Susannah York would in Altman's later *Images* and Shelley Duvall/Sissy Spacek in *3 Women* – and The Boy's act turns sour. In an uncomfortable sequence, the woman tries to take care of The Boy's 'needs' by finding him a prostitute. She enlists the help of a perplexed, reasonable businessman (Altman regular Michael Murphy) to find a call-girl (Linda Sorensen), then creepily watches what goes on. Also memorable is a scene in which Frances finally unburdens herself of her desires to the prone Boy and reaches out to touch him – only to find the pillows he has arranged in his bed to cover for his sneaking out at night to get high with draft-dodgers (it is 1969, after all). This triggers a descent into madness, which the intense, interestingly mannered Dennis manages disturbingly well.

Like most stories in this vein (cf: *Repulsion*), it ends with someone stabbed to death, but here the murder locks the now-cracked principles together forever. At nearly two hours, it has dull spots as Altman slowly zooms across rooms and characters retreat into private worlds inside their skulls as much as the drably luxurious old persons' apartment. With the always-welcome Luana Anders. Photographed by László Kovács.

13 GAME SAYAWNG (13 GAME OF DEATH) (2006)

Chit (Krissada Sukosol), salaryman in a Bangkok music company, is having a bad day after a troubled life. He's mixed-race, with an abusive and now absent Anglo father. His smothering mother is an economic drain who still thinks he's dating a singer who ditched him because he couldn't make her famous. When a workplace rival cuts him out of a sale, he complains and gets fired.

On the way out of the building, Chit takes a mobile phone call from an anonymous woman who tells him he's been selected for a net-based reality show. If he performs thirteen tasks of escalating difficulty, he can win increasing sums of money. The first task is to kill a fly with a rolled-up magazine; the second is to eat the fly. From this, most people – and the audience – would see where it was going, and baulk at task three: to make at least three children in a playground cry. Chit, of course, carries on: literally eating shit, served with a salad at a posh restaurant. Staying in the game puts him in desperate situations: a brawl on a bus with some roughs, hefting the corpse of a neglected (and breakable) old man from a well and (more difficult) getting his uncaring family to pay attention, battering his ex's abusive rock star boyfriend unconscious (the guy keeps getting up after being hit with a chair, prompting Chit to whine that he's getting tired). Even an innocuous errand – helping a little old lady secure her clothesline – turns gruesome as razor-wire stretched across a road leads to the mass decapitation of a bike gang.

While Chit sticks with the game, his androgynous colleague Tong (Achita Sikamana) realises what he's up to – which imperils his standing since it's a condition of play that no one else finds out what he's doing. To get past this, Chit is given a samurai sword and the choice of killing the girl or her beloved dog. After that, the film gets weirder as Chit realises these tasks have been designed to evoke specific memories of his miserable childhood. For the big prize, he gets a chance to execute the brutal, foreign father he blames for his miseries, though he also now has flashes of the few happy moments of his youth and wonders whether the man at his mercy is the monster he remembers. Meanwhile, Tong penetrates the lair of the game-runners and confronts a white-suited, philosophical lad who looks about fifteen and has a Bond villain cat. The debate about what exactly is going on gets cloudy and, like a sub-plot about a cop pursuing Chit because he has an inkling that this game has been played before, is less compelling than the simple situation of the antihero, who gets more and more rumpled, his white shirt stained with ordure and bodily fluids, as the day wears on. Directed by Matthew Chookiat Sakveerakul; who co-scripted with Eakasit Thairaat, author of the comic on which it's based.

13 SINS (2014)

'YEARS GO BY AND YOUR BITTERNESS WILL GROW IN PROPORTION TO YOUR ASS.'

A US remake of the Thai *13: Game of Death*, directed by Daniel Stamm (*The Last Exorcism*), who also co-wrote with David Birke.

An opening set piece has an elder statesman Australian poet recite dirty limericks at a posh testimonial and cut off a woman's finger, then be shot by a security guard while reaching for a mobile phone which has been giving him orders. This reframes the story to stress the vast conspiracy before we get about two-thirds of the original plot – which is tweaked to make its hapless hero more sympathetic. Insufficiently ruthless to work in insurance, Elliot Brindle (Mark Webber) pleads with his boss (Richard Burgi) not to fire him because losing health benefits means his autistic brother Michael (Devon Graye) will be institutionalised. He is furthermore stuck with a once-abusive, now-near-senile father (Tom Bower), an unreconstructed racist/sexist who needs to move in with Elliot, who has a black girlfriend, Shelby (Rutina Wesley).

On the way out of the building, Elliot gets a phone call from a mystery voice (George Coe) offering a huge payout if he completes thirteen sinful tasks… which start with swatting a fly and eating it. A new wrinkle is that the protagonist is competing with someone else to complete the game. His rival turns out to be Michael, who has an easier time since he has no sense of right and wrong. A deep backstory is that their father once won the game himself, but cracked up in the process since one of his tasks was killing his wife. At a crucial point, he cruelly commits suicide so the brothers are set against each other in a task to kill a family member. The hook is good and the family story strong, even if it does tip too many elements into the mix. An additional subplot about a cop (Ron Perlman) and an in-the-know bystander (Pruitt Taylor Vince) needlessly gets away from the protagonist's quandary. A nice reveal is that Shelby got the same swallow-a-fly phone call and simply told the game organiser to fuck off. A rare remake which makes a good double bill with the original: they start at the same place, but take individual, interesting paths.

31 (2016)

'They call me Doom-Head,' announces a cadaverous, chatty killer (Richard Brake) in bedraggled clown makeup – setting the tone for writer-director Rob Zombie's collage of moments, faces, sick jokes, lines of dialogue and items of carny décor from the history of exploitation. Like his first feature, *House of 1000 Corpses*, *31* is especially indebted to Tobe Hooper's *The Texas Chain Saw Massacre* and *The Funhouse* – but the frenzy of homage has worn so thin it seems less a fond hark-back to 1970s drive-in horrors and 1980s video nasties than a latecoming entry in the torture-porn cycle which peaked circa 2007 amid sequels to and imitations of *Hostel* and *Saw*.

After a prologue featuring Doom-Head and a doomed-to-be-beheaded clergyman (Daniel Roebuck), the film is entirely set on October 31ˢᵗ, 1976. A camper van of carnies are waylaid by minions of a triumvirate of English-accented decadents in Versailles finery – Father Murder (Malcolm McDowell), Sister Dragon (Judy Geeson), Sister Serpent (Jane Carr) – and set loose in an overfamiliar derelict factory full of dripping pipes, rusty traps and under-lit passageways. The abductors place bets on who will survive longest against ranting, giggling killer clowns with nicknames like Psycho-Head (Lew Temple), Sick-Head (Pancho Moler), Death-Head (Torsten Voges) and Sex-Head (E.G. Daily). Zombie untidily and incoherently kills off half his carnies before reaching the death maze, so the key players are Charly (Sheri Moon Zombie), Roscoe (Jeff Daniel Phillips), Venus Virgo (Meg Foster), Panda (Lawrence Hilton-Jacobs) and Levon (Kevin Jackson) – with a predictable order of disposal. Several villains are undone by a tendency to stop and make speeches at helpless victims who then fight back with unsurprising ferocity.

Zombie's strength is casting, going outside the expected pool of cult players to showcase McDowell (star of Zombie's *Halloween* remakes), Geeson, Foster and Daily, and securing character actor Tracey Walter and porn star Ginger Lynn to pop up as colourful cameo degenerates. Gaunt Brake, best known for shooting Bruce Wayne's parents in *Batman Begins*, chews on a rare lead baddie role, even if the script offers more string than meat. As ever, Zombie is less interested in his normals, and even regular star Sheri Moon Zombie – cast as final girl – has little to do but scream and stagger. Zombie's filmmaking career began with inventive pop videos for his band White Zombie and he can frame an interesting shot or layer in an unusual and affecting snatch of music, but after six features he still can't come up with a fresh story, write characters with more depth than their makeup or direct suspense-horror scenes that work. His enclosed, referential universe – one scene is a supposedly straight reprise of a comedy cannibal bit from *The Rocky Horror Picture Show* – is like the circus puppet display that's the keynote visual here: wooden people jerking repetitively and hacking each other to bits.

TOKYO 10+01 (2003)

A cheap skit on *Battle Royale* and other kill-game flicks from writer-director Higuchinsky, auteur of the more interesting *Uzumaki*. A neon-lit futuristic setting is established by anime-look cityscapes with the Tokyo Tower landmark broken, but action is mostly confined to a drab warehouse and environs – which, given that the premise involves a *Warriors* chase through urban warzones, makes a seriously inadequate arena. Eleven caricature criminals are introduced – with nicknames, stats and cartoon images – before they wake in the warehouse to be ranted at by hat-wearing Mr K (Eisuke Sasai), top minion of an ailing tycoon (Yoshiyuki Arashi) who has willed his fortune to the survivors of a chase-across-the-city contest. The group split into teams, but start getting killed off by a machine-gun-toting goon squad before they're even out of the building. Lead players Jingi (Kee) and Coco (Natsuki Katô) get a little background (Jingi has a flashback trauma), but most contestants are shrill caricatures (a teenage hacker, a yakuza wannabe, twin Chinese martial arts girls, a screaming drag queen, etc.). Rather desperately, it parodies elements of *Battle Royale* – an instructional video with a perky hostess (Makiko) – which were parodic in the first place.

247°F (2011)

The shark-themed *Open Water* (2003) set the 21st century besieged-holidaymaker template followed by the croc-themed *Black Water* (2007), the lion-themed *Prey* (2007) and the bear-themed *Bear* (2010). Dropping the wildlife, a spin-off cycle began with *Adrift* (aka *Open Water 2*; 2006), where holidaymakers are put in a perilous quandary by stupidity and blind chance. That led to *Frozen* (2010), which was *Adrift* on a ski-lift, and *247°F*, which is *Adrift* in a sauna. Many of these are based on true stories, which doesn't make them feel less contrived. This sauna, built by Uncle Wade (Tyler Mane) at his own chalet, *isn't* idiot-proof… prompting a whine of, 'Well, we shouldn't have let Michael near it then.'

A mandatory half-hour opening offers character building and setup. Jenna (Scout Taylor-Compton), survivor of a car accident which killed her fiancé, is medicated for claustrophobia. Best friend Renee (Christina Ulloa) prevails on her to spend a fun weekend at PaganFest with horny Michael (Michael Copon), who is pretty much a complete dick, and would-be writer Ian (Travis Van Winkle), a know-it-all who senses he's going to do something significant with his life (which marks him for death). The kids try the sauna, several times returning after dips in the lake. After an argument, Michael staggers off in a bad mood and the other three get stuck in the sauna because he knocks over a ladder. It's not much of a peril (the real-life incident involved discomfort but no fatalities) and Ian's rapid patter about heat stroke and the mechanics of a gas-fired sauna get tired quickly.

As in most of the films in this cycle – which extends to the more respectable *127 Hours* – the practicalities of trying to find a way out of the trap are gripping even if the characters are annoying. Chances are, if we were in the sauna, we'd be irritated with our friends too. Multiple freak-outs, near rescues, an explosion, an imagined escape and a fatality ensue, with the girls healing their fractured friendship in shared adversity. Written by Lloyd S. Wagner, from a story by Levan Bakhia and Beqa Oniani; directed by Bakhia and Beqa Jguburia. Made in Georgia (former USSR), where the incident happened, but set in the US.

TRAPPED (1973)

A memorable high-concept TV movie from writer-director Frank DeFelitta (author of *Audrey Rose*).

Amiable if shallow Chuck Brenner (James Brolin) spends a last day with stern ex-wife Elaine (Susan Clark) and their doll-pretty daughter (Tammy Harrington) before Elaine and her decent new husband (Earl Holliman) move to Mexico and he loses parental access rights. In Noonan's Department Store, Chuck wants to buy the girl a 'Billy-Jo' doll (they look cheap), but one has to be sent over from a depot and Elaine needs to get to the airport – so Chuck volunteers to stay behind and take a cab over with the doll. He only has a fifty-dollar bill and while the clerk (Ivy Jones) makes change, he goes to the men's room because it's the only place he can smoke (in 1973, smoking was allowed in toilets and TV movies couldn't have a hero who wanted to take a leak). Chuck is mugged and stuffed in a stall and the store closes. After hours, Noonan's is 'patrolled by attack dogs', which means guys in arm-guards and fencing masks let dangerous hounds roam the aisles (a ludicrous notion, even then – wouldn't they do more damage than burglars?). Chuck, concussed from the attack by muggers the dogs didn't deter, fights off the killer hounds, who don't have on-site human masters.

There are slightly too many cutaways to the airport and the family wondering where Chuck is and whether they should do or say anything, but the contrivance of the wounded man pursued around an eerily empty store by killer dogs is absurdly gripping. Maybe time for a remake with Josh Brolin.

13 TZAMETI (2005)

A spare, taut little *conte cruel*, shot (in cool black and white widescreen) in France by Georgian writer-director Géla Babluani.

Roofing contractor Sébastien (Georges Babluani) – whose family is in dire economic straits – realises he'll never see the money he is owed when haunted Godon (Philippe Passon), who has hired him to fix up a beach house, overdoses in the bath. Impulsively, Sébastien opens an envelope addressed to Godon, believing it will lead to a well-paid job. Finding a train ticket and a hotel booking, he follows directions which lead to a crossroads in the middle of nowhere and a ride with a saturnine chauffeur to a semi-derelict house thronged with wealthy, jittery men. Joining a group of thirteen contestants, Sébastien finds he is in a Russian roulette elimination game with high-stakes bets placed on his survival or otherwise. The game is run with impersonal professionalism by announcers and officials. A more conventional film might delve into backstories or demonise villains – as Babluani's American remake 13 (2009) does – but the shocked, sweating Sébastien is too startled to take an interest in anything but survival as he is shuttled through heats until a climactic duel with a thug who seems to be a champion in this game. The flics on the case, who close in on the game, are as sinister to Sébastien as the crooks who run the racket and the drab, everyday world glimpsed through train windows is ominous from the outset.

13, with Sam Riley as the hapless protagonist and Jason Statham and Ray Winstone as his rivals, works well when sticking close to the original script (down to a harsh ending), but over-eggs an unneeded sub-plot for guest stars Mickey Rourke and Curtis Jackson (mostly to justify putting them on the poster). In vibrant colour, with sinister work from interesting character faces (Alexander Skarsgard, Ben Gazzara, Michael Shannon, Ronald Guttman, David Zayas), it's one of the better US do-overs of a foreign-language hit, but the original is more effective.

UKM: THE ULTIMATE KILLING MACHINE (2006)

In 1994, director-writer David Mitchell made *The Killing Machine*, a direct-to-video quickie with Jeff Wincott and Michael Ironside; this Mitchell-directed direct-to-DVD effort – written by Tyler Levine and Tim McGregor – is vaguely a sequel, as another government conspiracy to create super-soldiers goes wrong. It's also as generic a piece of nonsense as ever was.

The army develop a Frankenstein process to equip recruits for modern warfare. Having had limited success turning a combat-hardened grunt (Simon Northwood) into an uncontrollable nutcase, the UKM project puts four enlistees into a program conducted in a facility which looks like a derelict warehouse with security doors. In a decent idea, two get the psycho dose and two a placebo, so there's theoretical suspense as to who will be a kill-crazy psycho but, as even the script admits, it's easy to guess.

Michael Madsen in his umpteenth time as the hard-bitten, world-weary, all-cliché military man makes you nostalgic for Michael Ironside. Slinky Deanna Dezmari is a dragon-lady mad scientist who uses what looks like a power drill to inject super-serum directly into the skull (setting up her own death scene). The grunts are a drunken barfly (Mac Fyfe) and a street person (Victoria Nestorowicz), who become de facto heroes (though she gets the UKM upgrade), an eager-to-please asshole (Steve Arbuckle) who becomes the main menace and a runaway waif (Erin Mackinnon) who dies early. The first act, with inductees catching on that something is amiss with their unusual basic training, has its moments – but the remainder is dispiritingly familiar running around corridors killing or getting killed.

UNKNOWN (2006)

Five indie character actors wake in an abandoned industrial facility outfitted with surprisingly high-tech security: Greg Kinnear has a broken nose, Joe Pantoliano is tied to a chair, Jeremy Sisto has been shot and handcuffed to a rail, Barry Pepper has a case of twitches and Jim Caviezel gets to be protagonist because he came to first. A leaky canister of toxic gas has afflicted everyone with amnesia. A too-convenient newspaper article and a mystery phone call suggest that the bewildered, hostile, uncertain folk are mixed up in a recent kidnapping – but no one knows whether they are innocent victim or vile crook. Meanwhile, breaking the chatty claustrophobia, the wife of the kidnapped businessman (Bridget Moynahan) pays the ransom to unambiguous baddies (Peter Stormare, Mark Boone Junior) and detectives (Chris Mulkey, Clayne Crawford) follow a tracer stashed inside the bag of money.

Matthew Waynee's script is in the line of high-concept calling cards like *Reservoir Dogs*, *Memento* and *Saw*, though music video director Simon Brand seems uncertain of its premise and keeps getting out of the factory to follow other threads. Of course, the trick is to keep us guessing who's who, and even a few fragmentary flashbacks don't tip things off too early: Sisto, who gets his memory back first, has a speech about a childhood incident which links him to Caviezel, then dies before he can say anything actually useful.

The last reel has a triple-reverse as someone's memories clear to reveal layers of truth – first that he's a kidnapper, then that he's an undercover cop, then finally that he's so crooked he came up with the whole idea. The one-two-three punch is clever, but reduces the film to gimmick and means the ending (which homages *Double Indemnity*) feels provisional. However, it's fun to watch the leads (who get character names like Jean Jacket, Rancher Shirt and Bound Man) demonstrate hysteria, suspicion, tentative friendliness, treachery, ranting and resentment as they form provisional partnerships or show what they believe to be their true colours.

VILE (2011)

> 'SO NOW WE HAVE TO CAREFULLY TORTURE OURSELVES? TWICE!'

Though its title is asking for abuse, this isn't quite a barrel-scraping exercise, though it is an utterly generic *Saw* variant.

Nick (Eric Jay Beck) and Tayler (April Matson) have a nice day in the country (though she hasn't managed to tell him that she's pregnant), but make the mistake of offering an older woman stranded at a gas station a lift to her car ('Don't you think you should ask before you volunteer to play taxi for some strange cougar?'). This leads to them waking in a basement with an assortment of similarly abducted folks with gadgets bolted to their heads. An array of instruments for inflicting pain are provided.

A video message (from creepy looking Maria Olsen) explains the premise: to harvest a chemical produced by pain in the brain, the group must torture each other until a quota is filled, enabling the manufacture of a profitable drug.

Screenwriters Beck (who gives himself a lead role) and Rob Kowsaluk string together scenes of fingernail pulling, scalding and abuse. One subject (Greg Cipes) has old scars and reveals himself as a masochist cutter, Tayler tries to help Nick by giving him painkillers which mean he doesn't yield his quota, a girl (Maya Hazen) shows a sadistic streak and starts going too far, and Tayler reveals she's pregnant and unwilling to risk her baby (though circumstances eventually prompt her to extreme, protracted self-harm). It's horrible (vile, even), but the drug McGuffin – frankly as ludicrous as the rationale for *The Tingler* – is almost funny. An unfamiliar but professional cast add to their showreels with moments of revelation between screaming and bleeding. Director Taylor Sheridan (hitherto a TV actor) puts it together competently.

WAR GAMES: AT THE END OF THE DAY (2011)

The cast of this Italian-made endurance horror are mostly British, but its greatest demerit is dubbing which sounds worse than anything stuck on a foreign film back in the day. It has a reasonably cool premise (cf: *The Zero Boys, Paintball*) as callow young folk, notably sisters Lara (Stephanie Chapman-Baker, who has a good look) and Monica (Valene Kane), play paintball in the woods and run into territory where Uncle (Lutz Michael) and a couple of ex-soldiers have got bored with sadistically hunting dogs and decide on a whim to go after kids instead. Why? Because that's what maniacs do in movies like these.

There's reasonable byplay among the squabbling players – one of whom brought a real gun, just in case – but none of the characters really register, perhaps because their voices seem beamed in from outer space. Monica goes missing and Lara spends the film determined to find her – though, when she does, her sister is hung up on ropes and Uncle has just cut her throat.

Final girl Lara puts on a gas mask, then executes Uncle with spine shots. Wandering off bloody and traumatised, she steps on a mine the killers planted earlier – though it ends with a click and ambiguity rather than an explosion. Not free of dumb stuff like the blonde who misses a point-blank shot at the machete killer, it layers on burbling indie songs for contrast with horror – listenable stuff, and perhaps a link to 1970s

Italian exploitation's use of weird MOR music. Written by Daniele Persica , Romana Meggiolaro and Cosimo Alemà; directed by Alemà.

WINTER'S END (2005)

An Irish entry in *Collector-Misery* captivity drama. Slacker photographer Jack Davis (Adam Goodwin) attends an open-air pop concert the film can't afford to show, gets drunk, has a brief argument with his more responsible married best friend (Donie Ryan) and returns to the field to find his car has been stolen. Farmer Henry Rose (Michael Crowley) lures him down a country road and knocks him out, then chains him in the barn. The cracked villain's plan is to have the victim impregnate his half-sister Amy (Jillian Bradbury) so that the 150-year-plus tenancy of the failing farm can continue. He says he'll let the lad go with a cash payout, but Jack is smart enough to realise Rose has to kill him to have a hope of getting away with it. Rose has a bit of range and depth in his crazy schemes, while the meek, dependant girl goes along for fear he will put her other brother, simpleton Sean (Paul Whyte), in an institution. Jack has to tell Amy, who has been cut off from TV and newspapers, that Ireland doesn't have 'institutions' in that sense any more and hasn't for years.

All stories like this follow a similar pattern: the victim goes from disbelief to pleading to bogus cooperation to desperate escape while the captor tries to hold together a scheme which keeps stumbling over the human element. This is well-enough written and acted to get past familiarity. A good surprise comes late in the day, as Jack cannily gets Rose to send out for an especially poncey Italian meal as a last supper – which turns out to be a signal to his best friend, a chef. The climax is protracted, with running about and hiding behind hedges plus shotgun waving and an obvious casualty – but the coda, which finds captive and 'wife' together four years later with a young daughter, is affecting and creepy. Written and directed by Patrick Kenny.

YOU BELONG TO ME (2007)

A gay-themed New York indie mystery which hinges on the ancient stereotype of a gay guy's overprotective, domineering mother. An abduction narrative on the *Misery* pattern, it lets Patti D'Arbanville play a *Baby Jane*-style monster diva

– though the mummified son (or son surrogate) who features in the climax also suggests a *Psycho* turnaround.

Puppyish architect Jeffrey (Daniel Sauli) is put out when his works-from-home editor flatmate Nicki (Heather Simms) barges into his bedroom to offload a yapping dog just as Jeffrey is beginning foreplay with one-night-stand René (Julien Lucas). Annoyed René heads out and Jeffrey tails him to his building, which is owned by Gladys (D'Arbanville), and spies a flat for rent. In semi-stalker mode, Jeffrey moves into the new apartment, ticking off Nicki and creeping out René, who lives with a regular boyfriend. Already on edge, Jeffrey notices things about the building and, in the mode of *The Tenant*, wonders what happened to the same name/different spelling Geoffrey who lived there previously and has disappeared.

For a while, the film alternates between uncomfortable – Jeffrey goes to a busy party at René's place and blatantly embarrasses himself mooning after the host – and mysterious, as he probes the building's decaying spaces. Then, he finds himself imprisoned in a secret room, the latest of several substitutes for Gladys's dead-of-AIDS son.

D'Arbanville underplays the crazy lady, though she has a few freak-out scenes, and Sauli makes the nervy Jeffrey – who actually does *need* a mother – into a normality figure rather than an incipient maniac. Writer-director Sam Zalutsky is torn between gay slice-of-life and shrieking melodrama, and doesn't go as far as, say, Paul Bartel in *Private Parts* to play up the 'horror house' aspects. Still, unusual.

CRYPTIDS AND CRITTERS

Bigfoot, Mermaids, Gill-Men, etc.

ABOMINABLE (2006)

One of the more entertaining Bigfoot/Sasquatch/yeti movies, this drops the sub-genre's walking-in-the-woods-with-occasional-gore rut for a fresher (if derivative) plot.

Wealthy outdoorsman Preston Rogers (Matt McCoy), crippled in a climbing accident, holes up in a mountain cabin to convalesce with oddly unsympathetic male nurse Otis (Christien Tinsley). Preston's notion of peace and quiet takes a hit when a squabbling, jiggling hen party occupies the cabin next door – though he isn't above using high-powered binoculars to ogle the new neighbours. While peeking thusly, Preston glimpses a monster snatching a girl. Otis thinks he's raving and the cops write his emails off as pranks. The beast gets bolder – ripping a naked girl through a window, grabbing another through the floorboards, snacking on human meat. The film mostly stays claustrophobic and cabin-bound: even the mandatory nudity, splatter and stalk-and-claw action is seen through binoculars. Eventually, final girl Amanda (Haley Joel) joins the wheelchair-bound hero to fight off the towering monster.

McCoy is excellent as an obvious riff on James Stewart in *Rear Window* – a former action man turned whining neurotic, who overcomes his fears in a burst of panic and rediscovers survival skills. Tinsley does double duty as monster designer, in partnership with tall makeup effects guy Michael Deak, who was Sasquatch on *Sabrina, the Teenage Witch* and has been inside creep suits ever since *Cellar Dweller*. Deak's impressive, ferocious beast boasts a huge scowling face reminiscent of vintage Paul Blaisdell (*Day the World Ended*) or even *The Brainiac*, but this retro-look abominable woodsman is unprecedentedly vicious, spilling more gore than even the penis-ripping Bigfoot of *Night of the Demon*.

Despite the narrow focus, there's room for veterans Dee Wallace-Stone (imperilled farm wife), Lance Henriksen and Jeffrey Combs (doomed hunters), and Paul Gleason (unimpressed sheriff). Writer-director Ryan Schifrin gets a family rate on a cut-above-the-budget-level score from his composer father Lalo.

ABSENTIA (2011)

'I'M GONNA SHOWER. I SMELL LIKE AN ARMPIT'S ASSHOLE.'

A slow-burning character-driven film with a terrific premise (developed in unexpected ways) and superbly engineered creep-out scares. Seven years after her husband Daniel (Morgan Peter Brown) seemingly dropped off the face of the Earth, Callie (Katie Parker) wanders a dowdy Los Angeles neighbourhood putting up missing person posters. Heavily pregnant by the cop on the case (Dave Levine), she has hallucinatory flashes of Daniel's spectral presence as she does paperwork to have him declared dead in absentia. Callie's recovered-addict Christian sister Tricia (Courtney Bell) has an odd encounter with an emaciated guy (Doug Jones) in an underpass – which leads to watch parts and other weird detritus being left in her bed. It's hinted that this is more than a missing person case: odd break-ins and disappearances in this ordinary area date back decades. Just after Daniel is declared dead, Callie goes out on a date with the cop… only to run into Daniel (who at first seems to be another hallucination) in the clothes he was wearing when he vanished and unable to explain where he's been.

Writer-director Mike Flanagan (*Oculus*) does well by awkward personal situations – not overdoing the backstory, but keeping it credible and uneasy. Has Daniel been kept in a cellar by a psycho, or – as suggested by reference to the Billy Goats Gruff – are trolls responsible? A more intriguing spin on the changeling theme than the *Don't Be Afraid of the Dark* remake with a distinctive blue-collar milieu. The unactressy leading ladies are both excellent. Among the first horror movies to explore the depopulated, economically damaged suburban spaces of post-crash America, later visited by films as varied as *The Pact, Only Lovers Left Alive, It Follows* and *Don't Breathe*.

BACKWOODS BLOODBATH: CURSE OF THE BLACK HODAG (2007)

'DID YOU EVER SEE THAT CRAZY SHITHEAD IN A HOCKEY MASK? THAT GUY AIN'T SHIT COMPARED TO THIS ASSHOLE!'

The only thing setting this shot-on-DV-with-a-no-name-cast effort apart from the pack is a mild but clever third act twist. Inspired by one of those Bigfoot-type local legends every American backwater supports, it's set in Oneida County, Wisconsin – home to the Hodag (Seth Chilsen), an egg-laying carnivore which has evolved to wear clothes (including a long slicker coat), use cutting tools and be generally indistinguishable from a dreadlocked human killer. Like a *Mimic* Judas bug, it resembles a wino… like the Reeker, it smells… like the Creeper, it rips off body parts.

A gang of junior *Big Chill* types who were at high school together spend the weekend at the proverbial cabin in the woods, to honour a pal who recently fell off a balcony. Most of the character stuff, which takes up a lot of time, is about Jessica (Angela Lowe) realising her jock former-boyfriend (Josh Mijal) is a dork and gravitating to sensitive photographer Mark (Jesse L. Cyr). The Hodag slaughters a couple of people – for various reasons, the woods are full of passersby who die in extravagantly gory if ludicrous manners (the blood looks like gallons of treacle) – but the monster isn't the only killer in the woods.

Flatly made, with minor step-printing and roaring to punch up the splatter, this is stuck with iffy performances, though writer-director Donn Kennedy tries to give characters unusual traits. Cooper (Travis Ruhland) is so focused on listening to 'the game' on the radio he is alarmed when the car is sabotaged only because it rules out a beer run, deems the fatal goring of a close friend less irritating that a lack of bratwurst and is so upset by his team losing that he literally doesn't care if he lives or dies.

BANSHEE!!! (2008)

Your basic adequate monster/slasher film. In a 1970 prologue, dudes with facial hair pick up a silent blonde hitchhiker (Jess Wakefield) who turns into a flickering CGI creature and kills them. In the present day, a bunch of unpleasant college kids camping in the woods are offed by the monster. It can impersonate other people, but isn't a good enough actor not to give off evil starey vibes when doing so. The body count rises so high that the survivors, most of whom don't last long, have to burst into a woodland home and hook up with new characters, including a hero (David McCarthy), an old-timer (Kevin Shea) and a lady cop (Kerry McGann).

The only surprise is that the dim blonde (Ashley Bates) turns out to be final girl, not the more sensible brunette (Iris McQuillan-Grace). The token black guy (Troy Walcott) is a dolt who plays stupid pranks even after a few of his friends have been ripped up in front of him. Little is made of the howling (the thing banshees are known for, as a rule) and a few Irish-American characters don't really explain why this Irish monster is in

Connecticut. Its weakness, stupidly, is loud, discordant noise: the hero fends it off with guitar twangs. A distant cousin of the *Jeepers Creepers* Creeper, this banshee has wings, a radiator-grille snarl and a bad attitude. Written by John Doolan, Gregory C. Parker and Christian Pindar; directed by Colin Theys (*Remains*, *Dead Souls*).

BIGFOOT (1970)

Among the first of many, many Bigfootsploitation movies, this drive-in hit boasts that it was filmed in mountain locales where Bigfoot has been seen – though it cuts between walking-aimlessly-in-the-woods footage and a cramped studio forest set. But for the dayglo outfits and twangy guitar score, it could be a 1940s jungle programmer. The creatures – theorised to be missing links – even seem to be wearing modified gorilla suits which could have been handed down from Charles Gemora or Ray 'Crash' Corrigan. In a long, slow preamble, pilot Joi Landis (blonde Joi Lansing) parachutes out of her stricken plane into the wilderness, strips out of a tight blue jumpsuit to reveal a low-cut minidress and is leaped upon by something hairy and scream-inducing.

The rest of the film has the Bigfoot family stalked by various factions: travelling salesmen/carny hustlers Hawks (John Carradine) – lots of dialogue, delivered with enthusiasm – and Briggs (John Mitchum) – porky comedy cousin with a fringe beard; a bike gang led by bandana-sporting Rick (Chris Mitchum) out to rescue an abducted momma (Judith Jordan); and a posse commanded by the sheriff (James Craig, of *All That Money Can Buy*). The plot features the stealing-women-to-breed gambit, with Lansing and Jordan decorously tied to posts serial-style, but Hawks' desire to capture Bigfoot alive so it can be exhibited prods it towards another familiar story (free paraphrasing of *King Kong* extends to 'It wasn't you, mister. It was beauty did him in.').

It's lackadaisically told. The biggest Sasquatch – a tall guy shot from below (Nick Raymond) – is killed offscreen by dynamite, suggesting either that a sequel was planned or director Robert F. Slatzer couldn't afford a proper climax. With cowboy star Ken Maynard, Russ Meyer veteran Haji as an Indian maid, pin-up Jennifer Bishop, former Munchkin Jerry Maren (as Child Bigfoot), son-of-Bing Lindsay Crosby (another biker), Memphis mafioso Del 'Sonny' West and Spike Jones stalwart Doodles Weaver (Sigourney's uncle).

BIGFOOT HOLLER CREEK CANYON (2006)

Another batch of unlikeable, squabbling students spend the weekend at a house in the woods and are slaughtered by a hairy monster. The characters are all stock: the bland blonde final girl (Anna Bridgforth), the faithful friend who has always loved her but never spoken up (Gentry Ferrell), the hot-to-trot Latina who has loud sex (Tammie Taylor), the beer-guzzling asshole jerk tool who gets killed first (Johnny Ostensoe), the under-characterised chick with a crush on the guy who only has eyes for the heroine (Mélisa Breiner-Sanders) and the panty-sniffing cheating ex-boyfriend who tries to fake sympathy (Justin Alvarez). Writer-director John Poague (*The Wickeds*) plays a backwoods red herring and guest star Ron Jeremy is an inept ranger who utters ominous warnings about killer bears, spies on kids having sex and gets his head stamped flat. The creature (Nathan Faudree) just shows up, prompting surprisingly little curiosity about its origins, and there's over an hour of teen soap idiocy before screaming and panicking takes over. Limbs are ripped off and severed heads dropped, but the shaggy monster sports the sort of hair-suit seen in these things since the early 1970s. No atmosphere, no suspense, no fun.

THE BLACKOUT (2009)

A low-budget monster movie harking back to the cheap *Alien* ripoffs of the '80s; the oily, snarly man-in-a-suit look of its CGI-augmented creatures evokes *Scared to Death*, *XTRO* or *Forbidden World* (in my book, a good thing). Jim Beck's script reaches even further into B-movie history by updating the premise of the fondly remembered *The Slime People* (1963).

On Christmas Eve, Los Angeles is struck by small earth tremors and noxious fumes leak from cracks in the ground. In an apartment building, LA types go through the usual round of whining, quarrelling and scheming while ignoring omens. Elizabeth (Barbara Streifel Sanders) and Daniel (Joseph Dunn) have a spat about Daniel's deadbeat brother Dylan (Ian Malcolm) crashing on their couch for the holidays, but the loser shows a heroic streak when their two kids go missing. Kyle (Tyler Armstrong) gets chomped by a monster in the basement while fetching a Christmas present, but his sister Ashley (Abigail Droeger) is trapped in a lift by intermittent power outages caused by seismic/monster activity. A party in the next apartment gets out of hand when monsters (spawned from trilobitish things which pour into the basement) start killing with scissor-tipped prehensile tails.

In disaster/monster movie fashion, characters die through gory attack, sacrifice, ironic fate and effects set piece. Performances are a little shrill, despite twinges of half-decent characterisation, but the Christmas setting is well used. The derivative critters have an interesting trait: they radiate an electro-magnetic pulse which shuts off lights (including torches) and other electricals as they get near. After an extended climax in the lift-shaft (always a favoured menace location), survivors escape the building to find a *Demons*-style apocalypse in the streets (which is frankly beyond the budget). Despite cavils, reasonable fun. Directed by Robert David Sanders (editor of *Postman Pat: The Movie*).

THE BOOGENS (1982)

> 'WHEN WE'RE IN THE MINE, THE RULES ARE SIMPLE ENOUGH FOR EVEN YOU GUYS TO UNDERSTAND: NO FUCKING AROUND.'

An old mine is reopened and unexplained subterranean creatures crawl out of the dark. This has much in common with the slashers of the early 1980s, but its body count is down to old-fashioned monsters rather than a psycho. It's surprisingly reticent about the 'boogens', who are only glimpsed in the final minutes – which means we never quite work out what they look like. They have bug-eyed round heads with big-fanged mouths and snake-like constricting tentacles (or tails) and crawl along the floor to chew victims' ankles before slicing necks or faces. The backstory is that the mine shut down in 1912, presumably after an earlier monster attack. In the spirit of *Friday the 13th*, a crazy old coot (Jon Lormer) has guarded the place these many years, warning folk not to reopen the place.

Much of the film is about young college graduate engineers Mark (Fred McCarren) and Roger (Jeff Harlan) and their girlfriends Trish (Rebecca Balding) and Jessica (Anne-Marie Martin) and contrivances whereby one of them can be killed but thought to be just out of town. The film might seem to dawdle in scenes where Jessica shows off her pool prowess or Trish cosies up to her guy, but Balding and Martin are winning. The eerie, monster-haunted mine and the snowy, craggy countryside give the fantasy a certain proletarian grit (cf: *The Strangeness*, *My Bloody Valentine*). Director James L. Conway improves greatly on his dreary SF films (*Earthbound*, *Hangar 18*).

THE BURROWERS (2008)

An excellent horror western – with a dour widescreen look – which comes up with a fresh monster whose depredations have an interesting historical rationale. Kink-kneed humanoid ghouls who immobilise their prey and bury them alive to fester till they're edible, the burrowers fed off buffalo until the white man hunted their natural prey to extinction... now they're after human meat.

In an opening riff on *The Searchers*, an isolated farm comes under attack. Assuming they're besieged by hostile Lakota, homesteaders retreat to the storm cellar – only for the creatures to come through the walls. A posse formed to rescue abducted Maryanne (Jocelin Donahue) includes Irish immigrant Fergus Coffey (Karl Geary), cool gunman William Parcher (William Mapother), tagalong kid Dobie Spacks (Galen Hutchison), ex-slave cook Walnut Callaghan (Sean Patrick Thomas) and John Wayne-style tough old hand John Clay (Clancy Brown). Unfortunately, the leader is vain cavalry officer Henry Victor (Doug Hutchison), more intent on fomenting a career-boosting Indian war than saving the girl.

Writer-director J.T. Petty (who made something interesting out of *Mimic 3*) doesn't take the obvious route: the odious Victor, whose moustache-trimming echoes Custer in *Little Big Man*, survives while better men don't and the repulsive monsters are only as dangerous as most human characters. Several times, Petty breaks an entrenched film convention and has horses shot dead – this ought to happen in every running cowboy battle, but how many other westerns make a point of it? In a striking image, an unknown woman is found buried alive on the prairie, one mad eye staring up out of the dirt.

CREATURE (2011)

This man-in-a-suit monster movie took a critical/commercial pasting on US theatrical release – achieving a record low turnout. That probably has as much to do with its bland, used-too-many-times title as inherent weakness. The pitch seems to be to do something like *Octaman* or *The Monster of Piedras Blancas* in the style of Eli Roth or Rob Zombie, with obnoxious characters and torture porn/ordeal elements.

Siblings Oscar (Dillon Casey) and Karen (Lauren Schneider) drive pals (Mehcad Brooks, Aaron Hill, Serinda Swan, Amanda Fuller) through the bayou en route to a supposed fun time in New Orleans. However, the duo – children of demented patriarch Chopper (Sid Haig) – are scheming to offer their friends to gator-man Grimley (Daniel Bernhardt), who wants to kill the men and mate with the women. Schneider gives the best performance, exuding backwater creepiness (a little like Patricia Pearcy in *Squirm*) with side orders of lesbian seduction and incest. Pruitt Taylor Vince, Wayne Pére and David Jensen sit about the shack/store leering, and a whole cult/clan turn up for the finale then fade into the swamp as the very buff Navy SEAL hero (Brooks) tussles with Grimley around a sucking sinkhole.

The impressive monster suit homages the lantern-jawed look of *The Alligator People* and the monster action is fun, though the retro-*Deliverance* angle is superfluous. Not great, but watchable. Written by Tracy Morse and Fred Andrews; directed by Andrews.

CREATURE FROM BLACK LAKE (1976)

> 'I'M GETTING MY SHOTGUN AND THEN I'M GONNA MAKE A RUG OUT OF THAT DAMN THING.'

Most Bigfoot features are set in the cryptid's traditional Pacific Northwest territory, but this slice of drive-in cryptozoology opts for Louisiana swampland. An aquatic Bigfoot leaps out of the water to kill an old-timer in the prologue, as if this were scripted as a fishier *Creature from the Black Lagoon* imitation but retooled into something furrier when *The Legend of Boggy Creek* put Sasquatch on the exploitation map. Jaime

Mendoza-Nava, who scored *Boggy Creek*, does the same here; a decade later, he'd do the same for the similar *Terror in the Swamp*.

Director Joy N. Houck Jr (*Night of Bloody Horror*) cameos as a Chicago professor who misleadingly declares that there have been no reported incidents of Bigfoot attacking humans (just after we've seen one) and sends students Rives (John David Carson) and Pahoo (Dennis Fimple) South to visit the reputedly monster-infested Black Lake. Agonising time is spent on cornball comic monologues about hamburgers, joshing in the local café and barbershop, run-ins with the sheriff (Bill Thurman) and almost anything but encounters with a creature who might be 'a mutant bear or gorilla' (or, equally, might not). The monster's roar is caught on tape, making a waitress drop a trayful of lunches when played back, while Orville (writer Jim McCullough Jr) narrates a flashback in which he is orphaned by a creature attack... but the shaggy-suited monster is barely glimpsed until the climax, then only seen in long-shot (most Bigfoot fiction films take cues from supposed actual footage of the critter and keep their distance) as it mangles Pahoo and tips Rives' camper-van down a slope.

In a bit of business reused in *Don't Go in the Woods* and commonplace after *The Descent*, one of the heroes accidentally stabs his stumbling friend while trying to fend off the monster; here, it's not a fatal wound – allowing for a happy ending, though the status of the creature is left ambiguous. Western veterans Jack Elam and Dub Taylor fill the quota of whiskery drunks whose monster stories are disbelieved. An early credit for distinguished cinematographer Dean Cundey (*Halloween*).

CURSE OF BIGFOOT (1975)

'WHY IT'S A MUMMY – COVERED WITH MUD!'
'WHAT A FIND!'

One of the odder (and, despite its shoddiness, more entertaining) Bigfootsploitation films, this repackages the 1958 semi-amateur effort *Teenagers Battle the Thing* with a new-made prologue to pass off its monster (a deformed or prehistoric Indian mummy) as Bigfoot. It does, admittedly, leave big footprints. A slow opening apes the usual creaky travelogue with droning narration, woodland ramble footage, poster-paint blood spilling on rocks and a full view of the tusked, poached-egg-eyed, gurning creature lurching through the woods in the spirit of 1950s creature design triumphs like *The Brainiac* and *From Hell It Came*. A long classroom lecture about legendary monsters is interrupted by a downer guest lecturer who sets up a flashback (i.e. all of *Teenagers Battle the Thing* in colour – though prints of the original circulating online are in black-and-white) by explaining that the expedition he is describing was so harrowing one survivor is an asylum inmate who can only express herself by screaming.

However, the traipse up into mountain country – led by the unfortunately named Dr Bill Wyman (Bill Simonsen) – has a low body count. All the kids seem relatively sane at the abrupt climax in which buckets of kerosene are thrown over the monster and it's lit up like a torch. Reams of woodenly delivered banter – the girl lamenting she's never allowed to do intrepid archaeology like the guys, the prof musing about primitive mummification techniques – pad it out and the rampage is just ordinary lumbering and screaming. Other attenuated productions: *Equinox, Terror in the Midnight Sun/Invasion of the Animal People, Monster a Go-Go!* and Jerry Warren Mexican mash-ups like *Attack of the Mayan Mummy*. Written by James T. Flocker; directed by Dave Flocker.

DEADLY DESCENT: THE ABOMINABLE SNOWMAN (2013)

A dullish Syfy monster movie, shot in Bulgaria, set somewhere else. Military guy Tanner (Chuck Campbell) has a grudge against the monster who killed his father. Drunken chopper pilot Foster (Adrian Paul) drops him on top of a mountain so he can hunt the beast (though he brings only one small gun). Rick (Nicholas Boulton), Tanner's CO, and Nina (Lauren O'Neil), his sister, mount a rescue mission which gets a bunch of disposable grunts killed. If Tanner had filed a monster-fighting plan before going up the mountain, all these people would still be alive and he'd still be an asshole. The *Critter*-mouthed, bear-bodied, knuckle-dragging furry monsters ('ugly Chewbacca') resemble the *Attack the Block* aliens with less glowy teeth. It has CGI monsters, snow, gore and helicopters, but a real avalanche. Scripted by Nathan Atkins (*S. Darko*); directed by Marko Makilaakso (*War of the Dead*).

LAS GARRAS DE LORELEI (THE LORELEY'S GRASP; WHEN THE SCREAMING STOPS) (1974)

This Teutonic-Hispanic hybrid from writer-director Amando de Ossorio draws on the myth of the Nibelung, but is a melange of werewolf picture and *She/L'Atlantide* immortal wicked queen story. A community on the Rhine, with at least some misty location work, is terrorised by a creature who strikes on the full moon, ripping victims (a young bride, a blind musician, etc.) apart with green rubbery claws (the effects are ropey but extreme, with exposed hearts, blood on nipples, torn-open ribcages, etc.). In a William Castle-ish frill, a few frames of red flash before murders – there's no horror horn or on-screen warning ballyhoo, so we can just take it as mystic foreshadowing.

The local girls' school, a *Lycanthropus*-style institute full of Euro-babes in skimpy outfits, hires hunter Sirgurd (Tony Kendall) to track the beast. He wanders around in safari suits non-colour-blind animals would see coming a mile off and banters with uptight teacher Elke (Silvia Tortosa), who hates him on sight and thus becomes one-third of a romantic triangle. The other angle is wildchild waif Lorelei (Helga Liné), who wears a fetching black-fringed bikini and is even more obviously the monster's alter ego than Barbara Shelley in *The Gorgon*. A goateed professor (Ángel Menéndez) demonstrates that an injection and a beam of artificial moonlight transforms a severed human hand into a barbed green version of the monster's claw. The lorelei, whose sidekick Alberic (Luis Barboo) hangs around in monk's robes, invades the laboratory to murder the scientist, but he obligingly tips acid over his own face, which melts away gruesomely.

In an impressive vaulted space under the Rhine, the lorelei – who resembles the *It! The Terror From Beyond Space* Martian in a black robe – has a collection of the skeletons of her previous human lovers. Also present are three Rhine Maidens in leopard-pattern bikinis who hiss, argue and catfight. Their plot purpose is to free Sirgurd from chains so he can rescue Elke before a bomb thrown in the river brings down the roof. Sirgurd stabs the lorelei with a handy semi-magic dagger (an offcut from Siegfried's sword) and the monster turns into a pale Liné. She breathes, 'We'll meet again in Valhalla,' before dying, then shows up in colour negative on a horse, galloping into the afterlife. It has choral music among the usual easy listening burble, a lot of beautiful women striking pin-up poses, vibrant 1976 fashions, video nasty-level gore (trimmed from those horrible 1980s video releases), a myth-science-cliché mess of a monster and a few moments of Rhine-ish lyricism. Great fun.

HYBRID (SUPER HYBRID) (2010)

> ### 'LET'S SEE A SHOW OF HANDS: WHO THINKS HECTOR AND AL WERE KILLED BY A MAN-EATING CAR?'

In the tiny sub-genre of blood-drinking car movies, *Hybrid* distinguishes itself by being loopier even than *Upír z Feratu* or *Blood Car*: the menace stalking a cavernous underground garage in Chicago is a giant squid with the chameleon ability of disguising itself to lie in wait for prey. In its usual habitat, this vampire cephalopod looks like a coral reef; here, it imitates a black sedan (which resembles a less classy model of *The Car*) but still occasionally sprouts CGI tentacles. In an especially surreal image, the car turns back into a writhing mass of tentacles visible under a semi-transparent dustsheet.

Ray (Oded Fehr), boss of the garage, is a prime example of the bad movie character type of Instigating Asshole. Everything the crass, selfish, money-grubbing bastard does makes things worse – putting (and keeping) everyone in danger, while provoking character conflict and tossing off cynical remarks. Heroine Tilda (Shannon Beckner), nice guy Bobby (Ryan Kennedy) and hot chick Maria (Melanie Papalia) all have a surprising wealth of information (gleaned from the Discovery Channel) and the actors manage not to look ashamed delivering speculative explanatory speeches between scenes of the car prowling, shapeshifting and stalking (it has red bloodvision POV).

The monster turns into other types of vehicles to fool victims, morphing into a pickup truck for one of many chase-through-the-garage stunt sequences. It even sneakily turns into a reassuring police car to lure Bobby into its front seat for crushing and digesting purposes. Only when trapped in a pit full of spikes does the car revert to its mollusc/squid/mouth-and-tentacles form. Written by Neal Marshall Stevens (aka Benjamin Carr), whose CV includes a lot of Charles Band movies (*The Creeps*, *Head of the Family*), *Thir13en Ghosts* and some *Hellraiser* sequels. Directed by Eric Valette (*Maléfique*).

HYPOTHERMIA (2010)

This minimalist monster movie from Glass Eye Pix shares themes with producer/bit-player Larry Fessenden's eco-horrors (*The Last Winter*, *Beneath*). Director-writer James Felix McKenney (*Satan Hates You*) delivers a solid central situation as contrasted families on an ice-fishing vacation are terrorised by a monster. The performances are good, with Michael Rooker cast against type as the calmer father so the less-familiar Don Wood can play the raving asshole. Sensible Ray (Rooker) and his dignified wife Helen (Blanche Baker) cringe when obnoxious Cote (Wood) shows up in a mobile home, blaring music, whizzing about drunkenly on a snowmobile and calling the unseen predator which has denuded the lake of fish a 'bitch'. The families at least try to get on – until Cote's son (Greg Finley) is killed and Cote begins ranting about revenge. Cote sneers when Ray mentions global warming as the probable cause of the monster's appearance, and there's a subtext about the way both misread nature. It sticks to its one location and offers 1970s levels of frothing gore, but the toothy amphibian man-suit worn by Asa Liebmann is only just above Larry Buchanan standards. Admittedly, McKenney doesn't let it appear on screen too long and not going the CGI route is at least refreshing, but the film gets giggles when the main menace appears – a shame, since the less-well-scripted *Creature* had the resources to deliver an effective gator-man.

ICE QUEEN (2005)

> 'THERE ARE SPECIES OUT THERE
> THAT CAN CHANGE GENDER OR
> EAT THEIR OWN YOUNG.'
> 'YEAH, THEY'RE CALLED LIBERALS.'

This quickie features a slightly out-of-the-rut monster (English model Ami Veevers-Chorlton), frozen in a glacier since the Pleistocene Era. The Ice Queen has blue skin, red eyes, claws, fangs, a below-zero body temperature, a tight cryo-suit with red tubes stuck out of it (which earns the soubriquet 'bad fashion bitch') and insides 'more akin to those of an insect' than a human being. She kills by regulation claw-slashing, but also by puncturing victims and freezing them from the inside – and is frisky around tedious hunk hero Johnny (Harmon Walsh), especially when he courts hypothermia by stripping down to his shorts and rolling in a snow drift. It's a *Doctor Who*-style chased-around-a-remote-base picture with squabbling, broadly drawn fools cooped up in a crushed ski-lodge after an avalanche caused by a plane crash caused in turn by the Ice Queen killing the pilot (Neil Benedict).

The preamble is littered with comedy/soap about the numbnuts hero being on the outs with girlfriend Tori (Noelle Reno) because she thinks he's grappled in a hot tub with silicone-enhanced bimbo Elaine (Jennifer Hill). Johnny also gets a hard time from his strict boss Audrey (Tara Walden), who takes offence at a homophobic joke (way to write a sympathetic character, guys). Mad scientist Dr Goddard (Daniel Hall Kuhn) does the *Thing From Another World* bit of trying to protect the rampaging monster from people who only want to save their petty lives and ignore benefits to science. Veevers-Chorlton (or 'Veveers-Chorlton' in the end credits) gives the Ice Queen personality, but the film underuses her: even Goddard never tries to communicate with the monster and the rationale for the transformation from normal-looking blonde to horror hag is shaky. It's cheaply beefed up with borrowed footage: a helicopter attack from Abel Ferrara's *Body Snatchers*, ski stunts from *Avalanche* (aka *Escape From Alaska*). Directed and co-written by Neil Kinsella (*2 Dead 2 Kill*).

INDIGENOUS (PREY) (2014)

> 'HAVE YOU SEEN THAT VIDEO OF THE TEENAGERS THAT WENT MISSING OUT HERE IN THE JUNGLE?'

This ordinary horror film has lovely Panamanian jungle locations and decent monster design, but middling script, concept and performance – and resorts tiresomely to herky-jerky, stop-frame jitteriness for its gore/action. It's among a bunch of films which might be considered post-found footage: an online clip of a monster attack is part of the backstory and another leaks out during the crisis, ridiculously good-looking tourists and their local hook-ups sometimes tote cameras and a lot of news footage fills in the story, but it's primarily a conventional narrative. College-age kids (Zachary Soetenga, Lindsey McKeon, Sofia Pernas, Pierson Fode, etc.), in Panama to surf and bar-hop, hear about an awesome waterfall in the middle of the jungle which isn't overrun by tourists because it's the reputed haunt of a *chupacabra* ('an evil spirit trapped in a half-human, half-monster body') – here depicted as a Nosferatu-look man-eating cryptid. Of course, screaming terror and death ensue. One decent idea has the story break and go viral while the standard plot is taking place, prompting worldwide reassessment of local legends (including traditional goatsuckers in Texas) and military action against many varieties of snarly creature. Ordinary as this is, the big reveal might make for an interesting sequel or series. Written by Max Roberts; directed by Alastair Orr (*From a House on Willow Street*).

IT WAITS (2005)

A standard monster movie from director Steven R. Monroe (*Sasquatch Mountain*, *House of 9*, the *I Spit On Your Grave* remake) and writers Richard Christian Matheson and Thomas E. Szollosi. A Native American archaeologist (Eric Schweig) ventures into a cave and frees an all-purpose monster after the manner of *Jeepers Creepers* (or, for older viewers, *Gargoyles*). The clawed Bigfoot lookalike turns out to have bat-wings and near-human cunning. Forest ranger Dani St Claire (Cerina Vincent), soaking in vodka after causing the death of her best friend (Miranda Frigon), cheers up a bit when her boyfriend Justin (Dominic Zamprogna) arrives at her tree-house workplace – then the monster attacks, slaughtering whoever happens past (and leaving Justin's severed head where she's bound to find it). Vincent gets to do more than her stock imperilled babe act (cf: *Intermedio*, *Seven Mummies*), but doesn't really convince as a guilt-ridden drunk or a Ripley-style survive-at-all-costs heroine. The monster (Matt Jordan – also in *Mansquito*) is just an angry, nasty brute. The woods look nice, but we've been here before.

THE LONELY ONES (2006)

A better-than-average spam-in-a-cabin movie, *The Lonely Ones* has a luxurious cabin, though it's stuck with video murk, inadequate sound and inconsistent acting typical of its budget range. Writer-director David Michael Quiroz Jr deserves points for unfamiliar monsters (his ghouls are reminiscent of the Carkers in Anthony Boucher's classic story 'They Bite') and unusual character interplay during a regulation normals-under-siege-through-the-night plot.

A crowd of college kids (too many, actually – half fail to register before they die) venture into the wilds to stay at a cabin owned by Tifa (Devanny Pinn). While indulging in soap-opera tangles, they ignore omens like anecdotes about sorority girls who disappeared in these parts (in the 1988-set prologue) and a gas station encounter with seething, brooding biker Blake (Jose Rosete). Pigtailed Rinoa (Heather Rae) is hung up on Cid (Vince Reign), a bipolar jock who's sensitive for a while but has cheated on her with Tifa. A couple of plots simmer for a reel or so until Luke (Ron Berg), a Zandor Vorkov lookalike with a mawful of fangs, shows up with a posse of 'feral ghouls' and fulfils a cliché by ripping off the head of the token black guy. Blake turns out to be a monster hunter tracking Luke's pack: he blasts Tifa, who bleeds green, spits out false teeth, and is revealed as a 'gatherer' ghoul whose job is to lure the unwary where they can be eaten. Blake organises the traumatised kids to defend the cabin, but only Rinoa is really enthusiastic about it. Escape attempts turn out badly (the ghouls go for *Night of the Living Dead* gut-gobbling) and the monsters are resisted with boiling water and kitchen implements.

The most unusual angle is that it keeps getting back to weird soap opera. Tifa, among people so long she's alienated from her own kind, still wants Cid as a lover. The dolt opts to betray the humans for her, though jealous Luke skins him on the mistaken assumption Tifa won't mind who's wearing the face of the bloke she fancies. Rinoa gets more pissed off and tough (undoing her bunches when she gets serious) and is in a position by the fadeout to take over Blake's anti-ghoul crusade. The last reel has too much agonised back-and-forth among ghouls and humans, but Quiroz at least gives his creatures a complicated attitude, internal dissents and quirks.

MAMMOTH (2006)

'WE'VE GOT AN ALIEN-POSSESSED MAMMOTH ON THE LOOSE AND IF WE DON'T STOP IT THE GOVERNMENT'S GONNA KILL ALL OF US.'

This SciFi Channel effort – set in Louisiana, shot in Romania – seesaws between outright spoof and straight (if silly) monster business.

Museum curator and job-absorbed single father Frank Abernathy (Vincent Ventresca) notices an alien artefact lodged inside a mammoth on display in a huge chunk of ice. When the doodad is extracted, the ancient animal thunders to life as a partially rotted zombie with a soul-sucking trunk(!) under the influence of hostile extra-terrestrial forces. The monster gets loose and attacks a teen 'pod party' (lots of kids tamely bopping to I-pods) and Frank has to step up and become a hero to his semi-estranged daughter (Summer Glau), hauling in his B-movie/UFO-conspiracy fanatic dad (Tom Skerritt) for help and hooking up with babe-look 'government stooge' Woman in Black (Leila Arcieri). A sub-plot features a Thing/Beast With Five Fingers alien-possessed, malevolent crawling hand.

Director-writer Tim Cox (*Larva*) tosses in sci-fi movie gabble as characters compare versions of *The War of the Worlds* or make frozen Han Solo jokes and there's a comedy score – but when characters get killed, it plays straight. It ends up with the usual fight in a disused industrial space. The CGI zombie mammoth is frankly too poor for a computer game, but it's still a unique creation.

MAN-THING (2005)

Often confused with DC's Swamp Thing, who debuted a few months later, Marvel's muck-monster *Man-Thing* was one of the horror-cum-superhero characters (*Ghost Rider, Werewolf By Night*) who emerged in the early 1970s after a ban on horror was lifted by an alteration of the Comics Code. Managing the lowest profile of the many Marvel properties brought to the screen since the late 1990s, *Man-Thing* is a shot-in-Australia, no-name-cast, straight-to-DVD quickie with more gore (and bad language) than most kid-friendly comics adaptations. The monster (Mark Stevens) is barely glimpsed for most of the picture, which concentrates on a new sheriff (Matthew Le Nevez) in a Florida backwater, caught between exploitative oilman Schist (Aussie icon Jack Thompson) and Native American activists. When he finally shows up, Man-Thing is an impressive, red-eyed creature, inspired by but not a simple lift from the comics design. As much menace as avenging spirit, Man-Thing kills a few sympathetic characters (growing trees inside their bodies) as it works its way through those responsible for siting an oil-drill in the sacred 'Dark Waters'. Dubbed-in Cajun accents sound phony, but director Brett Leonard gives it an eerie liana-choked, mossy, ugly-wet feel closer to the imaginary swamp of the comics than the actual locations used in the *Swamp Thing* films.

MEXICAN WEREWOLF IN TEXAS (2005)

Despite the title, this isn't a werewolf movie; it is set in Texas, though. The Mexican modern legend (scarcely 'urban') of *el chupacabra* (the goat-sucker) has featured in many films (*Chupacabra: Dark Seas, Legend of the Chupacabra, El Chupacabra, Bloodthirst: Legend of the Chupacabras*) and an *X-Files* episode ('El Mundo Gira'). Besides preying on livestock, this version of the monster gorily kills folk (a vet, a butcher) who have animal blood on them and contrivances (a leaky bag of monster-bait) get victims smeared to up the kill count. Teen heroine Anna (Erika Fay) sees capturing a *chupacabra* for bounty as a way of escaping her small town (Furlough, Texas). Monster hunter Cabot Speers (Wolfgang Metzger) thinks aliens stole his dog and the *chupacabra* is their escaped pet (he hopes for a prisoner exchange). Adding to the complications, the heroine's undertaker father (Mark Halvorson) sews together a suit of pelts and finds a meat-fork which matches *chupacabra* fang-marks, plotting to kill her boyfriend (Gabriel Gutierrez) and frame the monster. For a cheapie, this has more going on in acting and scripting departments than usual – though serious John Sayles-ish elements jar with Texan comedy hijinx. The attacks are all blurry gore and low-rent hair suit business. One witness says *el chupacabra looks like* a werewolf. As in most *chupacabra* movies, the monster isn't considered newsworthy if it sticks to its folkloric m.o. (sucking Mexican goats); it only gets attention by relocating to America and killing people. Written and directed by Scott Maginnis.

THE MONSTER (2015)

Writer-director Bryan Bertino (*The Strangers, Mockingbird*) likes to keep things simple – his preferred premise is a couple with a credibly uneasy, raw relationship suddenly threatened by a horror-movie monstrosity which forces them to work together. Here, as instanced by the blunt title, the setup is so basic it might have done for a short. Value is added by a committed performance from Zoe Kazan as a useless foul-up mom stranded in the woods with her sullen daughter when their car is sent into a spin by an already wounded wolf.

An economical setup establishes that Kathy (Kazan) is such a failure at looking after young Lizzy (Ella Ballentine) that the girl wants to live with her father. Throughout, small flashback scenes illustrate mother-daughter hostility as Kathy's lifestyle choices, which start with smoking in the car and escalate to an unerring preferrence for rotten boyfriends, put a strain on Lizzy's tolerance. These scenes push the envelope on dysfunctional family ties – mother and daughter shriek 'fuck you' at each other during an argument about Lizzy appearing in a school play – but Bertino gives snapshots rather than over elaborating, just as he presents the horror without too much explanation. We're never sure what the monster – an impressively toothy and wet-furred man-in-a-suit creation (stuntman Chris Webb) – is, though it might conceivably be related to the werewolf or Bigfoot family.

Like *The Strangers*, this mostly plays in real time at a single location – a stretch of lonely road. It's dark and wet, and emergency services show up only to become monster fodder as mother and daughter sort out their relationship between attacks and escape attempts. In the mid-2010s (maybe as the influence of *The Babadook* seeped through the genre), a surprising number of horror/suspense films featured mothers fighting to protect children (cf: *White Coffin, Under the Shadow, Monolith*). *The Monster* microfocuses on the theme with Kazan thoroughly unsympathetic as the spaced-out child-woman with red rat-tails and numbed resentful meanness going through a hard road to some sort of redemption during the ordeal. In most of these films, the imperilled child is a token – sometimes even a baby – but *The Monster* gives equal time to Ballentine as the deeply hurt Lizzy, who also finds inner resources as the big beast keeps coming back.

It's so simple some horror fans might resent its seeming lack of interest in the nature of its menace – but it's a very effective fright machine, with telling, spiky character touches. Scott Speedman, star of *The Strangers*, has a tiny cameo as Kathy's latest douchebag boyfriend.

NYMPH (MAMULA; KILLER MERMAID) (2014)

This Serbian horror movie from writer-director Milan Todorovic (*Zone of the Dead*) has a great found location, an interesting monster, moments of eeriness and horror and the sheer presence of Franco Nero going for it, even if the basic plot is thin, the younger performers uneven and there are few surprises.

A prologue has an attractive young couple in a Serbian resort stalked by a hooded killer (Miodrag Krstovic) who looks like the fisherman from *I Know What You Did Last Summer* and uses a sharpened anchor on a chain as his gimmick weapon. Then, fill-in scenes introduce American bikini girls Kelly (Kristina Klebe) and Lucy (Natalie Burn) on holiday – Lucy hopes to reconnect with her local boyfriend Alex (Slobodan Stefanovic), but is put off when he turns up with a fiancée (Sofija Rajovic). Boban (Dragan Micanovic), a slightly hyper friend of Alex's, encourages the gang to take a trip – against the advice of grizzled local Niko (Nero) – to an abandoned island fort, which turns out to be where the killer lives. Glimpsing a girl (Zorana Kostic Obradovic) trapped down a well, the kids attempt a rescue, but she turns out to be Scylla, an impressive mermaid who shifts between beauty-with-a-tail and fish-faced horror. A complex backstory reveals that Niko and the killer are survivors of a Soviet era military unit sent to the fortress.

It makes less of its monster than *Thale* or *Siren* (or even *Las Garras de Lorelei*), but there is blunt interest in the devotion of the dogged, rapt killer to the monster whose song only men can hear – since Kelly is the viewpoint character, we only have hints of what it sounds like. The use of CGI is sparing and effective, the killings are nasty and the fort offers impressive battlements and tunnels.

RED CLOVER (LEPRECHAUN'S REVENGE) (2012)

> 'YOU DON'T THINK IT'S PATHETIC THAT IT TOOK YOU BEING ATTACKED BY A MYTHICAL CREATURE FOR ME TO TALK TO YOU.'

Not a reboot for the *Leprechaun* series – that came with *Leprechaun: Origins* (2014) – but a Syfy small-town monster effort with a decent creature, a couple of okay performances, and some thought behind its mythology. However, a mean streak inhibits the fun.

Irish Channel, a Louisiana town founded by immigrants, is plagued by a boggart (Kevin Mangold) which looks like a midget *Swamp Thing* with fangs. The leprechaun is invoked when colleen Karen O'Hara (Courtney Halverson, who at least has red hair) picks a red four-leafed clover. The creature snatches gold teeth, coins and medallions while killing anyone it comes across. Karen has a backstory involving a sheriff dad (Billy Zane) and a drunk grandfather (William Devane), plus a wannabe boyfriend (Derek Babb) who looks stuff up online and discovers lucky horseshoes are to leprechauns what crucifixes are to vampires(!). The town founders kidnapped a leprechaun so they could find a gold seam and prosper from exploiting it – hence the revenge spree. There's a high casualty rate among comedy townsfolk, earnest sidekicks, total innocents and sleazy reporters.

Anthony C. Ferrante's script has self-aware touches: the heroine's traditional lament that she feels she's living in a bad horror movie is answered with, 'No, in a bad horror movie, the monster would kill everybody *but* you.' (which is, indeed, what happens); a tabloid hack (Gabriel Jarret) is famous for his sharknado story (later, Ferrante scripted the *Sharknado* films). Halverson is an appealing heroine and Devane adds class as the old-timer everyone ridicules whose rants about 'the little people' turn out to be right in every particular. Directed by Drew Daywalt.

THE SAND (2015)

> '*I DON'T WANT TO DIE WITH A DICK ON MY FACE.*'

Sadly, *Blood Beach* (1980) didn't found a franchise and it took thirty-five years for another movie to have a man-eating monster lurk under a sandy beach. While its menace is kin to the *Blood Beach* creature, the storyline of *The Sand* is closer to 'The Raft' episode of *Creepshow 2* or Larry Fessenden's killer fish picture *Beneath*; and the film fits into the cycle of small-scale peril pictures (*Open Water, Adrift, Frozen*, etc.). A bunch of college kids head to the beach for a graduation party. Heroine Kaylee (Brooke Butler of *All Cheerleaders Die*) is so ticked off when her nearly ex Jonah (Dean Geyer) hooks up with hottie Chanda (Meagan Holder) she doesn't notice cut-up Gilbert (Cleo Berry) fetching an alien/cryptozoological egg along with driftwood for the fire. The next morning, after a wild party montage, Kaylee and crush-nurturing Mitch (Mitchel Musso) are in a lifeguard station, Jonah and Chanda and dimwit Marsha

(Nikki Leigh) are in a car and Gilbert is stuffed in a barrel with a penis drawn on his face. Several characters who step onto the sand are sucked under and gruesomely dissolved by tendrils, prompting the realisation that piles of clothes strewn about are all that's left of the other party people.

The script by Alex Greenfield (*The Temple*) and Ben Powell (*The Aggression Scale*) knowingly sets up contrivances – most of the cell phones are in the trunk of the car to ensure party hijinx don't wind up on the internet, etc. – to limit characters' options and there's enough bad feeling in the group to distract them from the business of escaping a monster whose reach extends about twenty yards.

As in most movies in this cycle, escape or survival methods are improvised using whatever comes to hand and regular foul-ups add to the body count. A beach patrolman (Jamie Kennedy) comes by in thick-soled boots which protect him for a while, but he's more interested in haranguing the kids than being any help. Though well acted, smartly written and nicely directed by Isaac Gabaeff to ratchet up the tension, *The Sand* suffers from hit-or-miss CGI – even the lo-tech practical monster/gore effects of vintage Corman circa *Attack of the Giant Leeches* or Frank Henenlotter in his *Basket Case-Brain Damage* mode would play better than the glitchy, cartoony pixel-jumble which passes for a monster here.

SASQUATCH MOUNTAIN (2006)

This wander-in-the-woods quickie resurrects an old favourite Chuck Griffith/Corman plot (cf: *Beast Ffrom Haunted Cave*, *Creature from the Haunted Sea*) as crooks making a getaway after a robbery run into a monster.

In a *Blair Witchy* home-video prologue, happy father Harlan Knowles (Lance Henriksen) is widowed when his wife is attacked by a tall, shaggy, snarly Sasquatch (Tiny Ron) – turning him into an embittered obsessive out for revenge. The script (by Michael Worth, who writes himself a meaty role) gets crowded as too many characters find reasons to go into the woods and be crushed to death. Chief robber Travis Cralle (Craig Wasson) has trouble stopping his crew – a British thug (Raffaello Degruttola), a cowboy-hatted dude who thinks he's charming (Worth) and a tough-as-nails Asian woman who has survived abuse (Karen Kim) – from killing each other. Fleeing a small-town bank job, the gang crash into a vehicle driven by Erin (Cerina Vincent) – a babe running away from something unspecified – and have to take a hike, dragging the girl along as a hostage. Sheriff Harris Zeff (Rance Howard), Vietnam veteran Eli Van Cleef (Tim Thomerson) and (inevitably) Bigfoot-hating Knowles form a posse to track the crooks. The two groups take casualties and the survivors ally against the monster – but this particular violent, ambling thug doesn't seem all that formidable.

Director Steven R. Monroe, who had already put Vincent in the woods in *It Waits*, glues it together with minimal atmosphere or excitement. Some entertainment value comes from odd monologues which seem scripted to provide audition pieces and a fine array of crusty character actors. Henriksen played a different character called Harlan Knowles in the earlier Bigfoot drama *The Untold*, to which this is not a sequel; that had a follow up called *Sasquatch Hunters*.

SASQUATCH: THE LEGEND OF BIGFOOT (1976)

> 'WE KNEW THAT WE MIGHT CATCH SIGHT OF A SASQUATCH AT ANY TIME AND THAT KNOWLEDGE KEPT US ON THE ALERT FROM NOW ON.'

A dull nature hike with a near-constant drone of narration, this is typical of the 'In Search of Bigfoot' brand of cryptozoological 1970s drive-in schlock (*The Legend of Boggy Creek*, *Creature from Black Lake*, etc.) and not to be confused with the even drearier *The Legend of Bigfoot*. It includes a clip from the much-debated Patterson-Gimlin film – a core text of the Bigfoot myth which either shows the rare creature in the wild or a tall guy ambling in an ape-suit – but mostly spends time on the winding woodland trail with gabby narrator/team leader Chuck Evans (George Lauris) and a bunch of broad stereotypes (a comedy old-timer, a nervous cook, a skilled Native American tracker, a sceptic reporter). They encounter sundry non-mythical animals and take time to yarn around the campfire (passing on one tall tale from Teddy Roosevelt) to justify dramatised Bigfoot anecdotes. Occasionally, a shadow looms or a shaggy silhouette is shown on the horizon – but a proper monster shows up for a clumsy rampage in which no one gets killed and papier-mâché rocks feature heavily. The end credits run under a syrupy song ('High in the Mountains') about the lonely, man-shunning beast. Written by Ed Hawkins and Ronald D. Olson; directed by Ed Ragozzino.

SIREN (2010)

This brief, good-looking British horror film has lovely Tunisian locations, a fresh use of Greek mythology and an attractive cast… but falls down in the story department. Rachel (Anna Skellern) and Ken (Eoin Macken) are on a Greek island yachting holiday with Marco (Anthony Jabre), Rachel's ex – which leads to simmering sexual tension and resentment. They haul a dying man out of the sea and put ashore on an island to bury him. There, they come across enigmatic blonde Silka (Tereza Srbova), who doesn't say much but has a great singing voice. Oh, and it was mentioned earlier that this might be *the very island* where Odysseus encountered the sirens who lure sailors to their doom.

There are echoes of the 1970s (*Daughters of Darkness, Let's Scare Jessica to Death*) as normals let a weird woman into their lives and suffer for it. All three holidaymakers are drawn to Silka and have hallucinations featuring gore (or at least streaks of blood), but it's fairly reticent about sex, though the setup seems to suggest erotic thriller levels of action (it has too little story for a proper film, even at 76 minutes, but enough for a porno). The last act gets lively as the siren sings Marco to death in a decently staged scene which intercuts seductive crooning with bloodier screaming and dying. Performances are okay, with Skellern – first seen in a provocative red dress in roadside sex-play that pads out the film – a little better than the rest. Eerie moments, but slight overall. Written by Geoffrey Gunn and Andrew Hull; directed by Hull.

SKULLDUGGERY (1970)

> 'PAMAKAN – ISN'T THAT THE VILLAGE OF PROSTITUTION?' '…AND CANOE-PADDLING, OF COURSE.'

For decades, this was a hard-to-see film – and so tended to be known by a striking still of Pat Suzuki in a full-fur makeup (with visible nipples) as a 'Tropi', one of a tribe of missing links. As it happens, the film never allows as clear a look at Bud and Marvin Westmore's Russ Meyer-on-the-Planet-of-the-Apes makeup creation. *Skullduggery*, which might have been called almost anything (though it does include duggery with skulls), is an uncomfortable mix of jungle adventure, blunt satire and squeam-making sexual/racial politics. Its mood swings seem all the weirder thanks to resolutely mainstream production values and bland TV-movie style. Screenwriter Nelson Gidding (*The Haunting*) adapted Vercors' 1952 novel *Les Animaux Dénaturés* (aka *You Shall Know Them*) for Otto Preminger – whose wayward career was running to *Skidoo* and *Hurry Sundown* at the time – but the film ended up directed by Gordon Douglas (*Them!*, *Zombies on Broadway*), brought on after one day of shooting to replace Richard Wilson.

Paleoanthropologist Sybil Graeme (Susan Clark, in jungle kit by Edith Head) is in Papua New Guinea searching for fossil evidence of the missing link. Rogueish adventurer Douglas Temple (Burt Reynolds) and drunken pal Otto Kreps (Roger C. Carmel, in Harry Mudd mode) wheedle their way onto the expedition – by amusingly crippling one of the team (Edward Fox) – so they can stake claims on valuable deposits of minerals used in the manufacture of colour television sets. Sybil rebuffs macho Douglas for a few minutes then sleeps with him, which doesn't stop him trotting out sentiments like, 'If there's anything I can't stand, it's a brainy woman.' In the jungle, Douglas plants some bones he's brought along to keep the expedition in one place while he maps those deposits, a trick Sybil sees through at once but is only mildly annoyed by. Clark often got stuck with playing a humourless feminist/liberal shown up by a cheeky man's man – notably as the social worker in *Coogan's Bluff*. Here, her interactions with Reynolds – who unironically plays caveman in a movie which features *actual* cavemen – are painful. Dialogue runs to gems like, 'Is it possible, Douglas, that we've wandered into uncontrolled territory?'

After reels of arsing around in the jungle, which includes business with a tribe of bare-breasted women and Douglas cheerfully ordering a native guide to his death in taboo territory, the expedition discovers a tribe of hairy hominids played by crouched-over Japanese mimes. Sybil calls in her sponsor, industrialist Vancruysen (Paul Hubschmid), who shows up by helicopter and revives a cargo cult. After an abrupt transition, everyone exploits the chattering little Tropis: Douglas turns them into miners in pink dungarees who turn over wheelbarrow-loads of ore in return for canned ham; Sybil and colleagues try a selective breeding program, as Vancruysen sees the non-human but willing creatures as a source of slave labour; pidgin-spouting priest Father Dillingham (Chips Rafferty) wants to baptise the tribe *en masse*, but hesitates because it might be sacrilege; and Kreps may or may not have had drunken sex with Topazia (Suzuki), knocking her up; a local black native tribe invite the expedition to a feast and serve roast Tropi, which the Westerners baulk at eating. If Topazia and Kreps can have a child together, then the Tropis are legally human and have rights – but she has a miscarriage in a tacky Papuan Snow White-themed motel.

In a development demented even by the standards of this film, Douglas claims to have killed the baby and insists he be tried for murder. An intense Papuan DA (William Marshall) is pitted against Vancruysen's smooth mouthpiece (Alexander Knox) as a wise old judge (Rhys Williams) presides in a noisy courtroom. Expert witnesses include a racist Rhodesian boffin (Wilfrid Hyde-White) who argues the Tropis aren't fully human (before admitting he thinks that black people aren't either) and a Black Panther (Booker Bradshaw) who insists the straight-haired, pink-skinned Tropis are in fact prototype Caucasians. This descends into farce and the fact the wretched Topazia gets crushed to death while trying to escape isn't as sobering as the film would like it to be. Producer Saul David might have hoped to compete with *Planet of the Apes* in the science fiction satire-cum-adventure stakes. It has a fascinating subject (presented awkwardly) and a good non-star cast (Reynolds hadn't yet broken big), but is kind of a disaster… Still, it's a unique oddity.

THE SNOW CREATURE (1954)

Purportedly the first movie to deal with the Himalayan legend of the Abominable Snowman. A few hesitant moves in Myles Wilder's script prefigure Nigel Kneale's superior TV play *The Creature* (filmed by Hammer as *The Abominable Snowman*), but the film is a draggy 71 minutes. A mostly pointless Tibet-set first half ('The first days were uneventful, monotonous and tedious,' admits the narration) and an entirely conventional climactic rampage in Los Angeles storm drains bookend a half-reel of more interesting (if not actively good) material.

Stalwart botanist Frank Parrish (Paul Langton) and a hard-drinking photographer (Leslie Denison) embark on a Himalayan expedition in search of rare fauna (like Henry Hull in *The WereWolf of London*). English-speaking sherpa Subra (Teru Shimada) insists they hare off after a yeti who has abducted his young bride. Stuff happens and is talked about: the yeti kills a sherpa; everyone traipses several times through a snowbound Bronson Caverns; Subra corners a yeti who may or may not be the abductor (there's only one big yeti suit so it's a moot point) and causes the death of its mate and child; Frank insists on drugging the creature and carrying it back to civilisation. Scientist and snapper argue about whether to further human knowledge or make money, and the yeti is imported to California in a giant fridge. The monster is held up at the airport because officials can't decide whether it's human – and therefore an illegal immigrant – or an animal. While bureaucrats argue, the creature escapes, 'attacks' a trampy street woman, makes an appearance in a meat-packing plant and is pursued into the drains by the hero and the cops.

Questions of whether the creature is sentient or valuable are set aside as it is gunned down and forgotten so the film can sign off on an 'up' note as the cop on the case is told his wife has just had a baby. The yeti suit, seen only in shadow, reputedly contains lumbering giant Lock Martin (Gort of *The Day the Earth Stood Still*); it may be a re-dressed *Invaders From Mars* Martian outfit. A few of its appearances are effective (cinematographer Floyd Crosby stages one good shot of the beast lurking among hanging sides of beef), but most of the monster footage is recycled several times over, regardless of whether or not it cuts into scenes. Character business, like the photographer's alcoholism and the cop's impending fatherhood, pads the script to feature length. Performances are of the turn-up-and-say-the-lines variety. Directed by W. Lee Wilder (*The Man Without a Body*).

SWAMP DEVIL (2008)

Familiar CGI-monster-rampages-through-a-small-town nonsense from the SciFi Channel, shot in Canada by David Winning (*Turbo: A Power Rangers Movie*) with a thrown-together supernatural revenge plot that blends *Night of the Scarecrow* and *Pumpkinhead* without a whole lot of sense. Its strong suit is that the monster, who owes something to Marvel's Man-Thing and DC's Swamp Thing, is impressive: animated CGI vines and vegetation read better onscreen than SciFi's usual big snakes or wobbly dinosaurs. The film still wastes half the running time on characters shooting the monster long after it's established that bullets have no effect on it – there's even a sidetrack as one character heads back into town to pick up more useless shotgun shells and cannily has them put on his tab (he gets killed soon after, so doesn't have to settle the bill).

Melanie Blaime (Cindy Sampson, good in a nothing heroine role) is summoned by mystery misfit Jimmy Fuller (Nicolas Wright) to the town (Gibbington, Vermont) where her seemingly cracked father Howard (Bruce Dern) was once sheriff. A few old-timers have been killed, the monster is manifesting in the relatively unswampy woods (what was wrong with *Wood Devil* as a title?) and crusty old Howard eventually dishes out backstory about the killing of a child-murderer in the wilds (Dern brings acting muscle to this, justifying his presence). Jimmy turns out not to be a misunderstood hero but the resurrected villain – he shifts easily between snarling sadistic psychopath and his alternate form as long-limbed, human-shaped mess of trees, roots, vines and earth to spear, crush, throttle or pursue his one-time persecutors and their relations.

For some reason, the monster can't leave the region, which makes for odd suspense as wounded folks crawl towards the county line – and a satisfying (if provisional) finish as the old sheriff drives a pick-up into the monster and shoves it over the border, whereupon it turns back into dead mulch. However, a witch-woman summons the creature from its pool in a coda – though no sequel has come along. Written by Ethlie Ann Vare (*Black Swarm*) and Gary Dauberman (*BloodMonkey*).

THALE (2012)

Specialist cleaners Elvis (Erlend Nervold) and Leo (Jon Sigve Skard) mop up when corpses are discovered – though Elvis's delicate stomach renders him unsuitable for the job and their camaraderie is strained by the fact that each is keeping a secret (an illegitimate daughter, lung cancer) from the other. In a remote house, the duo cope with the body of an old man – seemingly a scientific researcher – rent apart by animals. In his secret basement, they find grubby recording equipment and a bath of milky fluid from which emerges a naked young woman, Thale (Silje Reinåmo). She has apparently been imprisoned by the dead man, though it develops he was keeping her hidden from authorities who have darker purposes. Capable of violence but also magical healing, Thale is a *huldra* – a forest spirit related to the shapeshifter of *The White Reindeer* – and has a back-wound where her tail was docked.

Most of this Norwegian film is a three-character piece as the two men cope with a creature who seesaws between threatening and helpless and plays on their own worries by reminding Elvis of his neglected paternal responsibilities and holding out to Leo the possibility of a cure. The *huldra*'s spindlier, CGI-assisted kin are glimpsed, suggesting a growing menace – but real threat is provided by the ruthless decontamination-suited

Scandinavian equivalent of the Men in Black, who capture and torture the hapless working stiffs to draw out the *huldra*, prompting a swift, inexplicit orgy of supernatural violence (akin to the swimming pool massacre of *Let the Right One In*). Written and directed by Aleksander Nordaas.

13TH CHILD (2002)

The sort of project which usually casts community theatre folk, this shoddy, video-look horror picture somehow landed decent name actors. Top-billed Cliff Robertson, miscast but game as a sinister hermit whose pet spider morphs into a giant horned monster, even co-wrote the script with producer Michael Maryk.

In a tricky but pointless structure, ex-cop Riley (Robert Guillaume) bugs his eyes in a padded cell as we flash back a few days to an investigation carried out by an FBI agent (Michelle Maryk) and bantering cops (Gano Grills, Christopher Atkins) at the behest of a Jersey D.A. (Lesley-Anne Down) whose father was Riley's partner and a victim of the legendary Jersey Devil. DNA analysis of a claw by a boffin (Peter Jason) shows the monster is a conglomerate of reptile, bat, spider, deer and human. The long-lived Mr Shroud (Robertson) is either related to the creature (which looks like a cheap *Alien* with antlers, but is at least tall and drooling) or casts his soul into the killer critter.

Riffing on the Jersey Devil cryptid legend, it trots out an incoherent 'explanation' for sightings of the bat-winged thing, which is here basically a big goon with a grudge, doing the bidding of a ranting maniac. It covers several styles, none effective – *Blair Witch*y wandering-in-the-woods, *X-Files* cryptozoology (self-important date, place and time titles), hokey demonology and old-fashioned slasher stalking. The end credits give the title as *13th Child, Legend of the Jersey Devil, Volume 1*. Directed by Steven Stockage.

THROWBACK (2013)

'CAN YOU CALL THE COPS AND GET THEM TO TASER THE SHIT OUT OF A GUY IN A TROPICAL SHIRT?'

This entry in the busy search-for-a-yeti field has a few things going for it, like the unusual Australian rain-forest setting (Australia's version of Bigfoot is called the Yowie), a prologue involving legendary dynamite-happy bush outlaw Thunderclap Newman (Andy Bramble), and a search-for-Newman's-gold storyline that adds a *The Treasure of the Sierra Madre* vibe. Most of all, the fact that it's not a found-footage film means reliance on having characters, a plot, editing, widescreen imagery (it claims to be 'filmed in yowievision'), a music score and other luxuries which used to be commonplace even in low-budget horror.

Writer-director Travis Bain sets it up with an 1825 sequence in which a nugget is stolen from a prospector by a crook who is then robbed by Newman only for them both to run into the Yowie (Warren Clements) and get gored. Things get slightly untidy in the present day as treasure hunters Jack (Shawn Brack) and Kent (Anthony Ring) follow directions in an old diary which leads them to Newman's cave stash. Larcenous, nastily British Kent tries to drown Jack and make off with the treasure, but Jack survives and teams up with disapproving forest ranger Rhiannon (Melanie Serafin). Aussie character star Vernon Wells appears in a funny vegetable disguise as a policeman on the trail of the Yowie, but most of the film is a feud between Jack and Kent, with each leaving the other for dead or in trouble with the monster.

Bush lore extends to finding a lost Portuguese mission and a cache of Newman's still-viable dynamite, but as with many Bigfoot-Sasquatch films, the story wouldn't be changed a whit if the menace were just a large angry bear. The monster is a letdown – its face is barely glimpsed, so it's mostly a marauding fur coat. Performances are fun, though.

TROLL 2 (TROLL I) (1990)

'THERE'S NO COFFEE HERE IN NILBOG! IT'S THE DEVIL'S DRINK!'

The show-your-superiority-by-laughing-at-miserable-rubbish approach to cinema has always stuck in my craw. Personally, I despise *Top Gun* or *Moulin Rouge* more than any famous schlock picture – and I'd rather watch *Plan 9 from Outer Space* than the average Academy Award Best Picture winner. This in-name-only follow-up to a mid-list Charles Band quickie, made in Utah by Italians (*Troll* was made in Italy by Americans), has climbed Worst of All Time lists. Undeniably poor, it is nevertheless entertaining, and has enough bizarre-even-in-this-context ideas to count as modestly original; it's certainly worthier and more amusing than Troma's would-be funny prepackaged cult movies.

The whitebread Waits family take part in a house swap and move to the sinister rural community of Nilbog. Young Joshua (Michael Stephenson) – advised in dreams by his dead, story-telling Gramps (Robert Ormsby) – knows from the outset that the Nilbogites, who have four-leaf-clover scars, are secretly goblins (or trolls – Llort wouldn't be as good a scary town name, though it sounds slightly Welsh). They are intent on suckering the family into eating bright green food which will effect a gross transformation into vegetables suitable for goblin consumption. Strict vegetarians, the monsters won't eat people until they aren't meat any more. On their first night in town, Joshua prevents dad (George Hardy), mom (Margo Prey) and sister Holly (Connie McFarland) from tucking into the food by peeing all over the table. 'You can't piss on hospitality!' shrieks dad, 'I won't allow it!' Strident, hectoring, peculiar performances from the local maniacs – especially Deborah Young/Reed as witchy harridan Creedence Leonore Gielgud – don't match the ranting, strained acting of the supposedly 'normal' characters. Director-writer Claudio Fragasso (aka Drake Floyd) favours zooms, non-stop electric organ music, green gloop, abrupt mood-switches and awkward dialogue which sounds as if it's been translated from Italian by a computer program and recited by actors ordered not to change a word. Sample exchanges: Joshua: 'Are you nuts? Are you trying to turn me into a homo?' Holly: 'Wouldn't be too hard. If my father finds you're in here, he'll cut off your little nuts and eat them. He can't stand you.'; 'Hey guys, did you hear that scream?' 'It was probably just Arnold, deflowering a Nilbog virgin.'

The MGM logo is peculiarly out of place on something like this, but Leo the Lion roars fore and aft and Louis B. Mayer must be sicking up green gunk in his grave. Freckle-faced, awkward leading man Stephenson grew up to make *Best Worst Movie*, an entertaining documentary about the production and afterlife of *Troll 2*.

THE UNKNOWN (CLAWED: THE LEGEND OF SASQUATCH) (2005)

In the woods, poaching redneck assholes led by obvious baddie Ed Janzer (Miles O'Keeffe, the film's 'name') are attacked by a barely glimpsed monster which rips out guts, etc. Much later, a large hairy corpse is found covered with maggots – and so we *perhaps* intuit the hunters got killed for accidentally shooting dead a relation of the monster, who spends most of the film lurking behind trees (in what looks like a puffy Andrew Duggan mask). Also up on Echo Mountain, haunt of the legendary Taku'He (the local name for Sasquatch), are four high-school kids. Sensitive, semi-geeky nice guy Richard (Dylan Purcell) and prank-playing jock horndog Jay (Brandon Henschel) are ordered to collaborate on a science project about endangered species and take along Jay's cute cousin Jenny (Chelsea Hobbs), who has a crush on Richard, and Shea (Casey LaBow), the token blonde airhead.

Though Jay keeps up idiot jokes well past the point of tolerance and camcorders everything *Blair Witch* style, the first surprise is that the kids are reasonably well written and played within broad stereotypes (Purcell's encounter with a bear is especially on-the-money). The second surprise is that none of the teens get killed: Taku'He is essentially peaceful unless disturbed and ultimately protects the kids from the film's real villain. It has moments of guts-pulled-out gore, but otherwise feels like a young adult story, with the moral that some people are worse than monsters (a flashback shows white settlers massacring Indians and trespassing on the sacred mountain). Director-writer Karl Kozak casts former teen horror stars Cooper Huckabee (*The Funhouse*) and Lee Purcell (*Summer of Fear*) in grownup roles.

YETI (YETI: CURSE OF THE SNOW DEMON) (2008)

On the principle that any sincere based-on-fact drama would be a whole lot better with a ravening monster in it, here's an imaginative spin on the Andes plane crash saga *Alive* in which would-be cannibal plane crash survivors fight over a pile of edible corpses with a hungry Abominable Snowman.

An American college football team (plus some girls) crash-land not in the Andes but the Himalayas. When one of the group (Elfina Luk) sets fire to the dead because she doesn't want anyone eating her brother, the monster comes after the living survivors.

The yeti (*gigantopithecus*, apparently) does CGI-assisted Hulk leaps, but is mostly a tall guy in a white, shaggy monster costume with a rubbery fang-face (it resembles a Marvel Comics villain, the Wendigo). The young, no-name, mostly Canadian cast – Josh Emerson, Ona Grauer, Crystal Lowe, Marc Menard, Carly Pope and Brandon Jay McLaren, with Peter DeLuise top-billed as a rescue guy unsubtly named Sheppard – aren't up to the dramatic demands of post-crash agonising and bickering (Adam O'Byrne is the weasel who hoards chocolate), but do well enough when pursued, abused and dismembered.

Full marks for the guy who splints his broken leg by tying a friend's frozen-stiff severed arm to his shin, and an extra tick for the avalanche which – just when it seems things can't get any worse – tumbles tons of snow on everyone. Written by Rafael Jordan (*Copperhead*); directed by Paul Ziller (*Beyond Loch Ness*).

FAMOUS MONSTERS

Frankenstein and Dracula

ALUCARD (2005)

Touted as 'the truest telling of Bram Stoker's novel ever to reach the screen', there's no faulting writer-director John Johnson's microbudgeted film for lack of ambition. Faithful if underfunded, this is the first *Dracula* adaptation to tip 'Dracula's Guest', a posthumously published 'deleted chapter', into the plot. It also features scenes and characters (Quincey Harker, the heroine's son) pruned even from back-to-the-book endeavours like the BBC's *Count Dracula* or Francis Ford Coppola's *Bram Stoker's Dracula*.

Johnson semi-updates the period and sets it in 'Nilbog' (a name copped from *Troll 2!*) rather than London (Nilbog still has a Piccadilly Circus, though). Johnathan Harker (Liam Smith) taps his journal into a laptop and Dr Seward (Jay Barber) has a mini-recorder for case notes, but clothes are near-period, blood transfusions are unhygienic and Victorian language is only occasionally salted with modernisms. This means losing a key element of the novel, which 'sells' supernatural elements by locating them in a recognisable, then-contemporary world bounded by railway timetables and newspaper reports. *Alucard* takes place nowhere: so, rather than trespass in a modern world, this vampire moves from one limbo to another. Johnson, who also plays Quincey Morris, does unusual things which respect the text: in the early castle scenes, Count Alucard is played by Hal Handerson as an old, bushy-bearded brute... but scraggle-haired, youthful Dino A. Muminovic replaces him for the vampire's subsequent limited appearances, including one full-frontal nude scene (though Handerson continues to dub the dialogue). Acting is competent on a regional-theatre level. Most of the cast assume mid-Atlantic accents, but David Harscheid and John VanPatten are surprisingly true to Stoker as a windily Dutch Van Helsing and a ranting Renfield. There's one good shock appearance from Renfield and a few well-realised key scenes, but the climax dwells oddly on a poorly staged kung fu tussle with gypsy henchmen before almost throwing away Alucard's death.

Another curious choice is that the bulk of the film is widescreen, but opening and closing moments are standard frame. A mostly effective ambient score gives way to campy rap over the end credits.

ALVIN AND THE CHIPMUNKS MEET FRANKENSTEIN (1999)

Around since the early 1960s, the sped-up voice novelty singers became a big-screen franchise in the 21st century after various made-for-TV cartoon series and features. Backed by Universal, this uses the copyrighted Karloff-look flat-headed Frankenstein Monster. In a black-and-white prologue, a torch-carrying peasant mob attacks the castle of Dr Frankenstein (Michael Bell), who dismantles the monster (voiced inevitably by Frank Welker) and takes a job in Hollywood on a studio backlot with a failing theme park. Alvin, identifiable by the huge A on his dress, and his backing singers Simon (glasses, smart) and Theodore (timid, stupid) get trapped on the lot overnight and encounter scary folk. Alvin, dosed with a Jekyll-and-Hyde potion, goes crazed at the premiere of *A Midsummer Night's Car Crash*. The Monster turns out to be nice and gets a job as a tour guide, while the wicked scientist's horrible fate is to be stuck in a 'Sammy Squirrel' costume and forced to sing a theme song to tourists. There are above-the-target-audience's-head jokes (a studio minion called Mr Yesman), but it's mostly running about and not very amusing shouting. Followed by *Alvin and the Chipmunks Meet the Wolfman*.

ARMY OF FRANKENSTEINS (2013)

> 'NO, THIS ISN'T RIGHT! YOU CAN'T GO AROUND SEWING CANNONS TO PEOPLE!'

Influenced by *Army of Darkness*, *Frankenstein Unbound* and *Abraham Lincoln Vampire Hunter*, this low-budget effort – not to be confused with *Frankenstein's Army* – has more ideas than it can comfortably explore even at a slightly protracted 108 minutes.

During the American Civil War, Union soldiers skirmish with a horde of multiple-exposed lookalikes for Universal's Frankenstein Monster (Eric Gesecus) – more the stout Lon Chaney Jr version than the lean Karloff model. In the present day, supermarket minion Alan Jones (Jordan Farris) has trouble proposing to girlfriend Ashley (Jami Harris) thanks to a weasely boss with a blatantly false moustache (blatantly false moustaches are a recurrent feature). Alan is abducted by Igor (Christian Bellgardt), a kid in steampunk goggles, and near-anagrammatical mad scientist Dr Tanner Finski (John Ferguson), who is obsessed with creating the creature Mary Shelley envisioned. Finski plucks out Alan's eye and implants it in his monster, then Alan throws a switch too early. Not only does the monster come to life, but a horde of duplicates from parallel universes are pulled into this reality and time-zapped (along with Alan and Igor) to the last days of the Civil War. That multiversal monsters are just a throwaway idea shows how busy the film is: an army of alternate monsters as conceived by other filmmakers, authors, illustrators, etc. would have been cool… but this shower are just shambling duplicates psychically linked to the original.

Alan falls in with his ancestor Solomon (Rett Terrell), who loses an arm and has a steampunk ray gun replacement sewn on by Igor. Alan sometimes sees through his absent eye, getting a monster POV. The prime monster is whisked off in a balloon with ex-slave nurse Virginia (Raychelle McDonald), who sees his innate sweetness and converts him to the cause of the North. Evil-bearded Southern officer Robert E. Walton (Thomas Cunningham) gets Finski's *Re-Animator* reagent from Igor and doses a lieutenant who becomes an oatmeal-faced hulk (Billy Bean). Though Igor insists the monsters aren't called Frankensteins, the label sticks as the army clashes with Confederates (presumably with the involvement of Civil War re-enactors). The finale has *two* monsters show up at Ford's Theatre on the night Booth (Christopher Robinson) is due to assassinate Lincoln (Donald Taylor).

Director Ryan Bellgardt – who co-wrote with Josh McKamie and Andy Swanson – doesn't have the epic resources necessary, but gives it a solid try anyway. Performances are broad, but the declamatory style works in context, there's a great deal of limb-ripping gore taken in good spirit, the fate of John Wilkes Booth is laugh-out-loud funny and the finale ties up *most* of the time-twisting plot.

BANDH DARWAZA (1990)

This Indian *Dracula* knock-off features a tall, cloaked, fanged, blood-drinking personage addressed as *nevla* (the master) or *shaitan* (demon or monster), but otherwise unnamed: as such, he might even *be* Dracula, rather than a local imitation. Star Ajay Agarwal looks and acts like an unholy mix of Robert Quarry's Count Yorga, a grown-up *It's Alive* baby (with prominent forehead veins) and Rondo Hatton.

Like some 1970s Hammer films, it winds up being a sequel to its own extended pre-credits sequence. In an eighteen-minute prologue, the infertile wife of a nobleman who is considering taking a younger secondary bride to secure an heir is advised by witchy servant Mahua (Aruna Irani, in a standout performance) to visit Kali Pahari (the Black Mountain), an evil region where the Master dominates a cult of fanatical, murderous followers. A bargain is struck – the Master will impregnate the wife, and if the resulting baby is a boy, she will get to keep it. Naturally, she gives birth to a girl, Kamya, and tries to back out of the deal, leading to her death and the (temporary) destruction of the Master.

Two decades on, Kamya (Kunika) is taken with often-shirtless nice (if smug) guy Kumar (Hashmat Khan). Kamya uses magic to influence Kumar while he is singing a love duet with his simpering sweetheart Sapna (Manjeet Kullar) – the nice, dull girl keeps turning into the exciting, wicked one in the choruses, disorienting the thick-headed swain. Torn between her titular and actual fathers, Kamya is instrumental in resurrecting the vampire. Fulfilling the 'Lucy' role, the doomed Kamya is more interesting (and sympathetic) than the good-looking, obnoxiously cheerful folk we're supposed to worry about.

A long, intermittently clunky film, this overuses insistent crash-zooms and hissing samples from Harry Manfredini's *Friday the 13th* score. However, the Master is one of the most *physical* screen vampires – crashing through the windscreen of a moving car, chasing victims around his palace and rising from the dead covered in dripping slime. Scripted by Dev Kishan and Shyam Ramsay; directed by Tulsi and Shyam Ramsay.

BATMAN/DRACULA (1964)

Supposedly, this was once a 54-minute film. Only a 21-minute extract survives... though the notion that Andy Warhol's underground films have fixed running times is speculative. Projected on walls during live happenings, these are moving pictures in the sense of ambient wallpaper rather than narrative cinema. Goateed, beatnik-look filmmaker Jack Smith (*Flaming Creatures*) sports a Satanic smile and a black cloak as the composite title figure. Much of the movie consists of him prancing about on a New York rooftop swirling the cloak in competition with Baby Jane Holzer. Though the credits are scored with a Batman-themed novelty song, most of the film is accompanied by early Velvet Underground music – with beat poetry/pornography overlaid ('The

Nothing Song'). Other music is by The Farmingdale Sound Machine, Thousands of Lives and Sun Ra. There are quite a few solarisations and superimpositions as Factory folk dance in place or stare out at the audience – even a cat gets a lot of close-ups. A vaguely pleasant watch since Warhol's friends seem to be having a better time than usual, but a puzzling artefact when dislocated from its original context. Note that Warhol was, as often, ahead of the curve: this was made before the 1966 *Batman* TV series – itself influenced by pop art and camp – helped the Caped Crusader cross over from comics star to mainstream pop icon.

THE BATMAN VS DRACULA (2005)

'I THANK YOU FOR CARRYING ON MY LEGACY IN ITS ABSENCE, BUT NOW THERE IS ROOM FOR ONLY ONE BAT-MAN IN GOTHAM.'

A feature spin-off from the animated series *The Batman* (2004-8), this is one of those ideas which had to happen sooner or later.

A youngish Bruce Wayne (voiced by Rino Romano) is pitted against an arrogant Dracula (nicely voiced by Peter Stormare), and Batman's just-starting legend is in danger of being eclipsed by the well-established image of the bat-man from Transylvania. Duane Capizzi's script works classic bat-villains into a Dracula story: searching for mob treasure in a Gotham City graveyard, the Penguin (Tom Kenny) discovers the vampire's staked and chained skeleton (transported from Transylvania) and bleeds on it, then becomes a Renfield-like minion; Dracula turns various Gothamites ('the Lost Ones') into semi-vampires, and the Joker (Kevin Michael Richardson) becomes an even-loonier, fanged, wall-walking albino. Assuming the pseudonym 'Dr Alucard', Dracula crashes high society, intent on ritually draining Lois Lane knock-off Vicky Vale (Tara Strong) to revivify his vampire soulmate, Carmilla Karnstein (hauled in from J. Sheridan Le Fanu). Batman synthesises a cure so he can restore humanity to recently turned vampires, but uses a sunlight generator to dust the Count (overcoming his superheroic reluctance to kill by reasoning Dracula isn't alive).

Though it has effective, spooky action and is decently scripted, the film is hampered by blocky, manga-look character designs carried over from *The Batman*, a less pleasing take on the comics material than the earlier *Batman: The Animated Series* or the later *Batman: The Brave and the Bold*. Directed by Michael Goguen.

BOLTNECK (BIG MONSTER ON CAMPUS; TEEN MONSTER) (2000)

A mild teenage horror comedy on the genial level of *Frankenstein General Hospital* or *Frankenstein: The College Years*, though Danny Elfman-style scoring, lightning strikes over Los Angeles and a Shelley Duvall appearance (even a dialogue reference to *Frankenweenie*) suggests an aspiration to Tim Burtonhood. Arrogant jocks (Justin Walker, Christian Payne) accidentally kill gangling Karl (Ryan Reynolds), a kid trying to crash a cool party. Student genius Frank Stein (Matthew Lawrence) resurrects Karl, substituting criminal grey matter for Karl's damaged brain. The monster becomes a Buddy Love-like mentor to stereotype nerd Frank, helping him make time with a teen princess (Christine Lakin), but also seems to run amok, stealing school funds for a party and perhaps attacking a co-ed. In an upbeat finish, it turns out Karl hasn't done most of the bad things he's suspected of, but still gets his original brain back for a normative wind-up. Pre-stardom Reynolds is okay as the innocuous monster, hiding scars under a hat, but Lawrence is an unimpressive lead. The end credits song samples the theme from *Mad Monster Party?*. With bits from Judge Reinhold, Charles Fleischer (the voice of Roger Rabbit) and Richard Moll (who played the Monster in the *Weird Science* TV episode 'Searching for Boris Karloff'). Scripted by Dave Payne (writer-director of *Reeker*); directed by Mitch Marcus (*The Haunting of Hell House*).

BONNIE AND CLYDE VS DRACULA (2008)

A low-budget genre mash-up, more indebted to *Billy the Kid vs. Dracula* than Seth Grahame-Smith. This Bonnie (Tiffany Shepis) is the dominant partner, dragging Clyde (Trent Haaga) on a crime spree which brings them into conflict with folks even worse than they are – serial killers, vampires, a pulp mad scientist. The film cuts between plodding crime hijinx – not on a level with the low-budget Roger Corman vintage car gangster films of the '70s – and the house of hooded, disfigured Dr Loveless (Allen

Lowman). In partnership with a currently enfeebled Dracula (Russell Friend), Loveless performs arcane experiments while terrorising his gamine-like oddball sister Annabel (Jennifer Friend, by a long stretch the best thing here). After an hour of this, Bonnie goes to the house looking for a doctor to treat gut-shot Jake (T. Max Graham) and gets bitten by Dracula, who grows young again and turns a houseful of guests into vampires. Given the title, there's disappointingly little gangsters-on-ghoul action... Dracula is throttling Clyde when Annabel accidentally opens a curtain and the archfiend tamely dissolves. At the end, human Clyde and vampire Bonnie are still on the road and Annabel goes off to become a hobo. Performances are all over the place, with Russell Friend especially ordinary as a long haired, growly, cowled vampire. Writer-director Timothy Friend hits on a unique mix, but this really ought to have delivered more.

EL CASTILLO DE LOS MONSTRUOS (1957)

Reference books tend to scramble the ingredients of this Mexican comedy. It is not a remake of *Abbott and Costello Meet Frankenstein*, though it does cop ideas from the American film, and – despite its impressive line-up of monsters (unmatched until *The Monster Squad*) – an awful lot of time is spent on shenanigans in town before it gets to the eponymous castle.

El Clavillazo (Antonio Espino) is a knockabout comic whose shtick consists of a very strange hat and an overlarge zoot-suit jacket, plus whiskery routines like miming a passionate serenade for his sweetheart Beatriz (Evangelina Elizondo) and being forced to mince when the radio segues to a female torch singer. Clavillazo, who uses his stage name for his character, pals around with gurning stooges who have one mannerism apiece. A typical bit of business has asylum-visiting El Clavillazo encounter another sane person, whereupon the 'normals' each warily assume the other is mad and attempt a nervous, soothing duet, interrupted by a real homicidal maniac whose mad act isn't far removed from the comedians' clowning. Meanwhile, in the castle introduced before the credits with atmospheric touches (clawed hands holding reins), scientist 'Dr Sputnik' and his scarred, hunchbacked minion make monsters. Posing as a kindly blind man, Sputnik kidnaps Beatriz (another burst of atmosphere, with eyes staring out from under a slouch hat) and uses hypnosis to convince her that she is his love, Galatea. The hero blunders out to the castle, confronts doctor and monsters, runs around a lot being stalked and almost strangled, and rescues the girl.

Germán Robles, Mexico's biggest horror star, does an act akin to Lugosi in *Abbott and Costello Meet Frankenstein* or Christopher Lee in *Tempi duri per i vampiri*, sending up his role in *El Vampiro* by skulking with cape and fangs. All the other monsters just lurch on and off quickly: a Gill Man patterned on the Creature from the Black Lagoon is devolved into a big dead fish, a Wolf Man is throttled by another beast from behind cell bars, a tall, thin butler in the Karloff Frankenstein Monster image melts to cogs and clock parts, and the vampire vanishes at dawn. Dr Sputnik is shot in the back by the dying hunchback after the usual rant ('Yes I'm mad, if it's mad to want perfection!') and El Clavillazo and sweetie are rescued by his idiot friends, who keep throwing the wrong switches (lowering a spiked roof, squirting gas or water) before getting them out of a booby-trapped cell. Director Julián Soler frames one or two things that look good in stills, but mostly stands back and lets the comedians jump up and down in desperate pleas for laughs which don't come, while action is staged in a primitive Mascot serial/ Jerry Warren manner. You've been warned.

DEAFULA (1975)

A unique oddity, *Deafula* is a low-budget, black-and-white vampire movie made by deaf director-writer-star Peter Wolf in Portland, Oregon. It's in Sign-o-Vision – characters use sign language with the audio equivalent of subtitles (voice-over which doesn't emanate from onscreen actors – though the dub for Dracula at least tries a Lugosi accent). The alternate title *Young Deafula* suggests a Mel Brooksian spoof and the title character looks comical in stills: boasting not only fangs and a Demon King goatee, but an enormous false nose on a par with *The Brainiac*. However, it's not a comedy. You can tell because it has a comic relief character, a bumbling British policeman (Dudley Hemstreet) imported to America because of his expertise on vampire cases. He isn't very funny, but his scenes are clearly supposed to be lighter than the angsty, brooding business he interrupts.

White-wearing, hirsutely blond Steve Adams (Wolf) periodically transforms Jekyll-and-Hyde-style and bites upwards of twenty-seven people to death. The curse affects his teeth, hair colour, nose and clothes (he sprouts a cape). In an origin close to Marvel Comics' Blade, Steve's mother (Katherine Wilson) was bitten by Count Dracula (producer Gary R. Holstrom) while pregnant. Deafula – he even calls himself by his nickname, which is more than Blacula did – is torn between two fathers, a minister

(James Randall) who signs his sermons and the arch-vampire. To cope with his problems, Steve consults Amy (Norma Tuccinardi), an unhelpful witch whose cringing minion Zork (Nick Tuccinardi) has tin cans instead of hands (in a signing world, the equivalent of having his tongue torn out). Scotland Yard's Inspector Butterfield teams up with a moustached cop (Lee Darel) to trap the killer. The detectives don't suspect their good friend Steve – though they have a long (signed) conversation about his habit of eating peanuts in their shells, later a significant clue. Dracula, for some reason, is interred in a nearby cave, where Deafula has a primal confrontation with his evil sire and his resurrected mother. After that, Deafula is overcome by religious décor in his father's church (cf: *Taste the Blood of Dracula*) and lies down dead (but purged).

Wolf stretches thin resources and tries for expressionist effects, but that papier-mâché nose and evil beard keep dragging the film to the level of *Dracula, the Dirty Old Man*. It's sincere in its commitment to the deaf community, even indicating in the end credits which of the cast and crew were hearing-impaired. Of course, Wolf couldn't hear the soundtrack and so can't be blamed for flat line readings (proper subtitles would have made more sense) and intermittently ominous piano score. Some action scenes – including the death in a hypnosis-induced crash of a bad biker – run silent. It'd make an interesting double bill with the even cheaper all-deaf British werewolf movie *Night Stalkers*.

DEAR DRACULA (2012)

A short (42 minute) CG animated kids' movie. Sam (voiced by Nathan Gamble), a mildly misfit kid whose best friend is a spider, wants a Dracula action figure rather than something more wholesome. Grandma (Marion Ross) tells him to write to Santa, but Hallowe'en is sooner than Christmas, so he writes to Dracula (Ray Liotta), who is hanging about his castle feeling sorry for himself because he's not scary any more. Encouraged by minion Myro (Emilio Estevez), the Count goes to whatever American suburb Sam lives in to brighten up his life… which means encouraging him to go to the party thrown by cute Emma (Ariel Winter), who likes a) monster movies and b) him. The mean kid who bullies (well, patronises – this avoids anything too upsetting) Sam dresses as a sparkly vampire and Dracula hypnotises him into acting like a chicken. That's pretty much it for plot, though Dracula also wins a Best Costume prize as an 'old-school vampire' and cheers up. Very cheap-looking, with old shtick done at length and a clunkily designed Drac. Still, over before it gets too painful. Written by Brad Birch, based on a graphic novel; directed by Chad Van De Keere.

DIE HARD DRACULA (1998)

'IT'S A WONDER WHAT GOOD FRESH BLOOD CAN DO, ESPECIALLY FROM SEXY GIRLS.'

Among the shoddiest Dracula movies ever made, this looks and sounds like shot-on-video porn; in fact, it's *less* well made than *Intercourse with the Vampyre* or *Muffy the Vampire Layer*. Writer-director Peter Horak – whose other credits are as a stuntman on major studio films from *Evel Knievel* to *Mystery Men* – secured locations on two continents (shooting in Prague and California), but the minimal sets where most of the action takes place are less impressive than the castles and countrysides.

Whiny drip Steven Hillman (Denny Sachen) loses girlfriend Julia (Kerry Dustin) in a rowboat accident and travels to Eastern Europe to forget his sorrows – though he wanders Prague streets by night shouting her name. He meets Carla (Dustin, with a silly accent), a lookalike for his lost love, but also falls in with Indiana Jones-costumed Van Helsing (Bruce Glover, the film's only 'name'). Van Helsing's ineptitude (failing to destroy the Count with a bullet to the heart) is copped from Richard Benjamin in *Love at First Bite*, leading to a running joke as various vampire-killing methods merely irritate Dracula. It's not funny, though some sequences – a dentist encouraged by Van Helsing to defang the Count – are theoretically jokey. There's mild domestic bickering between Dracula, who gets about his dungeon in a wobbly floating coffin, and Sonia (Talia Botone), an ashen-faced consort who slobbers blood into a wineglass as she desports herself on a grand piano. A sex scene between Steven and Carla is interrupted when Dracula flies into the room (like George Reeves as Superman) to abduct the girl (his mocking sign-off is a *To Have and Have Not* parody, 'Just put your lips together and suck.'). He transports her to his castle for some piano playing (these Draculas are very musical) and a dance, then bites her. Steven shows up for a swordfight – he chops off Dracula's head, but it sticks back on again. Carla, now vampirised, floats in greenlit fog pulling faces, and Dracula sees off the vampire slayers with zap-bolts from his fingers.

In the climax, a now-fanged Van Helsing (cf: *Sundown: The Vampire in Retreat*) persuades the dim-bulb hero it was all a dream. Dracula is played by three actors (Ernest M. Garcia, Chaba Hrotko, Tom McGowan) with different, if unimpressive looks (scraggly hair, tubby, dark glasses, bloated face, etc.) which might take cues from the Count's changeability in the novel (or the range of action figures inspired by Gary Oldman). A rare moment of invention has Van Helsing tormented by Dana (Nathalie Huot), who pops about the landscape like a staring refugee from *The Running Jumping Standing Still Film*. The music is repeated refrains from classical hits like the 'Blue Danube Waltz'.

LA DINASTÍA DI DRACULA (DYNASTY OF DRACULA) (1978)

A tired little Mexican vampire movie. In a 16th century prologue reminiscent of several Paul Naschy films, Gilles de Rais-type Satanist Antonio de Orloff (Kleomenes Stamatiades) is staked by the Inquisition near the Convent of Five Moors. Madame Kostoff (Erika Carlson), the villain's girlfriend, vows to bring him back. Three hundred years later, de Orloff's better-behaved descendants own the property. Baron Van Helsing (Roberto Nelson) arrives from Europe and tries to buy the estate. Along with the traditional tux and cape, the Baron has a remarkable Elvis 'do with attached sideburns and huge fangs. Dr Fuentes (Fabián), fiancé of heroine Beatriz (Silvia Manríquez), instantly pegs him as a descendant of Dracula.

Unusually, the film's Dracula (we never find out his real name or relationship to the famous vampire) is less important than de Orloff and his witch sidekick. The Baron claims the usual bunch of victims ('snakes don't drink blood') on the side, but spends most of his time working towards de Orloff's Walpurgisnacht resurrection. Dr Fuentes teams up with a priest (José Nájera) – the man of science has to convince the man of faith vampires are at work – to defeat the evil. The 'Lucy' figure is Beatriz's mother Doña Remedios (Magda Guzmán), who is vampirised and converted to the Baron's cause, but gets staked and has her mouth stuffed with garlic (a rarely filmed Stoker lick). Finally, de Orloff briefly returns from the dead in a cavern and the heroes see off the villains with a lot of fire.

Poorly directed by Alfredo B. Crevenna (*Bring Me the Vampire*), it deploys elementary special effects when the vampire suddenly appears or the witch turns into a dog. Single-named Fabián is the Mexican actor Fabián Aranza, not the American pop singer Fabian Forte. Nelson, bare-chested in his final face-off with the priest, is an ineffectual pantomime Drac, snarling and hissing for the kiddies.

DOCTOR DRACULA (LUCIFER'S WOMEN) (1975/1981)

An odd hybrid. In 1975, Paul Aratow made *Lucifer's Women*, a sex film in which John Wainwright (Larry Hankin) – a bearded academic who has written a book about reincarnation – somehow gets possessed by Svengali. Wainwright is mixed up with a Satanic cult led by another borrowed character, Sir Steven (Norman Pierce) from *The Story of O*, and out to get together with exotic dancer Trilby (Jane Brunel-Cohen, who is at least sufficiently beautiful).

In 1981, director Al Adamson and producer Sam Sherman shot extra scenes to replace more explicit sexual material so the result could be sold to television as *Doctor Dracula*. The resulting film includes Dr Anatol Gregorio (Geoffrey Land), a doctor possessed by Dracula, and Hadley Radcliff (John Carradine), leader of a cult seeking eternal life. Typical Adamson sloppiness is the inclusion of a take where Carradine loses the thread mid-tirade and breaks character. There might be a weird, workable idea in the notion of a fight between people possessed by competing fictional villains, but Gerald du Maurier and Bram Stoker aren't well-served by this throwdown between their famous creations. Mostly, people stand around looking glum and talking endlessly. Mike Raven lookalike Hankin, a real hambone, even argues with himself when Svengali's spirit detaches from its host.

Trilby does a butterfly-skirt dance, and long, dull Satanic ceremonies feature SnM drivel about some women being 'natural-born slaves' (perhaps input from 'technical adviser' Anton LaVey). In the end, thwarted Radcliff slumps over apparently dead and Dracula gets heroine Valerie (Regina Carrol) in a car to gloat about defeating the cult. She takes a bomb from her purse and blows them both up (stock footage under the end titles) to tidy everything up. A possessed or ghostly mother's really annoying croaky voice is the scariest thing here.

DRACULA (2006)

Three decades on from *Count Dracula* (1977), the BBC mounted another Christmas special *Dracula*. Screenwriter Stewart Harcourt, who refrains from using a single line of the book, seems to find Bram Stoker's plot under-motivated, so this Dracula (Marc Warren) is invited to England – much as he has to be invited into a house, perhaps – by Lord Arthur Holmwood (Dan Stevens). The glowering Singleton (Donald Sumpter), leader of a Chelsea-based cult, convinces Arthur that the Count can cure his syphilis. Though the Hammer-style cult serves Dracula well, he slaughters them all – following a lazy TV convention that villains murder their own lieutenants to underline their evil nature.

Like all three 1979 Draculas (John Badham's, Werner Herzog's *Nosferatu the Vampyre*, *Love at First Bite*), this presents Stoker's authority figures as inept imbeciles… so despairing surrender to the monster is inevitable. Different *oughtn't* necessarily mean worse, but all the characters are ill-served: after a single vampire encounter, Van Helsing (David Suchet) becomes a nervous wreck with a false beard, who keeps trying to run from the fight; Mina (Stephanie Leonidas) is weepy after luckless Jonathan (Rafe Spall) is left dead at the castle; Lucy (Sophia Myles) inherits Mina business like being forced to drink Dracula's blood from an open vein in his chest, but her vampire career is almost omitted – which means Myles doesn't even compete with her bitchy fanged turn in *Underworld*; and poor Dr Seward (Tom Burke) has to hold the story together by traipsing back and forth from London to Whitby.

Warren appears first with mud-pack makeup and nasty nails, then rejuvenates as a big-haired, shabbily-dressed creep. In a seldom-used bit from the book, he steals Harker's travel documents and clothes so he can pass for normal in England – which means he looks like a boring guy in tweeds rather than a threatening goth. Though he sports fangs and starey eyes, Warren's major Dracula assets are his hands: he is forever fingering people's faces and necks seductively, then ripping off heads. In a feeble finish, the Count is staked from behind; a single line ('Are you *sure* you pierced his heart?') sets up a last-moment reappearance as an aged derelict. Besides undervaluing the material, this does everything by halves – with poor CGI cliff-top castles and manors, unexciting tussles, listless performances from a good cast and uncommitted direction from Bill Eagles. A busy, unaffecting 90 minutes bereft of terror, romance and adventure, with a vampire king inches shorter than most of his enemies, this *Dracula* in every way lacks stature.

DRACULA (2009)

'TO EAT YOUR STEAK RAW ALLOWS YOU TO ABSORB THE POWER OF THE COW.'

This no-budget feature from writer-director-literally-everything-else George Anton (listed as 'procucer' in the end credits) would rate among the most obscure versions of *Dracula* if it weren't posted on YouTube for all to see. With chunks of what might be autobiographical material, it aims higher than, say, *Countess Dracula's Orgy of Blood* or *Lust for Dracula*, but lacks even the resources available to these softcore skits. Peculiar and oblique, it's further afflicted by budget-enforced blandness and a tendency to rant and ramble.

Demented Van Helsing (Gary Youst) vows vengeance against the king vampire and Dracula (Juan R. Caraccioli, barely in the film) bites a hooker in contemporary Los Angeles. Then Anton cuts to a hallucinatory, brief, violent domestic dispute – first of many barely connected vignettes of life on the margins of the city. Matt (co-writer Dan Martino), a struggling screenwriter working as a delivery guy, is pulled over by Officer Traxel (Greg Williams) and arrested for unpaid parking fines. In alternate versions of the follow-up scene, Matt is raped (inexplicitly) by the cop and has a philosophical chat in a cell with a convicted murderer. Matt delivers food to a Hollywood player (Derek Baker) who agrees to look at his script and, after persuading him to rewrite it as a vampire movie, buys it. In an edgy scene, Matt visits his parents in New Jersey; his mother (Kelly C. Ryan) indulges him while his father (Youst) cruelly crushes his dreams of making it in the movie business.

Not only does Youst play Van Helsing and Matt's father, but Baker turns up as Jonathan Harker and other actors play dual or triple roles. The Dracula-related scenes which fit around the story of Matt's Hollywood struggle might be figments of his work-in-progress screenplay. Fair enough, except even idly searching YouTube viewers most likely feel rooked if they click on a *Dracula* and get 82 minutes of whining from a wannabe screenwriter who never earned his father's approval. Familiar fragments are presented, recasting Harker and 'Reinfield' (Collin Sutton) as LA real estate agents and Lucy Westenra (Ginger Pullman) as a presenter on '*America's Hot Models*'. She's dating cop John Seward (Patrick Kaiser), short-fused asshole Holmwood (Alex Arleo) and some guy we never meet called Quincy who works with Mina Murray (Lala Hensely). Key scenes are referred to but not dramatised: we see Harker walking up to Castle Dracula, but not his meeting the Count and the vampire brides; Van Helsing persuades Holmwood to stake Lucy, but she is never a vampire on screen (or even bitten by Dracula); Reinfield eats flies in a hotel room but vanishes from the plot.

The tracking down and destroying of Dracula is omitted and the climax comes after Matt has sold his screenplay, reconciled with his father and become a Hollywood monster. A sudden conflict blows up with his former friend Vinnie (Ivan Crasci), one of the hot models, which leads to them taking their shirts off in the park and rushing at each other, with Matt flashing plastic fangs. It's better made than many an Asylum film, even if video effects are cheap (a blur to indicate possession, rudimentary split screen/multi-angle) and there's literally no action. The cast aren't amateurs (they mostly have real IMDb credits, albeit in 'third cop'-type roles) and do what they can with awkward dialogue ('Killing her? You know I could get arrested for this?'). Other works from the indefatigable auteur: *Sherlock Holmes* (2011), *The Passions of Jesus Christ* and *George Anton's Romeo and Juliet*.

DRACULA (2012)

> 'THANK GOD I HAD ENOUGH GARLIC FOR ONE BULLET.'

Though blessed (or cursed) with 3D, Dario Argento's second gothic horror classic remake – after his peculiar *Phantom of the Opera* – is surprisingly among the smaller-scale *Draculas*. Argento and several credited co-writers borrow heavily from Jimmy Sangster's tailored-to-a-tiny-budget script for Terence Fisher's *Dracula*, again summoning Harker (Unax Ugalde) to Castle Dracula to catalogue the Count's library rather than expedite emigration to far-off (and expensive) Victorian England. Action is confined to shot-in-Italy Middle Europe, though no country is specified, and most characters conveniently live in the shadow of the castle.

In one reasonably interesting innovation, this Dracula (Thomas Kretschmann, in a costume very like Louis Jourdan's *Count Dracula*) has a pact with corrupt town worthies, endowing schools and limiting his predation on the condition he is not defied. The best horror sequence comes when he contemptuously avenges himself on these treacherous minions. Like Hammer, Argento cuts costs by reducing Dracula's harem from three to one; indeed, buxom Tanja (Miriam Giovanelli) is a lift, down to the character name, from Anouska Hempel's hoyden in *Scars of Dracula*.

A new wrinkle, adopted especially for 3D, is that the Count manifests as all manner of vermin, including an owl, a cloud of flies and an alarming (female!) giant praying mantis. Pallid Asia Argento is a surprisingly subdued Lucy, upstaged by Giovanelli when turned into a vampire, while Marta Gastini's tagalong Mina is yet again a reincarnation of Dracula's lost love (if barely present in the film). Getting round the problem of Van Helsing's dodgy accent, Argento casts Rutger Hauer (the first Dutchman ever given the role), but the promise of a face-off between Kretschmann's Count and Hauer's Professor fizzles in a climax which is heavy on CGI but light on drama. Dialogue is high-flown but clunky ('I am nothing but an out of tune chord in the divine symphony,' laments Dracula) and Argento seems hampered rather than liberated by 3D. Claudio Simonetti's score makes nostalgic, eerie use of the theremin, which has fallen out of fashion as a signifier of unworldliness since the 1950s. Lesser Argento, lesser Dracula – but major mantis.

DRACULA EXOTICA (LOVE AT FIRST GULP) (1980)

Following his Lugosi imitation in *Dracula Sucks*, Jamie Gillis donned a natty blue-lined cape for this extraordinary X-rated item. Written and directed by Warren Evans (aka Shaun Costello), it's among the sleazier examples of a sleazy-enough form, but is the first Dracula movie with an 'origin' (oddly, Francis Ford Coppola's *Bram Stoker's Dracula* plumps for a very similar backstory). Slo-mo bat footage flickers under the credits as in Herzog's *Nosferatu*, then 'Leopold Michael Georgi, Count Dracula' narrates a flashback to when he was a frilly-shirted Romanian prince in soft-focus love with virginal, devout Surka (Samantha Fox). Dejected during an orgy, he drags Surka to the dining table to be mass-groped by the drunken throng. Overcome by lust, Dracula rapes the protesting commoner, who commits suicide – prompting the prince to 'curse and defy the laws of the church'. In return, God denies Dracula sanctuary in heaven or hell, gives him eternal thirst for blood and fans 'the burning fire of lust within' while condemning him 'never to be satisfied'.

Four hundred years later, Castle Dracula is a tourist attraction in Communist Romania (cf: *Love at First Bite*). Dracula's brides have been failing to bring him to orgasm for a century; they are played by Denise and Dianna Sloan, twins who one-up Madeleine and Mary Collinson in the ... *of Evil* stakes. Ungraciously, the Count has cockney minion 'Renfrew' (Gordon G. Duvall, doing a decent Peter Butterworth impersonation) pour holy water over them to clean house. He departs for New York, where Surka has been reincarnated as Sally Iancu (Fox again), an Irish-Romanian 'Federal Intelligence Bureau' agent whose boss (Eric Edwards) thinks Dracula is a Soviet spy. Arriving as usual on a fog-shrouded ship, Dracula has a Yorga-style fight with thuggish drug smugglers ('It seems that the ship carried a cargo even more dangerous than myself.'), who are worn out from an energetic sex session with Puerto Rican spitfire Vita Valdez (Vanessa del Rio). Vita stabs Dracula and steals his wallet, whereupon he turns her into a) a vampire and b) his secretary. An especially perverse sex-horror scene has Vita's naked corpse mauled in the morgue by a necrophile (Joel Kane aka Herschel Savage) who is surprised when – in a twist on a well-remembered scene in *Blacula* – she comes to fanged life and bites him. This is a rare instance of porn played for suspense: the punch line is delayed as ominous music drones while the morgue attendant has sex with the unresponding woman, who only shows her fangs after he's ejaculated.

Not content with being vampire, spy and 'cultural commissioner', Dracula becomes a Broadway producer – as a way to meet drinkable girls. Inevitably, Dracula and Sally get together: she shows up to audition and sings a traditional Hungarian song, and they have a romantic night-time-in-New York montage. Being in love stirs the Count's conscience and he can't bring himself to seek victims ('Who is less entitled to life than I?'). When Dracula and Sally finally have sex ('Now my love, redemption is at hand.'), the Count has his first orgasm since death – intercut with silent movie crashing waves and the ticking of a clock which stopped when he became a vampire. The treacherous Vita turns into a skeleton while pleasuring the equally treacherous Renfrew, and the lovers transform into 'doves of peace' to fly happily towards the rising sun – which is at least an ending we've not seen in a Dracula movie before.

Though *Dracula Exotica* has the expected silly comedy (an offscreen crash as Dracula flies through a window Renfrew forgot to open), it's weirdly serious about its vampire love story and intricate spy nonsense. It's nearly a 'proper film', with plot (too much of it, in fact) and characterisation (Fox plays Surka and Sally as different people – they even make love differently). Evans pumps in fog to stage striking gothic tableaux between grungy, rather unappealing sex scenes. Not exactly good, but also not just a rote sexfest with fang-flashes and cloak-swishing (cf: *Lust of Blackula*, *Out for Blood*, *Bite!*).

DRACULA: LORD OF THE DAMNED (2011)

This Canadian *Dracula* takes an approach somewhere between John Johnson's *Alucard*, with its faithful community theatre-level adaptation of the novel, and Guy Maddin's *Dracula: Pages from a Virgin's Diary*, with deliberately outmoded film techniques. In a distinctive theological take, the former Vlad Tepes has a messiah complex and sees himself as a saviour, though his victims have differing opinions. When the Count flees London for Transylvania, Mina (Amanda Lisman) diagnoses, 'He has to retreat to his cave to rebuild his delusions, lest he go mad with self-knowledge.'

Writer-director Theodore Trout plays Dracula – with stuck-on sideburns, fangs and a bat-symbol breastplate – as a ferocious, demented shapeshifter. The vampire appears as a golden youth (Ethan Jensen) to Van Helsing (Mike Grimshaw) and manifests other shadow-forms, including a Nosferatu muppet and an iron-faced Grim Reaper/ Ferryman. Quincy (Randall Carnell) diagnoses that Dracula isn't just a vampire but a wendigo. It uses cartoons for some special effects, has Terry Gilliamish animation and collage sequences, and is mostly in stressed black-and-white, with occasional tints and colour splashes. Some Stoker dialogue is flattened (the Count's introduction is, 'I am Dracula. Please come in.') and deliberately overheated lines ('Can he be destroyed – a dead mediaeval warlord whose evil is eternal?') add a sly camp touch, though this is mostly a serious attempt to make the old story disturbing again. This Dracula has a harem of *five* vampire wives, who are hauled off Harker (David McPherson) and given a peasant baby to tear apart gruesomely. Harker later wakes in the castle to find the child's mother (Alexandra Steinmetz) hanging dead outside his window.

A few Victorian social and sexual mores are interrogated – this Mina is Lucy's maid, and Lucy (Denise Brown) suffers guilt-induced madness for cheating on fiancé Dr Seward (Ian Case) and becomes a blood-boltered, glowing-eye-socketed harridan vampire quite unlike any other depiction of the character. The score drones, with a few classical (Bach's Toccata and Fugue) and goth metal selections, and a genuine handmade feel disarms criticism. Performances are good, if on the Canadian-accented side, and a real engagement with the material carries the film through rough spots and awkward passages. With Hal Hewett as Renfield.

DRACULA REBORN (2012)

> 'WHERE'S THE CRUCIFIX?'
> 'IF ONLY IT WORKED. THIS EVIL'S
> NON-DENOMINATIONAL.'

Less peculiar than George Anton's no-budget *Dracula* (2009), this bland vampire movie pulls the same gag (as does the gender-switched *Lust for Dracula*) of relocating the story to budget-friendly contemporary Los Angeles and sticking Stoker's character names (or approximations) on a variety of cops, docs, goons and victims. There's a lot of driving around, but no sense of urgency – and things pan out predictably.

Realtor Jonathan Harker (Corey Landis) sells a large disused industrial building in a bad neighbourhood to sinister, non-specifically foreign 'Vladimir Sarkany' (Stuart Rigby). It's hard to understand why Sarkany (only named as Dracula in the end credits) needs the empty premises since he already has a perfectly acceptable posh Malibu pad. Sarkany is seen as a CGI-faced vamp attacking Petra Hawkins (Christianna Carmine), another estate agent, before the credits. He demonstrates further undead cred by swiftly slaughtering three overage gangbangers who hassle him in his new lair. Reusing the reincarnation angle that's become a *Dracula* cliché, Sarkany owns a picture of a strange nude who exactly resembles Harker's British wife Lina (Victoria Summer). Ranting Quincy Morris (Krash Miller) pops up in the back of Harker's car, claiming Sarkany has seduced his girlfriend Lucy (Linda Bella) and turned her into a vampire (Amy Johnston). Jonathan and Lina visit the Sarkany mansion, where bald, waspish Renfield (Ian Pfister) is major-domo, to look at the picture. Their car stalls on the winding road home, forcing them to sleep in the open air – Lina wakes up with 'spider-bites' on her neck and Dr Joan Seward (Dani Lennon) diagnoses anaemia.

A military-looking Van Helsing (Keith Reay) barges in to kill two cops, Detective Holmwood (Preston Hillier) and Detective Varna (Charlie Garcia), who are mind-controlled by the vampire. He then co-opts Harker into a vampire hunt like the (perfunctory) finish of Tod Browning's *Dracula*. Van Helsing and Sarkany fight and, like the Van Helsings in John Badham's and Werner Herzog's films, the fearless vampire killer gets lifted up and impaled, with Sarkany pulling out and squeezing his heart. But Harker and Lina stake Sarkany back and front, only for (in another *Count Yorga, Vampire* touch) Lina to bite the hero ('I'll never forget you.') and, in a *Daughters of Darkness/The Hunger* sort of way, take over the vampire's home, wealth, minion and style. Rigby, a Birmingham brickie and professional Tom Cruise impersonator, rasps with a Terence Stamp British accent (Stamp was a stage Dracula) and stares into space often, and writer-director Patrick McManus makes the odd choice to overlay his face with marble pallor, blue veins, hollow cheeks and cartoon neon eyes in post-production.

DRACULA'S CURSE (BRAM STOKER'S DRACULA'S CURSE) (2006)

The casting of bland Australian horror regular Rhett Giles as a Van Helsing relative suggests this is a sequel to *Way of the Vampire* (aka *Bram Stoker's Way of the Vampire*), but writer-director Leigh Scott starts from scratch. Unlike the usual fare of The Asylum (home of *Snakes on a Train*, *Transmorphers*, etc.), it's not imitative of any specific blockbuster – which hardly makes it original since it borrows from *Night Watch*, *Blade: Trinity*, *Buffy the Vampire Slayer*, *Kindred: The Embraced* (and other role-playing games) and even *Way of the Vampire*. It feels even cheaper than most Asylum product – taking place almost entirely inside an abandoned warehouse where sneery types brandish toy weapons and snarl dialogue at each other.

Jacob Van Helsing (Giles), descendent of Abraham, leads a cadre of fearless vampire hunters which includes the foxy Gracie Johanssen (Eliza Swenson, who also wrote the music) and mystery man Rufus King (Thomas Downey). A vampire faction headed by 'The Old One' (director Scott), who has a top hat and long white hair, proposes a truce – vampires will stop preying on the unwilling if hunters stop killing vampires out of hand. Sceptical (obvious baddie) vampire Rafe (Jeff Denton) is in charge of enforcing the dictate on 'the clans'. This works for a while, but ambitious Countess Bathorly (Christina Rosenberg) won't get in line, hung up on the notion of drinking 'the pureblood' (from other vampires). After betrayals, reversals and double-crosses, it climaxes (spoiler) with a not-expected revelation that King is 'Lord Vladimir Drakulya'. Here, the vampire has done a deal with the Devil to live as a man (indeed, as a vampire hunter) provided he doesn't use his powers. However, he turns into a giant bat creature (in a fantasy wood) to impress on Bathorly (famous vampires all get extra letters in their names here) that she's not a good person, which means his deal is off and he has to go back to being a hissing fangy creature at the wannabe emotional curtain.

The martial arts fights and shootouts look like rough rehearsals and don't even get minimal assistance from, say, convincing sound effects. The no-name actors (Giles is the best performer here) all have porno/soap stridency as they rattle through reams of nondescript talk. It unusually features two distinct vampire strains: inhuman, makeup-buried *Nosferatu* creatures and regular folk with pointed teeth.

DRACULA'S GUEST (2008)

'YOU SHOULD BE ASHAMED OF YOURSELF... AND YOU CALL YOURSELF AN ADMIRAL!' 'HOW DARE YOU... I'VE FOUGHT IN THREE WARS... I'VE KILLED HUNDREDS OF FOREIGNERS!'

Writer-director Michael Feifer specialises in worthless serial-killer biopics (*Ed Gein: The Butcher of Plainfield, Bundy: An American Icon*); this stab at gothic horror is more ambitious – if hampered by an inability to hire actors who can do 19th century British or Transylvanian accents without sounding like utter prawns. Ostensibly based on the short story/deleted chapter 'Dracula's Guest', it's a melange of bits (and names) from the novel, earlier Dracula films and a version of Stoker's life even less fact-based than the Roger Corman-produced *Burial of the Rats* (where Stoker tangles with piratical rat-women on a trip to Russia). Like many low-budget 21st century attempts at period horror, it goes with ugly, desaturated colours (influenced by John Badham's controversial preferred transfer of his *Dracula*?) rather than attempt the rich look of Hammer.

A story which spans a continent and several countries seems to take place mostly on a California beach. Young, bearded, brogue-sporting Bram (Wes Ramsey) finds his girlfriend Elizabeth (Kelsey McCann) imprisoned in a cave near Castle Dracula. Through bars, she gives him sorry news that the Count has 'planted the seed of the beast in my body'. Then, we flash back to London where Bram has Jonathan Harker's job as 'a real estate agent' with offices in Baker Street. He is charged with finding a suitable property for a Mr Dracula (Andrew Bryniarski). The villain is undramatically introduced sitting in a chair in the office insisting – in his worst Bela Lugosi accent – on being addressed as 'Count'. Bryniarski's hulking Count has long black hair, the stuck-on goatee favoured by several of the screen's worst Draculas (Zandor Vorkov!), plastic fangs and a tendency to speak slowly. In a London park, the plot boils as characters stand awkwardly in a clump struggling through stuffy dialogue: Admiral Murray (Dan Speaker), Elizabeth's father, disapproves of Bram as a future son-in-law, which annoys the young lovers. Elizabeth runs off in a snit and Dracula smarmily transports her to Transylvania – though she puts up a spirited Victorian argument against being raped ('How dare you treat me as if you have my acquaintance. You do not!').

In the cave, Dracula recites extracts from the novel about his heroic past. There's nearly an interesting argument as Elizabeth dismisses Dracula's tales of mediaeval martial glory by telling him her father foresees tanks and aeroplanes making old-fashioned warriors obsolete. The Admiral comes from a line of vampire-hunters who have persecuted Dracula, so the Count's abuse of her is personal. Bram has adventures in France with scurvy, treacherous peasants offering a new flavour of bad accent – but duffs them up. He arrives on foot in Transylvania just in time to be warned that it's Walpurgis Night and the unquiet dead are around ('Oh, I see, suicides, how interesting.'). Bram survives a brush with three vampire women in the woods (this *might* be a trace element from the short story). Elizabeth sees Dracula flying overhead, but we don't. She whines further about 'his seed' (she mystically knows she's pregnant) and bad attitude ('You don't know what it is to have love inside your heart – I don't know if you even have a heart.'). Bram proves his heroism by climbing a cliff as a rinky-dinky organ score tries to give the impression the feat is more difficult than it plainly is. The Admiral shows up at the cave and tells Elizabeth she has 'abilities beyond your imagination' thanks to her special bloodline – though the Murray superpowers are never brought into play. Bram clambers into the castle – represented by a borrowed mausoleum – and waves a knife ('I'm an Irishman, and an Irishman never turns his back.') and Dracula swishes a fur-collared crimson velvet cloak, cackles like a panto villain, and uses powers of invisibility and/or telekinesis.

The Admiral ('I've a long history with Vlad the Impaler.') teams up with Bram, who rescues the girl. The savant has a slow, clumsy sword fight with the slow, clumsy vampire (who finds it hard not to get his sword tangled up in the cape) and manages to skewer the bastard – who gloats about reigning in Hell as he dies. The Admiral ('Without a head to wear a crown, you'll never reign anywhere.') drives a sword through the prone Dracula's heart (it looks more like his stomach) and announces that Bram and Elizabeth 'have an appointment in Westminster Abbey – to be married!'

Dracula disappears in a simple effect (no expensive putrefaction), but his cackle stays behind – and we're left to wonder whether Elizabeth's child will take after the vampire or vampire-hunting side of its lineage.

DRACULA SUCKS/LUST AT FIRST BITE (1979)

This relatively elaborate X-rated film exists in multiple, radically different versions. *Dracula Sucks* (95 minutes) offers surprisingly intense horror, restrained (if still hardcore) sex scenes and a range of kinks including necrophilia, incest and rat-fondling. *Lust at First Bite* aka *The Coming of Dracula's Bride* (74 minutes) has more explicit sex, enough dubbed-in jokes to make it a comedy and a surprisingly romantic variant ending. *Dracula Sucks* features old-time radio excerpts on the soundtrack, including a *Suspense* with Bela Lugosi, while *Lust at First Bite* has an eclectic selection of 1930s and '40s songs (Woody Guthrie, Spike Jones). The various softcore or censored cuts released in cinemas and on video outside the US are cut-downs of *Dracula Sucks*.

Set in the 1930s – as signalled by good costumes and a borrowed vintage car – this uses much of the script of the 1931 Tod Browning film with jokes tipped in (just like Mel Brooks' *Dracula: Dead and Loving It*). A running joke copped from *MASH* consists of absurd announcements ('Attention, attention, Dr Van Helsing please return the crucifix to the chapel.') over the tannoy at Dr Seward's Sanitarium. It can charitably be assumed the fake bat-on-a-string is an intended comic effect and David Lee Bynum's terrified black butler (who confuses Van Helsing with Van Heflin) is supposed to be a *parody* of a 1930s film stereotype. Full-bearded and dressed as a head waiter, with Lee-style red-lined cape, Jamie Gillis's Dracula is played fairly straight, with the oddly effective touch of dubbing tigerish growls over his snarls of anger or lechery. Cadaverous Reggie Nalder (minion to *Dracula's Dog*, Barlow in *Salem's Lot*) is a sinister Van Helsing – a rare case of a 'name' actor showing up in porn, albeit under an assumed moniker (Detlef Van Berg). Like other 1979 Van Helsings, this killjoy savant is essentially useless against the vampire ('I sure could use a cognac,' he muses, 'or a Quaalude.').

Good supporting performances come from Annette Haven as a suitably ethereal Mina, Serena as gloomy 'Lucy Webster', John Leslie as a pompous Dr Seward and (especially) Richard Bulik doing a committed Dwight Frye impersonation as Renfield (in *Lust at First Bite* he is billed as 'McGoogle Schlepper'). Notably bad is John Holmes

(*Sex and the Single Vampire*) as rampant 'Dr Stoker', who has a session with a vampire – the shot of the maid (Irene Best) sinking plastic fangs into the famous Holmes member is unique to *Dracula Sucks* – and winds up with awkward fang-scars. 'Ha-ha, Big Dick is sick!' crows an unsympathetic orderly (screenwriter William Margold). Paul Thomas, who later directed his own vampire porno *Out for Blood*, is a traditionally dim-witted Jonathan Harker; his frustrations at being engaged to a virgin for three years are relieved in the back of a yellow taxi by a blonde nurse (Dietrich-look Seka). Unusually, there's inexplicit gay sex as Dracula forces himself on Harker before seducing Mina. The climax is a long, piano-scored sex scene between Dracula and Mina in a cave. In *Lust at First Bite*, Dracula gets the girl ('Dracula has his new queen – she's found eternal sexual passion with her master.'); in *Dracula Sucks*, Van Helsing and Harker get there in time to expose him to sunlight.

Perhaps indicating something other than altitude, the end credits bill this as 'filmed at a castle in the *high* California desert.'

DRACULA: THE DARK PRINCE (2013)

There have been so many different approaches to Dracula that anything fresh ought to earn at least the token marks students get for writing their names at the top of exam papers. *Dracula: The Dark Prince* retells the old story in a new-ish genre – as a Dungeons & Dragons-style fantasy quest.

In 15th century Wallachia, Christian prince Dracula (Luke Roberts, with long blond hair) comes home to find his lieutenants have murdered his wife (Kelly Wenham). Upset, he renounces God and is turned into a vampire. One hundred years later (i.e. still in the nebulous Middle Ages), his castle retinue includes vampire concubines, sneaky Grand Vizier-type assistant Renfield (Stephen Hogan) and a warrior champion Wrath (Vasilescu Valentin), who boasts impressively silly horned armour. Sisters Alina (Wenham again) and Esme (Holly Earl), of an order of teetotal slayers, carry a casket through the woods. Swashbuckling would-be charming thief Lucian (Ben Robson) steals the precious cargo, the Lightbringer. Though he's disappointed it's just a big stick, it's actually a Swiss army staff with hidden compass and blade attachments which (get this!) turns out to be the weapon Cain used to slay his brother. It's most effective if wielded by a descendant of Cain (logically, well over half humanity) against a descendant of Abel (made princes by God, so Dracula is one).

Lucian falls for stereotypically feisty Alina, but has to be convinced by Leonardo Van Helsing (Jon Voight with tricorn hat, droopy 'tache and false nose) to join a trek to Dracula's invisible castle (the magic compass helps) to defeat the monster. Alina, of course, is the reincarnation of Dracula's murdered wife and warms to the handsome prince, which ticks off his hench-folk (remember the lesson of Arabian Nights films – never trust a Grand Vizier). Van Helsing's party of slayers – which includes a Brummie-accented Norseman who has a Greek character name, Andros (Richard Ashton) – scale a Carpathian mountain and break into the castle to confront the monster. It has biting, one or two naked set-dressing slave girls and cheapo CGI disintegrations, but is more low-rent fantasy action than horror and strains for romance as the heroine chooses between two unlikeable men. Supposedly set in a historical 16th century, it goes with costumes from several eras – the women mostly model leather cutaway britches. Even the character names taken from Stoker, history and *World of Warcraft* don't make sense.

British pretty-boy Roberts, a veteran of 217 episodes of *Holby City* who had a bit part in one of the *Pirates of the Caribbean* sequels, is among the screen's weakest Draculas. It's possible to sell a vampire as a tortured, romantic soul (though that Barnabas-*Blacula*-Anne Rice stuff got old in the 1970s), but Roberts' well-mannered weediness is scarcely imposing, especially since this Dracula is an idiot who repeatedly trusts the obvious wrong 'un in his inner circle. Written by producer Steven Paul (of the *Baby Geniuses* franchise) and director Pearry Teo (*Necromentia*).

DRACULA: THE IMPALER (THE IMPALER) (2013)

A minor horror film with much in common with Jean Brismée's 1971 *La plus longue nuit du diable* (*Devil's Nightmare*) – which also had seven tourists emblematic of deadly sins stranded in a castle with a witchy female custodian. Here, Veronica (Diana Busuioc) is the caretaker of the castle of Vlad the Impaler and seven American young folks – a greedy one, a lecherous one, an envious one, etc. – spend a week in the place to squabble, have sex and get killed so Dominic (Teo Celigo) can be possessed by the spirit of Vlad III (Gregory Lee Kenyon). Though he bites a chunk out of a neck at one point, the demonic Dominic seems not to be a vampire but some other species of supernatural troublemaker.

Director Derek Hockenbrough – who also co-wrote with Busuioc, Daniel Anghelcev and cinematographer Steve Snyder – has a good premise (*La plus longue nuit du diable* is a gem), but this cramped production keeps stumbling. The kids are supposed to be between high school and college, but look much older and are strident boobs fit only to be killed. It's all well and good making a misanthropic portrait of horrible folks getting their comeuppance, but this means it's impossible to care about their fates, work up suspense beyond the issue of who dies next or generate any spookiness. It has one unnervingly odd appearance by three hungry, wisp-draped concubines (Vera Nova, Jennifer Starr, Victoria Levine).

DRACULA 2012 (2013)

Dario Argento isn't the only filmmaker to get a 3D Dracula on the market. Malayalam writer-director Vinayan's contemporary reworking was made in Kerela, far from India's Mumbai-centred film industry. Roy Thomas (Sudheer Sukumaran) and his bride Lucy (Shradha Das) stop over in Romania en route to a London honeymoon and visit Bran Castle, a tourist spot associated with Vlad the Impaler. Out of curiosity, Roy performs a ritual summoning and Dracula shows up as a CGI Man-Bat lookalike, possessing him in a manner which evokes the opening of *The Legend of the 7 Golden Vampires*. In Roy's form, Dracula learns Malayalam and turns Lucy (who has been taking a bath with a towel modestly wrapped around her) into a vampire.

Assuming the name 'Professor William D'Souza', Roy/Dracula returns to Kerela and moves into the Warner Bungalow, a home (with crypt) found by Jonathan Harker analogue Raju (Prabhu), who is engaged to Meena (Monal Gajjar). That venerable glimpse-of-a-picture bit makes Dracula set his sights on Meena (yet again, the reincarnation of Vlad's wife), though he also goes after her Lucy-like sister Thara (Priar Nambiar). Guru Soorayan (Nassar), father of Meena and Thara and uncle of Raju, subs for Van Helsing, though he needs assistance from an Anglo-sounding set of locals – chubby Dr Paul Robinson (the Seward character) and police commissioner Benny Thomas (Roy's brother), plus some 'Romanian Bishops'. Dracula's arrival is the excuse for 'Prince of Darkness, I Love You', a non-diegetic pop video performed by bare-midriff Indian goths. The only other number is 'Parijatha Pookkal', a love duet for Raju and Meena that nametags flowers and puberty. Meena throws a smoothie in Raju's face in a mall to show how much she loves him, but Dracula – shirtless as often as Wolverine, with bulging veins and

Hammer-type fangs – cuts in, forcing her to drink blood from his chest.

The home stretch, derived from the novel, has vampirised Meena guiding the heroes to Dracula's hideaway, a jungle cemetery. A *fakir* Renfield character (Thilakan) gabbles about his master to distract the good guys, but they eventually open the right tomb. Blessed with divine kung fu skills thanks to the just-killed guru, Raju has a fight with the vampire. In Stoker's original draft, Castle Dracula collapses when its master is destroyed – this is the first film to dramatise that deleted scene as the death of Roy/Dracula causes Castle Bran to explode. A long two and a quarter hours, with too many CGI bats flapping in poor red-and-green 3D. Some sequences are clumsily comical and others unintentionally so, all the heroes (and villains, come to that) are arrant fools, a repetitive orchestral score keeps trying to insist it's exciting and a potentially interesting mix of religions simply adds to the confusion. Sukumaran's glowering Dracula aspires to tragic hero status, but just comes off as a creep.

DRACULA II: ASCENSION (2003)

Dracula 2000, essentially an unacknowledged remake of Hammer's *Dracula A.D. 1972*, was the first Dracula movie in three decades to have sequels, though Dimension Films stretched the budget by making two follow-ups back-to-back on cheap Romanian locales. *Dracula II Ascension* perversely passes Romania off as New Orleans. The smallest-scale instalment of the series, this spends most of its plot elaborately resurrecting an arch-villain who is only unleashed near the finale.

A man in black (Jason Scott Lee) who resembles the Gerard Butler Dracula of *Dracula 2000* stalks a white-clad woman (Jennifer Kroll) in a Czech street... but turns out to be vampire-hunter Father Uffizi pursuing the undead. In a neat, tiny moment, the woman's reflection is glimpsed in a window and Uffizi realises he's dealing with a brace of lookalike vampires (nostalgically labelled Twins of Evil in the credits) who can pose as each other's missing reflection. Then, picking up where the earlier film began, Dracula burns at sunrise and the body is taken to a nearby morgue where new characters fuss over it. The bulk of the film takes place in abandoned Eastern Bloc-style settings (a ruined mansion and a swimming pool) where crippled lecturer Lowell (Craig Sheffer), medical examiner Elizabeth (Diane Neal), a sinister Englishman (John Light) and some disposable students keep the barely revived monster (Stephen Billington) strapped down as they study his blood. Under orders from a cameo cardinal (Roy Scheider), Uffizi tracks the body and arrives just as the monster has thoroughly corrupted his captors.

It's an unusual and workable idea (derived from Hannibal Lecter) that Billington's blond, white-faced Dracula, at his weakest and most confined, is still an unbeatable opponent. The script flirts with a scientific rationale for vampirism before going back to the basic if unfashionable notion of Dracula as irredeemably damned and supernaturally evil. As with director/co-writer Patrick Lussier's *Prophecy* sequel, *Ascension* isn't short of clever little bits (it's a rare film to make use of the vampire's folkloric obsessive-compulsive disorder, a need to count spilled seeds or undo knots), though the cramped, cheapskate feel prevents it from being fully satisfying. Modish cynicism is all-pervasive, with characters mostly rotten before the vampire gets to them – even the apparent heroine is willing to sell a corpse for thirty million dollars.

DRACULA III: LEGACY (2005)

This concludes a trilogy director/co-writer Patrick Lussier began with *Dracula 2000* and *Dracula II: Ascension*. The Dracula of this saga regenerates and is recast (like *Doctor Who*), so each film offers a different take. The avowed model for *Legacy* is *Heart of Darkness*: vamp-hunting martial artist priest Uffizi (Jason Scott Lee) and guilt-ridden civilian sidekick Luke (Jason London) travel through a blighted, war-torn Romania towards the lair of a monster who has lost touch with his empire and become an ultimate couch potato, watching television while taking blood through intravenous tubes. It's a good idea, distinct from Gerard Butler/Dracula-as-Judas and Stephen Billington/Dracula-as-Hannibal-Lecter of *Dracula 2000* and *Dracula II: Ascension*, but Rutger Hauer/Dracula-as-Kurtz is a disappointment. Coming to the role after ineffectual stabs at king vampiredom in *Buffy the Vampire Slayer* and *Salem's Lot*, Hauer gives one of his less-committed performances.

However, this road to Castle Dracula has engaging diversions: a *Vampire Circus* homage with blood-drinking clowns and an impressive vampire on stilts; and business with vampire-hating rebels and human-harvesting minions out in the Romanian sticks shows a grander ambition than, say, the *subspecies* films. Luke's motivation is to save his girlfriend (Diane Neal), bitten in the previous film. The state he finds her in – addicted to other vampires' blood in an impressive, if discreet semi-lesbian orgy of fluid-exchange – is at least a new development in a crowded genre. Lee, fighting a Blade-like vampire infection, is defrocked to allow mild romance with 'EBC' newswoman Julia (Alexandra Wescourt). The Conradian finale sets up an ironic reversal which is a logical extension of the finish of *Apocalypse Now*, but also reprises Lee's fate in *Talos The Mummy*.

DRACULA 3000: INFINITE DARKNESS (2004)

A dopey concept, poorly executed. A thousand years in the future, where Christianity is forgotten but bad rap music is still around and people make remarks about *The Bionic Woman*, elements from *Dracula* are tipped into a cheap *Event Horizon* knock-off. Captain Abraham Van Helsing (Casper Van Dien) and his grumbling space-salvage foragers board the derelict spaceship *Demeter* in 'the Carpathian Galaxy' to find the crew dead. A recorded log from Captain Varna (Udo Kier) is ominous about a cargo of sand-filled coffins from 'the planet Transylvania'. Dracula (Langley Kirkwood), using the name Orlock, is a pantomime-cloaked, surprisingly inactive vampire. He turns doper 187 (Coolio) into the worst-ever black vampire, but *doesn't* murder everyone. In an *Alien*-related twist, Orlock lets heroine Aurora Ash (Erika Eleniak) escape, prompting everyone to suspect her – tying her to a chair in imitation of *The Thing* – until she reveals she's a bloodless robot/undercover narc.

There's a germ of an idea in pitting an ancient vampire against people from a culture that has forgotten what he is and how to destroy him, though computer files confirm that a wooden pool-cue will do the job (in 2950, pool cues were still made of wood, unlike in 3000, we are told) until the ship can be brought near enough a double star to flood it with sunlight. Oddly, this latter plan *isn't* the ending – which manages to run in rapid succession through *three* dud finishes: Dracula is defeated by having his arm torn off in a closing door and wanders off in pain, surviving horny crewman Humvee (Tiny Lister) discovers Ash used to be a 'pleasurebot' and lecherously throws her over his shoulder (among the worst-acted scenes in Dracula movie history) and Varna's tape message somehow blows up the ship. Being the worst Dracula movie made in a year with *Van Helsing* and *Blade: Trinity* is some sort of achievement. Written and directed by Darrell James Roodt, a South African auteur who alternates genre (*City of Blood*, *The Stick*) and dully respectable (*Sarafina!*, *Cry, the Beloved Country*).

DRAKULA ISTANBUL'DA (DRACULA IN ISTANBUL) (1953)

'WE SHOULD GO AND GARLIC THE CHESTS BEFORE MIDNIGHT.'

The Turkish commercial film industry has long since made a habit of tailoring famous stories for the domestic market (cf: *Tarzan Istanbul'da/Tarzan in Istanbul*) and a minor international cult prizes Turkey's ridiculous, eccentric imitations of *Star Trek* or *Superman*. Less well known is this sincere, surprisingly straight transposition of *Dracula* to contemporary Istanbul. Drakula (Atif Kaptan) retains his name, but all Bram Stoker's supporting characters get a Turkish makeover. Despite innovations like making blonde heroine Güzin (Annie Ball) a dancer who desports in a harem outfit and the downplaying of crucifixes as vampire repellent weapons (a lot of garlic is used instead), *Drakula Istanbul'da* is more faithful to Stoker than any other cinema adaptation until Francis Ford Coppola – though the cramped production misses the scope of the book and screenwriter Ümit Deniz turns an epic into the story of a creep who makes a pass at the hero's wife and is then properly seen off for it. Nevertheless, there are modest innovations – Kaptan, white-haired and balding, is the first screen vampire with fangs (indeed, his fierce canines look like tusks) and this is the first film to stage the memorable image of the Count crawling head-first down the wall of his castle.

Besides the use of garlic – and a plot-point which leaves Güzin briefly vulnerable because she can't wear a garlic necklace while dancing – this has its Van Helsing, Dr Eren (Kemal Emin Bara), stress that the stake through the heart is just to pin the vampire down till the subsequent decapitation finishes the creature off. Sadan (Ayfer Feray), the Lucy, and Drakula are both served this way, discreetly with no onscreen blood or head-lopping. Azmi (Bülent Oran), the Harker, travels to Romania to help the Count buy properties in Istanbul, is warned off by peasants, menaced over the dinner table by the mysterious nobleman, spooked by a hunchbacked minion with a false nose and insanely large moustache, vamped by a single bride and takes a spade to the vampire's head when he finds him bloated in his crypt. In Turkey, tailcoated and cloaked Drakula – who uses the pseudonym El Cross Abdullatif – transforms Güzin's dark-haired cousin Sadan into a child-hunting vampire. Turan (Cahit Irgat),

Sadan's Arthur fiancé, consults with Dr Eren and Seward-like Dr Afif (Münir Ceyhan). Together, they destroy her then seal nine out of Drakula's ten coffins with garlic. Azmi recovers from a nervous breakdown… and shows remarkable confidence when Drakula has the nerve to hypnotise his wife into giving him a private performance, chasing the cowardly vampire back to his hidden tenth coffin (in a local cemetery) and impulsively staking and beheading him, then breezing home to insist Güzin throw all the garlic out of the house and never even use it in cooking again. Directed by Mehmet Muhtar.

EMMANUELLE VS DRACULA (EMMANUELLE THE PRIVATE COLLECTION: EMMANUELLE VS DRACULA) (2003)

Behind an eye-catching title lies a softcore snoozer which was originally an episode of a late-night cable time-waster series, *Emmanuelle the Private Collection* – itself a footnote to the long-lived franchise derived from Emmanuelle Arsan's semi-autobiographical novel. The wicker chair is about the only connection to any previous incarnation of the sensual adventuress.

Emmanuelle (Natasja Vermeer), 'the world's most independent woman', attends a bachelorette party for Lucy (Mollie Green) with three friends whose character notes instantly give away the sexual routes they'll take: repressed Mary (Beverly Lynne), happily married Susan (hardcore star Kelsey Heart, billed as Kelsey) and incipient lesbian Jennifer (Valerie Baber). Mystery man 'Mr Robertson' (Ernesto Perdomo) turns up at the isolated house, claiming to have had a car accident. Emmanuelle, who has vampire-themed bad dreams, is suspicious, but the others are intrigued by his hypnotic power to give women spontaneous pleasure (cue cutaways to unrelated characters masturbating on sun-loungers). Robertson, aka 'The Dark One', humps and bites Lucy in the shower and she spreads vampirism (signified by fangs, goth makeup and fetish underwear) through the party. Emmanuelle fights back, presuming *The Lost Boys* rules apply so that if she kills the sire her friends will revert to normal. The goateed vampire turns out *not* to be Dracula but a mere minion. The real Count (Marcus DeAnda) shows up for a one-on-one with the heroine, pitting superior sexual abilities against each other in a sadly vanilla shag on the carpet.

The thin story is padded with flashbacks but keeps defaulting to achingly familiar minimal-contact sex scenes. Director 'KLS' (aka Keith Shaw) leaves in takes where the cast fumble lines and the script by Rafael Glenn (aka Rolfe Kanefsky) makes little of the clash of icons – though it drops hints that Emmanuelle (uncharacteristically a sexual killjoy here) has supernatural status of her own.

FRACCHIA CONTRO DRACULA (1985)

A feeble Italian comedy, built around unprepossessing, middle-aged Paolo Villaggio. The star is best known for a popular ten-film series in which he played a luckless clerk called Fantozzi – this finds him as a similar twerp called Fracchia, carried over from a TV series and the earlier *Fracchia la Belva Umana*.

Fracchia is so terrified during a horror film that he gets up and unamusingly tips over several rows of cinema seats. Like Jonathan Harker, this meek fifty-something virgin works as an estate agent. On the point of being fired by his boss (glowering Paul Muller), Fracchia has to take another fussy eccentric (Gigi Reder) to Transylvania because the fool wants to buy a five-bathroom house for a tiny sum. 'Count Vlad' (Edmund Purdom) has his castle on the market, but everyone in the inn flees at the mention of his name. A singing barmaid (Susanna Martinková) surprisingly comes on to Fracchia, telling him it's dangerous to be a virgin in this region. He leaves the room, but returns to find her in a clinch with the vampire, gets the wrong idea and mumbles without raising so much as a smile. Purdom's jowly, uncharismatic Dracula is an evening-dressed, cloaked Lugosi-alike, partnered by Ania Pieroni (the Third Mother of *Inferno*) as his slinky sister Oniria, who has terrible 1985 hair, but is still fabulous-looking.

With even less plot than, say, *Dracula Blows His Cool*, *The Vampire Happening* or *Mama Dracula*, this offers occasionally nice images courtesy of ridiculously overqualified cinematographer Luciano Tovoli (*The Passenger*, *Suspiria*) and a cameo from Romano Puppo as the Karloff-look Frankenstein Monster. The rote run-around-the-castle business winds up with a rooftop chase that finishes when Dracula impales himself on Fracchia's umbrella… then he wakes up back in the cinema – it's all been a dream! But a fanged Purdom is sitting behind him!

Directed and co-written (with Villaggio, Franco Marotta and Laura Toscano) by Neri Parenti, who had done several Fantozzi pictures and later had an Italian domestic success with the annual *Natale* films. Fracchia was never heard from again.

FRANKENSTEIN (1910)

This thirteen-minute epic from the Edison Manufacturing Company was the first *Frankenstein* film. Were James Whale or Jack Pierce, who collaborated on the look of the Monster for the famous 1931 film, aware of this? By the early talkie era, such things were already relics – but the built-up brow of the Edison Monster foreshadows Karloff's square head, albeit with a cloud of frizzy hair. The resemblance is more apparent in stills than the film – so Pierce and Whale needn't have seen the film to be influenced by it.

J. Searle Dawley – who dashed off films of *The House of the Seven Gables*, *A Christmas Carol*, *The Corsican Brothers*, *Tess of the d'Urbervilles*, etc. – was in charge of making this radical cut-down of 'Mary Shelley's famous novel', which isn't so much directed as staged. The camera is locked off and actors gesticulate and posture in front of elementary sets – scarcely a narrative advance on the conjuring trick films Méliès made before the turn of the century. Intertitles impose interpretations on scenes *before* they play out – 'Frankenstein is appalled at his evil creation' is at once bluntly accurate and subtly ambiguous (is the act of creation evil or the result?). Frankenstein (Augustus Phillips, mature for a med student) bids farewell to his sweetheart (Mary Fuller) and heads for college, where he discovers the secret of life and writes home that he intends to create 'the most perfect being'. In a study adorned with a skeleton in a chair, Frankenstein whips up a cauldron full of potion which he locks inside a cabinet – another reminder of stage magic tricks. In a sequence surprisingly similar to scenes in *Hellraiser*, the creature (Charles Ogle) takes form as flesh accrues to a skeleton. When the Monster comes out of the box, Frankenstein is upset by its hideousness and flees home to get married. The creature bothers Frankenstein on his wedding night, prompting a physical tussle between creator and created – the girl, surprisingly, is only lightly menaced, rather than (as in Shelley and Whale) the target. In an ending which predates *Nosferatu*, the Monster is struck by his own reflection and fades away; his image lingers in the mirror a few moments, until Frankenstein comes into the room and looks at the reflection, which becomes his own.

By 1910, *Strange Case of Dr Jekyll and Mr Hyde* was already the most-adapted horror story, and this plays up the doppelgänger theme of Shelley's novel. Aside from the creation (shot in reverse so the Monster *undissolves*), Dawley's most imaginative coup is business with a long mirror in which Monster and Frankenstein are several times reflected, with each catching sight of the other. Though a silent film, this Monster can clearly speak; so it's frustrating to have no idea what he is saying angrily to his creator when he barges into his house – is he voicing a legitimate grievance or making threats against innocent people? What actually happens at the end? Supposedly, the power of love dispels the Monster, but there's no fuzzy frame to suggest this might all be a dream – so we have to take what we see literally. Clad in rags, with spindly limbs, big shoulders and a *Struwwelpeter* hair-tangle, Ogle's Monster is a screen first, but all the characters are stick figures, since cinema had not yet evolved a way of telling rather than illustrating famous stories.

FRANKENSTEIN (1973)

'IF SUPERHUMANS ARE TO EXIST, IT IS CLEARLY OUR DUTY TO CREATE THAT LIFE IN THE LABORATORY.'

Having gained a gothic reputation with the soap *Dark Shadows*, producer Dan Curtis set out to collect the *Famous Monsters* set in back-to-the-book television adaptations of key horror texts, beginning with Jack Palance in a 1968 *Strange Case of Dr Jekyll and Mr Hyde*. Curtis's 1974 *Dracula* (also with Palance) was among his more elaborate efforts, but this companion piece, directed by Glenn Jordan, reverts to the production methods of *Dark Shadows*: mostly set-bound, shot on video, with a highly theatrical script (from Curtis and *Dark Shadows* writer Sam Hall) and soap-like emotional climaxes (some from the book, some new-coined). Made as a two-part serial for a late-night drama slot called *The Wide World of Mystery*, it's usually seen as a single two-hour film.

Victor Frankenstein (Robert Foxworth) toils with two short-lived assistants, Hugo (George Morgan) and Otto (John Karlen), to bring life to his cobbled-together creation, billed as 'The Giant'. Hugo suffers a stroke and donates body parts (but *not* a brain, oddly) to the project. The Giant (Bo Svenson) is initially a puppy-like toddler – rejected by his maker only after he has, in the first of several elements lifted from *Of Mice and Men*, hugged Otto to death. Curtis and Hall stay closer to the novel than many other adaptations (though this is not a production which can afford an Arctic expedition), but make significant tweaks: Elizabeth (Susan Strasberg) is to be the sister of Victor's nagging friend Henri (Robert Gentry), and Agatha (Heidi Vaughn), daughter of the family the Giant learns to speak from, is the saintly blind person who doesn't see the creature's scars (in the book, it's her father). Crucially, the killings are reworked to fit the interpretation of the monster as a Lennie-like innocent who doesn't know his own strength (the one exception, his most calculated murder, is off screen). Svenson, like Clancy Brown in *The Bride*, plays a self-pitying kid in a hulk's body; it's an acceptable reading, but the very physical actor isn't allowed destructive tantrums (he rampages carefully so as not to knock over the sets) or calculated malice. Not one of the great *Frankenstein*s, but a respectable, worthy try on limited resources.

FRANKENSTEIN (1994)

> 'IT'S BAD ENOUGH THAT SHE KILLED
> HER HUSBAND AND CHILDREN
> WITH AN AXE, BUT TO HAVE
> HER BRAIN STOLEN...'

Made the same year as the Kenneth Branagh film, this X-rated take on 'the classic story of eternal lust and endless passion' was written and directed by its star, Buck Adams. A long explanatory text pre-empts the 'story', what there is of it. Frederick von Frankenstein, great-great grandson of the original, resurrects his wife Christine (Rebecca Wild, a huge-breasted blonde with a Bobbi Flekman accent), though she now has the brain of Maria, a woman who went mad and killed her family with an axe. As in several Hammer films, Frankenstein's assistant is called Hans – here Hans Himmler (Tony Tedeschi), the schlub who procured the unsuitable brain. After a scene in a mad lab dressed with familiar cobwebby electrical props, this is mostly non-stop sex as the story stops dead for orgies around the rock pool of a Beverly Hills castle featuring doctors (Steve Drake, Tony Martino) and hookers (Felecia, Anna Malle, Lady Berlin).

Hans faints when he sees Christine – does the character name refer to *Frankenstein Created Woman?* – walking around, though that's just to set up his revival to have sex with a pretty redhead (Brittany O'Connell). Ambitiously, it opens and closes with sex scenes between the same performers, with Wild supposedly playing different personalities – which is slightly out of her acting range. In a perverse, unusual plot wind-up, Maria becomes the monster's dominant personality and demands sex from Frederick – who obliges, in self-hating fashion, just to have final contact with his wife's body. Within the confines of the format, Adams isn't a dead loss as director and manages some halfway decent acting. But it's a long way from the relative luxury of *Dracula Sucks*.

FRANKENSTEIN (2004)

Of many screen *Frankensteins*, this two-part Hallmark TV miniseries sticks closest to Mary Shelley's novel. Worthy and slightly dull, it's respectful of the themes, but seldom moving or frightening. Taking few liberties with the text, Mark Kruger's script tweaks things to make its antagonists more sympathetic. Crucially, the moment where 'Viktor' Frankenstein (Alec Newman) rejects his just-born creature (Luke Goss) – when the scientist really makes a monster – isn't as extreme as it needs to be to turn the creature into the murderous outcast required by the plot. The gaunt, bad-skinned creation also just isn't repulsive enough to count as a proper monster: he even passes among crowds at a hanging without exciting too much comment. Though not exactly a romantic ideal, Goss is by no means the hideous giant who spurs even good people to attack him on sight. Though the almost-apologetic murder of Elizabeth (Nicole Lewis) is well played, he never shows the Satanic, sadistic streak Shelley intended in her indictment of the way bad parenting produces monsters. Otherwise, it's typical Hallmark: carefully directed by former Amicus man Kevin Connor, clever in its use of Slovakia to pass for Switzerland, Germany and the Arctic Circle, and rounding up a quality supporting cast (Julie Delpy, Donald Sutherland, William Hurt, Ian McNeice, Jean Rochefort). Goss and Newman aren't bad, but this production won't let either Frankenstein or his Monster show the darks which make them great characters in the first place.

FRANKENSTEIN (2004)

'I TOLD HIM TO FIND HIS BLISS.
I NEVER THOUGHT HIS BLISS
WOULD BE CHOPPING
PEOPLE TO PIECES.'

A pilot for an unmade TV series, developed from a story/format by Dean Koontz, whose possessory credit has vanished. Directed by Marcus Nispel (who has never made anything that wasn't a remake), associate produced by Martin Scorsese(!) and scripted by genre TV veteran John Shiban (*The X-Files*, *Supernatural*), it's still rubbish.

Two hundred years after events which might or might not have inspired Mary Shelley, Deucalion (Vincent Perez), a shambling tall guy in an 18th century hoodie with a slight cheek-scratch the script tries to pass off as a hideous scar, has tracked his similarly immortal creator Victor Helios (Thomas Kretschmann) to pre-Katrina New Orleans. Helios creates a race of two-hearted supermen, one of whom becomes a self-hating serial killer called 'the Surgeon' – he cuts up people (including fellow creations) while incubating a monster baby. The perverse Helios keeps drowning and resurrecting consort Erika (Ivana Milicevic) and works with a cabal of highly placed allies, but never intersects with the A story. Deucalion – named wittily for the son of Prometheus – continually pops out of shadows to give mystery tips to tough but sensitive cop Carson O'Conner (Parker Posey). The heroine is kitted out with TV pilot baggage, including an autistic brother, a gossipy Irish housekeeper (even seen with a feather duster) and a doughnut-eating partner with a crush on her (Adam Goldberg). The killer is another cop, Harker (Michael Madsen), and the climax is a minor monster-on-monster fight, with the mad baddie thrown from a great height in a disused factory to be impaled.

Supposedly a reimagining of *Frankenstein*, this more closely resembles an outright steal from *Scream and Scream Again* – witness: the composite creations infiltrating power elites, the rogue creature leading a police chase, the mad scientist who is himself a product of his own lab. Posey, wonderful even in supporting roles in dud threquels like *Blade: Trinity* and *Scream 3*, gets a rare lead, but is given nothing to work with.

FRANKENSTEIN (2007)

Written and directed by Jed Mercurio, this *Frankenstein* has a contemporary (maybe near-future) setting, uses Shelley's character names, cites cutting-edge science (it's all about stem cells), slyly references previous adaptations and feels free to make up its own story while occasionally staging highlights from the novel. It's the approach of *Blackenstein* or *Doctor Franken*... but, before we write it off completely, also essentially what James Whale did in 1931. Given that the book is about issues which always feel current, from the dangers of untrammelled genius through parental responsibility to the problem of being superficially concerned with physical beauty, Mercurio was probably right to take this route and deliver – to quote an *X-Files* episode title – a 'post-modern Prometheus'. However, a general air of rush suggests the possibility of a miniseries proposal slimmed to ninety minutes-with-adverts.

Dr Victoria Frankenstein (Helen McCrory), whose surname is not mentioned in dialogue but glimpsed on a scientific paper, works on the Universal Xenograft Project for a university outfit called Windmill (referencing the climax of the Whale film) under Professor Waldman (Neil Pearson) and icy stereotype bitch Professor Pretorius (Lindsay Duncan). Against orders, Victoria grows a beating rubber heart from the stem cells of her terminally ill son William (Matthew Rault-Smith). The Windmill lab is a big concrete set with biohazard stickers and cast-iron scientific equipment, where as many scenes as possible are played to keep the budget down. A soap strand develops in Victoria's tussles with smoothly nasty ex-husband Henry Clerval (James Purefoy), who has a higher-tech biogenetics firm with evil government contacts. All this boils down to a strange tendency among *Frankenstein* adaptors to think the scientist needs personal motivation (an ailing or dead relative, usually) to tinker with the forces of life, rather than simply being an overreaching genius. As it happens, Frankenstein creates a Monster (Julian Bleach) by accident. After William dies and so can't benefit from a transplant (the fact that the artificial heart was bigger than his chest might have been a problem, even with a DNA match), the UX Project burbles on: vat-grown organs conglomerate and come to life during a power-cut which is, as science, less credible than Cartman's scheme in *South Park* to grow his own pizza parlour by accumulating aborted foetuses and piling them up next door to the restaurant he wants to duplicate. Still, monsters have to be made somehow.

Mercurio gets one thread right. The key scene in the Monster's development is not his creation, but the moment when he invades Frankenstein's home (emptying her fridge when she's not looking) and she reacts with a horrified scream because he doesn't meet her standards of beauty (he resembles a cross between the creatures from *The Creeping Flesh* and *The Funhouse*). However, the second half is a rush: the Monster (usually called 'the UX') racks up a body count (snapping a little girl's neck and offing most of Victoria's colleagues) and is captured by Clerval and the government, who strap him to a chair (cf: *Bride of Frankenstein*) and implant control devices which look like Karloff's neck-bolts. McCrory struggles valiantly to find a way of playing this, as Victoria begins to take a parental interest in her genetic offspring and tries (like the parents in *It's Alive*) to protect it, but the rest of the cast are stuck with barking duff, ominous lines and striking poses. A visit to a chilly beach where the Monster almost gets to be a child before men with guns show up tries for poignance, but mostly serves as a reminder of how much better ITV did with *Chimera* in 1991. The underlying material is so good the film can't help but strike sparks occasionally, but – like most things created by the Frankenstein family – it seems likely this stumbling, misshapen effort is not what was intended.

FRANKENSTEIN (NATIONAL THEATRE LIVE: FRANKENSTEIN) (2011)

A filmed version of Danny Boyle's National Theatre production of Nick Dear's adaptation of Mary Shelley's novel – though an audience is in evidence, the performance has been altered slightly (the monster is born with a bandage loincloth rather than full-frontal naked) for this recording. Two entirely separate versions exist, reflecting the conceit of lead actors Benedict Cumberbatch and Jonny Lee Miller alternating the roles of Victor and the Creature. For the record, I saw the one with Cumberbatch as the Creature.

Skipping the Arctic frame and Frankenstein's backstory, the play begins with the Creature coming to life, learning in a wordless ten-minute mime to get control of his body, before his creator casts him out into a cruel world that makes him crueller. The business of monster-making, dealing with grave-robbers and toiling in a mad laboratory is saved for later, when Victor is persuaded to try to create a mate for the Creature. Frankenstein has to fight to be a major player in his own story, since this is one of the most monster-centric versions of the tale. In an instance of colour-blind casting which makes the piece seem fable-like, black actors – George Harris, Naomie Harris – play Frankenstein's father and cousin Elizabeth. Traditionally a dull role, Elizabeth has a poignant sequence on her wedding night (the set momentarily evokes James Whale's film – a bit of misdirection since the monster is under the bed not outside the French windows) as she makes a human connection with the Creature while frustrated by her preoccupied bridegroom (who has, in fact, married her just to bait a trap), only for the Creature regretfully to rape and throttle her, howling, 'Now I am a man!' in anguish after completion.

This is *Frankenstein* as tragedy, with every chance the characters have for happiness ruined by outside forces, their own baser impulses or malign fate: it ends with both pressing on into infernal light across the snowy wastes.

FRANKENSTEIN (2015)

In Bernard Rose's filmography, this faithful-yet-radical adaptation of Shelley's novel – which also references James Whale's film versions – is less like *Candyman* and *Paperhouse*, his best-known genre films, than the low-budget, shot-on-DV modernised adaptations of Tolstoy (*Ivansxtc, 2 Jacks*) he made with star Danny Huston. Among the goriest *Frankenstein*s ever made, almost on a par with *Flesh for Frankenstein*, it relocates the story to contemporary Los Angeles and is as much essay on the text as straight-ahead horror film.

Rose splits the character of Frankenstein in two, with Victor (Danny Huston) and his wife (Carrie-Anne Moss) expressing different feelings about their creation (Xavier Samuel, the kid from *The Loved Ones*). Using a digital printer, the Frankensteins and their colleagues – including a waspish Dr Pretorius (Dave Pressler) – create a perfect human being, an adult-sized baby which Victor warily admires and his wife nurtures with hugs. However, as in *Frankenstein: The True Story*, the innocent's beauty is marred by tumorous growths and Victor wants to terminate him and start over again. In reference to Jack Pierce's Karloff makeup, the first boil looks like a neck electrode and the creature sustains a cranial drill scar across the forehead. Escaping the science facility, the creature has an innocent encounter with a little girl playing pooh sticks which goes awry when he tosses her into the water (like Karloff) then rescues her (as in Shelley), only to end up beaten by a Californian mob and violently apprehended by the cops. The trauma of the novel is reiterated when the caring mother visits the jail and denies knowing her creation, who takes the name 'Monster' from the insults of the crowd. Taken off by cops for summary execution, Monster escapes and falls in with a blind jazzman (Tony Todd), who – in a lift from *Of Mice and Men*, a common reference for Frankenstein films – looks after him until he unintentionally, through lust and rage and not knowing his own strength, kills a hooker (Maya Erskine) the beggar has paid to sleep with his protégé. Making his way back to the Frankenstein place by trudging along the freeway, Monster finds Victor has started an upgraded experiment – not a bride, but a doppelgänger – and his family reunion goes awry. Uniquely, the film ends with a depiction of the monster's self-immolation – planned but not carried out in the novel.

It might well be a dictum that in making a Frankenstein movie, the monster should be taller than the blind hermit – but Todd (Rose's Candyman) towers over the huddled-in-a-hoodie Monster, and Huston is similarly more imposing in stature than Samuel.

However, Samuel is among the best screen Monsters – beautiful yet progressively warped, inarticulate and violent (but reading prime passages from Shelley's prose in voice-over), tragic and childish (a little like Terence Stamp in *The Mind of Mr. Soames*) yet authentically savage and terrifying when he unintentionally (or intentionally) strikes back. Rose, who also scripted, spends little time on the mechanics of creation (we're told it took six months to print the eyes alone), but is acute about the social and emotional abuses which turn innocent Adam into a Monster. Like Danny Boyle's stage production, this *Frankenstein* starts with the creation – which Rose uses as a way of telling the whole story from the viewpoint of Monster. Huston and Moss are ambiguous, intriguingly contradictory figures: because the Monster doesn't understand, we never learn *why* Mrs Frankenstein rejects the creature she has mothered, and his sense of being outside society (having no friends, no property and no name) is reinforced when he peeps through a screen window and finds his creators indulging in foreplay.

The film's low-budget aesthetic, traipsing along highways from a clinical institution to scuzzy skid row, is deliberately desaturated. Rose was one of the first filmmakers to embrace Digital Video and there's a chasm between his achievements in the medium and the simply ugly look of many shoot-it-fast-and-cheap horrors. Rose admits a certain presumption – a word stressed in this script, which was the title of the very first theatre version of the story, *Presumption; or, The Fate of Frankenstein* – in using the single-word title, in cinema hitherto owned by Universal and Whale. He earns the right by delivering a significant contribution to the ever-expanding Frankenstein filmography.

FRANKENSTEIN '80 (MOSAICO) (1972)

A basic Italian gore movie, utterly humourless but ridiculous. Dr Otto Frankenstein (Gordon Mitchell), a morgue attendant in a large hospital, creates patchwork being Mosaico (Xiro Papas), who wanders around in a leather coat and hat looking like a slimmed-down, scarred Tor Johnson, murdering people and stealing their organs because his own body threatens to reject those sewn into him. Long-haired reporter Karl Schein (John Richardson) is involved in the plodding investigation. Otto keeps mildly rebuking his creation for the murders, then taking him back for more work. Despite the mad science, it feels like a regular *giallo* as the monster pulls out guts or has sex with a hooker before killing her (admittedly, there's a plot justification: he wants to find out if his new gonads work). The McGuffin is a jar of 'schwartz serum', a newly developed drug to counter tissue rejection. The characters have German names, perhaps to make it marginally more likely that a doctor called Frankenstein could be on hand. The effects stretch to rubbery severed heads (one in the fridge) and entrails. With Dalila Di Lazzaro (a Frankenstein monster herself in *Flesh for Frankenstein*) and Argento favourite Fulvio Mingozzi. The sole directorial credit of Mario Mancini, cinematographer of *Frankenstein's Castle of Freaks* and camera operator of *Blood and Black Lace*.

FRANKENSTEIN REBORN (2005)

Having done over Dracula in *Way of the Vampire*, The Asylum tackle the other great horror staple (copping a title from a kid-friendly 1998 Full Moon mini-movie) with Australian Rhett Giles following up his poor Van Helsing with a worse Frankenstein. Writer-director Leigh Scott credits Mary Shelley and uses her character names, but lifts mostly from *The Curse of Frankenstein* – albeit without expensive period trappings.

Dr Victor Franks (or 'Frank', as the end credits have it), accused of a string of murders he didn't commit, is interrogated by psychiatrist Robert Walton (Thomas Downey) and tells the story of his science project gone wrong, incidentally (as in the Hammer film) confessing to a killing the cops *aren't* charging him with. With colleagues Elizabeth (Eliza Swenson) and Hank Clerval (Jeff Denton), Franks creates nanotech solutions to medical problems. A paraplegic subject (Joel Hebner) recovers the use of his limbs (as in *Blackenstein*), but – thanks to Franks' kinks being passed along with the nanomeds – suffers violent, sexualised nightmares. When the kid asks to be unscrambled, Franks shoots him dead(!) to use as raw material for a lank-haired, messy-faced creature which will prove his theories, all the while relaxing with drugs and three-way sex with Elizabeth and another assistant (Christina Rosenberg). The monster escapes and kills people close to Franks, including Elizabeth – but the scientist gets him onside in a project to revive her, which means procuring fresh female corpses.

There's enough meaningless gore for an H.G. Lewis tribute, including Franks' corporate backer (Sarah Lieving) having her legs ripped off, but nothing disguises the fact that this takes place almost entirely indoors on minimal sets (the under-patronised nightclub where the scientists unwind is especially makeshift) as amateur-hour players knit brows and deliver earnest dialogue.

FRANKENSTEIN'S ARMY (2013)

Towards the end of World War II, Russian film student Dimitri (Alexander Mercury) is attached to a Red Army unit invading Germany. As per the rules of found-footage horror, he keeps filming when the squabbling soldiers get cut off in a scary situation. The troop moves into a deserted village where nuns have been massacred. The senior officer is killed quickly, prompting others to vie for command.

After a conventional start, the movie redeems itself with an orgy of steampunk splatter. Usually in found footage (as per *The Blair Witch Project*) there's no budget for onscreen monsters, so the threat remains unseen (or barely glimpsed). Here, doomed characters wander into a Shelleyish 'workshop of filthy creation' where unshaven Viktor Frankenstein (Karel Roden), grandson of the famous one, stitches parts of dead soldiers to rusty weaponry to create an array of killing machines. 'Only the Nazis would think of this,' gasps a Russian, though it turns out that the Soviets would sponsor Frankenstein if they could get hold of him. A meld of jerky-cam *Blair Witch* techniques and *Re-Animator* gore, this delivers a new twist on the Nazi zombie theme thanks to imaginative, disturbing monster design. A human head sewn onto a struggling teddy bear (Frankenstein's mum, apparently), clanking and grinding machines attached to arms and heads (these hybrids are zombots, according to the credits), a cerebral experiment where one soldier (Joshua Sasse) has half a Nazi brain and half a communist brain in his blood-spurting head, etc.

There's little plot – though a conspiracy element emerges as the cameraman turns out to have a hidden agenda to secure Frankenstein tech – and characterisations (bullying Russian, sensitive Pole, etc.) are basic. But it's gruesome fun and Roden brings gaunt presence as one of the movies' madder Frankensteins. In a rare subtle touch: filming style changes when cameraman Dimitri falls under the influence of a *director*, Frankenstein, and the funhouse/computer-game pell-mell of monster attacks calms down for nasty surgery and ranting mad science lectures. Written by Chris W. Mitchell, Miguel Tejada-Flores (*Beyond Re-Animator*) and director Richard Raaphorst.

FRANKENSTEIN'S GREAT AUNT TILLIE (1984)

One of the oddest Frankenstein films. The monster is merely a sub-plot in a story about the eponymous feminist heroine (Yvonne Furneaux, of Hammer's *The Mummy* and Fellini's *La Dolce Vita*). She comes to the Transylvanian village of Mucklefugger with the current Dr F (Donald Pleasence in a toupee) and his ageing-babe wife Randy (June Wilkinson, a British glamour model who uniquely managed to be a Windmill Girl *and* a *Playboy* playmate). Tillie plans to enter a car rally which hasn't thought to prohibit women contestants, but is distracted by a feud with a corrupt Bürgermeister (Aldo Ray) who has just closed a home for wayward girls. Tillie upholds the E.R.A. (Ermintrude's Rights Again), named for a heroic goatherdess whose statue stands in the square.

Created to be a perfect valet, the blue-grey Monster (Miguel Angel Fuentes, of *The Pumaman*) wanders in the background, copping gags from *Young Frankenstein*, while Pleasence and Wilkinson conduct their own strange love story. Pleasence, quixotically, delivers one of his more engaged try-anything performances, and seems to have improvised some of his dialogue. Great Aunt Tillie, who is semi-immortal, saves the castle from the Bürgermeister and prevents its sale to be demolished so petroleum can be mined from underneath it (when a steam car wins the rally, petrol prices plunge and the deal is off).

Written and directed by Myron J. Gold (who scripted the SF satire *The Monitors*), this runaway production was shot in Mexican woods with a peculiar mix of British, American and Mexican players. It wavers between comedy and pretension in a manner guaranteed to cause bafflement. Not to be confused with *Pehavý Max a strasidlá* aka *Frankenstein's Aunt*.

FRANKENSTEIN'S WEDDING... LIVE IN LEEDS (2011)

A massive theatrical/musical event staged at Kirkstall Abbey in Leeds in 2011, and broadcast live – not without problems – by BBC-TV. It wrestles with the oft-told tale and manages, with only a few flashback creation sequences, to cram much of the complicated plot around the spectacle of Victor Frankenstein's society wedding – which, in the context of the piece, is attended by a huge audience who are involved in the story at several junctures.

Not content with simply working up a modernised version of Mary Shelley, in which Victor (Andrew Gower) is a Northern-accented genius who intended to create a soulless, mindless human as a renewable organ donor, writer Chloe Moss adds in soap-opera sub-plots. Here, Henry Clerval (Andrew Knott) is a war hero army padre who tries to talk Elizabeth (Lacey Turner) out of marrying his best friend minutes before he's due to officiate at their wedding. Time is also wasted as Victor's father Alphonse (Mark Williams) reunites with the brother he was estranged from years before because of a stolen bicycle. In this take, Henry – always a useless drag of a character – is responsible for the carnage. When he finds out Frankenstein is working on a mate for the Creature (David Harewood), he convinces the scientist to strangle the female creature on the operating table (which makes him a pro-abortion clergyman) and thus triggers the killing spree in which he is the next victim.

All over the place tonally, it throws in broad comedy, bloody horror and whinging about scientific ethics. A succession of turns involving big dance routines and truncated performances of thematically apt hits like 'White Wedding' and 'Tainted Love' get in the way of the drama rather than enhance it. Early in the evening, several songs get underway – including a belter performed by maid of honour Justine (Jemima Rooper, a live spark wasted here) – only to be interrupted by Alphonse blustering onstage to put a stop to the revels. In the middle of the lumbering mess, Gower (slightly channelling David Thewlis) and Harewood (unusually cast – making the Frankenstein Monster an exploited black guy is an interesting notion) work hard to connect with these great characters, and – under the circumstances – acquit themselves reasonably.

Certainly no worse than some other TV takes on the material, it's an uncomfortable hybrid of theatre, cinema and television and not even committed to its musical or stadium rock elements. After a bizarre finale in which Victor is shot by a passing policeman, there's an impressive use of the setting as the Creature dashes into the cheering crowd and is lost among a sea of people. In a bit of circularity, the Creature's adventures among the homeless of Leeds evoke the mutating astronaut of the 2005 live-TV remake of *The Quatermass Experiment* – whereas the original *Quatermass* explicitly homaged earlier versions of *Frankenstein*. Directed by Colin Teague.

THE FRANKENSTEIN SYNDROME (THE FRANKENSTEIN EXPERIMENT; THE PROMETHEUS PROJECT) (2010)

Though it depicts stem-cell research in irresponsibly hysterical terms, this makes a fair fist of modernising Mary Shelley. Elizabeth Barnes (Tiffany Shepis), a scientist who sports a *Les Yeux Sans Visage* white mask, recounts her involvement with secretive illegal research sponsored by millionaire Dr Walton (Ed Lauter). In an underground facility ruled by chilly Dr Victoria Treville (Patti Tindall) and brutal security chief Marcus (Louis Mandylor), female runaways, illegals and drifters pay off debts by being impregnated through artificial insemination. They then have painful abortions so the fiendish Dr Treville can harvest stem cells for experimental use. When Kima (Zena Otsuka), impregnated by nice-guy Irish attendant David Doyle (Scott Anthony Leet), commits suicide after her abortion, Elizabeth tests a newly developed re-animation serum on her. Kima returns as an uncontrollable, feral creature and Marcus puts her down just as she shows signs of intelligence. When understandably aggrieved David tries to sue the company, Marcus shoots him, then argues that his dead tissue be used in further experiments.

The film gets more interesting when David is revived. As in *Splice*, the arc of test subject to monster is unusually complex: at first, he's a blank slate who has to be educated from infancy, but telepathic ability means he can construct a new personality (without an accent) from the minds of terrified people around him. Eventually, he becomes a cunning, murderous sociopath who works off grudges from his former life. Writer-director Sean Tretta (*Death of a Ghost Hunter*, *The Death Factory Bloodletting*) creates unusually strong character interplay and gets good performances from an unfamiliar cast (especially Leet and Tindall). Victoria is a cold bitch to everyone, but genuinely committed to mothering and protecting the monster, while the new David has healing powers but is also capable of ripping someone's jaw off on a whim. In a seldom-used Shelley plot lick, the creature becomes more cruel as he gets cleverer. In the end, after a killing spree, David cuts off Elizabeth's face to graft onto his own skull… she unmasks to reveal that she now looks like a traditional film Frankenstein Monster.

It has more ideas than it can cope with (to be fair, the same is true of the novel), including a possibility that this monster is a messiah and the last-reel involvement of the Catholic Church.

THE FRANKENSTEIN THEORY (2011)

As found-footage *Frankensteins* go, considerably less demented than *Frankenstein's Army*. Indeed, the use of a classic monster doesn't really differentiate it from the many 'in search of… *aargh* it got me!' films about aliens, psychos, Bigfoot or dinosaurs.

Just-expelled student genius Jonathan Venkenheim (Kris Lemche) has family papers which 'prove' Mary Shelley's novel was non-fiction and that he's the descendant of the mad scientist she called Frankenstein. Believing the Monster still alive in the Arctic, he corrals familiar young, disposable filmmakers to head North with him: director Vicky (Heather Stephens), camera guy Eric (Brian Zuckerman) and cameraman Kevin (Brian Henderson). After an uneasy interview with Clarence (Joe Egender), a Canadian druggie who claims he's encountered a giant creature ('A man who wasn't a man.'), they hire local guide Karl (Timothy V. Murphy), who cheers them up with a Quint speech about killer polar bears. Heading for the middle of nowhere, following a pattern of unsolved homicides and caribou migration, they meet the usual fate... the capable guide dies first, and then the rest, one by one. The film raises a possibility its monster isn't just a grunting, homicidal thug, but doesn't have the patience or effects/ makeup resources to deliver anything else.

Even a cursory reading of the book would suggest Venkenheim ought to try to make things right with the outcast creature his ancestor failed to take care of. Instead, there's a lot of trudging through snowy wastes (nice locations) with nightlight POV creeping and hysterical sobbing panic. The killings all involve crunchy sound effects. At the end, the fur-skin-clad Creature (Roger Morrissey) is glimpsed, carrying Vicky, possibly still alive, out of a yurt along with an old rag-doll he seems to have left there. Written by Vlady Pildysh and director Andrew Weiner.

FRANKENSTEIN VS. THE CREATURE FROM BLOOD COVE (2005)

A black-and-white parody of two generations of Universal Pictures monsters, stirring in mild gore and t&a with low-rent celeb cameos and exaggerated, amateurish performances. Dr Monroe Lazaroff (Larry Butler) creates a *Creature from the Black Lagoon*-type Creature (Corey J. Marshall). It escapes and terrorises Blood Cove, California, menacing or shredding the nude models who pose for photographer Bill Grant (writer-director William Winckler). To continue his experiments, Lazaroff and minions travel to Eastern Europe – where they run into a briefly seen Wolf Man (Butch Patrick of *The Munsters*, billed as 'Patrick Lilly') – to dig up the Frankenstein Monster (Lawrence Furbish). Imported to California, the Monster also escapes, briefly thinks Bill's assistant/love interest (Dezzi Rae Ascalon) is his 'bride', has several fights with the Creature and terrorises a titty bar... all the while troubled by the ghost of Victor Frankenstein (also Marshall).

Tension between respectful, affectionate homage to the *Famous Monsters* standbys and a perceived need to cram in enough toilet humour and silicon-bouncing to appeal to the Troma segment of the marketplace is ultimately fatal. With porn stars Ron Jeremy and Selena Silver, Lloyd Kaufman (who has succeeded Forrest J Ackerman as most ubiquitous cameo player in genre cinema), Raven De La Croix (*Up!*) and writer David Gerrold.

FRANKENSTEIN VS. THE MUMMY (2015)

'WHAT GOOD IS YOUR MAGIC AND ANCIENT SPELL NOW, PROFESSOR?'

On a contemporary American campus, young Dr Victor Frankenstein (Max Rhyser) – who has wanted to reverse death ever since his mother committed suicide – toils on the creation of an artificial being (Constantin Tripes), liaising with skid-row bodysnatcher Isaac (Robert MacNaughton), who kills random folks for their organs. Meanwhile, Egyptologist Professor Walton (Boomer Tibbs) sacrifices co-eds to revive a Mummy (Brandon deSpain) who was once an evil sorcerous pharaoh. Linking the stories is Naihla Khalil (Ashton Leigh), Victor's girlfriend, who is in Walton's department. Victor unwisely transplants Isaac's brain into his hulking, stringy-haired creation – creating an articulate, particularly vicious Monster, who ends up on a plot collision course with the Mummy.

Writer-director Damien Leone goes old-school with the title, rubbery makeup effects and loopy Universal-style premise and gets committed performances from Leigh, who speaks subtitled ancient Egyptian at one point, and Tripes, who gives an interestingly hateful, cunning reading of the Monster; possibly, they're channelling Yvonne Furneaux in Hammer's *The Mummy* and Lon Chaney Jr dubbed by Bela Lugosi at the end of Universal's *The Ghost of Frankenstein*. Tibbs seems to have been cast on the strength of a superficial resemblance to Universal's favoured high priest George Zucco. What lets the film down – besides cramped, dull settings and a baggily paced extended running time (115 minutes) – is Rhyser's bland lead. This Victor's project owes as much to *Re-Animator* as Mary

Shelley. He's written to seesaw between sneaky villain, Promethean visionary and misguided hero… but the shrugged-off performance hurts, where full-blown Jeffrey Combs or Peter Cushing or James McAvoy laboratory ranting might have held the whole thing together.

In the end (spoiler!), the Frankenstein Monster crushes the Mummy's dusty head – but then gets macheted by the heroine. Since the Mummy is vivified by actual gods and the Monster brought to life by galvanism, that's a big win for science over religion – very rare in American cinema.

FRANKESTEIN, EL VAMPIRO Y COMPAÑÍA (1962)

An unauthorised, fairly close remake of *Abbott and Costello Meet Frankenstein*, this features Mexican comedians José 'Ojón' Jasso and Manuel 'Loco' Valdés as handymen Paco and Agapito.

Agapito (a stout, stern Abbott) and Paco (a tall, rubber-limbed Costello) deliver supposed wax dummies of the 'Frankestein Monster' and 'el Vampiro' Conde Lorenzini (cadaverous Quintín Bulnes) to a wax museum. Minions of slinky mad scientist Dr Sofía (Nora Veryán) steal the figures. Soon, the monsters are up and about, with Lorenzini plotting to take over America and the scientist scheming to put Loco's brain in the Monster's skull. Just as the Wolf Man hectors Abbott and Costello, so a moustached creep who turns into *el Hombre Lobo* when the full moon shines pops up to nag the plot along.

Rather than emulate A&C's hysterical doubletalk, Jasso and Valdés incline to face-pulling '*¡Ay caramba!*' yucks. Though Bulnes makes a decent skeletal vampire in Lugosi duds, the stocky Universal-look Monster and the shaggy-faced Wolf Man aren't exactly makeup triumphs. Some Mexican horror films of the period, including director Benito Alazraki's *Muñecos Infernales/Curse of the Doll People*, have sumptuous art direction and expressionist camerawork: this just looks cheap and drab. Scripted by Mexican monster mainstay Alfredo Salazar, who worked on Aztec mummy, masked wrestler, *vampiro* and *bruja* movies.

FURANKENSHUTAIN NO KAIJÛ: SANDA TAI GAIRA (THE WAR OF THE GARGANTUAS) (1966)

Though the export version doesn't splice in Raymond Burr, this Japanese monster movie is radically different in domestic (Japanese) and US releases. The former, *Furankenshutain no kaijû: Sanda tai Gaira*, is a direct sequel to *Furankenshutain tai chitei kaijû Baragon/Frankenstein Conquers the World* (1965). The latter, *The War of the Gargantuas*, is a standalone: 'Frankenstein' is redubbed 'Gargantua', top-billed US star Russ Tamblyn horns in on extra scenes, and lounge singer Kipp Hamilton – who has only one (admittedly memorable) scene – is bumped up to second-billed 'special guest star'. Kumi Mizuno, held over from the 1965 film, has a different character name, and the only flashback to the youth of Frankenstein/Sanda/Brown Gargantua shows a creature which doesn't resemble the Frankenstein who took on Baragon or conquered the world last time round.

Even as *kaiju eiga* go, this is whacky. A giant octopus attacks a ship, only to be dragged away by a shaggy green piranha-mawed giant humanoid which proceeds to finish the job of sinking the ship and vindictively drowns sailors swimming away from the wreck. The climax of the Japanese version of the first film featured a similar octopus – but there's no other reason for the thing to be here: it's never mentioned again and Japan has enough on its plate with two giants to worry about other monsters at large. Suspicion falls on the feral Frankenstein/Gargantua raised by Dr Paul Stewart (Tamblyn) and Akemi (Mizuno), but they think the sea giant is a new menace since *their* monster was gentle unless provoked. Furthermore, shaggy footprints suggest that particular creature is hiding out in 'the Japanese Alps'. It turns out that the green monster generated from scraped-off cells left behind by the brown monster – *not* the living severed hand from the first movie – and takes its form because it grew in the sea. In the Japanese version, the authorities arbitrarily name the bad monster Gaira and the good monster Sanda; in the English dub, they are the more prosaic Green Gargantua and Brown Gargantua. Snarling, pissed-off Gaira, whose seaweedy hide breaks out in gruesome sores, terrorises more boats (a great shot has the monster peering up through clear waters). He even picks up and drops torch-singer Hamilton (after she's delivered the amazing dirge 'But the Words Get Stuck in My Throat') to put a damper on a pleasure cruise she's entertaining, then strides ashore at the familiar Toho tank and wades into the Japanese Self-Defence Forces.

Sanda, the Beatle-haired, less snarly monster, is at first sympathetic to his persecuted offshoot and tries to help, but the ungrateful Gaira just wants to smash things. Sanda remains devoted to Akemi, and catches her when she falls off a cliff during a Gaira-related landslide. When Gaira picks up and drops Akemi (a bit of *King Kong* business, often reprised) during a rampage in Tokyo, Sanda is motivated to take on the baddie in a destructive, no-holds-barred fight ranging through the city (many buildings are crushed) and out into the bay. A neat-o zap-cannon is deployed to harry Gaira and a new underwater volcano(!) puts an end to both creatures. Because humanoid monster costumes are more manoeuvrable than the typical big lizard/moth/lobster/turtle/walrus/sludge suits of Japanese monster fame, the battle between Gaira (Haruo Nakajima, longest-reigning Godzilla performer) and Sanda (Hiroshi Sekita – a good guy *kaiju* for a change: he usually fought Nakajima as MechaKong, Ebirah, etc.) is among the most exciting, fast-paced and brutal in the genre. It's also surprisingly nasty but jokey about the villain's people-eating ways: Gaira crams a girl into his mouth and spits out the flowers she was carrying; Sanda does an 'oh not again' double take at finding mountaineering clothes strewn about like discarded peanut shells near a bloated Gaira. Directed and co-written by genre specialist Ishirô Honda.

FURANKENSHUTAIN TAI CHITEI KAIJÛ BARAGON (FRANKENSTEIN CONQUERS THE WORLD) (1965)

Effects pioneer Willis H. O'Brien, the key creator of *King Kong*, spent much of his career failing to get ambitious projects backed in Hollywood. Among these was an outline for *King Kong vs Frankenstein*, which was sold overseas to Japan's Toho studios and rewritten (without O'Brien's participation) as *King Kong vs Godzilla*. Economically, Toho didn't entirely drop O'Brien's giant Frankenstein Monster concept, recycling it for this odd, lavish creature feature from the *Gojira* team of director Ishirô Honda and effects man Eiji Tsuburaya.

The setup is elaborate and contrived, but weirdly impressive: in 1945, with the Nazis on the point of defeat, the still-beating heart of the Frankenstein Monster is requisitioned from a German laboratory and sent to the Military Hospital in Hiroshima, where scientists intend to use it to breed a race of soldiers who can't be killed by bullets. Takashi Shimura, frog-faced star of Kurosawa classics (*Living*, *Seven Samurai*) and the first *Gojira*, has a cameo as the head of this project – which is terminated by the atom bomb. It's a truism that Japanese monster movies are profoundly influenced by the country's first-hand experience of nuclear war, but this is almost unique in using Tsuburaya effects to depict the *actual* atomic strike – with a wall of flame filling the screen and a vivid crimson mushroom cloud. 'Fifteen years later', guilt-ridden American scientist Dr James Bowen (Nick Adams) works with local sweetie Dr Sueko Togami (Kumi Mizuno) and ambitious colleague Dr Yuzo Kawaji (Tadao Takashima) to study long-term radiation victims. A perky girl finishes embroidering a cushion for Bowen before expiring offscreen. The film hurries, skipping from characters feeling sad about the doomed girl to visiting her grave on the one-year anniversary of her death, to get to the monster stuff, which is unique in both the Frankenstein filmography and the *kaiju* pantheon.

A feral boy (Kôji Furuhata), referred to as 'Frankenstein', lives near the ruins of the hospital. It's likely the monster heart has generated this body, though an alternate theory is that a starving orphan *ate* the heart and transformed (nevertheless, the script – if not the makeup – suggests he's Caucasian). After a radiation-induced growth spurt, Frankenstein becomes twenty feet tall. Wearing caveman skins, he sports crooked teeth (one ineptly blacked), a Karloffian brow ridge and a shaggy, greenish wig. Though a hulking innocent, Frankenstein is savage enough to eat animals raw; in a jarring sequence for a kiddie matinee picture, a class of schoolchildren find the explicitly rent-apart and gore-spatted remains of their pet rabbits. In another leftover from O'Brien, the monster has a *King Kong* relationship with kindly heroine Sueko: he tries to protect her and she speaks up for him even when her boss wants to write him off and harvest that unkillable heart.

The plot, when it finally arrives, is simple, yet blissfully loopy. Frankenstein hides in the woods, but takes the blame when *another* monster, armadillo/dinosaur/bulldog Baragon, pops up from beneath the earth (it's a burrower) to wreck various structures. There's no explanation of where Baragon comes from. It has a glowing horn (evoking 'The Dong with the Luminous Nose') and Godzilla-like fire-breath, and is basically a patchwork Toho *kaiju*. The army, the mob and scientific opinion take against Frankenstein, and pursue him into the woods to kill him – but when Baragon comes out into the open, only the more human monster can take on the other creature in a lengthy wrestling match. Pitting a humanoid giant against a man-in-a-suit monster compromises the illusion of miniature sets – but a climactic bout during a forest fire which echoes the holocaust of Frankenstein's creation is spectacular.

The 'international version' has a strange end: Frankenstein triumphs over Baragon only to be dragged into a lake by a floppy giant octopus which was barely glimpsed earlier

– not only is the last-minute new threat arbitrary, but the reaction of the characters ('He saved us… He's dead… Ho hum… Never mind… I'm sure he'll be dead.') is bizarre (the dubbed *Frankenstein Conquers the World* cut omits the octopus). In an early scene, Frankenstein escapes captivity by wrenching off his own hand (offscreen) to get out of a shackle – but the hand stays alive and crawls out of the picture. Before they turned into child-friendly free-for-alls, Toho monster movies mixed serious themes with outrageous hokum; somewhere in here is a parallel between Frankenstein's experiments and the unleashing of the atom bomb, but the stress is on colourful spectacle. Followed by *Furankenshutain no kaijû: Sanda tai Gaira/ The War of the Gargantuas*.

GRAF DRACULA IN OBERBAYERN (DRACULA BLOWS HIS COOL) (1979)

This obscure West German-Italian nudie horror comedy was made in 1979, but the English dub was done later (hence an onscreen copyright date of 1982), adding extra gags (rarely funny), including a last line which references *Raiders of the Lost Ark* without counting as a joke. Derivative of *The Playgirls and the Vampire* and *Uncle Was a Vampire*, it's an entry in the scrappy 1970s disco vampire cycle (cf: *Son of Dracula*, *Nocturna*, *Mama Dracula*).

Stan (Gianni Garko, billed as 'John Garco'), descendant of vampire Count Stanislaus (also Garko), opens a disco in the former dungeons of his German castle. Ignoring a campaign against licentiousness led by moralist busybody/Van Helsing family member 'Mrs Nutcracker' (Ellen Umlauf), Stan brings in a bevy of often-nude models to attract interest. In the cellar under the disco are the coffins of the Count and his consort, Countess Olivia (Betty Vergès), who feed on blood stolen by whining retainer Boris (Ralf Wolter). The noise of songs like 'Rock Me, Dracula' piques the vampires' interest and they mingle with the partygoers, prompting confusion between the Count and his lookalike descendant. The family come to a mutually satisfying arrangement that, in the most interesting development, quickly palls as Stanislaus and Olivia grow weary of an unlimited supply of willing necks.

Relentlessly jolly, this has the lederhosen-slapping broadness typical of 1970s German sex comedies. Debuting director Carl Schenkel (using the name 'Carlo Ombra') later made the fine stuck-in-a-lift thriller *Out of Order* (*Abwärts*), the TV movie *Bay Coven* and the Hollywood *giallo Knight Moves*.

HALÂL 'ALAIK (SHAME ON YOU) (1953)

This Egyptian imitation of *Abbott and Costello Meet Frankenstein* features lookalikes for the Frankenstein Monster, Dracula and the Wolf Man to recreate scenes from the American film, but they aren't really the famous monsters. Instead, they're a mummy, a hypnotist/mad scientist and an epileptic(!), presumably on the principle that the originals don't feature in Arabic pop culture.

The film features the hard-to-take comedy stylings of Ismail Yasseen (who has the Lou Costello role) and Abdel Fatah al Kasri (whose Bud Abbottiness extends to a pal who keeps yelling, 'Abdou'!). The comics gurn through hoary jokes ('Can you tell me how old you are?' 'Actually, I can't – because when I was born I was too young.') and react open-mouthed as scary people lumber at them. Initially, they work in an antiques shop, to which 'the mummy of Farfour Ben Bakhtour' (Muhamad Soubay) is delivered, but heroine Afiff (Lola Sarfi) gets them jobs as waiters in the home of her uncle, Professor Aasim. The self-styled Invincible One ('Mameluke') wants to transplant Ismail's brain into the mummy's head so he'll be easier to control. Aasim has enslaved Dr Mourad, Afiff's nattily moustached boyfriend, who sprouts Chaney Jr fur and fangs when he hears a wolf howl (one does, whenever convenient). Farfour wears an exaggerated Karloff mask and semi-Beatle wig, plus big boots and shabby clothes. Aasim sports a Lugosi cloak and hypnotic amulet, but also a devilish goatee and non-false crooked sharp teeth. He spends enough time in a coffin to recreate the opening scene of *Abbott and Costello Meet Frankenstein*, but is otherwise not a vampire even though he is described as looking like an 'affrit'.

The small-scale, drab film keeps its shadows to laboratory scenes, mostly playing out in well-lit, unatmospheric rooms. Director Essa Karama's sole clever bit of staging has the transformed Mourad stalking Ismail in a small courtyard where sheets are hung out to dry. In a surprisingly bloody moment, Mourad scratches the mummy's face and leaves claw marks; which is more than Universal dared in *Frankenstein Meets the Wolf Man*. Otherwise, it's the usual eek-a-monster stuff. In the climax, Farfour and Aasim plunge off a balcony to their deaths, leaving Mourad freed of his curse and eligible to settle down with the heroine (as in *House of Dracula*, which might be where the moustache comes from). The sign-off gag features the comedians spooked by the voice of the Angel of Death instead of the Invisible Man, but is the same basic idea.

...HANNO CAMBIATO FACCIA (1971)

Among the oddest, loosest *Dracula* adaptations, writer-director Corrado Farina's ... *Hanno Cambiato Faccia* takes cues from *Nosferatu* and shares blood with contemporaries like H.W. Geissendörfer's politicised *Jonathan* and Hammer's modish *The Satanic Rites of Dracula*. A political cartoon rather than a horror film, it's nevertheless creepier than Farina's later pop art *fumetti*, *Baba Yaga*. Indeed, its villain's fog-bound lair – a crumbling horror movie location outside but all-white ultra-moderne indoors – is among cinema's most unsettling Castle Draculas. The forested grounds are patrolled by nasty little white cars (1970 Fiat superminis) driven by thugs with white jumpsuits and matching crash helmets, a malign presence which prefigures the automotive pack of *The Cars That Ate Paris*.

'Dottore' Alberto Valle (Giuliano Disperati), a mid-level executive at the AAM motor company, is invited to meet his ultimate boss, Engineer Giovanni Nosferatu (Adolfo Celi). The hapless Alberto drives to the Nosferatu estate through Eastern European-looking country, with the usual taciturn peasants. A 1971 reinvention of the peasant who warns Harker about vampires is Laura (Francesca Modigliani), a hippie chick whose free-spiritedness is signified by a lack of blouse under the coat draped around her shoulders. Alberto enters the estate and is greeted by Corinna (Geraldine Hooper), Nosferatu's androgynous executive secretary (the actress is most familiar for taking a male role in *Deep Red*). As in all versions of Harker's stay at the castle, everything is ominous… warning signs include audio adverts for Nosferatu products triggered by sitting on a sofa or turning on the shower, and a clinical chamber stocked with babies (not food for the brides of this Dracula, but pledged from birth to his service). In a ledger, Alberto finds his own baby photograph…

Celi's plump, suave Nosferatu carries weight from the actor's role as Largo in *Thunderball*; note how many Bond villains have played Dracula (Christopher Lee, Louis Jourdan) or other arch-vampires (Christopher Walken, Grace Jones, Famke Janssen, Donald Pleasence). The tycoon's eccentricities include pistol practice with human-shaped targets which groan when hit. He has tentacles in every area of life – politics, the church, philosophy and (most of all) advertising. His minions screen black-and-white commercials (for aerosol LSD) and namecheck Godard, Marcuse, Asimov and Fellini to suggest the extent of his permeation of contemporary culture (*Baba Yaga* includes a similar crew of namedroppers and another dig at Godard, who featured a Professor Nosferatu in *Alphaville*). Playing golf in rough terrain, Alberto chances upon an abandoned cemetery where the head of a marble Jesus is buried under leaves and Nosferatu's tomb reveals he was born in 1801 but has no death date. Intercut seductions feature bloodless but symbolic neck kissing, and acolytes become vampires.

The cinematography by Aiace Parolin (*Keoma*) has some of the look of Giorgio Ferroni's *Night of the Devils* and moments prefigure Werner Herzog's remake of *Nosferatu* (which follows this in one of its amendments to Murnau/Stoker's plot), while Amedeo Tommasi (*The House of the Laughing Windows*) contributes a haunting, sinister-charming score. The point that rich and powerful people are like vampires isn't new – Karl Marx said the same thing in so many words ('Capital is dead labour that, vampire-like, lives only by sucking living labour, and lives the more, the more labour it sucks.') – but Farina makes it in an unusual way, depicting a gothically corrupt world.

HEISSE NÄCHTE AUF SCHLOSS DRACULA (HOT NIGHTS AT CASTLE DRACULA) (1978)

Obscure German vampire smut. A honeymooning couple visit Castle Dracula. Bride Eva (Gina Janssen) is spooked by red-bow-tied Graf Dracula (Mariano Perez) and a shuffling liveried retainer. Female cackling is heard throughout the manse – a borrowed, well-appointed heritage home like the ones in Jesús Franco's gothic films (Janssen was in Franco's *Sadomania*). In the kitchen, a maid masturbates with a carrot and a wooden spoon. A veiled 'Frau Grafin' prowls in a see-through train which slightly evokes Jean Rollin. The cook gets it on with the maid. The Grafin doffs the veil to seduce a silent, tall fellow who looks vaguely like the somnambulist of *The Cabinet of Dr Caligari*. The happy couple have sex, then dine with the Graf, whose hypnotic spell transports Eva into 'Dracula's dream' – a lengthy orgy featuring girls in coloured wigs and glitter and guys in masks smearing gold paint on each other and doing sexy things with grapes and champagne. Finally, insensible Eva is carried by that irritatingly slow servant into a room where a black guy is unchained to have sex with her. The Graf, who takes no part in any of the action, watches and narrates about bestial urges. Only at the very end does he reveal spindly fangs and bite the girl's neck – the shuffler puts the lid on the coffin, and it's all over with a soundtrack wobble and a fade-out. Directed by D. Laniger, which might be a pseudonym for Reginald Puhl.

HISTÒRIA DE LA MEVA MORT (STORY OF MY DEATH) (2013)

In late 18th century Switzerland, ageing rake Giacomo Casanova (Vicenç Altaió) is too distracted by pleasures of table, boudoir and chamberpot to write his memoirs. Continuing a seemingly endless grand tour, the Venetian drags his Sancho Panza-like manservant Pompeu (Lluís Serrat) to the Carpathians, where they put up with a dour, religious farmer (Xavier Pau) and his gaggle of desirable daughters. Loitering nearby is a rival alpha male predator, Count Dràcula (Eliseu Huertas). Having served both masters, Pompeu prefers the roving, emotional Casanova to the castle dwelling, boring Dràcula.

The premise sounds ripe for a gruesome comic romp like Paul Morrissey's *Blood for Dracula* or an exercise in archetype-mixing strangeness like Jesús Franco's *The Erotic Rites of Frankenstein*, but Catalan writer-director Albert Serra, prime exponent of 'slow cinema', favours long takes on digital video, non-professional actors, protracted scenes of everyday activity, poised tableaux and enigmatic, elliptical dialogue. Consequently, this isn't the Mr Sex Meets Mr Violence film you might expect from the potent collision of metaphorical historical and literal literary ladykillers. Casanova and Dracula don't meet until the finale, by which time night has fallen and it's too dark to discern precisely what passes between them. As seen by servants and victims, both incarnations of male desire are absurd, impotent and doomed (if not entirely unsympathetic).

Here, Casanova is a powdered, tittering coprophile given to moments of private hilarity or despair. He strains over his own heroic bowel movements and delves under a maid's skirts to prize an anus 'like a rosary of bon-bons' while encouraging her to defecate in his mouth (a scene presented with Peter Strickland-like tact). He breaks a window with his head during the single conventional seduction (less unnerving than the childish laughter which accompanies his amorous thrusts) and shrugs off the philosophical movements which are changing Europe ('Heads will roll.'). Dracula is a white-bearded, bouffant-haired presence who wheedles around the women he needs to bleed and utters cries of pain and terror on their behalf after biting them. In one of the character's oddest screen introductions, the camera finds Dracula – shown from behind, highlighting his finely sculpted black hair – sitting in long grass in daylight with a woman he is trying to inveigle back to his castle, 'where there is no place for Christianity' (just as Casanova quotes Montesquieu in saying Rome would be more beautiful without churches).

The women glumly submit to seducers – in one case, Casanova deflowers a girl with his fingers only for Dracula to steal in and lick up the blood – but their own agenda for 'wickedness' is more about escaping patriarchs, like the religious father (who, along with an ox, is the film's major sacrifice), than becoming playthings. The approach invites ridicule, and the film's length (144 minutes) and steady pace are patience testing. The longeurs, of course, are partially the point, forcing the viewer to strain to discern meaning and terror in darks between moments of wry, strange comedy. The epitome of a not-for-everyone film; its reception might depend as much on mood as taste.

HOUSE OF FRANKENSTEIN (1997)

This two-part miniseries dusts off the title of the 1944 Universal monster rally; the only remains of the original are the name 'Dr Niemann' (used on a minor character) and the idea of a plot involving the Frankenstein Monster, a vampire and a werewolf.

English-accented vampire Grimes (Greg Wise), proprietor of a House of Frankenstein nightclub, finances an Arctic expedition to recover the original Monster (Peter Crombie). The defrosted Monster goes unnoticed among Los Angeles derelicts and pals about with a World War II veteran who fulfils the plot function of blind hermit. Meanwhile, rogue cop Detective Coyle (Adrian Pasdar) investigates slayings by the so-called 'Raptor Killer' – Grimes transformed into a winged, bat-faced Greg Cannom-makeup beast who looks like Batman villain Man-Bat. Bitten by Grimes's werewolf sidekick, mousy Grace Dawkins (Teri Polo) becomes sexier within the limits of US Network Standards and Practices circa 1997 (i.e. tame next to Amanda Ooms' often-naked lycanthrobabe in *Wilderness*) and morphs into a wolf by night. After a long stretch in which Grimes ineffectually tries to murder Grace, a romantic triangle develops between cop, werewolf and vampire. Dr Kendall (CCH Pounder) does Van Helsing licks by handing out crucifixes, stakes and expository lectures.

With four hours to fill, this has to be busy, so the horror-monster stories are tied to cop operatics which bring the whole thing thuddingly down to earth. A succession of cliché supporting characters includes the ethnic partner who gets killed (Miguel Sandoval), the heroine's best friend who is turned into a slinky vampire (Jorja Fox) and the grouchy boss who doesn't believe subordinates' crazy monster theories. There is weird theology as Kendall alleges vampires fear crucifixes because they are fallen angels ('Their only natural predator is God.') and one unprecedented scene has a vampire repulsed when the hero's late mother's blessed ashes are thrown into its face. Despite pseudo-profound mumblings ('But we need our monsters, all communities in crisis do.') and lame jokes ('That's the trouble with immortality, you lose your edge.'), its worst failing is its pre-digested, filling-in-time-between-the-commercials, nobody-gave-a-damn feel. Written by J.B. White (*Hefner Unauthorized*); directed by Peter Werner (*Ruby's Bucket of Blood*).

HRABE DRAKULA (1970)

Though it drops characters (no Renfield) and threads (Lucy has just one suitor) to fit the sprawling plot into a trim 76 minutes, this Czechoslovakian television production is among the most faithful *Dracula* adaptations. Also, it's the first *Dracula* directed by a woman – Anna Procházková (who co-scripted, with Oldrich Zelezny).

As often, the Transylvania opening and closing are more exciting than the drawing-room drama: an effect underlined by the use of impressive snowbound locations for Castle Dracula and overlit studio sets for Victorian England. Jonathan Harker (Jan Schánilec), who sports impressive sideburns, is ensnared by a stocky, bearded Drakula (Ilja Racek), who greatly resembles Michael Lonsdale in *Moonraker* and wears *giallo* murderer black gloves and a traditional vampire cape. A Hammer influence is detectable in some fang-baring action, but vampires here are less physical beings: Drakula fades in and out of existence through simple superimposition, and the elaborately-dressed, tittering brides flit like ghosts. *Hrabe Drakula* includes key moments from the book unused or played down in earlier adaptations: the Count (and later Jonathan) climbing down castle walls, the brides torn away from their chosen victim but pacified with a squealing baby (offscreen), the active role of the Count's gypsy minions, the death of Lucy's mother (Marie Brozova) by her daughter's bedside.

In England, slightly mannish brunette Mína Harkerová (Klára Jerneková) embroiders a lot while the pompous Van Helsing (Ota Sklencka) and Dr Seward (Jirí Zahajsky) treat bitten blonde Lucy (Hana Maciuchová). Mina comes into her own leading the slayers in pursuit of the Count to his Romanian bolt-hole. Jonathan, recovering from traumatic amnesia, gets to despatch the king vampire by throwing a knife into his heart, whereupon he turns into a pile of ash. Not as impressive a sketch of *Dracula* as the similarly scaled British *Mystery and Imagination* version, but interesting.

JONATHAN (1970)

This radical repurposing stages moments from *Dracula* – the Count (Paul Albert Krumm) forcing a victim to drink blood from his chest, Jonathan (Jürgen Jung) assailed by the three vampire brides, the Count hauling the concubines off his guest with a cry of, 'This man is mine! and assuaging them with a peasant baby – but strips out most of the plot to couch the conflict between Dracula and Jonathan in political terms, with both alpha males eventually lost amid raving crowds of their followers. It is even an early entry in the alternate vampire world sub-genre, set in an 18th century where vampires who don't fear the sun openly rule.

Though director-writer Hans W. Geissendörfer takes cues from Hammer's *The Kiss of the Vampire* and a plot element (the creatures' vulnerability to running water) from *Dracula: Prince of Darkness*, he draws on sources as diverse as Kevin Brownlow and Andrew Mollo's *It Happened Here*, Miklós Jancsó's *The Red and the White* and Michael Reeves' *Matthew Hopkins, Witchfinder General* in staging tableaux of bloody oppression against chilly yet beautiful landscapes. Gorgeously shot by future superstar Robby Müller, the film cartoonishly equates Dracula with Hitler. This Count rants at assembled ranks of thralls and swans about in a stylish high-collared cape, but only rarely gets his fangs dirty – he has a cadre of brutal human thugs to enforce his rule and see off threats to his regime. Arthur Brauss, a familiar German hardman seen as Nazis in *Cross of Iron* and *Escape to Victory*, is among the sternest of these SS-like minions. The vampire congregation – choreographed as if taking part in a community passion play – includes a train of scarlet-robed decadents, the three traditional pale ladies and a flock of little girls in pink ballet outfits.

Student of a doddery Professor Van Helsing (Oskar von Schab), Jonathan – like Harker in Hammer's *Dracula* – comes to the area to overthrow Dracula's rule. He falls asleep in the coach and his bag of vampire-killing equipment is stolen and turned over to a hunchback who desecrates a store of confiscated crosses and communion wafers. Beguiled by the heroine (Ilona Grübel), who performs a musical number, Jonathan is captured by the vampires and treated brutally in the castle's dungeons. Many audiences will be more upset by the real onscreen stomping of a rat than the faked branding of the hapless, shirtless hero. The Professor's followers arrive *en masse*, reclaim the crosses and set about violently overthrowing the state, leaving still more corpses littered about the landscape. In an eerie, affecting finale, the Count and his last followers are herded into the sea by the cross-and-torch-wielding mob and destroyed, floating limply in shallow waters as an almost-forgotten Jonathan slumps on the beach.

A bitter vision of oppression and revolution, it's often shocking yet lyrical, ostensibly humourless but bitingly satirical, enacted by performers who sleepwalk as if hypnotised like the cast of Werner Herzog's *Heart of Glass* and scored with a mix of ominous easy listening from Roland Kovac and romantic classical selections from Edvard Grieg. Geissendörfer later created the long-running soap *Lindenstraße* for German TV and produced art-genre oddities *The Nine Lives of Tomas Katz*, *Berberian Sound Studio* and *Uncle Boonmee Who Can Recall His Past Lives*.

LADY DRACULA (1977)

This German vampire movie, from a story by blocky American star Brad Harris, isn't quite a comedy, but offers lumpen hijinx with panicky undertakers and a busy, funky score which is hard to take seriously. Eddi Arent, comic relief in dozens of Edgar Wallace movies, does prissy shtick as a copper working with Harris's he-man trench coat to investigate a spate of blood-related crimes. Director F.J. Gottlieb was an old *krimi* hand, too – with credits like *The Phantom of Soho* and *The Black Abbot*.

In a 19th century prologue, Dracula (Stephen Boyd), sporting his usual cloak-and-fangs look, bites a German Countess and is destroyed in his crypt by a stern band of clerical vampire-killers. An unusual touch in this oft-staged scene is that the priest has to uncross the vampire's arms, which lie over his heart, before staking him in the coffin with a broken spade handle, whereupon the vampire's outstretched arms sag as he does a slow dissolve to dust. Aside from token flashback snarls, Dracula is then out of the picture. In 1970s Vienna, workmen on a building site dig up a coffin (cf: *The Return of the Vampire*, the TV movie *Vampire*) and remove a valuable cross, freeing Countess Barbara von Weidenborn (Marion Kracht). Evelyne Kraft, the blonde goddess from *The Mighty Peking Man* (*Goliathon*), takes over the role from the angelic Kracht and swans about in high style, fitting into swinging modern society with red lip gloss (fangs optional) and a *Charlie's Angels*-coiffure, plus a wardrobe of fabulous, mostly yellow outfits (unusual colour scheme for a vampire). She commits a few murders, is upset by garlic dressing on steak, turns into a giant bat (not that impressive) and burns her hand on a cross. Torn by feelings for the clod hero, she tries to ethically source her diet by robbing a blood bank, but winds up biting a nurse anyway.

Arent, apparently playing himself, can't get anyone to take his vampire theory seriously and impales his own foot with a trick cane. Harris writes himself as irresistible to women but seemingly doesn't bother with a character name, playing a cop just known as the Kommissar – trading on Brad Harris's *Kommissar X* film series. After a scrappy last-reel fight, the hero pursues the vampire into a secret room, where she has a coffin with an automatically lowering lid. She pulls him in with her for a comical, abrupt finish. Arent makes a funny remark as a swingle-sung 'Lady Dracula' theme cuts in. Kraft's Lady Dracula should not be confused with Ingrid Pitt's *Countess Dracula*, Louise Fletcher's *Mama Dracula* or Sylvia Kristel's *Dracula's Widow* – or the distinguished personage's other various brides, daughters, fiancées, girlfriends, mistresses, groupies and hangers-on.

LEAGUE OF FRANKENSTEIN (2015)

Evidently, Alan Moore has fans in the adult entertainment industry. This British-made eight-part serial scrambles the cast lists of Moore's *The League of Extraordinary Gentlemen* and *Lost Girls* comics in a pulp-steampunk porn free-for-all which almost incidentally has some near-workable ideas (what if Wonderland and Neverland went to war?), but keeps stopping dead for mercilessly protracted, dully shot sex scenes.

In the early 20th century, genius Victor Frankenstein (Danny D) is distracted from bringing his dead wife Elizabeth (Tina Kay) back to life by an invasion from Wonderland led by the busty daughter of the original Captain Hook (Jasmine Jae). Besides his well-known work in the field of reanimation, this Frankenstein invents dimensional portals. When Peter Pan (Ryan Ryder) is an early casualty of the war, Frankenstein uses his heart to revive his Bride – though Pan gets it back for a happy ending (so to speak). Siding with Frankenstein are vampire-slayer Barbara Von Helsing (Franceska Jaimes), Alice of Wonderland (Mia Malkova), Tinker Bell (Sophia Knight), jungle adventuress Jane Porter (Jasmine Webb) and a tattooed-all-over Apeman (Rob Diesel). Vampire Lord Ruthven (Locus Grafenberg) makes a rare screen appearance too.

It runs to decent costumes and sets, primitive CGI and clumsy action, but the sex scenes – honourably excepting a silly, orgiastic take on the Mad Hatter's tea party – are mechanical, even when the participants *aren't* lightning-struck cyborgs. Asking porn stars to act is a risky venture, but Mr D (as Frankenstein *and* the Mad Hatter) delivers something like characterisation. Sienna Day's Wendy risibly whines, 'but you an't got your powers no more' to Peter in a broad Midlands accent. Written and directed by Dick Bush, who has also made X-rated versions of *Sherlock* and *Doctor Who*.

LEENA MEETS FRANKENSTEIN (1993)

Directed by Scotty Fox and written by 'L.S. Talbot', this X-rated riff on *Abbott and Costello Meet Frankenstein* has dim-bulb beauticians Leena and Nicole London visit the mansion of Count Dracula (Mike Horner), who plans to control the Frankenstein Monster (Jon Dough) and inaugurate an era of eternal evil. Larry Abbott/Talbot (Tony Tedeschi), the Wolf Man, is also in residence, along with gypsy wife Elena (Tina Tyler), while Betty Page-cum-Morticia-like Betty (Madison) is pack mother of the Count's wives (Brittany O'Connell and Paige Carlson) and preppy third-generation monster hunter Steve Van Helsing (Randy Spears) turns up to help thwart Dracula's plans.

Shot in black-and-white (except for the sex scenes), this is decked out with familiar jokes (at table, Dracula is upset by the use of the words 'steak' and 'cross') and ancient gags ('This is what they call going down for the Count.'), but makeup effects are surprisingly adequate. In a minor homage to *Nosferatu*, Dracula is destroyed after Leena distracts him past sunrise with sex, incidentally curing him of his evil instincts... though there's also a Hammer touch as her accidental opening of a curtain reduces him to ashes. London's major contribution is to seduce the Monster ('You know I like 'em big and dumb.') after being made up as a Halloween-level Bride of Frankenstein, while Tedeschi transforms from Wolf Man to human before his sex scene because Tyler doesn't 'want to take another flea bath'. Let's face it – more respectful of the Universal monsters than *Van Helsing*.

THE LIBRARIAN: CURSE OF THE JUDAS CHALICE (2008)

> 'SO SOMEBODY'S LOOKING FOR A CHALICE THAT RESURRECTS DEAD VAMPIRES AT THE SAME TIME DRACULA'S BODY'S GONE MISSING. THAT'S NOT GOOD.'

Following *The Librarian: Quest for the Spear* and *The Librarian: Return to King Solomon's Mines*, this is the best of three breezy, fantastical TV films about Flynn Carsen (Noah Wyle), who works for an immortal sage (Bob Newhart) in a New York library which houses artefacts like Excalibur, the Time Machine, the Spear of Destiny and Noah's Ark. The saga riffs on Indiana Jones, *National Treasure*, *The Da Vinci Code* and a shelf-load of classic literature and lore, but has its own modestly winning personality.

Flynn is fed up with the strain put on his private life by his secret job – his girlfriend dumps him with, 'Maybe some women are okay with the wild and unpredictable life of dating a librarian, but I'm not.' – and goes on holiday to New Orleans. Between jazz clubs and drinking, he falls into a mystery runaround involving voodoo queen Marie Laveau's tomb and pirate Jean Lafitte's ship in search of the Judas Chalice, an artefact made from the famous thirty pieces of silver, which ex-KGB baddie Kubichek (Dikran Tulaine) wants to use to resurrect Dracula so he can lead an unkillable army and retake Russia. Flynn gets involved with Simone Renoir (Stana Katic), a 403-year-old vampire chanteuse. It turns out that the bones in Dracula's tomb belong to a peasant, and the arch-vampire has been walking the Earth as crippled Professor Lazlo (Bruce Davison), who needs the chalice to restore himself to full power. Mild-mannered Davison joins a long line of unlikely actors (David Niven, Roger Daltrey, Robert Pastorelli, Adam Sandler) cast as Dracula, though his king vampire is supposed to be in disguise until the climactic fight, which features good use of disintegration effects and hollow-eyed zombie ghouls.

The series' signature cracked erudition runs to lifting theology from *Dracula 2000* about Judas being the first vampire – hence the aversion to crosses, silver, holy water and stakes made from a particular tree. The franchise took a rest before reviving as TV series *The Librarians*. Scripted by Marco Schnabel, based on characters created by David N. Titcher; directed by Jonathan Frakes.

LUST FOR DRACULA (2004)

Seduction Cinema's output of silly spoofs with lesbian softcore scenes (*The Erotic Witch Project*, *Gladiator Eroticvs*, etc.) occasionally switches gears to pretentious horror footnotes with lesbian softcore scenes.

Mina (Misty Mundae) is the unfulfilled, childish wife of pharma tycoon Jonathan Harker (Julian Wells, a woman apparently playing a man) and sister of vampire-hating Abigail Van Helsing (Shelly Jones). Dracula (Darian Caine) is in Los Angeles to liberate Mina with softcore sex. Another vampire (Andrea Davis) floats about with a schoolgirl acolyte (Casey Jones). It seems like several plots shuffled together as director-writer

Tony Marsiglia (*Dr. Jekyll & Mistress Hyde*) delivers the contractually required number of lesbian gropes, then just doodles.

Among the time-fillers: Mundae performing a heartfelt soliloquy to her imaginary baby 'Bat Bat', a sub-plot about unethical use of prescription pills, schoolgirl vampires who might be a Jean Rollin homage, characters who are radically different from scene to scene (Mina grows smarts and explains things at the end) and a few tiny vampire elements.

MINA MURRAY'S JOURNAL (2016)

A very contemporary take on *Dracula*, which not only updates Bram Stoker's journal entries and recorded case notes into vlog postings, but gives heroine Mina (Rosie Holt) an even more central role. Here, *she's* the estate agent who takes a trip to Transylvania – expecting a four-star Bucharest hotel with spa and pool – to hand-deliver contracts to Count Dracula, while boyfriend John Harker (Liam Dryden) stays home and frets. The bite-sized episodes mostly feature Mina talking to camera, though flatmate Lucy (Kate Soulsby) and Lucy's medical student admirer Jack Seward (Matt Hargreaves) start their own vlogs and chip in with concern for their friend and updates on the ravings of voluntarily committed mental Renfield, who eats insects and rants about the coming of 'the Master'.

Billed as 'Season One', this covers only the first section of the novel and is post-modern enough to get laughs from the fact that every viewer knows this story and is well ahead of Mina in picking up on what's wrong with her host in Romania, though the punch line reveals that she's canny enough to get past her own inclination to explain rationally and admit 'they totally are vampires'. Tone is generally sweet and witty, indulging the attractive, self-involved Mina – who is bisexual, but doesn't notice that Lucy has a crush on her – as she chatters, unaware of gathering shadows or the bat-thing lurking in the background. However, the story eventually darkens and there are moments of proper chill.

Dracula never appears on camera, though his 'brides' (Sara Parker, Sophie Parker, Steve Fitzgerald) barge into Mina's room in the castle, their vampire presence disrupting the image in such a way that it's possible they can't fully show up on video. It has a tonal and structural precedent in similar YouTube updates of Carmilla and Sherlock Holmes, but writer-director James Moran (*Severance*, *Cockneys vs Zombies*) gives it distinctive, dryly British character.

MONSTER BRAWL (2011)

> ## 'WHAT DO YOU THINK ABOUT LIVING IN A WORLD WHERE MONSTERS MUST FIGHT TO THE DEATH?'

An endearingly dumb high-concept picture inspired by *Frankenstein Meets the Wolf Man* in which a callow promoter stages monster bouts in a haunted cemetery. Fair dos for including one classical monster (a Cyclops) alongside Universal staples (a Mummy, 'Frankenstein', Lady Vampire, Wolf Man), oddities (Swamp Thing parody Swamp Gut and harridan Witch Bitch) and a Zombie Man (left over from a Pittsburgh outbreak, with a *Return of the Living Dead*-style military handler). It seems odd Dracula (at least) doesn't make the cut. The makeup jobs are functional but take the punishment dished out in stunt fights. It's a bigger problem that bite-size backstories don't give the monsters much character and they all do little more than grapple and roar, with narrator Lance Henriksen (as God) naming signature moves which aren't all that special.

It's kept going by funny, well-written, callous commentary from Buzz Chambers (Dave Foley) and Sasquatch Sid Tucker (Art Hindle, from *The Brood*), who give it a *Death Race 2000* vibe, parodying pompous, hectoring sports talk – with Hindle's commentary degenerating after he's bitten by a zombie, until he has to be 'put down like a dog'. There are some good jokes, like 'Frankenstein' ('Frankenstein's Monster, if you want to be a dick.') speaking only in quotes from Mary Shelley, the seemingly brainless Swamp Gut's subtitled environmentalist speech and a debate about whether Frankenstein is technically also a zombie.

So, the scores: Cyclops (Jason David Brown) defeats Witch Bitch (Holly Letkeman); Lady Vampire (Kelly Couture) defeats the Mummy (Rj Skinner); Wolf Man (Skinner) defeats Swamp Gut (Brown); Frankenstein (Robert Maillet) defeats Zombie Man (Rico Montana); after a longer bout with Wolf Man, Frankenstein takes the Heavyweight Championship belt. Written and directed by Jesse T. Cook, who co-directed *Scarce* with *Exit Humanity*'s John Geddes (who cameos as a zombie victim). Not even as bizarre as the average Mexican monster-wrestling film, but the concept of conflating classic monsters with wrestling personae is amusing.

MYSTERY AND IMAGINATION: DRACULA (1968)

As everyone who's ever tried to adapt Bram Stoker's *Dracula* into another medium has found, the novel is too sprawling to be easily reduced to eighty minutes of straight-ahead drama. However, this episode of the low-budget ITV series *Mystery and Imagination* (substantially shot in three days!) does interesting, even innovative things. It takes cues from the 1920s theatrical versions and the 1931 film and some business evokes Hammer, but telewriter Charles Graham and director Patrick Dromgoole make choices which prefigure the directions of subsequent Draculas with Jack Palance, Louis Jourdan, Frank Langella, Klaus Kinski and Gary Oldman. One clever shortcut – starting the action in Whitby and doing the Harker-goes-to-Transylvania/brides-of-Dracula shtick as a hallucinatory film insert flashback – even resurfaces in Guy Maddin's *Dracula: Pages From a Virgin's Diary*.

'Number 34' (Corin Redgrave), a wild-and-white-haired madman, gets out of his straitjacket and erupts through the upstairs windows, literally crashing a dinner party hosted by Dr Seward (James Maxwell). As the lunatic prostrates himself before his 'master', the camera pans to reveal the guest of honour is Count Dracula (Denholm Elliott), already ensconced in polite society. This Dracula has a black goatee, Vincent Price-in-*The Tomb of Ligeia* sunglasses and affects a garment which resembles a monk's habit as much as the traditional cloak. Elliott manages a Transylvanian accent which isn't a Lugosi imitation and delivers Stoker's speech about Dracula's ancient bloodline to an impressed Lucy Weston (Susan George). In Browning's *Dracula*, Renfield gets Harker's trip to the castle; here, Harker gets Renfield's insanity: Number 34 isn't Stoker's madman, but his hero – so altered even his own wife Mina (Suzanne Neve) takes a while to recognise him. In a striking scene, Dracula semi-possesses Jonathan – Redgrave spreads a blanket like a cape and taunts vampire-hunters in Elliott's dubbed voice.

A severely bearded Van Helsing (Bernard Archard) uses mesmerism to help Jonathan remember his Transylvanian ordeal. The brides are less sexy than usual, played as hissing, capering vermin. Unusually for 1968, when only Jean Rollin's *Le Viol du Vampire* was a precedent, one vampire is black, Nina Baden-Semper (later co-star of national embarrassment sitcom *Love Thy Neighbour*). While Seward and Van Helsing fuss over Jonathan, Lucy is repeatedly bitten by Dracula. Victims clearly enjoy being drained, though Elliott sports the nastiest fangs – rattier even than Max Schreck's – of any screen Dracula. Neve's married Mina, whom Lucy criticises as 'too governessy', is unhealthily repressed, allowing George a chewier role as flirt, invalid, corpse and vampire. Several often-dropped characters appear. Lucy's ailing mother (Joan Hickson) is the useless twit who breaks the garlic chain to allow the vampire into her daughter's boudoir; servants are usually blamed for this – here, a maid notes Dracula doesn't have a reflection, but thinks better of mentioning it to her employers. Swales (Hedley Goodall), Stoker's 'local character', gloats about lies told on gravestones ('She were a proper slut.') and establishes Dracula's British residence is a suicide's grave in the Whitby churchyard (almost all the action takes place in the asylum or the cemetery). A Carmilla-ish Lucy bites her friend before Dracula puts his own mark on Mina.

Seward has a Protestant English horror at Van Helsing's vampire-killing 'popery' (rosaries, crucifixes). In the climax, Van Helsing uses holy water to reconsecrate the suicide's grave and Dracula (who offers to share the knowledge of centuries if shown mercy) disintegrates in the dawn light. A wax face melts off a skull, with Elliott's face superimposed – a strikingly gruesome effect. Later Draculas belabour the point (subtly made here) that the vampire is more appealing than the stiff, prurient, uptight men arrayed against him. Maxwell goes too far with face-pulling in the finale, as Seward reacts to Dracula's disintegration as if it were simply a foul smell. As in Terence Fisher's *Dracula*, the wind blows away the Count's ashes, leaving only his ring. With a cynicism echoed by John Badham's *Dracula* and a bit of business used in the 1980 *Flash Gordon*, Mina picks up the ring, still enslaved to the Count. Under the end credits, Mina is seen with fangs, predating the punch lines of the Count Yorga films.

MYSTERY AND IMAGINATION: FRANKENSTEIN (1968)

This ITV drama stresses the *doppelgänger* theme by casting Ian Holm as both Frankenstein and his monster. The doubling spills into new-minted plotting about a sidelined vengeance-seeker who gets Victor mixed up with the Monster.

Scripter Robert Muller plays up Frankenstein's neurasthenic gutlessness in the scientist's initial rejection of his monster (billed as 'The Being') and general wavering. He's in a tizzy of self-recrimination even as innocent Justine (Meg Wynn Owen) gets her head chopped off for the murder of his brother Wilhelm (Frank Barry). Later, Victor takes a chopper to his unfinished female creation, though he knows this will spur the monster to more murders. Muller attaches the peripheral characters to the inn where Victor and Elizabeth (Sarah Badel) have their ill-fated wedding night, making this an odd instance of the British television tradition that all action should revolve around the local pub. When the unwelcome visitors call on Victor in the university town of Heidelberg (in the novel it was Ingolstadt), they lodge at the inn. The nice daughter (Morag Hood) of blind Felix (Michael Francis) works as a barmaid (her crippled brother hangs out too), minion Fritz (Ron Pember) gets drunk with the alcoholic sexton (Robert Hunter) who helps with body-snatching, and even fatherly lecturer Krempe (Richard Vernon) pops in regularly for schnapps and exposition.

The play harps on religion, simplifying Mary Shelley's use of Milton to engage not only with blasphemy but also poor parenting: Fritz declares he doesn't believe in God because no creator would have made him deformed, but Frankenstein isn't even interested in the argument as he concentrates on harnessing the lightning; the Being argues with initially welcoming Felix when he asks who God is and assumes from the devout answer that the blind man means Frankenstein (which prompts him to blaspheme that God is bad). Holm – later Victor's father in *Mary Shelley's Frankenstein* – relishes the meaty dual role. His Victor is an infuriating egoist who never finishes anything or considers the consequences, while the Being is effectively pitiful with a sly, mean streak. His sole moment of delight comes when he pulls on some torn old trousers, learning like a toddler to dress himself.

Directed, a trifle stiffly, by Voytek, better known as a production designer. Some of the (minimal) location work was done at Strawberry Hill, the gothic fantasy house Horace Walpole built with profits from the genre's first great success, *The Castle of Otranto*.

NOCTURNA (1979)

'Compass International – a new direction,' announces the trailer, 'on course for the '80s and beyond...' Well, maybe. This got lost in a 1979 Dracula movie glut – probably because, though literally in tune with the zeitgeist, it's not very good. In her original specialty as a belly-dancer, Armenian-born Nai Bonet had a scattering of '60s and '70s bit-parts in *The Beverly Hillbillies* episodes and *The Spy with a Cold Nose*; later, she established herself as a disco diva and took the trouble personally to produce this all-round star vehicle.

Nocturna (Bonet), Dracula's shapely granddaughter, forsakes vampirism for the love of a mortal (Antony Hamilton). The story (which Bonet wrote) is an excuse for her to strut in see-through shrouds, take a long nude bath, snap off comedy lines, command loving close-ups and dance more than humanly possible. Undoubtedly gorgeous and with a lovely smile, Bonet somehow doesn't project much personality. It doesn't help that Hamilton, ironically referred to as her 'straight mate', reads onscreen as both colourless and gay – scarcely someone to forsake her immortality for. Though hoary gags about 'a very good year' for blood are trotted out, writer-director Harry Hurwitz (*The Projectionist*) comes up with vampire business which would turn up in later movies or books. Hurwitz's 1970s New York scene amusingly features an earnest self-help group (Blood Suckers Anonymous), vamps who worry about their weight thanks to all the hypoglycemia around, and talk about 'coming out of the coffin'. Future Alex Cox regular Sy Richardson is 'R.H. Factor', a vampire pimp who pushes snortable blood and has a stable of bloodsucking masseuses.

John Carradine reprises his signature *Dracula* curtain speech from a coffin ('If I'm alive, what am I doing here? If I'm dead, why do I have to wee-wee?') before he fits in false fangs, Brother Theodore mutters bleakly as a treacherous minion, and Yvonne De Carlo riffs on Lily Munster (this Dracula is even called 'Grandpa') as the Count's nagging ex-girlfriend Jugulia Vein. A few bat transformations are done with cartoon effects dating back to Abbott and Costello, though sparkly disco lights are added. A ton of lively, disposable music comes from Gloria Gaynor, Vicki Sue Robinson and Moment of Truth, while classical interludes harking back to Olde Transylvania are reminiscent of Claudio Gizzi's *Blood for Dracula* score. With big-jawed Irwin Keyes (as Transylvanian Character) and Drew Barrymore's brother John Blyth Barrymore (as Punk Vampire).

ORLAK, EL INFIERNO DE FRANKENSTEIN (1960)

Inspired by then-recent Hammer Films *and* the classic Universal series, this Mexican film scrambles *The Curse of Frankenstein* and *House of Frankenstein* by opening with elderly Professor Carlos Frankenstein (Andrés Soler) languishing in jail. Glib rogue Rojas (Joaquín Cordero), Frankenstein's cellmate, helps the Professor escape and return to his cavernous laboratory (a nicely vaulted set). Frankenstein vivifies his headless creation Orlak (named for the character in *The Hands of Orlac*?), who sports a curious box-like contraption strapped to his shoulders until Frankenstein gives him a wax face modelled on Rojas (allowing Cordero to play both roles). Prefiguring the vengeance-seeking hypnotist of *The Evil of Frankenstein* and the remote-control creatures of *Dr Frankenstein on Campus*, Rojas – who has a list of victims already prepared – dominates

Orlak, whispering orders via a microphone built into wire-framed glasses. Orlak strides around in wide-brimmed hat and black cloak, attacking Rojas' enemies while the villain has perfect alibis. For instance, Rojas calls on elegant, piano-playing socialite Elvira (Irma Dorantes) while Orlak batters a dignitary in a strikingly staged sequence outside a stark, prow-like corner house.

Sub-plots bubble: scarred assistant Eric (Carlos Ancira) wants a new face, Rojas smarms around Elvira, Inspector Santos (Armando Calvo) is frustrated because he can't pin the crimes on Rojas, and Frankenstein is concerned by the progress of his experiment. For his next atrocity, Rojas has the lumbering Orlak murder a mother and baby. During a fraught conversation with Elvira's disapproving father (Antonio Raxel), Rojas grips his hands together just as Orlak's close on the crying baby's head (an inexplicit yet transgressive shock). Elvira, who has a faint moustache, finds Orlak lurking in her garden and takes him for Rojas, whom she inexplicably hasn't pegged as an utter rotter. The monster, confused by emotional backwash from his master, refrains from crushing her head. Some of Rojas' enemies catch on that they're in danger and beat him up, but Orlak arrives to order and kills them – crushing one against a wall with a table, after doing the traditional unfazed-by-a-hail-of-bullets bit. Orlak pays a call on the smitten Elvira, who wants to elope with him. In an imaginative moment, the monster crouches by a fire and expresses his inner torment as his wax face gruesomely melts. The silly goose screams and faints, and the monster – also as is traditional – carries her off. In a modest reversal, this monster doesn't find his own humanity until he stops looking normal and becomes physically grotesque.

The monster, one eye popped and the other halfway down his cheek, pursues Rojas, who has abducted Elvira. Santos saves the girl, who dangles from a balcony, while single-minded Orlak catches up with the villain. With his last gasp, Rojas uses the glasses to order Orlak to kill Santos and Elvira, but his control over the creature doesn't extend beyond death. Orlak runs off, pursued by stone-throwing peasants, and redeems himself by rescuing a girl we've never met from a fire(!) before willingly surrendering to the flames. Frankenstein and Santos exchange philosophical pleasantries about free will and the soul, ending with a heartfelt, 'Quien sabe?' Rafael Baledón (*The Man and the Monster*, *The Curse of the Crying Woman*) wasn't the best of the Mexican horror directors and *Orlak* doesn't have the production values of higher-profile efforts like *El Vampiro* or the truly demented tone of *The Brainiac* – but it is a fast, fun, occasionally poignant stab at monster melodrama.

THE PASSION OF DRACULA (1979)

In 1977, the John Balderston-Hamilton Deane *Dracula* had a successful Broadway revival with stylised Edward Gorey sets. Around the same time, Bob Hall (a comics writer who created *The West Coast Avengers*) and David Richmond wrote a hipper stage adaptation. Oddly, W.D. Richter's script for John Badham's 1979 *Dracula*, in which Frank Langella reprised his Broadway star turn, junks the Balderston-Deane for something closer to Hall and Richmond's take on Bram Stoker. This as-live television production of *The Passion of Dracula*, taped at the Ed Sullivan Theater, aired on a series called *Broadway on Showtime*.

Set in 1911, it limits the action to the drawing room of Dr Seward's sanitarium near Whitby and begins with Wilhelmina Murray (Julia MacKenzie) – Willie for short, not Mina – already mysteriously ill and her uncle Dr Cedric Seward (Gordon Chater), a Nigel Bruce-ish tubby moustached buffer, calling in Dr Abraham Van Helsing (Malachi Throne). Also on the case is accented Dr Helga Van Zandt (Alice White), an Austrian disciple of Freud ('Ze patient manifessted severe depression und recited Tennyson for two hours… It is not unusual in English women of her age.') who has an affair with married Lord Gordon Godalming (K.C. Wilson). Helga later transforms into a Morticia-Lily-look vampire. Newspaperman Jonathan Harker (Samuel Maupin) shows up to investigate because people hereabouts suggest a link between recent throat-ripped-out deaths and lax security at the asylum, which boils down to Renfield (Elliott Vileen) running about pursued by Jameson the butler (Brian Bell).

Cheaper and more soap opera-ish than BBC-TV productions of stage plays which ran as *Sunday Night Theatre* for decades, this limits its effects to one dissolve disappearance and a lot of spilled dry ice fog. Some theatrical coups – like the ringing of Dracula's voice in the dark as Van Helsing tries to hypnotise Renfield – don't translate to TV and there's much running to the French windows and peering offstage (or, indeed, shooting at that pernicious bat – 'I'll have you this time you flying bastard!'). Christopher Bernau, who created the role on stage, is a ranting, strutting, snarling Dracula – not the romantic figure suggested slightly by the title. After Willie has briefly vamped *him*, he gets bent over a footrest and staked onstage. The body count is low – even Renfield doesn't die in this adaptation. Throne and MacKenzie are good, but others veer between terribly earnest and knowingly camp. Studio director J. Edward Shaw adapts the stage direction by Peter Bennett.

PEHAVÝ MAX A STRASIDLÁ (FRANKENSTEIN'S AUNT; FRECKLED MAX AND THE SPOOKS) (1987)

An international smorgasbord, adapted from a Swedish children's novel by Allan Rune Petersson. A West German-Czech co-production with a multinational cast, it was made as a TV serial then edited into a hard-to-follow feature. A feel-good fable, it nevertheless has a ruthless streak unthinkable in a Western kids' film.

Red-headed orphan Max (Martin Hreben) flees a cruel circus and seeks refuge at Castle Frankenstein, where Henry F. (Bolek Polívka) has created beings with watery or fiery characteristics (Eddie Constantine, Tilo Pruckner). Albert (Gerhard Karzel), his newest monster, has a zip in his forehead *a la Young Frankenstein*; given a frozen genius brain, he comes to life as an amiable lunk with Hugh Grant dentition. The monster wants a mate and the bigoted villagers keep going on the rampage. A blacksmith-inventor tries to exploit the monster and Max tries to help Albert romance a winning chemist (Barbara De Rossi, of *Nosferatu in Venice*).

Also on hand: Count Dracula (Ferdy Mayne, reprising his role from *The Vampire Happening*), who can fly by day or night, the eponymous aunt (Viveca Lindfors, smoking cigars), a minion Igor (Jacques Herlin), a ghost lady (Mercedes Sampietro), librarian Mr Talbot (Flavio Bucci, of *Suspiria*), who might be a wolfman in the longer version (he's *the* Wolf Man in the book), and sundry circus/village characters who pop up to partner off with the leftovers at the end. Czech director Juraj Jakubisko (*Bathory*) is just a referee. Bereft of their original voices, the cast rely on their looks. Settings are on a level with the locations used by Jean Rollin or Jesús Franco for monster rallies and there's genuine affection for the characters, but it's still a mess – with obvious lacunae and a tendency to have people run around in panic whenever plots collide.

REVENANT (MODERN VAMPIRES) (1998)

Going against the late '90s trend for supercool vampire hunters (*Buffy the Vampire Slayer*, *Blade*, *Vampires*), this scrappy, engaging little picture presents Van Helsing (Rod Steiger) as a comic fanatic who hooks up with gangbangers to pursue his crusade. World War II-era vampire Dallas (Casper Van Dien), who cuts cigars on his teeth, returns to Los Angeles, though he is on the outs with Dracula (croaking Robert Pastorelli), who rules the undead from his nightclub empire. Dallas seeks Nico (Natasha Gregson

Wagner), a waif he turned twenty years ago, and effects a *My Fair Lady* transformation on her. Having lived as the Hollywood Slasher, a serial killer dressed as a hooker, Nico becomes an attractive, unpredictable young woman who reconciles her ultra-violent streak with childish joy in shopping and hanging out. Among Dallas's associates are Zsa Zsa Gabor-accented diva Ulrike (Kim Cattrall), genial Vincent (Udo Kier) – 'Let's get together and kill some people.' – and Richard (Craig Ferguson) and Rachel (Natasha Lyonne), who run an art gallery and jack up post-mortem prices by murdering the painters they exhibit. Rachel is eternally pregnant with a vampire baby.

Director Richard Elfman and screenwriter Matthew Bright, following their demented *Forbidden Zone* and *Shrunken Heads*, are loose cannon filmmakers, throwing in too many characters and sometimes reaching too far for sick humour. A tied-down Ulrike hurls racial abuse at the gangbangers, begging them to have sex with her so she can bite and infect them – Cattrall tries hard with this, but the scene pushes so many rape/race buttons it should come with multiple trigger warnings. However, *Revenant* has an appealing live-wire performance from Wagner and funny turns from most of the supporting cast. Steiger and Pastorelli deliver initially amusing if one-note readings of the roles of the great antagonists of vampire fiction. This Count has diversified, running a body-disposal service, while vampires have taken over California's most important political offices and live blatantly among self-absorbed humans who swarm in LA's all-night clubs and cafes and galleries. Among the favours Elfman pulls in are makeup effects from Rick Baker and a catchy score co-written by his brother Danny.

RITI, MAGIE NERE E SEGRETE ORGE NEL TRECENTO... (THE REINCARNATION OF ISABEL; THE GHASTLY ORGIES OF COUNT DRACULA) (1973)

The Italian title translates as *Rites, Black Magic and Secret Orgies in the Fourteenth Century*, which sounds as much like an encyclopaedia entry as an exploitation come-on. An astonishing, if slightly tiring exercise from out-there Italian horror specialist Renato Polselli, this reduces Mickey Hargitay, star demento of *Bloody Pit of Horror*, to blending in with a parade of grotesques, bizarros and tortured topless lovelies.

Isabel (Rita Calderoni), witch queen of the 14th century, was tortured to death by a mob. A modern-day cult, led by her reincarnated warlock lover (Hargitay – perhaps playing Dracula), wants to bring her back to life by sacrificing a collection of young women. The movie avoids mystery or suspense: we are told what is going on, then Polselli stages a series of scenes in which young women are tied to crosses, stripped semi-naked and mutilated via fakey-looking heart-ripping, breast abuse and eyeball-gouging. The grey-faced Isabel – a rotted hole between her naked breasts where her heart used to be – observes. Some characters find the warlock in his coffin, cuing the use of Bava-ish lighting effects, and the reincarnation is thwarted, which brings everyone back happily to life for a reprise of the comedy by-play which has occasionally interrupted the black magic rites/orgies.

It's hard to work out who's who until the show is nearly over, then it doesn't turn out to be very important (all those sacrificed girls are indistinguishable). The uninhibited if silly horror-sex is so shoddily presented it never approaches the transgressive – which is probably just as well.

SAINT DRACULA (DRACULA THE DARK LORD) (2012)

Officially a United Arab Emirates production, this was mostly made in the UK (with a British cast) by Indian writer-director Rupesh Paul.

Dracula (Mitch Powell) is a romantic swain looking for the reincarnation of his lost love (again!), who turns out to be novice nun Clara (Patricia Duarte). Whispering monk Benjamin (Daniel Shayler) is out to impale Dracula for his connection with a string of murders committed by a female vampire who might be one of his cast-offs. Powell, dressed in a red ruffle shirt, talks about love and God, while Benjamin and Clara exchange Bible quotations which consistently seem beside the point. In a long, colour-desaturated flashback, all the principles appear as mediaeval characters analogous to their modern roles. It seems the thwarting of Dracula's original love thanks to a jealous sister (Suzanne Roche) had something to do with his transformation into a blood-drinking immortal.

About an hour in, Paul includes a sedate musical number (in the Bollywood manner?) with Dracula striding through a pack of ballet dancers in black goth outfits. They return in white under the end credits, suggesting this might once have been a full-on musical (Clara's singing is talked about but never heard). Just as Clara and Dracula are about to marry, Benjamin appears to throw a large crucifix-handled spear through the vampire's heart – but Dracula has enough time to deliver a perhaps-blasphemous soliloquy to the figure of

Christ on the cross before dying. A Welsh castle and churches and municipal buildings in Liverpool and Manchester add production value and the cast strike poses which are impressive until they have to spout terrible dialogue in deadly earnest. One of the odder Dracula movies, it's still sluggish, monotonously acted and theologically dubious.

SANTO EN EL TESORO DE DRÁCULA (SANTO IN THE TREASURE OF DRACULA) (1968)

It's possible this started production as a period vampire movie and was reworked mid-shoot as a mod Santo picture. A cheapo *Time Tunnel* effect sends heroine Luisa (Noelia Noel) back in time to be menaced by Drácula (Aldo Monti) while the intrepid Santo (himself) stays in the present day. The scripted justification for this is that time travel is so gruelling a process only women can undergo it, but the time machine might just be a device to tie the story together. In the laboratory, Santo and his pals – including Luisa's boffin father (Carlos Agostí) and nerdy comedy relief clod Perico (Alberto Rojas) – use television to remote-view history as Luisa gets mixed up in a cut-down Dracula story. Adding to the bewilderment is that here Santo is not only a pro wrestler-cum-superhero, but a genius intent on clearing his name when the scientific community scoff at his claims to have invented a practical time machine.

In the past, a handsome Dracula confronts a Van Helsing type (Fernando Mendoza), smashes a mirror while quoting Stoker ('Foul bauble of man's vanity.') and introduces himself as Count Alucard (prompting a painful bit of mirror writing). He transports a Transylvanian treasure to a Mexican cave, accompanied by a gang of plump, silent vampire women in see-through shrouds (topless in the alternate version released as *El vampiro y el sexo*). He often turns into a flapping toy bat, and is strangely lit (seemingly from inside his cloak) whenever he looms with fangs. The past-set mini-story comes to an end with Dracula staked and Luisa returned to the present, where Santo battles a black-hooded villain who removes Dracula's stake to bring him back to life. This secondary evil mastermind plot is resolved with a sped-up fistfight in a graveyard, a chase in which the film is distorted to make the cars look bigger and an unmasking. In the actual finish, Santo and pals are trapped under a net in Dracula's caves, but the roof falls on the Count – cheating audiences of 'el enmascadero de plata' and 'el rey de los vampiros' grappling to the finish.

The utter casualness of the time travel angle is bizarre, and the disjunction between Universal-style vampire stuff and poverty row serial heroics makes this an even more disorienting experience than the average Mexican wrestling horror picture. Which is actually a recommendation. Directed by René Cardona.

SEVIMLI FRANKENSTAYN (MY FRIEND FRANKENSTEIN; TURKISH YOUNG FRANKENSTEIN) (1975)

This ramshackle Turkish production is a straight lift from Mel Brooks' *Young Frankenstein* – with almost all the gag sequences, characters, running jokes (the repeated offscreen horse's neigh) and plot turns feebly imitated. Even whole sections of Brooks' score are tipped in. Shot in colour, with arid Turkish locations standing in for Brooks' gloriously studio-bound monochrome Transylvania, it gives the impression that writer-director Nejat Saydam *only* knows *Frankenstein* through Brooks' parody. This monster is just a big, goofy guy without even a zip in his neck and Frederick von Frankenstein (Bülent Kayabas), who prefers to go by the name of 'Timur Frank', is a smarmy clod with a big moustache and an annoying fiancée. Without cultural context, it's hard to gauge precisely the level of humour, but the face pulling, double taking and falling over suggest it doesn't match the original mix of clever patter, affection for its subject and vaudeville low comedy.

SHARKENSTEIN (2016)

> 'I'VE NEVER SEEN A SHARK LIKE THAT BEFORE. IT LOOKS LIKE A GROTESQUE COMBINATION OF DIFFERENT SHARKS.'

This minimally budgeted quickie evokes Richard Cunha (*She Demons*), Jerry Warren (*Teenage Zombies*) and Ray Dennis Steckler (*The Incredibly Strange Creatures Who Stopped Living and Became Mixed-Up Zombies*) – with knowing tributes like naming the setting Katzman Cove after the producer of *Zombies of Mora Tau* and an odd pause as monster-savvy heroine Madge (Greta Volkova) lists Universal and Hammer Frankenstein films. A clunky black-and-white prologue even harks back to *Frankenstein Conquers the World* as the heart and brain of the Frankenstein Monster are sent out of Germany during World War II to be used in Nazi mad-science experiments.

Seventy-odd years later, a patchwork killer shark is given leftover monster organs by German-accented quack Klaus (Jeff Kirkendall). Struck by lightning, 'Sharkenstein' grows forelegs, forces itself sexually on an ex-porn star (Kathryn Sue Young) and is pursued by an angry mob with (topical touch) more guns than flaming torches. Heroic lifeguard Duke Lawson (Ken Van Sant) lures the monster to a lighthouse to be blown up.

J.K. Farlew's script and deadpan performances make the rampage surprisingly mundane, while director Mark Polonia relies too much on weak CGI rather than rubbery model-work. Even *Octaman* makes more of its monster than this. Brief cutaways of the crawling/swimming expressionless shark (which has a Karloff flat head, electrodes and scarred fins) give no sense of interaction with the fools it gets to kill. Withal, better value than *Shark Exorcist*.

SHISHA NO TEIKOKU (THE EMPIRE OF CORPSES) (2015)

19th century society is reshaped by the scientific innovations of Victor Frankenstein and Charles Babbage. An underclass of living corpses – revived by Frankensteinian injections and programmed with punch-card software generated by Babbage's giant computers – are soldiers, servants or suicide bombers. In 1878, boyish medical student John Watson reanimates a close (perhaps, very close) friend as a sad-eyed scribbler he names Friday (his official designation is Noble Savage 007). Blackmailed by one-eyed spymaster Walsingham (code-name: M), Watson and Friday are packed off to Afghanistan to retrieve Frankenstein's lost notes. Renegade Russian scientist Alexei Karamazov is using the notes in an attempt to recreate Frankenstein's original, unrepeated experiment and vivify an articulate monster with a soul (or, at least, intelligence). Also involved in a chase about the world – including spells in Tokyo and San Francisco before looping back to London – are British adventurer Frederick Burnaby (a historical character), bosomy American mystery gal Hadaly Lilith (an Edison-made automaton, working for ex-President Grant), the USS Nautilus (a nod to *The League of Extraordinary Gentlemen* as much as Verne) and the white-bearded original Frankenstein Monster ('the One').

This steampunk *anime* is based on a novel by Project Itoh which borrows from Bruce Sterling and William Gibson's *The Difference Engine* and my own *Anno Dracula*. It extrapolates a world dominated by Babbage's theories and fall-out from a famous monster's story and mixes real people with refugees from other Victorian fiction. The book (completed by Tô Enjo) was published posthumously, which might explain why the film's plot clanks as it waffles on weighty themes (what is a soul?) while speeding through incidents (several wars and mini-apocalypses) which might have benefited from more attention. Too often the main characters are on the sidelines of action, watching or taking notes while battles are fought or maddened zombies run riot (seemingly turning vampire by the amount of neck-biting on view). There are unusual elements, like the understated homoerotic bond between Watson (who doesn't hook up with his usual partner until an after-the-credits tag) and his corpse near-doppelgänger Friday, but the picture slips into an *anime-manga* rut as it boils down to a world-changing catastrophic event masterminded by a cackling villain and thwarted by straight-up good guys. A confusion of characters – including a Karloff-look flat-headed brute – clash at the Tower of London as a Big Magic Effect appears in the skies.

The animation is variable, with rich detail and backgrounds but some shaky character stuff (Hadaly's ridiculous breasts are rather disturbing). Scripted by Hiroshi Seko, Koji Yamamoto and Midori Goto. Directed by Ryôtarô Makihara.

THE SINS OF DRACULA (2014)

> 'YOU'RE NOT GOOD WITH PUNS, STICK WITH EVIL.'

Sometime in the 1980s, devout Billy (Jamie Dufault), star of the church choir conducted by Pastor Johnson (Carmine Capobianco), is persuaded by secular girlfriend Shannon (Sarah Nicklin) to join a theatre troupe. He is confronted by decade-specific stereotypes – Dungeons & Dragons addict Traci (Samantha Acampora), muso NuWave (Jesse Dufault), stoner Bandilli (Derek Laurendeau) and gay Lance (Aaron Peaslee). Producer Lou Perdition (Steven O'Broin) drops a proposed production of *Godspell* in favour of a musical called *Jonestown Jubilee*, but his grand scheme is to sacrifice his cast to revive bald, moustached, Lugosi-garbed Dracula (Michael Thurber).

Rhode Island auteur Richard Griffin (*The Disco Exorcist, Murder University*, etc.) has a track record with sly genre spoofs. Here, he draws on Hammer (like Christopher Lee in *Dracula: Prince of Darkness*, this Count maintains dignified silence… until a 'Marcel Marceau in *Silent Movie*' punch line) and the '80s likes of *Fright Night*, while envisioning a fundamentalist Christian scare movie pitching a good-natured churchgoing lad among stage folk he finds almost as threatening as vampires. The community theatre setting is appropriate since Griffin's best work has the feel of a good homemade production with talented if little-known actors giving it 110% and production values dependant on borrowed locations and general goodwill. He mostly stays away from the gross-outs – aside from anal impalement in the spirit of *2001 Maniacs* – endemic in low-budget comedy horror, daringly trying for subtler humour (Billy's prayer monologue is a hoot) and at least half-serious monster scenes.

Cast standouts are O'Broin, who combines Christopher Guest in *Waiting for Guffman* with Christopher Neame in *Dracula A.D. 1972*, and Acampora as the pedantic gamer whose costume is modelled on the outfit worn by Beverly Randolph in *The Return of the Living Dead*. The last reel reverts to *The Disco Exorcist* mode to bring on a Shaft-cum-Blade exorcist/vampire hunter (Jose Guns Alves) to team up with the Christian krewe to face the Prince of Darkness… which leads to an infernally witty punch line. Scripted by Michael Varrati.

STAN HELSING (2009)

'From the executive producer of *Scary Movie*', blares the DVD cover – trumpeting the directorial debut of Bo Zenga. A dispiriting addition to the crowded category of comedies which don't contain a single honest laugh, this shows how on top of pop culture it is by coming along five years after *Van Helsing*.

DVD rental store slacker Stan Helsing (Steve Howey) denies relationship with monster-hunter Van Helsing, and would probably resist any suggestion that his describing-porn-titles-over-the-phone shtick owes anything to Kevin Smith. On Halloween, Stan gets in a car with uptight ex Nadine (Diora Baird), fat black pal Teddy (Kenan Thompson) and Teddy's blonde dolt date Mia (Desi Lydic) to go to a party downtown. A detour to drop off some DVDs takes the quartet – all in silly costumes (cowboy, Indian, superman, stripper) – to a gated community built on the ruins of a burned-out horror film studio troubled by (barely) parodied franchise fiends Fweddy

(Ben Cotton), Needlehead (Charles Zuckermann), Lucky (Jeff Gulka), Mason (Ken Kirzinger, who played Jason in *Freddy vs Jason*), Michael Crier (Lee Tichon) and Pleatherface (Twan Holliday), plus a Hitcher (Travis MacDonald) who references *The Texas Chainsaw Massacre* rather than *The Hitcher*. Peculiarly, the most extended parody is of *Jeepers Creepers*, as the characters crawl down a pipe and find sewn-up victims in a cave.

It boils down to a karaoke contest between monsters (who riff on the Village People) and normals, with the fate of the town at stake. Leslie Nielsen is excruciating as a waitress – the point in *Airplane!* was that he played it straight, but at this end of his career Nielsen was just another rubbish rubberface doing fart gags and drag in a desperate pursuit of yocks that aren't there. The Frankenstein Monster (John DeSantis) appears as a gay pornstar, though Zenga's many gay references (including the Chucky-like Lucky being gang-raped by other dolls) are mostly confined to the deleted scenes. Three vampire women (the only Dracula element of this supposed *Van Helsing* skit) show up as pole-dancers. Bits for Michael Jackson and Barack Obama lookalikes don't count as jokes. Worse than *Vampires Suck* and *Transylmania* put together.

SUBJECT TWO (2006)

A *Frankenstein* variant which makes creative use of a budget that doesn't allow for much more than two actors up a mountain – a setting which evokes the snowy Swiss and Arctic scenes of the novel even as film's ultimate mad scientist is a scrambling of Mary Shelley's character name ('Dr Franklin Vick').

Adam Schmidt (Christian Oliver), a failing med student (significantly, his problem course is Ethics) is mysteriously approached by Dr Vick, who offers him a research position. Adam is ferried to the mountain by a nice, ambiguous blonde (Courtney Mace), then trudges through the snows to meet the supposed Vick (Dean Stapleton, uncannily like a younger Jack Nicholson). After a chat, the doctor throttles Adam, doses him with nanite soup and leaves him out in the cold. A day later, Adam revives from the dead. Over a course of experiments, Adam – Subject Two – is repeatedly killed and reanimated, turning into a self-repairing, apparently immortal being. Fumbling his way to treat agonising side-effects, Vick operates on his back, taking away his capacity to feel pain or, indeed, anything. The two debate the situation between experiments, and Adam decides he doesn't want to continue resurrecting after experiencing a range of deaths (shooting, strangling, bleeding, stabbing, bludgeoning) – though the process becomes automatic, and he rises even after a passing hunter pots him.

The last reel gets busy as Adam wanders off into the snows to evolve by himself while the abandoned researcher cries in vain to get him back into the program. Then, the nearly forgotten Subject One (writer-director Philip Chidel), a botch-job buried in the snow, rises and turns out to be the real Dr Vick, killed and dosed by a leery minion who didn't want to undergo the process. Shot on DV in trying conditions, it has a sense of snowy isolation and low-key performances persuasive enough to sell the wilder science. Things don't quite ramp up in the climax the way they should, with Chidel's gruff, makeshift Dr Vick ranting out of key with the two leads. It engages with Shelley's ideas as few Frankenstein films do, but also manages deadpan mad-science black comedy.

TALES OF DRACULA (2015)

A fond fan-made tribute to the Universal monster rallies of the 1940s, this is brief enough (75 minutes) not to become an ordeal – though amateur performances, lack of action (the Dracula vs Monster fight is a matter of mutual shoving), makeshift direction and incoherent scripting eventually wear thin. Originally conceived as separate short films, it cuts between sort-of sequels to unmade versions of the Dracula, Frankenstein and Wolf Man stories before loosely tying strands together.

The effect is closer to Al Adamson's piecemeal *Dracula vs Frankenstein* than avowed models *House of Frankenstein* and *House of Dracula*. Distinctly different traditions are evoked by its main monsters: werewolf Creighton Reed (Tom Delillo) is a Lon Chaney Jr lookalike, the Frankenstein Monster (writer-director Joe DeMuro) resembles the Karloffian slapdash of Hammer's *The Evil of Frankenstein* and the stringy-haired Dracula (Wayne W. Johnson) has a dissipated rock star look which has never really worked for the character (cf: *Van Helsing*, *Dracula: The Dark Prince*). Holding the thin story together is feminist mad scientist Victoria Frankenstein (Courtney Bennett), who uses a smear of Dracula's blood to make the Monster even more indestructible. She foolishly explains what she's done at length to the Count, who snaps her neck to prompt the final, inconclusive monster battle.

Delillo sports excellent Jack Pierce-look makeup, applied in nostalgic lap-dissolves, though his hapless Wolf Man Reed never quite finds a place in the story. In sub-plots, farmer's daughter Ilona (Greta Volkova) turns vampire and Professor Von Helsing (Mickey Ray) – the name harks back to *Dracula's Daughter* (1936) – broods about not destroying Dracula properly. Oddly absent from the mix are a hunchbacked assistant and a uniformed police captain. Made in black-and-white.

THIS AIN'T DRACULA XXX (2011)

The specific influence for this X-rated skit – to the extent of denying it in the trailer and pretending to be based on the public domain novel – is *Bram Stoker's Dracula*, though it owes as much to *Dracula: Dead and Loving It*. Voice-overs from assorted characters, trying various degrees of British accent, and inadequate CGI coach-to-the-castle and dog-jumps-off-the-ship scenes evoke the 1992 Coppola movie, and Dracula (Evan Stone) is introduced sporting the Gary Oldman-look two-white-buns hairstyle (later, in his only other appearance, he's in Lugosi-Lee evening dress). Most of the plot is dropped to make room for sex scenes: Jonathan Harker (Ryan Driller) and the vampire brides (Jennifer Dark, Bridgette B, Brandy Aniston); dark Mina Murray (Jessi Palmer) and redheaded 'Lucy Westerna' (Marie McCray); 'R.M. Rensfield' (Tom Byron, doing an acceptable Tom Waits-as-Brit accent) and a nameless blonde maid (Krissy Lynn); Arthur Holmwood (Joey Brass) and Quincey Morris (Alan Stafford) and vampire Lucy – Dr Seward (Jack Lawrence), as ever, is left out; and Dracula and Mina (she becomes a vampire after swallowing Dracula's semen). Andy Appleton plays Van Helsing, with authentic Northern British accent though he's supposed to be Dutch. The sets are small and fakey, but costumes are good. Directed by Axel Braun, an XXX parody specialist who has tackled sitcoms, superheroes and space opera.

TRANSYLMANIA (2009)

'I'M STARVING. ANYONE CRAVING SHEEP TESTICLE-STUFFED GOAT BALLS RIGHT NOW?'

Transylvania 6-5000 for the *EuroTrip* generation.

Stereotyped American college kids – some held over from the *National Lampoon's Dorm Daze* films – spend a semester in Transylvania and what you expect to happen does. Rusty (Oren Skoog) is a lookalike for vampire king Radu, who is out to reunite with his evil love, whose soul is in a music box and latches on to an innocent body (Jennifer Lyons) when music plays. Rusty has had an internet relationship with Draguta (Irena Hoffman), who turns out to be a hunchback whose dwarf mad scientist father Dean Floca (David Steinberg) plans on giving her a new body, which means *Thing That Couldn't Die* living severed head action for body donor Lia (Natalie Garza). Braggart Cliff (James DeBello) pretends to be a vampire slayer, but has to work hard when teamed up with real deal Teodora Van Sloan (Musetta Vander). There are jabs at *Bram Stoker's Dracula*, *Van Helsing* and *Buffy the Vampire Slayer*… and someone knows enough to call a character Edward Van Sloan. The *Young Frankenstein* Frau Blücher gag is revived, only to make it more hilarious for the 21st century a horse farts every time someone mentions Castle Razvan. A near-ingenious routine is muffed as Rusty and Radu do the Harpo-Groucho mirror gag from *Duck Soup* before Radu remembers he has no reflection – there's an idea here, but the filmmakers have no idea how to make it funny.

Crass, nasty stuff about female bodies sours even runabout silliness – with pole-dancing, bare-breasted babes (and a trio of vampire brides) to drool over and ughs of disgust at deformity (by comparison, the treatment of the hunchback girl in *House of Dracula* is sensitive) and stitched-up Frankenbabe bodies (a trace element of *Frankenhooker*). It has quality castle locations (also seen in the *subspecies* films and *BloodRayne*) and a rap version of 'Monster Mash' under the end credits. Written by Patrick Casey and Worm Miller; directed by David and Scott Hillenbrand.

LAS VAMPIRAS (1969)

This opens with John Carradine in a sports jacket, dubbed into rich deep Spanish, chatting about *vampiras*, explaining that Edgar Allan Poe believed in them and he does too. After animated credits and a long, dull wrestling match, beefy *luchador* Mil Máscaras – who changes his mask as often as the heroine of a Ross Hunter melodrama changes frocks, and augments his leotard with a sparkly Sgt Pepper jacket – reveals his sideline as an investigator of witches (*brujas*), UFOs (*OVNIs*), etc. He is currently interested in vampires because his latest ring opponent (a black man called Blackman) has been attacked by bats. When a girl is drained of blood, puzzled cops muse that this *'extraño caso'* might involve Dracula. With private eye Carlos Mayor (Pedro Armendáriz, Jr), another weird mystery specialist, Mil Máscaras investigates a spooky crypt and discovers the tombs of Count and Countess Alucard… a name he finds highly suspicious.

Meanwhile, in a well-lit lair, Count Branos Alucard (Carradine) – *not* Dracula under a pseudonym, apparently – rages and laughs hysterically in a cage while sporting a Disney villainess cape with a big stiff collar. Branos has been overthrown by sneering vamps in green leotards who all act like Lorena Velázquez in *Santo vs. las Mujeres Vampiro*, striking non-stop poses as they plot against humanity. Dissent among *las vampiras*, who hold regular choreographed dances, leads to a duel between Valeria (María Duval) and Aura (Martha Romero), who hiss as they jockey for command while extras flap their arms. Eventually, Aura lets *'el maestro'* out of his cage, and he seems ready to resume his throne as *'el rey de los vampiros'* until dominatrix Valeria (Dracula's widow, it seems) reduces him to an infantile, blubbering wretch. However, Branos gets his mojo back and abducts Carlos's girlfriend Marian (Maura Monti); in the sole nightmare moment of a silly film, Carradine leers as he walks towards the camera (representing a terrified cop), briefly genuinely evil rather than a doddering joke. Carlos and Mil Máscaras are mind-controlled to fight each other – MM wins (obviously). Marian is rescued from a coffin before she can be bitten and Mil Máscaras uses a flaming torch to set fire to the lair, burning the vampires. Carlos and Marian clinch and the cop on the case muses that the hero always runs off before he can be thanked. But Marian thanks him anyway. Thank you, Mil Máscaras. Really, thank you. Written by Adolfo Torres Portillo and director Federico Curiel.

VLAD (2003)

Another Dracula riff, further cementing the (debatable) identification of Bram Stoker's character with the historical Vlad the Impaler.

Romanian student Linsey (Monica Davidescu) is charged with returning a McGuffin amulet to Vlad's tomb. Along with two Americans (Paul Popowich, Kam Heskin) and a Brit (Nicholas Irons), she is in the Carpathians for vague academic purposes, sponsored by members of the secret Order of the Dragon (Billy Zane, Brad Dourif). In the woods, the kids have flashbacks to the hard times of Vlad (Francesco

Quinn) and the past leaks through in the shape of Ilona (Iva Hasperger), who speaks Chaucerian English and is fleeing the glowering prince, who CGI shapeshifts into a wolf and sports a batface but isn't quite a traditional vampire. Of course, Vlad is after the lookalike of his dead wife, but Renfield-type Mircea (Emil Hostina) wants him to restore the nation's glory and gets impaled for his pains.

The bigger names get killed off or written out early, too much dramatic weight falls upon the least-compelling performer (Popowich) and a late attempt to make the villain semi-sympathetic doesn't work (he may look cool, but he's still a murdering swine). However, its odd historical frills, a few patches of literacy (including a reprise of Stoker's 'you would pit your wits' speech), interesting secondary cast members (especially Irons, Davidescu and Hasperger), Romanian locales and general medieval romantic gloom are mildly distinctive. Written and directed by Michael Sellers.

WAY OF THE VAMPIRE (BRAM STOKER'S WAY OF THE VAMPIRE) (2005)

The Asylum's attempt to ride the *Van Helsing* coattails by casting an unshaven Australian pretty boy (Rhett Giles) as Stoker's little old Dutch vampire-hunter. Like Hugh Jackman's Gabriel Van Helsing, this Abraham Van Helsing is an immortal working for the church. In a black-and-white prologue, Van Helsing and a quickly-written-out band defeat Dracula (unimpressive Paul Logan). Foolishly, Van Helsing has left his wife in the care of Sebastien (Andreas Beckett) – either the son or a disciple of Dracula, depending on whether you believe the film or the trailer – who turns her, so the hero has to kill her.

The bulk of the film is set in present-day Los Angeles, mostly in large, deserted warehouses where Van Helsing and Sebastien hang out with their posses. Van Helsing, a blood specialist in a local hospital, trains some devoted churchgoers in the art of vampire slaying, while Sebastien keeps a low profile and insists his minions don't hunt humans. It winds up in a *West Side Story* showdown between the two bands, with Sebastien dead but Van Helsing still not free of his burden in that number two vampire Arianna (improbable but glamorous Denise Boutte) is still out there. Very, very cheap and poorly played, with scrappy fights and elementary horror. Scripted by Sherri Strain, Karrie Melendrez, Michael Stewart; directed by Sarah Nean Bruce and Eduardo Durão.

YAMI NO TEIÔ KYUKETSUKI DRACULA (DRACULA SOVEREIGN OF THE DAMNED) (1980)

A footnote to Dracula's film and comics careers, this animated feature finds screenwriter Tadaaki Yamazaki adapting a two-year run of Marvel's *The Tomb of Dracula* (largely written by Marv Wolfman) into a single, largely incoherent storyline. The process of making the film in Japan then dubbing it into English scrambles character names: Domini, Dracula's intended bride, becomes Dolores; Quincy Harker, wheelchair-bound head of the vampire-hunting band (born in the last pages of Stoker's novel) is now Hans Harker, though he still hangs around with Rachel Van Helsing (grand-daughter of...) and martial arts expert Frank Drake (Dracula's good-guy descendent); Mephisto, Marvel's main stand-in for the Devil (Peter Fonda in *Ghost Rider*), becomes plain old Satan; and Lilith, Dracula's fetish-garbed daughter-cum-nemesis, is now Leila in a sub-plot which seems set to spin off its own disco vampire serial-killer storyline but doesn't. Sadly, Blade didn't make the cut, though he was the comic's breakout character.

Opening narration explains that Dracula, King of the Vampires (indeed, Sovereign of the Damned), has left Transylvania for Boston, where a band of Satanists offer up Dolores as a bride for the dark powers. Dracula, easy to mistake for Satan in a certain light, snatches the woman, seems genuinely to fall in love with her and they have a human baby, Janus. Killed by the vengeful masked cult leader, Janus is miraculously resurrected as a golden angelic superhero (essentially, an anti-vampire who transforms into an eagle rather than a bat) and swears to end his father's evil reign. He doesn't, but does turn back into a baby. Harker, Drake, Van Helsing and a vampire-sniffing hound (kind of a straight Scooby-Doo) set out to assassinate Dracula, but repeatedly fail. For a stretch, thanks to divine intervention, Dracula assumes human form and nags Leila to bite him so he can become a vampire again. In Transylvania, he is bothered by zombie-like vampires who have defected to a new master – but gets his fangs back and reclaims his title after a fight with his rival. Finally, Harker skewers Dracula with a silver spoke from his wheelchair wheel and, for this film at least, ends his wicked life.

It has an *anime* look, with big eyes and winsome faces, but reproduces details of Gene Colan's comics designs (Dracula's pencil-flick moustaches, his layered cloak, Lilith/Leila's Vampirella-Barbarella cutaway costume). However, directors Akinori Nagaoka and Minoru Okazaki don't have the resources for first-rate work, and many scenes are barely a step above those 1960s Marvel cartoons which tried to bring Jack

Kirby or Steve Ditko strips to life with cut-outs and camera moves across panels. Still, the wayward storyline holds interest as it tries to wrestle Stoker's concept into Marvel's soap-superhero universe.

ZINDA LAASH (THE LIVING CORPSE) (1967)

Though it bears a 'based on the novel by Bram Stoker' credit, this *Dracula* variant opens with Jekyll-style mad scientist Professor Tabani (Rehan) drinking a potion to gain eternal life. He appears to die, but wakes up in his coffin as a vampire. As the first vampire picture from a country (Pakistan) with no vampire tradition, *Zinda Laash* is free to make up its own origin myth. It dispenses with Christian elements (which aren't even given Islamic equivalents), uses some familiar undead attributes (fangs, hating sunlight, etc.) and invents a few variations (hearts are stabbed with knives so they can bleed out the stolen blood).

After the setup, it becomes a Lollywood remake of the Terence Fisher *Dracula*. Moustachioed journalist Aqil Harker (Asad Bukhari) visits Tabani's castle to investigate a spate of mysterious deaths and has exactly the same experiences as John Van Eyssen's Jonathan Harker. The Vampire Bride (Nasreen), Tabani's transformed assistant, attempts to fascinate Harker with several dances before she flashes fangs; Nasreen even has a hairstyle like Valerie Gaunt's in *Dracula*. Drawing from the novel, Tabani (who wears a Lee-style cloak) placates the woman when he hauls her off the (short-lived) hero by handing her a baby to eat. It's inexplicit and the baby is a stiff doll, but it's still a shock. The Peter Cushing role is taken by Aqil's hardhead brother (Habib), though a bearded innkeeper does the Van Helsing bit of explaining vampire lore.

In black-and-white, inexplicit by Western standards, this has a contemporary setting (the final dash back to the castle is a car chase – making Tabani the first Dracula with a driving license). The odd interpolated nightclub song or dance on the beach amid a melange of borrowed music (including James Bernard, easy listening and Mozart samples) give it a peculiarly alien feel even as it reproduces familiar elements. Some sets are modelled on Hammer's (Bernard Robinson's trademark curly columns) so Fisher's camera angles can be reused. It climaxes with an extensive fistfight between good guy and vampire, which strays all over the castle (including falls down stairs into the crypt) and winds up with the praying hero accidentally knocking aside a shutter so blazing sunlight falls on Tabani and turns him into a skeleton. Directed by Khwaja Sarfraz.

FOUND FOOTAGE

AFFLICTED (2013)

> '*I'M JUST TRYING TO HARNESS THE POWER OF THE INTERNET TO HELP YOU WITH YOUR VAMPIRE PROBLEM.*'

A lively, surprisingly affecting video diary vampire movie. It has parallels with *Chronicle*, but directors/writers/stars Derek Lee and Clif Prowse take off in unexpected directions. They play characters with their own names, with clips from their teenage filmmaking efforts to establish their longstanding friendship. When Derek is diagnosed with a possibly fatal brain aneurysm, Clif resolves to accompany his friend on a round-the-world trip and document the tour on video. An unusual angle is that Clif uploads footage to the internet and gets feedback from friends and family, not all of whom think this jaunt is a great idea.

After sky diving and sightseeing, the guys hook up with friends (Zach Gray, Edo Van Breemen) in a band touring Europe, travelling from Barcelona to Paris… where Clif encourages Derek to hit on Audrey (Baya Rehaz) at a gig. Barging in on his buddy at the hotel, Clif finds Derek knocked unconscious and wounded in the arm. They continue to Italy, where Derek sleeps for unnatural periods, can't keep food down and sunburns terribly, but also develops super-strength, speed and agility. Clif tries to help his friend cope with the transformation and also documents it. Lee gives a remarkable performance, with understated makeup and bizarre bodily contortions, as he tries pig-blood and robbing a blood bank. He learns that only human blood satisfies and is compelled to attack his friend. Guilt-ridden and without funds, Derek returns to Paris to seek out the monster – keeping the camera rolling in tribute to Clif. He finds Audrey's Renfield (Benjamin Zeitoun), takes out an entire SWAT team and confronts his maker. She can't cure or kill him (even a stake through the heart doesn't work), but suggests he choose his victims more purposefully (she picked him because he was dying), whereupon he goes after a murderous paedophile. Under the end credits, a feral Clif revives as a vampire in Italy and begins killing tourists for blood.

The format requires elliptical storytelling, forcing the viewer to make plot connections even as the emotional spine – the friendship between serious Derek and joker Clif, and where it takes both men – depends on banter and flashes of concern. It stretches a low budget to locations in four countries and impressive stunt-work with agile *parkour* vampires.

ALONE WITH HER (2006)

Writer-director Eric Nicolas assembles this movie from grainy footage supposedly shot via hidden cameras carried or planted by bespectacled, sweaty Doug (Colin Hanks). Spotting Amy (Ana Claudia Talancon) walking her dog in a Los Angeles park, he decides to target her. In a creepy, plausible scene, he buys over-the-counter surveillance gear – telling a jaded salesperson he wants to check up on the nanny. He installs cameras in Amy's apartment and peeps on her intimate moments – on the toilet, in the shower, masturbating, gossiping with best friend Jen (Jordana Spiro), working on paintings. Arranging to meet Amy at a coffee shop, Doug uses insider knowledge of her music and film tastes to seem a kindred soul and eases into her life – offering or needing favours, disrupting a possible relationship with a workmate by poisoning her milk and spreading a rash-producing gel on her bedsheets. A series of contrived disasters (a stolen laptop which gets her fired, broken glass on her kitchen floor which temporarily puts her on crutches) allow him to come to the rescue. However, he also overhears that despite all he's done for her, he creeps Amy out. The latter stages default to familiar plotting – the best friend is as doomed as best friends always are in stalker movies (cf: Julianne Moore in *The Hand That Rocks the Cradle*, Anne Heche in *The Juror*) and when Doug finally gets a chance to score he turns out to be impotent (and murderous). Hanks is mostly in the shadows, which puts pressure on Talancon, who is stuck with a thinly written role: Amy never makes any connections between her run of bad luck and the guy she can tell is a lying maniac. A caption tries to sell it as a serious social issue film, but – despite the gadgetry – it's the same old psycho-targets-hottie plot.

ALTERNATIVE 3 (1977)

I caught the last half of this ITV mock-doc when it was first aired and was semi-fooled for five minutes before recognising the voice of Scott Tracy (Shane Rimmer) as one of the 'real' people interviewed. Like Orson Welles' *War of the Worlds*, *Ghostwatch* and *The Blair Witch Project*, it set off a huffy controversy about the ethics of using the form of non-fiction news reportage/documentary to tell a scary tale – though, as usual, the percentage of folks taken in was fairly low. The point is to sow seeds of doubt rather than whip up genuine alarm – a tactic always wilfully misunderstood by newspapers which habitually run irresponsible scare stories but throw fits when other media playfully or satirically get in on the act. In retrospect, the creepiest press response comes from the critic who could accept covert moon bases and life detected on Mars, but 'saw through' the scam because it depended on the ridiculous premise of climate change rendering Earth uninhabitable.

The 50-minute special purports to be part of bluntly titled documentary series *Science Report* (other episodes are elusive) and spins a dull story of the 'brain drain' (UK scientists lured to work overseas by more money and better facilities) into a suggestive thread about boffins who have mysteriously disappeared. An astronomer who dies in a Silkwoodesque car crash leaves a scrambled video eventually cleaned up (a precedent-setting *Blowup*-with-video trick later seen in *No Way Out*, *The Last Broadcast* and others) to show a joint US-Russian space probe landing on Mars in 1962 and something wriggling under the red dust. A drunken ex-astronaut (Rimmer) confesses that the Apollo missions were all for PR because there were bases on the moon well before Armstrong got there. The frightening aspect, informed by then-recent weather anomalies (the drought of 1976), is that the covert space program is a way off the planet for an elite few when climate change kills everyone else. This may have been the first time the case for global warming was put in a TV documentary, with a simple diagram and explanation of the term 'greenhouse effect'.

Hosted by newsreader Tim Brinton, it sometimes feels clunky – actors had yet to learn the trick of faking vox pops, and interviews with evasive or forthcoming witnesses are obviously scripted – though there are in-jokes at the plodding TV documentary mannerisms. The title is explained by a pipe-smoking don (Richard Marner) who admits the first two alternatives (reduce consumption or population growth) are unthinkable; it refers to 'getting the hell off this planet while we still can'.

THE AMITYVILLE HAUNTING (2011)

'IT'S NOT ENTERTAINMENT, AND WE'RE NOT PACKAGING IT AS SUCH.'

This Asylum knockoff welds the *Amityville Horror* plot to the *Paranormal Activity* format. Another family, so strapped financially that the only good-sized home they can afford is haunted, move into the DeFeo/Lutz house, though of course this doesn't spring for a location even approximating the famous gabled windows. Tyler Benson (Devin Clark), a teenage annoyance, insists on filming everything, and ex-military dad Douglas (Jason Williams) eventually puts up spy cameras which catch ghostly apparitions not noticed in real life. These ghosts show up on some but not all cameras – do they distinguish between .avi and .mpeg formats, or what? The teenage daughter (Nadine Crocker) is a troublemaker who sneaks off with boys, but her younger sister (Gracie Largent) makes friends with a dead kid no one else can see and mom (Amy Van Horne) whines even before paraphenomena kick in. As in *The Amityville Horror*, being haunted turns dad into a tyrant – he becomes a mad martinet barking military orders – and as in *Paranormal Activity* folk are mangled by invisible forces or possessed to kill. Directed sans credit by Geoff Meed.

ARE YOU SCARED? (2006)

A combined rip-off of *My Little Eye*, *Cube* and (mostly) *Saw*. A group of young folks who have applied to be on a reality TV show called *Are You Scared?* wake up in a disused factory and are forced to take part in gruesome stunts which invariably involve mutilation or death (and nasty gadgets). A disfigured mastermind (Brent Fidler) sits at a bank of screens, watching squirming, bleeding victims fail to deal with challenges which involve confronting 'their greatest fears' and being drilled, blasted, acid-burned or mangled. Heroine Kelly (Alethea Kutscher) realises the show-runner is her abusive father. Meanwhile, some cops who have covered previous crimes by the same culprit try to track down the killer. The most elaborate trap involves twins strapped to chairs with automated drills aimed at their skulls. Written and directed by Andy Hurst.

ARE YOU SCARED 2 (TRACKED) (2009)

Are You Scared was a melange of *My Little Eye* and *Saw*; this unrelated picture – bought up and released as a sequel – is *My Little Eye* and *The Most Dangerous Game*. It's a shame the original title was dropped, since its multiple meanings are the cleverest thing about it. Two couples yomp into the woods on what they think is a treasure hunt but have been suckered into a net-based snuff game. Masked madmen show up to torture and kill them at the behest of a growling controller (Tony Todd) who sits surrounded by screens, chatting with his tortoise or playing etch a sketch (which prompts him to try a Caribbean accent). When the kids find an old house in the woods, the fact that there's a severed arm on the table counts for less than the big pile of cash lying around – they keep thinking this is all a gag until much too late in the day. The horrors aren't that imaginative – the whiny one (Andrea Monier) is separated from the group, stripped to her undies, hung up and carved on (she actually says the stock torture-porn line 'Why are you doing this to me?'). The other three (Kathy Gardiner, Tristan Wright, Chad Guerrero) wander around the surprisingly big house, dodging killers, caught on camera ('I'm sick of being part of someone's game.') and trying to figure out an escape. Finally, the controller gives the survivor a lecture about kangaroos and philosophy. 'There's no worse predator on Earth than a human being,' the controller muses. 'This is one of the biggest underground websites in the world… you understand, it's bigger than porn!' It's not clear from the editing whether Todd was actually on set with the other actors. Written and directed by John Lands (no, *not* John Landis) and Russell Appling.

THE BAY (2012)

> 'I'VE GOT A TOWN FULL OF
> **DEAD BODIES.'**
> 'A SMALL TOWN. REALLY, I THINK
> WE NEED TO KEEP THINGS IN
> PERSPECTIVE HERE.'

Barry Levinson's found footage eco-horror tract spins a monster movie from the real-life pollution scandal that the Chesapeake Bay is 40% dead. Traumatised rookie TV reporter Donna (Kether Donohue – whose name rhymes with that of the star of the sub-genre's breakthrough, *The Blair Witch Project*) narrates to camera and in voice-over, purportedly assembling footage kept from the public since a 2009 disaster in the Maryland coastal resort of Claridge (the film was actually shot in South Carolina).

Inside the Chinese box structure are 1970s clichés like the mayor (Frank Deal) responsible for the pollution – a huge amount of steroid-laden chickenshit from his battery farm has been dumped in the bay – doing the *Jaws* thing by not calling off the 4th of July festivities even as the death toll climbs. The pollutants cause isopods – which start as leech-like grubs and turn into insectile crustaceans – to grow rapidly, eating people from the inside and the outside (as in *The Flesh Eaters*). The reporter wanders through the escalating disaster filming it. Other threads follow local cops responding to what are first thought to be murders, an overworked ER doctor who gets no help from FEMA or the CDC, a suffering teenager who yammers on her mobile phone as things get worse, and a yuppie couple with baby who cross the bay in a yacht to catch the fireworks display and turn up to find the town eerily abandoned.

Tipped in are events from a few weeks before, in which oceanologists studying the bay become early victims, showing that the authorities already knew what might happen and chose to ignore it. Sly humour, like the beauty queen who foreshadows her own bloody fate with 'I think it's every girl's dream to be Miss Crustacean,' and Donna's embarrassment over the tight trousers she was wearing that day (they are *very* tight), offsets the real anger, which relates to the US's patchy record in responding to anything from global warming to Hurricane Katrina. Screenwriter Michael Wallach co-wrote the story with Levinson and throws in some bitter ironies: the main villain dies in a regular car crash he would have survived if the emergency services weren't overwhelmed by monsters. A-lister Levinson, making one of his smaller personal projects, isn't too fastidious to hold back on jump scares – there's a good shock as yummy mummy Stephanie (Kristen Connolly) is surprised by a demented infectee in the back seat of the car she has requisitioned to escape.

BE MY CAT: A FILM FOR ANNE (2016)

This celebrity obsessed found footage redo of *Peeping Tom* boasts a relentless, committed performance from Romanian writer-director Adrian Tofei as a would-be filmmaker who talks non-stop to the camera in English. The film is supposed to be a video communiqué to the Hollywood actress Anne Hathaway, who Adrian wants in his dream project (and, perhaps, life). Adrian has engaged three actresses for what they think is an actual movie to show how he conceives of his realistic film *Be My Cat* – for a while, they're more annoyed that this isn't a real job than afraid of an unstable, filthy-teethed weirdo who is prepared to drug, bind and murder them to impress Anne Hathaway with his vision. The women (Alexandra Stroe, Florentina Hariton, Sonia Teodoriu) react differently and come to varied fates (Hariton, who commits the 'crime' of having put on too much weight to get into a Catwoman outfit, is treated worst), but this is Tofei's film throughout – which means viewers putting up with the all-too-convincing appalling creep well beyond when any character point has been made. Like many inside-the-mind-of-a-psycho movies, it wallows in male self-pity in a way that tends to support his view that his victims are little more than dolls to be dressed up or dissected. The film's final girl does (perhaps) talk Adrian out of killing her, but the improv chatter of the scene defuses any suspense involved.

BLACKOUT (2013)

Few studies of the found footage horror film pay much attention to the UK TV tradition of scaremongering mock-documentary, though *The War Game* and *Ghostwatch* are well known. Written and directed by Ben Chanan (*Cyberbully*), this Channel 4 feature postulates a cyber-attack on the United Kingdom which takes down the national grid. Backup generators come online for emergency services, but eventually fail – leading to tough triages at hospitals. Selected authentic news footage from riots and disasters fills in the picture of panic and rising savagery. Mini-stories are told by folk who record themselves even as batteries run low over the week without power. A girl survives a car crash and tries to persuade hospital authorities her brother isn't brain dead and unplugworthy… some louts record their thievery of cars and petrol… a single mother and child accept a lift from a plausible offender whose electronic ankle-monitor just turned off… and a middle-class self-sufficiency smuggo with a generator blogs an almost-pleased rant about how unprepared everyone else is. News gets out about his resources and he's besieged and robbed, evoking the classic *Twilight Zone* episode 'The Shelter'. In a hackneyed but bluntly effective climax, the lights come back on just as the now-deranged blogger is battering a derelict to death in a battle over scraps in a looted-out supermarket. It defaults to melodrama, which undermines the sober documentary angle but makes for more entertaining horrors. We don't see much of the authorities (a post-riots David Cameron speech is usefully recycled), but the *War Game* tradition is followed in suggesting that in a hypothetical crisis they would be overwhelmed and inept.

BLACK WATER VAMPIRE (2013)

Many horror films are inspired by *The Blair Witch Project*, but few are as close to being a remake as *Black Water Vampire* – though it eventually comes up with an onscreen monster and plays a different (if hardly original) game in the climax. Student filmmaker Danielle (Danielle Lozeau), who mentions in passing that she's taken one of those Christian vows of premarital abstinence, and her producer friend Andrea (Andrea Monier) drag cocky camera guy Anthony (Anthony Fanelli) and nervy asthmatic sound guy Rob (Robin Steffen) into the snowy woods around Black Water, VA, to visit a site where drained-of-blood dead girls have been found over the years. Raymond Banks (Bill Oberst Jr), a creepy local, was convicted of the killings and is interviewed being freaky on death row. In the woods, the filmmakers get lost, have to stay extra nights, squabble, find creepy signs (a sigil drawn on their tent and trees), split up, become hysterical, recriminate – until a Nosferatu-look creature (Brandon deSpain) is spotted hanging upside down in a tree. The last reel features a vampire cult and a perhaps-predictable fate for the virgin protagonist. Obnoxious chatter stands in for characterisation, but the woods look pretty. Written and directed by Evan Tramel.

THE BORDERLANDS (FINAL PRAYER) (2013)

This UK found footage film inclines more to ghostliness than wandering-in-woods, though the panicky climax goes underground (cave-like tunnels are a Brit-horror trope from *The Descent* to *Kill List*). Surveillance is set up by techie Gray (Robin Hill), a lay person working with a covert Catholic agency to investigate a supposed miracle in a West Country church (a cross falling over during a Christening). Deacon (Gordon Kennedy) is a dour, hard-drinking, non-collar-wearing priest traumatised by a bad experience in Brazil. Angry enough to punch out a local hoodie who gets on his (and our) nerves, Deacon is an interesting, articulate protagonist. Less delineated are a by-the-book superior (Aidan McArdle) and a veteran church ghost-chaser (Patrick Godfrey), while the local priest (Luke Neal) exits (from the tower) before his motives become apparent. The early manifestations seem a little mild and it's never clear why anyone would think something poltergeisting off a table counts as a miracle, but the talk is good. Gray and Deacon debate the weirdnesses and generally address the nature of faith and doubt. It's scare-light until the climax, which winds up with the leads swallowed by the earth as a tunnel becomes horribly organic. Written and directed by Elliot Goldner, with a hefty thanks to additional writers Sean Hogan and James Moran.

THE BURIED SECRET OF M. NIGHT SHYAMALAN (2004)

A problem arose when there was a two-hour documentary slot for a tie-in with a film (*The Village*) which wanted to keep plot details secret until its release – which was solved by this sly bit of metafiction. However, it's too long to be a good joke and too shallow to be much else. Director Nathaniel Kahn, coming off *My Architect*, is in Philadelphia to do a SciFi Channel doc on director-writer M. Night Shyamalan. He has trouble with the touchy, reticent subject – 'Night' walks off in a quiet huff but has his publicist (Ilana Levine, who played a similar role in *Tanner '88*) do the tantrum – and finds access blocked. Delving into the director's background, Kahn unearths personal material (a childhood drowning experience, a haunting, some symbolic crows) which relate to his best known films (no one mentions *Praying With Anger* and *Wide Awake*). It would be more effective if the film claimed *terrible* things about its subject (that he's a possessed alien supervillain who sacrifices people to gain success, say) rather than slightly spooky stuff. On the plus side, Kahn and Shyamalan (very subtly sending himself up) give naturalistic performances. Johnny Depp is funny as himself, dropping ominous hints about why he backed out of being in *Signs*.

THE BURNINGMOORE INCIDENT (REALITY KILLS) (2010)

> 'MR LANGFORD HAD NO WAY OF KNOWING HE WAS ABOUT TO TATTOO A KILLER.'

This found footage horror features relatively blue-collar characters rather than the usual whiny students, and at least tries to address the ethics of exploitative docutainment.

Family man James Parrish (Geoff Tate) has freaked out, got a weird tattoo, murdered his whole family and disappeared. *Gettin' Hammered*, a home improvement reality show, films an episode in the abandoned house in Queens where the anoraked killer is hiding. Quite a bit of time is spent on arguments among the builders and the film crew, which are occasionally credible: a workman is told he can't play his 'tunes' because music will make the footage hard to edit (expensive music rights aren't mentioned), the macho builders are embarrassed that they need a makeup girl. Then characters get bludgeoned or stabbed in the basement, and the rampage goes into overdrive after a building inspector (Vincent Palma, seizing a one-scene bit and taking it to the limit) tries to shut them down. Late in the day, the producer discovers he has footage of all the killings from the fixed cameras in the house and tries to get his appalled presenter to keep doing narration because this true crime racket is more lucrative than a home makeover show. Written by J. Andrew Colletti and director Jonathan Williams.

CAMP DREAD (2014)

With this post-modern slasher movie writer-director B. Harrison Smith (*The Fields*) riffs on the '80s likes of the *Friday the 13th* series (though its real reference, down to casting Felissa Rose as a scream queen, is *Sleepaway Camp*) while tapping into post-*Scream* concerns like reality TV. Despite opening and closing with audition tapes, it's not quite a found footage film – indeed, the characters *think* they're being filmed all the time, but might not be. Julian Barrett (Eric Roberts), once-successful producer-director of the *Summer Camp* series, hauls mixed-up teenagers out of rehab or the justice system ostensibly for a work-release counselling program, then tells them they're competing in a reality show extension of his film franchise with a million-dollar prize to the sole survivor. The nastiest twist – that Barrett has been paid by parents to murder inconvenient or unpleasant kids – is clever, signalled early on when the most sympathetic girl (Nicole Cinaglia) admits she is here because she killed the golden boy brother who was raping her and her parents took his side. Roberts is value for money in a more substantial role than his frequent take-the-cheque exploitation efforts. *Halloween*ie Danielle Harris has a guest turn as a sheriff who hasn't seen many horror movies, which sets up a funny, cruel punch line. However, the kids – required by the plot to be more unpleasant even than the usual slasher victims – still manage to be more irritating than interesting. The kills are acceptably gruesome, if not that inspired.

CLASSROOM 6 (2015)

Among the poorest found footage films, this lifts (as usual) from *Paranormal Activity* and *The Blair Witch Project* – but keeps sabotaging its own premise by over-employing zooms and shaky-cam jitters (well before the purportedly scary stuff starts), though the footage is supposedly shot for broadcast by an aspiring TV news team. After disappearances from 'Classroom 6, Building H' and rumours of portals to other dimensions, ambitious presenter Annie Monroe (Valentina Kolaric) takes psychic Jack Dogget (Mike McLaughlin) and a constantly complaining crew to spend the night without permission on school premises to document paranormal phenomena. Everyone argues from the outset and is remarkably bad at their jobs. The psychic's main investigative tool is throwing tennis balls into empty classrooms in the hope that a spook will toss one back. The backstory is vague, Annie and her associates have no interesting shades, and all the ramped-up hysteria and pointing-the-camera-at-the-floor gambits fail to disguise the fact that nothing frightening happens. Yet again, it's established at the outset that the characters have disappeared, so there isn't even a token interest in seeing who gets out of the school alive. Written and directed by Jonas Odenheimer.

THE DARKEST DAWN (2016)

A sequel to director-writer-star Drew Casson's found footage debut *Hungerford*, a small town invasion saga. Bigger in scope, this still sticks with first-person camera, borrowing from *28 Days Later* and *Cloverfield*, but closer in tone and achievement to *The Zombie Diaries*. Suburban Chloe (Bethan Leadley) gets a video camera for her sixteenth birthday and documents family life in fits and starts – until news comes in of strange happenings in Hungerford. Vast oblong spaceships appear in the skies, deploying death-rays and metal bugs which turn folks into killer zombies. Chloe and her nurse sister Sam (Cherry Wallis) are shocked when their father is zombified and quick-killed by the army, then get semi-abducted by the weasely, paranoid Bob (Stuart Ashen) – who takes them into underground tunnels and is plainly intent on exploiting them. The survivor band from *Hungerford* – Cowan (Casson), Adam (Tom Scarlett) and Kipper (Sam Carter) – show up, having abandoned their own filming, and the sisters team up with them to make their way through the ruins of London (impressively managed for the low budget) and out onto the Thames.

The alien enemy is a remote threat, and the protagonists have more immediate trouble with rotten humanity. Plot threads about a McGuffin device which might be the key to defeating the invaders, Chloe's unusual blood type and Adam's missing-in-action girlfriend Philippa (Georgia Bradley) are somewhat mangled in the telling. Leadley is excellent as Chloe, who keeps filming in the hope that her record will reach her lost mother, credibly veering from jaunty to demented in extreme circumstances, while the rest of the cast are hit-and-miss. Casson, who co-scripted with producer Jess Cleverly, goes for ruthlessness and shock, but that mode peaks in an early encounter with a band of thugs who use a child as a lure then play 'keep or kill' with the charitable souls they trap ('There are people upriver who make us look like fucking Pudsey Bear')… leaving the squaddies who are the main menace of the last half of the film without a new act, even as a wild-eyed, gun-toting creep (Jamie Paul) becomes the chief villain. It's implied that various baddies want to make sex slaves of the sisters, but the film is a little coy about the nature of their nastiness. A few quiet moments are less effective than the chaotic battle scenes.

DAYLIGHT (2013)

This found footage film plays an unusually complex game. Social worker Jennifer Bacon (Jennifer Borman) is accompanied by videographers David (David McCracken) and Josh (Josh Riedford) on a linked set of cases. Early on, Jennifer is bitten by a rabid child, then gets involved in the case of Susan Ellroy (Jeanine Cameron), a once-bright fourteen-year-old who has become hostile and self-harming. She seems to be in an abusive relationship with 'Mike and Gabe', who turn out not to be louts but archangels. Suspicious of an older priest (Patrick J. Andersen) involved in the case, Jennifer and the guys make connections to a failed exorcism, a comatose abusive priest, a boy who committed suicide and Sydney Irons (Sydney Morris), a little girl who appears to be possessed. At mid-way point, the recording is broken up by footage from a happier Sydney's birthday party – previously-taped footage showing through – and *Paranormal Activity* night-cam stuff taken by her sister (Gretchin Irons). With escalating chaos, backstory tumbles out at the isolated Irons home, the body count rises and the past starts to show up on film. It's mostly jittery camerawork, improv performances and a near-Shane Carruth level of storytelling-by-implication, but has solid scares like the sudden leaning-into-frame of a character not previously established as on site, the addition of CGI disaster and horror effects to shaky frames and a mass appearance by spooky kids. DP Kaidan Tremain shares the director credit with Joel Townsend and McCracken, who also co-wrote.

DAY OF THE MUMMY (2014)

'I CHARGE EXTRA WHEN A CURSED MUMMY IS INVOLVED.'

So… finally, a found footage mummy movie. Now there only needs to be a found footage invisible man movie and a found footage hunchbacked minion movie to complete the set. The bad news is that this is 76 minutes long and the mummy – a spindly, snarly, vicious bastard which looks great for a low-budget creature – doesn't show up until 62 minutes in. Previously, we've had wandering in the desert (pretty) and wandering in tunnels (yawn). Roguish Egyptologist Jack Wells (William McNamara) wears glasses-cam with an inbuilt transmitter and his boss Carl Rosencane (Danny Glover, playing his entire role sat at a desk) pops up in a small window in the corner of the screen to keep an eye on the expedition. Wells is looking for the tomb of the cursed Neferu (Brandon de Spain), who was mummified alive by his pharaoh brother, to get hold of a big valuable diamond (the Kodek Stone) interred with him. Producer Andrea Mornier plays a tough chick along for the trip. Egypt is played by Venezuela. Scripted by Garry Charles (*Cute Little Buggers 3D*). Directed by Johnny Tabor (*Eaters*).

DEMONIC (2015)

A catchall of 2010s horror styles: a haunted house/mass murder/demonic possession drama, with police procedural and found footage elements. It's also among a number of films in which finding footage is a part of the plot.

Cop Mark Lewis (Frank Grillo) and his shrink girlfriend Dr Klein (Maria Bello) investigate deaths in a house which was the site decades ago of similar murders. They view footage filmed by obnoxious director wannabe Bryan (Scott Mechlowicz), who nudges handsome plank John (Dustin Milligan), son of the survivor of the earlier massacre, and his girlfriend Michelle (Cody Horn) into a séance to capture paraphenomena digitally. The back-and-forth between the investigation and the evening-which-went-wrong is further complicated because the killings are a re-enactment of the earlier massacre. Mysteries involving John's mother and the credited previous killer are solved, and there's a tricksy misdirection as to who is wearing the glasses-cam on which the axe-slayings are recorded. In a beginner's screenwriting tic, random characters are well up on historical architecture, so they can explain porch gas lamps and milk-chutes to set up horror moments involving these features. Meanwhile, kids need parapsychology terms everyone who's seen a ghost movie knows explained to them.

Top-billed Grillo and Bello bring gravitas to roles strictly beneath their talents – Lewis and Klein, who call off a date to poke around the crime scene, aren't involved in the meat of the movie, which takes place earlier in the evening and is full of good-looking actors playing rote, annoying kids. Megan Park is the token sexy new-agey blonde believer, while Aaron Yoo is yet another Asian techie who gets killed early. These are all folks we've seen before – and in the case of the needlessly assholish Bryan, the heroine's ex-boyfriend who takes every opportunity to snipe at John, have long since lost patience with. Directed by Will Canon (*Brotherhorn*) from a script devised with Max La Bella and Doug Simon

THE DEN (2013)

For me, one of the least fun ways of watching a movie is a vimeo link, which feels a lot like sitting at a desk working. This is a rare case where it's the optimal viewing mode: *The Den* imitates a 76-minute computer desktop capture the way *The Last Horror Movie* imitated a rental VHS. Elizabeth (Melanie Papalia) has a grant to study online chat, focusing on a site called The Den. A parade of idiots (one NYC cycling-with-a-webcam stunt is great), pervs (real and muppet penises) and scammers gives way to a campaign of stalking. Witnessing live-streamed snuff, Elizabeth calls the cops but gets little help. Her remote-hacked computer switches on to record boyfriend Damien (David Schlachtenhaufen) going down on her – a clip then emailed to her course advisor (Saidah Arrika Ekulona) and the faculty approving her grant. Damien disappears and his apartment is stripped, but the police still don't take Elizabeth's paranoia seriously. Her laptop drive is wiped, her best friend (Lily Holleman) is snatched by a scarecrow-masked goon and shows up with slit wrists, and her pregnant sister (Anna Margaret

Hollyman) is menaced. Paranoia escalates, with creepy stuff glimpsed on screen while Liz happens to be looking away. Suspicion is cast around supposed allies like a cop (Matt Reidy) who disapproves of the unmarried sister being pregnant and a computer-savvy friend (Adam Shapiro) irritated by the jittery heroine's ingratitude. However, the big reveal is mundanely familiar (cf: *Cradle of Fear*, *My Little Eye*) and this boils down to yet another movie in which a woman is tortured (she does a spell in a *Saw*-like derelict bathroom with a webcam bolted to her head) for no real reason. With the next victim set up, a coda pulls back from the screen (objective camera style) to show a consumer selecting death clips from a menu of offerings. Co-written by Lauren Thompson and director Zachary Donohue.

THE DEVIL'S MUSIC (2008)

'IF THE DEVIL'S GOT ALL THE BEST TUNES, WHY DO ALL THE BOY BANDS FUCKING SUCK?'

Sometimes tagged a horror version of *This is Spinal Tap*, this is closer in tone and sensibility to *Bob Roberts*, asking the viewer to tease out a sinister storyline behind its music industry in-jokes. Band-members, PR folk, critics, psychologists and passersby are interviewed about Erika Spawn, an 'extreme' horror rock act fronted by Angela Lee (Victoria Hopkins). Shaky-cam footage documents the band's last European tour, when seemingly timid groupie Stef Regan (Lucy Dunn) stabs Angela/Erika during a concert, precipitating a burst of tabloid paranoia which urges the singer to become even more extreme. Erika, the sort of wild grrl who pulls a straight-razor on a TV interviewer, is contrasted with Robin Harris (Scott Thomas), an ex-boyband crooner who has become a middle-of-the-road entertainer (he pulls a rose on *his* interviewer). Following the old saw that Cliff would make a more devastating Antichrist than Elvis, dreadful events connected with Erika Spawn – which run to a nightclub massacre carried out by supposed fans – are part of a master plan by the covertly demonic Harris to ensure his rise to perhaps-political, perhaps-cultural power on an 'All Our Futures' platform.

Writer-director Pat Higgins (*TrashHouse*, *Hellbride*) constructs this especially well: the mock-doc trick, all the way back to *Citizen Kane*, is to give snapshots which make up a mosaic with vital pieces missing or open to differing interpretations. When she comes to believe Harris is behind the violence which has wrecked her life (but helped her record sales), Angela/Erika breaks into his home and tortures him on camera. News media which condemn the fake violence of her act are happy to run colour photos of her genuine bloody rampage 'in the public interest'. Hopkins and Thomas are credible in performance, interview and supposedly candid footage. Good work also from Dunn (quietly setting the camera to record her stabbing attempt from the wings), Cy Henty as Erika's intense manager Eddie Meachum (still astonished that his first reaction to the onstage attempted murder of his client was to ask her attacker if she was all right), Alan Ronald as the Scots drummer who doesn't take it seriously until too late, and (especially) Jess-Luisa Flynn as 'excellent bassist'/'nightmare human being' Adele Black who provides a sceptical, penetrating, funny take on the story while missing all the salient points.

DIGGING UP THE MARROW (2014)

In the TV series *Holliston* and witty little films shot for FrightFest, Adam Green plays a version of himself... Here, in an even more meta manner, he plays *another* version of himself, who has all his IMDb credits but is as dangerously obsessive about a documentary project as Heather Donohue in *The Blair Witch Project*. Drawing on an anecdote about an oddly obsessive fan of *Hatchet* and an art project by monster designer Alex Pardee, the film finds Green distracted from the work his company should be doing by William Dekker (Ray Wise), a retired detective who claims a society of monsters (human freaks who have crawled off to make lives for themselves) exists in an underground space he calls the Marrow.

In found footage style, the first expedition to a park after nightfall yields nothing which shows up on film. Dekker keeps saying things are moving in the shadows and spins anecdotes about creatures shown in artwork (by Pardee). Hints are dropped that Dekker has a son among the outcasts and that 'some of them' are dangerous. Just when it seems this is all sizzle and no steak, a physical effects creature makes a shock appearance. Green sticks with the project, though his business partner (Will Barratt) and wife (Rileah Vanderbilt) are sceptical or wary and his friend Kane Hodder dismisses the monster on video as special effects. The spine of the film is the shifting relationship between Dekker, a manipulative fraud but onto something, and Green, who wants to believe in monsters but often forgets that they are, after all, monsters. On learning that Dekker approached every other horror director in Hollywood (Tom Holland and Mick Garris play themselves) and was turned down, Green's reaction is priceless: feeling foolish at falling for something, showing a glint of pride at sensing a truth his peers missed, yet neurotically resentful that he was literally last on the list.

More monsters appear, springing several *Jeepers Creepers* surprises (a frill of snakes, a scary face with a silly mask tattooed on its bald head), evoking the creature outcast societies of *Nightbreed* and the *Basket Case* sequels. It gets serious near the end, as Dekker disappears from his rented house and is discovered in a cage underground, taking back everything he's said and denying that creatures exist, before presences manifest in Green's home. It's witty, pointed, makes interesting use of the docu-format, springs well timed scares and has nice practical effects monster designs. With Tony Todd, Lloyd Kaufman, Don Coscarelli, Joe Lynch and the late Dave Brockie (Oderus Urungus).

THE DINOSAUR PROJECT (2012)

This bluntly titled bit of *Blair Witch*ery – it's not even *The Dinosaur Diaries* – is a found footage 'lost world' movie. As in *The Lost World* (1960), explorers reach the land where dinos live by helicopter (then disabled, to keep the story going) rather than slog through trackless jungle, following a crumbly map, as in the 1912 Conan Doyle novel, which came at the end of the era when enough unexplored stretches of the globe remained to accommodate fictional lost worlds.

It opens with news footage about M'kele M'bembe, 'the African Loch Ness Monster', which might be a plesiosaur (it was a brontosaurus in *Baby: The Secret of the Lost Legend*). Indiana Jones hat-wearing cryptozoologist Marchant (Richard Dillane) leads an expedition into the Congo, with a wormy sidekick who shows signs of incipient psychosis (Peter Brooke), disposable film-crew folk and a guide who is blatantly trying to direct them to the wrong place. Marchant's fifteen-year-old techie son Luke (Matt Kane) stows away in the chopper, a development which feels like something from a 1950s kids' book. The boy's clashes with his stern father pad things out until the monsters show up, and then annoyingly keeps going. The found footage tendency to present self-absorbed, constantly chattering characters (fair enough – who else would film everything?) means these people stay focused on not-that-interesting personal troubles when any decent science fiction film would be going, 'Gosh, wow, dinosaurs!' or theorising why evolution has bypassed this region. It's unclear whether the locale here is a hidden valley, a government secret project or a time warp, but the upshot is the same – monsters!

Flying creatures any six-year-old would recognise as pterodactyls – which none of the cryptozoologists or palaeontologists care to name – flap at the helicopter and it goes down in a region swarming with prehistoric life. Though the CGI is just okay – above Syfy Channel, but a long way from *Jurassic Park* – there are still cool creatures: a horde of wing-walking, man-sized vampire bats are the standouts, but a plesiosaur shows up to eat someone and a baby dino (named Crypto) bonds with Luke and saves him from its hungry/angry parents by spitting all over him. The cast are all one-notey, even the dinosaurs – in theory, the plot is that the disapproving father and the rebellious son learn to appreciate each other in extremis (with each prepared to sacrifice for the other), but in practice so much time is spent on them being dicks that any reconciliation is beside the point since it's hard to care whether either survives. The spectacular locations would have benefited from being filmed properly. Written by Tom Pridham, Jay Basu and Sid Bennett; photographed by Pridham; directed by Bennett.

DIRECTOR'S CUT (2016)

An extraordinarily clever – yet wickedly accessible – exercise in runaway metafiction, this represents itself as a 'director's cut' (though it's more like an internet fan edit) with voice-over commentary from Herbert Blount (screenwriter Penn Jillette) of apparently middling *Se7en* knock-off serial-killer thriller *Knocked Off*. Adam Rifkin, the real director of *Director's Cut*, appears as himself, trying to direct the crowdfunded *Knocked Off* as major investor Blount constantly shoots behind-the-scenes footage he interpolates into the finished product. Aptly, *Knocked Off* is about a serial killer who imitates famous crimes by restaging them with new victims… but *Director's Cut* – which is loosely inspired by the 1982 quickie *The Last Horror Film* – shows how jolly-yet-creepy Blount disrupts the shoot by stalking and eventually abducting leading lady Missi Pyle to fashion his own version of the film which bluntly photoshops him in as a leading man and has her play scenes opposite him at gunpoint.

The *Knocked Off* sections are credibly ordinary and slick, with Harry Hamlin,

Hayes MacArthur, Lin Shaye ('The police captain is usually an angry African-American man, but we cast the old lady from *Insidious*.'), Marshall Bell, Nestor Carbonell and Gilbert Gottfried gamely playing as if they were in a direct-to-VOD time-waster. The contrived love affair between cops Winters (Hamlin) and Mabel (Pyle), which enrages the jealous Blount, is as formulaic as the guessable yet ridiculous whodunit angle (perhaps borrowed from nothingy 2005 thriller *The Lost Angel*) is an on-the-nose pastiche, amusingly skewered by the stalker's commentary (as he projects his fantasies onto Pyle and points out continuity errors, fudged plot points and non sequitur cameos). Teller, Jillette's silent magic-act partner, is hauled in as a red herring suspect and pressured to talk, only for Blount to comment, 'This is an in-joke,' before he opens his mouth. A funny strand involves the perils of crowdfunded movies as Rifkin grudgingly hands out dialogue to numerous 'producers' who have paid to appear onscreen – with a stunt- and effects-filled one-take massacre ruined by Blount's terrible delivery of his only scripted line.

Quite remarkably, Jillette creates a memorably grotesque villain in the mostly unseen Blount – whose skewed priorities are apparent as he slows down and freeze-frames ordinary shots of Pyle while fast-forwarding through an elaborate Charles Manson sequence and noisily chomping snacks over dialogue scenes. A self-deluded comic creation, Blount becomes genuinely sinister in the home stretch as he snatches Pyle and works more and more damage on the film to fulfil his fantasy. It's a black comic riff on *Misery* and *King of Comedy*, with up-to-the-minute technology – and explores fresh ground in finding horror and laughs in the way media can be co-opted by fans and remixed for varying purposes. The fact that the tall, long-haired, gravel-voiced, flamboyantly dressed magician stands out in a crowd so much that he's the worst possible film extra or stealth pursuer is funny, but Blount is unpredictable enough to be occasionally pathetic or chilling.

Rifkin has a background in exploitation (directing *Psycho Cop Returns* and *The Invisible Maniac* as 'Rif Coogan' during the VHS boom) and mainstream screenwriting (*Small Soldiers*, *Mouse Hunt*). His auteur ventures (*The Dark Backward*, *The Chase*, *Detroit Rock City*) have a shared universe revisited here (via the fictional Blump products). He often casts B-movie veterans alongside stars from the adult entertainment industry – who here include Bree Olson (from *The Human Centipede III*), Lexi Love and Sophie Dee.

THE DYATLOV PASS INCIDENT (DEVIL'S PASS) (2013)

> 'YOU FOLLOWED A STEP-BY-STEP PLAN THAT LED TO THE DEATHS OF NINE PEOPLE. WHAT DID YOU THINK WOULD HAPPEN?'

Finnish-born Hollywood action specialist Renny Harlin goes low budget for this found footage riff on a well-known Russian mystery from 1959 (which yanks in a well-known American mystery from 1943 by way of explanation).

In 1959, a group of Russian climbers led by Igor Dyatlov died mysteriously in the Ural Mountains. American student Holly (Holly Goss) takes a documentary crew to the spot where the tragedy occurred, hoping for answers. On the team are conspiracy buff Andy (Ryan Hawley), sound girl Denise (Gemma Atkinson) and experienced macho hikers Jenson (Matt Stokoe) and JP (Luke Albright). The *Blair Witch* template is followed exactly in the first two acts, albeit with more extreme weather. On the trail, GPS gadgets go haywire and the kids start getting on each other's nerves. Among the solutions discussed: aliens, yeti, psychological quirks exacerbated by the geography, uranium deposits in the mountains, Soviet era super-soldier experiments. Near the site, Holly finds a door in the mountainside, then the film breaks with the ambiguity and gets into the monsters-in-an-abandoned-facility kick familiar from the *Outpost* series and many other post-Soviet/Nazi exploitation films.

Inside the bunker, Harlin turns on the monster skills honed on *Prison* and *Deep Blue Sea* and a sudden turn involving the *Philadelphia Experiment* (no one mentions the movie) sets up a satisfyingly horrid snake-swallowing-its-tail fate for the survivors. The snowy wastes look great (there's one terrific avalanche), but it's still a slog to get to the bunker with squabbles replicating nearly fifteen years' worth of wandering-to-their-doom movies. The pale, fanged, emaciated, bamfing monsters are a trifle generic set beside the machine-zombie hybrids of the broadly similar *Frankenstein's Army*. Scripted by Vikram Weet.

EMERGO (APARTMENT 143) (2011)

A Spanish movie which does a pretty good imitation of being American, this offers the usual polter-phenomena, plus a thin mystery. Self-pitying Alan White (Kai Lennox), worried that his late wife is haunting the family home, relocates angry teenage daughter Caitlin (Gia Mantegna) and surprisingly well-balanced son Benny (Damian Roman) to a ratty flat in a mostly empty block – if there are neighbours, they're awfully tolerant of the racket – only to find that, as in *Insidious* and the *Paranormal Activity* films, ghostly bother follows them to the new address. Alan calls in slightly-too-glowery academic parapsychologist Dr Helzer (Michael O'Keefe) and his associates, who put up the cameras and get the paranormality on tape. There's much destruction, throwing things about and emotional trauma as it seesaws between blaming the sulky teenager and her scary dead mom (Laura Martuscelli). The twist ending is spoiled, on the DVD I saw, by an onscreen menu. Scripted by Rodrigo Cortés (director of *Buried* and *Red Light*). Directed by Carles Torrens.

LA ENTIDAD (THE ENTITY) (2015)

A Peruvian found footage horror film, which is not strikingly original enough in concept to earn an English-language remake. Aimless film student Joshua (Rodrigo Falla) is urged by his ex-girlfriend Carla (the striking Danielle Mendoza) to make a project about 'reaction videos', internet postings which show people reacting as they watch horrific true-life film clips. With irritating cut-up Benjamin (Mario Gaviria) and more serious Lucas (Carlos Casella), Joshua and Carla investigate a particular clip… only to find that the three people in it have died since witnessing an unspecified horror. The investigation leads them to encounter something nebulous in a graveyard, an escalating series of supernatural phenomena and a rising body count. The backstory involves a woman tortured to death by the Inquisition, and impossible film footage of this in which the various contemporary characters see their own faces when the hood is taken off the garrotted victim. An additional twist beside the familiar found footage doom of stirring up a paranormal hornets' nest and suffering the consequences is set up by a few sly looks and throwaway lines, but requires a flashback montage near the end to make the plot point stick. With broad strokes characterisations, decent half-seen demons and nice use of locations full of arcane clutter (a cavernous university library, the graveyard), it's still pretty rote. Directed by Eduardo Schuldt, scripted by Sandro Ventura from a story by Schuldt.

EPISODE 50 (2011)

> *'HEY GUYS, THE CELEBRITY GUEST STAR HAS ARRIVED, CATCHING GHOSTS WITH SHEER SCOTTISHNESS. ANY GHOSTS COME NEAR ME, THEY'LL BE KILT!'*

Not precisely a found footage film, this is in the same sub-cycle as the *Paranormal Activity* movies and *The Last Exorcism*: it begins as if composed of material shot for a paranormal reality show, but eventually shifts to more conventional objective filming. It harks back beyond its specific moment to *Legend of Hell House*, *Ghostwatch* and *Session 9*. A setup (Episode 49) establishes *Paranormal Inspectors*, a show hosted by Jack Kelley (Josh Folan) and Damon Brown (Chris Parry), who specialise in rational explanations for hauntings. A panicky householder is driven to bash his wife with a hammer under the apprehension that she's a spook, then they sit still (she bandaged in a way few real people would let themselves be filmed) as it's patiently explained that rodents, paint fumes, dodgy homemade wiring and the like are responsible. Then, in the *Hell House* lick, dying millionaire Andrew Worthington Jr (Jim Thalman) commissions the team to go into a decommissioned West Virginia insane asylum (aka 'the Gateway to Hell') which has a rep as the most haunted spot in America to establish whether there's a hell he'll be burning in for all eternity.

Onsite, the *PI* gang of sceptics run into the Academia Spirit Searcher's Club (ASSC), led by floppy haired exorcist Dylan Miller (Keithen Hergott), a rival team of 'believers' hired for balance. Besides the tensions and clashes between the two approaches to the supernatural – which echoes the Friends of Ghosts (FOG) and Scientific Measurement of Ghosts (SMOG) from the old *Avengers* episode 'The Living Dead' – the groups have internal dissents (arch-explainer Jack has a deeply buried trauma and possible psychic experience of his own to cope with) and alliances (the tech guys get together). As usual in these movies, and unlike the tiresome parade of creaks and mutterings that distinguish the uneventful real paranormal tabloid TV shows they evoke, things manifest at a rapid clip: a dead nurse with every bone in her body broken, the psycho Satanist patient who killed her (posing as a lost child ghost, in another *Hell House* bit). There are atrocities and killings – Andi (Natalie Wetta) is given shock treatment to get her to pay attention; medium Lysette (Eleanor Wilson) gets her neck snapped. Also, to shake things up, Kieron (Kieron Elliott) shows up doing a comedy Scots act and then just tries to get out of the danger zone.

Presumably because the location was available, there's an unusual late-in-the-day change. The Satanic portal the dead villain is opening with ritual killings isn't on this site but in the prison – now a museum – where he was confined before he was moved to the asylum, so the survivors hare over to meet their ultimate fate. The big problem is little is new here – even intriguing abandoned institution locations have been done over and over, let alone the mock-doc gimmick. It's reasonably well acted, has okay character beats and a couple of scares – but falls into the crowded too-late-in-the-cycle-to-have-much-impact file. Written by Ian Holt, from a story by directors Joe Smalley and Tess Smalley.

EUROPA REPORT (2013)

This post-millennial space opera is a rare found footage film justified in its technique, since space missions are indeed documented minutely all the time. A mission controller (Embeth Davidtz) narrates to camera, establishing that a private enterprise multi-national mission to Europa, the ice moon of Jupiter, has ended disastrously. The rest of the film has the video look and chattery tone of found footage but is sharply edited (a wealth of material from the mission has been transmitted back to Earth and assembled) and given the benefit of a decent, memorable score by Bear McCreary. Findings suggest the possibility of lakes under the surface of Europa which might support life, and the mission is supposed to check this out... There are no contrived conflicts among the crew, though they don't always agree on courses of action. A tense EVA scene pays off with dour Andrei Blok (Michael Nyqvist) saved despite a rupture in his glove while talkative, charismatic James Corrigan (Sharlto Copley) can't come back inside because he has toxic fuel smeared over his spacesuit... so he drifts off poignantly to his death. On the surface of Europa, things don't go as planned with the ice-drill and Katya Petrovna (Karolina Wydra) has to take an unscheduled surface walk which also ends badly. Fate – or possibly malign intelligence – doesn't want to let the ship leave, and the impressive climax has water spilling into the ship as the longest-surviving astronaut, pilot Rosa Dasque (Anamaria Marinca), diverts power from life support into the communications array so that the mission can at least send home the news that there is life outside the Earth, as demonstrated by a Cthulhoid squid-thing which overwhelms her. It's relatively sober, inventively cast (Daniel Wu and Christian Camargo complete the crew), credible in physical details and effects (the video-look, mimicking footage shot in space, is perhaps even more believable than the effects-heavy spectacle of *Gravity*) and has a good shock at the end. It is perhaps a little thin dramatically, taking its cues from Eastern Bloc SF of the 1960s rather than the hopped up American pulp tradition. Written by Philip Gelatt. Directed by Sebastian Cordero.

EVIDENCE (2012)

'OH MY GOD, IT'S AN ALIEN GORILLA! THAT'S SO SCARY!'

The first half of director Howie Askins' and writer-star Ryan McEvoy's *Evidence* is rote found footage wandering – though it takes off into new sub-generic areas for a busy, exciting climax that sprinkles flash-cut monster action between signature found footage shots like screaming women running ahead of camera through the woods with the cam-light glaring at their backs and jagged edits with low battery signage. Ryan (McCoy) is going camping with his girlfriend Abi (Abigail Richie) and best bud Brett (Brett Rosenberg) plus Abi's friend Ashley (Ashley Bracken) and shooting a non-specific documentary about their flyblown, grumbling antics in the wood. Omens pile up: a dead fish well away from water, a black bush in the distance that suddenly lopes, cries in the night, an armed and creepy passerby at the campfire. Then, however, after the RV is trashed and Brett goes missing, the film gets wilder, with briefly seen monsters (long-armed, glowy eyed, shaggy-coated things), mad science conducted at a remote facility, soldiers either fighting the monsters or rescuing civilians, zombie-like mad people, a pregnant woman in a basement spawning mini-monsters and extreme splatter deaths.

EVIDENCE (2013)

Another variation on the found footage premise, not to be confused with *Evidence* (2012). Writer John Swetnam sketched the idea in *Evidence* (2011), a short which he directed; presumably, he couldn't bear to change the title between that draft and this finished film, directed by Olatunde Osunsanmi (*WithIN*, *The Fourth Kind*) – though a caption at the beginning suggests it might have been called *The Unblinking Eye* at some stage. It opens like *Hostage*, with an elaborate CGI shot tracking through a freeze-frame junkyard in the aftermath of a massacre. In conventional filmmaking style, cops Burquez (Radha Mitchell) and Reese (Stephen Moyer) go over the footage found in cameras and phones discovered at the site. All this framing hints at how it's going to turn out. Ostensibly, director Rachel (Caitlin Stasey) is shooting a documentary about her aspiring actress friend Leann (Torrey DeVitto), which includes the embarrassing moment when her musician boyfriend Tyler (Nolan Gerard Funk) proposes to her in public just after she's starred in a play and is turned down. Tyler still shows up for a bus trip to Vegas, but the bus crashes in the desert thanks to a hidden trap. The driver (Harry Lennix) and other passengers – a mystery woman not on the manifest (Dale Dickey) who has a bag of cash, a runaway teenage conjurer (Albert Kuo) and a Russian dancer (Svetlana Metkina) – are stranded. A killer in a welding mask picks them off, and the footage fragments to convey the horrid deaths. Close analysis reveals a culprit, but the tagline ('Witnesses lie – the camera doesn't') suggests another solution. Even as the cops go over the footage, it leaks onto the internet and Reese realises it's edited to mislead – at the end, the mystery snuffmakers promise, 'You can be in the sequel.' It's half-clever, well acted in general and has nasty flashes of horror, but its cynical smugness is hard to warm up to.

EVIL THINGS (2009)

A *Blair Witchy* effort, with a tiny video surveillance twist at the end; it deviates from the template only to lift business (predator POV through greenish night-vision goggles as a lone woman gropes around in the dark) from *The Silence of the Lambs*. Miriam (Elyssa Mersdorf) and her four best friends head to her aunt's snowbound upstate New York house to celebrate her eighteenth birthday. Leo (Ryan Maslyn) brings along his camcorder and compulsively chronicles the trip, though one of his friends makes the well-stated point that no one would want to play back and remember much of what he films – Tanya (Torrey Weiss) is car-sick, for instance. On the road, the kids think a red van is stalking them. When Mark (Morgan Hooper) comes back from warning off the driver, he doesn't want to talk about it. The quintet go from best pals to bickering whiners when they can't find the house or, later, go on a woodland walk and get lost. In the last act, a video cassette is delivered which shows that the van-stalker has been filming them too, then person or persons unknown invade the house. It doesn't take the easy explicit murder route, and gets its best shocks from doors closing or lights going out. Enough grace moments show the kids aren't total bastards who deserve what's coming to them – default lead Cassy (Laurel Casillo) does a sustained impersonation of Leo's Italian mother which fills out the mostly unseen cameraman's character – and their squabbles and dumb moves are all too credible. It's presented as a piece of FBI evidence, so the conclusion is foregone. Written and directed by Dominic Perez.

EVP (2012)

This first person camera film begins with writer-producer-director-star Kevin Duncan explaining Electronic Voice Phenomena. To research a script on the subject, Duncan visits a haunted Scots cemetery with a cassette recorder to ask questions on the grave of a supposed vampire's victim. This takes six minutes, followed by an equally lengthy subjective shot which involves cycling out to the cemetery to do the experiment… which doesn't seem to yield results, though the protagonist (very seldom seen onscreen) does crack up in a way that suggests this might be a veiled adaptation of 'Whistle and I'll Come to You'. Duncan also admits to taking smart drugs and might just be having a breakdown. A psycho doppelgänger in a Pennywise killer-clown mask pops up very occasionally. The first person thing is hard to read – has the character strapped a camera to his head, or is this just the way Duncan shows his POV, which includes a lengthy period spent hiding under the bed where all his DVDs are stacked (he has empty shelves where they probably used to be) and a lot of wandering about the flat? The problem is that it's hard to relate to a character we see so seldom and this just emerges as an amateur Michael Snow movie, probing into space – messages are written in childish scrawl or drawing on the walls sometimes, and there might be a murder (just like in Snow's *Wavelength*). It's a demanding watch for meagre reward, though it deserves credit for working its nexus of art and exploitation and being relentless about it.

THE EXECUTION OF GARY GLITTER (2009)

'I DON'T THINK THEY REALLY SHOULD HAVE THE DEATH PENALTY, BUT I THINK HE SHOULD DIE.'

It's a British television tradition, all the way back to *The War Game*, to use science fiction to debate current events. Remembering the lesson of Orson Welles' 1938 *War of the Worlds* radio broadcast, this essay features onscreen announcements throughout that it's not a news program but a made-up story set in a parallel world where, after the Soham child murders of 2002, the UK government bowed to public pressure and reintroduced the death penalty for murder and child rape.

Paul Francis Gadd, aka pop singer Gary Glitter (Hilton McRae), is repatriated after serving a sentence for child sex offences in a Vietnamese jail (which happened in the real world). He finds himself on trial at the Old Bailey on what is now a capital offence (which is fiction). Presented as a fly-on-the-wall documentary, it's less insistent about seeming like non-fiction than other efforts in the sub-genre: lengthy, straight drama scenes have Gadd talking with his defence lawyer, John Carter (Adam James). The title tells you where it's going and the capital punishment issue is reduced to mad-eyed, fanatical women sloganeering on either side outside Pentonville Prison. The details of the execution are credible, presenting an antiseptic modern version of the brisk hangings shown in *A Short Film About Killing* or *Let Him Have It*, whereby a false wall in the death cell turns out to be a sliding door to the gallows. A just-promoted warder (Alan Brent) explains 'I'm called officially "a hanging technician"… words like "hangman" come with too much baggage.'

Talking heads Ann Widdicombe (a conservative politician), Miranda Sawyer (a music journalist) and Gary Bushell (a tabloid columnist) discuss pop and execution; a problem of celebrity culture is that – though they know it's wrong – many can't find it in themselves to hate convicted sex offender Gadd more than they despise Widdicombe or Bushell. McRae is persuasive as a Mandarin-bearded, jail-canny, unforthcoming Gadd, though writer-director Rob Coldstream isn't interested in – and probably couldn't get away with – an extended trial hashing over whether or not he's guilty enough to deserve the death penalty under the (let's not forget) made-up legal system in the imaginary country shown here. The most credible moment comes when a remix of Glitter's old hits and snippets from his testimony is a download hit on the day he is hanged; he is slyly pleased to learn in his death cell that he's number one again, then furious when he understands the context.

EXISTS (2014)

Blair Witch Project co-creator Eduardo Sanchez returns to found footage with a standard entry in the busy sub-sub-genre of found footage Bigfoot movies. Less distinctive than Bobcat Goldthwait's *Willow Creek*, *Exists* at least has a well-designed monster. After the usual teasing glimpses of something hairy, the film delivers actual action scenes. In a set piece reminiscent of the second *Jurassic Park* movie, Bigfoot jumps onto a car that has slid into an incline, lashing into helpless victims. A premise we've seen before has a gang of thoughtless, not-too-characterised kids drive into the woods in search of the mythical monster. They run over something unidentified, then Bigfoot besieges them in a cabin because (as is very guessable) his (or her?) child (Little Bigfoot) was killed. It has decent suspense and monster stuff and an escalating body count... but the kids lack the obsessive improv character feel of *The Blair Witch Project*. Written by Jamie Nash, who collaborated with Sanchez on *Lovely Molly*. Certainly not as imaginative a use of the cryptid as, say, *Abominable* or *Yeti Curse of the Snow Demon*.

EXORCISM (2014)

Too many found footage films mimic *The Blair Witch Project* by having a caption at the beginning that gives away the ending. *Exorcism* has captions which run all the way through the film, contradict each other, are riddled with misused apostrophes and include howlers like 'Chris's head was decapitated'. Rob Davies (Alex Randall), an obnoxious but believable low-rent filmmaker, sets out to shoot a movie called *The Exorcism Tape* in an isolated house where an exorcism was performed in the 1960s. In a found footage innovation, the real chronicler of the horrors is the guy hired to document the shoot with on-set B-roll. Rob makes the grandiose claim that he intends to take up where *The Exorcist* left off, but as a demon causes chaos on the set by possessing actors and crew in succession, the film feels more like yet another lift from *The Evil Dead*. The leading lady is even called Ash (Aisling Knight) and has a spell being under the influence of the demon before she is exorcised, when an actor (Rick Alancroft) reads pages from the *Exorcism Tape* script at her (which gets him possessed instead), so she can do the night-vision sobbing to camera. The acting is variable (to put it generously), a lengthy irrelevant party game of spin-the-bottle pads the running time to 73 minutes and all the characters are unlikeable assholes, but it has a few moments of near-cleverness as a possessed actress (Elise Harris) wanders into a scene and smears blood over the leading lady to the approval of the annoyed director ('That's what I'm talking about!'). Written and directed by Lance Patrick.

EXTINCTION (THE EXPEDITION) (2014)

The found footage film is now as formulaic and ritualised as, say, Hammer horror or 1980s slasher sequels. The menace varies, but the story structure is so set in stone that surprises are rare. Fifteen years on from *The Blair Witch Project*, foolhardy filmmakers still traipse into danger, squabble and joke through long build-ups, then run screaming from whatever is out to get them – but keep filming through the horrors. Scripted by director Adam Spinks and star Ben Loyd-Holmes, this pays lip service to credibility as cameraman James (Daniel Caren) argues with producer-presenter Michelle (Sarah Mac) that, despite the danger they're in, it's important to keep shooting, so survivors can take evidence of living dinosaurs in the Peruvian rain forest back to civilisation. James heroically dies for this principle, but he's also the mandatory irritating character who gets on everyone's nerves to make a bad situation worse. South African cryptozoologist Professor Howser (Loyd-Holmes) leads an expedition into the jungle – mostly filmed in Wales, which does a reasonable impersonation of Peru – but hints at an ulterior motive which never emerges. It almost seems a coincidence that the expedition runs into dinosaurs, which are well done practical puppets. At least one death occurs because someone who should know better relies on *Jurassic Park* for information ('So their vision *isn't* based on movement?'). There are early ominous bits with defecting or evasive guides, a sinister logging official and dangerous wildlife, but the last half of the film is just running from dinosaurs – Mac's bottom takes centre screen as the camera follows her clambering over rocks and up trees – with glimpses of gruesome carnage. This isn't even the first found footage dinosaur film, trotting along after *Tape 407* (which saves its monster budget for one shot) and *The Dinosaur Project* (which has more CGI).

FOUND FOOTAGE 3D (2016)

Producer-writer-actor Derek Mitchell (Carter Roy) browbeats director Thomas (Chris O'Brien) into shooting *Spectre of Death*, a derivative found footage horror film, in 3D – simply because it would be a first, free-associating that his screen character is a 3D enthusiast who shoots home video in stereoscope and even tapes two Go-Pro cameras together on top of the fridge to add dimension to surveillance inserts. Mitchell co-stars in the film with his estranged wife Amy (Alena von Stroheim), because he signed a contract before they split. Shooting at the proverbial cabin in the woods, the crew includes short-tempered sound man Carl (Scott Allen Perry) and horror fan PA Lily (Jessica Perrin). The key player is Derek's brother Mark (Chris O'Brien), who handles the B-roll (in 3D, of course) for the 'making of' documentary (which itself becomes found footage).

An exercise in Quaker oat-box metafiction, this pokes fun at particular failings of the found footage genre (including a dig at the they-keep-filming-because-they-need-the-light gambit of *Hollow*) and questions why anyone would want to tread the *Blair Witch Project* path yet again. An argument about Derek's preference for CGI over practical effects skips past objection 'but we can't afford good CGI' and when the spook shows up, it looks more like a black blur than a monster – the reason given in the context of this film for cameras rolling even as chaos descends is that the spectre ('What is this – a British film?') appears only on the recorded image, so characters can see it coming if they keep looking at the monitor.

Writer-director Steven DeGennaro opts to deliver the *Scream* of found footage – god help us, but someone will do the *Scary Movie* eventually – by sticking close to rules laid out in debates about the form ('everybody dies') and staging effective jump scares (a falling shovel) even as characters bicker about whether the tactic is cheap or not. Fearnet.com critic Scott Weinberg appears as himself, though it's not until his exit moment that much is made of his in-joke cameo as gruesome (and seemingly practical) effects start to litter the cabin. The usual paranormal persecution shenanigans play out, with personal drama decently sketched in as Mark (of necessity, the least-seen character) is protective (if slightly creepily) towards Amy as she seems to be drawn back into a relationship with the obnoxious Derek and pros Thomas and Carl complain about their producer's single-minded, unethical commitment to the doomed project.

THE GALLOWS (2015)

Four teens – jocks Reese (Reese Mishler) and Ryan (Ryan Soos), cheerleader Cass (Cassidey Gifford) and drama queen Pfeifer (Pfeifer Brown) – are trapped overnight in a high school theatre and bothered by the ghost of a student accidentally hanged twenty years earlier during a performance of a play which is being unwisely revived. Tired *Paranormal Activity* moments have folks tossed about or dragged into the air by invisible entities. The jock trio are intent on vandalising the set so Reese won't embarrass himself in the production, but Pfeifer isn't really strident enough to earn their dislike (she ought to be Tracy Flick from *Election*). The climax is (of course) a re-enactment of the fatal finale of the old play in which terrible actor Reese finally gives a real performance with a noose around his neck. This found footage horror has an impressive setting and a decent premise, but the kids are hard or impossible to like and the format of everything being filmed on phones sabotages the build-up of suspense. There ought to be a system as with 3D where you can choose a theatre showing the non-found footage version to avoid headaches. Plot lapses (the revival staging of *The Gallows* is exponentially harder to believe than the first Valentine's dance since the massacre in *My Bloody Valentine*) and found footage contrivances (sometimes the camera can't be held by anyone but keeps moving) break the spell, though the film has decent scares and a last reel twist or two. Written and directed by Chris Lofing and Travis Cluff, who did better with the viral clips that marketed the film than the movie itself. As a theatre ghost story, it was upstaged by *A Haunting in Cawdor*.

GERBER: ISTORIA DI MELISSA (THE GERBER SYNDROME) (2010)

This low-budget, Italian-speaking film from writer-director Maxì Dejoie contributes to two thriving anxiety genres of the 21st century: documentary horror/SF and pandemic paranoia. Its rough, grainy look evokes *[•REC]* but it engages in some of the medical issues of Steven Soderbergh's *Contagion*.

Gerber Syndrome ('I Morbo di Gerber') first manifests symptoms easily mistaken for the flu, but in the second stage infectees develop heightened aggression. They spread the disease by attacking, scratching and biting whoever gets in their way… before entering a terminal phase. Documentarians (played by the real filmmakers) track characters caught up in the bigger story: Dr Ricardo (Sax Nicosia), who starts to lose his objectivity when his student niece Melissa (Valentina Bartolo) is infected; and Luigi (Luigi Piluso), an employee of a private security firm controversially sub-contracted to round up victims. While Melissa's case runs its course, forcing her parents to make hard choices about treatment, Luigi is on the streets, troubled not only by his grim job but vigilante gangs who take advantage of the crisis to lynch the ill.

As upsetting scenes have the untreated infected cooped up in a drab quarantine centre, the film follows 1970s exploitation (*The Crazies*, *The Cassandra Crossing*, *Rabid*, etc.) by assuming the authorities will deal with the disease in the most ruthless manner imaginable. Bartolo gives the standout performance, shifting from bright, worried young woman to spitting harridan.

GRAVE ENCOUNTERS (2011)

> 'IT'S NOT FUNNY. THIS PLACE IS ABOUT AS HAUNTED AS A SOCK DRAWER.'

Since *Session 9*, there can't be a disused hospital or prison in the US that hasn't had a horror film shot in it. Directed and written by 'the Vicious Brothers' (Colin Minihin, Stuart Ortiz), this is essentially *Blair Witch* in a building. Lance Preston (Sean Rogerson), host of the show *Grave Encounters*, takes his small crew – cameraman TC (Merwin Mondesir), tech guy Matt (Ben Wilkinson), sound girl Sasha (Ashleigh Gryzko) – and an actor who plays a medium, Houston Gray (Mackenzie Gray), to the Collingwood Psychiatric Hospital, which has a rep for being haunted. Locked in for the night, they suffer mild phenomena – doors shutting, Sasha's hair being lifted – but things get weirder when the sun doesn't rise and the caretaker doesn't arrive to let them out. Breaking through the front doors or an emergency exit only leads to more corridors and passages, which shift when not looked at. Matt disappears while collecting his gear only to show up later in a hospital gown and gibbering, then falls down a lift shaft. Sasha has 'HELLO' carved into her back by an invisible force, perhaps a mocking response to all that 'Is there a spirit there?' and 'Show us a sign' stuff. Everyone wakes up after a snooze to find they have personalised asylum ID bracelets.

The arc is familiar as smug, cynical fakers – Lance bribes the new gardener to claim a supernatural experience ('I saw a ghost over there – it was really scary.') – learn their lesson during an ordeal. Lance, a rat-phobic, is reduced to clubbing and eating vermin, does the Heather speech-to-camera trick and is finally lobotomised by ghost doctors. It's full of borrowed bits, though the sources are eclectic: hands reach out of walls as in *Repulsion* (here, out of the ceiling too), a wheelchair moves (*The Changeling*), a ghost comes out of a tub filled with blood (*The Tingler*), spooks crawl on ceilings (*Exorcist III*), and CGI spectre mental patients and mad doctors with distorted mouths loom (the *House on Haunted Hill* remake). For such a derivative item, it proved surprisingly influential – followed by several virtual lookalikes (*Episode 50*) and a sequel.

GRAVE ENCOUNTERS 2 (2012)

A blockbuster hit on DVD/download/pay-per-view, *Grave Encounters* kicked off a cycle of near-carbon copy imitations – a phenomenon almost creepier than its haunted asylum/found footage premise. So, here's a sequel – scripted by the original's the Vicious Brothers (who have a funny cameo), directed by John Poliquin – which takes a fairly obvious route for a found footage sequel (not dissimilar to *Blair Witch 2*), as student filmmaker Alex Wright (Richard Harmon) gets obsessed with *Grave Encounters* and comes to believe it's real found footage released by an unethical producer to profit from tragedy. Trying and failing to find the original actors, he hooks up with the producer – who offers to finance a sequel, which means Alex and his friends go to the real haunted asylum from the first movie and the film turns into a rerun as CGI-face spooks off them one by one. Actor Sean Rogerson appears as himself, lost in the asylum for years like Ben Gunn and willing to sacrifice newcomers to get out. There seems to be an influence from *Diary of the Dead* in Alex's abandonment of his original student horror film project – a widescreen conventional slasher – to get involved in a reality scare show, with leading lady Jennifer (Leanne Lapp) going from mock scream queen to real victim. It's okay for what it is, even inventive within the confines of the mushroom-growth sub-genre. Extra points for the opening montage of vloggers reviewing the original film, not all favourably.

HEIDI SLATER (2015)

A tricksy British found footage exercise, which indulges a level of metafiction too far in playing its game. After a collection of audition snippets, as a wide range of women try out with the line, 'I am Heidi Slater,' we meet Heidi (Margot Mount), ambitious to present a documentary. With director J-P (real director Jean-Paul Bankes-Mercer) behind the camera and archly named Jeff Foley (Darren Harris) on sound, Heidi accompanies gruff Northern psychic Tobias Danzig (Tom Charnock) to a heritage site house supposedly haunted by the victims of a murderous chief constable. The initial setup is that Tobias thinks this is going to be a paranormal documentary but the team intend to expose him as a charlatan, though masks are continually pulled off so – at different times – it seems the shoot is designed to set up one or more of the characters for on-camera murder (and, in Heidi's case, rape). The guide (Steven Hillman) does ill-judged jokes and Danzig shows a genuinely nasty side – both seemingly coaxed into cruelty just because they're on camera. The number 'eleven' recurs and standard found footage chills (panicky runs through the dark, bodies tripped over, betrayals and to-camera meltdowns) are deployed even as the artifice is continually undercut by nods like clapperboards that identify this as 'Untitled Horror Film'. It may fall into the too-clever-by-half category, but the performances are very good for this level of filmmaking (especially Mount and Charnock) and it's even reasonably unsettling.

HOLLOW (2011)

This owes the usual debt to *The Blair Witch Project*, but also parallels the better-resourced *A Night in the Woods*, which also treads a haunted British wilderness with literary associations (there, Dartmoor; here, Dunwich) and uses the possible psychosis of the heroine's ex-boyfriend – whom she brings along on a trip with her current love interest – as a trigger for definite doom and possible supernatural influence. Yet again, characters are compelled to keep the camera rolling through a crisis – especially when witnesses ask for it to be turned off. A (perhaps imaginary) function of the specific camera model is used as justification: the light won't work unless it's also filming and these people are in situations where they need the gadget as a torch. Emma (Emily Plumtree), who has to clear out a large house in Suffolk inherited from her vicar father, takes along estate agent fiancé Scott (Matt Stokoe), long-time best friend James (Sam

Stockman) and James's recently acquired blonde single mum girlfriend Lynne (Jessica Ellerby). James is still in love with Emma and brings Lynne partly to flaunt and partly in the hope of tempting Scott to infidelity so he can pick up his favoured girl on the rebound. Also in the mix is an impressive ancient hollow tree with a bad history involving a monk-hooded figure and double suicides. Over a weekend of drugs, bad decisions and arguments, the trio are overwhelmed by panic. It's clear this will wind up with some or all of them dangling from the branches. Part of the genre deal is that no one is really likeable – seriously, anyone who would marry an estate agent, much less a pretentious one who insists on being called a 'property consultant', deserves what they get – but this doesn't make that crucial leap from squabbling to terror well enough to enlist sympathy with doomed, self-involved characters. The good stuff is location-specific: prowling around the tree, the ruined abbey, the crumbling (and dangerous) cliff. Written by Matthew Holt; directed by Michael Axelgaard.

THE HOUSES OCTOBER BUILT (THE HOUSES OF HALLOWEEN) (2014)

This mock-doc horror film suffers from foregone conclusion finale syndrome, with confusion about what is specifically happening but little doubt that doom is inevitable. There's also the other common failing of the form: young filmmakers, ostensibly playing themselves, who come across as too obnoxious to live and too clueless to put up with for ninety minutes before they get got.

However, it hits the documentary side of the mock-doc equation more than usual as five friends – director/writer Bobby Roe, token girl Brandy Schaefer, big beardy Mikey Roe, driver Jeff and surplus guy Zack Andrews – take off across rural America in an RV visiting the 'haunts' which spring up at Halloween, in search of fabled underground 'extreme' scare attraction the Blue Skeleton. Much of the film consists of visits to real spookshows, snippet-like interviews with folks who run them, and glimpses of their gimmicks – mostly ghost train rides with added heavy metal and chainsaw action (one features zombie paintball). Along the road, as Bobby gets more obsessive about the Blue Skeleton, the gang repeatedly run into creepy characters not affiliated with the haunts they are hanging around – a hulking clown (evil clowns are omnipresent at these things), a girl-woman with a cracked porcelain doll face, a shaggy suited 'feaster bunny'. It's obvious they're the Blue Skeleton crew and the filmmakers are being drawn towards doom, but they go along with it – not without arguments – on the assumption that the extreme scare will stop short of actual harm and death (spoiler: it doesn't).

The improv chatter and inconsistent characterisation undermine a quite clever idea – that these victims would willingly court peril in search of thrills out of a need to find a haunt that delivers the way the protagonist of *The Vanishing* (an influence) wants answers so much he's willing to die for them. The character licks are broad and mainly trigger bickering – Jeff's food fads, Brandy's sulk when taken to a horror-themed strip club – rather than engage us in the victims' quest for horrors. The Blue Skeleton crew are well conceived and creepy in initial appearances, but what happens when they get the filmmakers in their clutches is banal. Scripted by Roe, Andrews and Jason Zada; and sort of a remake of a same-titled actual documentary they made in 2011.

HUNGERFORD (2014)

This ultra low-budget found footage picture – co-written and directed by star Drew Casson, previously best known as the yob who gets his face punched in a highlight of *The Borderland* – has enough good moments to suggest the young auteur's potential, including a few accomplished special effects and some unusual character interplay. Casson returned, with more money, to continue the story in *The Darkest Dawn*.

Cowan Rosewell (Casson), a slacker teen living in the eponymous small town, starts a video diary as a college project, and begins chronicling the lives of his small circle of friends. A mystery explosion isn't enough to distract him from trying to get back with Janine (Kitty Speed), a girl he's keen on but hasn't called in six months. Cowan's on-probation housemate Adam (Tom Scarlett) resents being blamed when a girl seems to overdose at Janine's party – which scuppers Cowan's relationship possibilities, but also means resentment at home since Adam insists he wasn't to blame. Just as everyone is hung up on small issues, a possessed postman barges into the house and attacks Adam – surviving knife-wounds but felled by a deodorant spray that detaches a puppeteering bug from his neck. A weirdly credible stretch has Cowan, Adam, Adam's sister Philippa (Georgia Bradley) and oddly obsessive Kipper (Sam Carter) unsure what to do with the corpse, which they end up dumping in the bin just as a policeman shows up looking for drugs.

Hungerford society collapses as the alien infection – which owes a bit to Robert A. Heinlein's *The Puppet Masters* – continues and more and more possessees take to the streets. Getting over a found footage hump, there's a moment where Cowan realises that he is in the middle of epoch-making events and insists the gang keep filming everything. It has hit-or-miss local talent performances, some hasty scripting and obvious budget limitations, but manages a distinctive personality and a nice sense of escalating panic overtaking the community. Made in Hungerford by proud locals.

HUNTING THE LEGEND (2013)

Another found footage Bigfoot movie. Besides following a well-beaten forest track, it suffers from awkward performances and follows the *Blair Witch* template so faithfully that (unlike most competing efforts) it doesn't even deliver a glimpse of onscreen monster. Chris (Christopher Copeland) has been obsessed with Bigfoot since his hunter father vanished in the Alabama woods, perhaps killed by the creature. With long-suffering girlfriend Hannah (Hannah Wallace), best friend Jeff (Jeff Causey) and a hired cameraman (writer-director Justin Sealey) and sound guy (Alex Ballew), Chris mounts an expedition into Sasquatch-infested woods. Unlike the leads of most found footage films, the protagonist is less interested in making a movie – though he fits head-cams on everyone – than tracking and killing the creature who got his Dad, so the setup includes visiting a shady gun salesman to buy weapons and hiring a tracker dog (a nice idea which isn't developed). After chats with locals who have thing-in-the-woods stories, they meet a paranoid, aggressive hermit (Stan Copeland) who warns them off before disappearing. Then, the group get lost, find signs of Bigfoot activity (including the regulation big footprint), are freaked out by skinned rabbits hung from tree-branches, squabble a lot, threaten to quit and meet nasty fates. The obsessive, vengeful lead character is a minor innovation, but gun-toting Chris is as whiny, irresponsible and unlikeable as the anything-to-make-a-film nuts of most *Blair Witch Project* imitations and Copeland's performance veers between wooden and hectoring. The busy climax features an inevitable moment where someone tells someone else to shoot anything that comes through the cabin door and winds up blasted.

INNER DEMONS (2014)

Another possession-themed found footage/mock-doc horror film, with a stronger character through-line than usual. It's presented as material shot for a sensationalist documentary TV series that has an intervention format. Carson Morris (Lara Vosburgh), a teenage girl from a devout but non-fundamentalist Christian family, is a self-harming drug addict. The TV folks get the co-operation of her parents (Colleen McGrann, Christopher Parker) and a rehab/group therapy facility to follow her attempt to turn her life around. Director Seth Grossman worked on a TV show called *Intervention* which has the format of the fictional program here, and brings a cynical, insidery edge as the filmmakers express sham-sympathy for the subject, and make manipulative approaches to her family and the folks trying to help her. It emerges that Carson has turned to drugs in an attempt to cope with what she believes is a demon possessing her… and, in an unsettling development, getting clean will also allow the evil spirit more power.

There's a nice, credible treatment of this revelation – with the rehab counsellors taking the demon as a metaphor, some of the other patients being less sceptical (though they're all junkies, so who listens to them?) and producer Suzanne Tully (Kate Whitney) seizing on the possession angle to make this segment of the show stand out. Intern Jason (Morgan McClellan) forms a real connection with Carson – and, perhaps, the demon – which Suzanne is willing to exploit. It's also handy that Jason keeps filming when the family try to pull the girl away from the cameras.

Glenn Gers' script works hard on the backstory, involving Carson's travails at a school where her beliefs make her the butt of a joke Satanic ritual – which, of course, was preserved on a camera-phone – that has led to the present situation. As with many found footage films, the tricksy storytelling and faux-vérité business serve as excessive packaging for a tiny, familiar story. However, Vosburgh is good in a complex, ambiguous role and lends the old, old tale emotional impact – though speaking-in-a-deep-voice-while-staring-evilly should probably be retired as a way of representing demonic possession.

JERUZALEM (2015)

Scripted and directed by Doron and Yoav Paz, *JeruZalem* – purportedly Israel's first supernatural horror film – is a next-generation found footage picture, one-upping the tonally similar *Cloverfield* by having a protagonist wear a high-tech Google Glass device through an apocalyptic crisis.

On a trip to Israel, Jewish American princesses Sarah (Danielle Jadelyn) and Rachel (Yael Grobglas) hook up with handsome Christian archaeologist Kevin (Yon Tumarkin) and friendly Muslim guide Omar (Tom Graziani). When Sarah's bag is stolen, she loses her prescription glasses and has to wear her Google Glass all the time, sidestepping the why-keep-filming issue which dogs found footage movies. Ominous notes creep into the holiday fun, as Omar explains that a house they pass is an asylum for those suffering 'Jerusalem Syndrome', a species of madness brought on by being close to the vortex of religious conflict. Kevin becomes a ranting maniac when overcome by premonitions of doom and is dragged to the madhouse by soldiers. Demonic events on a Biblical scale erupt in the city. In the middle of escalating confusion and terror, Sarah tries to rescue Kevin, keep her infected-by-a-demon friend safe and escape ground zero through a labyrinth. Aspects of the Glass established early on as amusements – face-recognition software, a zombie-killing game and the music library – are deployed in more sinister context. A stunning final shot conveys just how much the apocalyptic catastrophe has changed the city and the protagonist.

Lead character Jadelyn is necessarily off screen almost throughout, which puts the acting weight on Grobglas and Tumarkin, who go from fun-loving young folks to haunted, desperate and perhaps possessed. Filming on the fly, the Paz brothers gained access to locations throughout the city; the ever-heightened tensions between factions on the streets and in the shrines of Old Jerusalem add to the unsettling feel. It has humour, often at the expense of clueless Americans, but goes all-out for the monstrous in its fast-paced, hectic latter stages.

LAKE MUNGO (2008)

This Australian mock-doc seesaws between the paranormal and human evil exposed. After the death-by-drowning of teenager Alice Palmer (Talia Zucker), her no-nonsense dad Russell (David Pledger) claims to have seen her ghost in her old room. When her brother Matthew (Martin Sharpe) shows photos and even videos which hold her image, her mother (Rosie Traynor) refuses to believe the girl is dead, even after an exhumation and DNA test. Psychic Ray Kemeny (Steve Jodrell) gets involved, but there's an about-face a few reels in as Matthew admits he's faked most of the ghost photographs. Then, one of the photos shows an all-too-human presence – a next-door neighbour (Scott Terrill) creeping into the dead girl's room, trying to retrieve a videotape of her having perhaps-coerced sex with the couple she babysat for. The supernatural comes back again, as the family dig up 'treasures' Alice buried at the desolate Lake Mungo (no water in sight) and find a mobile phone recording of her encounter with an apparition that seems to be her future dead self. Writer-director Joel Anderson uses manipulated home video footage and doctored photos to eerie effect, but also implants creepinesses in talking heads scenes, as various witnesses don't quite 'fess up or tell contradictory stories. For instance, the psychic never mentions to the family that Alice consulted him when she was alive. A deceptively mild piece, with the almost-reassuring interview scenes gentling us into glimpsed, ambiguous, sometimes-redacted found footage horrors.

THE LOST COAST TAPES (2012)

> 'I'M SORRY, MISS CONWAY, YOU JUST CROSSED INTO AN AREA OF SASQUATCH THEORY I FIND VERY DIFFICULT TO TAKE SERIOUSLY.'

Mid-list found footage horror. Even the 'it's not the monster you were expecting' punch line has been done several times since the *Blair Witch* parallel *The Last Broadcast*. TV journo Sean Reynolds (Drew Rausch), crawling back from a nervous breakdown, thinks he's landed a career-restarting scoop when crusty old guy Carl Drybeck (Frank Ashmore) offers to show a Sasquatch corpse to a news crew for a cash payment. Savvy African-American techs know too much to go looking for Bigfoot and shift the job onto Kevin (Noah Weisberg), a jittery geek who seesaws between excitement and terror. The crew is completed by sceptical Darryl (Rich McDonald) and Sean's credulous, spiritual girlfriend Robyn (Ashley Wood), who's into all the weird stuff 'that ruined your career in the first place'. Things follow the usual course – bickering, ominous hints (Drybeck insists the crew be hooded so they don't know the location of the wild woods), possible hoaxes, myth-making monologues. The terror escalates as all routes out are blocked by felled trees, the gang split up to be eaten/splattered by unseen monsters, and the last survivor apologises to camera for getting everyone killed. At the end, Sean gabbles, 'It's not Bigfoot' as a weird light show surrounds the cabin (alien abductors?) and is killed by something bipedal with cloven hooves (a demon?). Scripted by Bryan O'Cain and Brian Kelsey; directed by Corey Grant.

THE MIRROR (2014)

A fairly posh found footage effort, in which upscale young Londoners set up cameras to observe a supposedly haunted mirror in the hope of winning a prize from the (real) James Randi Foundation for proof of the paranormal. Nothing in particular manifests from the looking glass – which is less fearsome than the one featured in *Oculus* – but Matt (Joshua Dickinson) increasingly falls under the influence of dark forces or has a very bad mood. He turns on his pretty girlfriend Jemma (Jemma Dallender) and oddly obsessed filmmaker best mate Steve (Nate Fallows). The camera records Matt walking in his sleep, prompting him to remember his childhood somnambulism and become cagy and defensive. With a camera strapped to his chest, he takes to wandering with a knife, and becomes hostile to the whole project. Though there are brief trips outside for gory murders, writer-director Edward Boase mostly stays inside the well-appointed apartment, and has the camera turned off – perhaps by supernatural means, perhaps through deliberate sabotage – for stretches when plot events are happening. The cast are solid – Dallender, after turns in *Community* and *I Spit On Your Grave 2*, is becoming a typecast victim in low-budget horror, but brings bite to the lengthy relationship scenes, hinting at cracks in the trio's friendship before the horror starts. It concludes with the inconclusive caption many found footage films deploy in lieu of plot resolution.

MR JONES (2013)

Though it doesn't completely work, this has interesting spins on familiar material, seguing at some point from found footage to subjective hallucination. Bipolar-but-medicated Scott (Jon Foster) and his understanding (very hot) girlfriend Penny (Sarah

Jones) retreat to a cabin in the woods to work on their relationship and get their heads together with nature. Scott films the process as part of a documentary project with a vaguely therapeutic subtext. After a few months, the couple get bored and fidgety with the wilderness idyll and a creepy neighbour steals Scott's backpack (which has their car keys in it). They venture into the thief's hitherto-unnoticed home and find disturbing scarecrows made of trees and bits of bone. Scott is eager to explore while his girlfriend is wary, but as soon as she sees the scarecrows things in reverse… she recognises them as the work of famous, high-priced, yet mysterious and reclusive artist 'Mr Jones' (Banksy and JD Salinger are name-checked) and insists Scott's documentary shift focus to the Jones phenomenon. Scott goes to New York in sped-up sequences to interview artists, critical commentators and the recipient (Ethan Sawyer) of a scarecrow who has burned it and is still traumatised. In fragments, it emerges that Jones' art has a purpose, marking a border between waking life and dreamworld, and that his celebrity is just a side-effect (also a good joke about the elaborate art direction of *The Texas Chain Saw Massacre* – what if gallery owners started exhibiting and selling Leatherface's work?). Back in the woods, Penny encounters the masked Jones (Mark Steger) and gets a sense of Lovecraftian encroaching dread. When Scott returns, he takes a baby scarecrow from an elaborate arrangement, which puts time out of joint: the car won't work, the sun doesn't rise, and his mind fractures along with the world and the narrative. The ending is too pat, but the route there is interesting and disturbing. Written and directed by Karl Mueller.

MOCKINGBIRD (2014)

Three video cameras are delivered as wrapped mystery gifts – to 'the couple', suburbanites Tom and Emmy (Todd Stashwick, Audrey Marie Anderson), 'the woman', college student Beth (Alexandra Lydon), and 'the clown', live-at-home loser schlub Leonard (Barak Hardley) – with cards instructing them to keep filming at all times. Each thinks they've won or are competing in a contest and are initially unconcerned. Indeed, given how well established the conventions of found footage horror are, it's a stretch that they ignore so many bad omens and go along with it. An escalation of nastiness – including that old favourite, the creeper videotape delivered to the household where it was covertly shot – and threats of death if they turn the things off eventually convince them they are in trouble, but they still keep the cameras on and obeying instructions.

Writer-director Bryan Bertino made the simple, effective *The Strangers*; here, he uses similar tactics as folks are terrorised by unknown sadists. There is even a similar reveal as it turns out the manipulative villains are kids, headed by the creepy Jacob (Spencer List, who has similar nasty brat roles in *Offspring* and *Bereavement*). In the climax, the victims are brought together in a room full of red balloons so they can panickily murder each other when a simple conversation would lead to a happier ending. It makes good use of unsettling classical music and performances are decent – Hardley gets the most leeway as the loser who embraces becoming a clown and partaking in supposedly money-winning stunts like having strangers film him being punched or kicked in the nuts – but it's a rote exercise in the same old stuff.

MUIRHOUSE (2012)

An Australian found footage film with the high concept that it's mostly shot in a real haunted location – a gimmick also used in the British *Paranormal Diaries* films. A drawback is that the Monte Cristo estate is maintained as a museum, so paranormal investigator Phillip Muirhouse (Iain P.F. McDonald) has to crack up when tormented by unseen entities without breaking anything antique. It opens with Muirhouse wandering dazed and naked, then does scene-setting as we follow him on a tour where he films at all the sites in his *Australia's Most Haunted* book and winds up at the Monte Cristo. It assumes more familiarity with the history of the place than non-Australian audiences might have and so the backstory – which involves an abused mentally handicapped child, a stern religious woman who died in her own chapel, and other vaguer atrocities – is barely sketched. Muirhouse, against advice, spends the night alone in the mansion and goes mad thanks to jiggery-pokery beyond the edge of the frame or while the green night-vision is on. Chairs are supernaturally put on tables, which isn't that terrifying, and McDonald gets hysterical very quickly for someone who supposedly has experience with places like this. Written and directed by Tanzeal Rahim.

OPEN WINDOWS (2014)

Like *The Den* and *Unfriended*, this found footage mutation represents itself as a capture of a computer desktop screen, with multiple windows, Skype calls, emails checked, linked audio and video files, and faux-interactive trickery to further an unfolding drama. Like *Grand Piano*, it's a Spanish-made suspense mystery with Elijah Wood on a long call with a psychopath, forced to jump through hoops. Nick Chambers (Wood) runs a website devoted to Jill Goddard (Sasha Grey), star of a science fiction film franchise, and has won a bloggers' contest to interview her over a meal in an Austin hotel during a promotional event. However, he is called by mystery voice Chord (Neil Maskell), who says the actress intends to break their date and enlists him in a plan of petty revenge, which escalates as Nick realises Chord intends to do much worse than release a sex tape online. While toting his laptop and trying to rescue the woman he has got deeper into trouble, Nick is in contact with a group of initially masked French hackers who believe they are aiding a legendary cyber-vigilante and fall into a disagreement when it seems that Chord is their hero rather than Nick. Like writer-director Nacho Vigalondo's other twisty essays in limiting premises (*Timecrimes*, *Extraterrestrial*), it embraces technical challenge but also has a tightly focused, if far-fetched and tricky, plot (which slightly echoes Vincenzo Natali's *Cypher*) to recommend it.

OUTPOST 37 (MANKIND'S LAST STAND) (2013)

Writer-director Jabbar Raisani's UK-South African science fiction/action film has a certain Neill Blomkamp influence. A documentary crew follows a military unit policing an area between Pakistan and Afghanistan troubled by the left-behind remnants of a recently defeated mass alien invasion. As in Blomkamp's films (and *Monsters Dark Continent*), the science fiction overlaps real-world issues... the mostly American grunts are as worried by local insurgents as aliens, which means it takes them a long time to catch on to the twist SF-savvy viewers will cotton immediately: the wave of shambling suicide bombers who attack OP37 are mind-controlled by implants in the back of their necks. In a slightly racist development, a Yank soldier who gets an implant (Matthew Holmes) is able to resist orders and give the game away – implying that the locals who become killer zombies are weak-willed feebs.

It tells a small, significant story in a larger war narrative, with the platoon the film follows taking losses as they realise the engagement they're fighting with 'the Heavies' is potentially the start of the second wave invasion. Even the documentarian gets caught up in the action, badly wounded and staying behind to trigger the bomb that destroys the aliens' satellite-jamming station. It's a straight-up gung-ho picture, almost in the vein of expensive pro-war efforts like *Battle: LA* or *Battleship*. Cliché grunts are valorised at the expense of turbanned folk whose lands they've invaded to protect the planet (it's supposed to be funny when they kill goats and funnier when a local goatherd tries to get compensation for a flock slaughtered by the Heavies), and big stomping, snarling armoured baddie aliens aren't worth getting to know anything about. It's well put together, with the familiar intercut interviews, jittery camerawork during firefights (the image pixelates when aliens fire zapping weapons) and good effects.

Better than the average Syfy dud, it is still slightly strident and monotonous. Adrian Paul cameos as a general, but the all-male cast are mostly competent hulk no-names (Joe Reegan, Reiley McClendon, Michael Dube, Justin Munitz). The green kid (Sven Ruygrok) who gets teased about his Mom but really wants to earn the respect of his fellows does indeed get poignantly killed. A post-credits coda hints at the ironic approach of *Starship Troopers* as the wounded who have lost hands and legs are fitted with prosthetics and sent back into battle. Co-scripted by Blake Clifton.

THE PARANORMAL INCIDENT (2011)

> 'IF I HAVE TO SPEND A WEEKEND IN A SHITHOLE TO GET AN A, IT'S BETTER THAN DOING ANY WORK, EH?'

Following *Grave Encounters*, another found footage paranormal investigation of a disused asylum picture. Despite a frame story (objective cinema style) which has a conspiracy angle, as the sole survivor (Oliver Rayon) is interviewed by a female agent (Amanda Barton) as part of what turns out to be a shadowy government cover-up (complete with *Mission: Impossible* fake hospital room), this is the same shtick over and over, even more poorly realised and with whiny, inconsistent, annoying characters. Students – on some nebulous parapsychology course with no apparent adult supervision – spend a weekend in Odenbrook Sanitarium, site of a supposed mass patient suicide. What happens is the usual stuff (EVP, flickering patient ghosts, hair mussed by invisible presence, voices of dead relatives, dragged screaming into dark corners, maps that don't make sense) in the usual style (shaky handheld, green night-light) with the usual arguments and recriminations. One dude (Brett Edwards) is along to piss people off and do all the wrong things, and a bunch of pretty girls (Nadia Underwood, Sabrina Villalobos, Chelsea Vincent) run about in tight outfits getting panicky. Written by Chris W. Freeman and director Matthew Bolton.

POPULATION ZERO (2016)

This mock-doc mystery thriller is constructed around a real-life legal quirk which has never been put to the test. If murder is committed in a sliver of Yellowstone Park, a killer could theoretically walk free because the US Constitution guarantees trial by jurors resident in the jurisdiction – but only bison live there, so it would be impossible to empanel a jury. Co-director Julian T. Pinder, playing himself, is drawn to the case of Dwayne Nelson by a mystery email and sets out to document the crime. Nelson is supposed to have shot three young men hiking in the park after a trivial argument, then immediately turned himself in and confessed before slipping through the loophole to serve only a token sentence on the minor charge of carrying a firearm in a state park. The first half achieves remarkable verisimilitude, as interviews with grieving relatives and lawyers on both sides of the case ring true. Without too much fuss, the film also establishes the eeriness of the park and sketches a climate of fear in the small town where Nelson lived. Cowboy-hatted, earnest Pinder becomes obsessed with the case, occasionally arguing with sceptical co-director Adam Levins about how deep he is getting in… and convenient revelations suggest Nelson was playing a longer, cannier game than anyone suspected, with the film itself part of his strategy. It benefits from mostly grounded, muted performances from interview subjects. Even Pinder's corner-cutting and dramatic overemphasis is believable, touching on a complicity between cold case documentarians and sometimes-dubious subjects. Pinder chews over all accounts of the case, fretting that everything is too neat – then spots a contradiction which leads him to greater insight. This smacks of neat scripting rather than reality, as the second half abandons strict credibility to expose a larger game of vengeance. Inspired by 'The Perfect Crime', an article by Michigan State University law professor Brian Kalt.

RESURRECTING "THE STREET WALKER" (2009)

The entertainment industry mock-documentary seems to be a category of British low-budget horror. Writer-director Ozgur Uyanik's film has much in common with Pat Higgins' *The Devil's Music*, Ross Birkbeck's *Showreel* and Guy Decker and Gavin Boynter's long-in-the-works *Nitrate*. Outside horror, Simon Ubsdell's *That Deadwood Feeling* and Mark Withers' *Bare Naked Talent* also use the format, suggesting a lot of exasperated film industry types (like the runner protagonist of *Resurrecting "The Street Walker"*) boil over with anecdotes, resentments, and bright ideas. They're in a position to borrow offices as locations, use available equipment and hope the results cut together into something which tells a story.

Marcus (Tom Shaw) agrees to shoot a documentary following school friend James (James Powell) from minion to auteur, and keeps cameras rolling as James falls under the spell of an unfinished, perhaps-cursed film he tries to retrieve from obscurity. Working as coffee fetcher, script reader and photocopier operator in the office of producer Mike Lowrie (a convincing Hugh Armstrong), James turns up footage from *The Street Walker*, a horror movie abandoned in 1985. The director died shortly after Mike invested in the film and the cans have been gathering dust ever since. Spouting his philosophy that 'You've got to go for what you want to go for, do what you want to do... before some big fucker comes along with a hammer and hits you on the head,' James works to get Mike to sign off on allowing him to finish the film. He also goes into a personal spiral, kicked out of his upper-middle-class parents' home for not having a proper job and settling down, and bridling under the sharp tongue of development exec Trish Thistle (Lorna Beckett), who always calls him 'shitface' and complains about his ineptitude at menial tasks he plainly believes are now beneath him. So, it's obviously going to end in tears when Mike advances James a budget to shoot a new ending for *The Street Walker*, but puts Trish in charge as a producer.

Resurrecting "The Street Walker" opens like one of many documentaries about the video nasties kerfuffle of the 1980s, presenting familiar titles, headlines and posters. This explains why *The Street Walker* was such a doomed venture, though Uyanik fudges things by making the unfinished film in black-and-white to contrast with the in-colour vérité and talking heads. The 'plot' of *The Street Walker* has a thuggish Michael Elphick lookalike (Gwilym Lloyd) pick up girls (who wear an assortment of retro clothes and hairstyles), whom he drugs, ties up and kills. He meets a girl who seems nice, but she stands him up when they arrange to have a date – and the film runs out before anything like an end. Uyanik doesn't take the obvious course of revealing that the footage consists of snuff movies, though James (and Marcus, come to that) show surprisingly little interest in tracking down the cast and crew to find out their stories. However, James comes to believe someone died on the set of *The Street Walker* and the reshoot is troubled by what seems to be more than bad luck. Filming the vital scene is nearly a disaster when the cast and crew are locked in as a fire breaks out, and the actress cast in the key role dies of an apparently random asthma attack. James gets more out of control and pointedly harangues Marcus as he sees that the documentary he hoped would be a triumphant DVD extra about how he overcame the odds to become a filmmaker is more likely to be one of those gripping accounts of a floundering freak ruining his life while failing to make anything (cf: *American Movie, Overnight*).

It's clear where *Resurrecting "The Street Walker"* is going, which makes the closing scenes less horrific or affecting than they might be. However, Uyanik's film has much going for it, especially in performance and character. Acting is usually the most problematic area of scraped-together-through-favours films, but Parker is a compelling lead, sympathetic in his movie brat commitment but subtly off-putting in the way he treats everyone around him. His rants against the constraints imposed by his family and lowly job are authentically rebellious, but tinged with a sulky sense of entitlement which shows he's an incipiently dangerous posh bloke. Hugh Armstrong, the cannibal from *Death Line*, is so credible as a Wardour Street denizen that I thought he was a real film industry figure playing himself in a fictional context (lots of mock-docs have people do this). We only get hints about the original auteur of *The Street Walker* and possibilities that the film's sinister influence persists. Even in his paranoid frenzy, James doesn't consider that someone apart from his snippy boss might not want the film finished, though we suspect his shoot was sabotaged (and his star killed) by people who want the project to stay dead. A potent addition to the list of 'cursed movie' films: *The Hills Run Red, Cut, Slaughter Studios*, etc.

ROUGH CUT (2013)

A documentary account of the remaking of a film that doesn't exist. The backstory is that writer Mike Harte and filmmaker Jamie Shovlin cut together *Hiker Meat*, a pastiche 1981 exploitation movie, by using clips from dozens of 1970s and '80s films. We don't see that much of *Hiker Meat* (for copyright reasons?), though there's a *Los Angeles Plays Itself* vibe to a sequence of a heroine wandering woods at night, composed of several different actresses in several different landscapes. The bulk of the film follows Shovlin as he remakes *Hiker Meat* with a real cast, effects, borrowed classic cars, locations (England subbing for either California or Italy posing as America), midge attacks, music (from Euan Rodger), etc. Some interview subjects, like Harte (explaining how many aspects of the film arise from the randomly chosen date of August 1ˢᵗ) and Rodger, seem to be sending it up. Others act as if they are simply making a low-budget horror pastiche (*Hiker Meat* sounds a little like *Invasion of the Blood Farmers*). We see the staging of a few key effects shots – an exploding house modelled on a bit from *The Sender* and a shadow monster out of *Deadly Spawn* – and the technicians are simply doing their jobs, but there's a suggestion that the whole thing is a kind of exquisite corpse project. Shovlin actually set out to make this film, *Rough Cut*, and only filmed a few sequences of the otherwise non-existent *Hiker Meat* remake. Oddly absent, for instance, are creative clashes… even when a valuable old vehicle is in a minor accident that will probably be costly, no one loses their temper. The only complaints are about midges. It slots into that *Amer-Berberian Sound Studio* trend of appropriating exploitation elements for art purposes, but is a little more handmade and less focused. Still, an interesting watch.

SHOPING-TUR (SHOPPING TOUR) (2012)

This Russian excursion sets the familiar warning against going on holiday in an unusual quarter of the world; after so many films in which Westerners are menaced in the former Soviet bloc, it's refreshing to see unwary Russians set upon by friendly Finns. A credibly annoying teenager (Timofey Yeletsky) keeps his cameraphone rolling on a trip he's taking with his attractive, recently widowed mother (Tatyana Kolganova) and their bickering has an often-nasty edge, because they find it easier to scratch each other than deal with the loss of the husband/father. On the coach, the kid is appalled to find out that this is a shopping tour rather than what he might think of as a holiday. In the middle of the night, the coach is taken to a seemingly deserted superstore and the tourists are let loose in its aisles – only the kid notices blood and finds a corpse in a customers-not-allowed area. Finns attack bloodily, and mother and son argue about whether they're vampires or cannibals. Writer-director Mikhail Brashinsky manages a balancing act between genuinely felt terror – as the estranged pair bond while trying to survive – and bizarre satire in the Nordic vein of *Troll Hunter* and *Real Exports*). It's revealed that on one day everyone in Finland eats a foreigner – though they're perfectly nice the rest of the time (and mostly vegetarian, if prone to suicide and alcoholism). The phone is taken from the kid at one point and Finns happily talk about their murderous tradition, but the main characters return for a finale which offers a gruesome way out of their predicament and a break with subjective filming in an impressive pull-back shot. Kolganova is especially strong in a well-written role, often turning away from her son's annoying camera to avoid showing how deeply hurt she is; the mother-son dynamic is an unusual choice in this sort of horror, adding freshness to the much-used format.

THE SIGIL (2012)

> 'WE'RE MAKING A DOCUMENTARY. SUNDANCE, MAYBE.' 'FUCK YOU, MAN! SUNDANCE WON'T MATTER IF WE'RE DEAD!'

One of the weakest found footage horror films. The plot is workable, a twist reasonably set up and the meld of Satanism and cover-up potent, but execution is poor. People who don't like *The Blair Witch Project* or *Paranormal Activity* often label them amateurish; *The Sigil* shows how professionally crafted those films are. Some months after a bunch of corpses are found in a Los Angeles home, a small group – Devan (Devan Liljedahl), sister of one of the dead, and wannabe filmmakers Brandon (director/co-writer Brando Cano-Errecart) and Nate (co-writer Nathan Dean Snyder) – show up to make a documentary. As they poke about the house, a plausible neighbour (Brittney Daylee) agrees to put up the filmmakers – who didn't even book a motel – overnight. Matt (Matthew Black), the neighbour's brother, has been traumatised by events next door, but his sister is blithe about coping with his seizures. In the house, the kids find Satanic stuff and the dead brother's journal, which bigs up 'Luke LaVey' as a Satan-worshipping covenmaster responsible for all the evil. So, which of the characters is secretly the wicked Luke? The camera wobbles, bloody handprints are seen on the ceiling, everyone screams, and the trio – who have soapy arguments about their differing agendas – suffer the usual non-specific ghastly fates. Exposition delivered via Google, the new millennium's go-to narrative shortcut, is clumsily overused as characters have to look up what a sigil is and the connotations of the name Baphomet.

SKINWALKER RANCH (SKINWALKERS) (2013)

I must be weakening. This is yet another found footage film which doesn't even try to make sense and has a mixed ability cast (pros like Jonathan Gries and Michael Horse among the unknowns), but I warmed to its catch-all weirdness and a few decent character moments amid the panicky shouting. In an area known for cattle mutilations and lights in the sky, a small boy goes missing. A team of paranormal documentarians despatched by a mysterious foundation film everything, including regular reappearances by the child's fleeting spectre. In an unusual development, the rancher (Gries) keeps having to remind the investigators that he's more interested in getting the missing kid back than investigating the amazing unknown. Lots of stuff happens, which puts it ahead of most walk-in-the-woods or watch-the-sheet-twitch films… a giant wolf-like dog attacks, vehicles are crushed by invisible forces, a spindle-legged alien wanders about, possessed or changeling kids with psychic powers prompt investigators to severe self-harm, a U-Matic tape from the '70s reveals that the investigators' backers were here before and bad things happened which the current team haven't been told about, more folks disappear in bright lights, and a UFO puts in an appearance. Directed by Devin McGinn (*The Last Lovecraft*); scripted by Adam Ohler.

SOMEBODY'S THERE (THE PIGMAN MURDERS) (2015)

A surprisingly common but elementary found footage horror mistake is to open with a long series of captions which give away the whole (thin) story. This purports to be a record made by a professional videographer (Marius Puodziunas, the credited cinematographer) of a trip to Galway taken by seven Dublin pals in honour of a deceased mate – originally as a memento for the dead guy's family, but eventually uploaded to the internet as snuff. Over half the film is frittered away on maundering to-camera speeches about what a great bloke the deceased was and bickering which extends to one unexplained fight… before the lads are attacked and killed in the wilderness by a couple of grunting bad guys wearing pigs' head masks. Galway looks nice, but these wild woods aren't especially threatening. At that, it's not even the worst found footage horror film made in Ireland – that would be the hideous rape-and-possession fest *The Inside*. Written and directed by SPK (Sean Patrick Kenny).

THE TAKING (THE TAKING OF DEBORAH LOGAN) (2014)

Many possession dramas, all the way back to *The Exorcist*, revolve around children – with demonic manifestations which mimic puberty or adolescent rebellion. In *The Taking*, the possessee is a senior citizen and evil influence is mistaken for signs of dementia.

Student Mia Hu (Michelle Ang) and her two-man documentary team – voluble and easily spooked Gavin (Brett Gamble) and usually-behind-the-camera Luis (Jeremy DeCarelos) – move into the large rural home of retired Deborah Logan (Jill Larson), a spirited if frail old lady diagnosed with the early stages of Alzheimer's. Deborah's daughter Sarah (Anne Ramsay) needs financial and practical help which the filmmakers can give. Omens mount up: snakes in odd places, irrational outbursts, night-time wanderings, the re-activation of a long-disused telephone switchboard. *Paranormal Activity*-type paranormal activity leads Mia to connect Deborah's alarming behaviour with the disappearance decades earlier of local child murderer Desjardins, who attempted an immortality ritual with his killings and might be possessing Deborah to complete the job. In a rare lead, character actress Larson projects disturbing intensity as the likeable old stick who transforms into a haggard witch, augmented by subtle makeup effects. Deborah goes from afflicted and affecting to possessed and dangerous, sicking up earthworms and taking on disturbing snake qualities, including venom spitting and a distending maw.

Director Adam Robitel, who co-wrote with Gavin Heffernan, makes all the jittery characters distinctive – Sarah is a hard-drinking lesbian who isn't quite out with her mother – without distracting from escalating terror. The first hour is mostly confined to the isolated home, which has cavernous recesses suitable for exploring by the thin beam of the camera light; Luis comments on the property's many attics and basements, where creepy secrets are stashed. The finale moves to a hospital where Deborah/Desjardins grimly sets sights on an ailing, eerily compliant little girl, and into confining caves, where the final confrontation takes place. It signs off with an effective, creepy touch very much in the 1970s possession movie tradition. Produced by Bryan Singer and Jeff Rice.

TAPE 407 (2012)

The USP of this found footage horror is an impressive crash seen from inside a plane going down. The rest is more familiar business as survivors wonder why help doesn't turn up and something unseen (until the final frames) picks them off. Structurally, it parallels *The Grey* (I assume *Lost* DNA in the mix somewhere) – though the usual downbeat resolution means you don't get any probing of human nature beyond the basic observation that people in a crisis are whiny and annoying. Found footage convention is that everyone will die, so characters' struggles are always provisional. Leads Trish (Abigail Schrader) and Jessie (Samantha Lester) are teenage sisters who bicker over the camera and make a nuisance of themselves on the plane – though the mandatory loose cannon is Charlie (Brendan Patrick Connor), an aggressive drunk who's rude to the flight attendant (Samantha Sloyan – who gives the best performance, but dies early) in the air and never stops complaining or saying the wrong thing when they're on the ground. So much time is spent coping with his spats and panics that the characters can't focus on the monster until it's too late – I'm beginning to think that including folks like this in horror movies is just a way of padding out thin menaces. In an abandoned town, survivors find an old radio. The operator they reach is oddly insistent about getting them to go back to the wreckage – despite the monster which has been killing them off – to fire a flare. It's plain the Evil Government (or Corporation) responsible for this area (The Mesa Reserve) want them to die, so the only ongoing mystery is what kind of monster is out there. Eggshell fragments are found and a scaly tail glimpsed, but not until the end – and after the fate of the heroines is settled – does a full-on (genetically engineered?) dinosaur appear. Some dialogue rings true, but a lot is just chatter. Directed and written by Dale Fabrigar and Everette Wallin.

THE TAPES (2011)

Why would filmmakers who don't know how to spell 'Beelzebub' make a devil movie? Set in snowy Whitstable, this is a basic found footage film. Danny (Jason Maza) and Nathan (Arnold Oceng) set out to record a *Big Brother* audition tape for Danny's girlfriend Gemma (Natasha Sparkes). Hearing rumours from a barmaid (Mandy Lee Berger) that a gruff farmer (Lee Alliston) holds swinger parties, the lads drag Gemma to an isolated, near-dilapidated farm in the hope of getting saleable video of orgies. While trespassing, the dolts find tarot cards, pig heads, demon symbols and a torture rack. An hour in, they start being taken and sacrificed – in a pretentious spin on hostage videos, Gemma is forced to read out a statement on the part of 'the Brothers of Beelzebub' (she can't pronounce it either) before vanishing. Most of the film is wandering about and shrill arguments – and interview snippets with people unaccountably upset that the horrible lead characters are missing or murdered. 80 minutes that feel like a month. Scripted by Scott Bates; directed by Bates and Alliston.

388 ARLETTA AVENUE (2011)

This surveillance/stalker movie at least gives some thought to who might make or edit the footage. An unseen character stakes out the title address in Toronto, installing mini-cameras in the home – then the car and workplace – of householder James (Nick Stahl), a young ad exec married to grad student Amy (Mia Kirshner). A campaign of harassment begins with a compilation CD of golden oldies in the car and odd little japes – the weirdest of which is the substitution of James's cat with a near-identical but different animal. After frayed nerves (and past troubles) prompt a near-row, Amy disappears, leaving a note which means the cops won't take her vanishing seriously. James gets more hysterical and the stalker gets more invasive. Thinking over his life, James remembers Bill Burrows (Devon Sawa), a former friend he bullied at school, and looks him up to see if he's responsible and make an awkward attempt to apologise. Realising James is only sorry because he's under pressure, Bill snaps, 'You're still an asshole.' More extreme attacks (a severed cat's head, computer footage of Amy in a basement) lead James to turn up at Bill's apartment with a knife. Of course, the stalker has picked on James at random – the implication being that a campaign like this would turn up anyone's guilty secrets. Writer-director Randall Cole gets a higher-profile cast than usual for a found footage film. Former teen stars Stahl and Sawa are excellent – their scenes together are uncomfortable, understated and quietly creepy. It fits in with too many similarly styled films (cf: *Alone with Her*, *Evil Things*) to be outstanding, but is well crafted and reasonably disturbing. Its punch line is among the instant clichés of the sub-genre: a DVD filed with others labelled with addresses, and the prowler staking out a new home.

THE UNFOLDING (2015)

The new wrinkle in this British found footage haunted house story from writer-director Eugene McGing is that it's set in autumn 2016 against the backdrop of an international crisis which leads – inevitably, given how much time is spent on radio news broadcasts – to nuclear war, with low-budget visual burnouts to signify the larger cataclysm. While everyone else is concerned with this vaguely detailed news event, obsessive researcher Tam Burke (Lachlan Nieboer) drags his girlfriend Rose Ellis (Lisa Kerr) to a very haunted house in Devon with the usual MO of putting up surveillance equipment and recording psychic phenomena. After a brief visit to Dartmoor for location shots around Hound Tor, most of the film is set inside the house. Old and imposing, it has an interestingly remodelled, white-painted interior which looks more liveable than most movie haunted houses. There's a mystery as to the source of the haunting, which gives a slight *Legend of Hell House* overtone, and a medium (Kitty McGeever) and a professor (Robert Daws) show up to help with exposition. Kerr, the most interesting presence, takes the Pamela Franklin role of becoming emotionally invested in the haunting. The spook stuff is the usual (telekinetically stuck-in-the-walls cutlery, etc.), with the low-budget frill that the phenomena tend to switch off cameras when anything really impressive is going on. The thematic link between the psychic investigation and the coming war is vague and half-hearted, especially when set beside pointed uses of the ghost story for social comment by Nigel Kneale in *The Road* and Don Taylor in *The Exorcism*. As a British found footage picture, it struggles to find its own identity between *A Night in the Woods* (also set on Dartmoor) and *The Borderlands* (another West Country psychic investigation). Still, it's sincere and has good moments.

UNFRIENDED (2015)

Stalker thrillers *Open Windows* and *The Den* extend the found footage setup to take place entirely on computer desktops, and a Skype-based haunting surfaced as early as 2002 (*The Collingwood Story*), but this surfs the 2015 social media zeitgeist most pertinently. A group of teens are haunted online by Laura Barns (Heather Sossaman), an alpha bitch who committed suicide after a humiliating video – of her drunkenly fouling herself – was posted. A year on, Laura's dead account reactivates and she hooks into a chat among her former friends: Blaire Lily (Shelley Henning), on whose screen the film takes place, her boyfriend Mitch (Moses Jacon Storm), alpha male dick Adam (Will Peltz), snarky girlfriends Jess (Renee Olstead) and Val (Courtney Halverson), and chubby cybergeek Ken (Jacob Wysocki). The avatarless intruder controls computers and people through supernatural and psychological manipulation, bringing out the group's who-betrayed-who secrets in a truth game, then moves on to murder. That the original crime of posting the video was spurred by Laura's nastiness takes the edge off the complicity of the friends in her death, though they all turn out to have been vile to each other. It inventively uses features of the web for creepy effect – buffering to allow only glimpses of the gorier horrors, a moment when what seems a frozen image turns out to be a girl shocked into paralysis – but mostly consists of the young cast shouting at each other as the horror ramps up. It hangs so much on its gimmick that its potent thematic content (cyber-bullying, slut-shaming) seems like freight rather than the point, but has a certain up-to-the-moment grip. *Friend Request*, a non-found footage film, tells a similar story. Written by Nelson Greaves; directed by Levan Gabriadze.

UNIDENTIFIED (2013)

An odd mash-up, similar to but less successful than *Willow Creek*, *Unidentified* wraps typical found footage horror around a chunk of improv comedy. It starts as a mock-doc spin on *The Hangover* as SF/comics geek Jodie (Eric Artell), who nags everyone to join his YouTube channel, takes a camera on a trip to Las Vegas with three friends – problem gambler Nick (Eddie Mui), affable slob Dave (Colton Dunn) and characterless Jeremy (Parry Shen) – because Nick's wife (Beth Alspaugh) wants her husband's behaviour documented. En route, the gang stop off in a UFO-themed diner where a weirdo tells stories about all the Sasquatch and aliens he's run into while drunk. In Vegas, the film defaults to frat comedy situations – the mobster loan shark who won't get repaid, the nerd who chats to a girl not realising she's a hooker, the high-stakes poker game for Downs' syndrome players Nick cheats his way into only to lose all his cash. While fleeing into the desert, the film skips genres and the last reel is all weird phenomena, cult conspiracies, alien-seeming pustules and summary executions. There are a few jolts and some chat feels real, even if the people aren't terribly engaging. Written and directed by Jason Richard Miller, from a story he co-devised with cast members Mui and Shen from a concept by Mui.

VAMPIRE DIARY (2006)

While shooting a rambling documentary about the goth scene, videographer Holly (Morven Macbeth) is smitten with Vicki (Anna Walton), who turns out to be 'a real vampire'. The pair fall into an obsessive relationship, with Holly filming the photogenic predator and enabling her continued existence, even if it means a string of her friends being bled dry and lightning raids on blood banks. Vicki, raped by a shadowy male vampire (Richard Stanley!), is pregnant with a ferociously hungry creature. Modish in its video diary form, this patches together threads from many earlier films (cf: *Vampyres*, *The Addiction*, *Razor Blade Smile*). The appearance of a real vamp in a goth milieu is one of those obvious ideas which comes up every few years. Gravel-voiced Keith Lee-Castle, who plays the goth DJ who becomes Vicki's first willing victim, was in a fairly similar *Urban Gothic* episode, 'Vampirology' (and the kids' show *Young Dracula*). Walton has a good vampire look; she went on to mini-horror stardom (*Hellboy II The Golden Army*, *The Seasoning House*, *Soulmate*, *Cherry Tree*). It tries for a low-key, credible world, but falters as the plot straggles to the seaside for a monster birth finale and predictably perverse coda. Directed by Mark James and Phil O'Shea.

VAMPIRES (2009)

The Belgian vampire community invites a film company to chronicle their lifestyle; the first two crews sent out are killed by bloodsuckers who can't control themselves, so this feature is dedicated to them.

This mock-doc inevitably evokes *Man Bites Dog* even as it prefigures the better known *What We Do in the Shadows*. The wittiest angle is that the self-interested, petty-minded subjects are awful in ways which have nothing to do with their vampirism. Patriarch Georges Saint-Germain (Carlo Ferrante) is annoyed by his voracious if goofy wife Bertha (Vera Van Dooren) and studly, vain, know-nothing son Samson (Pierre Lognay). Rebel daughter Grace (Fleur Lise Heuret) wears pink clothes and tan makeup, and attempts suicide because she wants to feel human. The household has a 'meat' girl – an ex-hooker (Benedicte Bantuelle) on tap for blood, who also performs Renfield chores (these vampires are slightly useless – having no idea they can get to London on Eurostar). In the basement lurk Elisabeth (Selma Alaoui) and Bienvenu (Batiste Sornin), a hidebound, snobbish 19th century couple, who scheme to get the Saint-Germains moved out so they can live upstairs and not have to sleep in upright coffins. Belgian vampire society is run by sulky eternal child Little Heart. When Samson dallies with the master's pouting cougar wife Eva (Alexandra Kamp-Groenvald, of *Dracula 3000*), the Saint-Germains have to relocate to Canada. There, sham liberal arch-vampire Jean-Paul (Julien Doré), an extra in *Battleship Potemkin*, insists they work for a living and try to integrate. A funny skit on vampire romance has Samson hook up with a Quebecois goth girl he can't understand and become a terrible but enthusiastic busker. Grace, in the film's sole moment of poignance, gets her wish and becomes a real girl... only to wander off, cold and alone, to an uncertain future.

It has clever vampire lifestyle gags, with Grace delighted at the gift of a pink coffin for her deathday. A service industry, including a canny human funeral director eager for repeat custom, enables these predators to survive. The police bring unwanted immigrants to the door (the middleman is surprised George can speak the victims' language) and ungrateful vampires whine about having to eat black people all the time. It has mock-doc crudities and *longeurs*, but quite a bit of the writing and playing is priceless, especially when vampires flirt or reveal their nasty selves in to-camera interviews. Directed and co-written (with Frederique Broos) by Vincent Lanno, who also plays the unseen director-interviewer.

THE VISIT (2015)

Writer-director M. Night Shyamalan ventures out of his comfort zone with a found footage psychological thriller made for the medium-budget Blumhouse shingle.

Shy teenager Becca (Olivia DeJinge), a budding filmmaker, and her younger brother Tyler (Ed Oxenbould), an obnoxious white rapper whose overconfidence belies a terror of dirt and a tendency to freeze in a crisis, set out to document a trip they are making to the snowy backwoods to spend a week with grandparents they've never met. Still unable to cope with her parents' marriage break-up, Becca hopes to find out why her mother (Kathryn Hahn) left home. Greeted at the station by Nana (Deanna Dunagan) and Pop Pop (Peter McRobbie), the kids are taken to an idyllic farmhouse without WiFi and treated to biscuits and folksy charm… but rapidly catch on that there are many things wrong. Incontinent Pop Pop collects his full diapers in a shed and gets dressed up for a costume party at odd times of day. He also recalls being fired from his factory job for claiming to see something white with yellow eyes. Nana has 'sundowning syndrome' and goes feral after dark, clawing and crawling around naked. She gets under the house and plays tag/hide and seek with the kids in creepy-aggressive mode, dodges questions by throwing scary fits and sometimes sits in a rocking chair laughing to keep her terrors at bay. Oh, and the kids aren't allowed to go into the basement because of mould.

It's not so much that there's a twist coming – here, the penny hangs suspended for a long time after audiences have guessed the reveal, nudged by hints delivered by a couple of visitors who show up when the old folks are mysteriously not around, only to drop at the climax when the mechanics of terror are fully engaged and the sinister gameplay (a manic game of Yahtzee) is ramping up. The kids aren't terribly likeable, but aren't stupid either, and both are acute psychologically: Tyler deflects criticism by pointing out his sister's neuroses and Becca interviews Nana cleverly by asking her to tell stories rather than reminisce, only to be bombarded with a fairy tale-alien abduction fantasy that would in an earlier MNS film turn out to be true but is here as sad-creepy as the delusion of the paranoid in *They Look Like People*. Dunagan and McRobbie, you-know-the-face bit-part actors, score substantial maniac roles and are both plausible and terrifying – as much for the moments when they show self-awareness, express sympathy or calmly explain what's wrong with their other half as for the insane leers and sudden jumps. The climax, of course, confronts both kids with their worst fears – making for shocks that demonstrate Shyamalan retains a knack for springing scares.

WILLOW CREEK (2013)

As performer and director, Bobcat Goldthwait is usually eccentric (cf: *Shakes the Clown*) – so it's odd that this horror movie so strictly adheres to the found footage formula, following exactly the plot and production template of *The Blair Witch Project*. It's not even the first Bigfoot-themed found footage film. As this acknowledges, the Bigfoot legend goes back to scraps of 1968 home movie footage ('the Patterson-Gimlin film') purportedly showing the American yeti wandering away from some backpackers. Here, Bigfoot-believer filmmaker Jim (Bryce Johnson) and his sceptical actress girlfriend Kelly (Alexie Gillmore) drive to Willow Creek to shoot a documentary at the site where Patterson and Gimlin shot their film. They interview locals, visit the Bigfoot Museum and diner (and stay at the Bigfoot motel) and talk a lot about the legend and its provenance. This is light and chatty, with fun-poking at Bigfoot-themed folk songs and other cryptozoology fan trivia, but once out in the pretty wilderness – after an encounter with an unfriendly, threatening local who tells them to turn around and drive home – things turn scary. The highlight is a nineteen-minute inside-the-tent take as the couple go from social embarrassment (he proposes marriage and she avoids saying yes) to terror as off-screen activity suggests evil intent… It's slightly too obvious Goldthwait (who voices whatever it is that's out there) is just poking the tent with sticks to get a reaction, but the performers deliver a sustained crescendo of fear. A problem, as usual, is that there's nowhere to go but a downer ending… a nude woman, previously seen on a 'missing' poster, is glimpsed and the couple come to a presumably horrible fate (is Kelly taken to be Bigfoot's mate?) as the camera is abandoned.

WITHOUT WARNING (1994)

Made in the same format as the nuclear terrorism thriller *Special Bulletin*, this asteroid disaster movie starts with an extract from a typical cable thriller then interrupts the broadcast for a breaking news story. An asteroid on course for the North Pole splits into three pieces and smacks down in Wyoming, Lourdes and the Gobi Desert. News anchor Sander Vancoeur (as himself) and science correspondent Dr Caroline Jaffe (Jane Kaczmarek) host the coverage, which gets complicated when a dazed little girl survivor in Wyoming and a rescued skier in France start gabbling in the same form of tongues. Another asteroid turns up, to be shot down by USAAF fighters with nuclear weapons as the Pentagon uses the incident as an argument for the implementation of the Star Wars missile shield. Of course, the unlikeliness of two asteroids on the same path stirs up debates, with scientists from SETI arguing that alien intelligence is involved. The population of an entire town vanishes and asteroids are aimed at Beijing, Moscow and Washington. They are shot down, but general rejoicing is interrupted when monitors show an entire storm of Earth-killers on the way. As the world ends, there's the now-familiar cut to static. There is a deliberate echo of Orson Welles in the Halloween setting and contrived awkwardness to simulate the rushed quality of emergency news, with scientists breaking rank and correspondents getting emotional (Kaczmarek has an embarrassing address to her daughter at home when things look bleak). A passable contrived shocker, but silly. We are supposed to believe our rash first shot causes the war and the aliens were only trying to be peaceable (deciphered, the gabble turns out to be our Voyager message played back). Any intelligence that keeps a swarm of killer meteors in reserve as they make pacifist overtures by hurling hunks of rock at a planet surely can't complain at not being welcomed. Arthur C. Clarke pops in from Sri Lanka for a genial if stiff cameo. Also with Dennis Lipscomb, Phillip Baker Hall, John de Lancie, Bill Clinton. Directed by Robert Iscove. Written by Peter Lance.

THE WOODS (BIGFOOT TRAIL) (2013)

> 'YOU DIDN'T BELIEVE HIM ON THE WHOLE "WE SHOULDN'T GO THERE" SHIT DID YOU?'

Yet another Bigfoot found footage movie. *The Blair Witch Project*, still the template for the form, was inspired by pioneering 1972 Bigfoot film *The Legend of Boggy Creek*, so it's only natural multiple coat tail-riders should send documentarians wandering into woods in search of Bigfoot and getting Sasquatched. The twist here, if it is a twist, is that protagonist Mark (writer-director Mark Bacci) and sometimes-reluctant partner Rebecca (Rebecca Davis) set out to make an exploitative hoax documentary (Mark airily admits you don't even need to show a monster on screen to get noticed) only to run into the real thing. This means much of the running time is taken up with squabbles as Mark directs an increasingly annoyed Rebecca as she reacts to various hoked-up signs of Bigfoot activity. As usual, the early stages include encounters with supposed experts (all with plaster-casts of Bigfoot tracks) and an ominous bearded local who warns the outsiders away. The backstory involves the killing of a hiker and the disappearance of his wife, suggesting a parallel with the superior *Willow Creek*, which isn't carried through since the creature (a briefly glimpsed monster suit which resembles *Trog*) is more interested in killing interlopers than snatching a potential bride-of-Bigfoot. A frame story involves a friend of the vanished couple (Aliyah O'Brien) confronted with the recovered footage – and a recorded phone call from the hysterical Rebecca – and shruggingly admitting she doesn't know what to make of it all. The woods look nice, the people are grating and the monster works better when barely seen. Utterly generic.

HARD CASE CRIME

THE ACE OF HEARTS (1921)

Gouverneur Morris's novel was inspired by the 1919 Red Scare, but this Lon Chaney vehicle downplays politics in favour of Mabuse-like supervillainy. The subversive organisation (run by a stereotypical bearded anarchist called Ratovich) is more like R.L. Stevenson's eccentric secret society the Suicide Club than a revolutionary cell. Since no commie in a 1921 film (or a 1952 one, come to that) could be motivated by political conviction, the members are all neurotics and bizarros.

Chubby idealist Forrest (John Bowers) and femme fatale Lilith (Leatrice Joy), drawn to radicalism by a lack of love in their lives, reform when they fall for each other. Agents surround fat cat Mr Morgridge (Hardee Kirkland) disguised as a portrait painter, waiter, etc., to observe at first-hand his plutocratic rottenness. Having tagged Morgridge 'the man who has lived too long', the society sit around their hideout while Lilith deals cards. The eventual recipient of the ace of hearts is obliged to assassinate the tycoon. The task falls to Forrest, who sours on murder when he and Lilith start smooching. The lovers repent, but worry the boss (Raymond Hatton, billed as 'The Menace') will have them killed if they try to quit.

Chaney plays long haired fanatic Farralone, who has the star's usual case of unrequited love for the heroine. In one scene, he stands outside in the rain looking at embracing shadows on the blinds, petting a small dog, torn between helping and killing. The film would play better if he were *more* torn, since the dog nuzzling reveals what a softie Farralone is. When he draws the ace of hearts, he takes one of his own bombs to a meeting and sets it off, destroying the gang. A newspaper account suggests his severed arm is found clutching the card, but we only see a limb stuck out of the rubble. The lovers go free to sunnier climes. Directed by Wallace Worsley, one of Chaney's regular collaborators, this is frankly a miss: interesting plot angles are neglected in favour of self-sacrifice and a plodding romantic triangle, though the card-dealing gambit prods Worsley to work up some suspense.

AKP: JOB 27 (2013)

Every so often, some bright spark – in this case, writer-director Michael L. Suan – gets the idea of doing a film without dialogue. A Japanese hit man (Tyce Philip Phangosa) goes to America for a job and falls for a hooker (Roxanne Prentice), which prompts him to grow a heart. His newfound sensitivity comes out when he slaughters a roomful of goons who've been nasty to his girlfriend and hesitates to fire when his target gets out of a car cradling a little girl. In *Le Dernier Combat* (or *Deafula*, for that matter), there was a reason for the cast to be mute; here, it's just odd. Love scenes are elaborately banal (walks on the beach, through cornfields) though Suan stages a few neat sight gags (the hero putting an annoying dog in a dustbin, a game of peekaboo in the field). With this approach, characters have to be archetypes, but really there've been too many super-cool but inwardly sentimental assassins and beaten up, beautiful hookers in regular genre movies to bother with this pair. It is stylish and makes good use of a wide selection of music (Nat King Cole figures heavily), but faintly boring, like watching non-stop pop clips or adverts.

THE BIG NIGHT (1951)

> 'THAT'S HOW IT IS WITH SOME MEN. THERE'S ONLY ONE WOMAN IN THE WORLD FOR THEM... AND IF IT'S THE WRONG ONE, IT'S TOUGH.'

A minor Joseph Losey noir from his pre-exile Hollywood period, this is an adaptation of a novel (*Dreadful Summit*) by one of my favourite lesser-known writers, Stanley Ellin (who co-scripted with Losey). It's stuck with a mixed-blessing performance from John Barrymore Jr (later John Drew Barrymore) in a difficult mixed-up teenager role: terrible in some scenes, affecting in others. It has a great hook: bookish George LaMain (Barrymore), jovially bullied by street roughs and patronised by barflies, seethes as big-shot sportswriter Al Judge (Howard St John) walks into a saloon with some cronies and humiliates George's father (Preston Foster), forcing him to strip to the waist ('show me skin') and submit to a brutal caning administered with the columnist's walking stick. As in *The Killers*, the victim accepts his fate, spurring an investigation. George takes a gun and spends the night running around the city, intent on avenging his father. He collides with lowlifes – a drunken writer (Philip Bourneuf), a bogus cop (Emile Meyer) and an understanding, slightly older woman (Joan Lorring) – before catching up with Judge and learning harsh truths. Black singer Mauri Lynn has a great little moment (one of Barrymore's good scenes) as George sees her in a club then out on the street and blurts out how good she is and – unusually for a film of this vintage – gasps that she's beautiful, 'even if you are a...' The word isn't said, but Lynn's eyes tell the story. Robert Aldrich is recognisable in a bit as a fight fan and Dorothy Comingore has one of her rare post-*Citizen Kane* roles. Hugo Butler and Ring Lardner Jr contributed to the screenplay, perhaps influenced by the similarly structured Clifford Odets-scripted *Deadline at Dawn*.

IL BOSS (THE BOSS) (1973)

Just as *Dawn of the Dead* inspired zombie flesh-eating and *Apocalypse Now* boosted jungle warfare, *The Godfather* made mafia movies saleable in Italian exploitation, though a mini-cycle of violent gangland pictures let filmmakers deal with Italian as opposed to Italian-American crime. Fernando De Leo's tough melodrama is one big kill-off, with only Henry Silva left standing. Orphan hit man Lanzetta (Silva) is introduced firing rocket-propelled grenades from the projection booth into a bunch of slavering crooks who are about to look over the latest skin-flicks from Denmark ('Jesus doesn't like porno movies.'). Melende (Howard Ross) and Cocchi (Pier Paolo Capponi), the nasties of a rival faction (Camorra rather than Mafia), kidnap Rina (Antonia Santilli), daughter of quivering Don Giuseppe (Claudio Nicastro). Godfather Don Corrasco (Richard Conte, who had been in *The Godfather*) orders Lanzetta and smoother mobster Pignataro (Marino Masé) to bring her back alive if possible but shut down the situation anyway, even if it means killing everyone else. Rina is given a hard time by her kidnappers for taking part in student protests, gets drunk (on the inevitable product placement J&B) and enthusiastically lets her captors gang-bang her, before having an affair with Lanzetta and getting machine-gunned through a door; De Leo claimed 'only a conformist' would object to this characterisation. The token cop (Gianno Garko) is corrupt, too, so – by default – Silva's rootless killer emerges as the only honest man in town. There's a nice ritzy Riz Ortolani score.

CAGED (1950)

'AT LEAST WE GOT HONEST MATRONS IN HERE. WHEN I BRIBE ONE, SHE STAYS BRIBED.'

A key women-in-prison film, much tougher than its exploitative descendants. Fresh fish Marie Allen (Eleanor Parker) arrives quivering and pregnant after her unemployed husband is killed botching a gas station hold-up. With a gutless mother who won't leave her stepfather to take in the baby and no job prospects, Marie doesn't make parole and learns from cons and warders to become a callous survivor. Agnes Moorehead is cast against type as liberal, reforming Warden Benton, but the prison is ruled by Harper (Hope Emerson), the female answer to Hume Cronyn in *Brute Force*. The gross matron reads romance magazines, nips booze and gobbles chocolates, and takes bribes from organised crime. She loves nothing more than forced head-shaving and the rubber hose, unless it's psychological torture like strutting in trampy clothes before a date and gloating about men in front of a cage of sex-starved dames. It's only a matter of time before someone (Betty Warde) kills Harper with a fork ('Kill her kill her kill her... Kindly omit the flowers,' Marie snarls).

In a hardboiled ending, Marie doesn't swear to go straight but takes a deal from 'vice queen' Elvira (Lee Patrick) for parole. Putting on lipstick, she gets into a car with two men, presumably to become a call girl; the warden knows she'll be back. Parker is extraordinary, seething on the edge of a breakdown and then – head shorn ('Thanks for the haircut.') – becoming a monster. Director John Cromwell relies on close-ups of Parker's face – as when she looks through the bars at a fur-coated prison visitor, out-staring the nervous woman. Oddly, one of the tougher elements probably wouldn't have raised an eyebrow on first release: pregnant Marie virtually chain-smokes. With Ellen Corby as a daffy murderess, Jan Sterling as a CP ('common prostitute') and Jane Darwell. Written by Virginia Kellogg, with presumably well-researched con slang ('on the flip', 'freeside').

THE CAPTURE (1950)

Despite its contemporary setting, this flashback-heavy rural noir from director John Sturges falls in with (and slightly prefigures) the 1950s trend for surrogate father/ cowboy anguish (*Shane*, *Hondo*). It stumbles a little because Lew Ayres, whose screen image is sensitive rather than hardboiled, doesn't seem tough enough to be a haunted protagonist. He even sings cowboy songs.

Wounded Lin Vanner (Ayres) staggers into a Mexican hut to tell a priest (Victor Jory) how he came to be in a bad spot. When supposed payroll thief Tevlin (Edwin Rand) takes off through the desert, oil company man Lin joins a posse to track him down. Lin shoots Tevlin, not realising he is trying to surrender, and he bleeds to death without revealing where the loot is or even admitting guilt. Troubled at having killed a man – after starring in *All Quiet on the Western Front*, Ayres became a pacifist and stuck to it even when it was inconvenient for his career – and wanting to solve the mystery, Lin looks up Ellen (Teresa Wright), Tevlin's widow. He takes a job on the neglected family ranch, where he discovers that the marriage was rocky and becomes a hero to the dead man's son (Jimmy Hunt, of *Invaders From Mars*). In arch-melodrama style, Ellen discovers Lin killed her husband and their bitter confrontation ends in a clinch and a wedding… but Lin can't leave things alone and a burst of sleuthing leads him to deduce that Tevlin was a patsy for an inside job. Things take a fatalist turn as everyone Lin encounters somehow winds up dead; for a nice guy who doesn't want violence, he semi-accidentally racks up a major body count. The irony runs deep ('Don't you understand… it was in the cards from the very first?') as the hero ends up on the run, wounded in the arm like his wife's first husband so he can't put his hands up to surrender.

Niven Busch's script, from his own novel, is a mix of rote melodramatic soap and challenging, frank material. The lead characters are given some depth and the milieu (oil displacing cattle) is important, but quality aspirations mean it grips less than a straighter action movie. During a shootout finale, there's time to talk about fate and an unconscious desire for self-destruction, which is all very well… but sillier than significant. The Busch-scripted *Pursued* and the Sturges-directed *Bad Day at Black Rock* have a more satisfying balance of suspense and serious drama. There's too much music from Daniele Amfitheatrof, especially guitar/trumpet themes to remind us this is Mexico.

THE CHASE (1946)

Based on Cornell Woolrich's novel *The Black Path of Fear*, this is among the most literally nightmarish *films noirs*… with a long, revoked central section which might or might not actually be happening. The frame story, which involves amnesiac blackouts, seems no more or less unreal than the dream. Ex GI Chuck Scott (Robert Cummings), down on his luck in Florida, picks up a fat wallet in the street. After buying a meal, he takes the wallet to an address listed inside. Grateful owner Eddie Roman (Steve Cochran), frankly astonished at the sucker's altruism, hires Chuck as a chauffeur. Sleek gangster Eddie – introduced cuffing his manicurist (Shirley O'Hara) across the face for making his cuticles bleed – is married to fragile, terrified Lorna (Michele Morgan). The first act establishes Eddie's craziness, as he uses an odd device in his car to control the speed from the backseat while the hero drives, while Peter Lorre oozes wry menace as his sidekick Gino.

In a Lewtonish horror scene, a boat-owner (Lloyd Corrigan) who refuses to sell ships to drug-importer Eddie is locked in a wine cellar with an unseen dog. It rips him to pieces as a bottle of Napoleon brandy bleeds into a gutter. Chuck and Lorna run off to South America, but bad things happen to them in crowded, claustrophobic studio sets representing Cuba. In a nightclub, Lorna takes a fatal dagger to the back on the dance floor. Chuck looks incredibly guilty, but insists the hear-no-evil monkey-hilt dagger he bought from sinister Madame Chin (Nina Koschetz) has been switched for a see-no-evil monkey. Chuck evades the cops and goes on the run, nearly wriggling free of the frame… then we loop back to Chuck waking up earlier in the day. Now, the situation pans out differently, with Eddie backseat driving his car into a train while racing the fugitive lovers to the docks. As to what happened really, it's a noir shrug about whether or not it matters. Woolrich may have been sending up his own convoluted plotting, including characters with names like Job and Midnight; David Lynch's *Lost Highway* seems built on fragments of memories of this film. Scripted by Philip Yordan (*When Strangers Marry*); directed by Arthur Ripley (*Thunder Road*); cinematography by Franz Planer. Producer Seymour Nebenzal worked with Lorre on *M*.

CROWN V. STEVENS (1936)

One of Michael Powell's quota quickies, this isn't a courtroom drama but a London-set proto-noir. Naive clerk Chris Jansen (Patric Knowles) goes to money lender Julius Bayleck (Morris Harvey) so he can buy an engagement ring. His snippy, shrill girlfriend (Mabel Poulton) dumps him for a wideboy (Billy Watts), keeps the ring ('I've got to have something to remember you by.') and leaves him with a debt he can't pay. Visiting Bayleck after hours to plead his case, he finds the man dead and Doris (Beatrix Thomson) behind a curtain with a smoking gun. The next day, Chris's skinflint boss Stevens (Frederick Piper) sends him to fetch an account book from his home and he discovers the murderess is his employer's wife – a former showgirl irked that Stevens won't support her in a life of luxury. Chris has pangs of conscience and Doris starts thinking another murder might solve her problems.

Based on Laurence Meynell's novel *Third Time Unlucky*, it's a story Alfred Hitchcock would have played for suspense. Hitch would have had the hero suspected of the murder, but Powell lets Chris off the hook too easily, especially after he gets together with the winning heroine (Glennis Lorimer). The dramatic interest is in the Stevens house, with bitter arguments between stern, cheapskate husband and downtrodden, would-be flighty wife. Things are skewed by a *terrible* comedy turn from Davina Craig, typecast as a lopsided, whining maid who throws hysterical fits at any improper suggestion; she does the same act in *Sweeney Todd*, *Tangled Evidence* and *The Black Abbot*. Googie Withers and Bernard Miles have early roles as a successful gold-digger and a plodding copper.

DANGEROUS VOYAGE (TERROR SHIP) (1954)

'GAMMA RAYS. SOUNDS ABSURD, DOESN'T IT?'
'WHY NOT. IN THESE DAYS OF ATOM BOMBS AND FLYING SAUCERS, ONE CAN EXPECT ANYTHING.'

Vernon Sewell – who directed, wrote the original story and provided the main location for this – was always happy on a boat; he captained the supply ship for Michael Powell's *Edge of the World* and often chose maritime subjects. Like *Ghost Ship* (1952), *Dangerous Voyage* is an oddly casual mystery of the sea which stars Sewell's own yacht, the *Gelert*. Vast things are at stake, but no one seems that fussed so long as they can mess about in boats and shrug their way towards genteel romance. Disappearances, reappearances and deaths are treated as mildly puzzling rather than world threatening. Typical is a comedy scene in a French police station where the goodies complain they've been shot at and local *flics* assume they want to apply for a gun license.

Yank-in-Britain Peter Duncan (William Lundigan), author of pulp thrillers, has a mind to buy a small boat and likes the look of one on offer from brother and sister John and Joan Drew (Vincent Ball, Naomi Chance). They admit it's mystery salvage. Finding the craft in distress in the English Channel, they towed it ashore only for the sou'westered crew to disappear. The trio investigate, tracing the yacht to the French shipyard where it was built and looking up its last registered owner, English artist Vivian (Jean Lodge), in Paris. The story drifts back to England, where Vivian – sister of a missing atomic researcher – shows up in the water with baddies after her. A kindly copper (Kenneth Henry) explains it's down to a theft from a nearby research laboratory (a lump of uranium derivative 'about the size of a pea'), which was concealed in the mystery boat's oversize mast. The difference between a sloop and a ketch is a key clue to the location of the stolen fissionable material, but seagoing Sewell assumes everyone in the audience knows *that* and doesn't bother to explain.

Peter, Joan and John start sporting gamma ray burns which don't worry them too much, even after a boffin with a geiger counter detects trace radiation on their boat. An eccentric touch, prefiguring Joseph Losey's *The Damned*, is provided by a self-declared genius sculptor (Beresford Egan) who runs a pub and makes strange artworks: a chunk of lead from an abstract is used to conceal the McGuffin. The finale echoes the same year's *Kiss Me Deadly*, but suggests Sewell did little (or no) scientific research: goodies aboard the *Gelert* close in on the fleeing spy (Peter Bathurst), who shoots at them and somehow triggers 'a small atomic explosion'. This raises an impressive (if small) mushroom cloud, but doesn't make all of Southern England and Northern France uninhabitable for generations.

DEATH IS A WOMAN (1965)

A sun-struck little crime story, with a lower-case cast, an odd 'how did she do it?' angle (the title kind of gives away whodunit) and a sense of not quite firing on all cylinders... though it springs for what passed for X-certificate material (naked breasts in one scene) in the mid-'60s and winds up with an ear-abusingly dire Denis Lotis theme song ('Francesca').

Posh undercover man Dennis Parbury (Mark Burns) is infiltrating a crooked casino on an unnamed island played by Malta when both its bosses are killed. We see Francesca (Patsy Ann Noble) gun down the first boss (Michael Brennan) after her dimwit fancy man Joe (Shaun Curry) has beaten him up, but the senior crook (William Dexter) is killed by a dagger thrust in a locked room with an inaccessible but open window (hint: Francesca is holding a speargun while posing in a bikini on the poster). Dennis is joined by fake fiancée Priscilla (Wanda Ventham), whose main contribution to the sleuthing is distracting cleavage, but feral slut Francesca self-destructs without much prompting – and Joe goes through a fling with a bar girl (Caron Gardner) and a fight with a sailor before getting his scuba air pipe cut by Francesca just before she is busted for retrieving a cache of heroin.

Director Frederic Goode made the oddly touristy, untypical vampire movie *The Hand of Night* – which also featured Terence de Marney, who steals scenes here as a tramp informer who swaps his false teeth for booze. Anita Harris pops up to sing a song in one of several club scenes. Scenery and the cast look nice, but it's low on energy. Noble, an Australian pop singer, had been set dressing on *The Benny Hill Show* and went on to *Carry On Camping*, then a run of US TV guest shots (as Trisha Noble) and a bit in a *Star Wars* prequel; she gets a build-up here, but doesn't show much personality as a venomous villainess whose deeper character flaws we have to take on trust. Scripted by Wally Bosco.

DECOY (1946)

This obscure Monogram B is worthy of comparison with Edgar G. Ulmer's low-rent masterpiece *Detour* (1945). It doesn't have auteur pedigree, since director Jack Bernhard made few and little-seen films (his most famous credit is the dinosaur movie *Unknown Island*), and the leading lady – and at the time Mrs Bernhard – who gets an 'introducing Miss Jean Gillie' credit didn't follow her extraordinary showcase with anything at all (she previously had done bits in a few minor British films I now want to track down because she's in them) and died in 1949 aged thirty-three. The shot-in-a-week haste shows in cramped, chatty mid-film scenes (this 76-minute movie would play better at 65), but Gillie's Margot Shelby is the most unrepentant monster woman in noir (because of her British accent, she's a precedent for Peggy Cummins and Jean Simmons in later films) and *Decoy* boasts one of the wildest scripts (by Nedrick Young, from a story by Stanley Rubin) in the genre.

A terrific opening shot has a bloody handed, zombie eyed goon in a dishevelled suit (Herbert Rudley) loom up in a foul mirror above a dirty sink in a gas station washroom. He hitches a ride to San Francisco, where he staggers into Margot's suite and shoots her even as she kills him (it's as if he's already dead but needs killing again – a theme in the film). In walks a snappily dressed, shady character (Sheldon Leonard) we take for a gangster (Leonard seldom played anything else), but who turns out to be cop Sergeant JoJo Portugal, who has the dying woman recount her story. In *Double Indemnity* and others, the man ensnared by a killer dame provides the voice-over; here, the woman explains how she used a series of disposable guys. Margot is the girlfriend of Frank Olins (Robert Armstrong), a convicted murderer who is going to the gas chamber without revealing where he's stashed the loot from a heist. He's too smart to tell her where it is, so she's scores funding from another gangster (Edward Norris) to pull off a daring rescue. By seducing Craig (Rudley), the prison doctor, she has the corpse smuggled out after the execution and revived with the magic-sounding (but real) drug 'methyl blue'. Olins draws a map and gets killed permanently. Margot goes after the loot, leaving dead, broken and damned men in her wake. In an amazing finish, we return to the storytelling and Margot asks the cop to come 'down to my level for a change'… As spellbound as everyone else, JoJo lowers (for a kiss?) and she laughs in his face.

In the words (later) of Billy Wilder, 'I've met some hardboiled eggs in my time, but you – you're twenty minutes.' Like *Detour*, this makes a virtue of low budget – the sets seem made of chipboard, and even Margot's prized furs look ratty. Gillie is blankly beautiful with her hair up or down and her line readings vary (to suggest duplicity or just the limits of her acting talent?), but she's devastating. That laugh is among the most chilling gotchas in the movies. It has its great minor grotesques: the whore's maid who keeps a wary eye on the parade of stupid men, the morgue attendants bickering about big words (the seeming dummy corrects his smarter pal on the pronunciation of 'dichotomy'). The punch line is that twice-dead Olins has the last laugh – he's given his killers directions to a box containing one single dollar: 'To you who double-crossed me… I leave this dollar for your trouble. The rest of the dough, I leave to the worms.'

DILLINGER AND CAPONE (1995)

Made on the relative cheap for Roger Corman's New Horizons, this has an interesting high concept (objectively, it's a fresher take on gangster legends than *Public Enemies*) and star performers (Michael Sheen, F. Murray Abraham) who might usually be out of Corman's range – perhaps signed on because screenwriter Michael B. Druxman (*The Doorway*) offers meaty takes on gangland icons. It opens at the Biograph Theater in 1934 and spells out what is only hinted at in the Corman-produced *Lady in Red*, that the fellow gunned down as John Dillinger was the gangster's brother (brilliant casting for Joe Estevez). In 1940, Dillinger (Sheen) is living on a farm under the name 'John Dalton' and married to Abigail (Catherine Hicks), who knows he has a past but not how big it is. Just out of prison after his tax evasion rap, Capone (Abraham) has Abigail and her son (Michael Oliver) kidnapped to pressure Dillinger into pulling a job, heisting missing millions from a hidden vault in his old Chicago HQ. The town is now run by nasty Lou Gazzo (Anthony Crivello), who has a good meet-horrid scene tormenting and killing a weasely rat (Clint Howard), but Capone has dreams of getting on top again, though he has delusional spells when he shoots hookers or imagines Eliot Ness coming for him. Dillinger and a *Ruggles of Red Gap* won-in-a-bet English butler, Cecil (Stephen Davies), recruit old associate George (Don Stroud, from Corman's *Bloody Mama*) and punk kid Billy (Sasha Jenson) for the robbery, and a pair of comically venal FBI agents (Jeffrey Combs, Michael C. Gwynne) get on their trail. A decent, twisty robbery story with multiple complications, it takes time to let Sheen play a mellow Dillinger, angrily advising young crooks not to become murderers, and give Abraham quality mad scenes as a ranting, syphilitic Scarface Al who nevertheless has lucid, even touching moments. Directed by John Purdy (*Unabomber The True Story*).

DRIVE A CROOKED ROAD (1954)

'SHORTY, AS LONG AS YOU'RE GETTING
WITH IT, YOU GOTTA GET IT RIGHT.
THAT IS NOT A GOOD LOOKIN' DAME.
THAT IS THE ATOM BOMB.'

An understated, effective character study-cum-film noir from underrated director Richard Quine, who also co-wrote with Blake Edwards. Ace driver and mechanic Eddie Shannon (Mickey Rooney) is self-conscious about his shortness and a car-crash scar. He is ill at ease with workmates who cat-call passing women in a display of lecherous yet pathetic machismo that is perhaps even more uncomfortable now – the leering and face-sticking through a soundproof window makes the guys seem like sad creeps, but the women easily ignore (or provoke) them. Slick out-of-towners Steve Norris (Kevin McCarthy) and Harold Baker (Jack Kelly) spot Mickey racing. Steve sets his stacked girlfriend Barbara (Dianne Foster) to ensnare the boob, inviting him to boozy parties in a Malibu beach house, then cajoling him into being getaway driver for a bank hold-up in Palm Springs. It takes time on character stuff before getting to the crime, and Quine-Edwards write great brittle patter for the icily jovial hoods (Harold is a needling wiseass, Steve more subtle)… saving suspense for the last-reel heist, which (as in *Gun Crazy*) stays outside the bank with the waiting driver then delivers a rattling single car action scene as Eddie drives fast through town and along a bad road to get on the highway before road blocks go up. Inevitably, Eddie has the crashing post-robbery realisation that the girl (who has conscience pangs) has suckered him and Steve and Hal try to rub him out. Rooney, more often a show-off maniac in this phase of his career (*Baby Face Nelson*), plays it tight and interior, showing put-upon Eddie's growing confidence as Barbara takes an interest in him as taller guys literally talk over his head.

ENRAGÉS (RABID DOGS) (2014)

This remake sticks close to the plot of Mario Bava's *Cani Arrabati*, but amps up the style: the setting is nebulous (French crooks on the run on Canadian locations), significant flashbacks occur in a surreal scarlet-lit corridor and a folk ritual detour features a

Wicker Man-style bonfire and bear-skinned revellers. Assured and gripping, it misses the grit of the rougher, more grounded (*very* Italy-in-1974) original. The opening heist is complicated (in an updated touch) by an Occupy protest outside the bank and a dropped can of teargas. A quartet of robbers face off cops and snatch hostages. The competent boss (Pierre Lebeau) is wounded and chooses to go down in a hail of bullets so his comrades can get away, but Sabri aka Little Chief (Guillaume Gouix) isn't as able to control the panicky Manu (Franck Gastambide), who has ineptly killed a hostage, and scarred psycho pretty boy Vincent (Francois Arnaud), who is immediately more interested in fondling the surviving female hostage (Virginie Ledoyen) than escape. Ditching their stolen van, the thugs invade a car driven by a buttoned-down, desperate guy (Lambert Wilson) who has an unconscious four-year-old girl in the back and says he's driving her to a hospital for a kidney transplant.

Captions announce the passing of time as the ill-assorted crew try to leave the city, with thwarted escapes, cop checkpoints, friction between the robbers and the ticking clock of the ailing girl. Writers Yannick Dahan (*La Horde*), Benjamin Rataud and director Éric Hannezo – the source is credited as a Michael J. Carroll short story from *Ellery Queen's Mystery Magazine* ('Man and Boy') – keep upping stakes on the Bava version, but tend to blunt the suspense: if a scene in *Cani Arrabati* involved squirming to get away from an obstacle, there's gunplay here and incidental characters get shot dead. It piles on the situations – a stroke-ridden old woman recognises the robbers from a TV broadcast and desperately rings the bell for her carer as one of the thugs advances on her, then is left helpless when the nurse is caught in the crossfire… a ranting, shotgun-toting garage proprietor also sees that news show and is gunned down by Sabri. Among the '70s holdovers is the fact that female characters are useless or comatose, and their horrible treatment by the men in the car is just the way things are.

EYEWITNESS (SUDDEN TERROR) (1970)

'I CAME HERE FOR A HOLIDAY. I GOT A FRONT-ROW SEAT FOR AN ASSASSINATION AND A FREE RIDE WITH WALTER MITTY.'

Made between *The Window* (1949) and *Cloak and Dagger* (1984), this uses the Boy Who Cried Wolf premise as a vehicle for leading kid actor Mark Lester in the wake of his success in *Oliver!* (1968). Lester is good as Ziggy, a fanciful lad whose imagination is encouraged by his doting grandfather (Lionel Jeffries), but the film doesn't trust its star and builds up Jeffries' (terrific) role as a crotchety, whimsical yet tough ex-officer while also devoting time to the scenic delights of Malta, playing an unnamed island state. Killer cops Paul and Victor Grazzini (Peter Vaughan, Peter Bowles) stage a JFK-look motorcade assassination, ostensibly to help unsympathetic Sean Bean-soundalike police chief Galleria (Jeremy Kemp) stage a coup and impose martial law. Ziggy sees the killers strike, but his sister Pippa (Susan George) won't listen. Even when the grandfather starts reasoning things through it's too late since Ziggy has left the house during curfew and the baddies are after him. The Grazzini brothers are particularly vile villains: besides the original hit on a visiting African Head of State (Tom Eytle), they murder Ziggy's preteen friend (Maxine Kalli), dump a confederate (John Allison, in fabulously louche clobber) off a cliff, shoot a monk (Jeremy Young) and kill the family's sternly devoted housekeeper (Betty Marsden).

A tiny bit, as Jeffries plays a bagpipe record while rigging up Molotov cocktails to see off villains who are invading his fortress home, parallels *Straw Dogs* to a surprising degree, down to the casting of Vaughan and George. Director John Hough – whose future *Twins of Evil*, Maltese-born Madeleine and Mary Collinson, have a tiny unbilled bit – overdoes zooms and odd angles, but stages a terrific final chase along the cliffs. It keeps skittering away from British *giallo* mode to play conspiracy, eccentric character comedy, young romance and hard action. It's full of great British or British-resident faces: Joseph Furst, David Lodge, Robert Russell. Blond, handsome Tony Bonner (*Creatures the World Forgot*), cast as nice guy Tom Jones, must have expected a leading man career, but his heroics are superfluous since Jeffries handles the fighting. A weakish punch line has Ziggy see an aged Hitler in a restaurant, complete with moustache. Jonathan Demme co-ordinated music, which includes grooviness from Van der Graaf Generator. Co-produced by Irving Allen and Paul Maslansky. Scripted by Ronald Harwood (*The Dresser*) from a novel by John Harris (writing as Mark Hebden).

FIVE STAR FINAL (1931)

A rattling, angry Warner Brothers/First National yellow-press exposé from a mini-cycle of cynical newspaper pictures initiated by the stage and screen success of *The Front Page*. Also based on a play (by Louis Weitzenkorn), this is as vicious in its depiction of the circulation-chasing staff of a big-city tabloid as the more famous property – but a lot less indulgent, playing for shocking melodrama rather than nasty laughs.

Joseph Randall (Edward G. Robinson), editor of the struggling *New York Gazette*, is pressured by smarmy proprietor Hinchecliffe (Oscar Apfel) and a strong-arm circulation man to cut front-page coverage of the League of Nations and play up 'shopgirls in trouble'. Following orders, Randall rakes up the twenty-year-old scandal of Nancy Voorhees (Frances Starr), who was exonerated by a jury after shooting her caddish lover. This upends the new life Nancy has made with loving, respectable husband Michael (H.B. Warner). Jenny (Marian Marsh), Nancy's innocent daughter (who didn't know her own backstory until the presses rolled), is engaged to a well-connected young man (Anthony Bushell, later director of *Terror of the Tongs* and a co-star in the TV *Quatermass and the Pit*). Though he has a wisecracking voice of conscience in a wry, lovelorn secretary (Aileen McMahon), Randall unleashes his dogs – who include predatory blonde news-hen Kitty Carmody (Ona Munsen) and sordid bogus reverend T. Vernon Isopod (Boris Karloff!).

Blaring headlines cause Nancy to crack and her prospective in-laws huffily squelch the wedding. Following an unproductive afternoon trying to get the publisher or the editor on the telephone, she and her husband commit suicide. As luck would have it, Kitty discovers the bodies and Jenny learns her parents are dead by seeing their corpses on the front page. After that, even Randall knows he's gone too far. The powerful if hokey finish finds Jenny ('Why did you kill my parents?') and Randall delivering impassioned *j'accuse* speeches to the pompous bastard proprietor. Made in the late prohibition, pre-code era, it's full of illegal but tolerated speakeasy tippling. Dialogue is smart and cynical: when a cub reporter tells the secretary he's thinking of changing his name, she advises against it because 'New York is too full of Christians as it is'. T. Vernon Isopod (a splendid character name) is reputed to be dangerous for a woman to share a taxi-ride with. Karloff, in a rare credible non-horror role, is a leering dog-collared lech expelled from divinity school for sexual impropriety. Marsh, the very lovely Trilby of *Svengali*, has a role which could seem bland or shrill, and runs with it – more than holding the screen against Robinson (not easy) in their big confrontation. Like a sad number of 1930s 'social issue' films, it depressingly seems as relevant now as on first release. Scripted by Byron Morgan; directed by Mervyn LeRoy.

GANGSTERS (PLAY FOR TODAY: GANGSTERS) (1975)

Shot on film, this is an unusually cinematic entry in the BBC's flagship drama anthology series *Play for Today*. Directed by Philip Savile (*The Boys From the Blackstuff*, *Count Dracula*) from a teleplay by Philip Martin (who writes himself a juicy bad-guy role), *Gangsters* prefigures the hardman crime dramas found more often on ITV in the 1970s (*The Sweeney*, *Out*, *Fox*), but uses Birmingham locations rather than the familiar streets of Shepperton. It's a little more blatant in using the gangster genre to present a portrait of contemporary Britain, paying attention to the city's cultural and racial mix. Pompous 'community leader' Rafiq (Saeed Jaffrey) extorts protection from illegal immigrants or rats them out to the authorities, while young, vicious and black Malleson (Paul Barber) rises in a crime scene dominated by white hoods like mid-level mastermind Rawlinson (Martin).

A *Get Carter* hook has just-out-of-jail ex-SAS hardnut Kline (Maurice Colbourne) trying to avoid being murdered by the family of the gangster he served time for killing. In alliance with the mysterious Khan (Ahmed Khalil), Kline dismantles the crime empire of the Rawlinson brothers, who have taken over the cinema he co-owned with untrustworthy McAvoy (Paul Antrim). It's now a club where cowgirl strippers perform to the theme from *The Good, the Bad and the Ugly*. White (Rolf Day) and Indian (Mohammed Ashiq) comics spew endless Pakki and blackie and stupid Irish gags which are more aggressive than funny. Material like this was commonplace on TV in 1975; now, it's more shocking than the nudity and violence which got license-payers writing in to *Points of View*. Kline hooks up with Dinah (Tania Rogers), a stripper who used to be Malleson's girlfriend, but also gets close to Anne (Elizabeth Cassidy), a Rawlinson minion who uses her houseboat to distribute drugs. Anne goes through painful withdrawal as Kline withholds heroin to get information (he's tipped it in the kitchen bin, but she salvages some from the messy food wrappers); this is paralleled by an equally upsetting, mercifully curtailed scene as Malleson uses the electrical wires of a hairdryer to torture a tied-to-the-bed Dinah for the goods on Kline.

The sustained chase/action/fight finale ranges across a city full of spectacularly ugly concrete locations and goes almost parodically far in its brutal thuggery. This was among the first TV dramas to depict immigrants and second-generation black or brown Brits in anything more than 'social problem' terms. Khalil and Rogers are weaker as decent people than Jaffrey and Barber are as bastards, while Paul Satvendar (as Rafiq's debt collector) has the most outrageous sideburns on 1970s television. There are a lot of knowing winks, especially in the cowboy-movie references later picked up by *Life on Mars* ('My name's John Kline not John Wayne.'), but this isn't light-hearted – in the opening credits, Colbourne (who has one of the great battered TV faces) is introduced with a frozen snippet as he takes a heavy blow to the face. The follow-up series became increasingly bizarre, pulpy, baroque and satirical.

THE GIRL HUNTERS (1963)

An oddity on several levels. As Mickey Spillane adaptations go, it might be conceptually weirder than *Kiss Me Deadly* – to which it could be seen as an answer film – though its cheap dullness renders it a harder watch than Robert Aldrich's nuclear noir. In an act of authorial fantasy Raymond Chandler or Ian Fleming could only dream of, Spillane plays his private eye hero Mike Hammer, groping dames and battering hoods like a big kid acting out. He also had a hand in the screenplay – which is full of thug dialogue ('they'd be picking fragments of your skull out of the woodwork with needle-nose pliers') and assumes complete familiarity with the hero's previous adventures. When the film starts, Hammer has been a cracked alcoholic for two years, grieving for missing secretary Velda. She turns out to be working undercover as a commie-smasher in Russia(!), but never quite arrives, as if the reunion were being saved for a sequel.

Cop Pat Chambers (Scott Peters), Hammer's best friend, beats him up and dries him out for a new case. Hammer investigates a Russian spy called 'the Dragon' who turns out to be a team led by Laura Knapp (Shirley Eaton), the bikini-clad widow of a McCarthyite red-busting senator (presented, implicitly, as a good guy). With a misogynist glee that's somewhat tired this late in the game, Hammer beds the bad girl then dupes her into blowing off her head with a stopped-up shotgun (offscreen, of course). Made in England by journeyman Roy Rowland (*The 5,000 Fingers of Dr T*), with cut-in establishing shots of New York's sprawl and no-name ex-pat supporting actors. Lloyd Nolan gets huge special billing because he's the only semi-familiar face.

Spillane's Hammer is stiff and unattractive, leaden in line-readings but flip with bits of business like forcing a smarmy hood to eat a bullet or telling a nurse to lick her lips (a setup for him smacking a kiss on her later, after asking, 'Are your lips still wet?') and pitched literally head over heels when socked. With his trench coat and dead eyes, he could almost be in a Godard film – but everything else is makeshift.

THE HOODLUM (1951)

> 'IT'S TOO LATE, VINCENT. WHAT CAN MOMMA DO – GO TO THE ELECTRIC CHAIR FOR YOU?'

Director Max Nosseck and tough guy star Lawrence Tierney had a hardboiled hit in *Dillinger* (1945). This follow-up replays 1930s gangster clichés in a 1950s context, heightening family melodrama to cartoonish levels (Tierney's real-life brother plays his character's brother) to set up a powerful climax.

Nogoodnik Vincent Lubeck (Lawrence Tierney) is paroled from prison, because his old Momma (Lisa Golm) pleads on his behalf. He takes a job working for his brother Johnny (Edward Tierney) in the gas station Johnny bought with his share of their father's insurance (Vince's went on lawyers). It's plain from the get-go that Vince is rotten all the way through, and only his mother doesn't notice. In short order, Vince forcibly seduces and impregnates his brother's girl (Allene Roberts) and just shrugs when she jumps off the roof because he won't marry her. He annoys customers by mouthing off and sets his sights on robbing the bank across the road, using a nearby funeral parlour to get round a roadblock. A confederate claims a transient's body as a relative so a funeral can be arranged at the time of the hold-up, which turns into a shootout and a mass betrayal (even Vince's gang can't stand him and try to kill him). Vince, on the run, seeks shelter with his finally disillusioned mother. Golm has a great deathbed speech about what a heel Vince is, and Tierney crumbles before her... Then, in an EC comics poetic payoff, the finally wise Johnny drags his brother out to the city dump where they used to live so he can get shot and join the rest of the garbage.

Sam Neuman and Nat Tanchuk's forceful script bluntly has no patience with or sympathy for the title hoodlum – it's explicit that Vince is lousy and Johnny saintly, though they had exactly the same upbringing. Tierney simmers and snarls so much it's astonishing when the parole board listen to his mother, but he has the charisma to make his winning of Johnny's dimwit fiancée horribly credible. It's a cheap, defiantly sleazy little picture (much is made of the literal and figurative stink of the dump) with a grotesque streak in the sham-funeral angle, précis-like montages (newspaper headlines, shootouts and car crashes) to cover major plot turns, and one of Lawrence Tierney's most killer performances. Edward Tierney is stuck with the nice guy weakling role – the other Tierney sibling, Scott Brady, might have brought more to the turning-worm finale than he does.

HOT BOYZ (GANG LAW) (2000)

'THERE WAS A TIME WHEN THE FUTURE LOOKED SO GOOD... NOW I'M ON A DEAD-END PATH, CRASHING TOWARDS MY DESTINY.'

A once-in-a-lifetime team-up of over-the-hill straight-to-video superstars (Gary Busey, Jeff Speakman, C. Thomas Howell) and tagalong rappers (Snoop Dogg, Mystikal, C-Murder). Kool (Slikk the Shocker) drifts away from crime through devotion to martial arts and rap, but discovers the Man has it in for him when girlfriend LaShawna (Shireen Crutchfield) is busted on a murder rap after witnessing the killing of a black undercover cop by a crooked white cop. Tully (Busey), the hardass in charge of the investigation, promises to help out if Kool goes undercover with his homeys and gets close to a gang Tully wants to bust. An inevitable rap soundtrack is slathered over equally inevitable drek dialogue ('Our daughter should be in a college dorm not some jail cell,' 'Pregnant? I can't let you have our child in jail,' 'Wait a minute, don't do anything stupid.'). Action scenes (car chases, a drugs bust, shootouts) are on a level with a 1970s TV cop show, down to the sub-Lalo Schifrin stock themes. LaShawna dies after a brutal jail beating inflicted by the crooked cop, so the last act is Vengeance City. Slikk, whose brother Master P writes and directs (and co-stars), is no better or worse than any other rapper-cum-actor. The name-on-the-cover stars get little to do: Busey has a 'comic relief' bit with a stripper, Howell is a secondary cop, Speakman a chunkily Seagaled-out guru and Dogg barely registers until the last half-hour when the rappers get together in a vigilante gang to rip off the baddies. This arrant self-aggrandisement fantasy weirdly ends up with most of the good guys killed in a shootout in the proverbial abandoned warehouse – oh, all right, a drugs factory *disguised* as an abandoned warehouse.

THE KILLER WITHIN ME (2003)

Written and directed by character actor Jesse Vint (*Chinatown, Silent Running, Bobbie Jo and the Outlaw*), this mean-spirited shocker sets out a right-wing agenda defused by half-smart scripting and playing. It tries to be about something besides sheer nastiness – and its cartoon ending is memorable in concept, if not execution.

Charismatic sociopath Steve Padevik (William Benton) smarms his way out of prison on parole and takes to murdering former associates. Writer Danny Flanagan (Corbin Timbrook), whose latest book is about the redemption of ex-cons, argues that society is responsible for the creation of all criminals. At a reading, Danny (who looks alarmingly like horror writer Dennis Etchison) is harangued by a woman who cites the film's real-life inspiration, the case of Jack Abbott – a killer set free after lobbying by Norman Mailer who quickly murdered again. From that, it's obvious where the film is going. Danny is called by old friends and asked to shelter their son Steve, whom they paint as a likely victim rather than a cold killer. Danny's daughter Stacy (Stacie Doss) moves in with her mother Cassandra (Lydie Denier) to avoid Steve, but the young man woos her with fake sensitivity. Though Vint sets out to bash liberals, Danny isn't depicted as a naïve sucker: he sees through the kid's attempts to toady or manipulate even as he tries to give him the benefit of the doubt and encourages him to read Thomas Malory. Danny wants Steve to pick up concepts of honour, but Steve reads the King Arthur story as an argument for putting his enemies to the sword.

A good twist comes when Danny tries to back out of his agreement and realises his friends are terrified of their kid, and have a useless restraining order out against him. In the finale, Steve duct-tapes Danny to a chair at gunpoint, lectures him about what a gullible fool he is, then shoots him in the head. Danny survives but Steve kills Stacy (the film's sacrificial victim) so Danny revokes his bleeding heart position in the most blatant fashion imaginable… building a pyre of his wishy-washy book and burning the little bastard at the stake. Benton is white trash menace incarnate, a character type who made a comeback in the 2000s (cf: *Cold Creek Manor*, *The Lost*) usually to justify a 'furious vengeance' finale. Timbrook is more shaded a wrong-headed lead than the script seems to require, but it still boils down to the reactionary saw that 'a liberal is a conservative who hasn't been mugged yet.'

KILL ME TOMORROW (1957)

> 'THIS IS A BUSINESS, CROSBY,
> NOT A PLAYGROUND FOR
> IRRESPONSIBLE DRUNKS!'

Released in the same month as *The Curse of Frankenstein*, this is typical of director Terence Fisher's pre-horror efforts: a stodgy Brit noir built around a fading American star, with a wildly unlikely plot (from writer Robert Falconer) and little action or excitement. Crime reporter Bart Crosbie (Pat O'Brien – so faded he has to be cast as a drunken burnout), who caused the death of his wife by reckless driving, is reduced to interviewing pretentious revue star Bella Braganza (April Olrich), whose chatter of Stanislavsky and ideals suggests Marilyn Monroe. Meanwhile, crooks Heinz Webber (George Couloris) and Waxy Lister (Freddie Mills) run a diamond-smuggling racket out of a coffee bar where Tommy Steele (playing himself) belts out a couple of numbers ('Are You Ready, Rebel?'). This must have dragged some teeny boppers in to be bored by the stolid middle-aged lead. Bart's son has a movie eye disease which will kill him if he's not flown to Switzerland for an operation pronto. Going to beg money from the editor (Ronald Adam) who has fired him, Bart arrives just as the baddies shoot the newspaperman to quash an exposé. He contrives a situation whereby he'll confess to the crime if they pay for the flight to Switzerland… only the police inspector (Wensley Pithey) isn't convinced. Nosey reporter Jill Brook (Lois Maxwell) interferes, prompting hugely sexist outbursts from the unreasonable hero. It ends with a dash to the airport and a scuffle on the runway. With Robert Brown, Richard Pasco, Peter Swanwick and Al Mulock.

LIGHTS OF NEW YORK (1928)

'WAIT A MINUTE, HAWK, YOU'RE A HOUND FOR CHICKENS, AREN'T YOU?'

Most early talkies now sound odd because of the lack of background music, but this Warner Bros gangster drama – the first actual all-talkie, since *The Jazz Singer* only had songs and a line or two of dialogue – is nearly through-composed, with a somewhat intrusive score which underlines the histrionics. There are some sub-Jolson nightclub warblings too, because that must have been expected. Nice guy Eddie Morgan (Cullen Landis) and partner Gene (Eugene Pallette) have sunk their dough into a barbershop, only to find out that it's a front for a speakeasy run by slick-dressed bootlegger Hawk Miller (Wheeler Oakman). Hawk also smarms around Eddie's girl Kitty (Helene Costello) and gets shot, putting Eddie in a bad position – Gene tries to pose the corpse in the barber chair and give him a shave to conceal the corpse from the cops – until Hawk's girl Molly (Gladys Brockwell) owns up to plugging the hood. Crosby (Robert Elliott), the detective on the case, is willing to go easy on Molly because the gangster was wanted dead or alive for murdering a cop.

Despite the title, and a snatch of neon stock footage scored with 'Give My Regards to Broadway', it's studiobound and shot on the West Coast so lacks any New York atmosphere (scenes in Central Park are cramped, but the nightclub set looks good). Writers Murray Roth and Hugh Herbert set the tone for the talking gangster movie: there's too much sentimental speechifying ('I've lived, and I've loved, and I've lost!' wails Molly), but for the first time the tough, snarling patter of the urban hood was heard. The breakout line was Hawk's ominous instruction to hit men Sam and Tommy (Tom Dugan and Guy D'Ennery) to 'take him for a ride', which stayed in the language as a euphemism for execution for decades – though, ironically, the film doesn't stretch to showing a car or even a murder. Though horribly moralistic – at the end, Crosby orders the kids to get on a train out of town to the country where there's trees, fresh air and no organised crime – it's hardboiled in its own pre-code way, with plenty of broken laws. Directed by Bryan Foy.

MACHINEGUNNER (1976)

Written with a harder edge than usual by Bob Baker and Dave Martin (who created K-9 for *Doctor Who*) and produced and directed by HTV's busy Patrick Dromgoole (who made almost every West Country TV drama of the 1970s), this one-off TV movie casts Leonard Rossiter as Cyril Dugdale, a sleazy Bristol private eye whose Welsh accent comes out under pressure. Dugdale is a near-comic creation, but also a noirish beaten-up loser who triumphs against the odds. Rossiter gets laughs, but plays the shamus for real – his horniness and racism are truer to the times than much more-lauded drama of the period – and tough, brutal, sordid elements aren't skimped (Rossiter even has a nude scene). Someone must have decided it was too much of a downer since it's stuck with a jaunty comedy score that would have been more appropriate on an extended episode of *On the Buses*. The plot, rooted in what was going on at the time, is excellent: a property developer rents houses to 'undesirable' immigrants to drive out the long-established population, then evicts the recent tenants from overcrowded homes to make way for demolition and expensive developments. Cool black lawyer Felicity Rae Ingram (Nina Baden Semper, allowed to play a complicated character) hires Dugdale to snap photos of developer Jack Bone (Colin Welland) committing adultery, ostensibly for a divorce action but actually to shake the house of cards conspiracy because Bone is boning the wife (Kate O'Mara, also very good) of the kingpin behind the scam (Ewen Solon). It winds up with a fight in a meat-packing warehouse, and Dugdale pestered by an ex-wife, friends who've got beaten up, former clients and the like, but still not copping off with the girl whose life he's saved. 'Machinegunner' is supposed to be local slang for debt collector (first I've heard of it) – the misleading title probably didn't help the show's chances as a series pilot.

MOONRISE (1948)

> 'IF YOU WENT INTO ALL THE REASONS WHY THAT ROCK STRUCK JERRY'S HEAD, YOU MIGHT END UP WRITING THE HISTORY OF THE WORLD.'

Directed by veteran Frank Borzage (known for romantic early talkie melodramas) and scripted by Charles F. Haas (from a novel by Theodore Strauss), this rural man-on-the-run story stresses redemption, transcendence and poetry within the paranoid, violent, haunted world of noir. After an impulsive murder, the protagonist is harried by the authorities and his own conscience, but gets a shot at happiness with a sweet, unconventional love interest. The subject would have suited the neurotic male beauties who monopolised antihero roles in the '50s and '60s (Clift, Dean, Brando, Beatty) – there's even a scene in which an alienated youth puts his foot down on the accelerator in a semi-suicidal thrill ride prefiguring hot-rodders and chicken runs to come. However, bruised-looking Dane Clark is a convincing backwater rough (do we really believe Clift as a working class no-good in *A Place in the Sun*?) whose firecracker temperament makes him credible as a possible psycho-killer.

An expressionist opening shows that Danny Hawkins (Clark) suffered extreme bullying as a child because his father was hanged for murder (as it turns out, he killed the doctor who botched his wife's treatment and caused her death). The young man has his eye on schoolteacher Gilly (Gail Russell), but is needled by the local in-crowd. When Jerry (Lloyd Bridges) pushes Danny too far, he is battered to death with a rock and dumped in the woods. Terrified he'll be caught, and – worse – that this will confirm what folks have been saying about his bad blood, Danny is also liberated by his crime. With nothing to lose, he makes a play for Gilly, who turns out to be an equally complex, unpredictable character. In a marvellously played sequence, Danny takes Gilly to a decayed mansion (prefiguring *Rebel Without a Cause*) and is at once delighted and disturbed when she starts role-play, adopting a Southern belle accent and asking him to dance. By going off into her own fantasy, she breaks his image of her, but also shows she might be attainable. The canny Sheriff (Allyn Joslyn) gently asks Danny questions which set him up to manufacture a case against another suspect (which he can't quite bring himself to do). Billy Scripture (Henry Morgan), a childlike deaf mute Danny has protected, finds and keeps a knife that could link Danny with the crime.

In another set piece, Danny takes Gilly to a county fair to forget his troubles, but becomes jittery over the course of the evening – to the extent that he thinks the Sheriff is following him by sitting in the next car on the Ferris wheel and hysterically tries to get off the moving contraption. Danny reaches the point where most noir killers would become unredeemable, throttling the innocent fool in his shack, but is horrified by his own actions and stops just in time. In a wonderful, heart-tugging moment, Billy

(Morgan doesn't plead for extra sympathy the way most character actors cast as Lennie types do) is appeased by a gentle pat and smiles weakly at the man who has nearly murdered him. Rex Ingram is one of the occasional dignified, saintly black father figures who crop up in '40s films – a trapper (inevitably named 'Mose') who calls his dogs 'mister' because 'there isn't enough respect in the world'. He realises Danny's guilt early, but has faith the boy will eventually turn himself in. Ethel Barrymore is at the end of a run through the swamp as Danny's grandmother, bringing out the backstory in a scene which leads to an understated, affecting finish. Beautifully filmed, with as many misty fantastical stretches as harshly lit shadows, played with exceptional sensitivity by the non-star cast, this is a hugely underrated minor classic.

IL MOSTRO DELL'ISOLA (THE ISLAND MONSTER) (1954)

If a Randolph Scott film called *Gunfighters of Tombstone* turned out to be a romantic comedy set in Holland or a Jenna Jameson film called *Jenna Screws a Football Team* turned out to be a cartoon manual about DIY carpentry, the stars' fans would be as fed up as Boris Karloff's admirers are to track down this obscure runaway credit and discover it's not a horror film but a flat melodrama about an undercover cop infiltrating a gang of drug smugglers on the Italian island of Ischia. Pompadoured, slick-moustached Lieutenant Andreani (Renato Vicario) is assigned to bust the drugs ring. His nagging wife (Patrizia Remiddi) goes one better than nagging wives in other cop movies (cf: *Donnie Brasco*) by turning up on the island with their purportedly adorable moppet daughter, blowing his cover when she sees him making up to shady nightclub singer Gloria (Franca Marzi) to get in with the crooks. Benign old Don Gaetano (Karloff) runs a children's hospital, and is even more blatantly the mystery man behind the drugs ring than typecasting suggests.

Karloff – who spent more time on TV, radio, the theatre and gramophone records than movies in the 1950s – could play all manner of roles. He could easily have given even this tosh a lift – if the English language release weren't appallingly post-synced (it's the kind of track where a full-grown woman puts on a squeaky voice to play a child) and the star dubbed by someone doing a poor Karloff impersonation. Bereft of his voice, the only interest comes from seeing the bow-legged sixty-something mess around undoubled in small boats and doing the odd scowl. The kid is abducted and, in what was obviously supposed to be a big scene, Mrs Andreani goes to Gloria to plead for help, castigating her for being so unfeeling in letting a child be taken from her family. Because she once had a child, who has usefully died, the good/bad girl relents and helps out, which naturally means she has to take a bullet and be redeemed.

I can't understand the thinking behind writer-director Roberto Bianchi Montero's project. Would it have been so much trouble to do a rewrite and make a film about, say, an island devil-worshipping cult with Karloff as high priest (even the kidnapped kid angle would make sense if sacrifice was intended) and deliver a movie that could justify its title? Or else call it something like *Island of Drug Smugglers* and honestly sell the film to fans of cut-rate European crime movies? Karloff waited three years to make another film: *Voodoo Island*, which is among his worst, but at least delivers voodoo, zombies and killer plants.

THE NEIGHBOR (THE NEIGHBOUR) (2016)

Marcus Dunstan – who usually works with co-writer Patrick Melton – paid his dues with script work on the *Feast* and *Saw* series, then turned writer-director on the solid horror film *The Collector*, which was successful enough to merit a sequel (*The Collection*), but hasn't blossomed into a franchise. However, Dunstan carries over the lead of those films, Josh Stewart, into this rural noir thriller, which also follows *The Collector* in a mini-cycle of recent pictures in which 'ordinary, decent' criminals find themselves up against far worse folks (cf: *No One Lives, Don't Breathe*).

Army vet John (Josh Stewart) is semi-unwillingly working for his Mississippi drug boss uncle, Neil (Kenny Barr), and planning with loyal wife Rosie (Alex Essoe, of *Starry Eyes*) to cut out as soon as they're well setup enough to get away from the genial yet plainly monstrous gangster. When John notices a trash-bin rolled into the middle of the road, he makes the neighbourly gesture of putting it back in place – and the soft-spoken homeowner Troy (Bill Engvall) comes round with cold beers to quiz him about tracks on his property, setting John's antennae twitching… though it's telescope-snooping Rosie who spots Troy murdering a guy who seems to be escaping from his basement and realises the neighbour and his sons (Luke Edwards, Ronnie Gene Blevins) are running a lucrative, sinister racket from their home. Then, Troy notices Rosie has noticed, and John comes home to find his wife missing and all clues pointing across the road.

A tough cowboy crime picture in the spirit of *Blue Ruin* or *Cold in July*, this has an action-oriented, serial-style plot of physical threat, peril and escape as folks in desperate situations take more desperate measures. It has twists, some guessable – like who is in on Troy's racket – and some out of left field, but what works best is the fierce bond between the married leads, with Essoe a gutsier heroine than usual and the underrated Stewart simmering credibly as a not-bad guy in a bad business up against terrible people in a worse one. Dunstan and Melton know from their *Saw* days how to turn the screws, and there are any number of uh-oh moments – including a fight in a shallow grave full of raw mystery meat which leads to the death of the one character sensible enough to de-escalate the situation – and gruesome payoffs. Engvall, usually a redneck comedian, tones it down and manages menace as a bad guy patriarch. A smart, tough, bleak little suspense picture with just a sliver of heart.

NID DE GUÊPES (THE NEST; THE WASPS' NEST) (2002)

This slick, exciting French film landed writer-director Florent Siri a Hollywood gig (*Hostage*). It's ironic that another French director (Jean-François Richet) did the official remake of *Assault on Precinct 13*, since this 'homage' is truer to the original. It opens, like the Carpenter film, with various sets of characters on a collision course. Albanian mafia boss Abedin Nexhep (Angelo Infanti), arrested in East Germany, is being conveyed to the Hague in an armoured car by a multi-national troop of armed professionals. A gang of multi-ethnic drop-out thieves prepare a raid on an out-of-the-way warehouse loaded with electronic gear, and are set up to clash with the night security guards. In the shadows, an unstoppable horde of ready-to-die thugs in wasplike gas masks want to rescue Nexhep. Each group have their own complicated internal relationships and frictions, highlighted when the cops survive an assault by the Albanians and take refuge in the warehouse just as the crooks have tied up the guards and are lifting the stash. Heist man Nasser (top-billed Samy Naceri) is incapacitated early, which means his less capable lieutenant Santino (Benoît Magimel) has to take over, while girl crook Nadia (Anisia Uzeyman) becomes committed to taking a stand when she finds out that the villain specialises in mass rape and forced prostitution. Leadership of the cops falls to tough Helene (Nadia Fares) and middle-aged guard Louis (Pascal Greggory) shows the most competence.

Some characters crack and prove cowardly, some die heroically, some die pointlessly, and the Lecter-like villain starts talking to make things worse, even killing one of his captors with his fingertips. It has confidence with widescreen action, but keeps up the edgy inter-character business Carpenter did so well, with a Euro twist as characters of different nationalities and ethnicities are holed up in an archetypally anonymous, characterless locale. Among the few knowing nods to Hollywood action is a nicely humorous a capella version of the *Magnificent Seven* theme.

OFFBEAT (1961)

A matter-of-fact British B picture – scripted by playwright Peter Barnes (*The Ruling Class*) – which puts forward the quite subversive notion that professional crime might offer a more honourable, fulfilling way of life than the straight and narrow.

In an attention-getting scene, ex-MI5 man Layton (William Sylvester) carries out an efficient one-man bank robbery… then reports to Scotland Yard. After the death of an undercover policeman on this case, the spy has been seconded to take the identity of no-good Steve Ross and infiltrate a well-organised heist gang. In his new persona, Layton befriends genial crook Hemick (John Meillon) and secures an introduction to business-like planner Dawson (Anthony Dawson), who ropes him in on a jewel robbery. Blurring the line between sleuthing and entrapment, Layton suggests how to get round vault security by digging from fake roadworks ('Better not work too hard or somebody'll get suspicious.') and begins an affair with gangland hanger-on Ruth Lombard (Mai Zetterling). The mini-*Rififi* job is carried out – with tunnel collapses, near-disasters and improvised solutions to last-minute snags – but it becomes apparent that the protagonist has genuinely found camaraderie in crime and warmed more to his crooked confederates than the chilly, high-handed coppers who are running the operation. Will he run off with Ruth and his share of the loot? Or turn in his new mates and take cold comfort in a commendation? After the well-staged robbery, a tight series of ironies blow Layton's cover and leave him bereft as he has to revert to a real identity which seems hollow even to him.

Sylvester, a regular B leading man (*Hand of Night*, *Devils of Darkness*), earned movie immortality as Dr Floyd in *2001: A Space Odyssey* – but the unheralded, tiny *Offbeat* (very clever title) gave him his best role, fully taking advantage of his lightweight, not-quite-there screen presence. Zetterling, always a classy and challenging performer, tempts and needles the compromised hero with sly, feline grace. With familiar faces Neil McCarthy, John Phillips, Ronald Adam and Joseph Furst. Directed by Cliff Owen (*The Vengeance of She*).

THE PENALTY (1920)

Flatly directed by Wallace Worsley, who lacks Tod Browning's knack for the grotesque, this melodrama nevertheless offers one of the great Lon Chaney performances. After a street accident, a lad has his legs amputated below the knees by perhaps-incompetent surgeon Dr Ferris (Charles Clary). Decades later, Blizzard (Chaney) is master of the San Francisco underworld, at once a plain and simple gang boss and a demented anarchist who intends to foment large-scale terrorist atrocities. With leather buckets on his stumps and an apartment adapted to his needs with strategic hand-holds, Blizzard gets around well enough. Among his quirks is selecting mistresses who can work piano pedals by hand while he pounds away in mad virtuoso mode. Things are complicated by Secret Service agent Rose (Ethel Grey Terry), undercover as Blizzard's latest pedaler, and Barbara (Claire Adams), daughter of the surgeon who did him wrong. Barbara, who fancies herself a sculptor, advertises for someone evil-looking but magnificent to pose for a bust of Satan(!). To bring off his long-planned revenge, Blizzard gets the model gig – intent on blackmailing Barbara's father and another surgeon (Kenneth Harlan) into transplanting functional legs stolen from a nimble live donor.

Strange as the premise is, it gets wilder when the doctors perform not a leg transplant but a brain operation. It turns out Blizzard is evil not because he's embittered about losing his legs but because a concurrent head injury impaired his inherent nobility. Cured, he becomes a saintly pianist, woos and wins the girl, and all his crimes are forgiven by the law… but confederate 'Frisco Pete' (James Mason) back-shoots him while he's at the piano and he dies, musing, 'Fate chained me to Evil – for that I must pay the penalty.' There are flashes of grim humour (Blizzard delivers a speech about his grand plans then sneers at his mistress 'but you won't be here to see it unless you pedal better'), but the unbelievable twist is played straight. Even Chaney can't make the reformed Blizzard credible after he has so enthusiastically played nasty. The rest of the cast are stiff as underwritten, one-note characters, and some promised excitements – like the big anarchist uprising – never come along. Chaney wore a harness to pull off an entirely successful illusion of leglessness, but didn't feel the need, as he would in later vehicles, to add scars or wigs, which gives him a chance to show off a splendid unadorned scowl. Based on a novel by Gouverneur Morris.

PICCADILLY THIRD STOP (1960)

'SNATCHING PRESENTS FROM A WEDDING RECEPTION? THEY EVEN BLACKBALL YOU FROM BORSTAL FOR THAT.'

This caper film aspires to be a British *Asphalt Jungle* – an ex-military safecracker (William Hartnell) ogles teenage sweater girls and muses about foundation garments in an echo of Sam Jaffe's paedophile mastermind in the American film – but its toffs-gone-wrong milieu isn't as pointed as *The League of Gentlemen*. It dawdles in the setup, but comes into focus for the robbery finale. The splendidly named Dominic Colpoys-Owen (Terence Morgan), a posh but shady rogue, lifts earrings at a wedding he's crashed by virtue of palliness with upper class feeb Toddy (Charles Kay) – whose cropped-haired live-in girlfriend Mouse (Ann Lynn) doesn't really fulfil her plot function of making the duo seem less gay. Dominic cops off with Serafina (Yoko Tani), daughter of an ambassador of a fictional South Sea island nation. When she mentions her father has a hundred grand in used bills in a safe, Dominic can't resists putting together a raid – though it's plain that irritable, toff-hating Yank Joe Preedy (John Crawford) is liable to pull a double-cross, prompting Dominic to hook up again with Joe's wife (Mai Zetterling) to arrange a triple-play. Dennis Price suavely runs a gambling den and Ronald Leigh-Hunt turns screws as the copper who breaks the case. The robbery involves digging into the Embassy basement from the Underground, which takes longer than expected. Trains are running again when the time comes for a getaway – a falling-out leads to deaths by third rail and car crash to ram home the crime doesn't pay message. It's full of fun supporting people (especially Lynn, Hartnell and Price), but the leads are weak. The most interesting character bit – Joe's fuming hatred of 'chinless' British aristos ('I'd put 'em all down the mines. Knock some spunk into 'em.') – isn't especially well developed, though there's a nice gag when Dominic dryly points out that a particular useless 'nancy' happened to have climbed Everest. Scripted by Leigh Vance, who went from *The Frightened City* to US TV (*Mission: Impossible, Hart to Hart*). Directed by Wolf Rilla (*Village of the Damned*).

PIGGY BANKS (2005)

An offbeat serial killer road movie. Brothers John (Jake Muxworthy) and Michael (Gabriel Mann) seem like genial twenty-something slackers. John comes home to their latest shared apartment to find grinning Michael spieling suggestively about an attractive neighbour girl and his irresistible urge to break their self-imposed rules. Michael seems to be talking about lothario-like sexual activity (which, in fact, *is* part of his plan), but is really referring to the brothers' way of getting through life by extortion, theft and murder. The girl is dead and in a trunk, and – in a setup which prefigures *The Hamiltons* – the 'responsible' brother has to go along with his crazier sibling as they uproot from comfortable accommodation, move on to the next town and scope out more targets.

In narrated flashbacks, John explains the brothers learned their lifestyle from a father (a well-cast Tom Sizemore) who taught them that people are 'piggy banks'. When they need money, they 'break one open'. Dad favoured home invasions, but the sons prefer to charm young women, getting their PINs before killing them. The cosily psychotic setup is shaken when Michael brings home Archer (Kelli Garner), a freewheelingly frank bisexual who is entertaining enough for the brothers to keep around a while. After a few hours, it becomes obvious they have left too many loose ends and Archer will inevitably find out what they do, whereupon John regretfully bludgeons her with a pipe-wrench. Later, when Michael tries to murder him in reprisal, John kills his brother in self-defence. Heading across country to tie up loose end Gert (Lauren German, of *Hostel Part II*), the half-sister their father had with another family, John discovers Michael has been there before him (and probably killed their father) and that Gert (a long-haul trucker) is willing to take him into her bed and might have a genuine relationship with him.

The trajectory of the plot is canny: controlled stone-killer John, who we sense might be more redeemable than his impulsive brother, breaks the habit of a lifetime by opening up to his sister-lover, with an inevitable nasty (if ambiguous) surprise in store. Gert has also been taught to solve problems with homicide, albeit with a do-gooding vigilante streak. It has much squirmy material (children as accessories to murder, brother-sister incest, Dad's amoral code of survival), but is tactfully filmed and acted, with only glimpses of horrors (whimpering bound-and-gagged home-owners stashed in closets or around a breakfast table). In contrast with, say, Rob Zombie or Eli Roth, this probes the humanity of horrible people without excusing or glamorising evil behaviour. Directed by Morgan J. Freeman (*American Psycho 2*); written by Kendall Delcambre.

POCHI NO KOHUHAKU (CONFESSIONS OF A DOG) (2006)

An all-encompassing indictment of police corruption. Cop Takeda (Shun Sugata) starts out as a big, bear-like loveable family guy; Sugata looks like the sort who would be employed inside a Godzilla costume rather than leading a *Goodfellas*-length crime epic. Promoted to detective, Takeda is lured into a system of taking bribes, hassling civilians, kicking upstairs and nest-feathering. The emphasis is on hierarchy, as lowly crooked cops are expected to sacrifice themselves loyally to cover for extremely corrupt, sinister superior officers. The nice guy turns sour as he is expected – for instance – to be grateful when his boss offers to name his newborn daughter, contributing to the death of his marriage to decent, dutiful Chiyoko (Harumi Inoue). An American film might end with a hero bringing down the main crooked cop (*Internal Affairs*) or becoming a man of integrity pariah (*Serpico*), but this concludes with the Chaplinesque device of an editorial speech addressed directly at the audience. In a stylised prison cell after his fall, Takeda admits to being a dog all his career and finally goes down on his knees and barks, too.

The only difference between sympathetic characters and villains is that the former are ashamed of their corruption. The smooth, well-connected cop who rises under the chief's patronage and is deemed a suitable son-in-law benefits from a system which crushes the less photogenic Takeda – but an extraordinary fantasy outburst near the end shows he too is eaten up inside by going along with it. Scenes show petty abuses of power – hassling a pretty girl who asks for directions, out of boredom as much as the possibility to extort sex – or indulgences which spell long-term doom. The main opponent of police corruption isn't a man of integrity, but flashy, grudge-holding semi-hood Kusama (Junichi Kawamoto), who nags meek journalist Kitamura (Kunihiko Ida) – we see the system whereby police press releases are handed out and uncritically parroted – into working in vain to uncover ill-doing. Controversial (of course) on its home territory. Written and directed by Gen Takahashi, from a story by Yu Terasawa.

THE POT CARRIERS (1962)

British prison movies are rare; though not really a comedy, this is closer in tone to *Porridge* than *The Escapist, Silent Scream* or *The Criminal*. Rainbow (Paul Massie), a nice young man, is sentenced for assault after a fight with a guy hitting on his girlfriend (Carole Lesley). He's sent down because he used a handy knife, but gets a short sentence because he called an ambulance and tried to help the wounded man. Inside, he falls in with Red Band (Ronald Fraser), so-called because of the armband he wears as a trusty, and a group of mildly lovable misfits whose idea of a big score is a complicated heist which gets a side of gammon out of the kitchens and passed on to effete fence-chef Smooth Tongue (Dennis Price). A slightly gay-seeming squealer (Alfred Burke) gets Red Band stripped of his authority (and remission) and sent to solitary, and is punished by having scalding water tipped over his legs. Fraser, in a rare lead, is a prototype for Ronnie Barker's sitcom con: an unrepentant, unmalicious crook who keeps up the fiddles because he just needs to stay busy inside even when it's against his own interests. It's realistic rather than grim, with a long line of men slopping out and a sense of the dullness of prison life (in the kitchens, warders keep rattling off orders of 'diets' which end with 'four muslims, one diabetic, one Jew'). There are no evil warders or even really bad convicts. Based on a play, it only shows the outside world under the opening and closing credits. With many familiar Britfilm faces/voices: Paul Rogers, Davy Kaye (weasely little Jewish crook), Eddie Byrne, Campbell Singer, Patrick McAlinney, Neil McCarthy, Vanda Godsell, Windsor Davies, Martin Wyldeck. Written by T.J. Morrison and Mike Watts. Directed by Peter Graham Scott.

THE RIDDLE (2007)

A weird mystery with enough sub-Peter Ackroyd elements to stand out in the crowd, this is also sloppy, overlong and stuck with a clumsy finish in which the surviving cast gather on the banks of the Thames and the hero's dilemma is solved by a secondary character changing sides for no reason. Reporter Mike Sullivan (Vinnie Jones), who specialises in greyhound races, latches onto a crime story when much-loved pub owner Sadie Miller ('50s starlet Vera Day) is murdered. A corrupt cop (PH Moriarty) tries to bury the case and Mike's boss (Vanessa Redgrave!) fires him when he tries to stick the course. He gets inside help from a police PR (Julie Cox) and takes a strange tangent when the manuscript of a lost autobiographical Charles Dickens novel about murder and blackmail turns up in the pub basement. A trash-picking tramp (Derek Jacobi) weaves in and out of the story – he turns out to be Dickens himself, either a ghost or hanging about corporeally to get his book back. Also in the mix is property developer Don Roberts (Jason Flemyng), out to make a killing on inside information about where the Olympic Village will be sited (topical for 2007) – plus bit parts for Gareth Hunt (in his final role), Mel Smith and Kenny Lynch. Jones doggedly sleuths through the case, despite being doped by a shrill femme fatale (Clemmie Myers) and sharing scenes with nice-to-see-but-what-the-hell-are-they-doing? supporting players. The Dickensian flashback and the modern-day story are both workable, but don't quite shuffle together properly. Written and directed by Brendan Foley.

THE RIVERSIDE MURDER (1935)

Claire Haines (Judy Gunn), the heroine of this crime story, is a disenchanted critic eager to get into the exciting world of crime reporting ('Writing film notes isn't much of a job.'). This suggests aggrieved moviemakers out to tweak noses; reviewers of the day probably snorted as much as reviewers of *Lady in the Water* did in 2006 at M. Night Shyamalan's idea of a snotty film critic. This British murder mystery, based on a French novel (André Steeman's *Les Six Hommes Morts*), isn't otherwise memorable, though it has amusing turns from Basil Sydney and Alistair Sim (in his film debut) as, respectively, the perspicacious and plodding coppers delving into a standard uppercrust killing. Financier Robert Norman (Aubrey Mallalieu) is shot before an important meeting, and suspicion falls on businessmen who were about to enter into a deal with him (in the 1930s, British films enjoyed murdering or castigating financiers). Suspects include sometime Dr Watson Ian Fleming (not the writer) and future Quatermass Reginald Tate. Entertaining enough, but terribly stagebound, with exits and entrances and cut-glass talk in the drawing room. Directed by American Albert Parker, who made silent star vehicles for John Barrymore (*Sherlock Holmes*) and Douglas Fairbanks (*The Black Pirate*), but slipped to British quota quickies when talkies came in.

THE SCOTLAND YARD MYSTERY (THE LIVING DEAD) (1934)

This brisk, matter-of-fact British crime movie – scripted by Frank Miller from a play by Wallace Geoffrey (*The Perfect Woman*) – runs to enough understated macabre elements to justify retitling as *The Living Dead* for American release and being sold as a semi-horror film ('Not a ghost! Not a vampire! Not a zombie! What is the Living Dead?').

As in *Dark Eyes of London*, it's all about insurance fraud – a suspicious succession of seemingly healthy folks succumb to heart attacks and heirs cash large cheques. Commissioner Stanton of the Yard (Gerald du Maurier), impatient with polite British police methods, carries a gun and would like to use 'the Third Degree' in interrogations. The villain of the piece is smug, jolly Dr Masters (George Curzon), who divides his time between charitably treating the poor in the East End ("'E's a white man, 'e is. Never charged me nuffin' that time my husband ran up against my flatiron.') and consulting with the police as forensic examiner. He tags along with Stanton on the investigation, all but admitting his guilt and needling the copper as exhumations reveal books instead of corpses in the dead men's coffins.

It turns out that Masters has devised a serum which can induce catalepsy. When the jig is nearly up, he injects Stanton's abducted daughter Mary (Belle Chrystall), stashing her in his modernist private morgue and withholding the antidote – though his devoted wife Irene (Grete Natzler) reveals the secret when Stanton threatens to rough up the handcuffed, still-arrogant culprit ('While my daughter's life's in danger, regulations mean nothing to me.'). The finale features a dash to the airport and an attempted escape by plane. Masters tries to evade justice by taking his own serum, only to be undone when the last of the antidote is lost in a shootout. In a splendid punch line, his dying words are, 'Cheer up, darling. I'm heavily insured.' With Henry Victor (*Freaks*) as a jittery, disposable minion. Directed by Thomas Bentley (*Silver Blaze*).

THE SILENT PARTNER (1978)

In the lead-up to Christmas, disaffected schlub Miles Cullen (Elliott Gould), a teller in a shopping mall bank, realises Harry Reikle (Christopher Plummer), who is loitering in a Santa Claus suit, is planning a hold-up. When the bandit makes his play, Miles hands over some cash but steals a much larger sum for himself – then tidily stashes his loot in a safety deposit box, concealing the key in a jar of jam in his fridge. When the violent Reikle realises what Miles has done, he tries to pressure him into coughing up the cash and Miles takes countermeasures which escalate the feud.

Smartly scripted by Curtis Hansen (*LA Confidential*) from Anders Bodelsen's novel *Think of a Number* (previously filmed in Denmark in 1969) and directed with unassuming skill by Daryl Duke (*Payday*, *Slither*), this unashamedly Canadian thriller evokes the Patricia Highsmith template (cf: *Strangers on a Train*, *Ripley's Game*) in its dangerous, sexually-charged relationship between an amateur criminal and a stone sociopath. Gould and (especially) Plummer are outstanding as complex antagonists. Miles is a '70s version of Jack Lemmon in *The Apartment*, coerced by a glad-handing boss (Charles Kirby) into posing as the boyfriend of his mistress Julie (Susannah York). Miles has a crush on Julie, who needles him about his silly hobby (tropical fish). Reikle is unpredictably violent, and not even a terribly good hold-up man – Miles pegs him because he makes two abortive tries before pulling off the initial robbery – but is terrifyingly tenacious. The strangest aspect of the film is that Reikle almost admires his 'silent partner' – his menacing phone calls are flirty as well as scary. Miles thinks he solves his problem by leading the cops to Reikle, who is wanted for a very nasty assault on a hooker in a sauna, but his cleaning lady throws away the jam-jar… and Elaine (Céline Lomez), an ambiguous mystery woman, comes into his life to shake things up further. When Reikle reappears, horrors escalate (including a memorable beheading-by-fish tank) and the climax finds the robber returning, in eerily credible drag, for another crack at 'his lucky bank'.

It's a perfect blend of character comedy and dark suspense, and the abrupt seesaws into extreme-for-1978 violence keep it unpredictable as the partners plot against each other.

STRIP TEASE MURDER (1961)

One of the most temptingly titled B pictures from the vast backlist of the Danziger Brothers, the closest the British film industry came to Monogram. It's no *Cover Girl Killer*, but offers an hour of almost surreally genteel sleaze. Most of the film takes place in the Flamingo Club, presumably in Soho, where alcoholic, loud-check-suited stand-up comic Bert Black (John Hewer) provides dreadful patter between turns and polite patrons sit in nicely arranged chairs while lithe dancers peel decorously down to G-strings and pasties. Bert wears a battered funny hat and harps on about his former top-of-the-bill status, but the fatherly club manager (Michael Peake) gently reminds him he's only on to give the girls time to change costumes.

'Thirty if she's a day' stripper Rita (Ann Lynn) is ticked off when her gangster boyfriend Branco (bald, glowering Kenneth J. Warren) dumps her for younger, blonder, brassier, peculiarly accented rival Angelin (Vanda Hudson) and blackmails him about his dope ring. Most gang bosses would hire a cosh-boy or a gunman to ice the tart, but Branco calls in batty boffin Perkel (Peter Elliott), who wants a human test subject for his remote-control zapper (which uses then-new and exciting transistor technology, prompting several references to Sputnik). In the dressing room, Rita and Angelin have a mild hair-pulling fight over Branco. Rita gets sacked, so Diana (Jean Muir), who is secretly married to Bert, goes on in her place and is electrocuted. Everyone (including the useless plods) says it was an accident, but Bert lays off the booze and turns 'tec to track down the murderers, aided by stage door-keeper Lou (Leon Cortez). Meanwhile, Rita and wicked waiter Rocco (Carl Duering), still trying to muscle in on the dope racket, kill Branco – without needing to hire a mad scientist – to get his black book of drugs contacts. Perkel is lured to the club on the pretence of giving a demonstration to investors, and nabbed as he is about to repeat his experiment with an unwilling Rita, who has had a deadly microphone cellotaped to her hand by the stern hero. After it's all over, Bert admits he doesn't feel all that much better.

Paul Tabori's script would be utterly conventional without its minor science fiction content, and director Ernest Morris (*The Tell-Tale Heart*, *The Return of Mr Moto*) films almost all of it in long, dull master shots. Furthermore, Hewer is a boring hero, the appealing Muir dies before she can do more than a) her act and b) show off her cute bobbed hairstyle, and talented, interesting Lynn should have been given more scheming, shrewish rottenness scenes. The obscure Elliott, who has a bit as a blacked-up Indian professor in *Night of the Demon*, is man of the match as the amoral, dotty, bland professor, who creates his human bug-zapper device in a Highgate lock-up. Perkel excites Lou the doorman's suspicions by showing up as a flat-capped electrician to tamper with the microphone in the afternoon and again as a patron in evening dress to perform the murder experiment in the evening – though Lou forgets to mention this during the perfunctory investigation (just another routine stripper electrocution, it seems). In a realistic touch, inept scientific assassin Perkel still wants paying, even after offing the wrong ecdysiast.

LES VAMPIRES (1915)

A fabulously weird ten-episode serial from writer-director Louis Feuillade, whose pulp fictions were loved equally by popular audiences who enjoyed thrills and pretty girls and high-brow surrealists who relished savage anarchy.

The Vampires – a band of black-clad, gloating criminals – terrorise Paris, opposed by determined journalist Guérande (Édouard Mathé) and comical sidekick Mazamette (Marcel Lévesque). Perhaps because Feuillade kept falling out with leading men, the gang lose three leaders (and one rival crook arch-enemy) during the story. The breakout star is Musidora as the body-stockinged, sexy, maniacal, murderously devious Vampire No. 2, Irma Vep (crude animation rearranges the letters of her cabaret poster to unpick the anagram). She follows crook Fantômas and vigilante Judex, lead characters of earlier Feuillade hits, in her penchant for proto-supervillain gear, augmented by effective disguises. Early episodes pit Guérande, a newsman who can get astonishing cooperation from the police at a flash of his press card, against Le Grand Vampire (Marcel Aymé), a Fantômas-type troublemaker who goes so far as to murder the hero's dancer fiancée (Stacia Napierowska) with a poison ring in the second episode (perhaps because her batwing outfit mocks vampires). The Grand Vampire has Guérande kidnapped and put on trial by a Vampire Inquisition, but the infiltrating undertaker Mazamette – a bald, beaky eccentric who would fit into Hergé's universe – helps him escape, leaving the Vampires' Inquisitor under a hood to be executed by his fellows. The Grand Vampire also has to put up with trouble from Juan-José Moréno (Fernard Hermann), a rival gentleman thief who not only beats the Vampires to scores, but woos and wins the faithless Irma.

Everything gets a shake-up when the Grand Vampire is killed and Moréno hanged (offscreen between episodes), and a sleek bourgeois nicknamed Satanas (Louis Leubas) reveals himself as the *real* leader of the Vampires, only to be arrested within two episodes and kill himself in prison. His successor is poison specialist Vénénos (Frederik Moriss), who takes a rather larkish approach to crime – after one coup, he throws a party at which he does a high-kicking celebratory dance and reveals his fiendishness by drawing a cruel caricature of Mazamette (shooting an eyehole with a pistol) to amuse his fellow Vampires. Irma (who, it is implied, devotes herself to a succession of criminal lovers), Mazamette and Guérande are around throughout. The hero gains and marries a new love interest (Louise Lagrange), and Mazamette proposes to a maid (Germaine Rouer) whose husband is an incidental victim of a poison plot, but the tone changes as episodes unfold.

This serial feels made up on the hoof: early on, the Vampires seem to be a fearsome secret society, with disguised members among the Establishment and perhaps some great anarchist purpose; by the end, they are just a jovial crew of apache lowlifes with little ambition beyond loot. Despite their initial fearsomeness, the gang are all apprehended in a slapstick pile-up after Guérande sabotages their getaway balcony. Much of the action takes place before stage flats (recycled so the same wallpaper shows up in many venues), but Feuillade gets out on location for scurrying up walls and across rooftops (the Vampires use a 1915 version of parkour) and ambitious chases in which the camera is on a moving car. More genial and, perhaps, self-aware than *Fantômas* and *Judex*, as if everyone were beginning to tip the wink to the audience – which makes it a precedent for an entire strain of larkish action cinema (from Fairbanks and Flynn to Willis and Schwarzenegger), delivering the delights of high melodrama alongside an admission it can't be taken seriously.

VILLAIN (1971)

'Meet Vic Dakin', claimed the poster, 'Then wish you hadn't.' If Richard Burton had made more films like *Villain* and fewer like *Cleopatra*, he would be higher-rated as a screen actor. Burton's London hard man Vic seems to be both Kray Twins rolled into one, and the battered-and-boozed, mean-eyed star is as distinctive a gangster for Britain as James Cagney was for America or Alain Delon for France.

A conniving tough who gets a witness out of the way by telling her to make a cup of tea while he cuts her boyfriend's face off, Vic also shows the traditional sentimental streak by taking his dear old mum (Cathleen Nesbitt) to Brighton every weekend and bridles at a world grown soft ('We should never have abolished national service.'). Vic's fatal mistake comes in moving from his established protection racket into armed robbery, not to expand his empire but because he feels middle-aged flabbiness coming on and wants to get back into action to impress his sometime love interest, rent boy-cum-pimp Wolfe Lissoner (Ian McShane). It's a paradox of enlightenment that few gay characters in contemporary films are as unpleasant or interesting as Vic Dakin – in a telling moment, he orders his partner to keep the noise down during violent sex so as not to wake up mum. Made just after *Get Carter*, *Villain* similarly updates British gangland conventions into a '70s of flares, sideburns and seedy clubs – but without even the icy glamour of the righteous avenger Carter to rise from the muck as a movie hero.

Written by sitcom specialists Dick Clement and Ian La Frenais (with a rewrite by Al Lettieri, more familiar as a hood actor in *Pulp* and *The Getaway*), its dialogue sounds more authentic than that of TV's *The Sweeney* (it may be the first use of the word 'wanker' in a movie) and the plot is a neatly turned anecdote which pays off with a Burton speech ('Who are you looking at?') that prefigures Al Pacino's great restaurant rant in *Scarface*. Director Michael Tuchner, who defected to US TV after this striking first film, marshals an awe-inspiring collection of British character actors later lured to sitcoms, cosy TV detectives or double glazing adverts: Joss Ackland as an ulcer-ridden gang boss, Nigel Davenport and Colin Welland as determined plods, Donald Sinden as a sleazy MP caught in an extramarital orgy, Tony Selby and Del Tenney as minders, Fiona Lewis as a high-class topless tart. The London crime locations are acutely observed and brilliantly used: the bungled smash and grab in an industrial estate is a treat, with Burton blinding a driver by squirting him with a Jif lemon and a booby trapped suitcase full of cash extruding five-foot steel arms. Burton is creepy in a fascinating in-depth performance, consumed with hatred for ordinary citizens ('Stupid punters – telly all week, screw the wife on Saturday.') as he self-destructs by relying on weaklings who fall apart when the pressure is on.

HIGH ADVENTURE

Lost Kingdoms and Fabulous Voyages

ALABAMA JONES AND THE BUSTY CRUSADE (2005)

'THE NEXT DAY, THE
SLAVE-TRADERS WERE RAPED
BY THEIR OWN CAMELS...'

A soft-core snoozer from busy, mostly annoying director Jim Wynorski (billed as Harold Blueberry). It has an Indy logo, outdoor locations and some hats... but little patience for actual parody. Alabama Jones (Katie James), Oklahoma Jones (Nikki Nova) and California Jones (Cheyenne Silver) walk through a pleasant tropical landscape (Hawaii) in search of 'the idol of Punani', taking frequent time outs for lengthy minimal-contact (mostly lesbian) sex. They run into Luna the Jungle Queen (the very beautiful Aria Giovanni); hard-drinking, hairy (false-bearded), eye-patched, mock-Scots-accented safari guide Jungle Bill (screenwriter William Williamson); 'some random gorilla' (an old-fashioned suit); a giant red CGI scorpion; a Tarzan-type Jungle Man with a print skirt and '70s hair (Scott Styles); a glowing transparent stripping Princess of the Apes (Sunny Leone); and British-accented 'Amelia Airhead' (Kelle Marie), who crashed near the Fountain of Eternal Youth seventy years ago and has apparently been sitting bored in a field ever since. 'Funny' interview snippets with the cast run under the end credits, revealing that Katie James thinks Versailles is in Italy.

ANTINEA, L'AMANTE DELLA CITTÀ SEPOLTA (JOURNEY BENEATH THE DESERT) (1961)

This Italian-made version of Pierre Benoît's much-filmed novel *L'Atlantide* brings the lost civilisation saga up to date for the early 1960s in the manner of Irwin Allen's *The Lost World* and Hammer's *She*... by dropping most of the philosophy, ramping up the villainy and adding machine-gun battles, a helicopter crash and a climactic A-bomb test that brings down the chandelier (and cavern roof) to destroy the remnant of Atlantis which has persisted for millennia in the Sahara desert.

Directed by Edgar G. Ulmer (though Frank Borzage and Giuseppe Masini also had a hand in it), it's tangential to the Italian *peplum* cycle, as demonstrated by Anedeo

Nazzari in a Grand Vizier-type role, Gian Maria Volonté as a cruel overseer and scenes of slave revolts, exotic courtroom dance routines (with snakes) and bare-chested muscle action from Robert (James Westmoreland, billed as 'Rad Fulton'), the heroic stud outsider who services Queen Antinea (Haya Harareet) but is eventually disgusted by her cruelty ('Yes, you love me! You filthy beast!'). Macho Robert, thoughtful Pierre (Jean-Louis Trintignant) and expendable John (Georges Rivière) are brought down by a desert rainstorm while trying to warn some nomads about the bomb test and find themselves unwilling guests in Atlantis. Usually, the queen has her cast-off lovers preserved as artworks; here it's the luckless would-be escapee – who takes the least interest in her – who gets dipped in gold. Palestinian beauty Harareet, who had a showy role in *Ben-Hur*, is the screen's sexiest Antinea – with red hair, taut tummy exposed by startling costumes, a heavy lidded pout and a pet leopard (which Robert strangles with his bare hands in one of the less likely scenes). However, she's written as rather a drip. Each new Antinea is a reincarnation on the Dalai Lama model (only with less spirituality and more seething sadistic nymphomania) and the queen's mentor Tamal (Nazzari) is ticked off that she's rejected him in favour of promiscuity – though it seems a bit extreme to let the whole city get nuked to end her wicked reign. Zinah (Giulia Rubini) is the slave girl who gets away with Pierre as he flees, making it to the safe zone before the mushroom clouds rise.

After the skimpy budgets Ulmer was used to in his Hollywood career, this adequately financed Techniscope production must have seemed luxurious – but the results are slightly less lively than his best PRC efforts (*Detour*, *Bluebeard*), though on a par with his later American credits like the surprisingly similar *Beyond the Time Barrier*. Music by Carlo Rustichelli (*Blood and Black Lace*).

L'ATLANTIDE (1921)

The Frenchman Pierre Benoît's novel *L'Atlantide* (*Queen of Atlantis*) (1919) is an obvious imitation of H. Rider Haggard's *She*. In Haggard's much-filmed book, immortal queen Ayesha rules the Ancient Egyptian lost city of Kôr somewhere in the heart of Africa beyond deserts, jungles and mountains; Holly and Leo, adventurers from the outside world, are smitten by her beauty despite her cruelty, while a servant, Ustane, falls for Leo and is killed by the jealous queen. In Benoît's take, *apparently* immortal queen Antinea rules a surviving city of Atlantis concealed by impregnable mountains deep in the Sahara desert, and Saint-Avit and Morhange, two French foreign legion officers, are smitten by her beauty despite her cruelty, while a servant, Tanit-Zerga, falls for Saint-Avit, but dies in the desert while helping him escape after he has been driven by mad love (*amour fou* was big news in France in 1919) to kill his best friend. Haggard's tale has a more memorable finale, but Benoît delivers set pieces of his own, notably Antinea's red marble library where the mummies of her former lovers (she has a preference for military men) are kept along with first editions of the great books of the world, and the *classic* dying-of-thirst-in-the-desert-struggling-towards-the-well-that-turns-out-to-be-dry-wandering-off-maddened-towards-a-mirage trek.

Jacques Feyder's 1921 *L'Atlantide* is an ambitious 164-minute epic. The first act is hard going, prefacing an elaborate flashback structure. Survivor Saint-Avit (Georges Melchior, hero of *Fantômas*) puts off recounting his strange experiences while Feyder relishes the opportunity to show off North African locations. Once into the adventure, things pick up considerably. Stacia Napierkowska's Antinea isn't the all-conquering siren the script needs; a slim dancer when Feyder cast her, she infuriated the director by gaining thirty pounds before shooting started. It's a peculiarity of the plot that the anti-heroine doesn't actually *do* much beyond sit imperiously on a throne and ensnare passing officers. More interesting is Marie-Louise Iribe's Tanit-Zerga, who narrates an outstanding flashback-within-a-flashback about the desert raid which destroyed her village. One Leone-worthy shot has a single rifleman spying on the unwary settlement from a dune, joined by an army on camels who loom up over a ridge as if appearing out of the sands.

The tangle of insane loves around Antinea prompts Melchior to effective but extreme torment, as he is possessed to kill his friend Morhange (Jean Angelo) with what looks like a miniature croquet mallet. He breaks free of his obsession and escapes Atlantis with the aid of Tanit-Zerga and a noble, surprisingly unstereotyped Arab nomad, Cegheir ben Cheik (Abd-el-Kader Ben Ali). The punch line is wonderful: after listening to Saint-Avit's story of misery, suffering, death in the desert and terrible cruelty, all the other officer wants to know – having fallen under Antinea's spell, even by hearsay – is 'What about HER?' In the end, doomed men wander back into the desert, where the queen waits eternal (albeit with the latest Paris fashions brought in by caravan) and her lovers' sarcophagi fill up the niches in her fabulous library. A super-production in its day, this was one of the first adventure pictures to combine elaborately art-directed massive sets (its still-impressive Atlantis mixes classical and art deco motifs) with spectacular locations.

L'ATLANTIDE (1932)

The first talkie production of Pierre Benoît's novel went one better than Universal's *Dracula* by being made three times in three languages, with the same star (Brigitte Helm) and director (Georg Wilhelm Pabst), but different supporting casts. The French *L'Atlantide* has Pierre Blanchar as Saint-Avit and Jean Angelo reprising his 1921 role as Morhange; the German *Die Herrin von Atlantis* has Heinz Klingenberg and Gustav Diessl (Jack the Ripper in Pabst's *Pandora's Box*); the English *The Mistress of Atlantis* has John Stuart and Diessl again. The interesting Tela Tchaï is Tanit-Zerga in all three, though this take on the character is squarely in the tradition of 'disposable native girlfriend' as seen in many 'exotic paradise' films.

Given that director and star are major figures, *L'Atlantide* is a little flat: its script seems like an 89-minute cut-down of the silent film, and the abbreviated running time exacerbates rather than solves plot problems. The film takes too long to get to Antinea, then escapes from her fascinating clutches too soon to get on with thirst, madness and suffering in the desert. Pabst minimises fantastical elements: Napierowska's Antinea is either an immortal or one of a long line of queens who keep their land separate from the outside world; Helm's is the grown-up daughter of an Arab chieftain and an 1890s can-can dancer (Florelle, in all three versions) who stars in a lovely, petticoat-tossing flashback with overtones of the saucy backstage scenes of *Pandora's Box*.

This Atlantis is disappointingly just another North African city, without many 'lost civilisation' trappings. However, the remake still indulges in riotous flights of erotic fantasy. Helm – following inhumanly wicked roles in *Metropolis* and *Alraune* – is a cool, elegant, lethal queen, given to posing beside a huge statue of her sphinx-like face. She effortlessly seduces hapless Frenchmen, trounces Saint-Avit in a game of speed chess with an erotic undercurrent and actively orders her next lover to kill her last rather than rely on insane jealousy to get the job done.

L'ATLANTIDE (1972)

This French television adaptation of Pierre Benoît's novel is a very strange beast. Most takes on the material are romantic, exotic pulp adventures ranging from epic (the 1921 silent) to cut-price (Siren of Atlantis). This stylised, peculiarly conversational piece opens and closes with stark desert sequences, but takes place mostly in a very large, sumptuously appointed cavern. In other adaptations, Atlantis is a populous city in the Sahara ruled by perhaps-immortal queen Antinea; here, the lost civilisation consists entirely of the lair of the queen (glamorous dancer Ludmila Tcherina, decades on from *Tales of Hoffmann*), who has her blue-faced dead lovers preserved in mummy cases, an array of art and literature from the outside world strewn around, a wardrobe of seriously mod outfits, items of art direction (a huge door) that would suit an opera stage or a *Flash Gordon* serial and more yellow, red and orange throw pillows than an entire branch of Habitat circa 1972. It resembles Diabolik's hangout in Mario Bava's film. As usual, French officers Saint-Avit (Denis Manuel) and Morhange (Jacques Berthier) blunder in from the outside world and fall under the queen's influence – with Saint-Avit compelled to murder his friend, then making a break for freedom with Antinea's abused servant Tanit-Zerga (Marie-Christine Darah). In the strangest touch, Tanit-Zerga is tormented during a lesbian-inflected dance as Antinea scratches her bare shoulder with talon-nails while almost kissing her. Short on action, it mostly consists of Frenchmen discussing civilisation with the Queen – like *Lost Horizon*, the book is as much a philosophical novel as a fantasy. It's striking, strange and often gorgeous, but the chat becomes wearisome since all the characters are dramatic cutouts: Tcherina and Darah are vivid presences, while the enraptured intruders are inert. Hero Manuel only comes alive when lost in the desert in the climax. Written by Armand Lanoux and director Jean Kerchbron.

AVENTURA AL CENTRO DE LA TIERRA (ADVENTURE AT THE CENTRE OF THE EARTH) (1966)

An expedition into the bowels of the Earth searches for secrets about man's origins. Early on, familiar *One Million B.C.* stock footage illustrates the kind of dinosaurs which might be found, but the dimetrodon-iguanas are a feint. This *centro* is home to Black Lagoon knock-offs who take scratchy, lechy interest in top-billed diva Hilda (Kitty de Hoyos). Stalwart elderly Professor Diaz (José Elias Moreno) presses on, while discontents simmer in the group of *muy macho* adventurers. The usual surprisingly well-lit caves are wandered around, with intermittent hoked-up suspense scenes. The party have individually to cross a rope hand-over-hand above a deep gorge with bubbling lava at the bottom; no one does anything professional like clipping a safety line to the rope, which allows bobbling bats-on-strings to pester a hanging fellow who takes a dive into the goop and waves a mangled hand as he goes under.

Director Alfredo B. Crevenna stages odd moments well (a monster seen first as a set of mad staring eyes plays better than a full-on man-in-a-suit). As in the 1959 film of the Jules Verne story this obviously imitates, the expedition finds the temple of a forgotten civilisation, but it's just a backdrop to monster melodrama. A lizard-man who provides the creature action for the first half is skewered on a stalagmite, replaced in the plot by a winged, hairy demon-bat monster surprisingly like the ones in the later TV movie *Gargoyles* (or the feature *The Bat People*). Both have that goofy Mexi-monster look, sort of imaginative, sort of endearing, mostly silly. That goes double for a giant *Missile to the Moon* spider which chomps down on one explorer's head with pincers in surprisingly bloody but still ridiculous style. The doggily endearing tone is kiddie matinee, but with flashes of shock and gore.

Though it starts off as a Verne adventure with a melodrama streak, it turns into a body count monster picture as scientists are bloodily mauled and Hilda is abducted (to a lair that looks *very* Black Lagoon, especially since an underwater swim is needed to get to it) by the bat-thing. The monster offers her a live rat for dinner, which at least makes him more gallant than the lizard thing. When this fails, he tries a dead snake – even ripping it in half and chewing one end to show it's good. The ungrateful miss just faints (again) and young Dr Rios (Javier Solis) pops up to gut-shoot the creature, who still has enough spit to be on the point of killing the hero when Hilda pleads for the life of 'mi amor' and gets the beast to refrain from slaughter, finally winning him some sympathy just before the army show up and blast him (and his cavern) to bits.

LE AVVENTURE STRAORDINARISSIME DI SATURNINO FARANDOLA (1915)

This Italian silent film is a feature rather than a serial, but consists of four episodes (with at least one actor taking multiple roles). Based on an illustrated novel by Albert Robida, spoofing Jules Verne and his SF/fantasy/adventure contemporaries, it's an engaging skit.

In the first episode, our hero is cast adrift from a sinking ship as a baby and raised on an island by monkeys played by acrobats in blackface and tailed body stockings. Saturnino, played by Marcel Fabre (who also co-directed, with Luigi Maggi), grows up disconsolate at his lack of tail. He paddles off and saves a ship from pirates, is made captain by the rescued crew and instantly gets a trouble-magnet wife, Mysora (Nilde Baracchi). Swallowed by a whale while her husband is prising a pearl from a giant clam, Mrs F is mistaken for a mermaid by a grasping Australian explorer collecting marine animals for Melbourne Zoo. The professor keeps Mysora in a tank, with the stage puppet-whale and a bizarre squid thing. Saturnino calls his monkey friends to assault the villain's stronghold and save the girl. This would be enough incident for many films, but Saturnino has three adventures to go: finding a stolen white elephant in Siam in competition with a torture-happy police chief; rescuing African princesses from cannibals and then (disguised as bears) from gorillas; and getting mixed up in a war between 'North and South Milligan' (an evil 'Phileas Fogg' is behind it) which ends with a battle in the clouds between aerial warships.

An all-action entertainment spectacle in its day, this finds many excuses for getting showgirls into tight trousers (a parade of Siamese Amazon warriors, etc.). Baracchi, the heroine who constantly needs rescuing but looks as if she could take care of herself, is so muscular she might be intended as a joke at the expense of frail wisps like Pearl White. Fabre, who has a dashing grin and an amusing manner, is a still-unusual hero: impossibly brave, devoted and daredevil, but funny with it. The effects are Méliès-style – relying as much on stage apparatus as camera tricks. The climactic air battle, with balloons deflating and combatants falling from the clouds, is almost eerie – though the solemn score added by modern distributors might reframe a comic sequence as tragedy since the rest of the film is cheerfully parodically bloodthirsty.

CHITTY CHITTY BANG BANG (1968)

This overblown adaptation of Ian Fleming's children's book is one of the pastel-coloured ordeals of the late '60s – at once an attempt to emulate *Mary Poppins* (which is presumably why it's a musical), a proto-steampunk Victorian-Edwardian contraption spectacular (*First Men in the Moon, Doctor Dolittle, Those Magnificent Men in Their Flying Machines, The Great Race*) and producer Cubby Broccoli's stab at making something of those non-Bond Fleming rights. Director Kenneth Hughes is too lumpen for the material; it needed Richard Lester or, closer to hand, Lionel Jeffries. The enthusiastically charmless script feels like additional dialogue man Richard Maibaum rather than credited Roald Dahl – though a big scene (with a forgettable song, 'Toot Sweets') takes place in a Ken Adam-designed confectionary factory.

Single father Caractacus Potts (Dick Van Dyke, wisely not attempting a British accent this time) is a feckless inventor (and, ahem, crackpot) with a daffy ex-army dad (Lionel Jeffries), two shrill stage-school kids (Heather Ripley, Adrian Hall) and no mention of a wife (presumably dead). The kids want him to marry Truly Scrumptious (Sally Anne Howes), whom they've just met and who keeps getting driven into a muddy pond, but also buy and restore a former racing car they play in at a junkyard. He works on the car, named and sung about as Chitty Chitty Bang Bang. On a picnic, Potts spins a live-action yarn about the kingdom of Vulgaria, bad Baron Bomburst (Gert Frobe), the Child Catcher (Robert Helpmann) and a revolution which is the equivalent of the animated sequence in *Mary Poppins*. The Sherman Bros contribute variable songs: 'Hushabye Mountain' and 'The Old Bamboo' are quite good (though note the American vocab), but others are excruciating ('Truly Scrumptious', the Frobe-Anna Quayle ootchie-kootchie-fest).

Adam's design is fabulous and the pimped-out car worthy of Dinky toy immortality (it not only flies, but transforms into that most 1960s super-vehicle, a hovercraft), but the film just plods. It has that surefire sign of a failing comedy, characters who laugh at the onscreen antics, plus sped-up slapstick and burbling comedy music guaranteed to freeze the smile off your face. Some recall Helpmann as terrifying, and he's a great Dahl idea – but the blobby nose undermines him. Among a large, struggling cast, those (James Robertson Justice) who don't have to do German accents come off better than those who do (Benny Hill). With Desmond Llewellyn, Victor Maddern, Barbara Windsor, Arthur Mullard, Stanley Unwin (sorry – that patter of his was never funny!), Gerald Campion, Max Wall, Richard Wattis, Peter Arne and a young, unbilled Phil Collins. It's a toss-up as to whether *Doctor Dolittle* is worse.

COBRA WOMAN (1944)

'NO DRUG-SOAKED BRAIN COULD DREAM UP THE HORRORS OF COBRA ISLAND!'

Sometimes, popular culture is incomprehensible. How to explain the 1940s superstardom of Maria Montez? Devoted audiences, and Universal Pictures, rated her as the screen's greatest beauty (especially in Technicolor). Her Dominican accent supposedly suited her for South Sea Island and Arabian Nights princess roles, which let her dress up in skin-tight sarongs, bare-midriff two-pieces or (as here) a shimmering cobra-patterned high priestess sheath-dress (augmented by extraordinarily silly headgear).

Director Robert Siodmak and screenwriter Richard Brooks (working with Gene Lewis, from a story by W. Scott Darling) were men of taste and ambition, but they can do little with Montez (in a dual role, yet) or her held-over supporting cast (stiff hero Jon Hall, Sabu in a reprise of his *Thief of Bagdad* rogue), plus Lon Chaney Jr (star of Siodmak's *Son of Dracula*) as a tongueless brute and (worst of all) Koko the sarong-wearing chimp (who takes a proprietary interest in Sabu's ass in the fade-out joke). In the film's uncharted seas, native cultures borrow from India (snake worship and turbans), Polynesia (a touchy 'fire god' in the volcano) and Beverly Hills nightclubs (a religious rite requires the high priestess to shimmy up to a big cobra). Sweet Tollea (Montez) is kidnapped on the eve of her wedding to local clod Ramu (Hall) and spirited off to Cobra Island. Ramu crosses the seas, along with stowaways Kado (Sabu) and Koko, to get her back. In an odd twist, sinister kidnapper Hava (Chaney) is a good guy (though he kills a guard with a cobra-venomed stabber disguised as a flute) working for the just and wise queen (Mary Nash). The elder stateswoman wants exiled rightful heiress Tollea to replace her evil twin sister Naja (Montez, narrowing her eyes) as high priestess. Naja and baddie Martok (Edgar Barrier), who sports a turban which makes him look a complete dick (phallic symbols abound), extort gold from the people. They pettishly decree that more and more folk walk up the steps and jump into the volcano to appease the fire god. Naja's snake dance (which is a stunner) stirs the congregation to cobra gestures which are the best made-up salute in the movies until the wave of *The Wave*.

Montez is barely present as the good girl and isn't good as the bad girl, and their face-off is no triumph of special effects. The wicked high priestess is one of those villains stupid enough to step backwards out of a high window after she's missed throwing a javelin at the heroine at point-blank range. In the busy climax, Tollea bungles her takeover of the island because she's too scared to do a proper cobra dance and Kado uses his blow-gun (yes, another phallic symbol) to kill the snake. This so angers the fire god that the volcano blows and everyone panics until Hava tosses Martok into a pit of stakes to appease the fickle deity. Tollea doesn't even stick around to be the new queen, but runs off with her doltish fiancé, leaving the task of setting up a government and belief system to – get this! – a teenage handmaiden (Lois Collier) with no experience or claim to the throne. The Technicolor is gorgeous – with white marble sets that show off garish costumes and glowing skin-tones – and the kitsch irresistible. In the 1940s, audiences – rubes and cynics alike – loved Montez movies; now, they look like artefacts from a lost civilisation.

CONFESSIONS OF AN OPIUM EATER (SOULS FOR SALE; EVILS OF CHINATOWN) (1962)

Not especially entertaining or exciting, Albert Zugsmith's effort is bizarre: a 1902-set San Francisco Chinatown tong war/sex slave melodrama with high-flown Vincent Price narration (yoking in Thomas de Quincey's 1820 memoir as source material) and a major role for an ageing midget courtesan (Yvonne Moray).

In a long, dull sequence, abducted Chinese girls (some of their stunts are shot backwards, which is at least weird) are put ashore on that beach seen in Roger Corman's 1950s films. Rival Chinese factions get into a scrappy machine gun mêlée which climaxes with the apparent death of crusading editor George Wah (Richard Loo). Enter Gilbert de Quincey (Price), a seafaring adventurer with a philosophical bent. The star can handle waffly baroque voice-over narration in his sleep, but sailor-hatted, two-fisted *cheongsam*-chasing Gilbert reads more like a Mitchum or Bogart role and Price is fairly ridiculous in fight or smooch scenes. With Chinatown fenced off for a tong war, Gilbert murkily investigates Fu Manchu-like mastermind Lin Tang – actually slinky Ruby Low (Linda Ho) – the big figure in the 'Chinese bride auction' racket. In tunnels under Chinatown recalcitrant 'brides' (including the cheery, chatty midget) are kept in cages, starved to death so they aren't technically murdered (to avoid subsequent hauntings of their husbands). It climaxes clumsily with multiple unmaskings (Ruby is given away by her high heels). Gilbert and Ruby's death clinch has them literally dive head first into a sewer to be swept away by a torrent the actors could obviously escape if they wanted to.

At Universal in the 1950s, Zugsmith produced lasting cult films directed by other people (*The Incredible Shrinking Man, Touch of Evil, High School Confidential*); in the 1960s, he went independent as a producer-director on exploitation movies only a shade less sleazy than, say, Russ Meyer's efforts (*Sex Kittens Go to College*, *The Private Lives of Adam and Eve*, *Psychedelic Sexualis*). Here, he might have decided to make an old-fashioned sex slave picture (they were big in the 1920s – though the frisson was usually white girls sold to China, rather than Chinese girls abused in America) and, seeing how Price's star was rising in literary horror, thrown in the de Quincey tag and irrelevant shocks (insistent zooms to a decayed corpse on the beach, skulls floating in the opium dream scene) to copy Corman's AIP-Price-Poe style (albeit in drab black and white). In contrast with Hammer's comparable *Terror of the Tongs*, which is full of stuck-on eyelids and fake accents, the film at least casts Asian actors in varied roles. Only Moray is made up to look oriental (as she says, 'Pretty Chinese midget hard to find.'), while Philip Ahn, June Kim, Victor Sen Yung, Richard Loo and Linda Ho must have seen their meaty roles as a refreshing change from endless one-scene bits in mysteries and war films. Gaunt Terence de Marney has a creepy cameo as an addict who bogarts Price's pipe in the joss house; this references de Quincey's actual title (*Confessions of an English Opium Eater*) even as the actor's name curiously echoes the author's (though the character is a smoker, not an Eater). Ubiquitous dwarf Angelo Rossito (*Freaks*) gets more to say than usual as the paperboy who announces the tong war. Some plot elements seem to have inspired John Carpenter's *Big Trouble in Little China*.

CURUCU, BEAST OF THE AMAZON (1956)

Much hatred piled on this vilified quickie is down to a trailer and (fantastic) poster which promise a jungle monster movie like *The Creature From the Black Lagoon*. Instead, the beast – which resembles a giant parrot with fangs and feathery claws – is unmasked as an understandably pissed-off tribesman trying to scare whitey out of the jungle. If it were called *Adventure in the Amazon*, it probably wouldn't be despised – but no one would much like it either. Novelist-screenwriter Curt Siodmak (*Donovan's Brain*, *The Wolf Man*) had a brief career as a writer-director in the 1950s, apparently through sibling rivalry with more talented brother Robert (*Phantom Lady*, *Cry of the City*, etc.). This delivers all-cliché characters, a ton of wildlife footage and colourful on-location Argentine scenery, but little excitement.

When the beast slashes natives working for an American concern deep in the jungle, trouble-shooter Rock Dean (John Bromfield) investigates. Rock is among the most unreconstructed, unlikeable macho thug heroes in cinema – told that heroine Andrea

Romar (Beverly Garland) is a qualified nurse, he snarls, 'I know the type... Can't get a man, so she chooses a career,' before he even meets her. Surprisingly, she agrees to a date with the caveman, which is an excuse for a lengthy cabaret number from Larri Thomas. Rock spends a whole evening putting smarmy moves on Andrea while yawning when she tries to talk about her important research. Prefiguring *Medicine Man*, Andrea wants to come on the expedition in search of drugs that might be useful in cancer treatment. Rock puts up a token resistance ('I can think of a lot of places to take a woman... the jungle isn't one of them.') before consenting. Most of the film consists of encounters with Amazon denizens (piranha, spiders, buffaloes, a snake) and Garland gets to do a lot of screaming.

The monster plot is undramatically resolved when Rock bonks the beast on the head and the mask is doffed to reveal native guide Tupanico (Tom Payne). He gets one hilarious line ('I'm sorry I can't offer you both a chair, but my tribe doesn't know how to weave chairs.') and patiently explains that contact with civilisation has been a disaster for his people. It has lurid moments (an arm dangled into the river eaten to the bones by piranha), and the punch line has a good Indian, whose life the heroine has saved with an appendectomy, give Rock and Andrea a series of exotic presents, culminating in Tupanico's shrunken head. On this trip, Siodmak also shot *Love-Slaves of the Amazon*.

DARK STREETS OF CAIRO (1940)

> 'I'M HORRIBLY UPSET. WHAT'S THE MEANING OF THIS OUTRAGEOUS MURDER?'

Stock footage from *The Mummy* (1932) represents the discovery of 'the seven jewels of the seventh pharaoh', while mummy series villain George Zucco plays fez-sporting Cairo crook Abbadi, luminary of a nationalist cult called the Secret Defenders. Sets (an Egyptian redress of the Universal backlot village from *All Quiet on the Western Front* and *Frankenstein*) and props (mummy cases, artefacts) are also recycled from the studio's monster movies. Yank adventurers Dennis Martin (Ralph Byrd) and Jerry Jones (Eddie Quillan) spar verbally with Swedish sweetie Ellen Stephens (Sigrid Gurie) and Brooklyn-born harem-girl knife thrower's assistant Maggie (Yolande Donlan, as Yolande Mallott) rather than crack on with finding the stolen gems. Both love interests are mixed up with wrong 'uns: Ellen's nutty Swedish Baron father (Lloyd Corrigan) is Abbadi's potential buyer and Maggie's knife show partner (Henry Brandon) is the cult's hitman. Inspector Joachim (Rod LaRocque) plays chess with Abbadi, symbolising an ongoing friendly battle, and the villain's wife (Katherine DeMille) is working for the law. It's reticent about horrors (we're told people have been stabbed, but not shown the corpses) and even at 59 minutes is padded with much running through secret passages accompanied by score excerpts from *Son of Frankenstein*. However, it is lightly likeable pulp nonsense. With Sig Arno, Nestor Paiva, Dick Botiller and Steven Geray as bogus Egyptians and a lot of dumb American put-down-the-foreigners shtick, including a native who whips out a camera to snap a picture of a tourist and a fez-wearing character who turns out to be an American refugee from a Shriners' convention. Written by Alex Gottlieb (*The Strange Case of Dr Rx*); directed by Leslie (Laszlo) Kardos (*The Man Who Turned to Stone*).

THE FORBIDDEN TERRITORY (1934)

Dennis Wheatley's novel *The Forbidden Territory* (1933) introduces characters who feature in his better-known *The Devil Rides Out* (1934). The books have the same plot: the Duc de Richeleau and a protégé save a young man who has fallen in with a bad lot; they face a persuasive, repulsive villain and rescue a beautiful foreign girl who falls for one of the heroes (and hints at the sexiness which lured him into trouble in the first place). *The Devil Rides Out*, of course, is about Satanism. *The Forbidden Territory* is about Soviet Communism.

This adaptation, scripted by Alma Reville (Mrs Alfred Hitchcock), changes all the names and makes the Duc equivalent the father of the two heroes. Roving Rex Farringdon (Anthony Bushell, of the TV *Quatermass and the Pit*) hares off to Russia in search of Tsarist treasure, and is sent to a Siberian prison after loitering near an aerodrome where new super-science warplanes are tested. Sir Charles Farringdon (Ronald Squire), a wily old gent, and his stalwart son Michael (Barry MacKay) match wits with Commissar Leshkin (Gregory Ratoff), who plays with his cigarette in odd ways (was this thought to be a Russian trait – Leslie Banks does it as Count Zaroff?) as he politely hinders the heroes' investigation and later plots their execution. Singer

Valerie (Binnie Barnes) and ex-princess/teacher Marie-Louise (Tamara Desni) help the Farringdon boys out. The jolly romps involve ditching the Intourist spy (Boris Ranevsky) to go to Cossack cabarets, scrounging a sleigh (and, later, boots) to dash through snowy forests, pole-vaulting over an electric fence to steal a plane and hiding in a fake hayrick to be smuggled over the Romanian border.

Hitchcock considered directing the film, but it ended up with American Phil Rosen (*Return of the Ape Man*). It's not as sophisticated or exciting as Hitchcock's British spy-chase thrillers, and it's not as lavish a depiction of Stalinist Russia as Zoltan Korda's similarly plotted *Knight Without Armour*.

GREEN MANSIONS (1959)

'WE FOUND THIS ON THE BODY OF AN IMPETUOUS POLITICAL REFUGEE WHO WAS FOOLISH ENOUGH TO BELIEVE THE NATIVES' CHATTER OF GOLD AND A LOST VILLAGE.'

W.H. Hudson's 1904 bestseller was popular for generations; its heroine Rima the Bird Girl features in a Jacob Epstein bas-relief in Hyde Park and (weirdly) joined in the DC super hero stable via the 1970s *Super Friends* show. Comparable books like *She*, *The Lost World*, *Tarzan of the Apes* and *Lost Horizon* have been filmed many times, but this MGM CinemaScope production is the only screen version. The novel mixes romance and racism as embittered Venezuelan Abel falls for Tarzan-Mowgli-Peter Pan nature child Rima (full name: Riolama). Sole survivor of an extinct, nebulously conceived people, Rima lives in peace with animals and can't abide cruelty to them. The central relationship is so spiritual no miscegenation can be thought to have taken place between the white man and the perhaps-dark girl.

Director Mel Ferrer might have been more suitable in front of the camera, since Anthony Perkins is odd casting as cynical adventurer Abel – son of a minister murdered in a revolution, seeking gold to fund revenge. One of Ferrer's occasional films as a director, this was a showcase for his then-wife Audrey Hepburn as a lithe, athletic, supernaturally serene Rima. Dorothy Kingsley's script tidies up the book, and spectacular location filming (augmented by studio jungle) gives scope and grandeur – though there should be more difference between regular jungle and Rima's semi-enchanted habitat. Hepburn has more chemistry with animal co-stars than the uncomfortable Perkins, who croons a love song in a scene (surprisingly, taken from the book) which ought to be camper than it is. Sordid, cruel, ignorant, evil or disreputable folks from outside highlight the jungle idyll: Nuflo (Lee J. Cobb), Rima's supposed grandfather (and actually her abductor); Kua-Ko (Henry Silva), a buff, grinning killer native who nurtures murderous impulses; Don Panta (Nehemiah Persoff), a river-trader with several underage native wives; and Runi (a weirdly cast Sessue Hayakawa), a stoic chieftain.

The novel ends with Abel facilitating genocide of a tribe after Kua-Ko burns the Bird Girl to death. The film makes do with the villain drowning after a fistfight with the hero, and ventures further into fantasy. Rima, like a jungle plant which dies and resurrects elsewhere, appears unburned to the hero, summoning him back to nature.

THE ISLAND AT THE TOP OF THE WORLD (1974)

Directed at a competent plod by Robert Stevenson, this family friendly 'lost race' picture was adapted by John Whedon (Joss's grandad) from Ian Cameron's novel *The Lost Ones*. Disney product squeaky cleanliness sets it apart from competition like *The Land That Time Forgot* or the Harryhausen Sinbad films: blonde Viking heroine Freyja (very lovely Agneta Eckemyr) isn't ogled the way Caroline Munro was in adventure outings and proper monsters are sadly lacking (out-of-character killer whales don't count).

In 1907, Professor John Ivarsson (future newsreader David Hartman) and Sir Anthony Ross (Donald Sinden, over-emphasising everything) mount an expedition to find Ross's son Donald (David Gwillim), who went missing while traipsing north from Greenland in search of the whales' answer to the Elephants' Graveyard of early Tarzan films. Captain Brieux (Jacques Marin), a peppy stereotype Frenchman, has invented and built the colourful airship *Hyperion* (with all the brass trim and polished wood you expect) and insists on bringing his pet poodle on the trip (in the spirit of the *Journey to the Centre of the Earth* duck and the *City Under the Sea* chicken). In the Arctic, the crew take on Oomiak (Maku), an Eskimo who speaks of the 'demons' who took Donald; Mako overplays the broad cringing when airborne, but Oomiak turns out to be a true stalwart who 'fights like a bear' when trouble starts.

After a reel of aerial wonders (overhead shots of icebergs, various whales rushing happily to their dying grounds, lovely matte paintings of skies and mountains, model shots of the dirigible edging past ice floes), the explorers discover a temperate land warmed by volcanic upheavals inhabited by a colony of lost Vikings, and the drama becomes elementary. Donald lives with nice Vikings (especially the girl), but the colony is ruled by nasty flame-eyed high priest Godi (Gunnar Ohlund), who decrees the outsiders be burned to death. Saved from sacrifice, the adventurers make a break for safety – which involves serial-style action sequences on ice floes (with the whales), a flaming zeppelin crash which does away with the baddie, and much could-have-been-a-ride-at-Disneyworld sliding and falling through caverns and across seas. This sorely misses the breed of character actor who enlivened Disney's *20,000 Leagues Under the Sea* or even Irwin Allen's *Five Weeks in a Balloon*.

LEGEND OF THE LOST (1957)

This melodrama looks spectacular, but fizzles – with a trio of miscast stars (virtually the only characters onscreen for 90% of the movie) and a Ben Hecht-Robert Presnell script which is over-familiar (yet again, *Treasure of the Sierra Madre* is plundered) and ponderous.

In Timbuktu, Paul Bonnard (Rossano Brazzi, bizarrely typecast as French after *South Pacific*) hires drunk Joe January (John Wayne, whose company produced) to guide him into the Sahara on the trail of his long-missing father. Corrupt policeman Dukas (Kurt Kasznar, whose ham suggests a more light-hearted adventure) shows Bonnard around the souks, where Dita (Sophia Loren) picks his pocket. The forgiving Bonnard stays up all night to talk the semi-hooker out of her unwholesome lifestyle; that we don't hear the inspirational speech suggests even the writers thought it a hard sell. Reformed, Dita insists on joining the desert trip. After a mirage marginally less silly than the one in *Road to Morocco*, Bonnard reveals his humanitarian father spent his life searching for the lost city of Ophir. He now intends to find the place and spend its fabulous treasures on an institute of good works in the family name. Joe sneers at the dupe for embarking on a treasure hunt in trackless sands, but they find a lost city – only it's not Ophir, but Timgad (built and abandoned by Trajan's legions). Bonnard finds his father's skeleton, along with those of a guide and an Arab girl, and realises they killed each other, and he has always known his father was no idealist but a sensual treasure hunter. Following an inscription in the dead father's Bible, Joe lowers Bonnard into a cave full of 'dirty bats' to find treasure buried under a thousand years of guano. Bonnard, of course, goes mad – coming close to raping Dita, convinced the others are out to rob and kill him (repeating his father's tragedy), and heading off into the desert with all their supplies.

Henry Hathaway became one of Wayne's favoured directors (*North to Alaska*, *The Sons of Katie Elder*, *True Grit*, etc.), which shows the Duke had a measure of loyalty, since this was not a roaring success (it's similar in plot to Hathaway's superior Gary Cooper western *Garden of Evil*). Wayne stretches his image in a 'Robert Mitchum' role (a cynical drunken reprobate who comes through in the end), but isn't convincing in boozy bastard scenes; Brazzi is all over the place as a saint-cum-sociopath, impressing in neither incarnation (there's no sense he could ever be a threat to John Wayne); and Loren, unutterably lovely in Technicolor, is ludicrous as an Arab and has no chemistry with either co-star (like many sex bombs, Loren tended to be mismatched with leading men). An attempt at 'Italian'-style sensuality within the rigid conventions of 1950s American cinema was doomed: Loren plays her big nude scene with a vast donkey standing between her and the oglers in the audience as she pours water over herself. The film is watchable mostly for Jack Cardiff's desert vistas (with winds riffling dunes in Techniscope) and eerie views of the abandoned city (a truly spectacular Libyan location, Leptis Magna) in the middle of 'three thousand years of sand'.

MYSTERIOUS ISLAND
(JULES VERNE'S MYSTERIOUS ISLAND) (2005)

No one has filmed *20,000 Leagues Under the Sea* and then recast the star in a sequel based on Jules Verne's follow-up novel, though most versions of *The Mysterious Island* assume (justifiably) that Captain Nemo is famous for prior adventures with the *Nautilus*. In 1997, Hallmark had Rod Hardy direct a two-part *20,000 Leagues* miniseries with Ben Cross; nearly a decade later, they had Russell Mulcahy take a similar bash at *Mysterious Island* with Patrick Stewart as the renegade genius. The novel reveals Nemo's backstory as an Indian prince, but here he's Caucasian. Stewart wears something that looks as much like a turban as a watch cap and has a speech (accompanied by a bathetic burst of sitar) about how he was born an

Englishman but considers India his country and was justified in sinking British warships because his wife and daughter were killed in 'the Indian Revolution'. The ethnicity was an afterthought: in the first book, Verne assumed Nemo was Polish and harrying the Russian Navy; by the second, his publisher told him his many Russian readers would prefer the antihero be an anti-British Indian (his many British readers apparently didn't mind).

The script by Adam Armus and Kay Foster (Hallmark's *King Solomon's Mines*) borrows from the 1961 Cy Endfield-Ray Harryhausen version. The Union and Rebel castaways (heroic captain Kyle MacLachlan, proud non-slave Omar Gooding, curly-moustached Southern con man Jason Durr, short-lived bigot Nate Harrison) who board a balloon in a storm and float out of Libby Prison Camp in Virginia in 1863 are joined by surplus womenfolk (Gabrielle Anwar, Danielle Calvert). Nemo's island is overstocked with monsters (giant praying mantis, mosquitoes, rat, cobra, ants, geckos, scorpion) who pester folks. Nemo plans to bully the world into abandoning warfare (echoing Vincent Price as Nemo imitator Robur in *Master of the World*) by developing a nuclear weapon using rare element thorium (which he casually claims is responsible for the giant monsters) and making war too terrible to wage. Engineer hero Cyrus Smith (MacLachlan) figures this will just make war more terrible and refuses to help, whereupon Nemo puts the survivors outside his electric fence at the mercy of the monsters, leading to sub-Harryhausen-style poking-sticks-at-optical-effects-creatures and an alliance with separately stranded pirates Ben Gunn-look Atherton (Christopher Stephens) and teen pin-up Blake (Tom Mison). Troublemaker Bob (Vinnie Jones, doing an amateur cockney Robert Newton) needs both parts of an amulet as a treasure map, which prompts a deal of swashbuckling and sword fighting. Giant squid tentacles polish off the pirates (dragging down Bob after Nemo has totalled his ship with a bazooka), while a giant treasure-guarding spider teaches Pencroff (Durr) a valuable lesson about not being greedy by killing him.

Early on there's mention of an unstable volcano, which renders the eventual climax guessable: terrible CGI lava and flames erupt, destroying Nemo's life's work (and Nemo) while survivors paddle off in a rowboat. The show struggles to fill two feature-length episodes – but this is one of many 2000s productions truly scuppered by overindulgence in CGI rough draft effects which seem more pathetic even than the feeblest gorilla-with-a-space-helmet or baggy-rubber-iguana-suit-and-toytown-set efforts of yesteryear.

NABONGA (1944)

A PRC low budget is crippling enough for a mad scientist movie set in a dark house, but is catastrophic for this jungle picture. Snippets of laughably alien stock footage recur, while actors part the same foliage thicket over and over again. In a Tarzan setup, a plane crashes in the jungle (of course, we don't see it). Fugitive embezzler Stockwell (Herbert Rawlinson) murders the pilot then entrusts a strong-box full of cash and prop jewellery to his young daughter Doreen (Jackie Newfield – daughter of director Sam), who has already pulled an *Androcles and the Lion* act to ingratiate herself with a shaggy gorilla (Ray Corrigan). Some years later, grown-up Doreen (Julie London) wears a sarong and hangs out with the apes (or rather the one ape we see), but avoids jungle-girl stunts. Ray (Buster Crabbe), son of a man who committed suicide in disgrace after the embezzlement scandal, is intent on finding and returning the stolen goods. Trailing Ray are no-good Hurst (Barton MacLane) and blowsy Marie (Fifi d'Orsay), intent on finding and keeping the loot. The film's only interesting stretch is a chat between Ray and Doreen, who has 'no idea about right and wrong', in which she good-naturedly but stubbornly refuses to see his point about returning her treasure. PRC always went for chat over action: there's a sped-up fistfight or two and the gorilla snarls a bit, but this is mostly setup after setup of characters talking to each other, without even inserts or close-ups to punch up the conversation. London is fresh and interesting, but given too much conventional glamour makeup and hairstyling for her wild-innocent role. The others have been here before and know they'll be here again. Tiny features of interest: Tobo (Prince Modupe), Crabbe's black sidekick, is dignified and treated as an equal; screenwriter Fred Myton makes the heroine the daughter of a villain (as he did in *The Mad Monster*).

SHE (1925)

This expensive silent version of Sir H. Rider Haggard's romance sticks closer to the novel than subsequent adaptations – and trumpets that Haggard himself wrote (or at least signed off on) the intertitles. Business from the book usually omitted shows up: the African cannibal tribe (played by Caucasians with shaggy wigs) who put white-hot pots on victims' heads, the unveiling of Ayesha (whose beauty is such that any man who sees her is instantly smitten), the stairs worn down by two thousand years of the queen's footsteps and the teetering rock on the route to the eternal flame. Sadly, despite an international cast and lavish production values, the direction (G.B. Samuelson and Leander De Cordova) is terribly unimaginative, with an over-reliance on fixed camera long shots, staid cutting and theatrical gesturing.

Cambridge Professor Holly (Heinrich George), nicknamed 'the Monkey', takes his strapping adopted son Leo Vincey (a somewhat mature, bewigged Carlyle Blackwell) on an expedition to the interior of the Dark Continent, where a lost civilisation (of which we see disappointingly little) is ruled by the immortal Ayesha (Hollywood's Betty Blythe, heiress to Theda Bara's vamp roles and see-through pagan wardrobe). Along the way, Leo – one of the feebler heroes of the age – falls ill and picks up a native wife, Ustane (Mary Odette), who has to be disposed of by Ayesha, after a staring and gesticulating session. Ayesha recognises Leo as the reincarnation of Kallikrates, the lover she murdered in a jealous rage and whose mummy she sleeps beside.

The story is so well known the film feels no need to explain key events: in the climax, in the one scene everyone remembers, Ayesha steps into the flame that confers immortality to encourage the timid Leo and dwindles undramatically in an optical effect. No title explains that a second dip in the fire has reversed the immortality conveyed by the first and anyone who didn't know the book might assume Ayesha has just caught fire and burned to death. Blythe, with her 1920s bob, is stuck in a virtually unplayable role – the unveiling works in the novel, but all George's stunned eye-rolling and falling to his knees in pantomime desire can't convince us of the gorgon-like effect of Ayesha's beauty if the queen simply looks like a fairly pretty flapper who doesn't mind extensive semi-nude scenes (she strips but lets down her Godiva hair for the flame-bath). Next to the silent *L'Atlantide* or the 1935 *She*, this feels unambitious and antique – stuffy when it should be delirious, inadvertently comic when it needs full-blooded fantasy and melodrama.

SIREN OF ATLANTIS (1949)

'YOU MUST EXCUSE HIS RETICENCE. THE QUEEN HAD HIS TONGUE CUT OUT.'

Having backed two European versions of Pierre Benoît's *L'Atlantide*, producer Seymour Nebenzal assumed it'd work again as a vehicle for dropped-by-Universal exotica star Maria Montez. An expensive flop, credited to Gregg C. Tallas – who tidied up after Arthur Ripley (*Thunder Road*) and John Brahm (*Hangover Square*) took turns actually directing it – this is usually written off as doomed by the passing of the vogue for Montez's peculiar, monotonous screen presence. The real problem is that this would-be epic fantasy has much philosophising and dreaming out loud, but precious little action or adventure. It uses desert footage from the 1931 Brigitte Helm version, boasts no huge fantastical sets or effects (this is the dullest Atlantis on film) and runs a scant 76 minutes. Chunks of plot are missing, prominent actors aren't billed, characters come and go without explanation and it has that unfinished, shiftless feel associated with the oeuvre of Allan Smithee. Value-for-money hams Henry Daniell and Morris Carnovsky enliven early scenes, then vanish from the film – because they were only added as afterthoughts.

It's framed by a court martial at a French fort in the Sahara. Lieutenant St Avit (Jean-Pierre Aumont), sole survivor of an expedition sent out in search of a missing archaeologist, is charged with murdering his superior officer Captain Morhange. Flashbacks explain that the expedition found Atlantis in the high desert (swallowed by a sea of sand, rather than a sea of sea as in Plato's story) and that St Avit's woes are the fault of bewitching, mythically voluptuous Antinea (Montez). It's not clear whether the Queen is an immortal or one of a line of same-named tyrannical seductresses descended from Cleopatra and Marc Antony (though they presumably post-date the sinking of Atlantis by millennia). She retains her trademark habit of keeping the corpses of cast-off lovers around encased in gold (work done by a sculptor whose tongue she's had cut out) and maintaining a small harem of handsome men (all have wandered in from outside this easily visited lost kingdom) who are insane for love of her. St Avit is seduced in a game of chess, where Montez's clipped pronunciation of 'check' is used to cue rhythmic edits, and quarrels jealously with Morhange, who has intimate chats with the wicked, if slightly stiff queen. St Avit believes his superior officer is cutting in on him, but celibate monk wannabe Morhange tries to argue Antinea out of her evil ways by talking about God.

Trial concluded, St Avit is given an amulet from Atlantis by a Tuareg visitor – which confirms to us that his story is true, as if we doubted it – and tries to get back to the Queen, only to die in the desert (he's a murderer, remember – so the Breen Office won't let him escape) during a sandstorm and have the dunes bury him in a poetic final image. A possible feature of interest is that, though the vogue for studio exoticism had passed by the end of the war, this connects such confections as *Cobra Woman* and the complicated, contemporary femmes fatales of film noir. St Avit drinks a toast to the Queen before he even knows she really exists, hoping she's as beautiful and immoral as her legend would have it, and is then driven to kill his best friend by mad love for her; sadly, Aumont – who really married Montez – doesn't convincingly play the sort of obsession which drives noir fall guys to off rich husbands of deadly dames.

TERRY AND THE PIRATES (1940)

'I KNOW WHAT IT MEANS TO BE GRABBED BY THAT GORILLA.'

Milton Caniff's adventure strip and this movie serial are key influences on *Raiders of the Lost Ark*. The strip is notable for an exoticism and sexiness toned down in this Columbia matinee effort. The Dragon Lady, Caniff's slinky good bad girl, is played by Sheila Darcy as the somewhat matronly ruler of a lost race in the Asian jungles.

Terry Lee (William Tracy), a boy photographer who gasps 'gee willikers' all the time, keeps dragging adult hero Pat Ryan (Granville Owen) into trouble. Terry and Pat arrive in Wingpoo, outpost of someone's empire, where an American-sounding crooked Governor (William Irving) is in the pocket of half-caste, singsong-voiced baddie Fang (Dick Curtis), a low-rent Fu Manchu. Terry's archaeologist father (J. Paul Jones) has headed off into the jungle in search of the lost tribe, which Fang disapproves of – since he wants to use scrolls and a record-player rigged in 'the idol of Mara' to depose the Dragon Lady and get his hands on a fabled treasure. In his evil retinue are the usual henchmen (Jack Ingram is the top hand) who sometimes dress up in leopard hoods to spook the natives… plus Bongo, an all-purpose gorilla who gropes almost everyone at some point or other – though his main job is to crush Fang to death at the end, so the heroes don't sully their hands by killing him. The heroine is Normandie Drake (Joyce Bryant), whom Terry disses as a girl, even though she has much more spunk than the quite hysterical junior hero. Comedy relief stooge heroism comes from native magician 'Big Stoop' (Victor DeCamp) – which I heard as 'Big Stupe' – and bald Connie (Allen Jung). Aside from silly accents and eyebrows, Fang, the Dragon Lady and the bulk of the natives seem very white – and the gang are pretty much the same bunch of varmints who'd be rustling in a western.

Over fifteen chapters, there are a lot of back-and-forth captures, escapes, death traps (crushing walls, a flood, volcano, explosion, human sacrifice), etc.; a weird spoiler effect is that the cliffhangers are followed by a précis of next week's episode which always reveals that the heroes survive and blows the surprise of the next peril. Most of the performances are shrill and/or wooden (John Ince is especially dreadful as the High Priest). Scripted by Mark Layton, George Morgan and Joseph Levering; directed by James W. Horne.

DAS TIGER VON ESCHNAPUR (THE TIGER OF ESCHNAPUR) (1959) / DAS INDISCHE GRABMAL (THE INDIAN TOMB) (1959)

Fritz Lang returned to Germany in the late 1950s – admittedly, after his studio options dried up – and threw himself into recapturing the glories of his pre-Hollywood career. Before *The 1000 Eyes of Dr Mabuse* (1960), he had a huge domestic success with this pair of films (the first ends with a trailer for the 'even more thrilling sequel') based on a script and novel by his late ex-wife Thea von Harbou. A remake not of one of Lang's German silents but a two-part 1921 epic by rival Joe May, it's a fantasy gloss on an already fantastical vision of India (von Harbou was one of those oddballs who supported Hitler because he supported Gandhi). It's vague about when it's set: the 1921 film was contemporary, with telephones and cars, but this omits all but a few trappings (the hero's brother-in-law's horn-rim glasses) of modernity. It might be set in the 19th century, but – if so – where are the British? If it's after independence (and partition), why are we in a province where the Maharajah has the power of life and death over everyone? It blends location scenes with studio-built fantasies which only distantly relate to India (Debra Paget dances in Vargas pin-up gear before the vastly bosomed idol of an unnamed goddess) and a cast of Germans in boot polish play Indians of all castes.

Virile architect Harald Berger (Paul Hubschmid) comes to Eschnapur to design hospitals and schools for progressive Maharajah Chandra (Walther Reyer). He falls in love with half-European dancer Seetha (Paget), whom he rescues from a tiger. Chandra also loves Seetha, and his envious older brother Ramigani (René Deltgen) sees this as a way of overthrowing his rule – with aid from Chandra's bearded, blustery former brother-in-law Padhu (Jochen Brockmann), who resents his late sister's jewels being bestowed on a low-born dancer, and bald, sinister yogi Yama (Inkijinoff), who wants to keep Seetha pledged to whatever sect he is in. In Part One, the triangular relationship plays out and the cliffhanger has the lovers fleeing into a sandstorm. Chandra tells architect Rhode (Claus Holm), who is married to Berger's blonde sister (Sabine Bethmann), to set aside plans for modern amenities and instead build a magnificent tomb for the woman he loves but hasn't murdered yet. Part Two offers more suffering, a rebellion, a *Metropolis*-like flood as water pours into the palace, and redemption – Chandra takes a whipping and gives it all up to become an ascetic, since his brother is the real villain in the family – though a few plot-threads get washed away.

It has its moments of stern camp, when Paget or Luciana Paluzzi (as Seetha's handmaid) are smouldering (these dances aren't like anything else in the movies). There are also theatrical coups, like the appearance of zombie lepers in the dungeons, a fakir who murders the unwilling audience volunteer by piercing her basket with swords, fights with tigers (real and stuffed) and a wavery fake cobra which must be danced into submission. If the men are lost and stiff, it's hard to imagine other actors doing any better: the hero vanishes from a long section of Part Two, and doesn't seem that much more stalwart when he comes back. It has a gorgeous, enchanting artificial colour scheme (photography by Richard Angst).

UKRADENÁ VZDUCHOLOD (THE STOLEN AIRSHIP; LE DIRIGIBLE VOLÉ) (1967)

Like Karel Zeman's better-known *An Invention of Destruction*, this is a pastiche of several Jules Verne tales – mostly *The Mysterious Island* (complete with the *Nautilus* and Captain Nemo) with elements from *Five Weeks in a Balloon*, *The Children of Captain Grant* and others. It combines live action with animations in the style of 19th century illustrations, and has a funny, stiff attitude to the dawn of the modern age. After a montage of children annoying grownups through the ages, we arrive in 1899 and a variety of anarchic kids wind up drifting off on an airship which was on show at an exhibition. On the mysterious island, all the Ns on things make them wonder if Napoleon lives here. An intrepid newspaper photographer and a sneaky spy look for them. There's a rush to get the secret of the gas used in the dirigible (supposedly non-flammable, though it goes up in flames at the end) and some communist-era digs at capitalism as a banker issues fraudulent balloon stock. Pirates dressed like cowboys are also after the children and gruesomely wound each other (one fellow pokes his finger through the bullet-hole in his chest) along the way.

It has a lot of inventive, silent movie-style gags, often poking fun at the manners of the 1890s: the servant girl who looks for a place to set down a tray before opening a door and finding a perfect perch on her master's head; the stock swindler calmly making a pile of the bricks thrown through his window by an angry mob. An oddity is that the children aren't very likeable, sometimes coming off like tricksters (they steal the balloon) or acting pompous ('Musketeers are over, this is the century of technology,' a junior snob tells a boy whose hero is d'Artagnan). The adult world, apart from two token romantic leads, is corrupt and stifling, with a hypocritical prosecutor who gives the parents of the thieves a hard time in court, only to be exposed as the father of the ringleader. The look, using woodcuts and cut up vintage illustrations, prefigures Terry Gilliam's animations. Zeman enjoys the Verne-style flying machines, which are rowed through the air by uniformed soldiers.

SECRET AGENT MEN
(AND WOMEN)

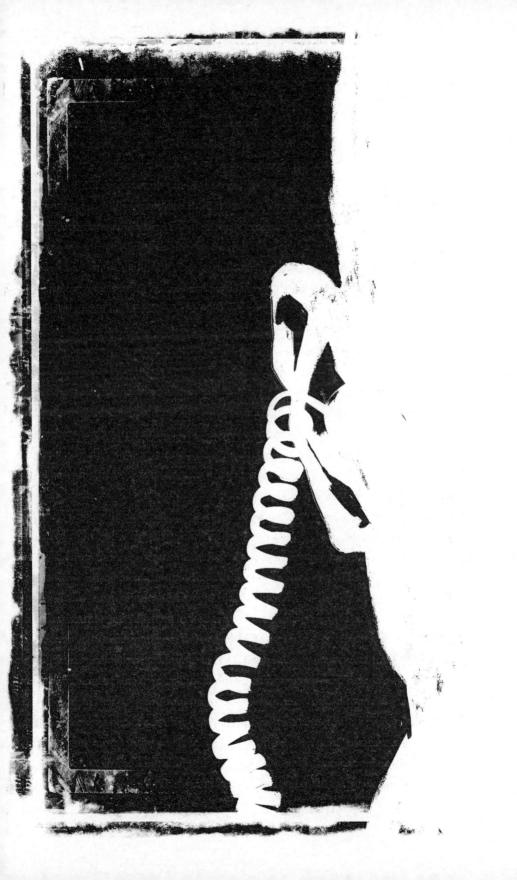

AFTER TONIGHT (1933)

'OH IF THIS CRAZY WAR GOES ON FOR ANOTHER MONTH, I WON'T HAVE A CHAIR TO SIT ON.'

In the early 1930s, glamorous female stars liked playing spies torn between love and duty during the Great War: Greta Garbo (*Mata Hari*), Marlene Dietrich (*Dishonored*), Fay Wray (*Madame Spy*), Madeleine Carroll (*I Was a Spy*). Here, Constance Bennett is Carla aka Karen aka K-14, a Russian spy posing as an Austrian nurse who falls for intelligence officer Rudy Ritter (Gilbert Roland). It seems he'll have to arrest her for a 'five minute trial' and execution, but a confederate pops up to shoot him in the arm so she can escape. When they reunite after the war at the Swiss train station where they first met, she's dragging an unexpected child – who she says is her niece, though the pre-code implication is clear. It borrows from the stories of Martha Cnockaert and Edith Cavell – though one Carla Jenssen sued the studio claiming her life had been plagiarised – but goes for wistful suffering rather than grim tragedy. The happy ending didn't help: *After Tonight* was a famous flop in its day. Spies who bravely faced firing squads went down better with audiences. Like many of these films, it's about a section of the war (Austria vs Russia) Americans were remote from to allow sympathy for both sides – though there's something about the way the hero aggressively tries to pick up a desperate woman in the meet cute scene that's more creepy than charming. Directed by George Archainbaud (*Her Jungle Love*).

AGENTE S 03 OPERAZIONE ATLANTIDE (OPERATION ATLANTIS) (1965)

If this Italian-Spanish 007 clone had an appealing leading man and a director on a par with Mario Bava (or even Antonio Margheriti) it would have cult status. As it is, it's just odd.

George Steel (plank-like John Ericson), international agent of something or other, is lured off a long-haul flight to Japan which sets down in Rome and recruited by a uranium concern to investigate doings in North Africa. It is rumoured that survivors of ancient Atlantis(?) sit on top of huge deposits of the mineral. Steel flirts with air hostesses and adventuresses and gets into fights and chases, then decamps to the Sahara. The plot channels the much-filmed *L'Atlantide* (those desert Atlanteans) and 'secret superscience realm' serials like *Undersea Kingdom* or *The Phantom Empire*. Weirdoes in fetish wetsuits use meteor minerals to power brainwashing or torture devices. The chief baddie peels a facemask to reveal he's the cartel exec who hired Steel in the first place. All this happens in the middle of the film, which returns to Rome for more routine chases and fights and resolutions which don't solve anything, plus a dizzying wind-up that seems to reset the whole thing to start all over again. A sub-plot involves women (and the hero) being packed in trunks and freighted to other countries in airplane cargo holds.

Given the promising mash-up of Euro-spy and lost kingdom pulp adventure, it's woefully unimaginative: wilder art direction, costuming, music and character acting were needed. With a young Erika Blanc. Co-scripted (with Victor Auz, Jose Lopez Moreno and Vinicio Marinucci) and directed by Domenico Paolella aka Paul Fleming (whose c.v. includes peplum, spaghetti western and nunsploitation).

BIG JIM MCLAIN (1952)

Unbelievably, Britain's Channel 5 prefaced a (rare) afternoon screening of this lunatic right wing propaganda film with a proud announcement that they'd awarded it their 'universal rating' and considered it 'exceptionally suitable for family entertainment'. Our heroes are investigators working for the House Un-American Activities Committee: staunch Big Jim (John Wayne), to whom it's a job which has to be done, and apoplectic Mal (James Arness), who lost a stretch of intestine fighting in Korea and literally can't stomach red subversion. At a ludicrous hearing, a slick 'professor of economics' dodges the 'are you now or have you ever been' question by pleading the Fifth Amendment and smugly returning to his well-paid job to poison more young minds; in real life, Fifth-pleaders were often jailed on contempt charges and universities had blacklists more extreme than the movie business.

Jim and Mal take a Hawaiian vacation that's actually a probe into a communist cell. Jim has a bizarre romance with Nancy Vallon (Nancy Olsen) – the script writes her up as 'a knockout', but she's frankly a bit dowdy – in which romantic banter often turns to politics as she tries to understand her doctor employer in psychological terms (basically, saying he's a communist because no one likes him) only for Duke to pooh-pooh this head-examining and write leftists off as rats who should be put down. A few ex-reds have redeemed themselves by becoming two-fisted squealers (a character type unique to McCarthy era movies) or, in an extreme case, a nurse in a leper colony. Hans Conreid does an excruciating comic turn as a mad academic to get some laughs in between the editorial. Veda Ann Borg is a blonde landlady who admires Jim's six-foot-four frame ('Seventy-six inches – that's a lot of man!') and insists on being dated before she coughs up info on the conspiracy. Creepy British-accented, foreign-named Sturak (Alan Napier) kills Mal and gets away with it by pleading that pesky Fifth Amendment.

The ending is unusual but inevitable in what was perceived as wartime: Big Jim half-loses the battle, but returns to the fray, determined to expose more reds and change the constitution so it doesn't protect traitors (even Senator McCarthy didn't harp on this as much as the movie does, because no one put up a fight about the constitutional rights of accused communists). Of course, the CPUSA is represented as a foreign agency in total thrall to Stalin. Awkwardness extends to the use of non-actors like police chief Dan Liu in imitation of the documentary style of some thrillers (*T-Men*, etc.). Its naiveté is camp, but you can't help remembering all the people ruined in American purges, or thinking that just as the Devil had the best tunes Marx had the best screenwriters. Written by James Edward Grant (*Miracles for Sale*), Richard English (*The Flying Missile*) and Eric Taylor (*Son of Dracula*); Directed by Edward Ludwig (*The Black Scorpion*).

THE BROKEN HORSESHOE (1953) / OPERATION DIPLOMAT (1953)

'HERE'S A TIP FOR YOU. NEVER HOLD ANYTHING BACK FROM THE POLICE – EVEN FOR THE BRIGHTEST OF BROWN EYES.'

These were the first British TV-spin-off films, both adaptations of six-part thrillers written by specialist Francis Durbridge. The BBC TV productions were broadcast in 1952, in the Saturday night slot later taken by the better-remembered Quatermass serials. In *The Broken Horseshoe* on TV, medical hero Mark Fenton (a surgeon properly titled Mr Mark Fenton, not Dr Mark Fenton) was played by John Robinson, the second Professor Quatermass. In the movie – directed by Martyn C. Webster, scripted by A.R. Rawlinson – he's gruff transatlantic Robert Beatty, who didn't make a strong enough impression to be carried over to the sequel, when Guy Rolfe took over (Robinson was replaced in the TV series too, by Hector Ross). Butchers Films didn't make a fuss about these films being linked, and few supporting cast carry over. Indeed, the Scotland Yard brother-in-law (Peter Coke) of the first story is mysteriously absent from the second, when he might have come in handy, though Fenton's odd habit of not going to the police when he trips over corpses renders moot any official status he might have. In both films, Sister Rogers (Janet Butler, Patricia Dainton) helps out.

In *The Broken Horseshoe*, a patient (Ferdy Mayne) leaves an envelope with Fenton, telling him to post it if he doesn't come back in a week. Calling on the address given, Fenton finds the patient dead, but doesn't alert the cops because a mystery woman (Elizabeth Sellars) he fancies is mixed up in the case. It seems to be about refugees from the Eastern Bloc, but is actually to do with an international horse race doping ring run by a slimy non-specific foreigner (Roger Delgado, nicely evil) and a mystery higher-up who is pretty blatantly one of Fenton's hospital colleagues. Given that the plot depends on Elizabeth Sellars being the sort of instantly ensnaring looker Rita Hayworth or Ava Gardner might not be beautiful enough to play, Beatty's Fenton comes over as more of a twit than a hero. With George Benson, Ronald Leigh-Hunt, Hugh Kelly, Toke Townley and Vida Hope.

Operation Diplomat is co-scripted by the returning Rawlinson and director John Guillermin, already showing action skills which would lift him from Tarzan films to *The Towering Inferno*. Shorter than the first film, with a more interesting leading man, its plot is just as silly. Fenton is snatched off the street to operate on a mystery man, who turns out to be a kidnapped diplomat (James Raglan) due to be smuggled out of the country by spies. It has good London location scenes, including a rooftop chase with a crook (Sydney Tafler) pursuing a nurse (Lisa Daniely) and a finale on the docks as Fenton has to stop the victim being loaded onto a Polish ship in a crate. Dainton, who played Durbridge's series character Steve Temple in *Paul Temple Returns*, is a plucky assistant; she and Rolfe could easily have carried the series further if there had been more Mark Fenton adventures. The culprit is again obvious. With Anton Diffring as a disgraced doctor, Avice Landone, Ballard Berkeley as the Yard Man, and Michael Golden.

D.E.B.S. (2004)

At once an Austin Powers-style superspy parody (especially targeting the *Charlie's Angels* films) and a sweet-natured lesbian romantic comedy, this merits comparison with *Brokeback Mountain* in presenting a non-heterosexual take on a standard movie genre… but is primarily concerned with being fun.

A hidden test in the American SATs system selects schoolgirls with an aptitude for secret agent work to become D.E.B.S. (the acronym is never quite explained), who wear fetish plaid miniskirt outfits and alternate sorority hijinx with missions against supervillains. Heroine Amy Bradshaw (Sara Foster) has a 'perfect score' she is upset to learn is due to her abilities as a liar. Depressed after a breakup with her Homeland Security boyfriend (Geoff Stults), Amy joins mousier best friend Janet (Jill Ritchie), gung ho team leader Max (Meagan Good) and French-accented sex addict Dominique (Devon Aoki) in staking out a meeting between deadly international villain Lucy Diamond (Jordana Brewster) and top Russian hitwoman Ninotchka (Jessica Cauffiel). The meet turns out not to be the start of a criminal plot but a blind date set up by Lucy's henchman (Jimmi Simpson), which turns out badly as the couple don't hit it off and everyone starts shooting. Amy and Lucy meet cute in battle and comfortably gay Lucy hits on surprised but not unwilling Amy, who then gets an unearned reputation as the only agent to survive an encounter with the villain. Thereafter, it's a fast-paced, inexplicit, silly teen romance with appealing (if non-threatening) leads and nicely developed secondary plotlines. Amy strains her relationships with close friends to get together with a villain who is willing to reform for her but tempted to use a giant death-ray to sink Australia if things don't work out.

Written and directed by Angela Robinson (expanding her short film), it stretches minimal resources to deliver a widescreen action movie feel with CGI computer read-outs, teleport effects and a plaid force field. Holland Taylor and Michael Clarke Duncan are the heads of the secret organisation.

THE DELTA FACTOR (1970)

Veteran Hollywood director Tay Garnett and paperback bestseller Mickey Spillane went into partnership on this cheap thriller, perhaps hoping for a franchise. Considering they were both known for sex and violence (Garnett made *The Postman Always Rings*

Twice), the smattering of nudity and brutal punch-ups are expected, but it is ripe with attitudes and clichés well past their sell-by date. A tagline over-sells the thrills: 'Mickey Spillane. His Gut-Ripping!... Face Splattering!... Adventure Turns a Caribbean Paradise Into a Bullet-Riddled Island of Hell!'

Manly crook Morgan (Christopher George), currency smuggler and jail-breaker, is offered twenty years off his sentence to pull a job for the government, rescuing a political leader from a prison in the corrupt island nation of Nuevo Cadiz (sort of an imaginary version of Batista and/or Castro Cuba). Morgan teams up with agent Kim Stacy (Yvette Mimieux, in an array of wigs and midriff-baring outfits) and they have to get married (for real) as part of the cover story. The mission often takes a back seat as the thug hero makes grim advances to the girl, who holds him off with a gun, but eventually warms to him. 'There's no law against a man raping his wife,' Morgan smarms, which Spillane might actually believe; later, when Kim admits she likes him after all, he coos, 'Oh, you mean I won't have to rape you,' and she responds with a heartfelt, 'I love you, Morgan' (a line only Spillane could think an actual woman would say). Nuevo Cadiz is replete with bugged hotel rooms, across-the-street snipers, moustachioed secret policemen in dark glasses, a swarthily corrupt dictator, sultry femmes fatales (Spillane's wife Sherri plays a chanteuse/informant who gets throttled by a black-gloved subjective camera) and a bucketful of sub-plots, but the film spends a lot of time hanging about the hotel rather than getting on with the action. Diane McBain is a blonde trying to avoid the police chief (Joseph Sirola), Yvonne DeCarlo is a New York madame in the film only so an early scene can be set at a party with underdressed call girls (a naked woman on an inflatable chair is the supposed epitome of decadence) and Ralph Taeger is the hero's services buddy and fixer.

George, well cast as a shady hero, seems embarrassed by Spillane's attempts at amusing hardboiled banter (when a hotel employee asks what's happened to his suite after a bomb has gone off, he snarls, 'Woodpeckers.'). The appealing Mimieux is stuck with another of the run of thankless roles she suffered throughout her career; Kim is supposed to be a super-competent secret agent, but the sexist hero doesn't give her any shooting, driving or fighting to do and her only function in the action climax is as a hostage. You can tell how out of date the filmmakers were by the resolutely non-groovy hero's 1950s suit and tie outfit (only the women dress as if it were 1970) and red Volkswagen. The stock music also sounds like a leftover from an earlier decade, not to mention the spray-on suntans and moustaches of the Nuevo Cadizians. After a not especially inventive jailbreak-cum-revolution, which at least makes use of an impressive prison location, there's an okay car chase along winding roads and across fields. The VW takes a battering, but proves almost as reliable as Herbie until it explodes in a ditch.

ESCAPE IN THE FOG (1945)

This San Francisco-set wartime spy movie has an odd, semi-fantastical premise, but soon defaults to standard duplicity and heroics. Eileen Carr (Nina Foch) is an unusual heroine for the era: a Naval officer suffering from combat fatigue who has started having prophetic dreams. She meets cute with the cheerful federal agent, Barry Malcolm (William Wright), she has seen in a dream being attacked by Nazi spies, who want to get hold of a list of Chinese underground fighters they want to turn over to 'the Japs'. Barry isn't fazed by this psychic stuff and goes about his business. Higher-up Paul Devon (Otto Kruger, in a rare Allied role) doesn't pay attention to the dream talk, so Eileen heads for the foggy bridge where she has envisioned the attack taking place and intervenes to save the hero's life. Everyone is surprisingly accepting of Eileen's seer act, but also not terribly interested in it. I assumed that Aubrey Wisberg's script would eventually have a rational explanation, but the heroine's ESP is just dropped as she becomes the usual hostage for the shootout finale. It has odd wartime wrinkles, like a young Shelley Winters as a female cabbie who has to wait for two more passengers (evil spies, natch) to join the hero and heroine before she can drive them out on the town and a clash of secret services whereby the Navy don't want to admit they have a remote-controlled ship passing under a bridge at midnight just as Barry was throwing the McGuffin off it. With Konstantin Shayne and Ivan Triesault as accented baddies. Directed at a fair old clip by Budd Boetticher.

THE FEARMAKERS (1958)

'WHAT KIND OF A CHANCE DO YOU THINK A BRAINWASHED PSYCHO LIKE YOU WOULD HAVE OF CONVINCING ANYONE OF ANYTHING?'

Immediately after *Night of the Demon*, director Jacques Tourneur and star Dana Andrews made another jittery, paranoid movie… but this politicised film noir has not accrued any reputation, probably because its McCarthyite politics were already uncomfortably out of date. The odd thing is that, though it's a red scare movie along the lines of *The Iron Curtain* (another Andrews effort) or *Big Jim McLain* – ending with a Korean war vet punching out a traitor in front of the Lincoln Memorial and vowing to take a stand before 'that committee' – it's actually an acute, prophetic and chilling indictment of the way American politics have gone in subsequent decades.

POW Alan Eaton (Andrews), tortured in Korea, is repatriated. Wearing a rumpled trench coat that looks as if he's slept in it, he returns to the small research/PR firm he thinks he owns to find Jim McGinnis (Dick Foran), a glad-handing subordinate, claiming his partner sold the outfit to him just before he died in a road accident. Alan is indignant, but easy to shoo off because he has torture-induced crack-ups. He takes a job with his old firm at the request of a senator (Roy Gordon) who realises McGinnis is being paid by a fellow-travelling anti-nuclear campaigner (Oliver Blake) and a shadowy political fixer who seems to be an enemy of democracy (but could as easily be right as left). As usual, neurotics and eccentrics pop up as instruments of international communism – a burly braggart (Kelly Thorsden), a trampy forger (Veda Ann Borg), a thick-specced, weak-chinned statistician (Mel Tormé) – but the business about how market research or opinion polls can be skewed or faked is as resonant now as ever and the rising anger that political power can be sold like soap-flakes or a TV show still burns.

Surprisingly little is made visually of the hero's PTSD, though he cracks up at just the wrong time to keep the plot going twice. It looks cheap, with back-projected locations and a weak female lead (Marilee Earle), but Andrews is excellent as ever – his weathered good looks appropriate for the tortured veteran. Scripted by Elliot West and Chris Appley from a novel by Darwin Teilhet.

THE GAY DIPLOMAT (1931)

'IF I LET PERSONAL FEELINGS GET IN THE WAY OF MY WORK, I'D HAVE STOOD IN FRONT OF A FIRING SQUAD LONG AGO.'

It seems perverse that thickly accented Ivan Lebedeff was given film star build-up in an era when established silent stars with poor voices were thrown aside. Legend has it that Lebedeff cheated the preview system by faking cards from audience members claiming he was the next Valentino, and the poster claimed 'a world of film fans voted him a star'. After this flop, he was relegated to bits and Bs; and he's even third-billed in this, his supposed breakthrough. The title, like *The Gay Divorcee*, now provokes snickers, but showbiz insiders would have picked up on its connotations in 1931. A story by an uncredited Benn W. Levy (*Blackmail, The Old Dark House*), a playwright who had a Hollywood spell, becomes a stagey-seeming script by Doris Anderson (additional dialogue by Alfred Jackson), though director Richard Boleslavsky (*Rasputin and the Empress, The Garden of Allah*) throws in dark, expressionist touches like a scuffle with the camera close on shadowed faces.

During WWI and before the Revolution, Russian Captain Orloff (Lebedeff) is wounded, prompting a mass sigh from pretty nurses because he's so handsome (he has a very neat moustache). His St Petersburg boss sends him to Bucharest to weed out a female spy, confident in his way with women. He falls in love with Countess Diana Dorchy (Genevieve Tobin), suspect number one, and forces Baroness Alma Corri (Betty Compson), the real spy, to out herself to save the Countess's life when the embassy spymaster (Purnell Pratt) orders a euphemistic assassination ('dealt with in the customary way'). It's mostly chitchat, with eavesdropping and the odd shooting. With Arthur Edmund Carewe as an 'enemy' spy (the Germans don't get mentioned). Tobin, bright and funny despite silly dialogue, and Compson are better than Lebedeff; these days, they're as forgotten as he is.

HAMMERHEAD (1968)

After Ian Fleming became a bestseller, many authors launched espionage/adventure series with Bond-ish continuing macho stud agents. During the James Bond movie craze, producers bought movie rights to these franchises and placed bets on Donald Hamilton's Matt Helm, James Leasor's Jason Love or John Gardner's Boysie Oakes (*The Liquidator*). Even the venerable Bulldog Drummond was called out of retirement and Bonded up. James Mayo's Charles Hood featured in a run of paperbacks, but had a one-time-only big-screen shot in this cheapish, if decently mounted, well-cast British picture. Hollywood veteran director David Miller (*Billy the Kid*) had a career renaissance in the 1960s, delivering his lifetime best work (*Lonely Are the Brave*). But, like Vince Edwards' wooden Hood, with *Hammerhead* the stolid Miller comes across as an incurable square paralysed with middle-aged anxiety by mod surroundings.

The plot is standard stuff. Hammerhead (Peter Vaughan), a megalomaniac criminal millionaire (and collector of pornography), is plainly a low-rent Bond villain: he has a yacht but no lair, and the merest snatch of a theme song. He schemes to substitute a lookalike for a diplomat (Michael Bates, in two roles) to get a copy of some McGuffin papers. Edwards is a dead spot, but everyone else is great value. Hood meets a contact at a Chelsea 'happening' where goateed pop artist Vendriani (Douglas Wilmer) sloshes ketchup on a girl and puts her into a giant burger bun (among other sillinesses, most involving near nudity) before the humourless police raid the place and start a riot (we're supposed to think of Andy Warhol, but it's more like a sequel to the Dennis Price scenes in *The Rebel*). Sue Trenton (Judy Geeson, having more fun than in the entire rest of her career), a wild arty hippie chick in a minimal outfit, latches on to Hood. He gallantly helps her evade the police, whereupon she keeps popping up on his mission, which involves an extended trip to Portugal. Edwards' stony expression almost cracks into irritation as this ditz keeps reappearing to compromise and annoy Hood. Vaughan is a good villain, at once cultured and crass. Beverly Adams (Lovey Kravezit in the Dean Martin Matt Helm films) makes something of the traditionally disposable role of Ivory, the villain's two-timing girlfriend; in Bond films, this character is usually fed to piranha, but Ivory gets her own back, firing a spear gun through Hammerhead's helicopter-borne getaway sedan chair.

Also on board: Patrick Cargill and William Mervyn as Hood's bowler-hatted contacts, David Prowse as Hammerhead's hulking bodyguard (the Oddjob role), Diana Dors running an arty strip-club in Lisbon (featuring Hammer starlets Maggie Wright, Veronica Carlson and Penny Brahms), Jack Woolgar as a snivelling ex-jockey/informer/comedy-pathos sidekick killed to give the hero a personal motive for doing his duty, Kenneth Cope as a running-joke motorcyclist in a stuck-on Portuguese moustache, Kathleen Byron wasted as the diplomat's wife, Tracy Reed (*Dr. Strangelove's* Miss Foreign Affairs), Patrick Holt, Joseph Furst and Windsor Davies. It takes a while to get to the Hitchcockian caper in which the diplomat is replaced by the double during a concert, which constitutes the meat of the story and a decent suspense beat. Supporting player Bates (who is terrific here) becomes the default star for a long stretch when the villain is behind the scenes and the hero busy elsewhere.

INTERNATIONAL GORILLAY
(INTERNATIONAL GUERILLAS) (1990)

> 'YOU FOOLS! IF IT WAS SO EASY
> TO KILL SALMAN, ONE MAN
> WOULDN'T HAVE MESSED WITH A
> BILLION MUSLIMS!'

This Pakistani action-comedy (with serious scenes) attained passing notoriety when the BBFC baulked at certificating it on the grounds that it libelled author Salman Rushdie. It was passed for UK release when Rushdie, an admirably consistent freedom-of-speech advocate, said he wouldn't sue anyone over the silly movie, realising a) it would then be a huge bootleg hit (not that it had much of a British legal release) and b) he had more to worry about with the *fatwah* (kill order) issued against him by the Ayatollah Khomeini on publication of his novel *The Satanic Verses*.

For most of its running time, *International Guerillas* presents Rushdie (Afzaal Ahmad) no more seriously than, say, *The Naked Gun* does the Queen – with the added fillip that clean-shaven, thick-haired, blazer-sporting, cigar-puffing older-Jerry Lewis-lookalike Ahmad in no way resembles the bearded, bespectacled author. Rushdie heads a SPECTRE-like cabal of crooks, mercenaries and blasphemers determined to wipe out Islam through blasphemy and lives in splendour in an island palace surrounded by disposable guards. He is introduced spaghetti western-style with close-ups of his hands as he personally beheads righteous would-be assassins who have been caught attacking his island. Wiping his enormous sword with a hankie, he tastes Muslim blood and announces, 'Every time the blood of those who love Mohammed has spattered my chest all gods above and below have got scared.'

Later, the vile villain lures the happy family of guerrillas – cop Mustafa (Mustafa Qureshi) and his vigilante bandit brothers Javed (Javed Sheikh) and Ghulam (Ghulam Mohiuddin) – into a trap by announcing that he intends personally to inaugurate the world's largest casino-cum-disco. The guerrillas crash the opening dressed in Michael Keaton Batman suits(!) to find multiple Rushdies present – a bunch of ringers in *Mission: Impossible* masks. Not only does Rushdie capture the heroes, but he phones Mustafa's devout wife and lures her into danger too, intent on killing the whole clan to affront Mohammed. He is so evil that, like Dracula in *Taste the Blood of Dracula*, he can only be defeated by divine intervention... in the astonishing climax, floating volumes of the Koran manifest to zap him into fiery oblivion.

Along the way, director Jan Mohammed throws in endless poorly staged chase and fight scenes as if this were a simple low-rent *A-Team* knock-off, plus comedy with guerrillas in drag cosying up to fake sheikhs (who turn out to be genuine Islamic assassins), the last-minute conversion of Salman's Jewish security chief and his sister Dolly (Babra Sharif) to Islam (they switch sides in mid-battle), and disco numbers from hip-shaking cop Shagutta (Neeli) which stress the weird paradox of identifying disco (along with gambling and alcohol) as unislamic but devoting whole reels of film to songs. The guerrilla brothers even have a singing duel in their introductory robbery-of-a-nightclub scene, which is part of the *fifty-minute* pre-credits sequence.

The only scenes which touch on reality are a sub-plot in which Mustafa's children are shot dead by corrupt Pakistani police as they righteously demonstrate against Rushdie. 'I've never asked you for anything, but can I ask you for something now?' says Mustafa's dying daughter Baby. 'I want Salman Rushdie's head.' In real life, five people were killed by the police during a mass demonstration against *The Satanic Verses*, the first casualties on an unamusing round-the-world death toll caused by cynical manipulation of Muslim outrage by folks who far more deserve to be caricatured as supervillains than a British novelist.

It's acutely uncomfortable when the comedy guerrillas – and their mum – turn to camera and deliver straight-faced speeches about how Rushdie deserves to die for his crimes ('We'll mutilate your evil face so bad that even Satan won't be able to recognise you.'), which – even in this film – are fairly nebulous. Underlying the nonsense is a belief that, yes, a writer should be murdered and that folks who set out to claim the bounty on his head are admirable and beyond criticism. It's as if an American movie of the 1960s depicted Martin Luther King as a cackling child-rapist and cast the Rat Pack as heroic Ku Kluxers who take him down with the aid of super-powered Jesus. Clumsy even by Lollywood standards, with over-reliance on jerky zooms, posturing performances and hack editing, this has curiosity value – but even that wears thin over a long 167 minutes.

THE KREMLIN LETTER (1970)

John Huston's spy boom entry is, like *Beat the Devil* and even his contributions to *Casino Royale*, so peculiar it seems an attack on the genre. In an early scene, an Admiral (Huston) tells Navy man Charles Rone (Patrick O'Neal) he has been seconded to intelligence because of his trick memory and language skills. The hero is treated as if he were being dishonourably discharged, as the Admiral snarls at the whole concept of espionage. The spying world, neither as drab as le Carré nor as fantastical as Fleming, is simply hideous here, down to one of the nastiest last-frame twists in any film. Rone comes on like a superspy, to the extent that you first wonder why Huston didn't cast Steve McQueen or James Coburn. Then, it turns out he's trapped in the plot, and O'Neal's slightly weasely suavity is entirely apt. We're used to Bond's lovemaking being sold as part of his espionage tactics; Rone actually has to become a male prostitute while undercover in Moscow.

The plot, from Noel Behn's novel, is ostensibly about retrieving the title document, a letter from a US official offering support to Russia in the event of war with China, but it's a trickier game, involving thought-dead spy Sturdevant, who is manipulating the mission for his own reasons. Rone is brought in by Ward (Richard Boone, dyed blonde, folksy and jovially hateful) to recruit a freakish team: a terminally ill bogus minister (Dean Jagger), a hairy British-Mexican pimp known as the Whore (Nigel Green), drag artiste gay art dealer Warlock (George Sanders) and a safe-cracker called the Erector Set (Niall MacGinnis), who has retired and is replaced by his daughter (Barbara Parkins), who can open a safe with her bare feet in a neat demo stunt involving a time-bomb. On the other side are a self-hating sadist (Max von Sydow) married to the tramp ex-wife (Bibi Andersson) of a man he's tortured to death, a dope-addicted commissar who's playing all sides with equal cynicism (Orson Welles, of course) and a wavery family man (Ronald Radd) pressurised because his beloved daughter is vamped by a black lesbian (Vonetta McGee) at art school in New York.

One of those exercises in which East and West are equally corrupt and ruthless, and spies have no real allegiance to their masters anyway, this is also a black comedy that turns nastily serious. With plenty of lived-in faces: Lila Kedrova, Micheál MacLiammóir, Raf Vallone, Sandor Eles, Marc Lawrence, Cyril Shaps, Christopher Sandford, George Pravda.

MADAME SIN (1972)

This was planned as a TV pilot (producer Lou Morheim gets a 'created by' credit, though he didn't write the script), but it's anyone's guess how they expected a villain-centred show which kills off its ostensible hero in the climax of the first episode to get picked up; however, in 1972, I'd have tuned in every week to see Bette Davis get the better of some new guest good guy. Shot in the UK with US stars (Davis, Robert Wagner) and high-quality British support (Denholm Elliott, Dudley Foster, Gordon Jackson, Alan Dobie, Roy Kinnear), it straddles downbeat, cynical *Callan/IPCRESS* espionage with fantastical mod business out of Fu Manchu or *The Avengers*.

Down-and-out (i.e. unshaven) agent Tony Lawrence (Wagner) is slobbing around London against a touristy backdrop of red buses and green parks, miserable because his wife Barbara (Catherine Schell) apparently died on a botched mission. He is approached by Malcolm DeVere (Elliott), a well dressed but ineffably seedy fixer, who wants him to work for 'a private individual'. He says no, then is drugged by some passing nuns (one is Gabriella Licudi, of *Unearthly Stranger*) and airlifted in a helicopter by a sneering goon (Foster, adding a leering touch of puckish perversity to a standard minion role) to the well-preserved Scots mansion of Madame Sin (Davis). This apparently Chinese mastermind and sponsor of sciences has a lab full of mad boffins (Frank Middlemass, Arnold Diamond, Charles Lloyd-Pack) devising superweapons in her high-tech basement. Madame S wants Tony to help her brainwash a navy man (Jackson) so she can steal a nuclear submarine for some cackling revolutionary beards. She convinces him to go along first by showing evidence that his former boss (Paul Maxwell with an amazing moustache) sent Barbara off to be tortured and then, when he sees through that, producing the lady herself and revealing she's signed up with Sin. The major gadget gimmick is a gun which uses directed sound as a weapon – it's versatile enough to instil false happy memories (and piano virtuosity) in a troubled servant (Pik-Sen Lim) and temporarily deafen Tony as he's trying to blow the whistle. A good, Hitchcocky moment has deaf Tony bully a tourist (Kinnear) into making a vital phone call, which is complicated because he can't hear whether the authorities are alert enough to take action.

Davis has blue eyeshadow rather than the false eyelids Christopher Lee favoured in oriental mastermind roles. She clearly enjoys herself in high camp outfits – and her presence prompts other players to raise their game. The caper itself is a bit dull, with much dashing across the landscape pursued by helicopters. After thwarting Sin's plans,

Tony is ready to settle down with Barbara when she announces she's carried out her mistress's orders and poisoned him – whereupon, in a turn I wasn't expecting when I saw this in the cinema on its theatrical release, he chokes to death and his widow leaves the corpse to rejoin Madame Sin, who might have been the dead hero's mother to boot. With Burt Kwouk (inevitably), David Healy, Al Mancini, John Orchard and Barry Moreland (as an early hologram – though the script calls it a holograph). Produced by Morheim (*The Outer Limits*), Wagner, Lew Grade and Julian Wintle (*The Avengers*), explaining the mix of US and UK film and TV traditions thrown into the mix (Morheim and Grade competed with flop Titanic projects in 1979-80, *S.O.S. Titanic* and *Raise the Titanic*); directed and co-written by David Greene (*Sebastian, Godspell*, the Redgrave sisters' remake of *What Ever Happened to Baby Jane?*).

MISSIONE SPECIALE LADY CHAPLIN/ OPERAZIONE LADY CHAPLIN (SPECIAL MISSION LADY CHAPLIN) (1966)

'TO FIRE THESE SIXTEEN ATOMIC MISSILES, ALL I HAVE TO DO IS THROW THAT SWITCH ON THE WALL OVER THERE. THE WHOLE CONTINENT WILL BE BLOWN UP.'

A nun (Daniela Bianchi) drives up to a monastery with a basket of linen, takes out a machine gun and wipes out a bunch of false monks then ventilates a computer. Under the credits, accompanied by an unforgettable Bruno Nicolai song sung by Bobby Solo, she strips out of her habit to disclose a bathing suit. This is couturier-cum-assassin Lady Arabella Chaplin. Her boss is an above-suspicion millionaire with the entirely reasonable-sounding name Kobre Zoltan (Jacques Bergerac), who raids sunken submarines for missiles to sell to an unethical government and keeps pet scorpions to fight on a tabletop to entertain wealthy guests. Enter American agent Dick Malloy (Ken Clark) – still wearing a trench coat with the collar turned up in a decade when spies were generally cooler, snappier dressers. His irascible boss Heston (Philippe Hersent) sends him to fathom the international mystery, which means a shootout in a deserted Spanish corrida, chatter at a New York heliport, a trip down below by bathyscaphe, the theft of rocket fuel in London, a Paris fashion show, a secret missile base in Morocco, etc.

This international (France-Italy-Spain) co-production is one of many Euro efforts made in imitation of the Bond movies, usually with a surplus 007 actor or two in the cast. Bianchi, more fun as a bad girl than as the romantic interest in *From Russia With Love*, gets to be a mistress of disguise (besides the nun, her best act is as a disabled old lady in a tricked-up wheelchair with guns in the armrests). Clark is a dud hero – so many of these films imported blocky B-reject Americans to play secret agents, missing the fact that Bond was British and suave as well as tough and sexy. Many trimmings are Bondian: a hook-handed henchman, black polo-neck-clad judo choppers, villains shoved against equipment to be electrocuted, the mad millionaire's novelty pet, the traitor killed by choking inside his getaway car after he's served his purpose. Delightful tech includes bubble-carapace attack helicopters and a remote-viewing underwater drone. Among the supporting lovelies are exploitation regulars Helga Liné (always best as a slinky woman of mystery – here, she represents the country which wants to buy the missiles) and Evelyn Stewart (aka Ida Galli).

Zoltan discovers Lady C is dallying with Malloy (like Pussy Galore, she switches sides; in fact, like Pussy Galore in the novel, she seems to stop being a lesbian as well) and tosses her out of his aeroplane. Luckily, she has a concealed parachute, her favourite machine gun and a theme tune which plays whenever she's being awesome. She's shooting it out with Zoltan's minions in the desert when who should swim ashore but Dick with a spear gun and some bombs. Like a macho thug, Dick slaps her unconscious to be solo at the wheel during a jeep chase to the ship where the weapons of mass destruction are stashed. Hero and baddie have a tolerably athletic punch-up in the burning hold and Zoltan gets fatally stung by one of his scorpions and dies laughing (a less wooden hero than Dick Malloy would have something amusing to say about this). Malloy and Heston bicker about the killer babe: 'What about that Chaplin girl. She's been nothing but a heap of trouble and you know it.' 'But she's still a lot of woman.' 'Ah, you're my best man, but woman-crazy!' At the end, Dick slaps handcuffs on Arabella… but not necessarily to arrest her.

The third 'Dick Malloy' movie, following *Agente 077 Missione Bloody Mary* and *Agente 077 dall'oriente con furore/Agent 077: Fury in Istanbul*. Note that an injunction filed off his serial number. Directed by Alberto De Martino (*Antecristo*, *Holocaust 2000*) and series regular Sergio Grieco (as Terence Hathaway).

MISTER JERICO (1970)

This sunny UK TV movie was evidently a pilot for a series Patrick Macnee might have sailed into after the 1969 cancellation of *The Avengers*. It's easy to see why that didn't happen: the star isn't well cast (or in great shape), one would-be regular (Marty Allen) is excruciating, and ITC's international market wasn't ready for a show about a sympathetic con man. Even if Dudley Jerico only rips off rich rotters (Herbert Lom takes the role here), he seems like a selfish bastard hiding behind Macnee's post-Steed ragged charm. Directed by Sidney Hayers (*Night of the Eagle*) from a script by UK TV pros David T. Chantler and Philip Levene, it has strategic Mediterranean locations to augment the usual studio-bound exotica, but is still cheap and cramped, especially beside glossy big-budget capers like *Dead Heat on a Merry-Go-Round* and *The Thomas Crown Affair*.

Jerico dresses in a more 'with-it' fashion than Steed, which means plump Macnee has to squeeze into brightly coloured shirts and foulards, but is so shifty you'd think he'd find it hard to dupe his marks. He's out to rook millionaire Victor Russo (Lom), who owns one of a set of fabled Gemini diamonds, by substituting a fake then selling the owner back the real one as if it were the long-lost twin. Complications arise because another trickster (Connie Stevens) is trying the same stunt. Russo helpfully shows Jerico how his security system works in a setup for the heist, and has a couple of rent-a-goon minions to provide physical threat. Allen is whiny tagalong sidekick Wally: following his teaming with Steve Rossi in *The Last of the Secret Agents?*, this was his last shot at big-screen stardom, and no wonder. Stevens, unexpectedly, comes off best in three different personae (at least one dubbed by the versatile Nikki Van Der Zyl); it's hard, obviously, to pull off mistress of disguise roles, since contrasting wigs and specs don't work as well as Martin Landau's false beards and noses, but Stevens' makeup and mannerisms sell the possibility characters wouldn't recognise the mousy blonde secretary and the dark-haired mystery woman as the same person.

LE MONOCLE RIT JAUNE (THE MONOCLE) (1964)

The third and final entry in the 'Monocle' series starring puggish Paul Meurisse (the sleazy husband of *Les Diaboliques*) as French intelligence agent Théobald Dromard, aka 'the Monocle' (created by the novelist Rémy). *Le Monocle Noir* (1961) and *L'oeil du Monocle* (1962) are noirish stories overshadowed by World War II, but – with 007 influence setting in – this is more freewheeling. Dromard is assigned to Hong Kong and Macao (good use of locations and authentic crowds) to thwart an Asian cult out to foment global war. The plot isn't much (a nuke in a coffin smuggled by junk to detonate next to a US warship), but it's an eccentric, wilfully French wild ride with some post-modern moments. 'Get ready, my friend,' says the Monocle, approached by thugs on a picturesque location, 'unless I'm mistaken, we're starting a fight sequence.' Dromard retains his regular sidekick, steak-and-*frites* bruiser Poussin (Robert Dalban), but also picks up socialite British spy Valérie (Barbara Steele, unflatteringly filmed), international fixer Elie Mayerfitsky (Marcel Dalio) and junior stiff Frédéric (Olivier Despax). Dromard reveals a nice line in French snobbery when dealing with Hong Kong's British intelligence agency; told France isn't at war with the English, he muses, 'One is never really at peace with them, either.' The film keeps throwing up weirdness: at a Chinese meal, the Monocle and allies are fed drugged fish (with lit-up eyes) and become drowsy as Asian baddies enter in slo-mo, doing the finger-clicking Jet dance from *West Side Story* forwards and backwards with added martial arts tumbling. Michel Magne's jazzy, inventive score is weird throughout – including strangled licks that prefigure Ennio Morricone's more extreme efforts. The punch line seems to find the Monocle literally turning Chinese, illustrating (in black and white) the title's racial pun ('rit jaune' means a sour or mirthless smile). Directed by Georges Lautner.

O.K. CONNERY (OPERATION KID BROTHER) (1967)

Only in 1967... only in Italy... could an entire movie, with a reasonably healthy budget, be built around the fact that Sean Connery's younger brother was sort of interested in acting. Of the (many) imitations of the James Bond series, this – even more than the Charles Vine movies, which sold themselves as the adventures of the second best secret agent in the world – is most outrageous in lifting from the parent megafranchise. It's also loopy Italian exploitation which shares personnel with the classic *Diabolik* – though director Alberto De Martino (*The Antichrist, Holocaust 2000*) is a plodder next to Mario Bava.

Neil Connery, who refused to shave a neatly trimmed beard which makes him look more like a villain than a hero, plays Neil, the brother of the coyly unnamed best secret agent in Europe. He's not a professional spy but a plastic surgeon who uses Tibetan hypnosis as anaesthetic (and for memory recovering purposes) who is also a champion archer and all-round playboy. Connery, whose infernally catchy Ennio Morricone-Bruno Nicolai theme song warbles 'OK Connery' wherever he goes, is approached by Commander Cunningham (Bernard Lee) and Miss Maxwell (Lois Maxwell) of the British Secret Service to fight Thair (Adolfo Celi), Number Two (codename Beta) of the SPECTRE-like evil organisation THANATOS. Thair plans to use a device (based on misuse of an 'atomic nucleus' and radioactive rugs manufactured by ailing blind people in North Africa) to disable every mechanical or electronic component in the world. Mildred (Agata Flori) is Thair's all-the-way-evil girlfriend and gets killed, while Maya (Daniela Bianchi) goes the Pussy Galore route and switches sides (along with her troupe of girl sailors) after receiving serious smooching from Dr Neil and discovering her boss intends to kill her off as a loose end. With guns, planes and cars not working, Connery and archery club pals in Robin Hood/William Tell hats invade Thair's underground lair with old-fashioned bows and arrows.

Yes, the casting is that blatant, with Lee and Maxwell in basically their regular 007 roles, and Bianchi (*From Russia With Love*) and Celi (*Thunderball*) doing Bond girl and Bond villain shtick honed to perfection in the official series. Even Anthony Dawson, the to-be-murdered Alpha of THANATOS, was in *Dr No* and (without credit) played Blofeld in movies where the villain stroked his cat in the shadows. Celi finds an escape dinghy built into his yacht in imitation of the boat gadget from *Thunderball* and a baddies-sat-around-the-plotting-table set piece echoes *Goldfinger* and *Thunderball*. Pop-eyed Connery (dubbed by a bland American) hasn't got the charisma to carry off the role of himself, let alone prove a credible threat to his big brother (he's rather more relaxed in *The Body Stealers*). However, *O.K. Connery* is a hoot for its non-stop parade of astounding outfits (Celi has a red leather jumpsuit with shoulder pads), weird plot turns (Connery poses as a blind Arab to infiltrate the evil rug factory and foment a rebellion, good guys dressed as van Gogh have a gunfight in an orchard with bad guys in red berets and matching pullovers), gadgets (a flick-knife that shoots a blade across the room, machine guns hidden in the ceiling), eye-popping candy colours and a general attitude of what-the-hell… In the Bond films, Maxwell's Miss Moneypenny spent all her time quipping and pining in M's outer office; De Martino at least gets the actress in the field to mow down THANATOS goons with a machine gun disguised as a sheaf of hay.

Outstanding contribution: costume designer Gaia Romanini. Also with Franco Giacobini as a comedy relief agent called away from his wedding, Ana María Noé as an imitation of Lotte Lenya's Rosa Klebb, and a lot of pretty girls. Story and script mostly by Paolo Levi (*7 Women for the MacGregors*, *The Killer Reserved 9 Seats*), with Frank Walker, Stanley Wright and Stefano Canzio.

OPERATION C.I.A. (1965)

> 'YOU'RE FAR TOO PRETTY TO BE AN EXPERT ON BIOCHEMISTRY AND AGRICULTURE.'

This original script by Bill S. Ballinger (*The Strangler*) and Peer J. Oppenheimer (*Nashville Girl*) feels like a faithful version of Donald Hamilton's Matt Helm spy novels – which were more grounded in reality than the Dean Martin films. It has added curiosity value as – along with *The Quiet American* and (sort of) *The Ugly American* – one of the few films to look at the trouble spot of Vietnam before American involvement became a major issue. It suggests that he-man spy Burt Reynolds' foiling of a plot against the American ambassador more or less puts an end to communist evil in 1965. Mark Andrews (Reynolds) is sent to Saigon to replace an agent blown up by a scooter-bomb. He proves bizarrely inept – getting mugged in a massage parlour/bath house (the first of several scenes in which women take off his shirt) within a few hours of arriving. A trip up country with a French agent (Danielle Aubry), who is also untrustworthy, involves a minor skirmish between the Vietcong and the local army (no American military presence is mentioned) and the last third is an extended location chase. Perennial Filipino bad guy Vic Diaz has a showy bit as a mincing, giggling commie, but most of the supporting cast are oddly dubbed apparent amateurs. Directed by a post-*Thing* Christian Nyby and shot in Thailand.

OPERATION: ENDGAME (ROGUES GALLERY) (2010)

> 'IT WAS YOU. YOU WERE HAVING PHONE SEX WITH THE DEVIL.'

On the day of Obama's inauguration, Fool (Joe Anderson) turns up at a new job with a black ops organisation of spies code-named after tarot cards. The Devil (Jeffrey Tambor), chief of the bureau, is murdered by persons unknown. He puts Operation: Endgame into effect, requiring his agents kill each other off. Since staff must leave guns, knives, etc., outside the sealed complex, killings are performed with office equipment (guillotine blades, a shredder, document spikes, etc.). Sort of a mash-up of *Salt* and *Office Space*, with an elimination game angle, this has a strong, off-kilter cast (Rob Corddry, Zach Galifianakis, Adam Scott, Brandon T. Jackson, Beth Grant, Bob Odenkirk, Ving Rhames), a leavening of cynical conspiracy wit (a house-clearing operation so the new government won't have the baggage of the old one) and funny lines and performances, but it's a near-miss rather than a modern-day answer to *The President's Analyst*. The direction (Fouad Mikati) isn't as sharp as the writing (Sam Levinson, Brian Watanabe) and the plot doesn't really have any place to go. However, it has relishable characters – with especially good, odd female psychos: Ellen Barkin's psycho cougar, who hasn't worn a dress this short since the day they killed Benazir Bhutto, Emilie de Ravin's cutesy girly homicidal loon, Maggie Q's svelte High Priestess. Throughout, doings are observed by jaded, gossipy surveillance guys (Tim Bagley, Michael Hitchcock) who keep up a funny commentary on the action.

THE RETURN OF MR MOTO (1965)

> 'OUR ONLY PROBLEM IS SATAN'S CIGARETTE.'

In the 1960s, with Bond fever in full swing, there was a general scramble to find spy-related film franchises – hence this revival for John P. Marquand's Japanese hero, unseen on screen since World War II ended Peter Lorre's series. The British-made film feels like an average episode of a UK TV show of the period, with a guest cast who have résumés full of shots on *Danger Man*, *The Saint*, *The Baron*, etc. Man-of-all-ethnicities Henry Silva presumably landed the lead on the strength of his turn as a martial arts-proficient Korean villain in *The Manchurian Candidate*; he mostly plays Interpol agent I.A. Moto as a snappily dressed, tough-talking regular guy, but spends the last reel in a wispy disguise beard doing a sing-song Japanese accent. Oddly, he does little of Moto's signature karate chopping – the film is light on anything like action. Moto is called to London by an old friend in the oil industry (Gordon Tanner) who is promptly killed by an ex-Nazi sadist (Martin Wyldeck). While investigating, Moto uncovers intrigue surrounding oil concessions in the Middle East; the script is prescient in envisioning the great battleground of the future, with the far-sighted Moto realising the great powers should pay more attention to the oil business. The villains (Marne Maitland, Brian Coburn, Anthony Booth, Denis Holmes) are obvious about it, but an above-suspicion English aristo (forgotten *Carry On* regular Terence Longdon) is fingered as a culprit in the last reel in a concession to Moto's old detective style. In a cynical twist, it turns out that the friend Moto is avenging was also in on the scam. Heroine Sue Lloyd is wasted and Harold Kaskett puts on boot polish as a typical British film and TV oil sheik. Directed competently, if without inspiration by veteran Ernest Morris (*The Tell-Tale Heart*).

SPIONE (SPIES) (1928)

This sleek, entertaining late-silent super-production was a run for cover by Fritz Lang after the monumentally expensive, ambitious and demanding *Metropolis*. It's not cheap, but returns to the thrills of the *Dr Mabuse* movies, with pulp devices harking back to Feuillade (a trainwreck like the one in *Fantômas*) and forward to Bond. The hypnotic villain is not Mabuse, though Rudolf Klein-Rogge again plays mastermind, but a literal no-one (Nemo the Clown) who most often appears as calm, wheelchair-bound Haghi, director of a bank which fronts for an organisation of (communist?) spies. Haghi sports Hitlerian slick hair and a Lenin-Trotsky goatee, but claims to be rich as Henry Ford (though he pays much less tax).

The German-based spy is out to secure a copy of a secret treaty between Britain and Japan, which – if publically known – will cause war in Asia! His favoured methods involve seductive female agents, guilt-ridden Russian Sonja (Gerda Maurus) and ephebically amoral Kitty (Lien Deyers). On Nemo's case are a counter-espionage agency which employs numbered operatives, notably dashing Number 326 (Willy Fritsch), first seen in disguise as a tramp inveigling his way into the office of his M-like boss (Louis Ralph) to unmask a secretary as a Haghi minion. Later, 326 cleans up and becomes a dapper charmer, winning over Sonja, who works with him against her former master. Halfway through, it's shown that 326's bosses also employ Nemo the

Clown... therefore most of this back-and-forth of spies is an utter charade. Sometimes, Haghi goes to great lengths to get information Nemo must already have, perhaps to keep his double life going.

Like most of Lang's silent work, it's a film of remarkable moments and scenes rather than coherent plot: still-life glimpses of the opium-soaked private life of the blackmailable wife of a diplomat who suffers through an awkward interview with the insistent Haghi; an overhead shot of a boxing match which pauses between rounds as couples in evening dress cluster round to dance; a disgraced Japanese diplomat (Lupu Pick) assailed by the guilt-spectres of murdered couriers who were only carrying dummy treaties (newspaper strips in impressive sealed envelopes) while he let Kitty walk off with the real one, and committing a reverential hara-kiri; Sonja struggling wildly with the chair she is tied to as Haghi shares 'the secret of my life' with her by rising from his wheelchair and slipping out, leaving her to be overcome by poison gas; a wall covered with *Metropolis* posters on the noirish streets where waifs and well-born rotters conduct the business of spying; Fritz Rasp's improbably waxed moustache as a disgraced and disgraceful Colonel selling out to the enemy; Deyers' erotic dishabillé writhing as she simultaneously excites the diplomat's pity and lust, worming her way into his trust; and 1928 high-tech communications gadgets which convey the latest news to the spy-master as he sits in his modernist office, wreathed by cigarette smoke and attended by a blandly sinister nurse he gives orders to in sign language.

In an extraordinary finish, Nemo goes on stage as armed police close in, and performs his strange act – which involves shooting at oversized puppet insects – while taking pot-shots at his enemies backstage and in the auditorium. Finally, laughing insanely, he shoots himself in the head and collapses ('curtain down') while the audience applauds wildly, thinking it's all part of the show – which, in Lang's terms, of course it is.

THE SPOOK WHO SAT BY THE DOOR (1973)

'DON'T QUIT UNTIL YOU EITHER WIN OR YOU DIE.'

Most 1970s blaxploitation films had token politics, but focus on individualistic superspades who weren't liable to join the Black Panthers – Shaft respects his militant brothers, but has his own agenda. Directed by Ivan Dixon and scripted by Sam Greenlee (from his own novel) and Melvin Clay, this is a more committed, angry, speculative exercise.

A smug white Congressman (Joseph Mascolo), behind in the polls with the Negro vote after a law and order speech, arbitrarily crusades against the all-white intelligence services. This forces the CIA to recruit black applicants, then put them through intensive training designed to make them all drop out before graduation – with a hulking white karate champion showing up to demonstrate why none of them are worthy to be in his beloved Company. Most of the class flunk, but Dan Freeman (Lawrence Cook), who keeps his head down and applies himself, literally stays the course, and graduates in a spare ceremony where he sits alone among rows of empty chairs and is congratulated as a credit to his race by the sole official present. Given that few of the cast are familiar, even among the black talent pool of 1970s exploitation films, Cook's quiet, tough Freeman (he proves his black belt is as good as the bear-like instructor's) emerges from the crowd as a central figure as the character does. More obviously charismatic types flunk, and when called a 'Tom' for working so hard Freeman doesn't argue or fight back.

Of course, the CIA put this trained agent to use by giving him a fancy job title that boils down to working the xerox machine – a detail which doesn't quite ring true: 1970s intelligence agencies would have had a lot of work for a black agent, especially in the FBI's COINTELPRO program to infiltrate the counterculture or the CIA's campaigns against communists in Angola and other African states. After five years, Freeman resigns to become a social worker in Chicago. He trains street gangs in insurgency tactics learned at the CIA, steals state-of-the-art hardware to replace their feeble weapons (he advocates resisting the draft but also recruiting 'Nam vets) and plans a multi-city uprising to take over the ghettos. Dawson (J.A. Preston), Freeman's black cop friend, only realises what Freeman is up to when there's open war on the streets – and Freeman feels forced to kill him, making the point that revolution won't just be a question of offing hated whiteys.

Informed by the Watts and Chicago riots (the unnamed Mayor is clearly a Daley figure) and the rise of the Black Panthers, *The Spook* is at once a program for African-American revolution and a prophecy of worst-fears-fulfilled for white conservatives ('We're going to turn the American dream into the American nightmare.'). Generations on, it remains a potent set of arguments and surprisingly good drama.

SERIAL KILLERS

AND COPS

ANAMORPH (2007)

A *Se7en*-inspired murky, overwrought, pretentious serial killer movie. Obsessive-compulsive cop Stan Aubray (Willem Dafoe with an unflattering haircut) partners with loser Carl Uffner (Scott Speedman) when corpses posed like artworks suggest either Stan shot the wrong man in closing the case of 'the Uncle Eddie Murders' or a copycat is working out a tapestry of revenge. The murder-as-art thing has literally been done to death, but *Anamorph* offers impressive *trompe l'oeil* mutilations: an upside-down corpse behind a wall with a pinhole to create a camera obscura effect, a dismembered body hung in a mobile so the pieces form a swooping heron shape (or something – maybe Rodan, the flying monster?). An ex-junkie (Clea DuVall) who was friends with a victim Stan didn't save and an eccentric art dealer (Peter Stormare) are suspects – but the killer (spoiler) turns out to be… just some guy (Don Harvey)! The title refers to that elongated-skull-in-the-Holbein perspective trick, and points to a development whereby prophetic pictures are concealed in crime scenes. Co-written and directed by Henry Miller.

THE CALLING (2014)

Small town police chief Hazel Micallef (Susan Sarandon) has a bad back and a drink problem. She bickers with her live-in mom (Ellen Burstyn – only fourteen years older than her screen daughter, she looks like Sarandon's grandmother), but earns the respect of wary colleague Ray Green (Gil Bellows) and is adored by just-transferred gay detective Ben Wingate (Topher Grace), who does legwork on a mystifying series of murders.

When Donald Sutherland – 100% more engaged by a cameo in a little thriller than a leading role in the *Hunger Games* franchise – popped up as a priest to dispense Biblical backstory, I had a tiny flashback to *The Rosary Murders*. *The Calling* is the 21st century version of those chilly Canadian films of the 1970s and '80s which hauled in anyone with a Canadian passport to fill out the supporting cast. Its 'nothing special' feel is rather endearing. The premise is at once familiar and ridiculous (a merciful serial killer tries to resurrect a dead brother by ritually despatching twelve devout disciples who have reasons to want to die) and a passive-aggressive approach to suspense makes it obvious that the 'villain' (soft-spoken Christopher Heyerdahl) isn't out to hurt anyone who doesn't want him to. The story moves with wintery torpor unpunctuated by car chases and explosions, only to trip over oh-come-on-now plot turns (a bunch of corpses with mouths frozen so that when looked at in succession they are uttering a Latin prayer). It ends with an ambiguous miracle. Scripted by Scott Abramovitch, from a novel by Inger Ash Wolfe; directed by Jason Stone.

CHRISTOPHER ROTH (2010)

Apart from a torture stretch mired in 'why are you doing this?' cliché, this Belgian-Italian *giallo* is solid – with tricky misdirection for those who think they can spot where the story is headed. As befitting a film with a Stephen King/Richard Bachman stand-in protagonist, it evokes *The Dark Half* and/or *Misery* and/or *Secret Window*, then takes another tack.

Juan (Joaquim de Almeida) writes inside-the-mind-of-a-killer books under the pseudonym 'Christopher Roth'. Piqued by a review which says he's gone stale, he shocks his publisher (raspy octogenarian Ben Gazzara) by moving to remote Umbria with loving wife Catherine (Anna Galiena) to work on a book celebrating the small joys of life. In an obligatory ominous note, the idyllic house is beyond cell phone reception. The couple are imperilled when they wander into the path of a boar hunt and Catherine is annoyed at being scared, admitting she used to be a proficient boar-hunter herself – setting up something for later. Juan learns a serial killer called 'the Boar' (who adds tusks to naked corpses) is active locally. His neighbours are suspicious: widower Erik Cardelli (Francesco Guzzo) is a big Christopher Roth reader, and his kids are weird – Giovanna (Jessica Bonanni) has an odd dislike of hearing her name aloud and hidden-away, boar-scarred Filippo (Inigo Placido) might have been shaped into a Christopher Roth-type monster by cruelties and mishaps.

Stylised *giallo* killings (effects by veteran Gianetto di Rossi) might represent reality or Juan/Roth's *idea* of reality (a red-spattering murder in an all-white bathroom). Eventually, Juan is hung up by the Boar (or our best suspect – any or all of the main characters might be or have imagined the Boar) and forced to confront the horror of his books. The ending, indeed the whole film, is open to interpretation as a *Usual Suspects* exercise in tale spinning. Written and directed by Maxime Alexandre.

CHUGYEOGJA (THE CHASER) (2008)

Ex-cop Eom Joong-ho (Kim Yoon-suk) runs a struggling vice ring. Several of his girls are missing – he believes poached to sell abroad. Mi-jin (Seo Yeong-hie) makes a date with Young-min (Ha Jung-woo), who might be part of the abduction ring. Joong-ho orders her to go home with him, then call with the address so he can come over and beat answers out of the client. However, soft-spoken, boyish Young-min isn't a rival pimp but a serial killer who has usurped a large, gated home by murdering the owners. The place is tricked out as a killing den, with bricked-up windows and an array of shackles and torture tools.

The bulk of the story unfolds over a long night as all three characters get deeper into trouble. Mi-jin follows orders and Young-min seems to give her chances to contact Joong-ho or simply leave – only there's no phone reception from the bathroom and the house is locked. The girl is gagged, tied and helpless, but Young-min is frustrated when church friends of the homeowner show up wondering where he is. They aren't fobbed off with an explanation and recognise a starved dog on the grounds (later, it digs up corpses). After impulsively killing the interlopers, Young-min has to get rid of their car. While driving away, the killer has a fender-bender with Joong-ho, who is searching for Mi-jin and realises – thanks to a distinctive phone – he has his hands on her abductor. Young-min tries to run and Joong-ho gives chase in a gruelling *Dirty Harry* urban action sequence. Both are dragged to a police station where, a third of the way through the film, the killer calmly owns up to the murders.

However, that evening, the Mayor of Seoul has been pelted with shit by a protester and the police are pressured to deal with this silly crisis – which eventually means the battered Young-min, who stops short of telling the cops where Mi-jin is but admits she might still be alive, is released. In an unsettling, grim development, the hooker breaks free and runs to a nearby store just as Young-min, whom the proprietor knows and trusts as a local, drops in for cigarettes. As in the less melodramatic, based-on-fact *Memories of Murder*, the bureaucracy and self-serving image-consciousness of South Korean police are shown to be a hindrance to justice. Dirty ex-cop Joong-ho, a cynical slob who almost grows a heart as he exercises detective skills, is better suited to bringing in the killer than the proper authorities.

The police aren't totally inept. A detective tailing the released murderer is shattered when he kills the shop owner and snatches Mi-jin; she knew about his *calculated* killings, but isn't prepared for sudden, pragmatic murders committed to cover his tracks. The antagonists are subtly played – without too much backstory, we get a sense of how ex-cop and killer have come to this crux as the plot takes turns (admittedly relying on cruel coincidence) to bring them together. Reticent with ultra-violence, it lets the horrid, heavy clunk of the killer's canvas toolbag on the bathroom floor and his home improvements (hooks, etc.) tell a sordid story. Scripted by Hong Won-chan and Lee Shinho. Directed by Na Hong-jin.

CIMARRON STRIP: KNIFE IN THE DARKNESS (1968)

Like the longer-running *The Virginian*, the single-season (1967-8) western series *Cimarron Strip* consisted of feature-length episodes. The adventures of Marshal Jim Crown (Stuart Whitman) exhibit a social conscience (courtesy series developer Christopher Knopf) and take history more seriously than the average *Gunsmoke* knock-off. This episode, scripted by Harlan Ellison to make use of the Jack the Ripper research he did for 'The Prowler in the City at the Edge of the World' (from *Dangerous Visions*), is a western bookend for the SF Ripper of Robert Bloch's *Star Trek* script 'Wolf in the Fold' (just as the Ellison story is a sequel to Bloch's *DV* contribution 'A Toy for Juliette').

The episode has a horror look, well handled by director Charles R. Rondeau; indeed, the regular title sequence of Crown riding cheerily in broad daylight seems out of place since the rest of the show takes place at night (fog machines working overtime). As Cimarron Strip suffers unnatural fog, 'dance-hall girl' Josie (Jennifer Billingsley) causes a scrap between admirers at an after-dark hoedown in 'Pony Jane's saloon'. Angry, lecherous Tal St James (David Canary), who acts so suspiciously he *has* to be innocent, pulls a knife and is talked down. Josie wanders off and is stabbed by a mystery man. Suspicion hovers around locals: the widowed town doctor (Karl Swenson), the only expert surgeon in these parts, has been spending time at Pony Jane's; Indian Shadow Feller (Ron Soble), an expert skinner who courted the dead woman, is most likely to be lynched; and Peddigrew (Don Hamner), a knife-sharpening tinker, loiters to eye the lovelies. Crown's younger sidekick, newspaperman Francis Wilde (Randy Boone) – his older pal is a stereotype Scot, Angus MacGregor (Percy Herbert) – makes a connection with the Ripper case. Shadow Feller is seized by a mob, but ruled innocent when a woman (Victoria Show) is killed while the Indian is in their clutches.

Ellison's research kicks in as Tipton (Patrick Horgan), a moustachioed member of the Whitechapel vigilance committee (and brother of one of the victims), arrives, having tracked the killer west. Wilde receives Ripper letters, pastiching the originals (Ellison also writes saltier cowpoke language than most pre-*Deadwood* TV westerns). Because of his British accent, Crown suspects Tipton, but the late-arriving culprit is soft-spoken Enoch Shelton (Tom Skerritt), who claims not to be a misogynist but a social reformer. He kills (as per a remark of George Bernard Shaw's) to draw attention to slum conditions – though Skerritt plays Shelton (very well) as a nasty, self-justifying sadist. An ironic finish has the killer stalked and slaughtered by Shadow Feller and other 'savages', who leave his corpse draped over a rock. With Jill Townsend as Crown's regular girl (imperilled but saved), Jeanne Cooper as Pony Jane and Grace Lee Whitney (*Star Trek*) as another frou-frou *dame*. Though the theme is by Maurice Jarre, the incidental music is by Bernard Herrmann.

COVER GIRL KILLER (1959)

> 'DOC, IF YOU WERE TO COMMIT SUICIDE AT ONE O'CLOCK IN THE MORNING, WOULD YOU PUT ON A BIKINI?'

An anonymous maniac (Harry H. Corbett, years before *Steptoe & Son*) is introduced peering at hideous publicity photos of strippers outside a Windmill-type London revue. Disguising himself with a raincoat, thick specs and a greasy wig, the madman murders the brazen hussies who appear on the cover of *Wow* magazine. The cramped, tatty theatre (the big number is 'She's the Showgirl With the Most to Show') and the drab layouts of *Wow* embody the mix of genteel anguish and pathetic sleaze which characterises British porn, and the cheapness of this brief B picture (61 minutes) adds to its throwaway authenticity.

Posing as a TV producer or an ad exec, the killer lures cringingly inadequate models to cramped locales where he overdoses them with morphine (an odd murder method ditched for plain strangulation and gunfire). His purple passages ('Surely sex and horror are the new gods in this polluted world of so-called entertainment.') sound a lot like self-loathing on the part of writer-director Terry Bishop. The killer is tracked by *Wow*'s Canadian archaeologist publisher Mason (Spencer Teakle), terribly well bred showgirl June (Felicity Young) and Inspector Brunner (Victor Brooks).

There isn't enough plot for a 25-minute short, so the investigation keeps turning up almost-interesting one-scene characters: sad, drab men who moan about lost women from retirement homes in Torquay or two-room dumps in Fulham; an actor (Denis Holmes), set up to be mistaken for the killer, who is dragged off by Scotland Yard angrily whining ('I've been an actor for twelve years, my face is well-known – I was with the Old Vic.'). A very similar plot is trotted out in *The Playbirds*.

11TH VICTIM (1979)

Director Jonathan Kaplan started with Roger Corman (*Night Call Nurses*) and drive-in action (*Truck Turner*), moved into indie drama (*Over the Edge*), had a varied '80s mainstream spell (*Project X*, *The Accused*) and settled into episodic television (*ER*, *Without a Trace*). This Movie of the Week interestingly straddles the glen-plaid style of 1970s network television and the Corman school of socially engaged exploitation.

Small-town news anchor Jill Kelso (Bess Armstrong) is reading copy on air when she recognises from a flashed-up picture that the eleventh victim of the Hollywood-based 'Lakeside Killer' is her sister (Marilyn Jones), an aspiring actress who wound up doing porno reels and 'outcall modelling'. Driven to investigate undercover, Jill falls in with her sister's roommate Sally (Pamela Ludwig), who lives the same kind of life (and is thus doomed to get murdered at the end of the second act). The case leads Jill to a sleazy model agency run by Spider (Eric Burdon!) and the Starwood disco, where girls get hit on by porno stud/obvious suspect Red Noble (David Hayward). A background bartender (Kaplan regular John Kramer) seems likely to be the real killer, but the mildly unexpected finale has Jill's investigation curtailed when a freeway chase-siege leads to the apprehension of a random suspect (William H. Burton) who might or might not be the Lakeside Killer.

Ludwig, who should have had a bigger career, steals the film as a disco era waif with enormous hair and a quiet snarl. For a TV movie, it has a lot of Los Angeles sleaze atmos: the apartment with broom-handle batters around the light fitting because a drummer lives upstairs, the groovy fuck-pads (one is supposed to have been a former Howard Hughes starlet nest), the underage kids hanging out on Hollywood Blvd. With

Harold Gould as a Wambaugh-wannabe cop more interested in his unfinished book than arresting a killer, the always-welcome Dick Miller, appealing New World starlet Tara Strohmeier, and Kasi Lemmons. Written by Ken Friedman (*Johnny Handsome*).

ELLERY QUEEN: DON'T LOOK BEHIND YOU (1971)

This pilot for an *Ellery Queen* TV series partners trench-coated but trendy Peter Lawford as a British Ellery with grouchy American Harry Morgan as his cop uncle. Ageing playboy Lawford is smarmily wrong (Jim Hutton eventually took over) and it's hard not to squirm as he smooth-talks his way onto the water-bed of heiress Celeste (winning Stefanie Powers): the payoff is that the burst bed floods her apartment while they're making out – a comic punch line to an otherwise grim serial murder case.

Adapted by Ted Leighton from the Queen novel *Cat of Many Tails*, it opens with the killing of a projectionist during a pastiche underground movie. Then, a succession of victims – each younger than the last – are strangled by the Hydra, who favours blue rope for boys and pink for girls. The murderer is working through the files of babies delivered decades earlier by Dr Cazalis (E.G. Marshall), now a prominent analyst. While a classic whodunit, the film draws on the recent or ongoing Boston Strangler and Zodiac. As New York is terrorised by the Hydra, protestors and commentators give cops a hard time. It's one of those mysteries where the main suspect is so blatantly innocent, even when seemingly arrested in the act, that the real culprit is obvious.

Director Barry Shear (*Wild in the Streets, Across 110th Street*) delivers a jazzy '70s vibe which parallels the Italian *giallo*, with stylish décor, groovy characters (potential victim Skye Aubrey runs an off-Broadway improv theatre, suspect Coleen Gray is an uptight maniac), eccentric clues, a hip score (Jerry Fielding) and stalk-and-kill suspense scenes.

LE FOTO DI GIOIA (DELIRIUM) (1987)

'I MARRIED BECAUSE I'D FALLEN IN LOVE AND FOR NO OTHER REASON. NEVER ONCE DID HE ASK ME TO STOP MODELLING IN THE NUDE.'

Well-upholstered Serenda Grandi served an apprenticeship in Italian sleaze cinema (appearing in *Anthropophagus* as 'Vanessa Staiger') before Tinto Brass's *Miranda* made her a mid-'80s sexpot *grande dame*. Here, she plays Goia – Gloria, in the English dub – a retired nude model who owns *Pussycat* magazine and is the focus of a *giallo* plot.

A demented killer who has bizarre subjective camera hallucinations murders models who have replaced Goia in the magazine, and sends her photographs of corpses posed against huge pin-ups of her earlier, nakeder work. Suspects abound: a wheelchair-bound peeping tom/rifle enthusiast in the next villa (Karl Zinny), a gay photographer (David Brandon), a perhaps-too-devoted assistant (Daria Nicolodi), an impotent and incest-fixated brother (Vanni Corbellini), a rival porn tycoon (Capucine!) and a mendacious ex-boyfriend (George Eastman). The usual plodding inspector (Lino Salemme) tuts disapproval, victims (Katrine Michelsen, Sabrina Salerno) pose nude and wear weird head prosthetics (a cyclops, an insect) before being cut up, and the Gianfranco Clerici-Daniele Stroppa script (from a story by Luciano Martino) plays shopworn tricks to keep the mystery going. Grandi is, of course, ridiculous but oddly endearing. Excuses are found to get her unclothed on the run from a maniac whose motivation seems to be fury she's given up modelling ('I want to see you naked one more time!').

Lamberto Bava makes an interesting hash of the weirder elements (the hallucinations enliven the first half of the film and are then dropped), but only briefly makes suspense work. It's strangely good-humoured (Eastman's fickle lover deadpans over the phone that he's not in Rome with the Colosseum in the background) and well paced enough to be entertaining. Among its extremely '80s aspects are horrible costuming and hair, ghastly luxury tat décor and an electronic Simon Boswell score.

FRANCESCA (2015)

This Argentine *giallo* homage takes authenticity so far as to be acted in Italian and set in a landmark-free version of Rome in an early '70s of reel-to-reel tape recorders and fetishist killers. While the directors of *Berberian Sound Studio*, *Amer* and *The Love Witch* draw on the visual and aural textures of *giallo* to explore personal concerns, Luciano Onetti offers straight-up pastiche. It's not about anything except how much Luciano Onetti, who co-scripted with Nicolás Onetti, loves Sergio Martino, Dario Argento and Luciano Ercoli. In an element more in tune with the *giallo*-influenced *Se7en*, the murders are all references to Dante's Inferno – which also inspired the killings in one of the BBC's *Messiah* series – as well as the long-ago death or disappearance of the title character, daughter of suspicious poet Vittorio Visconti (Raul Gederlini). The killer is a woman (or dressed as a woman) and has a striking variation on the traditional mystery slasher outfit, melding *The Bird With the Crystal Plumage* and *The Red Queen Kills 7 Times* looks: red leather gloves, hat and coat, and a veil. Inspector Moretti (Luis Emilio Rodriguez) and Detective Succo (Gustavo Dalessanro) catch the case and deduce the Dante connection from pennies left on the eyes of the corpses. Onetti takes pains to evoke 1970s cinema, accepting the limiting factors of his chosen form: stock characters (all subservient to the twisted mystery), convenient plot turns and a mechanical parade of revelations (all the way down to a final unmasking in the last frames).

GIALLO (2009)

Dario Argento has directed disappointing-to-disastrous movies for twice as long as he made remarkable-to-brilliant cinema. His decline is starkly evident as Japanese tourist Keiko (Valentina Izumi) and French model Celine (Elsa Pataky) take taxis in the rain through the streets of Rome. Similar scenes in *Suspiria* and *Inferno* are bravura set pieces, mixing image and music to perfection. Here, the taxi rides *aren't* red herrings (the cabbie actually is the killer), but the effect is flat, an unwise reminder of lost glories.

The maniac (Adrien Brody, billed as 'Byron Diedra') has the puffy-faced, big-nosed, all over makeup job look of Gregg Henry as the Indian in *Body Double*. Known as Giallo because jaundice gives his skin a yellow tinge, he also sports a Rambo wig/headband combo. He abducts beautiful foreign women and disfigures them while they're chained to a table in his lair (a disused gasworks). Giallo also masturbates while looking at images of mutilated women on his PC, mumbles incoherently, flashes back to his miserable origins as a hooker's cast-off kid and keeps regular hospital appointments. Lone, unconventional cop Inspector Enzo Avolfi (also Brody) works out of a basement and specialises in bizarre cases. Linda (Emmanuelle Seigner), Celine's worried sister, follows Enzo around as he does his sleuth thing. If Giallo is an extreme version of the misogynist loons who stalk in *The Card Player* or *Sleepless*, Enzo is a riff on *Dexter*. After slaughtering his mother's murderer, young Enzo was caught red-handed by a cop patron (Robert Miano) who set him on a path to usefulness and killing killers off the books. Brody, who alone seems in on the joke, is hilarious as Enzo gives a hardboiled precis of his origins. After Enzo makes a hash of heroism, the relationship sours: he walks away miserably while Linda shrieks that he's a useless asshole. It's possible there's irony here.

Argento complains that this was re-edited against his wishes, so it might not be all his fault; then again, it's marginally less terrible than *Mother of Tears*, which he was happy to sign. It's almost beside the point to carp about the repeated abuse-of-pretty-women theme, since the over-familiar torture scenes don't even manage a sado-erotic charge. Maybe more offensive is the reuse of the Rondo Hatton convention that disfiguring diseases produce serial killers. Co-written by Argento, Jim Agnew (*Tokarev*) and Sean Keller (*Mammoth*).

HORSEMEN (HORSEMEN OF THE APOCALYPSE) (2009)

A rare non-remake from Michael Bay's Platinum Dunes horror-mill, this *Se7en*-style serial killer thriller is entirely derivative, drawing on the Book of Revelations (already mined by TV miniseries *Messiah* and *Detective*). *Horsemen* has the feel of a project embarked upon hopefully, but trimmed and dumped when it didn't turn out well. After reshoots (with Chelcie Ross replacing Neal McDonagh in a key role), it clocks in twenty minutes shorter than a preview cut.

Workaholic, widowed detective Aidan Breslin (Dennis Quaid) neglects his absurdly sensitive teenage son Alex (Lou Taylor Pucci) and lets his younger boy Sean (Liam James) pore over crime photos. Author of a book on dental criminology (cool!), Breslin is consulted when a plateful of teeth are found on a frozen pond. Breslin's priest (Paul Dooley) isn't too annoyed by the cop taking calls during mass to withhold theological insight into Revelations-quoting graffiti ('come and see'). Kristin (Ziyi Zhang) – the adopted daughter of victims who have been suspended on *A Man Called Horse*-cum-*Hellraiser* S/M hooks – seems sweet, but shocks the cop by producing a plastic bag containing a fetus ripped out of her mother. She seems to confess to the murders, motivated by sexual abuse perpetrated by her creepy father (an under-used Peter Stormare, fresh from the similar *Anamorph*). However, the junior psycho – who taunts from behind bars like a combination Hannibal Lecter and Dragon Lady – is only one of a killer quartet who have colour-coded rooms and identify with the Four Horsemen of the Apocalypse. Next up, in a self-contained vignette, a tormented gay kid (Patrick Fugit) rips out his own heart while forcing his literally hung-up homophobe brother (Eric Balfour) to watch.

As was obvious all along, the case comes home as Breslin is chained to a theatre seat while Alex dangles in front of him. In self-defeating plotting, the brat steams and suffers every time a family outing is interrupted by a call to a crime scene – but he can scarcely blame dad for cutting out when he's *personally responsible* for the murders which ruin his family life. Even Alex admits the scheme (hatched in group therapy) would have been blown if only his dad bothered to go into his room, which is spray-painted white in honour of the pale horseman Death. Quaid, with a shaggy haircut, is grimly determined to get it over with. Pop promo maven Jonas Akerland (*Small Apartments*) directs from a script by David Callaham (*Doom, The Expendables*).

INDAGINE SU UN CITTADINO AL DI SOPRA DI OGNI SOSPETTO (INVESTIGATION OF A CITIZEN ABOVE SUSPICION) (1970)

It's often noted that Michelangelo Antonioni's art films *L'avventura* and *Blowup* are key influences on the development of the *giallo*. Elio Petri's Best Foreign Language Academy Award© winner is surprisingly overlooked, but also fed the commercial genre. A satire on Italian corruption, it's a strange cop/killer movie with political bite and a jaded, vicious view of affluent, trendy Roman life.

An opening pastiche *giallo* sequence (prefiguring the use of the style in *Amer*) also feels like a *Columbo* first act. A buttoned-down, conservative man (Gian Maria Volontè) turns up at the apartment of his exotic mistress Augusta (Florinda Bolkan) and she asks him how he's going to murder her today. He cuts her throat in bed with a razorblade, then meticulously arranges the scene to incriminate himself – with strands of his tie under her fingernails, strategically placed fingerprints and fetishistically stolen jewels. Only then does Petri let on that the killer is the departing head of the Rome Homicide Police, just promoted to the political section, where he is expected to treat radicals as harshly as he does killers. The murder turns out to be an extension of his hobby (restaging famous crime scenes with Augusta), but also an elaborate thumb-snooking act of self destruction which puts his old colleagues in a bad light.

Bolkan is so completely a *giallo* character that she went on to star in several pure genre films, and the killing has kinky elements – the cops leak to the press that no underwear was found in the apartment, not because a perv has stolen it but because she didn't wear any. A terrific, unnerving Ennio Morricone score ramps up suspense, but the film veers into black comedy and plays as an inverted version of Kafka's *The Trial* in which a blatantly guilty man literally can't get arrested. Volontè is smoothly cruel, but cracks interestingly as the film goes on – fantasising forces of judgement gathering in his apartment to point out the obvious clues. Very demanding, very rewarding.

THE LODGER (THE PHANTOM FIEND) (1932)

In *Gosford Park*, Ivor Novello (Jeremy Northam) cringes when the Maggie Smith character makes a cutting remark about his failure in this remake. Well she might: the Welsh-born matinee idol is notably weaker in the lead than he was five years earlier in the Alfred Hitchcock adaptation of Marie Belloc Lowndes' Jack the Ripper-inspired novel.

The Buntings – a fussy, busy lower middle-class London family – let a room to weedy, sinister Bosnian Michael Angeloff (Novello). Circumstantial evidence mounts to suggest that he is 'the Avenger', a serial killer responsible for cutting girls' throats in telephone boxes. However, Daisy (Elizabeth Allan), the family's daughter, is intrigued by the haunted soul, much to the ire of her smugly jovial, very British reporter boyfriend (Jack Hawkins). The Hitchcock silent is a fluid, daring work – forced to tell its story visually. This talkie is set-bound, chatty and stagey, and director Maurice Elvey refrains from suspense or horror until the last reel. Tiresome comedy from the heroine's windy know-nothing dad (A.W. Baskcomb) slows things down considerably. Typical is a protracted inquest in which an angry coroner rules, 'You can not be heard,' and the troublesome idiot assumes the dignitary is deaf and rabbits on loudly at length.

As in the earlier film, the script breaks with the book – and the 1944 Hollywood version, which set the story in Victorian times and turn the Avenger back into Jack the Ripper – by building up suspicion against the lodger (who returns to his room bloody-handed after a murder) then revealing he's not guilty. In the finale, the heroine thinks she sees Angeloff in the fog and taps his shoulder, only for a mad-eyed lookalike to turn round and menace her. The lodger, fleeing a hostile mob while handcuffed, intervenes and throttles the insane killer – his own brother – with his chain. Novello's affected, non-specific foreign accent sounds silly and his sighing, over-melodramatic angst would have seemed old-fashioned a decade earlier. The performance seems all the worse set next to Allan (*Mark of the Vampire*), who is bright, natural and appealing in a stock role. Elvey inherits themes from the Hitchcock film – the small-minded bigotry of a range of London types, prurient fascination with horrid murder, the 'wrong man' element which resonates throughout Hitch's filmography – but does little with them.

The American title comes from a speech in which a Scotland Yard official compares the killer to an Eastern European vampire. Scripted by actor Miles Mander (*Pearl of Death*) and critic Paul Rotha (*The Film Till Now*), from an adaptation by H. Fowler Mear (*The Triumph of Sherlock Holmes*).

THE LODGER (2009)

> 'TAKE YOUR DAMN PILLS. NOBODY'S GOING TO RENT THIS PLACE IF THEY THINK THE LANDLADY'S A LUNATIC.'

A contemporary-set adaptation of the Marie Belloc Lowndes novel, this is now about a Jack the Ripper copycat in West Hollywood (which is, we're told, the size of 1888 Whitechapel) and has a tricksier, ambiguous assignment of guilt.

Writer-director David Ondaatje takes an opportunity to play Hitchcock games. He recreates shots from the 1927 film, but also references the Master's canon via a *Blackmail* knife bit, a *Vertigo* track-and-zoom, a *Psycho* rocking chair simile, a *Strangers on a Train* following-feet sequence etc. Not exactly a substantial work, it benefits from a decent cast and a nice line in understatement. Here, Ellen Bunting (Hope Davis) is a neurotic with a glowering, neglectful husband (Donal Logue) and an imaginary son... and the film teases the possibility that suave lodger Malcolm Slate (Simon Baker) is a projection of her own fantasy. The resolution doesn't quite establish whether Ellen is the Ripper or not since – after her split personality has been diagnosed *Psycho*-style (Rebecca Pidgeon is the shrink) – a coda has the lodger renting new digs.

On the case are a couple of contrasting cops, Chandler Manning (Alfred Molina), who obsesses about the Ripper, and Street Wilkenson (Shane West), who everyone thinks is gay but isn't. Also with Philip Baker Hall (gruff superior), Rachael Leigh Cook (Manning's imperilled daughter) and Mel Harris (the cop's institutionalised wife). Davis, one of the most underrated actresses of her generation, is the best thing here; her fractured Ellen is interesting, sexy, poignant and, at the end, just a little terrifying.

THE LOST ANGEL (2005)

The principle interest of this loopy thriller is blonde Alison Eastwood cast as the kind of break-the-rules, blast-'em-first, bugged-by-bureaucracy cop her father used to play – though we don't remember Dirty Harry pressuring a suspect (C. Thomas Howell) by lap-dancing him in the interrogation room.

Another religious nutjob (cf: *Se7en*, *Resurrection*, *Messiah*) crucifies associates of deaf Father Kevin (John Rhys-Davies), scrawling bloody graffiti in cuneiform(!). Inspector Billie Palmer (Eastwood) and sidekick Julian (screenwriter Nicholas Celozzi) gun down a deadbeat arsonist (Darcy Laurie) who is nevertheless innocent of these murders. The lowlife survives and schemes to abduct and burn Billie's goth schoolgirl sister Sand (Claire Anstead). The backstory is that a home invader killed the girls' mother and (implicitly) molested Sand; the heroine has sworn to be a hard-bitten, gun-under-the-pillow bitch forever to keep the kid safe. Father Kevin, world-renowned expert on cuneiform, is amazingly unhelpful and seemingly untroubled by the deaths of his organist, secretary, etc. Another priest (Judd Nelson) hangs around, being suspiciously co-operative.

It plods entertainingly, with Eastwood giving value-for-money snarl, until a third act which suggests Celozzi wanted to give himself an acting workout and a few seedy jollies. After saving Sand, Billie insists on having Shannon Tweed-like sex with her willing, tagalong partner… Then, it turns out the cuneiform killer is a snitch (Rob Van Meenan) who has been giving Julian tips all along… *Then*, when Billie shows up at a meet between Julian and the murderer, the script pulls the old there-was-only-one-of-them-there-all-along reveal and Celozzi grandstands through the finale as a split personality whose alter ego is fluent in ancient writing. Directed adequately by Dimitri Logothetis (*Slaughterhouse Rock*).

M (1951)

In 1951, the idea of Joseph Losey remaking 1932 classic *M* was greeted with as little enthusiasm as the idea of Gus Van Sant remaking *Psycho* was in 1998; consequently, this effective psycho-thriller is vastly undervalued.

Fritz Lang's Berlin-set story is transplanted to Los Angeles, with the Bradbury Building for once playing itself. Released mental patient Martin Harrow (David Wayne) has a catalogue of giveaway movie-psycho traits: devotion to a dead mother, hatred of an abusive father, vaguely gay mannerisms, a kink about decapitating small clay dolls, a shoe fetish, and an urge to kill children not from paedophilia ('They weren't outraged or violated.') but to protect them from a corrupt grownup world. The character is over-egged, but Wayne – especially in his breakdowns – is effectively pathetic. With a tin whistle instead of Peter Lorre's whistling habit, Harrow plays pied piper and victims follow him out of pity rather than through cajoling. Losey contrasts the maniac with smoothly ruthless crime boss Marshall (Martin Gabel) and pragmatic cop Carney (Howard Da Silva), who are both on his trail. He is also shadowed by drunken lawyer Langley (Luther Adler), forced to plead his case, and brutal second bananas Lieutenant Becker (Steve Brodie) and Pottsy (Raymond Burr), who channel their perverse streaks into law enforcement or professional crime.

Losey follows Lang for two-thirds of the film, then goes his own way by making set pieces of Harrow's capture by the criminal community and near-lynching in an underground car park. The chase, with juvenile delinquents tipping off racketeers, winds up in the Bradbury Building, which Losey uses as well as 'Demon with a Glass Hand' (*The Outer Limits*). Thugs methodically break into every room while Harrow cowers in a locked doll manufacturer's office, his putative victim trying to help him as he breaks his whistle on the door then claws at the lock with bloodied hands. The trial is framed in a new way: the mob boss forces trained drunk Langley to speak up for the killer because he wants the crowds gone so there'll be no witnesses to this rub-out. Marshall guns down the lawyer himself just as the cops arrive, angered by Langley's rant about the kinship between killer and crooks, indicting society in the evil everyone wants to attribute solely to the madman. It's melodrama, with political undertones (an accusation of communism is flung). Scenes of innocent men attacked because they are seen with children interestingly prefigure the abuse panic that, decades after McCarthyism, became another excuse for American witch-hunting.

An interesting cast of non-star faces includes many blacklistees and oddballs: Karen Morley (*The Mask of Fu Manchu*), Norman Lloyd (*Saboteur*), Glenn Anders (*The Lady From Shanghai*), Walter Burke (often cast as sinister leprechauns), Norman Lloyd, John Miljan as Blind Balloon Vendor, Jim Backus as The Mayor, Janine Perreau (*Invaders from Mars*), Sherry Jackson (*The Mini-Skirt Mob*), Madge Blake (Aunt Harriet on *Batman*), George Barrows (Ro-Man from *Robot Monster*) and William Schallert as a dragnet-rounded neurotic. Written by Leo Katcher (*Party Girl*) and Norman Reilly Raine (*The Adventures of Robin Hood*), with additional dialogue by Waldo Salt (*Serpico*).

MURDER! (1930)

Alfred Hitchcock's second sound thriller isn't marked as a cornerstone like his first, *Blackmail*. Indeed, *Murder* isn't widely seen at all, because a single dated aspect confines it to the vaults. The self-hating murderer's motive is to prevent a malicious gossip from revealing to heroine Diana Baring (Norah Baring) that he's a half-caste ('Ah-ha, he has *black blood*,' elucidates an amateur detective). As it turns out, being mixed race is the least remarkable thing about him (and Diana knows anyway). Handel Fane (Esme Percy), a drag trapeze artiste given to fits of homicidal fury, appears screamingly gay but is supposed to be obsessively in love with Diana – though keeps quiet when she's condemned to hang for the crime he committed.

Ostensibly, it's a mystery. Sir John Menier (Herbert Marshall), a theatrical knight doing jury service at Diana's trial, is pressured to convict. Unsatisfied with the verdict and naturally falling in love with the girl in the condemned cell, Sir John becomes a sleuth, taking detective hints from the 'Mouse Trap' scenes in *Hamlet*(!), and sets about snaring Fane, the only other suspect. Hitchcock always professed to be impatient with whodunits; he skips through the mystery (i.e. no superfluous suspects or red herrings) to get to technical challenges and peculiar perverse quirks which interest him. In many ways, it's an advance on *Blackmail* in its innovative use of the sound and certain sequences are as striking and strange as the justly famous 'knife' routine in the earlier film. It opens with a long pan across a row of windows (typical Hitch is the shapely silhouette of a woman undressing), with heads poked out as the title cry goes up, and sundry busybodies crane to get on the scene of the crime. In the jury room, we get Hitchcockian satire of small-minded ditherers and resentful time-servers – a middle-aged man who initially votes to acquit because he fancies the accused and a daffy spinster who veers from believing the girl innocent on the grounds that she was in a fugue state when she killed to writing her off as a homicidal maniac. Sir John, the sole *Twelve Angry Men*-style hold-out, presents arguments only to be battered by a literal chorus chanting, 'What's your answer to that, Sir John?' in unison as they pose oppressively around him. The verdict and sentence are delivered offscreen as the camera stays in the jury room while a functionary ignores the momentous matters and tidies away teacups and papers.

While shaving and listening to *Tristan and Isolde* on the wireless, Sir John's interior monologue (voice-over was a daring new idea in 1930) blends with Wagner (performed by an offset orchestra) to become a singspiel aria. Hitchcock regretted the loss of some of the purely visual aspects of silent cinema, and is as concerned with inventive pictures as sound effects. In the climax, the camera is fixed up on a trapeze with the guilt-ridden killer, the background blurring behind him as he swings through the air. Then, flash-images of the innocent heroine appear and he chooses to hang himself in the Big Top to finish his act (Hitch cuts in a reaction shot from a horrified clown).

The astonishingly wayward plot is derived from *Enter Sir John*, a novel by Clemence Dane and Helen Simpson. It presses buttons which excite the young auteur: murder in a theatre (we stay in the wings, *Noises Off* fashion, as policemen interview witnesses who keep having to dash or stagger onstage to do their bits), an innocent accused who is also a slender female in bondage, class consciousness centring on the titled hero, audiences flocking to lurid spectacles, and a killer with a broken mind who dresses as a woman (and also, almost as significantly, a police constable). An array of eccentric supporting actors includes Miles Mander, Una O'Connor and Donald Calthrop.

MURDER ROCK (MURDEROCK – UCCIDE A PASSO DI DANZA; MURDER ROCK – DANCING DEATH) (1984)

'IT'S PRETTY NATTY. HE'S GOT AN ARMANI JACKET.'
'YEAH, AND NO HEAD.'

Made at the end of Lucio Fulci's burst of gory creativity, this bizarre, cynical *giallo* tips elements of *New York Ripper* and *Lizard in a Woman's Skin* into the passing vogue for sexually charged dance drama (one apt alternate title is *Slashdance*). 1984 was a bad time to make any kind of musical, and this is stuck with painful porno-disco from Keith Emerson and grind-the-air pelvic thrust choreography. The closest Fulci comes to aptly melding genres comes when the first victim strips off everything but her iconic leg-warmers before walking naked into the shower where (of course) she is killed. Dance scenes are shot in a cramped studio and semi-darkness that doesn't conceal anyone's embarrassment. Among the worst horrors on offer are white people breakdancing, fluffy hair and sweaty mist, an agonising earworm theme ('Tonight is the Night') and ghastly fashions. Earlier *gialli* benefit from the collision of horror-thriller imagery with the fab interior design, costuming and music of the 1960s and '70s; this is hobbled by the modes of a crasser decade.

While not as misogynist as *The New York Ripper* (few films are), it's crass enough. Killings involve a subjective camera creeping up on female dancers and pressing chloroform over their faces, then exposing their breasts so a jewelled hatpin can be thrust slowly into their hearts. Lieutenant Borges (Cosimo Cinieri), whose name might reference the Argentine author, ambles about crime scenes as ex-dancer Candice Norman (Olga Karlatos) – the martinet who runs the troupe – begins an affair with drunken actor George Webb (Ray Lovelock), whom she dreams is the murderer. 'You dream that somebody kills you and you actually go out looking for the guy?' Some clues (the old man's-jacket-buttoned-the-wrong-way-to-indicate-a-woman-is-wearing-it bit) seem held over from an earlier style of whodunit. Red herrings include Claudio Cassinelli as a buttoned-down lech and Silvia Collatina (Dr Freudstein's ghost daughter) as a wheelchair-bound teenager with a photography fetish who takes a semi-helpful picture when her nanny is murdered. Karlatos isn't as compelling a neurotic central figure as Edwige Fenech or Florinda Bolkan. It has a few nice street scenes of New York circa 1984. Written by Fulci, Gianfranco Clerici (*Cannibal Holocaust*), Roberto Gianviti (*Beatrice Cenci*) and Vincenzo Mannino (*Miami Golem*).

MÝRIN (JAR CITY) (2006)

A dour, spare Icelandic thriller which has a familiar outline (weary middle-aged cop tracks a semi-sympathetic killer while coping with his pregnant junkie daughter), but is awash with potent local colour. To non-Icelandic sensibilities, the scene of the hero tucking into his favourite take-out food (cold sheep's head, with the eye forked first) is more gruesome than the mangled corpses and violent incidents.

Nasty recluse Holberg (Thorsteinn Gunnarsson) is found dead in 'A typical Icelandic murder – messy and pointless.' After a seemingly senseless bludgeoning, a ton of physical evidence is left around the victim's smelly, porn-littered flat. Veteran Inspector Erlendur (Ingvar E. Sigurdsson) sleuths glumly, assisted by vegetarian wimp hotshot Oli (Björn Hlynur Haraldsson) and canny middle-aged Elinborg (Olafia Hronn Jonssdottir). The victim was a long-time lowlife who managed to duck out of rape charges in the 1970s, and fathered children who carry a hereditary disorder which means that girls die at a very young age. The killer is Orn (Atli Rafn Sigurdsrdon), one of Holberg's spawn, grieving father of a just-dead little angelic girl. Working in a genetics research institute, Orn has access to data which allows him to track his biological father. Because of its tiny, isolated population, Iceland is the site of much genetic research: the English language title refers to the facility where interesting anomalies (including the killer's aunt's brain) are preserved in jars.

Also mixed up in the complicated backstory are imprisoned thug Ellidi (Theodor Juliusson); another layabout no one has seen in decades, who turns out to be the cause of the smell in the dead man's flat; various old ladies who might have been raped in the 1970s (a blackly comic montage has cops making discreet enquiries among old dears); an ancient, famously crooked cop; and Eva Lind (Ágústa Eva Erlendsdóttir), the hero's distracting drug addict daughter who makes a handy hostage when crooks come after him. It avoids Iceland's scenic splendours to concentrate on grim, chilly, bleak, sordid locales with folks as wrapped up emotionally as they have to be in woolly jumpers to get through the day. Written and directed by Baltasar Kormákur, from a novel by Arnaldur Indriðason.

NIET VOOR DE POESEN (BECAUSE OF THE CATS; THE RAPE) (1973)

An interesting Low Countries *giallo* directed by Fons Rademakers ('Mother' in *Daughters of Darkness*), who also co-scripted with Hugo Claus. Based on a Holland-set novel by English crime writer Nicolas Freeling, it was shot in English and features a mix of British and Dutch actors (including pre-*Emmanuelle* Sylvie Kristel). Freeling's books feature Amsterdam cop Inspector Piet van der Valk, familiar from a British TV series with Barry Foster (its irritatingly catchy theme tune was a Euro-hit for months). Foster's van der Valk was a middle-aged, home-making Maigret-type (his wife is co-sleuth in some stories), but Bryan Marshall plays him as younger and studlier. Though it's established that the hero is married, nearly his first move on an out-of-town case is shacking up with call girl Feodora (Alexandra Stewart), who becomes his prime informant.

In a *Clockwork Orange*-style opening, a gang of dissolute youths steal a car and set out to burgle and vandalise the apartment of an antique dealer. The husband is forced to watch as five of the six thugs rape his wife. The one who refuses to join in is told, 'The Cats won't like it.' This clue leads van der Valk to a seaside town which is home to the Ravens, a rich-kid gang, and the Cats, their bike-riding elite girlfriends. In the strangest scene, the Cats lure a recalcitrant Raven to the sea by stripping naked and skinny-dipping with him (Kristel has sex with the lad underwater), then set upon him like killer mermaids until he drowns. Freeleng's inspiration becomes apparent when van der Valk deduces that the prime mover in the evil-doing is Jansen (Sebastian Graham Jones). The Manson soundalike owner of a gaming arcade/hangout, Jansen has filled their heads with weird, lunatic philosophy.

The film seesaws between vicious and cosy, with familiar British faces (Edward Judd, George Baker) and old-fashioned sleuthing (a significant clue is a talking parrot who quotes the title) co-existing with exploitation-style shock sequences and a seamy, stylised take on the kids' made up cult. The Ravens and the Cats are dropped surprisingly early, almost absolved of responsibility for their own crimes, in favour of a face-off between van der Valk and Jansen. Marshall (*Quatermass and the Pit*, *I Start Counting*, *The Long Good Friday*) is moral but macho (he even has a full-frontal nude scene) and Jones (whose only other major role was as 'John Pentacle', nemesis of the hero magician in the TV series *Ace of Wands*) is a louche Pied Piper of Evil. Stewart is good as the gun-toting hooker who saves the day just as Jansen has promised to stamp on every one of the hero's ribs.

THE PLAYBIRDS (1978)

> 'TO A DERANGED MIND, IT WOULD SEEM LIKE THERE'S THREE FORCES OF EVIL – SEX, WITCHCRAFT AND HORSES.'

Inept on several different levels, this is nevertheless strangely fascinating – and, in producer-as-auteur terms, a deeply personal film for 'pornocrat' David Sullivan. The plot, derivative of *Cover Girl Killer*, follows a *giallo*-style maniac in a deerstalker, who strangles girls who pose nude in *Playbird* magazine and scrawls numbers on their foreheads in lipstick.

Plods Holbourne (Glynn Edwards) and Morgan (Gavin Campbell) don't seem too worked up about the murders, even when a saucy model (Suzy Mandel) Morgan is personally guarding is killed on his watch. A higher-up (Windsor Davies) wants results and a roomful of advanced-for-1978 computers prints out profiles of perverts ('We're looking for a sex maniac, not a creeping Jesus.'). Eventually, the Yard hits on the bright idea of getting a policewoman to go undercover as a model. After a couple of embarrassing audition strips, Sergeant Lucy Sheridan (Mary Millington) gets the job, working first in a massage parlour then experiencing the casting couch of *Playbird* publisher Harry Dougan (Alan Lake). Dougan is a stand-in for Sullivan (the real publisher of *Playbird*) and a wedge of the film is wasted on Sullivan's real-life enthusiasm for horse racing, plus documentary shots of the printing and distribution of top-shelf mags and grudge-holding whines about censorious hypocrites (an anti-smut crusader is a peeping tom) and police ineptitude.

The murders, which most films would treat as set pieces, are staged by director Willy Roe as clumsily as the photo shoots, tame orgies, stripteases, police investigations and horse races. Much of it is tasteless, even for the '70s: a starlet wakes to find a masked intruder in her flat and says, 'Oh goodie, I'm going to be raped – I've never been raped before.' The punch line is that he just kills her. A last-reel death is more imaginatively conceived than the run of stranglings and seems tipped in from another film: during a photo shoot of a trussed-up naked witch a killer throws a can of petrol on her prop bonfire and produces an instant inferno.

Millington, then Sullivan's star pin-up/sex symbol, can't even say a line like 'Oh really?' with conviction. The film is built around her, but still treats her as utterly disposable. It's established that Lucy has self-defence skills, but when the killer comes for her in a coda – *after* a scene which shows him being arrested – she puts up no fight and is left throttled naked in the bath. With an array of British film/TV regulars: Derren Nesbitt, Kenny Lynch, Sandra Dorne, Ballard Berkeley, Dudley Sutton (as a religious fanatic who misspells Isaiah on his sandwich board). Written by George Evans and Roe, under the names Bud Tobin and Robin O'Connor.

THE PLEDGE (2001)

Friedrich Dürenmatt's spare novella *Das Versprechen* is a variation on his script for the film *Es geschah am hellichten Tag/In Broad Daylight* (1958), with which the author wasn't satisfied. The book has been adapted into Italian and German television movies (*La Promesa*, 1979; *Es geschah am hellichten Tag*, 1997), an English-language Dutch thriller (*The Cold Light of Day*, 1996) and this American art film, which transplants the story from frozen Switzerland to seasonally snowy Nevada. Its chilly, stately (i.e. long and slow, but not in a bad way) tone prefigures the later-popular nordic noir mode.

On the day of his retirement party, homicide detective Jerry Black (Jack Nicholson) vows on his 'soul's salvation' to Margaret Larsen (Patricia Clarkson), mother of a murdered (and raped and mutilated) little girl, that he will bring the killer to justice. His showboating former protégé (Aaron Eckhart) and easygoing boss (Sam Shepard) happily accept the forced confession of a disturbed suspect (Benicio Del Toro) who commits suicide, apparently convinced of his own guilt. But Black connects dots with earlier, unsolved cases involving girls who resemble dead Ginny Larsen (Taryn Knowles). Though he retires, Black doesn't let go, buying a run-down gas station and fishing shop (from Harry Dean Stanton) in the middle of a triangle formed by the crimes and fixating on a drawing left by Ginny in which she is being given 'porcupines' by a 'giant'. Black falls in with an instant family, credibly battered diner waitress Lori (Robin Wright Penn, with a missing front tooth) and her little girl Chrissy (Pauline Roberts). Nicholson plays it ambiguously, suggesting Black's depth of feeling for Chrissy (whom he recognises as a potential 'fourth angel'), but also the calculation of using her as bait (buying the child a red dress like the others wore).

Director Sean Penn teases with red herrings: Mickey Rourke in a one-scene bit as the father of a girl whose body was never found, and literal giant Tom Noonan (the Tooth Fairy of *Manhunter*) as a lay preacher who makes spiritual overtures to Chrissy (his mother also makes suspect porcupine novelties). After an exquisitely twisted finale, a wrecked Black is left outside his gas station, ranting at himself, having lost everything through his pledge but not saved his soul or caught the killer. Penn usually favours intensity as a director, but plays it cool here, with careful attention to landscapes, weather and character detail. A signature scene has cops striding through a chicken coop to investigate amid unconcerned clucking birds. With Vanessa Redgrave (Norwegian grandma), Helen Mirren (shrink). Scripted by Jerzy Kromolowski and Mary Olson-Kromolowski (*In the Electric Mist*).

RESURRECTION (1999)

This reunites director Russell Mulcahy with *Highlander* star Christopher Lambert (who also co-wrote with Brad Mirman). Cajun cop John Prudhomme (Lambert) relocates to Chicago after the accidental death of his child, which has caused a spiritual crisis (David Cronenberg is his soft-spoken priest). He becomes obsessed with a serial killer who spends the six Fridays leading up to Easter taking body parts from 33-year-old males who have the names of apostles – to reconstruct the body of Christ. Leland Orser (who was in *Se7en*) has the traditional role of the grim cop's funkier partner: instead of getting killed, as is traditional, he winds up shot in the leg by his own men thanks to a sneaky trick on the part of the maniac – an indignity is that when his limb is amputated, the killer raids the hospital and steals it for his gruesome devotional artwork. Like *Se7en*, it's full of driving rain, miserable gloom, pans across arrays of religious-philosophical matter, cops looking agonised, dollop-like domestic scenes to highlight the plot, unlikely deductions; unlike *Se7en*, it falls mostly flat.

THE RIPPER (1985)

'YOU KNOW IT'S KIND OF WEIRD, HAVIN' JACK THE RIPPER IN OUR TOWN AFTER ALL THESE YEARS, KILLIN' PEOPLE.'

In the mid-'80s, Oklahoma-based director Christopher Lewis pioneered the shot-on-video gore movie, scoring a rental hit with *Blood Cult*, which was more like shit-on-video. *The Ripper*, his second effort, is a marginal improvement. It's awkwardly acted, as visually dull as the porn tapes of the same era and its story doesn't make a lick of sense, but it's better-paced than *Blood Cult*, manages interesting character beats and is among the first films to talk up (generally accurate) pop-culture trivia. A student complains that a Trivial Pursuit question card confuses *Emmanuelle 2* with *Emmanuelle Joy of Sex*, a professor teaches a class on true crime cinema and talks about Jack the Ripper movies with reasonable erudition (we know he's troubled when he gets called out for citing Christopher Lee when he means Christopher Plummer) and the characters watch *Blood Cult* (and sneer at it).

A Victorian fantasy prologue involves a horse-drawn cab whose driver has one of the worst cod-cockney accents in film and the first of many graphic throat-slittings. In the present day, lecturer Richard Harwell (Tom Schreier) buys a distinctive ring which might once have belonged to the Ripper, then keeps falling asleep at the times a top-

SERIAL KILLERS AND COPS

hatted, cloaked dastard is slashing and gutting local women. Harwell asks a historian colleague about the choice of victims and is told it's because all contemporary women look like Victorian prostitutes, which is frankly bizarre – though everyone in this movie is stuck with ghastly mid-'80s fashions and hairstyles. Harwell is pestered by a fan student (Wade Tower), who seems to have a crush on him but becomes an avenger when his own girlfriend (Andrea Adams) is disembowelled.

Finally, Harwell's dance teacher girlfriend (Mona Van Pernis) is lured to a foggy warehouse where she is menaced by literally moustache-twirling, scleral-contact-lensed guest star-marquee name Tom Savini as a seemingly immortal Ripper. When shot by the cops, the Ripper turns back into Harwell – so he isn't that immortal really. Is Jack the Savini extending his life through sacrifice, possessing the professor via the ring, a manifestation of Harwell's film-crime-obsessed id or just showing up to kill people simply because Lewis wouldn't have a movie if he didn't? You be the judge. Scripted by Bill Groves.

THE RIPPER (1997)

Made in Australia, far from the British press who might take offence at the premise, this is another unlikely historical fantasy on the most overexposed unsolved mystery of all. Robert Rodat's script absurdly alleges that Edward Albert Victor (Samuel West), the Prince of Wales, was the Ripper. Like several earlier screen Rippers, he hates prostitutes because he's caught syphilis from one (a quack cure leaves him smelling of apricots), but more interesting is a neurosis about the impotence of his family in an era when they are no longer required to take on the French in battle. Inspector Jim Hansen (Patrick Bergin), a Whitechapel-born copper, is taken under the wing of police commissioner Sir Charles Warren (Michael York) and works on improving himself by learning the eleven ways of tying a tie (the suspect adjusts his neckwear for him). Hansen is tempted by a genteel arranged romance with Evelyn Bookman (Essy Davis, of *The Babadook*), but gets steamy with Irish working girl Florry Lewis (Gabrielle Anwar), the only witness who can identify the killer. Royal physician Sir William Gull (John Gregg), not a suspect for a change, is an unhelpful witness. With cramped period sets, a few borrowed stately homes and few touches of atmosphere. It's a bit of a plod, but performances are okay. Even West does his best with an impossible role as the horse-burning, self-hating, waspish weed-cum-mass murderer. Directed by Janet Meyers.

THE RIVER MURDERS (2011)

> 'WE'VE INTERVIEWED ALL YOUR SO-CALLED FRIENDS BACK TO HIGH SCHOOL. SOME OF THEM DON'T LIKE YOU VERY MUCH. OTHERS THINK YOU'RE A KIND AND GENEROUS MAN. NOT ONE OF THEM ADMITS TO BEING A HOMICIDAL MANIAC.'

The first names of the above-the-title stars of this serial killer movie are Ray, Ving and Christian – which coincidentally turns out to be a description of the murderer. Detective Jack Verdon (Ray Liotta) has a tough time when female corpses show up with crosses carved in their tongues and rings shoved up their vaginas. The victims are mostly his old girlfriends, though his mother(!) and his wife's one-time lover also fall victim (the last development is almost amusing – as it initially seems likely the gadabout cop had a one-night stand with a guy). FBI agent Vuckovitch (Christian Slater) makes snarky remarks and gruff boss Langley (Ving Rhames) barks orders. It's revealed early on that clean cut Jon Lee (Michael Rodrick) is the killer. The hero's long-lost, presumed-aborted son, he's out for a Biblical vengeance – and started by cutting up his own mother. The hero's late-in-life marriage to a chef (Gisela Fraga) is maundered about – she gets pregnant and is thus rendered unkillable, though it's easier to like the cop partner (Sarah Ann Schultz) pegged as doomed as soon as she mentions their one-time fling. There's a Pacific Northwest vibe, with several corpses found in the river (less relevant than the title suggests). Scripted by Steve Anderson. Directed by Rich Cowan.

THE SPORT KILLER (KILLER'S DELIGHT; THE DARK RIDE) (1977)

Inspired by the crimes of Ted Bundy and the Zodiac Killer, this sunshiny, cynical California-set serial murder *policier* is a lesser entry in a '70s cycle which includes *Dirty Harry*, *The Arousers*, *The Centerfold Girls* and *Don't Answer the Phone*.

Misogynist mama's boy Danny (John Karlen, sweating and blubbing or leering like an Andy Milligan or HG Lewis villain) prowls near a small-town swimming pool, disguised in cool shades and an assortment of hippie wigs and stuck-on moustaches. He picks up hitchhikers, verbally abuses them for being skanks (like his mother), strips them nude for fondling, then breaks their necks and dumps the bodies. Intense, under-supported cop Sergeant Vince De Carlo (James Luisi) and his psychoanalyst mistress Dr Carol Thompson (Susan Sullivan) set out to trap the killer, aided by Vince's swinger sidekick Detective Mike 'Mighty Mouse' Mitelman (Martin Speer). It has a mellow-groovy score (Byron Olson) and an air of being seamy yet laid back, with pretty victims (Eddie Benton, Hilary Thompson, Sandy Alan, Keli Sils) cheerfully climbing into the creep's van. A mean-spirited undertone suggests the filmmakers think the killer isn't far wrong about the permissive society. De Carlo's cowboy-hatted boss (Al Dunlap) says the case is low priority because a congressman's son was just blown away by bikers and all the department's resources are diverted. The fact that the married hero is having an affair his wife (Sharon DeBord) never finds out about just lies there unaddressed. De Carlo even puts his girlfriend in danger by getting her to go undercover as a lounge singer(!) and pick up the maniac. The bungled sting operation leads to Carol getting strangled and a flip freeze-frame finish in which De Carlo hugs the sobbing apprehended killer and shoots him in the gut.

Both leads were supporting regulars on crime shows (Karlen on *Cagney & Lacey*, Luisi on *The Rockford Files*) and this has a '70s TV feel, despite the odd flash of nudity. With George 'Buck' Flower as Pete the Witness. Screenwriter Maralyn Thoma's other credits are on soaps (*General Hospital, Santa Barbara*); she might have tipped in pre-written adultery and family squabble scenes to pad this out between killings. The sole director credit of Jeremy Hoenack, who spent the rest of his career as a sound editor, mostly in TV.

SUSPECT ZERO (2004)

Hollywood hired-gun screenwriter Zak Penn, who has a pile of *X-Men* and *Avengers* credits, broke into the business with one of those legendary 'blacklist' scripts. It circulated for about a decade – getting plaudits as one of the great unmade projects – before being filmed, after a credited rewrite by Billy Ray (*The Hunger Games*) and rumoured tinkering from Ben Affleck(!) and Paul Schrader. Director E. Elias Merhige, following *Shadow of the Vampire*, gives this fantastical serial killer thriller a strange, interesting tone which limited its commercial chances. Affleck and Tom Cruise were attached during development, but the less box-office Aaron Eckhart stepped in; Cruise remains an uncredited producer and his cousin, busy creepy character guy William Mapother, shows up.

FBI burnout Thomas Mackelway (Eckhart) is assigned to a backwater office, where he connects seemingly unrelated murders: a famous fugitive he failed to take down, quiet types who turn out to have human faces in their spare suitcases or dead kids buried in their yards. Gradually, Mackelway realises he is tracking Benjamin O'Ryan (Ben Kingsley), who has the gift of spotting uncaught serial killers. Both are seeking the perhaps-mythical title character, a murderer so cunning he's invisible to the authorities. At first, it seems O'Ryan is a fantasist who makes up stories about being a former FBI agent and is a refugee from a halfway house for the insane... but as Mackelway gets closer to him, entering into partnership to go after the bigger game, he starts believing there has been a cover-up and O'Ryan is the survivor of a 'remote viewing' ESP program with genuine psychic powers.

Eckhart and Kingsley spark off each other, but the actual plot plods, Carrie-Anne Moss is (as too often) wasted in a token FBI suit/love interest role and the home stretch is vague rather than terrifying. A lesser entry in the *Manhunter-X-Files-Se7en-Millennium* serial killer/sleuth gloomfest stakes.

THR3E (2006)

To enjoy this twisty thriller, you have to get past a title which – besides the dual irritation of using a number for a backward letter – invites derision by offering a less-than-half-the-value version of *Se7en*.

Police psychiatrist Jennifer Peters (Justine Waddell) survives an encounter with 'the Riddle Killer', a mad bomber who blows up her brother to make a point. The next intended victim seems to be theology student Kevin Parson (Marc Blucas). Persecuted by a phone prankster and harried with bombs, Kevin confesses that, as a kid, he locked a bullying older child in a warehouse and left him to die rather than risk harm to his friend Samantha. The grown-up Samantha (Laura Jordan) wants to help her protector, but a turn of events prompts her to wonder whether – after an horrendous upbringing in the home of a mad aunt (Priscilla Barnes) – Kevin hasn't fractured his personality. Glimpses of long-haired maniac Slater (Bill Moseley, as cannily cast as Philippe Nahon in *Haute Tension*) set up absurd but entertaining revelations which ought to be obvious from the title. Given the proliferation of 'imaginary friend' and 'embodied multiple personality' stories in the wake of *Fight Club*, this isn't too hard to see through – though it has more complications to deliver, with one alternate persona being a Riddle Killer copycat who spurs the heroine to spot the real murderer.

Scripted by Alan B. McElroy (*Halloween 4*, *Wrong Turn*, *Left Behind*), from a novel by Ted Dekker (a Christian horror specialist, though there's little religious content beyond the protagonist's study course); directed by Robby Henson (*The Visitation*).

URGE TO KILL (1960)

This Hitchcockian melange must have seemed quaint in the year of *Psycho*, harking back to the British boarding house claustrophobia of *The Lodger* and drawing on the Christie case (*10 Rillington Place*). Someone with white gloves (a perverse touch) strangles women in a London suburb. Suspicion fuelled by local prejudice falls on manchild Hughie (Terence Knapp, overdoing it), who tootles on a mouth organ. Affable Charlie Ramskill (Howard Pays, suitably weasely), a model lodger Mrs Willis (Margaret St Barbe-West) thrusts her unmarriageable daughter Lily (Anna Turner) at, is the real killer. Echoing Uncle Charlie of *Shadow of a Doubt* and prefiguring the tie-killer of *Frenzy*, Charlie is not only a misogynist psycho but a calculating creep who frames the innocent fool by giving him the white gloves. Fortunately, canny Superintendent Allen (Patrick Barr) spots loose details and tags the culprit – who huffily tries to get out of it until the copper reveals one of his victims has survived to accuse him. The murders are tamely staged, with Yvonne Buckingham and Laura Thurlow walking up to camera, recognising someone they don't feel threatened by and gloves reaching into the frame to throttle them (this from Anglo-Amalgamated, the outfit which simultaneously unleashed *Horrors of the Black Museum* and *Peeping Tom*). The scenes of hateful gossip down the caff, with bigots tutting 'shouldn't be allowed', play well, and a good suspense sequence has Charlie woo Lily just as she twigs that he's the murderer. With Wilfrid Brambell as a prissy lawyer, *Blue Peter* presenter Christopher Trace as a sergeant, Ruth Dunning as the landlady and Rita Webb as Charwoman. Written by James Eastwood from a novel (*Hughie Roddis*) and play (*Hand in Glove*) by Gerald Savory (who scripted the BBC's *Count Dracula*). Directed by Vernon Sewell, whose tight little B thrillers (*The Man in the Back Seat*) tend to be stronger than his better-known horror films (*The Curse of the Crimson Altar*).

YOU CAN'T STOP THE MURDERS (2003)

'CONSTABLE RAYMOND, CAN WE JUST ASK A FEW QUESTIONS ABOUT THE MURDER?... HAVE YOU FOUND THE HEAD?'

This ingenious, deadpan Australian comedy mystery has a dynamite premise, but the mean old music rights-holders wouldn't let it use the soundtrack it really needs to take fire. In the nowhere town of West Village, Australia, a serial killer murders a biker, a construction worker, a sailor, a cowboy and an Indian… and the dimwit police heroes realise he only has a cop to go before he's completed a set of the Village People (and spelled out YMCA with severed body parts). Local slacker policemen Gary (Gary Eck) and Akmal (Akmal Saleh) spend most of their time in a speedtrap on a road with no traffic, but the high-profile case means the Christian police chief (Richard Carter) calls in maverick Sydney cop Tony Charles (director Anthony Mir), who has a line in Don Johnson jackets, obnoxious bullshit and trigger-happy psychosis.

Eccentric suspects include a bereft guy who insists the search for his lost dog should have priority because he reported it missing before the murders started; Sebastian (Peter Callan), Gary's line-dancing arch-rival in a subplot which must have been about disco before the filmmakers found out they couldn't put the Village People where they belong (on the soundtrack); the short-fused butcher (Bruce Venables); the terrifying costumed deliveryman who turns up as a 'Love Panda' and spooks the local newswoman (Kirstie Hutton) Gary likes; a postal worker (Steve Rodgers), embittered because he feels the Village People should have included a mailman in their line-up; a near-silent work experience girl (Megan Drury) who shows signs of usefulness; and near-identically-named bike gangs (the Vandelas and the Vandelos) who rumble because their mail gets mixed up.

Eck, Saleh and Mir wrote it, and their back-and-forth patter has a nicely dry, absurdist edge, with small-town silliness as the killings mean a low turnout for the Village Fun Fest ('People don't have as much fun when there's murders.'). It has a makeshift look, and is surprisingly restrained about gore and camp ('It hasn't been substantiated, but there's a very strong rumour that all the Village People are gay,' comments a junior cop). It doesn't fire on all cylinders, but keeps up a constant stream of funny stuff.

WEIRD HIPPIE SHIT

ALBA PAGANA (MAY MORNING) (1970)

> ## 'YOU'RE INSULTING ITALIANS JUST BECAUSE I WENT TO BED WITH FLORA.'

An opening caption on this strange shot-in-England Italian drama thanks the staff, students and people of Oxford for their participation and stresses the film's intent to be an accurate representation of their behaviour (and fashions) – which is rather alarming since it fits between *Accident* and *The Riot Club* in depicting cruel, sinister and nastily comic goings-on between the rowing practice, tutorial sessions, punting and formal orgiastic behaviour. 'Better May Ball than last year?' asks a languid musician, after the evening has ended in gang-rape and casual murder. 'I don't know,' responds his chum, 'I was bored stiff.'

Handsome Italian student Valerio (Alessio Orano) struggles academically at Rufus College (he also gets told off for walking on the grass), but secures his place by becoming a rowing blue. Dark forces are aligned against him, represented by foppish scholar Roderick (John Steiner, later a spaghetti exploitation regular) and prejudiced tutor Finlake (Ian Sinclair). Needled into breaking taboo by refusing a 'sconce' (a challenge to drink two quarts of beer) and 'rusticated' (expelled), Valerio gets his own back during the May Ball by involving his tutor's strange wife (Rossella Falk) in fondling a drunken girl (Micaela Pignatelli). At the trippy after-party, Valerio helps the band rape Flora (Jane Birkin), who is Finlake's daughter and Roderick's girlfriend (two musos strum and toot throughout all the sex and violence). Flora has been making trouble by alternately trying to seduce Valerio and stirring feeling up against him – after the rape, she seems willingly to make out with him, then pushes him in the river and has the versatile if too-easily-led band batter him with oars until his presumed death.

Early on, there's a suggestion that Valerio is an admirable outsider in the stuffy college – he points out that students in other universities protest social issues while Oxonians argue about wearing black gowns over hippie outfits – but he comes across as a supercilious, unscrupulous creep who deserves the treatment he gets. Almost all reviewers seem to think Valerio is a working-class outsider, but he drives a white sports car and reads onscreen as European aristocracy pitted against upper-crust Brits. With a groovy song-based score featuring The Tremeloes, a riot of purple shirts and floppy scarves, an effective air of languid decadence and some tricksy touches (a key seduction scene is played out in a single shot of a distorting round mirror). Written by George Crowther, Fulvio Gicca and director Ugo Liberatore.

ALEX IN WONDERLAND (1970)

If remembered at all, this tends to be cited as the sort of self-indulgence only possible in the wake of *Easy Rider*. There's a fractured surrealism – evoked in the movie itself – in MGM bankrolling a hippie art movie which is also a self-conscious reworking of *8½*. As the hero strolls across the lot, we see a 'Mr Chips is Here!' banner in the background, announcing the Peter O'Toole musical (a *far* bigger flop than this), and it's supposed to be jarring that Peter Fonda's framed picture is up beside Burt Lancaster's in the studio corridor.

Paul Mazursky, whose previous hit (*Bob & Carol & Ted & Alice*) hardly earned the right to make what was dubbed '*1½*', plays the long-haired studio exec (with a caged monkey in his huge, den-like office) who throws ideas at long-haired filmmaker Alex Morrison (Donald Sutherland) in genial desperation, suggesting he go to Paris to read the galleys of a book (a Robert Evans anecdote) or take a Chagal lithograph from the office for inspiration. Sutherland is physically different enough from Mazursky to blur the autobiographical elements, though this oot-and-aboot Canadian has a Jewish New Yorker mother (Viola Spolin). Scenes of Alex's home life (with wife Ellen Burstyn and daughters, one played by Amy Mazursky) and noodling-around with affluent counterculture friends are rambling but also have a ring of truth. The unwisest decision was to echo *8½* (which Alex tries to explain to his daughter) with 'Fellini-esque' dream sequences involving clowns, clerics and hordes of extras dressed as the maestro (Angelo Rossito is credited as 'Fellini #1', which puts him ahead of cameoing Federico, who politely directs Alex out of his editing room). Though the fantasies are spurious, they sometimes have blunt force: a stretch of tarmac littered with choked corpses, naked African dancers surrounding Sutherland on a beach, the Vietnam war exploding in downtown Los Angeles to the tune of 'Hooray for Hollywood' and a musical ride with Jeanne Moreau (as herself).

Much is so obvious it's possible it was never meant seriously (a Jewish mother complains her son never calls), but some era-specific elements were worth getting on film for posterity. Alex rushes home enthusiastic about his acid trip, wanting to play the tape of his stoned mumblings to his sceptical wife, and is pissed off that she doesn't want to share his experience. It winds up with pretty (but real) Californian school kids staging a pageant about racial equality on a sun-drenched schoolyard as parents applaud while Fellinis, giraffes and other fantasy refugees blur in the background. Then Alex rambles about the big house he's buying and wonders what he'll be like at the end of the thirty years it'll take to pay off the astronomical $89,000 purchase price. Most of the film projects Alex mulls over did later get made: biopics of Lenny Bruce ('The only person who could play Lenny Bruce is Lenny Bruce and he's not available.') and Malcolm X, a modern western with Anthony Quinn as Navajo Man (*Flap*), a love story about a girl with a heart transplant (*Return to Me*). Mazursky didn't get *8½* out of his system, and took another bash at it in 1993 in *The Pickle*.

ANGEL UNCHAINED (1970)

Soulful biker Angel (Don Stroud) quits the Exiles/Nomads 'sickle gang' and exchanges leathers for denim to settle down on a dirt-scrabbling commune with hippie chick Merrilee (Tyne Daly). The pacifist commune – run by mild-mannered longhair Tremain (Luke Askew) – is repeatedly hassled by dune-buggy-riding, cowboy-hatted townies. Angel goes the *Magnificent Seven* route and calls in his old gang, now run by Pilot (Larry Bishop), to run security. Naturally, the bikers act the way the Mexican farmers were afraid the Seven would – getting drunk, cutting up, stealing hallucinogenic cookies from an old Indian (Pedro Regas) and brawling with each other. The three-way face-off is resolved when the townies attack en masse and the dropouts rally together to defend their patch. A martyrdom rams home the message that bikers and hippies should be friends.

Director Lee Madden (*The Night God Screamed*) and screenwriter Jeffrey Alladin Fiskin (whose major credit is the masterpiece *Cutter's Way*) don't bring as much to the bike gang genre as Roger Corman (*The Wild Angels*), Richard Rush (*Hells Angels on Wheels*) or Joe Viola (*Angels Hard as They Come*). A further drawback is a weird brass-heavy score no real biker would put up with (plus horrible songs). Stroud, whose thinning hair gets wind-whipped since he's too cool to wear a crash helmet, is less impressive as a good guy than as a villain in *Coogan's Bluff* – so he's upstaged by dry Bishop (later the director of *Trigger Happy* and a bit-player in *Kill Bill Vol.2*), foaming Bill McKinney (the 'squeal like a pig, city boy' man) and chubby-crazy Neil Moran (as Magician, a top-hatted biker with drugs in the pouches of his conjurer's cape). In an unconventional bit, Shotgun (McKinney) puts rough moves on Merrilee, who sees him off easily, then Angel steps in to protect his woman in a fight which he loses, incidentally destroying the cabbage field the commune depends on. Daly isn't a typical movie flower-child, but – on the whole – the hippies in this film are more believable than the bikers or the rednecks. As bikesploitation goes, a bit tame – most of the plot-motivating violence takes place off screen, and even the drug-taking boils down to a chocolate chip trip. It has the mandatory shots of a bike convoy cruising two-abreast and stretches to a few good stunts – especially a flying buggy colliding with a shack.

...ARTEMIS..8..1..(1981)

> 'VIRGINITY, CASTRATION, PREGNANCY. ALL THE ONE GODDESS?'

A BBC-TV one-off, scripted by David Rudkin (*Penda's Fen*), directed by Alastair Reid (the David Hemmings *Dr Jekyll & Mr Hyde*). Wildly ambitious and not a little pretentious, it explores a great deal of fascinating material, and literally wanders all over the map to come to grips with heady, earthy, primal material.

On a fog-bound North Sea Ferry from Denmark to England, leonine organist Dr Albrecht von Drachenfels (Dan O'Herlihy, made up to look like the villainess in *Vampyr* crossed with William Hartnell in *Doctor Who*) encounters a musicologist, Gwen Meredith (Dinah Stabb), and intones several ominous statements. A pagan artefact smuggled in pieces on the ferry prompts a random selection of passengers to suicide, transforming their loved ones into semi-possessed stalkers. On a mystic plane represented by a blasted tree-stump and some sand, the angelic Helith (Sting) and the demonic Asrael (Roland Curram) talk about the possible resurrection of their goddess mother, Artemis (aka Diana or Magog). Gideon Harlax (Hywel Bennett), a science fiction writer with paranormal interests, starts finding clues to a vast conspiracy in his array of IBM typewriter 'golf balls', before being drawn by Gwen into investigating Von Drachenfels, who is under Asrael's sway but trying to resist performing a concert/ritual which will perhaps raise the goddess. Meanwhile, Gideon's gay friend Jed Thaxter

(Ian Redford), a film studies lecturer, talks about *Vertigo*, cuing the manifestation in a library of a Hitchcock Blonde (Ingrid Pitt!) only Gideon can see.

For a lengthy chunk of the second half of the three-hour film, Gideon is mysteriously transported to an unnamed European country (perhaps an alternate Britain) in the grip of an apocalyptic upheaval; this echoes the settings of some 1960s Ingmar Bergman films (*Shame*), but might also be a vision of a post-Artemis future. Back in the present, Gideon and Gwen try to stop Von Drachenfels' final improvisation in a church scene which rather surprisingly quotes from a couple of Christopher Lee's Hammer Dracula deaths. Not all of the epic works (lines like, 'Being gay isn't the end of the world,' drop with a thud) and it has several slow spots, but it's a rich, rewarding tapestry of weirdness. Some of the character scenes, as when Gwen needles Gideon for his emotional timidity or the cop-out angelic deliverances of his novels, are blisteringly well written and acted. Rudkin, as ever, finds strangeness within the commonplace: noting a sign on the back of a van that promises 'Rolls… Stamps… Punches… Dies', Gideon muses, 'The life of a man.' Daniel Day-Lewis has a tiny bit as a student.

BARN OF THE NAKED DEAD (TERROR CIRCUS) (1974)

Alan Rudolph directed this grindhouse item between the hippie art movie *Premonition* and the Robert Altman-produced *Welcome to L.A.* Given Rudolph's later distinction, the presence of Andrew Prine (*The Centerfold Girls*, *Simon King of the Witches*) and a strange premise (plus a wonderful come-on title), it's a shame *Barn of the Naked Dead* isn't more exciting.

A gaggle of showgirls (Manuela Thiess, Sherry Alberoni, Gyl Roland) are driving to a Vegas gig. Ignoring a leering gas station attendant who warns them about radiator trouble, they drive off into the desert, furthermore taking 'a real neat shortcut', and are stranded. Andre (Prine), a seemingly nice young man, comes along and offers to let them phone for help from his homestead – a farm littered with derelict circus cages (plus a few animals). The girls end up chained in the barn, where Andre keeps about a dozen young women. He treats his captives like animals, and tries to train them as circus acts. They aren't naked at any time – though most of them end up dead. The central image is striking, as much for the ricketiness of the barn as anything else, but the villain's scheme depends on his victims being instantly pliable. The sort of showgirls who appear in Roger Corman films of the period would have escaped and sought bloody revenge by the second reel.

Andre's father, mutated by proximity to A-bomb blasts, lives in a shack on the property, occasionally stumbling out (seen as a pair of staggering legs) to terrorise girls. Late in the day, his oatmeal-covered monster face is revealed. Prine makes the most of high-flown lunatic dialogue – but none of the girls get a look-in and cutaways to the showgirls' agent (Chuck Niles) nagging the authorities are just filler. It slightly prefigures *The Hills Have Eyes* by linking 1950s nuclear tests with backwoods mutant folks.

BETWEEN TIME AND TIMBUKTU: A SPACE FANTASY (NET THEATRE BETWEEN TIME AND TIMBUKTU) (1971)

This Canadian TV movie takes elements, characters, lines and jokes from various writings by Kurt Vonnegut, Jr. – mostly the novels *The Sirens of Titan*, *Player Piano*, *Cat's Cradle* and *Mother Night*, the play *Happy Birthday, Wanda June* and the short story 'Harrison Bergeron' – though not much from his best-known book, *Slaughterhouse-Five*, which was in production as a major motion picture at the time.

Everyman Stony Stevenson (William Hickey) wins an advertising slogan contest and his prize is to be the sole astronaut of the Prometheus-5 mission to a 'chrono-synclastic infundibulum', which sends him careening through time and space to drop in on various Vonnegut characters and scenarios. Done obviously on the cheap, this uses educational film clips and stock footage for its space voyage (the end credits are over an eerily reversed rocket launch) and cuts away to deadpan comics Ray Goulding and Bob Elliott as news anchor Walter Gesundheit and astronaut Bud Williams Jr comment in dry, banal terms about the mission. Williams has never lived down the moment when he set foot on Mars and announced that the red planet looked like his driveway – which is why, following Soviet space program director Sergei Korolev's dictum that they should have sent poets not pilots into orbit (paraphrased by Carl Sagan in *Contact*), the supposedly imaginative (actually pretty inarticulate) contest winner has won a seat on the prized mission.

Rather than dramatize the books, many scenes have Stevenson talk with characters who dish out satirical philosophy – with Kevin McCarthy (*Invasion of the Body Snatchers*) and Hurd Hatfield (*The Picture of Dorian Gray*) as the deliberately fraudulent prophet

Bokonon and irresponsible scientist Dr Hoenikker (inventor of the apocalyptic Ice-9) from *Cat's Cradle*. The joke dystopia 'Harrison Bergeron', which has been remade three times, gets a relatively straight adaptation. The climax visits the shuffleboard-playing Heaven of *Happy Birthday, Wanda June* (which was also filmed in 1971, by Mark Robson – with Hickey in another role), where Stony meets the cheery little dead girl (Ariana Chase) who doesn't mind being killed by an ice cream truck on her birthday, and Adolf Hitler (Page Johnson).

In its flip, thrown-together, scurrilous manner – borrowing from early Brian De Palma (*Greetings*; *Hi, Mom!*) and Monty Python, as well as *The Twilight Zone* – this 'special' captures much of the tone of Vonnegut's fashionable-in-the-'70s work, even its sometimes-infuriating whimsy. Written by David Odell (*The Dark Crystal*), David R. Loxton (*Overdrawn at the Memory Bank*) and director Fred Barzyk (*Countdown to Looking Glass*); showing unusual respect for written science fiction, Barzyk and Loxton co-directed another low-budget mind-bender, the well-remembered TV film of Ursula K. Le Guin's novel *The Lathe of Heaven*.

THE BIG CUBE (1969)

The hook for this weird melodrama is 'Lana Turner on acid'. Directed in Mexico by Tito Davison from a script by TV hack William Douglas Lansford (*Starsky & Hutch*, *Star Trek: The Next Generation*), this clueless vision of the freak-out set (no one involved took a trip on anything other than Pan Am) is compounded by admirably insane last-reel plot turns.

Legendary stage star Adriana Roman (Lana) retires to marry macho tycoon Charles Winthrop (Dan O'Herlihy), though playwright Frederick Lansdale (Richard Egan) is also in love with the mature leading lady. Adriana tries to be sweet to Charles' pettish daughter Lisa (Karin Mossberg – excruciatingly terrible), but the brat resents daddy's remarriage and falls in with a bad crowd. The bizarre middle-aged idea of 'the Now Generation' is further out of touch even than *The Happening* or *Riot on Sunset Strip*. Lalo (Carlos East) paints scary fish and Bibi (Pamela Rodgers) comes on like a sociopath Ann-Margret, but creepiest of the crew is lounge lizard Johnny Allen (George Chakiris). Expelled from med school for cooking LSD, Johnny latches on to Lisa with an eye on the family fortune. When Charles is lost in a yacht accident, Lisa vacillates between sympathy for her widowed stepmother and the desire to punish her.

Johnny slips ailing Adriana doses of acid, and the diva's bad dreams get worse when recorded messages urge her to suicide.

For most films, saving Lana from a hallucinogenic murder plot would be enough for a climax… but this follows through with a spell of traumatic amnesia (the star certainly couldn't complain she wasn't being asked to act). The still-devoted Frederick proposes to cure Adriana by (get this!) writing a play about her recent life in which she will make her theatrical comeback in the hope that applause will bring her memory back. Two minutes after suckering Lisa into marriage, Johnny gropes Bibi (who has cool midriff-baring outfits) and tries to palm his new wife off on Lalo. Lisa divorces the slimeball and helps Frederick with his cracked scheme. Not only is Adriana cured of amnesia and acid flashbacks, but the play is a hit! Johnny ends up on a terminal bad trip in the den of 'the Queen Bee' (Regina Torne), crawling over the dirty floor scrabbling for sugar cubes.

Turner – a beauty, if never much of an actress – conducts herself with frozen, glamorous dignity. The trip scenes are beyond her (as written, they'd be beyond Meryl Streep or Sarah Bernardt), so she just bugs her eyes and wanders about in a nightgown. ©Oscar˙ winner Chakiris is aptly loathsome as the acid gigolo, but is such an obvious villain it would take a character as thick as Lisa played by an actress as bad as Mossberg to go along with him. Possibly Turner insisted the stepdaughter be a nonentity, rather than risk being outshone even by the low-wattage of, say, Sandra Dee or Diane Varsi. O'Herlihy and Egan are stolid, dependable and faintly ashamed. With wild and crazy music from The Finks, psychedelic pop art titles and set dressing, amazing if ridiculous fashions and a streak of stubborn squareness. Trashy but fun.

BLACK MOON (1975)

In writer-director Louis Malle's dream vision, an air of sexual threat coexists with whimsy and a machine-gun massacre kicks off a tale featuring magic creatures and talking animals. In green, wet French forests gorgeously shot by Sven Nykvist, a literal war of the sexes is fought between brutal gas mask-wearing factions. After running over a badger (evoking *The Texas Chain Saw Massacre*), Lily (Cathryn Harrison) drives through countryside, witnessing atrocities on both sides. A male soldier in a firing squad grieves over one of a row of shot-dead women, suggesting backstory otherwise never addressed – if this is even happening outside of Lily's head (which it might not be – a few objective shots strip fantastical elements from her world). Fleeing the male army, Lily seeks refuge in a cluttered gothic farmhouse where a bedridden old woman (Therese Giehse) babbles, alternately attacking the girl and imploring her for succour. Twins – mannish Alexandra Stewart and androgynous Joe Dallesandro, who both also seem to be called Lily – maintain the place, where an anarchic herd of naked children live with swarming animals.

At the wheel of her car, Lily seems a young woman; stripped of vehicle and the hat she's used to hide her long blonde hair, she is a child again. She struggles Alice-like with size: in a brilliantly contrived shot, she reaches across a table for a glass of milk which turns out to be a huge vase. Lily's adolescent pompousness is undermined by the old woman – who cackles when her knickers keep falling down and sneers at her flat chest (after which, she keeps her top button undone). Lily is warily attracted to the bird-like Dallesandro (who can't talk but can sing) and alternately menaced and tempted by a rough unicorn (no thin-limbed Disney ideal, but a shaggy Shetland pony with a dangerous horn). The film ends with Lily moistening her nipples – as Stewart has done – to suckle the crone, prefiguring the moment when Susan Sarandon lemon-cleanses her breasts in Malle's *Atlantic City U.S.A.* Striking weirdnesses crop up along the way – a burst of *Tristan and Isolde* performed by the feral children, the old woman's arguments with Humphrey the Rat, and the twins acting out a painting involving the decapitation of an eagle.

As an exercise in dream-logic and female adolescent reverie, *Black Moon* is worth filing alongside *Rapture*, Jonathan Miller's melancholy BBC *Alice in Wonderland*, *Valerie and Her Week of Wonders*, *The Company of Wolves* and *Pan's Labyrinth*. Harrison (*Images*, *The Witches of Pendle*) is excellent as the grave, withdrawn, slightly irritable heroine.

BLOOD AND LACE (THE BLOOD SECRET) (1971)

Pitched as an entry in the 'horror hag' cycle, with film noir regular Gloria Grahame as a middle-aged menace, this is also an early slasher film. In a POV stalker sequence, someone holding a hammer centre-screen sneaks into the bedroom of middle-aged slut Edna Masters (Louise Sherrill) and batters her (and her current lover) to death before setting a fire. Ellie (Melody Patterson), Edna's blonde teenage daughter, is dumped at a hellhole old dark house orphanage. Directress Mrs Deere (Gloria Grahame) talks to her dead husband and keeps the corpses of runaways in the freezer, putting the cold bodies in infirmary beds whenever there's an inspection so she can keep receiving their monthly $150 keep.

Also in residence are a clutch of mixed-up, disaffected kids – including a young Dennis Christopher and nymphet Terry Messina – and gurning handyman Tom Bridge (Len Lesser). Tom has a sinister catchphrase ('you get my drift') and can chop off a kid's hand with a cleaver-throw. That severed hand is stuck in a suitcase and forgotten until, late in the day, the case is opened for a predictable but effective shock. A killer in a burn-victim mask stalks the orphanage (looking like a stockier Freddy Krueger), a girl is tied up in the attic after an escape attempt (Mrs Deere torments the thirsty victim by drinking a glass of water in front of her) and the directress's cracked backstory (which involves cryogenics) gets equal time with Ellie's twisted family history.

Scripted by Gil Lasky – who has several odd items on his CV (producer of *Spider Baby*, writer of *The Night God Screamed*) and directed by one-shot Philip S. Gilbert, *Blood and Lace* has bright colours, flatly sunlit exteriors and a staid, swift TV-movie look which presents excesses in almost surreally matter-of-fact fashion. Choppy editing and clumsy staging defuse the extensive gore, but the acting is surprisingly solid. Grahame is splendid (and even underplays mania), Lesser seethes entertainingly as an all-round scumbag, the kids are more than competent, and familiar character faces Vic Tayback (overbearingly amiable cop) and Milton Selzer (corrupt orphanage official) seize chances for depravity with relish. A queasy, unusual resolution has two unmasked murderers settling into a warped, possibly incestuous relationship.

BLOOD FREAK (1972)

A one-of-a-kind cheapie, but still faintly dull. Nice guy biker Herschell (Steve Hawkes) is lured away from Christian girlfriend Ann (Dana Cullivan) by her loose-living sister Angel (Heather Hughes), who gets him hooked on something smokeable (more than pot, we're told). His life degenerates further when he takes a job on a turkey farm and eats a bird dosed with experimental formula. Thanks to the superdope or the genegineered bird or a combo of both, he sprouts a turkey monster head and rampages, gorily dismembering a victim. After the transformation, the monster (seen only in flashcuts which don't disguise how ludicrous it looks) visits Ann, who just lies there and waits for him to produce a note explaining who he is (which she patiently reads).

It feels like a sincere if ridiculous Christian anti-drugs tract rewritten as a lurid trash-horror picture, with H.G. Lewis-style gore (a leg sawed off). Wild parties involve sitting around toking to musak, while supposed horror scenes feature Lewisian locked-down camera and night-for-night murk. Director Brad Grinter appears as a narrator with a smoker's cough, though ex-bootleg Tarzan Hawkes muscles in on a producing-directing credit.

BREAD (1971)

An hour-long oddity from sexploitationer Stanley Long (billed as $tanley £ong), built around pop festival footage. It usefully shows what British kids looked like en masse in 1971, but has no pretensions to being *Woodstock* (or even *Glastonbury Fayre*). It's similar in plot to *The Ghost Goes Gear*, as teenagers stage a concert in the grounds of a stately home. Coming home from the Isle of Wight festival, a bunch of longhairs (Anthony Nigel, Peter Marinker, Dick Haydon, Noelle Rimmington, Liz White) pitch a tent on the lawns of drunken, perpetually furious aristo Rafe (Michael McStay), who doesn't look much older than them. They agree to paint his house, but decide to hold a free festival on the grounds instead. A feeble attempt to make a skinflick ('There's the maid having it away with your old lady, and you didn't know she was on a big lez scene…') to raise seed money stalls when they realise no chemist will develop the film. Eventually, big name bands Crazy Mabel and Juicy Lucy (the script admits they aren't exactly the Beatles) are secured and the lawn is overrun by hairy hordes. Rafe is still angry at the end, as the gang leave the stage in his garden – but there's no telltale post-festival rubbish heap. It quarter-heartedly tries to qualify as a sex film, but plays mostly as a hippie-era travelogue.

CANDY (1968)

'Is *Candy* faithful?' asks Orson Welles in a one-line trailer voice-over. A giggly female voice answers (mendaciously), 'Only to the book.'

Terry Southern's brand of satire transferred perfectly to the cinema in *Dr Strangelove* and screenwriter Buck Henry admirably worked from a cult novel in *Catch-22*, but Henry's adaptation of Southern and Mason Hoffenberg's *Candy* is dreadful. It would have made sense to cast Peter Sellers as all the men who have approximate sex with heroine

Candy Christian (blonde, lovely, blank Ewa Aulin). Instead, a roster of huge talents fail to be funny in pot-shots at easy targets: Richard Burton as drunken Welsh glamour poet MacPhisto, Ringo Starr as Mexican gardener-priest Emmanuel (with insulting funny voice), Walter Matthau as hawkish General Smight, James Coburn as celebrity surgeon A.B. Krankheit, John Huston as medical money-man Dr Dunlap, Charles Aznavour as a hunchbacked master crook who scales walls like Spider-Man, Enrico Maria Salerno as Warholian film artist Jonathan J. John, Marlon Brando as gurning guru Grindl and John Astin as Candy's lobotomised everyguy dad and lecherous hipster uncle.

A Franco-Italian co-production (a significant alternate title is *Candy e il suo pazzo mondo*), this suffers because French director Christian Marquand seems not to notice that the book is about America. Candy epitomises the sort of corn-fed teen princess played by Ann-Margret in *Bye Bye Birdie* or Tuesday Weld in *Rock Rock Rock* – so the very Swedish Aulin is just wrong for the central role. It has pop art sets, costumes and music (Steppenwolf, Dave Grusin, 'Magic Carpet Ride'), plus Doug Trumbull off-Earth effects, captivating Euro-women (Anita Pallenberg, Elsa Martinelli, Marilu Tolo, Florinda Balkan, Lea Padovani, Nicholetta Machiavelli) and Sugar Ray Robinson as Burton's chauffeur – but despite having all this stuff and all these people, it drags.

CURSE OF THE HEADLESS HORSEMAN (1972)

A rambling oddity from 'John Kirkland' (aka Leonard Kirtman, of *Carnival of Blood*), this is far from good, but has a decent mystery plot. While *Carnival* has a New York/Coney Island twang, this is a 'south-western' offering with hippie overtones. Clean-cut medical student Mark Callahan (Marland Proctor) inherits a run-down Wild West Show, but only gets the deed to the land if he can make it turn a profit. A collection of 'yeah man' youths squatting on the place volunteer to pitch in, to the disgust of a scar-faced caretaker (who also provides ominous narration). Bad stuff happens… one unfortunate is splattered by blood thrown by the title spook (who actually has a head even if it isn't attached to his neck) and then shot in the arm with what ought to be a blank; a girl freaks out on acid and is terrorised by the perhaps-imaginary spectre; a lecherous hippie strikes gold and tries to buy the ranch, then gets caught in the horseman costume. Several plots are juggled, and the last act springs some surprises – and also unusually deals with the emotional fall-out of the villain's unmasking. It has folky-hippie songs and probably authentic commune atmosphere, even if characters only get one distinguishing feature apiece (a girl called Yo-Yo has a yo-yo). In different scenes, the horseman is a real ghost, a drug vision or one or other of the baddies in disguise. Warhol superstar Ultra Violet shows up, toting a vintage Superman lunchbox

DAY THE FISH CAME OUT (1967)

Inspired by a 1966 kerfuffle when the US military mislaid a couple of nuclear weapons in the sea off Spain, this stodgy satire is set in the then-future year of 1972. Pilots Tom Courtenay and Colin Blakely spend most of the film hopping about jagged rocks in their underpants, struggling with a complete lack of material, while a US army investigator (Sam Wanamaker) poses as a hotel tycoon to buy up half the unpromising Greek island of Karos. While the lost bombs are smuggled off the island in a coffin, a box containing 'Object Q' falls into the hands of a poor goatherd (Nikolaos Alexiou) and his wife (Marlena Carrer). They try to break into it in the hope of untold riches, using a stolen chemical drip to get through the shielding. Inside are some ugly eggs which, when thrown into the water supply, become apocalyptically deadly. Candice Bergen shows up late in silly outfits as nymphomaniac Electra Brown and beguiles an ill-cast Ian Ogilvy, but at least adds life to a picture which could do with more bright sparks. Director Michael Cacoyannis (*Zorba the Greek*), at the end of his brief vogue, evenly distributes his lack of sympathies, depicting Greek islanders as grasping caricatures while blanding out American 'invaders'. There's a distant echo of *Whisky Galore*, but to little effect. 'Futuristic' bits include garish plastic outfits, a raucous computerised tourist centre and an enthusiastic but jerky dance craze.

DIONYSUS IN '69 (1970)

A valuable record of the state of fringe theatre c. 1968, this is also a curiously personal work from Brian De Palma. To record the Performance Group's anarchic production of Euripides' *The Bacchae*, a 'happening' directed (in a collaborative sort way) by Richard Schechner, De Palma trains two cameras, roughly on the cast and the audience, and presents the images in parallel throughout – his most extreme use of his signature split-screen effect, and even more committed to the process than the 'DuoVision' thriller *Wicked Wicked*. A moment in the hectic climax of *Phantom of the Paradise* – as a rock fan (William Shephard) writhes alongside the bleeding Phantom (William Finley) – is an arcane in-joke about *Dionysus in '69*, where Dionysus (Finley) writhes alongside the torn-apart King Pentheus (Shephard).

Aside from the antagonists, few of the other characters are differentiated – with the performers fitting together *Human Centipede*-style or disporting themselves with abandon, including members of the audience in their antics, and creating creepy vocal effects. There is a lot of nudity and it winds up with the spilling of much stage blood – but the black and white film is surprisingly unsensationalist about its shocking elements. Certainly not free of modish self-indulgence (when the violence starts, Dallas and Vietnam are namechecked), but as legitimate a way of mounting Greek drama – scarcely known for down-to-Earth realism – as any other. Claiming to be Dionysus reborn, Finley says he's done something no one else ever has: found a way to end this play. Announcing his candidacy for the Presidency ('A vote for Finley in '68 will bring you Dionysus in '69.'), he is borne out of the performance space into the streets on the shoulders of actors and audience members. His platform is total freedom, but a freeze-frame finish catches what looks like a Nazi salute.

DRIVE, HE SAID (1971)

Jack Nicholson's directing debut. Not a box office success or a critical favourite, *Drive, He Said* has fallen into obscurity – probably because of its plotless, disenchanted, slightly remote approach to campus activity and unculty lead actors. But it's interesting.

Hector (William Tepper), a college basketball star (one of Nicholson's lifelong enthusiasms) for whom 'the game isn't jive', is contrasted with roommate Gabriel (Michael Margotta, of *Wild in the Streets* and *The Strawberry Statement*), for whom it's 'staying after school in your underwear'. Hector has an affair with Olive (Karen Black), wife of a desperate-to-be-hip professor (Robert Towne), but has a more complex relationship with his unstereotyped coach Bullion (Bruce Dern). Gabriel stages literal guerrilla theatre by invading a game. He acts crazy to avoid the draft, but it spills over into his real life and he ends up being taken to an asylum (a hint at *One Flew Over the Cuckoo's Nest*?). Neither protagonist is especially engaging and, though solid, neither performer has the Nicholsonian flair which might have made them fascinating. Did Nicholson, who co-scripted with novelist Jeremy Larner, write roles he knew he could make work, then find other actors couldn't? Black's bored character gets credibly fed up with all the men in her life (they're all big demanding kids) and Gabriel's treatment of his girlfriend (June Fairchild) is an uncomfortable, horribly convincing reminder of how politically active '60s radicals could treat women worse than conservatives did and be self-righteous about it.

Gabriel's final acts are more disturbing than revolutionary: invading Olive's home – perhaps to terrorise and rape her, perhaps as another act of radical theatre (she seems unsure, laughing as well as screaming, but doesn't like it either way) – then breaking into the science lab while naked and liberating the creepy-crawlies. In contrast to this meltdown, Hector just plays basketball: the game scenes are free of sports movie clichés, and dependencies, resentments and rapports between coach and players are interestingly explored. It has non-obvious music – the theme is a Philip Glassish track by 'secret master' Moondog, a composer who chose to live on the streets for decades. Other aspects of counterculture cinema: as much male as female nudity, future TV stars in bit parts (Michael Warren of *Hill Street Blues*, David Ogden Stiers of *MASH*, Cindy Williams), acting roles for behind-the-scenes folk (Towne, Henry Jaglom, co-producer Harry Gittes), restless, chattery, join-the-dots plotting, and a sense that this is 'about America' rather than some irritating people doing inconsequential things.

EGGSHELLS (1969)

The Texas Chain Saw Massacre (1973) was Tobe Hooper's second feature. His first was this essay in (presumably) group autobiography made by (and about) hippieish students sharing a house in Austin in 1969, vaguely tuning out from reality. A 'ghost' haunts the house – he might be a scrawny, sword-wielding youth who doesn't interact with other characters – but this is in no sense a conventional haunted-house film. Or anything like a narrative movie.

Authentic, dazzling American underground document of the era or pretentious student nonsense protracted to feature length? Maybe both. As a time capsule, it's evocative and invaluable. The bulk of IMDb comments are from people who saw it at the time and knew the people in it (someone has done a *Return of the Secaucus 7* 'what happened next' listing, which notes, 'The Revolution never came!). Liable to befuddle and irritate many fans of Hooper's later work, but taken in the right mood (perhaps an altered state), it's fascinating. Certainly, some dialogue scenes run longer than an audience's patience, while time speeds up and slows down in a mesmeric manner at once seductive and monotonous. The question of What It All Means is moot – though Reichian perspex domes and a weird self-constructed machine give the story shape. It's also a strong visual: a gizmo with four hairdryer/electric chair headpieces sucks up four characters and reduces them to a liquid which pours out of a tap. The script is credited to Hooper, but the chatter sounds improvised. Like *Medium Cool*, it includes unstaged footage as the actors (in character) take part in an anti-Vietnam War demo or a sweet open-air wedding/party.

The prime mover is 'Toes', played by moustachioed Kim Henkel (screenwriter of *TCM* and Eagle Pennell's *Last Night at the Alamo*, and director of one of the *Chainsaw* sequels), presumably a stand-in for 'Tobe'. Everyone else uses their own first names. Allen Danziger, one of the doomed *TCM* kids, is the only known face, but Ron Barnhart, Pamela Craig, Sharon Danziger, Mahlon Foreman, Amy Lester, David Noll and Jim Schulman are all fresh, natural and credible even in freak-out scenes. Couples sit in the bath and bitch about their housemates or parents or the war, and occasional scenes play like sketches. A long wedding dress fitting has two guys from different sides of the frame with different political agendas try to squash the dress-up pleasure of the bride; typical of the masculinist downside of the counterculture, but also a witty conceit. 'Experimental' sections reminiscent of Mike Jittlov's animations (*The Wizard of Speed and Time*) show the imaginative framing/editing of *TCM* (and the sound/music design of Wayne Bell) was already a part of Hooper's repertoire. In a sequence which foreshadows a joke in *Ed Wood*, a single setup in the house's hallway is held for a succession of snippets as different people at different points pass through. A room is painted as if in animation, with no painter visible (the ghost?), the swordsman fights himself, a literal trip is taken (step-framing thorough a car journey) and musical numbers set an editing pace for general noodling-about bits and bobs.

Ponder the youthful ambitions – and skills – of a director who could make *Eggshells* and *The Texas Chain Saw Massacre*, envisioning a future in which both filmmaking modes were commercially and artistically viable. Another revolution which didn't happen.

FATA MORGANA (1971)

Werner Herzog claims this is science fiction: a documentary about a struggling planet made by an alien film crew. Fair enough – and it's an odd addition to the *Mondo Cane*-inspired demento documentary cycle. This impressionist collage plays well as ambient cinema, but is a strain to sit through under other circumstances. Repeated shots of aeroplanes coming in to land encourage the viewer to see shapes (mirages) in jet wash. Footage shot mostly in Africa is soundtracked with epigrammatic readings (Mayan creation myths, etc.) and hypnosis-assist music cues (Bach, Leonard Cohen). It has a restless, looking-out-the-window feel (many of the shots are travelling) as it finds huge derelict vehicles abandoned in the desert, pokes around the decaying bodies and bones of cattle, looks at unending sand dunes, etc. A cheery boffin in a wet suit talks about turtles and 'The Golden Age' is illustrated by a woman pounding an upright piano as a fellow in goggles plays the drums and vocalises brass instruments. At 78 minutes, it's not an ordeal (watched in a half-daze, it's soothing and only vaguely creepy). I recommend watching it with the director's commentary adding another layer of aural mystery.

FORBIDDEN ZONE (1980)

The debut feature of writer-director Richard Elfman, then partner – with composer brother Danny (*Batman*, *Nightbreed*, etc.) and future writer-director Matthew Bright (*Freeway*, *Ted Bundy*) – in the performance group The Mystic Knights of the Oingo Boingo. Reproducing the style of the Mystic Knights' stage shows, this scabrous black and white fable feels like a 1930s Fleischer Betty Boop cartoon redone under the influence of John Waters, the Three Stooges, *Flesh Gordon* and Terry Gilliam's Python animations.

In cardboard-cutout Los Angeles, the Hercules family live in a house with a (forbidden) door to the Sixth Dimension in the basement. Rebel daughter Frenchy (Marie-Pascale Elfman), who comes on like a punky Simone Simon, attends a chaotic high school where grownup pimps and gamblers have gunfights with drag act teachers. She ventures into the Forbidden Zone, which is ruled by wicked Queen Doris (Susan Tyrrell, in one of her frequent freak roles) who has stolen the king (an enthusiastic Hervé Villechaize) from the rightful ruler (Viva). Frenchy excites the queen's enmity and the king's interest. To the rescue come her Boy Scout brother (ancient vaudevillian Phil Gordon) and manic Grampa (Hyman Diamond), plus Bright (billed as 'Toshiro Boloney') as sexually confused twins.

With Joe Spinell as a horny sailor, Gisele Lindley as an always-topless Princess, 'The Kipper Kids' (Brian Routh and Martin von Haselberg) evoking Gilbert and George or *Beano* and *Dandy* and Danny Elfman as a white tuxedoed Satan. The most fun comes from the music, often vintage material remixed by Danny Elfman: Cab Calloway is fed through the mill, plus astonishing one-offs, like a commuter number called 'Pico and Sepulveda', Josephine Baker's 'La Petite Tonkinoise' and 'Yiddische Charleston'. Its geniality defuses potentially offensive material: Bright being tossed into a cell to be gang-raped by Arabs ('Oh beat me up, kill me, fuck that asshole.'), ethnic caricature ('What's a nice Jewish boy like you doing in the Sixth Dimension?'), Waters-style sexual eccentricities, etc. One of King Fausto's theories ('She's French and that's simple... therefore she's of the master race – a direct descendant of God, just like me.') prefigures *The Da Vinci Code*!

GAS! – OR – IT BECAME NECESSARY TO DESTROY THE WORLD IN ORDER TO SAVE IT (1970)

'WHAT WAS THAT, A BOMB?' 'NO, IT SOUNDED MORE IRONIC THAN THAT.'

Scripted by George Armitage, later director of *Miami Blues* and *Grosse Pointe Blank*, Roger Corman's hippie apocalypse comedy offers freewheeling radicalism and many scenes of good-looking dropouts cruising the desert in cool vehicles – including an Edsel and a fleet of tricked-out beach buggies.

In a cartoon opening, a bioweapons mishap ('This will screw up our perfect safety record.') leads to the death by rapid ageing of everyone over twenty-five (not shown in upsetting detail). Survivors either replicate the world of their elders, as a Texas football team becomes a marauding horde and the Hells' Angels take over the golf club, or try to find a better way, heading for a pueblo which is the oldest inhabited community on the continent ('In case you hadn't noticed, *we've got America back*,' jeers an Indian as he returns all the gifts, from smallpox to the English language, given by white people). Like Corman's *The Wild Angels*, *Gas!* skewers the hypocrisies of its rebels, though this is considerably less of a downer. It's genuinely moving that long-haired pacifist drifter Coel (Bob Corff, later voice coach to the stars) argues for co-operation rather than conflict ('We've tried it your way for 10,000 years.').

Given the way approximately every other post-apocalypse movie ends, it's a shock when invading goons, set to sack the peace-loving commune, see the point that co-operation trumps the violence of everything from *Le Dernier Combat/ The Last Battle* to the *Mad Max* sequels. This change of heart means a vibrant orange van which has trailed our heroes throughout opens to free the reborn idols of the era (or at least people wearing giant carnival heads representing them) – Lincoln, Gandhi, Kennedy, MLK and Alfred E. Neuman.

An influence on Stephen King's *The Stand*, this 'south-western' apocalypse riffs slightly on Godard's *Weekend* for its aimless grubbing amid pop-culture detritus. A comic shootout consists of young men yelling names of cowboy stars at each other, with black Ben Vereen apologising after he cites Jim Brown with, 'He was the only one, man!' Young talents show their playful sides: Cindy Williams riffs enthusiastically about pop music (though Coel responds that the 'sound of the sixties' was a rifle shot), Elaine Giftos takes charge of (and defuses) a rape scene in a manner your collective will still argue about, Bud Cort adheres to whichever faction will help him get laid and Tally Coppola (later Talia Shire) picks up slack. Among less familiar faces, Alex Wilson is strong as the exasperated warrior leader giving pep speeches to his horde ('Frankly, I don't know if you're good enough to sack El Paso.'), while Bruce Karcher rides in on a chopper as a gloomily optimistic Edgar Allan Poe with a raven on his handlebars and Lenore on the pillion. Country Joe and the Fish appear in concert. Trimmed by AIP head Samuel Z. Arkoff, with whom Corman angrily parted company, it remains under-appreciated and charming.

GET TO KNOW YOUR RABBIT (1972)

> 'AT ONE TIME, I THOUGHT THE TAP-DANCING MAGICIAN CRAZE WOULD MAKE A LOT BIGGER SPLASH THAN IT DID.'

In the wake of *Easy Rider*, studio suits often greenlit films indicting their own way of life – then interfered so much that the 'kids' they were hoping would be the audience didn't show up. On the strength of his counterculture comedies *Greetings* and *Hi,*

Mom!, Warner Brothers signed Brian De Palma to direct Jordan Crittenden's script about a mid-level executive who drops out of the rat race only to find the rats follow and sour his dreams of freedom.

Donald Beeman (a too-bland Tom Smothers), a toiler in 'the servo-mechanism industry', takes lessons with the Great Delasandro (an under-used Orson Welles) to become a tap-dancing magician. He abandons the nine-to-five for a life on Greyhound buses, appearing in small-town bars and strip joints with his conjuring act. Exec Mr Turnbull (manic John Astin) so relies on Beeman doing all his work (he even has a bomb threat phone call transferred to Beeman's line) he becomes a homeless bum when his underling quits. When Beeman takes pity on Turnbull and gives him a sinecure as his manager, Turnbull creates TDM (the Tap-Dancing Magician Corporation), a huge enterprise which enables other stressed-out execs to take Beeman's escape route but threatens to suck the original drop-out back into office dronery.

A troubled production, it flopped like such similarly pitched fables as *The Magic Christian, Who is Harry Kellerman and why is he saying these terrible things about me?* and *"Fools"* and De Palma looked to thrillers and horror to build a career, though he has sometimes strayed back to satire (*Home Movies, Wise Guys*, even *The Bonfire of the Vanities*). Typically for its time, the hero's spiritual journey involves thinly characterised, rather shrill pretty women who do nudity. Katharine Ross, the de facto leading lady, plays a character called Terrific-Looking Girl; it's to her credit that she makes something daffy, sexy and interesting of such a thinly written part... having learned something from being the plot token in *The Graduate*, she fights for screen space. De Palma – open to interesting actresses like Jessica Harper and Margot Kidder in the '70s and Noomi Rapace and Rachel McAdams in the 2010s – at least gives Ross room to be interesting. Suzanne Zenor and Samantha Jones get character names (Paula and Susan), but are stereotyped as Beeman's status-obsessed original girlfriend and a party pick-up ('I don't know how to ask you this, but how long have you been a cheap broad?' 'Well, it's an off and on thing.').

Allen Garfield, the sole hold-over from De Palma's indie films, has a weirder-than-funny scene as an oddly obsessive brassiere salesman in desperate, doomed search of a good time at a 'five-day party' which is as crowded as the Marx Brothers' *Night at the Opera* state room yet strangely silent and joyless. Veterans Charles Lane and Hope Summers pop out of a cupboard as Beeman's parents, and there are bits for M. Emmet Walsh (a *young* M. Emmet Walsh?) and Timothy Carey. Some De Palma flourishes survive: while Beeman and his girlfriend have breakfast, a near-identical couple are seen through two window frames playing a near-identical scene in the apartment opposite. Plus, he plays with split-screen and stages an overhead shot looking down on separate rooms.

GODMONSTER OF INDIAN FLATS (1973)

'BY ALL RATIONAL THEORY, THE
EMBRYO SHOULD BE DEAD. THE
TIME HAS COME TO ADVANCE IT
TO THE EXAMINING TABLE.'

A unique combination of mutant monster movie, eco-western, small-town melodrama, community theatre art movie and sly satire from enterprising, uncompromising writer-director Fredric Hobbs (*Alabama's Ghost*). Judging from stills of the monster or clips of its rampages, the film would seem to be on a level with such triumphs of inept creature creation as *Robot Monster* or *Sting of Death* – or worth lumping in with 1970s spawn like *The Milpitas Monster*, *Slithis* or *ZaAt*. Actually, the misbegotten shambling sheep-thing ('I can't accept this concept of intelligence – I say it's a damaged mongoloid beast!') is just an element of a stranger drama.

Shot on tourist attractions in the old west mining town of Virginia City, Nevada, *Godmonster* cuts between laboratory, where geneticist Clemens (E. Kerrigan Prescott) raises the shaggy sport with the help of Basque farmer Eddie (Richard Marion) and assistant Mariposa (Karen Ingenthron), and town, where patriarchal historian Mayor Silverdale (Russ Meyer stock company member Stuart Lancaster) and all-in-black bad guy Maldove (Steven Kent Browne) give the runaround to black executive Barnstable (Christopher Brooks), emissary of interests out to buy up and reopen the Comstock lode mine. The western-style villainy gets farcical as the dudish black guy is framed for the shooting of the sheriff's dog (leading to an elaborate, guilt trip-inducing funeral) and abducted from jail by a black-hooded secret society while the sheriff (Robert Hirschfeld) tucks into a huge meal without concern.

Near-lynching and dirty real estate deals are put on hold during the creature rampage, and the grasping mayor becomes enthusiastic about capturing the pathetic monster – which is roped by cowboys – and putting it on show in a cage perched on the town dump. The shadow of *King Kong* falls over the finale, as a huckster tries to exploit the monster – but Hobbs takes his story in unexpected directions, weirdly comic, but also oddly melancholy. An 'only in the '70s' original.

GONKS GO BEAT (1965)

A uniquely peculiar artefact from the British pop music boom. Out in space, the Great Galaxion (Jerry Desmonde) worries about Earth. All the serious interstellar ambassadors are busy, so huffing foul-up Wilco Roger (Kenneth Connor, with a space helmet) is despatched and told that if he fails to get things sorted out he'll be reassigned to Planet Gonk.

Gonks (humpty dumpty cushions with vestigial limbs) were a short-lived toy craze: it's likely they were written into this half way through production, since they are irrelevant to the story, pop up only in surreal cutaways (a dance scene with young folks swinging gonks around in the dark) and never actually *go beat* (at least in *The Ghost Goes Gear*, the ghost *goes gear*). Wilco is zapped down to Earth and finds the rival island communities of Beatland and Balladisle in a state of Cold War, with young folks brainwashed by tutors Reginald Beckwith and Pamela Brown (in a bodystocking) to express themselves only through their society's favoured music form. An uneasy truce is maintained by the A&R Man (Frank Thornton) who judges the annual Golden Guitar competition.

Inspired by 'that writer Shake-something', Wilco recreates the plot of *Romeo and Juliet*, bringing together a beat boy (Iain Gregory) and a ballad girl (Pamela Donald) who fall in love and win the competition with a beat-ballad fusion combo 'It Takes Two to Make Love'. Terry Scott is dithery as the pompous, inept Prime Minister of Balladisle. Guest turns include Ginger Baker (who takes part in an impressive mass drum-off), the Nashville Teens, Elaine and Derek and Lulu and the Luvvers. Director Robert Hartford-Davis and producer/cinematographer Peter Newbrook (known for horror films like *Corruption* and *Incense for the Damned*) cobbled together the script, which is thinner even than *Just for Fun* or *It's Trad, Dad*. Sadly, most of the tunes are as bland as the jokes are flat – though a few scenes (guitarists standing up in sports cars) are weird enough to seem like proto-pop videos.

GOODBYE GEMINI (TWINSANITY) (1970)

Director Alan Gibson made this after working for Hammer on the *Journey into the Unknown* TV series and *Crescendo* but before *Dracula A.D. 1972* and *The Satanic Rites of Dracula*. Based on Jenni Hall's novel *Ask Agamemnon*, *Goodbye Gemini* is a Swinging London indictment that's also one of a run of British 'private universe' psycho movies revolving around close-knit, semi-incestuous family relationships (*Our Mother's House*, *Mumsy, Nanny, Sonny & Girly*, *The Cement Garden*).

Twins Jacki (Judy Geeson) and Julian Dewar (Martin Potter), whose childish and ritualised relationship excludes everyone except a teddy bear called Agamemnon, arrive in the Big City. After Julian maliciously sets up a landlady to take a fall down stairs, they join a Chelsea ménage with all-in-white ponce Clive Landseer (Alexis Kanner) and his semi-deb semi-girlfriend Denise (Marion Diamond). Clive introduces the twins to his decadent, predominantly gay circle at a houseboat party hosted by Nigel Garfield (Terry Scully), where they attract the interest of 'progressive' MP James Harrington-Smith (Michael Redgrave) and the bitchy envy of outrageous art critic David Curry (Freddie Jones). Jacki, marginally more attuned to the outside world, is constantly fending off Julian's drunken, incestuous gropings. Clive, pursued for a bad debt by bookie Rod (Mike Pratt), makes overtures to both twins, but hauls Julian off to a seedy hotel for a session with a couple of tarts who turn out to be drag queens, then threatens to show Jacki photographs he takes of the orgiastic goings-on unless he turns rent boy to pay off Rod. After this lengthy setup, the film detours into looniness. Sidestepping the blackmail angle, because Denise tells Jacki everything anyway, the twins convince Clive to take part in a test, whereby he bets he can tell the difference between them. The siblings get up in white sheet ghost outfits which show only their eyes and appear to Clive, who can't make up his mind which is which and gets a sword through his neck. After this, Jacki has temporary amnesia and Julian goes completely off the rails. The ending is a tragic liebestod by gas tap.

Though not as unbelievable as the Chelsea of *Dracula A.D. 1972*, the Cheyne Walk set of *Goodbye Gemini* offer eye-offending fashions (Kanner's sheepskin trench coat, Pratt's floppy scarf, Jones's black furry coat, Geeson's fawn velvet loon pants) and studied wild settings (a pub with a drag stripper, the houseboat party) not to mention significant details like a poster for *Hair* and a Christopher Dunning soundtrack which includes very 1970 songs ('Tell the World We're Not In', 'Nothing's Good and Nothing's Free'). Kanner, the top-hatted 'Kid' in the freak-out last episode of *The Prisoner*, has major sideburns and an Irish/American (as opposed to Irish-American) accent as a character described as 'ectoplasm with appetite'. His Clive is so flamboyantly rotten he eclipses the bland psychosis of Potter (fresh from *Fellini Satyricon*) as yet another blond, sexually ambiguous, mad murderer (cf: *Peeping Tom, Straight On Till Morning, Twisted Nerve*). Geeson is okay as the timid lead, but gets lost as Gibson goes overboard on the weird camera angles. There are the usual mad twin scenes with mirrors and identical poses, but Geeson and Potter – though both blonde – don't really click as screen siblings, undermining the premise. Scripted by Edmund Ward, who later wrote Kanner's director-star outing *Kings and Desperate Men*. With familiar faces Peter Jeffrey (inevitable plodding police inspector), Terry Scully, Joseph Furst, Brian Wilde and Hilda Barry.

GOOD TIMES (1967)

A real archaeological artefact, *Good Times* is mostly of interest to anyone who wants to see a parade of fashions Austin Powers would reject as too garish to be seen on the street in. The nothingy plot has then-married Sonny and Cher, playing themselves as a one-note bickering sitcom couple, signing up with sinister tycoon Mordicus (an impeccable George Sanders) to make a movie but not wanting to do the mouldy rags-to-riches hillbilly script on offer. Sonny has a series of sketch-like fantasies in which he casts himself as a Wild West Sheriff (who runs around town in a *High Noon* parody as all his deputies hand back their badges to avoid the big gunfight), the Lord of the Jungle (wrestling bored lions and living in a tree penthouse with sidekick Zora) and hard-boiled dick Johnny Staccato (he wears two trench coats over his many holstered guns and another trench coat). Sanders, of course, pops up in each fantasy as a black hat who is out to get Sonny.

In the story, Cher is supposed to be less interested than Sonny in making a movie – which might well have been the truth, since she mostly lies around doodling outrageous fashion designs or contributing strange sung-through-the-nose vocals as poor goofy Sonny does all the hard work flogging life into skits which had most likely been rejected by the Monkees. The finale finds Sonny and Cher standing up for integrity and refusing to make a bad film even if it means they're blacklisted all over town – a lesson it's a shame that they (especially Cher) didn't take to heart.

Mordicus is so taken with their young free spirit that he doesn't destroy them professionally – for which we can all be grateful.

Astonishingly, the feature directorial debut of William Friedkin – who fills the screen with colour, action and gaggery after the manner of the then-hip *Batman* show while focusing on screaming outfits which remain among the darnedest things you ever saw.

GROUPIE GIRL (1970)

> 'OH LET'S SPLIT NOW BEFORE IT
> GETS TO BE A REAL DRAG.'
> 'NO, HANG ABOUT,
> IT MIGHT GET KINKY.'

A slice of up-to-the-minute tawdriness co-scripted by director Derek Ford and Suzanne Mercer, purportedly based on her own groupie experiences. Teenager Sally (Esme Johns) stows away in a rock group's transit van to get a lift to London, losing her virginity to one of the lads while the others are in an all-night caff. Waking up in a shared pad, she pretty much becomes furniture. In a signature moment, self-involved star Steve (Donald Sumpter) shoves Sally out the window of a moving van to offload her on another passing group, underlining her commodity status and incidentally causing one of those fatal crashes pop stars were wont to have. A comic bit is based on Mick Jagger's then-famous drugs bust, as Sally eats a lump of hash as the coppers show up. She nearly gets together with seemingly more sensitive Wesley (Billy Boyle), who might actually care about her – but his manager (Richard Shaw) orders him to get shot of her. Left with some money on a country road, Sally might as well go home. Ford tries some Richard Lesterisms, like opening credits written on a psychedelic van. Sexploitation business includes Steve having a three-way with the Collinson Twins, a dress-ripping backstage cat-fight and a decadent society party lorded over by an old queen where posh reprobates get it on with novelty hair band invitees in a make-an-animal-noise pair-up game. With Neil Hallett, James Beck, Ken Hutchison and Opal Butterfly as made-up band Sweaty Betty. Successful enough to inspire Lindsay Shonteff's superior *Permissive*.

HAPPY BIRTHDAY, WANDA JUNE (1971)

One of the first big studio movies to go almost unreleased, this odd, awkward film of a play by Kurt Vonnegut, Jr. was faithfully scripted by the author himself, scoring his only credit as screenwriter. Director Mark Robson, a journeyman with a career that ranges from *The Seventh Victim* to *Peyton Place*, doesn't show much of a knack for satire.

The action takes place almost completely on a big apartment set festooned with animal heads, with cutaways to Heaven where dead Wanda June (Pamelyn Ferdin) and a Nazi war criminal (Louis Turenne) play shuffleboard. Updating the story of Ulysses' return, Penelope (Susannah York – lovely but miscast) copes with two suitors – liberal wimp doctor Norbert Woodley (George Grizzard) and fawning macho vacuum cleaner salesman Herb Shuttle (Don Murray) – before her long-lost soldier/hunter husband Harold Ryan (Rod Steiger) returns, dragging along his sad-sack sidekick Looseleaf Harper (William H. Hickey). Harold's son Paul (Steven Paul, who would grow up to found the *Baby Geniuses* franchise) idolises his father while he's away, but is less happy having to live with him.

It's an attempt to tackle the era of Vietnam and making love not war with characters who seem like refugees from *The Dick Van Dyke Show*. Grizzard's pacifist doctor is a particularly weird representative of the counterculture (a longhair in a bar is more credible – one of the few additions to the play). Steiger is almost the whole show as a Hemingwayish man's man raging against the world, but also hurt by it as he becomes more brutal and obnoxious, pre-emptively alienating his wife, son and even his devoted but dim pal. Hickey, who met another version of Wanda June that same year in *Between Time and Timbuktu*, is on the money as the guy who dropped the Bomb on Nagasaki and now feels like a chump for following orders.

HEX (CHARMS, THE SHRIEKING) (1973)

This biker/art/western/horror hybrid is the only feature credit for director Leo Garen, whose CV includes directing episodes of *I Dream of Jeannie*, acting in Norman Mailer's *Maidstone* and scripting minor films (*Band of the Hand*) and TV movies (*Inflammable*). His co-writers have similar odd form: Doran William Cannon wrote hip films for older auteurs (Otto Preminger's disastrous *Skidoo*, Robert Altman's admirable post-*MASH* flop *Brewster McCloud*), Vernon Zimmerman directed exploitation (*Unholy*

Rollers, Fade to Black) and Steve Katz went into 1980s bubblegum TV (*The A-Team, Hardcastle and McCormick*).

The setting is Nebraska in the early 1920s. The back-of-nowhere on-the-road milieu almost excuses the hippie hairstyles, but the faces and attitudes on view scream '1973'. A gang of scruffy WWI veterans ride into town on army surplus sickles and get into a grudge race with local lout Brother Billy (future Grizzly Adams Dan Haggerty), whose souped-up Model T Ford is customised like a dragster ('It ain't fair,' he whines, 'I lost speed missin' that old lady.'). The bikers fetch up at an isolated farm run by strange sisters Oriole (Tina Herazo, who changed her name to Cristina Raines and starred in *Nashville* and *The Sentinel*) and Acacia (Hilary Thompson). As in other horror westerns of the time (*The Beguiled, Shadow of Chikara*), violent men meet their doom thanks to witchy womenfolk. Giblets (Gary Busey) foolishly makes aggressive moves against naïve Acacia. An owl rips his face off and Oriole won't let his comrades bury him on her property. Spells whittle down the gang: bike mama China (Doria Cook) has an imaginatively shot bad trip by the waterhole, Jimbang (Scott Glenn) suffers when a pistol he has personally restored blows up, and mute 'half-breed' Chupo (Robert Walker Jr) becomes possessed and turns on gang leader Whizzer (Keith Carradine).

Drive-in audiences expecting something like *Werewolves on Wheels* must have scratched their heads, and elements (the twanging mouth organ/jew's harp/kazoo music score) were horribly dated even at the time. But *Hex* is still fascinating and unusual. The performances, from future stars and future nobodies alike, are all strong, with scenes between Busey and Glenn an object lesson in over- and underacting: Busey does everything but grab the camera and shake it, while Glenn barely changes expression and steals every moment. Photographed with an acid haze by Charles Rosher (*The Cat Creature, Three Women*).

HI, MOM! (BLUE MANHATTAN) (1970)

Brian De Palma's sequel to his counterculture hit *Greetings* strings together satirical/ political sketches like some crossbreed of Godard and *The Groove Tube*. Voyeur Jon Rubin (De Niro) rents a rattrap apartment purely because it affords him a *Rear Window* view of a highrise that affords him a chance to create 'peep art', financed by a porno entrepreneur (Allen Garfield), which spins off into a series of subversive gestures which are at least as much down to personal kink as political or artistic endeavour.

After Hitchcockian gazing, which foreshadows the De Palma of *Sisters* and *Body Double*, Jon sets up the elaborate seduction of dippy Judy Bishop (Jennifer Salt) – she nods sagely when he says 'tragedy is such a funny thing' – timing things perfectly to get their sex on film, though her embarrassing ardour puts him in the awkward position of having to delay the action twenty-five minutes. The tripod droops at the crucial moment, aiming into another apartment. A long segment in black and white is supposedly a National Intellectual Television broadcast of *Be Black Baby*, a theatrical happening in which white liberal audience members are blacked up, force-fed soulfood by whitefaced black performers, robbed and raped and beaten and then disbelieved by a cop (De Niro), only to leave happy and enthusiastic about 'understanding the black experience'. More disturbing than funny, the segment almost prefigures Michael Haneke's grim lectures (the rape humour also points the way to future De Palma controversies).

After bombing a commune to get on TV in his army uniform, urban guerrilla Jon ends the film with its title, said to camera… here, De Niro flashes what might be an embryo Travis Bickle. With Gerrit Graham, Paul Bartel, Charles Durning (billed as 'Durnham'), Lara Parker (*Dark Shadows*), Ruth (later Rutanya) Alda and enough sex or pseudo-sex scenes for Troma to re-release it as *Blue Manhattan*.

IDENTIKIT (THE DRIVER'S SEAT) (1974)

> 'WHEN I DIET I DIET AND WHEN I ORGASM I ORGASM. I DON'T BELIEVE IN MIXING THE TWO CULTURES.'

Based on a novel by Muriel Spark, this peculiar Italian art movie from director/co-writer Giuseppe Patroni Griffi enshrines remarkable work from star Elizabeth Taylor. She was mocked by critics and camp followers for her hideous hairstyle, ghastly fashion sense and embalmed makeup in this film, though these are choices as perfectly considered as her looks in *Cleopatra* or *Who's Afraid of Virginia Woolf?*

Lise (Taylor) picks out a garish psychedelic dress for a special trip, then has a tantrum in the shop when told the fabric is stain-resistant. The film is full of off-kilter non sequitur moments which play games with Taylor's diva status: Lise marches past long queues at an airport and declares, 'It's a bomb,' while showing her handbag to security staff, is alternately solicitous and high-handed with everyone she meets, and brandishes a trashy paperback as if signalling a blind date who's days overdue. Intercut with Lise's careening around are scenes of the police grilling people she has come into contact with, though it remains ambiguous whether she's victim or perpetrator of the crime under investigation. On the plane, Lise is happy to be seated next to quiet, handsome young Pierre (Maxence Mailfort), but he dashes off to another row when boorish Bill (Ian Bannen, grinning like a fiend) joins them and aggressively chats her up. In the city, Lise runs into both men again… and also a widow (Mona Washbourne) who turns out to be Pierre's concerned aunt, plus a stereotypically randy mechanic (Guido Mannari) who tries to take advantage of the discombobulated heroine in the aftermath of a petrol bomb attack on a sheik's limousine.

Some weirdnesses are explained away: the Antonioniesque absence of people on the streets and in a shopping mall turns out to be because people are staying indoors during a terrorist bomb campaign. Other details – a woman asking which of two paperbacks is likely to be 'the more sadomasochistic', Lise fondling souvenir paper knives, the precise nature of Pierre's panic – only make sense after the final encounter, in which the dress gets stained and a knife used in a foggy park. Spark's black joke is to darken the cliché of the middle-aged woman coming to Italy to be seduced by a younger man by having a protagonist seeking not romance but death then be annoyed to run into rapists rather than murderers. A unique casting coup is that Andy Warhol, no less, appears briefly as a white-suited English milord.

THE INSOMNIAC (1971)

At 44 minutes, this is either a long short or a short feature. The only fiction work of writer-director Rodney Giesler, it's an extended fantasy of escape and repression – perhaps more memorable for its unsettling stretches than its somewhat banal message.

An unnamed middle-class family man (Morris Perry) lives in a London tower block and suffers from sleeplessness. He reads a significant children's story about a dragon who lives in two worlds (one idyllic, one horrid) and isn't sure which is a dream. Paradoxically at once sleepless and dreaming, he finds himself driving through green, lush countryside. He encounters well-dressed, sinister figures with reflective dark glasses – a pair of policemen and a jovial type who asks for a lift to a party where vampirish folk chatter grotesquely behind tight curtains and get violently angry when the light is let in. He coaxes a cool blonde (Valerie Ost, from *The Satanic Rites of Dracula*) away into the countryside. She takes off her glasses and they both take off their clothes to enjoy X-certificate sex in a pond. This erotic natural bliss is jarred when the dreamer wakes up in King's Cross. Tuxedoed tormentors from the dream pursue him across urban wasteland between gasholders and kick his clothes in the canal, then jeer at his muddy nakedness. The blonde drifts back to the sneering haut bourgeois creatures. The man is returned to his home by a policeman, and his wife (Patricia Leventon) is – quite properly – fed up with his straying, even if only in fantasy; after all, she lives where he does, and furthermore has to put up with his self-pity and dreams of blonde posh crumpet.

It's very of its time. Now, the urban desolation looks almost quaint – though the dinner jacketed remain sinister.

JOANNA (1968)

Between singing novelty hit 'Come Outside' (with Wendy Richard) and directing the doomed *Myra Breckinridge*, Michael Sarne wrote and directed this richly coloured Swinging London widescreen picaresque. Starlet Geneviève Waïte (Bijou Phillips' mum) is Joanna Sorrin, a free-spirited, well-off blonde from Frome who comes to the city as an art student and gets mixed up with various men. The most substantial episodes involve terminally-ill aristocratic drop-out Lord Peter Sanderson (Donald Sutherland, doing the most peculiar voice) who hosts an unending party (cue: trip to North Africa) and slightly shady black immigrant Gordon (Calvin Lockhart) who gets hassled by the fuzz – mostly for having too nice a flat and a white girlfriend. Waïte is alternately irritating and appealing, and Sarne carefully shows how much damage her fun-loving lifestyle wreaks, with a tolerant Granny (Marda Vanne) furious and tearful at her callous disregard and the shocked wife of one of her pick-ups shattered as Joanna blithely skips out after a one-night stand. A musical reprise finale in a railway station might have been an influence on *Slumdog Millionaire*. Rod McKuen's songs are lightweight, but the fashions and décors are groovy. With the very beautiful black model Glenna Forster-Jones (in an interestingly unstereotyped role), Anthony Ainley, Fiona Lewis, Sibylla Kay, Jenny Hanley, Richard Hurndall, David Collings and Caroline Munro. Produced by Michael S. Laughlin, who later directed *Strange Behavior* and *Strange Invaders*.

THE LOVE WITCH (2016)

Chic, poised, sensual Elaine (Samantha Robinson) – fleeing San Francisco and a relationship which has ended badly (especially for her lover) – settles in a quiet Northern California town. The community is open-minded enough to support a well-established witch coven among quaint ladies' tea shops and go-go dance bars. Augmenting her natural attractions with love philtres and witch bottles (mystic artefacts which involve urine and used tampons), Elaine sets out to find a suitable new man. This leads to legal complications since those she seduces tend to disappoint the next morning, and her cast-offs are inclined to sudden death by heart failure or suicide. She acquires a nemesis in realtor Trish (Laura Waddell), wife of one of her victims, but perhaps meets a match in macho cop Griff (Gian Keys), who investigates cases in which she is implicated but is still susceptible to her (literal) charms. Lord Bernard (Bernard Bullen) and Mandy (Dani Lennon), the coven's leading lights, pass their circle off as a renaissance fayre to lure Griff into a form of binding ceremony, but also wonder whether Elaine isn't too self-obsessed for the good of their relationship with non-pagan locals who only need a few rumours to form a traditional 'burn the witch' mob.

Following *Viva*, a pastiche of psychedelic sexploitation, all-round auteur Anna Biller immerses herself in an artificial world inspired by 1970s soap opera, TV movies, Italian and American horror films and post-hippie colour-supplement Wiccan glamour to create a wholly engaging straight-faced melodrama with barbed feminist footnotes. Besides directing, writing and producing, Biller edits, supervises the music (mixing her own compositions – including songs – with selections from *giallo* soundtracks after the manner of Tarantino or Hélène Cattet and Bruno Forzani), acts as production designer and set decorator (down to hand-crafting props) and supervises costumes (doing an awards-quality job). Almost the only gig she doesn't take is cinematography, but M. David Mullen (*Jennifer's Body*), shooting on 35mm film, fully enters into her mindset: primary colours pop so that odd props (an apple-red cigarette carton) take on sinister meaning. About the only filmmakers who have previously attained this level of control over their visions are Russ Meyer and Wes Anderson; the fact that *The Love Witch* evokes both their self-enclosed universes but with a uniquely female viewpoint suggests the freshness and strangeness of Biller's imagination.

Though a little too languid at two hours, *The Love Witch* is appropriately seductive. The deliberately muted performances of a cast selected because they look like 1970s models – with a nice throwaway about *The Stepford Wives* – are a dead-on match for

Biller's on-the-nose dialogue exchanges and ritual-like scenes of witch cults, tea parties and pole-dancing. It's a shock half way through when Trish pulls out a mobile phone and, later, DNA analysis of fluids used in a witch bottle leads Griff to Elaine – because otherwise this would seem to be set in the period it evokes. Like Cattet and Forzani (*Amer*, *The Strange Colour of Your Body's Tears*), Biller does more than resurrect a chic, cool bygone film style. Biller counters many of the underlying assumptions of the male-directed exploitation films she evokes (*The Mephisto Waltz*, *Simon King of the Witches*, *All the Colors of the Dark*) even as Elaine is ultimately shown to be a genuine monster for the unsisterly treatment of other women which goes along with her relentless romantic self-interest.

MORE (1969)

A Euro-hippie trip from Barbet Schroeder, chronicling the unfortunate involvement of just-graduated German youth Stefan (Klaus Grünberg) with pixieish free spirit Estelle (Mimsy Farmer). Grünberg follows the girl from Paris to Ibiza, where she is mixed up with Dr Wolf (Heinz Engelmann), a sinister German who amuses himself throwing swastika-hilted daggers and turns out to be a drug supplier. Stefan starts out with half a conscience, willing to join a friend in light housebreaking but unhappy that his partner has ripped off Estelle to finance the job. He also disapproves of Estelle's supposedly prior heroin use – but himself samples multiple drugs and gets hooked enough to wind up in an unsanctified grave. Farmer's Estelle is enigmatic and eye-catching, but protagonist Stefan is a prig who turns into a drag. With pleasantly stoned soundtrack burbling from 'the pink floyd' and sun-struck Nestor Almendros photography of the then-exotic isle. It manages drugginess without cliché effects by becoming as fixated as tripping characters on mercury swirling in a pan. Farmer scores a credit for helping out with the 'final dialogue'.

MURDER A LA MOD (1967)

For decades, *Murder a la Mod* was impossible to see, and studies of director Brian De Palma had to skip his feature debut. Now it slots in place as a key work. Given that it was barely a step up from a student film, *Murder a la Mod* is astonishingly confident and points the way to the politically engaged crazy comedy De Palma of *Greetings*, *Hi, Mom!* and *Home Movies*, but also the icy, tricksy slasher De Palma of *Sisters*, *Dressed to Kill* and *Body Double*. A 'screen test' sequence, in which girls (including Jennifer Salt of *Sisters*) are nagged to disrobe by an offscreen director who tries to get an undefinable reaction out of them is reprised in *The Black Dahlia*, down to De Palma again voicing the unseen director.

Murder a la Mod owes debts to film student set texts like *Rashomon*, *Psycho* and *Peeping Tom*, but has its own spiky identity. It plays and replays a sequence of events to give radically different points of view on the seeming and/or real death of actress/ model Karen (Margo Norton). She is involved with Chris (Jared Martin, later a star of Lucio Fulci films), a self-involved film student making a skinflick at the behest of cigar-puffing, sunglasses-sporting producer Wiley (Ken Burrows), an early incarnation of the hustlers played by Allen Garfield and Paul Williams in *Greetings* and *Phantom of the Paradise*. Chris is callous and ambitious enough to exploit his girlfriend for his movie, whether it be showing her naked or using footage of her genuine death. This theme recurs in *Blow Out*, where a sound man uses his girlfriend's death scream on a cheap horror film. De Palma was already examining his own tendency to subject women to staged indignities 'for the good of the film'. At one point, Karen, bloody and wrapped in plastic, lurches into frame looking like Sissy Spacek in *Carrie* – or Stefania Sandrelli's in *Suspiria*, come to that.

But *Murder a la Mod* isn't just a psycho-horror film: it's NYC student *nouvelle vaguerie*, with an anarchic comedy twist and a catchy, campy theme sung by William Finley (later the mad composer of *Phantom of the Paradise*). Otto (Finley) loons about in leather trousers, multiple layers of clothes and a weird moustache – getting a fake ice pick used as a film prop mixed up with a real one, despite the frame freezing and onscreen tags identifying which is which. Seemingly mute, this combination holy fool/imp of the perverse mutters interior monologue on the soundtrack when his viewpoint takes over. When Otto first attacks Karen, she is irritated at being smeared with ketchup; the next time, she's gruesomely stabbed in the eye in the first of De Palma's shock murder scenes. Some supporting performances are rough, but De Palma already has a knack with interesting actresses; Norton (who never acted again) is fresh, natural and engaging, grounding the film between Martin's unsympathetic cool and Finley's gooning.

PERMISSIVE (1970)

> 'I THOUGHT HE LIKED ME.
> I THOUGHT HE WAS MARVELLOUS
> UNTIL HE LEFT ME
> LYING ON THE FLOOR.'

An odd, distinctive aspect of the 1970s British sex film is a tendency to be exploitative yet miserable. Flesh is bared glumly and drugs give downers but no highs, like an illustrated *Daily Mail* editorial. The Wardour Street mix of salaciousness and sneer is encapsulated in the double-edged title of Lindsay Shonteff's pop scene exposé, though it would have been even more flavoursome under the working title, *Suzy Superscrew*.

The trailer ('in the backstabbing backroom world of the groupie girl') as much as admits *Permissive* is an imitation of Donald and Derek Ford's successful *Groupie Girl*, but the film is also a missing link between Ken Loach's *Family Life* and Pete Walker's *Cool It, Carol!* Suzy (Maggie Stride), a frail, longhaired girl in a duffel coat, arrives in London from the provinces (of course she doesn't have a regional accent). School friend Fiona (Gay Singleton) brings her into the entourage of hairy group Forever More – a real act, who would mutate into the aptly named Average White Band. Fiona, semi-exclusive girlfriend of bearded singer/songwriter Lee (Alan Gorrie), gives Suzy fabber clothes and protects her from feral harpies in maxi-dresses competing for temporary status as alpha shag. When the group go out of town and the promise of crash-space at another groupie's pad evaporates, Suzy dosses on bomb sites with spaced-out busker Pogo (Robert Daubigney). Pogo has an 'episode' in a church and gets run over in the street, driving Suzy back into the orbit of Forever More and their odious tour manager Jimi (Gilbert Wynne).

The sad sad story is predictable; in *nouvelle vague*-ish manner, Shonteff continually cuts in flash-forwards which show what will happen to all the characters, defusing horrors (Fiona's razorblade suicide in the bath) with foreshadowing glimpses. Suzy becomes a ruthless, calculating slut-bitch and sleeps her way through the band, displacing Fiona with zombie-like git Lee. Superscrewed over, Fiona sits miserably in the park for a while (to the accompaniment of Forever More's whinily memorable 'Sylvester's Last Voyage') and has a low-wattage *All About Eve* confrontation/cat-fight with Suzy. Coldly rejected by Lee, Fiona cuts her wrists in the bath as the group are leaving the hotel. Suzy nips back to fix her makeup, and finds Fiona dazed and bloody but still alive. The girls exchange a look, and Suzy leaves without saying anything, shutting the door on her (dying?) ex-friend. For a moment, the impassive Stride is truly frightening.

Shonteff (*Devil Doll*) goes for grim but credible: hotel suites where there's nowhere to sleep because all spaces (including the toilet) are taken by groping couples; post-coital chat ('You weren't much good last time.') in narrow single beds; folk-rock-scored wandering around bleak, bomb-damaged London; ominous pronouncements ('The graveyards are full of indispensable people.'); inexpressive, callous, barely-awake musicians (Gorrie, not an actor, is perfect) and hard-eyed hangers-on (the band are real musos, the girls mostly glamour models – including Madeleine and Mary Collinson, the *Twins of Evil*, who had been in *Groupie Girl*); too many people piling into a transit van for an out-of-town gig; leg-stretching larks in copses by the motorway under slate-grey skies (this is as much of a road movie as Britain can manage); groupies who spend concerts loitering in the dressing room for pole position ('I gave the manager a free screw to get back here.') and are bored by the endless fiddling of studio sessions (the girls never say whether they like the band's *music*); suede jackets, green smock-shirts, scarves used as headbands and purple paisley see-through blouses; cheap hotel tea services and ridiculously large joints. Jeremy Craig Dryden's script notes that – besides sexual availability – a groupie's duties extend to cooking, washing, hotel booking and carrying gear like an unpaid roadie.

UN POSTO IDEALE PER UCCIDER (OASIS OF FEAR, DIRTY PICTURES, AN IDEAL PLACE TO KILL) (1971)

'IT'S NOT JUST A HOLIDAY. WE'RE DEDICATED MISSIONARIES BRINGING THE GOSPEL OF SEXUAL FREEDOM TO DARKEST ITALY.'

Throughout a career in Italian exploitation, Umberto Lenzi turned from genre to genre, often making films in batches to ride a current vogue (gory cannibal, twisted *giallo*, western, tough cop, masked mystery man, war movie). This falls in with a bunch of Lenzi movies which seem to *want* to be interchangeable (*Orgasmo* aka *Paranoia* and *Paranoia* aka *A Quiet Place to Kill*) and straggles from freewheeling hippie drop-out movie into an it's-all-a-plot plot about rich folks trying to get away with murder.

English longhair Dick Butler (Raymond Lovelock, in a shagadelic Union Jack jacket) and his presumably Swedish girlfriend Ingrid Sjoman (Ornella Muti, whose character name is probably an homage to the director of *I Am Curious – Yellow*) bum about Europe, financing their protest-and-freakout lifestyle by making and selling smutty pictures (the astonishingly beautiful Muti has a body double for these). After evading Italian cops – yes, this suggests an English guy is more sexually liberated than any Italian, a notion possible only in a brief 1967-73 window – and getting ripped off by bikers, the couple semi-invade the remote villa of older, elegant, neurotic Barbara Slater (Irene Papas), who is married to a seldom-seen NATO official, and get round her with a series of tame-ish sex games. But, of course, there's a murder scheme in the offing.

The finish, maybe inspired by producer Carlo Ponti's wish to do something like *Easy Rider*, has the youngsters killed when their car goes off a cliff in a police chase. Lenzi finds interesting things to point his camera at – a Copenhagen red light district location, Muti bending over in brief yellow shorts, cinema vérité hippie hanging-out, the elegant villa décor – but loses grip on the story. This is a half-hour *Alfred Hitchcock Presents* plot spun out with red herring suspense sequences (including a bird attack in an aviary) and exploitation padding (like the 'dirty pictures' angle). The cast is interesting: Papas makes a change from Carroll Baker (star of *Orgasmo* and *Paranoia*) as the older mystery woman, and the faintly repulsive Lovelock is well partnered with Muti. A poppy, swingle score – including a jangling theme song – adds kitsch value, even as it cuts against the sexiness and the suspense.

PUFNSTUF (1970)

'WHAT IS IT ABOUT YOU
ROTTEN GOOD GUYS?
YOU ALWAYS WIN!'

Despite the presence of a post-*Oliver!* Jack Wild, this feature spin-off from Sid and Marty Krofft's kids' TV series *H.R. Pufnstuf* is utterly bizarre to British eyes (Krofft shows didn't play in the UK). Even without the notionally countercultural presence of Mama Cass(!) in warty makeup as Witch Hazel, the title's drug reference suggests a kandy-koloured trip for preteens of the Woodstock Nation.

Monkee-mopped lad Jimmy (Wild) is hassled by Yank brats who joke about him being 'kicked out of jolly old England'. He meets and befriends a talking flute (made of gold and encrusted with jewels) who guides him aboard a talking boat for Living Island, where dragon H.R. Pufnstuf (voiced by Allan Melvin) is mayor and (of course) everything is alive. As in Oz, trouble comes from a resident witch: Witchiepoo (Billie Hayes) wants to wrest the valuable bauble from the newcomer (Hayes even cackles like Margaret Hamilton). Jimmy makes fast friends of performers in oversized baggy felt costumes, who help him hang on to the flute. Witchiepoo wants to win 'Witch of the Year' from the Boss Witch (Martha Raye), but Jimmy and his pals are all about liberating that freakin' flute.

A hippie tree talks about trips, uses the expression 'bummer' and lets Jimmy get away with saying, 'It beats the knickers off band practice'; either rigid censorship of kids' films was slipping or blue-pencillers hadn't kept up with dope slang and British expressions. To the uninitiated, the denizens of Living Island are an annoying, inept lot – sweaty performers dressed in colourful garments that only vaguely resemble spiders, gophers, birds or clocks or whatever they're supposed to be. Several aerial bombing scenes in which Witchiepoo does flyovers on a broomstick with a sidecar and pelts the Pufnstuffers may be a Vietnam reference. A long routine involves the Good Guys persuading the villain that her castle is on fire by having the useless Googy Gopher import smoke from a heavy smoking fireplace. They show up in their official position as the fire brigade and rob the place, which is ethically dubious as well as crack-brained. The songs are horrible, horrible, horrible and it looks like Technicolor puke. Directed by Hollingsworth Morse (*Daughters of Satan*).

PUSSYCAT, PUSSYCAT, I LOVE YOU (1970)

'ARE YOU SURE WE'RE DOING THE RIGHT THING.'
'TRUST ME, IF I DIDN'T THINK IT WAS RIGHT I WOULDN'T SUGGEST A DOUBLE SUICIDE.'

This less-remembered semi-sequel to *What's New Pussycat?* climaxes with a pre-*Blazing Saddles* chase across movie sets, affording a valuable glimpse of filmmaking in Italy c. 1970 ('Rome wasn't made in a day, but these spaghetti westerns are.'). Playwright Fred C. Dobbs (Ian McShane) lives in Rome with wife Millie (Anna Calder-Marshall) and spends afternoons with mistress Ornella (Beba Loncar), but feeds the fantasies of his scalpologist (Severn Darden) with tales of other sexual escapades – and in neurotic dreams is romantically pursued by Milton the gay gorilla (Janos Prohaska). Its would-be sophisticated references (pop art, Fellini) are strained, but it has a few funny lines ('If all the pills you took were outside instead of inside of you, you'd look like a beaded dress.').

With Gaby André (*The Strange World of Planet X*), Marino Masé (*Lady Frankenstein*), Ian Trigger (short chiropodist), Joyce Van Patten (stern wife joke), John Gavin (movie star Grant Granite), Veronica Carlson (therapist at a weight loss spa called Battle of the Bulge), Madeline Smith, Katia Christine (*5 Dolls for an August Moon*), Richard Harrison (a cowboy actor), Janet Agren, Paul Muller (a guru) and Karin Schubert (*Bluebeard*). Lalo Schifrin's score includes 'Groove Into It' (not as big a hit as Burt Bacharach's 'What's New Pussycat'); a destructing typewriter in-joke excerpts Schifrin's *Mission: Impossible* theme. Cinematography by Tonino Delli Colli. Written and directed by Rod Amateau (*Daddy-O*, *Son of Hitler*, *The Garbage Pail Kids Movie*).

REFLECTIONS OF EVIL (2002)

There's a reason the title sounds like a 1970s TV movie. Director-writer-star-distributor Damon Packard's self-indulgent, mercilessly long (138 minutes) effort is obsessed with that genre, time and form: padding 'action' out with commercials from the '60s and '70s which hawk the ABC *Movie of the Week* or *Night Gallery*.

A sequence set on the Universal lot in 1972 involves touring the set of *The Omega Man* – passing the ground where the bodies were buried in *What Ever Happened To Aunt Alice?* – and loitering as young Steven Spielberg pisses off the veteran crew assigned to *Something Evil*. Sounds interesting? Well, in parts. Too much of it has the enormously obese Bob (ordinarily fat Packard bulked out by padding, multiple layers of clothing and many sets of headphones) wandering LA streets, hawking crap watches, yelling 'I'll fucking kill ya' at people (many yell back) and stuffing himself with junk food despite the complaints of his shrill mother. Scenes of a girl in a nightdress wandering past modern buildings perfectly mimic 1970s TV style, but they're outweighed by irritating rambles.

A great deal of the film has street people snarling and snapping (and dogs doing the same), with sound effects ramped up to underline the we're-all-dogs point. The film revolves around the Universal tour and finishes with a strange sequence snatched inside the *E. T.* exhibit and a conceptually funny-sick bit as a ghost takes a notional *Schindler's List* ride. For what was presumably a homemade film, it's undeniably ambitious and has moments of inspiration and invention. Typical of Packard's repurposing is the opening – a generic Tony Curtis intro for a 'classic' PD video release with strategic but obvious redubbings. The cruellest joke may be the 'to be continued' sign-off. Rumours of a 280-minute version persist.

O RITUAL DOS SÁDICOS (O DESPERTAR DA BESTIA; AWAKENING OF THE BEAST) (1970)

> 'MY WORLD IS STRANGE, BUT IT IS WORTHY OF ALL THOSE WILLING TO ACCEPT IT, AND NEVER AS CORRUPT AS SOME WOULD HAVE IT. MY WORLD, MY FRIEND, IS MADE OF STRANGE PEOPLE, BUT THERE ARE NONE AS STRANGE AS YOU!'

Brazilian writer/director José Mojica Marins introduced top-hat-and-talons alter ego Zé do Caixão, an atheist undertaker set against morality, in *A meia noite levarei sua alma/At Midnight I Will Steal Your Soul* (1963) and *Esta Noite Encarnarei no Teu Cadáver/This Night I Will Possess Your Corpse* (1966). This footnote has Marins appear as his famous character (and himself) in snippets which punctuate a picaresque ramble through 1960s high/low life. In heavily shadowed framing sequences, Marins argues with a psychiatrist and other worthies in a minimalist TV talk show. For half the film, these humourless stiffs rant about the dreadful state of morals, cuing vignettes spotlighting obvious and unappealing decadence. Mostly, it's topless nightclub dancing to Brazilian mutant beat music, with drug taking and fetishist/s-m orgies: a naked girl on a chamber pot ogled by a roomful of men, a lass in school uniform fingered by another crowd, a slim starlet surrendering to a gross producer, a hippie-look Jesus violating a woman with a tree-branch. *Another* TV show puts Marins on 'trial', with *cinema novo* director Glauber Rocha as witness for the defence. Evidence is presented of Zé's high pop-culture profile: posters, comics, a TV show, a cinema screening *Esta Noite...*, even a novelty samba record. Is Zé part of the trends this film exploits and condemns or does he stand above it all, pouring scorn on hippies and junkies?

In the climax, four characters take part in an LSD experiment and agree to focus on Zé. They pass out of the film's black and white reality to enter his weirdly coloured world. In this set piece, Zé walks down human stairs, faces of chattering grotesques turn out to be painted on bottoms, more unclad women are whipped and Zé rants about the nature of something or other. The twist is that the psychologist admits he gave his subjects distilled water rather than LSD: the visions came from their own psyches. Written by pulpster Rubens F. Lucchetti rather than Marins, it is significantly more pretentious than the earlier films, as if the director were trying to deliver artier elements some perceived in his rawer, more personal work. The tag, as Marins watches a minor drama on the street (a boy picks up a girl and drives off, watched by her friend from the pavement), perhaps thinking of a story to be spun from this tiny incident, is a clumsy conflation of the finishes of *8 ½* and *L'Eclisse*.

The first Zé films are rural gothics; this moves to bustling Sao Paolo, where Zé himself is practically overwhelmed. I suspect someone told Marins the hell scene of *Esta Noite...* was like an acid trip, inspiring him to capitalise on the association. Nothing here suggests deep thought about drugs (or, indeed, anything else). It rambles, with amazing moments buried in *longeurs*, but is a unique mix of Jean-Luc Godard's *Tout Va Bien* (Rocha's other 'acting' credit) and *Wes Craven's New Nightmare*.

ROMA DROGATA... LA POLIZIA NON PUÒ INTERVENIRE (HALLUCINATION STRIP) (1975)

The selling-point of this cop-vs-hippie picture is an elaborate (and impressive, if silly) acid trip sequence from the viewpoint of weird, wealthy young Rudy (Settimio Segnatelli) – his mother (Eva Czemerys) and her maid still give him elaborate baths, though he's nearly twenty – featuring body-painted writhing dancers as bird- or snake-people hatching out of a plastic tent, incestuous and/or homoerotic fantasies and his semi-animated transformation into a leafy landscape – and climaxes inevitably with suicide.

Otherwise, this is a cynical portrait of politically active, sensation-seeking young folks and their superficial, rich elders. A plodding copper (Marcel Bozzuffi) investigates a seemingly trivial crime (the theft of a snuff box) which gives him a shot at a big-time drug dealer, and the chance to disapprove of almost everyone he meets on the case. Bud Cort, wide-eyed and strange-looking as always, is Massimo, a hanger-on with a rich girlfriend (Annarita Grapputo), gets deeper in trouble as he tries ineptly to help his fickle friends. By 1975, the Corman-style trippiness was already dated, but this has decent psychedelic rock chanting, eye-popping mod-hippie fashions, some on-the-streets *vérité* demo footage, and a sense of restless Roman life. In disenchanted, conspiracy theory fashion, dogged cop and would-be revolutionary are both inconvenient to a ruthless establishment (which includes the catholic church, who pressure the cops to put Rudy's death down to whiskey rather than LSD).

A few striking vignettes puncture the pretensions of radical types – a middle-class drug offender snubbed by young criminals in prison, rich young dropouts patronise the butler who serves them spaghetti – but the cop delivers blunt speeches about irresponsible parents too. Like many 1970s cruelty-of-society pictures, it ends with a protagonist shot (by a pet shop managing hitman) and lying dead, ignored in the gutter as life goes on unheeding. Scripted by Vincenzo Mannino (*The New York Ripper*), Josè Sanchez, and one-time-only director Lucio Marcaccini.

A SAFE PLACE (1971)

> 'YOU'RE PRETTY AND SAD AND WEIRDER THAN HELL.'

Produced by BBS – the outfit which spear-headed a youthful movement in American cinema with *Easy Rider*, *Five Easy Pieces* and *The Last Picture Show* – this was the debut of writer-director Henry Jaglom. He took six years to make another film (*Tracks*), but didn't click commercially until *Sitting Ducks* gave him a brief vogue. Many find Jaglom's later personal movies indulgent; he usually strikes me as interesting, if slightly whiny.

Counterculture cinema tended to get hung up on rebellious, violent macho men. Like *The Rain People* and *Alice Doesn't Live Here Anymore*, *A Safe Place* admirably goes against that grain by spotlighting a woman, though fragile and neurotic seem the easiest descriptions of these heroines (see also *Diary of a Mad Housewife*, *Images* or even *Let's Scare Jessica to Death*). The always-adventurous Tuesday Weld is mercurial and mesmerising as Susan aka Noah, who drifts about New York being enigmatic, remembering or fantasising about magical childhood abilities, courted by a nice-guy rich-kid drop-out (Philip Procter) and a handsome heel (BBS regular Jack Nicholson). In an odd choice, Jaglom cuts away to stoned, blissed-out folk listening to Bari (Gwen Welles) talk about a dissociative experience – as if the protagonist were split into several personas (we see Susan as a little girl too) or Weld left the project before filming a key scene.

Sleight of hand is repped by Orson Welles stalking as an accented magician, looking much as he does in Brian De Palma's *Get to Know Your Rabbit* and his own *F for Fake*. The dope-fuelled, fractured conversations are credibly enervating, setting up pointed moments as Noah repeatedly tries to get men to be quiet and listen. The familiar hippie-chic freak look has New Wave or Cassavetes technique applied to longhairs, but Jaglom puts Vera Lynn, Charles Trenet and Dooley Wilson on his soundtrack (well before Woody Allen rooted through his jazz collection), rather than the contemporary sounds of *Easy Rider*; at the time, this was fresh, though some tunes ('La Mer' was heavily featured in *Tinker, Tailor, Soldier, Spy*, for instance) have been so often reused as to become cliché.

SECRET CEREMONY (1968)

Based on a Marco Denevi short story – adapted several times for Argentine and Spanish television – this mystifying, underrated exercise in gothic dress-up, role-play and old dark house camp is a female-oriented counterpart to director Joseph Losey's breakthrough film *The Servant*. In place of a male servant-and-master relationship, it has a mother-and-daughter axis, but its psycho-drama also plays out in a London mansion which embodies the mental and physical decay of the ruling classes. In contrast to the cool, Expressionist black and white of *The Servant*, this offers gloomy colour cinematography from Gerry Fisher, prefiguring his work on other mansion-set movies (*Malpertuis*, *Blind Terror/See No Evil*). Production design by Richard Macdonald (*Something Wicked This Way Comes*) and art direction by John Clark (who decorated the tonally similar *Performance*) add mod touches to the traditional olde junke shoppe aesthetic (magpie aunts actually raid the place for portable tat to sell in their antique shop). The striking location (Debenham House, Holland Park) was later used in *Carry On Emmannuelle* and *The Wings of the Dove*.

It opens with what seems a meet-weird on the upper deck of a London bus between two strange women who – it transpires – are already in the midst of an extended game. Earthy, mature Leonora (Elizabeth Taylor) has descended into alcoholism and prostitution after the death of her child (and the breakup of her marriage), but found a place in the orbit of fragile, infantile Cenci Englehard (Mia Farrow), who has managed to get Leonora to take the place of her dead mother amid the funereal splendour of a house stuffed full of designer knickknacks. Hannah (Peggy Ashcroft) and Hilda (Pamela Brown), the dead mother's sisters, occasionally visit to gossip, chide and steal – exploiting the enormously wealthy, apparently demented Cenci. The family money comes from her dead father Gustave, but a satyr-bearded, flower-presenting wicked stepfather is in the mix. Albert (Robert Mitchum, off his usual beat), a randy and perhaps paedophile academic, may have been an earlier partner in Cenci's fantasies. He constitutes a leering, eccentric threat to the oddball idyll and also gets the funniest line: 'I couldn't rape a randy elephant – I'm much too tentative.'

Like *The Servant* – deliberately evoked as the women take a trip to the seaside and Losey pauses to overhear a snatch of conversation from the next table – this follows shifts of power in a co-dependent or symbiotic relationship between a wealthy neurotic and an adaptive hanger-on, though here the viewpoint character is the outsider and the unknowable manipulator is the home-owner. *Secret Ceremony* – like Losey's other Liz Taylor charade *Boom!* – is indulgent of its stars (who parade in amazing outfits and have theatrical meltdown scenes), in contrast with the firmer control Losey had on *The Servant*'s James Fox and Dirk Bogarde. It was also evidently a troubled production, as anything involving Mia Farrow and Elizabeth Taylor in 1968 was bound to be. A creepy, disjointed film, it finds neither Taylor nor Farrow completely on form. When Cenci becomes by turns more childish (stuffing a toy frog up her dress to simulate pregnancy) and adult (abandoning the game of neurosis to appear rational during her craziest stretch), Farrow seems in the dark about her character's mental state. The seaside trip, which uses Dutch locations, shows why Fisher might have attracted the attention of *Malpertuis* director Harry Kümel: a ring of wicker beach chairs arranged like stooping megaliths is an especially memorable image. Losey also makes careful use of sound – with a disturbing array of 'noises off' throughout, and an eerie score (incorporating the occasional *ondes martenot* ululation) from Richard Rodney Bennett (*The Witches*)

SEPARATION (1968)

This British art film was once dismissed by critics who loved this sort of thing with subtitles but thought it pretentious or derivative for an English-language movie to evoke Antonioni, Godard, Resnais and Fellini. Jane (writer Jane Arden) is separated from her bespectacled, smarmily analytical Husband (David de Keyser) and has great sex with a young Lover (Iain Quarrier, in an extended take on his male pin-up role from *Cul-de-Sac*) while her personality fractures. The separation also involves several women – Arden made up as an Agatha Christie granny (though reading John Dickson Carr) and a blonde Woman (Ann Lynn) who might be Jane's alternate personality. It has a Procol Harum score and Warholish effects – lava lamp projections on disintegrating photographs, and mostly black and white visions of anonymous London locations (a women-only swimming bath, a depopulated park) with vividly coloured sci-fi-looking inserts. Directed by Jack Bond.

STRAIGHT ON TILL MORNING (1972)

Though *Straight on Till Morning* wound up on a 'Women in Terror!' double-bill with the formulaic *Fear in the Night*, it must have seemed a prestige project for producer Michael Carreras and Hammer Films. Rita Tushingham was not only a star but a proper actress, and director Peter Collinson was fresh from mainstream items like *Up the Junction* and *The Italian Job*.

Brenda Thompson (Tushingham) reads aloud a 'once upon a time' fairy tale she has written as the camera pans over a grim-oop-North row of terraced houses in Liverpool. The naive girl tells her mother (Claire Kelly) that she's pregnant and sets out for London 'to find a father for my baby, someone who'll love us both'. In the Smoke, Brenda falls in with a swinging, jaded crowd, getting a job at a boutique run by Jimmy Lindsay (hairy, sunglasses-sporting Tom Bell) and renting a room from Caroline (headband-wearing blonde Katya Wyeth). She is also obviously a provincial clod ('I don't go out very much.') and is upset when Joey (a post-*Likely Lads*, pre-*Whatever Happened to...* James Bolam), a bloke she likes, cops off with Caroline. Walking the streets of Earls Court, she impulsively kidnaps Tinker, a dog whose owner Peter (curly haired, girly mouthed Shane Briant in a sheepskin coat) she bumps into in a newsagent. She takes the dog back and winds up moving in with the strange young man, who is a psycho killer with a Peter Pan fixation. A gigolo who lives off and kills a succession of older women (and tapes their deaths), he insists on calling Brenda 'Wendy' and having her do his washing and cleaning, in return for which he promises to knock her up. All would be fine, but Caroline and Mrs Thompson insist on investigating Brenda's 'disappearance' – Peter lures Caroline into bed with suggestive come-hither looks and takes a stanley knife to her – and Brenda upsets him by shopping for psychedelic gear and a feathery wig. Musing 'children's stories are cruel', Peter locks Brenda in his room and plays back the tapes of his previous murders, including that of the dog, sending them both into hysterics. Later, he seems to have added her death to his collection. Film over – with one of Hammer's rare completely downbeat fade-outs.

Awash in turn-of-the-decade fashions, music (Annie Ross, who plays one of Peter's Wendys, sings a title song) and mores, *Straight on Till Morning* was dated when it came out. Thirty-year-old Tushingham had played many roles like Brenda since *A Taste of Honey* and had sent them up in *The Knack* and *Smashing Time*. Brenda's mannerisms are so irksome it's no wonder she hasn't got any friends – she's also stuck with a hair style which must seriously cut down on her peripheral vision. Briant, in what was supposed to be a star-making role after supporting psychosis in *Demons of the Mind*, has an acting showcase as Peter (his real name is Clive), but narcissist good looks and shallow pouting make him a less compelling, frightening or sympathetic figure than Carl Boehm in *Peeping Tom* or even Tony Beckley in *The Fiend*. Collinson is never content with just one scene – everything has to be intercut with something else: Caroline seducing Joey with Brenda pumping coins into a cigarette machine; Caroline being murdered with Brenda getting a facial mud-pack; Caroline arriving at work late with Caroline having sex (she does this a lot). All with jarring edits and music cuts, as if the director knew scenes weren't strong enough on their own and needed jazzing up. The film is a visual riot anyway: with white plastic chairs, rickety filigree stairs (prefiguring Collinson's remake of *The Spiral Staircase*), eye-offending outfits, a disco-lit boutique and Caroline's boots and hat. Scripted by John Peacock (*The Smashing Bird I Used to Know*).

SUNBURST (SLASHED DREAMS) (1975)

This came late to the self-actualisation boom of the 1970s and sat around in obscurity before being released to video in the '80s with a burned-in retitling on the back of bit-player Robert Englund's *Elm Street* notoriety. It's primo noodling self-indulgence, but not without interest. How many counterculture exploitation flicks feature '20s crooner Rudy Vallee (seemingly as himself) talking about old-time radio?

On campus, a classroom discussion (Peter Brown is The Professor) ponders, y'know, heavy stuff. Straight Jenny (Kathrine Baumann, a Miss Ohio whose credits range from *The Thing With Two Heads* and *99 and 44/100ths % Dead* to *Harry O* and *CHiPS*) expresses dissatisfaction with her gilded life. She admires dropout Michael, who has gone off to find himself in the woods. Her nasty, preppy b.f. Marshall (Ric Carrott) is pissed off at her attitude, but more sensitive and (it has to be said) manly Robert (Peter Hooten, later TV's *Dr Strange*) 'gets it'. After a bad scene (in all senses of the term) at the frat pool where a pledge is humiliated, Jenny and Robert head into the woods to find Michael finding himself. A reel or so features wandering in the wilderness accompanied by folk rock songs from Roberta Van Dere, then the kids discover Michael's seemingly abandoned shed. Skinny dipping in a mountain lake is interrupted by Levon and Danker (co-writers James Keach and David Pritchard), caricature sleazy rednecks (Keach sports a piratical scar) who do fractured imbecile semi-comedy. Later, the scumbags invade the cabin and the generally amiable tone turns nasty for what sets out to be a *Deliverance/ Last House on the Left/ Straw Dogs* rape scene – but blows over quickly as the rapists fall out and leave without killing the kids or even (seemingly) fully raping Jenny. This might be accidental, but it's also possible that the attack is a realistic depiction of a kind of sexual assault rarely bothered with onscreen. Jenny is traumatised and Robert has to reassess his pacifism (earlier, he turned down Vallee's gift of a hunting knife), but the film doesn't take the expected revenge route.

Michael (Englund) shows up and, contrary to the star's later image, helps Jenny get through trauma with passages from Khalil Gibran, herbal tea (oddly, these hippies never do or even mention drugs) and general kindly sensitivity. A real problem for the movie's prospects was that even longhair audiences preferred to see, say, Billy Jack kicking rapist ass than a victim coaxed to healing with philosophy. Levon and Danker argue in the woods. Robert finds them, and a non-contact knife/axe-waving fight ends with the bad guys muddied, humiliated and run off as if they were comedy goons rather than vile rapists. It ends with a hippie group hug (Robert's laughing/crying at his lapse into violence is oddly credible), more swimming, soundtrack warbling, Gibran-quoting and the leads walking hand-in-hand into a soft-focus sunset (or sunburst). With Anne Lockhart. Produced and directed by James Polakof (*Satan's Mistress*), whose credit reads 'created by'.

TAM LIN (THE DEVIL'S WIDOW) (1971)

> 'ARE YOU AFRAID OF HER?
> SHE CAN'T KILL YOU.'
> 'SHE'S RICH. SHE MAY HAVE
> BOUGHT A LICENSE.'

Perhaps the purest example of folk horror, this is a horror film based on a folk tale. Its soundtrack even features folk rockers Pentangle, whose accompaniment is a precedent for the score of *The Wicker Man*. Roddy McDowall's sole film as a director could only have been made at the turn of the 1960s into the '70s, but fits into a British sub-genre of modern-dress retellings of traditional stories (*A Canterbury Tale, Penda's Fen, The Company of Wolves*).

William Spier's script draws on 'The Ballad of Tam Lin', a narrative poem by Robert Burns, and the folk song 'Carter Hall': Tam Lin, a youth in thrall to the Queen of the Fairies ('who, in the centuries before pantomime, was reckoned a dangerous lady'), becomes Tom Lynn (Ian McShane), latest young lover of wealthy widow Mrs Michaela Cazaret (Ava Gardner). Tom leaves his patron's mansion and her charmed circle of beautiful acolytes for love in a caravan with a vicar's daughter. At this insult, Mrs Cazaret turns magically spiteful ('I'm going to have you put down.') and sics her 'second coven' – black-clad, much-nastier minions – on him. In the finale, Tom is drugged and set loose, with the coven pursuing him through the misty grounds of Carter Hall, the Cazaret estate (somewhere on the border between Scotland and England).

Apart from McShane, a good-looking plank in an unplayable role ('I live in a bloody daze.'), the film is distinguished by witty performances, especially from Cyril Cusack (deliberately cast to echo his role in *Gone to Earth*?) as the vicar, and cast-against-type Richard Wattis as Elroy, Mrs Cazaret's 'rancid old queen' secretary/consiglieri. There's a Lady Bluebeard chill as Elroy tells Tom about predecessors who have mostly perished in motor accidents. Showing a post-mortem photo he took himself, Elroy muses, 'You wouldn't believe, would you, that a face could spread so wide.' In gowns by Balmain, Gardner is glamorous and imperious as Mrs Cazaret, though it's odd that McDowall didn't cast his close friend Elizabeth Taylor (who plays a similar role in *Boom*). 'The children' are a once-in-a-lifetime mix of Britfilm dollies of both sexes: the heroines of three successive Hammer Draculas (Jenny Hanley, Stephanie Beacham, Joanna

Lumley) appear, along with Bruce Robinson (*Withnail & I*), Linda Marlowe (*Big Zapper*), Julian Barnes (*The Haunted House of Horror*), Sinead Cusack, Peter Hinwood (*The Rocky Horror Picture Show*) and a squeaky Madeline Smith ('I'll swallow anything as long as it's illegal').

The first hour, as Tom and Janet (Beacham) drift into a soppy freeze-frame-and-slo-mo hairspray commercial love affair, makes background use of paisley-clad, languid, well-spoken drop-outs as party extras. Lumley delivers sly non sequiturs ('Life is an illusion, therefore nothing is permanent... I shall go to Sweden.') and Pamela Farbrother has a spooky moment as a tarot-reading seeress panicked in the middle of a parlour game when she accidentally touches the orange-tinted glasses Tom has borrowed from Mrs Cazaret and foresees a horrible fate (but for whom?). The wild-hunt climax evokes the primal savagery of *The Most Dangerous Game* and *The Hound of the Baskervilles*, with hallucinatory special effects as Tom sees himself as a red-lit bear struggling through the undergrowth, imagines his hand turning into a constricting giant snake or sees water turning to fire. McDowall captures a particular kind of modish decadence, and perceives the darkening of psychedelic hedonism into Satanic cruelty.

THERE'S ALWAYS VANILLA (THE AFFAIR) (1971)

George A. Romero's second film, made with many of the creatives who worked on *Night of the Living Dead*, is the odd man out in his CV: a vaguely counterculture-ish, diffident look at the relationship between smart, directionless, no-longer-a-kid Chris (Raymond Laine) and smart, vulnerable model-actress Lynn (Judith Streiner).

Originally conceived as a short acting showreel for Laine, it mushroomed into a feature Romero claims wasn't really finished because writer Rudy Ricci left the project before finishing a script. Romero, always a skilled editor, imposed some shape in post-production, adding Chris talking to camera about his life and times and significant vox pops about a contraption-like piece of Pittsburgh public art (the Ultimate Machine). Some scenes are credibly uncomfortable and catch the restless, fractious vibe of the times, as when Chris runs into his estranged but amiable father (Roger McGovern) in a go-go bar and sets him up with a hippie chick... some stretches feel autobiographical on the part of Romero and his ad industry colleagues, as when Lynn appears in a commercial for Bold beer produced by sinister-looking ad guru Michael Dorian (Richard Ricci)... and a few moments go for outright satire, as when Chris lands a gig at an ad agency with caricature execs and is given the trial job of selling an army recruitment campaign to a draft-resisting generation.

A radical mood change comes in a sequence where pregnant Lynn visits a back-street abortionist – but doesn't go through with the operation; suddenly, Romero uses the tilted angles, dark shadows and jagged cutting of his 1970s horror films. Streiner appeared (under the name Judith Ridley) in *Night of the Living Dead* and Laine showed up again in a Chris-like role as the feckless lover of the witch protagonist in *Jack's Wife* (aka Season of the Witch). It'd make an interesting hippie-phase-of-horror-auteur triple bill with Brian De Palma's Greetings and Tobe Hooper's *Eggshells*.

TOOMORROW (1970)

Alien anthropologist 'John Williams' (Roy Dotrice) has lived on Earth for centuries, making Ford Prefect-like reports on uninteresting human achievements. Beamed up to a *Barbarella*-style lightshow ship (expensive effects work from John Stears), John reverts to grey alien form (now cliché, then a fairly new-minted look) and learns the Alphoid race is dying from a lack of exciting vibrations. Luckily, Toomorrow – an Earthling pop group – has just invented an electronic instrument ('a tonaliser') which will keep the Alphoids going. A collaboration of the Beatles, Mozart, Elvis and Spike Jones couldn't possibly live up to the universe-saving rep bestowed on Toomorrow, so their pleasantly forgettable, hardly-cutting-edge-even-for-1970 tones can't hope to convince. That said, the ambition of the script (by David Benedictus and director Val Guest) and its saving-a-species-with-rock-music concept plays better (who knows what aliens dig?) than if the film had suggested Toomorrow might have a number one hit or cheer up a sickly child or sell some albums. The most unbelievable scene has the bland combo wowing seemingly unstoned crowds at a 'pop festival'. The bizarre SF content is no more important to *Toomorrow* than, say, the space ambassador business of *Gonks Go Beat*. A middle-aged attempt at a 'happening' youth film built around a cobbled-together-for-this-movie group, it's as concerned with student protest sit-ins as saving the Alphoid race.

Don Kirshner (who co-produced, with Harry Saltzman) had form with prefab pop as music supervisor for The Monkees (and had another stab at this sort of thing with a busted pilot for a series about a pop group in the old west, *The Kowboys*). The pop template had changed since The Monkees, so Toomorrow has a blonde girl and a black dude for more diverse appeal. Tunesmiths Ritchie Adams and Mark Barkan don't come up with songs on a par with The Monkees' catalogue and Guest doesn't give the young folks (who use their own first names) much to play with in comic or drama scenes. Olivia Newton-John, who toiled for a few more years before becoming a proper star, is the bright-eyed girl singer with a mild antipodean twang (she calls someone a 'drongo'). The rest of the band, who didn't go on to anything like stardom, are Karl Chambers (hat-wearing drummer – described by *Variety* as 'a lively Negro skinbeater'), Benny Thomas (lead guitar, banjo, vocals) and Vic Cooper (sax, keyboards, organ, tonaliser). There are tiresome, footage-eating troubled romances: Benny with a faculty member (Tracey Crisp), Vic with a ballet dancer (Imogen Hassall, of Guest's *When Dinosaurs Ruled the Earth*) and Karl with a stunning, terribly thin, slightly nude model (Kubi Chaza) who gets the script's worst line ('I'm all for integration, but not with my cat!') *and* has the worst dialogue delivery.

The band hustle to play an eight-minute slot at the Round House introduced by disc jockey Stuart Henry, vaguely take part in a student protest (no mention of a war or anything – the issue that prompts the sit-in is student-faculty representation on committees dominated by bureaucrats, which sounds surprisingly credible) and are kidnapped by spaceship to save the Alphoids, which they manage with a couple of tunes before zapping back to Earth where it might all have been a dream but then again probably wasn't. With Margaret Nolan (Dink from *Goldfinger*) as an alien innocent who doesn't realise she's been given the body of a sex bomb – she wanders about as if expecting this to turn into a raunchier film, like, say, *Diary of a Space Virgin* or *Outer Touch*. Composer Hugo Montenegro – known in the UK for his hit cover version of *The Good, the Bad and the Ugly* and an album of music from *The Man From U.N.C.L.E.* – provides the jolly, tonaliser-heavy incidental music. *Toomorrow* is inoffensive and has little to say, but remains a fascinating relic from a period when hopeless entertainment industry squares tried to get hip and hook an affluent but disaffected youth audience. Costumes, hairstyles, aliens, spaceships, disco lights and student décor provide acute visual reminders of the precise two weeks (in September 1970) when the film was in cinemas.

THE TOUCHABLES (1968)

> 'DE SADE AND HEROIN WILL BE IN ONE YEAR... VIRGINITY AND COCOA THE NEXT.'

A Swinging London movie with a cool pedigree: director (and writer of the story) Robert Freeman designed Beatles LP covers and titles scenes for Richard Lester films; the script is by *Likely Lads* co-creator Ian La Frenais and *Performance* co-director Donald Cammell (and his brother David). It has *Performance* parallels (gay s-m gangsters, polysexuality, groovy communal pads), but is more trendy romp than serious freak-out.

The touchables are a go-go girl gang in miniskirts and fab gear, with individual looks: rifle-toting boss gal Sadie (Judy Huxtable), bewigged 'immigrant' Melanie (Ester Anderson), continental Busbee (Monika Ringwald, billed as Marilyn Rickard) and pixie-ish Samson (Kathy Simmonds). Abducting a dummy of Michael Caine from a party – the host is velvet-dressed, archly named Nigel Bent (Simon Williams) – is such fun they decide to kit up as nuns and kidnap live pop star Christian (David Anthony). They take the pretty boy to a fab home – a lakeside geodesic blow-up bubble with scatter cushions and a circular bed – for bondage games and (implied) beaucoup sex. When he gets tired and tries to escape, Sadie shoots Christian in the head and Samson revives him with a kiss.

It winds down with a chase (a bubble car features briefly), a punch-up, and the dome deflating. With Melanie dancing in silhouette as montage is projected on her, ballet-dancing wrestler Rikki Starr, Joan Bakewell as an Interviewer asking Christian about 'fashionable morality replacing traditional morality', and music from Nirvana (the old one) and Roy Redmond (covering 'Good Day Sunshine').

THE TOY BOX (1971)

> 'THERE IS ECSTASY IN MURDER. YOU CAN FEEL YOUR OWN BLOOD EXPLODING WITH EACH STAB.'

Made on the cusp of hardcore, this is a weirdie: a sex film spiced with surrealism the way other exploitationers became roughies by adding violence.

Donna (Ann Myers) drives to an isolated house (without exterior shots of the car or even the house she's going to). She remembers turning from virgin secretary to depraved exhibitionist when Ralph (Evan Steele aka Sean Kenney of *The Corpse Grinders*) gave her a vibrator as a birthday present. Later, this turns out not to have happened, but we're expected to have forgotten or not care. Donna and Ralph arrive at the house of Uncle (Jack King), a fat, bearded, open-mouthed voyeur who pays people to perform 'tricks' (oddball sex acts) with toys from 'the toy box'. At the moment, he's dead but enjoying his wake as swingers and hippies have an orgy with the occasional time-out for a trick. Laura (an uncredited Uschi Digard) does an odd number as her breasts are grabbed by a Thing-like box-dwelling hand; she is further groped by what might be a horny MR James spook (arms underneath or animating bed sheets). A chunky guy dressed as a butcher does a necrophile act with two girls. A drive-in movie make-out session pays off with decapitation. A couple in antique clothes have a soft-focus romantic picnic, which gets nasty as the guy puts on a mummy mask and the girl spears him repeatedly with a pitchfork.

After this, Ralph fails to convince the locked-in guests that Uncle intends to kill them. In a fog-filled basement lurks Sally (Deborah Osborne), a redhead who has grown (via *Village of the Giants* effects) into a giant space immortal. She mentions that Uncle (who resembles a *Star Trek* villain) runs a toy store on a planet where depraved humans are a valuable drug. 'Your species on this planet are free and easy, but on the planet Arkon, you are expensive and illegal.' Ralph has more explained to him by Uncle ('We are in a fourth dimensional plane of darkness so immense that your undeveloped brain cannot conceive it.'), who ultimately admits he's just a bighead projection. The real alien mastermind is Donna, who intends to wipe everyone out except Ralph, who she's taking along when the house 'transteleports' (a *Rocky Horror Picture Show* precursor?) so she can enjoy tormenting him forever. The orgiasts die pawing the windows and the house fades out.

Strange enough to be intermittently compelling, it doesn't quite have the low-budget invention of Russ Meyer or Radley Metzger (or even Jesús Franco) to go with its undoubted imagination. How did the original raincoat audience like it? With Marsha Jordan (*Count Yorga, Vampire*). Written and directed by Ron Garcia (later director of photography on *Twin Peaks: Fire Walk With Me*).

WONDERWALL (1968)

'THE CYCLE OF PISCES IS COMING TO AN END. THANKS FOR EVERYTHING, PROFESSOR – IT WAS BEAUTIFUL.'

Best remembered for George Harrison's score. His Beatley raga-music hall-rock burbles are okay, but it's not one of the great psychedelic soundtracks; the use of music in *Performance, Blowup, Easy Rider* or even *Scream and Scream Again* is stronger. Director Joe Massot has a speckled career: he was kicked off Led Zeppelin's *The Song Remains the Same*, made *Space Riders* with Barry Sheene, and wrote *Zachariah* and the *other* film called *Universal Soldier* (1972). It has unusual writing credits – story by Gérard Brach, script by G. Cain (Guillermo Cabrera Infante) – and carries over star Jack MacGowran and significant bit-player Iain Quarrier from Roman Polanski's Brach-co-scripted *Cul-de-Sac* and *Dance of the Vampires*.

Professor Oscar Collins (MacGowran) spends his days peering at germs through a microscope and ignoring colleagues (Richard Wattis, Bee Duffell). He lives in a clutter of books, newspapers, stuffed animals and butterfly displays. A pinprick hole in the wall creates a camera obscura and the silhouette of model Penny Lane (Jane Birkin) is projected into his flat. Obsessed, he makes more holes, peering into the magical swinging world of Penny and her photographer boyfriend (Quarrier). He dreams his way into her surreal-seeming life and – ultimately – breaks in to save her when she attempts suicide. There's something annoying about the association of books with deadness (where are the kids' books – surely, they'd have Vonnegut and Heller and *New Worlds* on their shelves and see-through tables?) and the quotations on the professor's bookshelves seem as with-it as the colourful décor next door. A thread skewers the fantasy, showing what the professor *doesn't* see – Penny with a cold or washing stockings in the sink – but it's mostly whimsical dress-up-and-play with hippie clothes. Quarrier seems to be in the same wardrobe he had in *Dance of the Vampires*, where he played a 19th-century gay vampire. A little of MacGowran's Beckettesque dithering goes a long way and his voyeur/fantasist is borderline creepy – though you can't argue with Birkin (or even Quarrier) as enviable ideals. Cleaning lady Irene Handl does the same shtick as in *The Rebel*. It has fantastical touches, like the butterflies which come to life when their case is smashed (and become cartoons). With Anita Pallenberg and Beatrix Lehmann.

WORK IS A 4-LETTER WORD (1968)

> 'THERE WON'T BE MUCH BLOOD
> TO SPEAK OF, JUST AN AGONY
> AND AN ACHING AND YOU
> NOT BEING ABLE TO DRAG YOURSELF
> ALONG THE WET PAVEMENT.'

Directed by Peter Hall – who has only flirted with the cinema, usually (as here) with stage adaptations – this offers a once-in-a-lifetime screen coupling of David Warner (in *Morgan – A Suitable Case for Treatment*-mode for one of his rare top-billed roles) and Cilla Black (not – frankly – much of an actress). The corporate comic dystopia slightly prefigures the tone of *Brazil*, but the outcome is more benevolent and hippie-dippy.

In the future, automation has eliminated most work, but full employment is mandatory so people must do non-jobs for limited times a week. Pinstriped Valentine Brose (Warner) wants to slack off, but needs a steamy, hot atmosphere to raise his favoured strain of hallucinogenic mushrooms. Thrown out of a Turkish bath, he applies for a job as a night-sweeper in a power station with steamy boilers which is owned by the omnipresent Dice Company. Betty Dorrick (Black) nags Val into marriage and he makes her honeymoon at the power plant. On site, Brose wants his wife to do his actual job – and kip in a hammock slung between pipes – while he cultivates mushrooms. This leads to a chaotic trip as the sensible characters get high, lose inhibitions and giggle while a computer melts down. Val himself seems so spaced out he doesn't really need to sample his own supply.

Like many dystopiae, it ends up with the lead characters wandering into a sylvan wilderness (an English wood) away from the nasty city. The funniest caricature is stuffy old Establishment figure Reverend Mort (Alan Howard), a short-tempered vicar who repeatedly throws Val out of church ('I'm gonna tell God about you,' complains the aggrieved party). Clanking slapstick (it's no *Modern Times*) has Warner scooped up by a bulldozer or an automatic lift in the factory and Black falling over in oil while a busy mickeymousing score (Guy Woolfenden, with electronic assistance from Delia Derbyshire when it gets trippy) tries to make it seem funny. Not that pointed a satire, it does envision an unusual, slightly Dickian future of leisure, uselessness and drugs. Written by Jeremy Brooks (*Our Mother's House*), from Henry Livings' play *Eh?* Cinematographer Gilbert Taylor also shot *Dr. Strangelove* and *A Hard Day's Night*; Kubrick (Warner wears a *Clockwork Orange*-like phallic false nose for his honeymoon) or Lester (*The Bed Sitting Room* is funnier and more biting) might have done better with the material. With John Steiner (junior exec), Zia Mohyeddin (mad scientist) and Tommy Godfrey. Black sings the title song.

ZACHARIAH (1970)

Advertised as 'The First Electric Western', the endearingly pretentious *Zachariah* prefigures such genre oddities as Jodorowsky's *El Topo* and Alex Cox's *Straight to Hell*. The story is the archetypal one about friends who become gunslingers and must inevitably face each other in the finale, but it's treated here as if it Meant Something Deeper – which means that after enjoying 75 minutes of violence, we can all agree peace and love and harmony is on the whole better for children and other living things.

Curly haired farm boy Zachariah (John Rubinstein) and eternally grinning apprentice blacksmith Matthew (Don Johnson) are fast friends who run away from home to join a gang of outlaws known as the Crackers (hippie folk-rock collective Country Joe and the Fish). These apparent 19th-century westerners tote electric guitars and have stage happenings at one end of town to distract from the bank robbery at the other. The boys hook up with Job Cain (Elvin Jones), an all-in-black master gunfighter who is also an ace drummer (his solo is impressive), then drift apart. Zachariah has a liaison with Old West madame Belle Starr (Pat Quinn, not to be confused with Patricia Quinn) in a town consisting of fairground-style brightly painted wooden cut-out buildings (a gag reused in *Blazing Saddles*), then gets rid of his outrageous all-white cowboy outfit to settle down on a homestead and grow his own dope and vegetables. Matthew, of course, goes for black leather after outdrawing Cain, and comes a-gunning for the only man who might be faster than him… but the message is once these kids have killed everyone else they can still make peace with each other and the desert or something, man.

Aside from Beatle-haired teenage Johnson making a fool of himself over-emoting to contrast with Rubinstein's non-performance, the film offers a lot of beautiful 'acid western' scenery and excellent prog rock or bluegrass music from the James Gang, White Lightnin' and the New York Rock Ensemble. Comedy troupe The Firesign Theatre (Phil Austin, Peter Bergman, David Ossman, Philip Proctor; huge on album in 1970) provided the script, which explains satirical touches like the horse-and-buggy salesman (Dick Van Patten) spieling like a used-car dealer and the madame's claim to have had affairs with gunslingers from Billy the Kid to Marshal McLuhan.

WILDLIFE

Fish and Reptiles

AATANK (1996)

Though touted as the *Bollywood Jaws*, this is mostly a melodrama (with inevitable songs) set in a fishing village where gang-leader Alphonso (Amjad Khan) inflicts injustice on all and sundry… especially after hero Jesu (Dharmendra) discovers a pearl bed which turns the place into a boom town. Things get considerably fishier an hour or so in when a giant man-eating shark barges into the movie, perhaps to avenge the violation of the pearl bed. In an eye-opening change of mood which would only feature in a Hindi film, Suzy (Nafisa Ali) – pretty wife of the hero's foster brother (Vinod Mehra) – is eaten by the shark seconds after she's sung a very cheery song while frolicking happily in the waves. Even this sudden death doesn't switch the film's tracks, as more songs and much strangely comic byplay intervene before the finale gets out on the water for a collage of bits from Jaws (plus the helicopter scene from *Jaws 2*) as Jesu, his girlfriend (Hema Malini), a brave cop (Girish Karnad), a Caucasian Robert Shaw-lookalike (Tom Alter) and other interested parties put to sea to go after the shark. The effects scenes run to bobbing miniature boats and an impressively toothy but blatantly fake giant shark model which bleeds profusely over Jesu as he stabs it to death. Substantially shot in the 1980s, but not completed and released until 1996. Directed by Prem Lalwani and Desh Mukherjee.

ANACONDAS: THE HUNT FOR THE BLOOD ORCHID (2004)

More like a rip-off than a sequel. A horde of credited writers (Hans Bauer, Jim Cash, Jack Epps Jr, Ed Neumeier, Michael Miner, Daniel Zelman and John Claflin) blithely proceed on the assumption that anacondas live in Borneo (they're a South American species). A jungle orchid might yield a drug with astounding regenerative properties, but only blooms once every seven years. An expedition of disposable scientific and business types hire a macho deadbeat (Johnny Messner), the only captain willing to take them upriver during rainy season before the end of the blooming week. The cast squabble to pass the time, with *Coronation Street* refugee Matthew Marsden as an unethical British-accented scientist-entrepreneur and Eugene Byrd as a hysterical, pop-eyed African-American who might as well be Willie Best in a baseball cap. Having eaten the orchids, local anacondas grow to giant size – but disappointingly refrain from killing anyone for too much of the running time. Towards the end, the creatures do away with some (but not enough) characters. A crocodile and a numbing poisonous spider are in the mix, though sadly aren't orchid-enlarged. With CGI creatures on a par with *Blood Surf*, relentlessly terrible dialogue, a plot which strays all over the map, and unexciting scares, this piffle makes the full-throttle hokum of *Anaconda* seem classic. Directed by Dwight H. Little (*Halloween 4*, *Free Willy 2*).

ANACONDA 3: OFFSPRING (2008)

'YOU WILL DO YOUR JOB OR THE ONLY THING YOU'LL BE SUPERVISING IS A PROCTOLOGIST REMOVING MY BOOT FROM YOUR RECTUM, DO YOU UNDERSTAND?'

The *Anaconda* series settled at its proper level with a DtDVD/cable threequel toplining David Hasselhoff, directed (back-to-back with *Anacondas: Trail of Blood*) by cinematographer Don E. FauntLeRoy (*The Stepford Husbands*, *Jeepers Creepers*). *Anaconda* was high-grade nonsense with name actors; *Anacondas: The Hunt for the Blood Orchid*, from which this picks up plot elements, coasted to a minor cinema showing on name recognition alone. Aside from being appended to a franchise, this time-waster resembles any of a dozen CGI snake efforts shot in former Warsaw Pact countries (*Boa*, *Python*, *Boa vs Python*, etc.).

In a hard-to-identify country (played by Romania), dying zillionaire bastard Murdoch (John Rhys-Davies) sponsors one of those scientific projects to create mutant monsters in the hope of curing a terminal illness (cf: *Deep Blue Sea*). When the snakes get loose, hard-bitten Hammett (the Hoff) leads a small (very soon much smaller) group of gun-toting mercenaries on a mission to kill them before a pregnant hundred-foot female spawns enough littler snakes to swamp the country. There is much wandering in the woods and derelict industrial buildings, with doomed characters observed in yellowy distortovision POV between regular snake attacks. Hasselhoff plays a vicious scumbag antihero rather than a straight-up good guy, which might be a back-reference to Jon Voight's mad snake-hunter in *Anaconda*. Mostly, it borrows from *Aliens*: ass-kicking science babe Amanda (Crystal Allen) snarls, 'Happy trails, slimy bitch!' at a genetically engineered mother snake who uses her spear-like impaling tail like the Alien Queen does, while preppy, treacherous company man Pinkus (Ryan McCluskey) does Paul Reiser's act.

ANACONDAS: TRAIL OF BLOOD (ANACONDA 4: TRAIL OF BLOOD) (2009)

> 'DESTROYING THE FLOWERS AND MY RESEARCH IS THE ONLY WAY I COULD ATONE FOR WHAT I DID.'

A direct follow-up to *Anaconda 3: Offspring*. Researcher Amanda (Crystal Allen) is still wandering the countryside (now identified as Romania) trying to atone for the way the miracle cure serum she extracted from those orchids (remember *Anacondas: The Hunt for the Blood Orchid?*) has made snakes grow very big and attack people. The project is funded by ailing millionaire Murdoch (a returning John Rhys-Davies), who doesn't care how many innocent bystanders (or his own aides and hired goons) get chomped so long as he gets his medicine. Moments after he has benefited from the cure, the CGI big snake ironically chomps him to death.

Mostly unknown actors pose as hardboiled mercs – with English speakers upfront, but Romanians filling out the list of victims – as they tromp about fields and woods until the fakey snakey gets them. The new wrinkle here is that the anaconda's regenerative powers are upped by the serum, so it can grow a new head if its original is blown to bits. Sadly (or not), this doesn't apply to John Rhys-Davies – his head presumably dissolves in the monster's gut. Directed (again) by Don E. FauntLeRoy and written by David C. Olson. The series went on hiatus until *Lake Placid vs Anaconda*.

AVALANCHE SHARKS (2013)

> 'I'M SORRY ABOUT THAT. A MAN SHOULD BE ABLE TO LIVE IN THIS COMMUNITY WITHOUT SNOW SHARKS EATING HIS DOG.'

The come-on synopsis can't be bettered: 'a bikini contest turns into a horrifying affair when it is hit by a shark avalanche'. A rare combination shark and Indian curse movie. Spirit Sharks (local name: skookums) prey on annoying skiers and bikini girls at a mountain resort where miners once massacred Native Americans. So, this is basically *Shark Manitou*, which would have been a cooler title if this didn't want to remind you of the tiresome *Sharknado* saga. The plot is kinda *Jawsy* but with a shrug, as if all the pieces were picked out by writer Keith Shaw (*Malibu Shark Attack*) and director Scott Wheeler (*Transmorphers: Fall of Man*) and just dropped. The Sheriff (Richard Gleason) wants to close the slopes, the mayor (Benjamin Easterday) needs them open to get out of debt, a Marine (Alexander Mendeluk) takes charge, a pretty biologist (Kate Nauta) is still traumatised by the loss of her parents to snow sharks twenty-five years earlier, a permatanned idiot wants the Sheriff's job (Eric Scott Woods). The attacks (terrible CGI) are brief, bloody and have no impact: walk-on joke extras and major characters are offed equally abruptly. A lot of dead footage fills space between the horrors. With Gina Holden, who also has *Dracano* and *Sand Sharks* on her resume.

BAIT (2012)

An Australian mashup of *The Mist* and *Malibu Shark Attack*, and – as such – reasonably entertaining. A shark attack prologue leaves lifeguard leading man Josh (Xavier Samuel, *The Loved Ones*) traumatised. In an only-in-the-movies trope, Josh has a news clipping about the most horrible thing which ever happened to him pinned up in his flat to fill in backstory. Having broken off his engagement to Tina (Sharni Vinson, *You're Next*), sister of the guard who died in his place, he takes an away-from-the-beach job in an underground supermarket.

Snarly manager Jessup (Adrian Pang) fires Kyle (Lincoln Lewis), boyfriend of shoplifter Jaimie (Phoebe Tonkin), and calls her cop father (Martin Sacks) to make an arrest. Then, Josh runs into Tina with her new boyfriend (Qi Yuwu) just as hold-up men Doyle (Julian McMahon) and Kirby (Dan Wyllie) arrive to rob the store. To cap off a bad day, a tsunami floods the market, washing in a very hungry shark.

The situation is ridiculous, but disaster movie conventions are deployed infallibly. The group tries to cope with the situation, improvise solutions (shark armour made from shopping baskets), handle lesser crises (sparking wires nearing the water), show character (estranged daughter and father bond, good crook is heroic while bad crook is rotten) and scream and/or die at regular intervals. Written by Russell Mulcahy and John Kim (with input from four others); directed by Kimble Rendall (*Cut*).

BENEATH (2013)

Evidently an 'entertainment' from director Larry Fessenden rather than an auteur work, this terror-by-fish cable-TV movie manages one-bad-day-on-the-lake suspense rather than the escalating-series-of-attacks found in the average *Jaws* ripoff. As in 'The Raft', the Stephen King story done in *Creepshow 2*, teens are stranded in the middle of a remote lake by a monster and turn on each other as they try to survive.

The major quirk is in using a big practical robot fish instead of CGI, which means the detailed creature has more personality and really displaces water (one thing cheap CGI never gets right). The monster isn't terribly lifelike (it evokes the fish from *The Singing Ringing Tree*), but is a rare contemporary creature with Cormanish presence. The stuck-in-a-boat kids are high school football hero Matt (Chris Conroy) and his overshadowed brother Simon (Jonny Orsini), Matt's blonde girlfriend Kitty (Bonnie Dennison) and the slightly ethnic decent kid Johnny (Daniel Zovatto) who has a crush on her, Kitty's friend Deb (Mackenzie Rosman) and nerdy Zeke who films everything (Griffin Newman), as if an earlier script draft wanted to be a found-footage film. On the lake, the fish bites Deb's arm and she bleeds out – what's horrid is that she's savvy enough about anatomy to realise how badly she's wounded – and the jocks lose the oars battering the creature. There are votes on who gets tossed or jumps in to distract the monster while the determined-to-survive folks paddle with their hands. Johnny has an amulet which protects him from the monster – though this is only proven when it doesn't eat him after he's semi-accidentally died.

The kids are obviously rotten – and their betrayals and cruelties come out in a crisis – but performances are good and everyone has some depth. The revelation that Simon is smart enough to land a scholarship to 'the University of Get the Fuck Out of Here' would usually make him the hero – but it develops that he's also a sociopath. Mark Margolis adds value as the mandatory ominous old-timer who issues an unheeded warning at the beginning and turns up again to say he told 'em so at the end. Scripted by Tony Daniel and Brian D. Smith (*Flu Bird Horror*).

BERING SEA BEAST (DAMN SEA VAMPIRES!) (2013)

> 'UNTIL NOW, THE GREAT WHITE SHARK WAS THE WORST THING KNOWN TO MAN. WHATEVER THIS IS IS EVEN WORSE.'

I'm not 100% sure what these 'damn sea vampires' are supposed to be. They look like CGI spawn of the goofy creatures which used to fight Gamera. The manta ray-bat-leech hybrids (deadly in the sea, on land and in the air) envelop victims with their spiny 'wings' and exsanguinate them with big toothy Pac-Man mouths. The Brook Durham (*Mammoth*) script is just another sea monster quickie, with the odd time-out to talk up the privilege and difficulty of single fatherhood.

A family dredging concern in Alaska discovers a submarine gold field but disturbs the DSVs (who appear in local legend), so the beasts switch dietary preference from seals to people. Donna (Cassie Scerbo) and Joe Hunter (Jonathan Lipnicki) want to avenge their crusty captain dad Glenn (Kevin Dobson), who dies in a chestburster scene. Deckhand Owen (Brandon Beemer) just wants to earn enough to support his son (who, mercifully, we never meet), marine biologist Megan (Jaqueline Fleming) gets over her enthusiasm for the new species while devising ways to kill them (in vampire mode, bright light is 'their kryptonite') and claim-jumping baddie Thorne (Lawrence Turner) makes the situation worse and pads out the running time with treacherous conniving. Directed by Don E. FauntLeRoy (*Lightspeed, Snakehead Swamp*).

BERMUDA TENTACLES (2014)

> 'OKAY CHIEF, WE'RE SURROUNDED BY TENTACLES. WE'LL HAVE TO SHOOT OUR WAY OUT OF HERE.'

So, Air Force One flies into a storm over the Bermuda Triangle and President DeSteno (John Savage) is jettisoned in one of those *Escape From New York* pods. US navy

Admiral Jane Hansen (Linda Hamilton) is stuck with know-all Chief Petty Officer Trip Oliver (Trevor Donovan) as head of the dredge-up-the-prez detail. Their old beef about her by-the-book policy and his dead best friend is set aside when giant biomechanical tubeworms rise out of the water and tower over the fleet, occasionally stabbing sailors. The tentacles are attached to a city-sized alien craft which has been on the bottom of the sea for years, collecting all those missing ships and planes. DeSteno is about to authorise a nuclear attack on the US to save the rest of the world when Trip volunteers to go on a solo bombing mission into the heart of the alien thing. Guess whether it works?

It seems like another Syfy derivative – after *American Warships* – of the less-than-stellar blockbuster *Battleship*, right down to casting an R&B artist (Mya Harrison) as a trim naval officer whose job is to agree with the hero. Stirring music, wooden acting, dire dialogue and a general air of high-stakes urgency cover the fact that it's a bit ordinary. Though it's nice to see Hamilton as a middle-aged authority figure, she's stuck with a killjoy characterisation. Savage, used to this sort of thing, overacts entertainingly. Also joining the missing-in-action-but-resurfacing-on-Syfy brigade is Jamie Kennedy as the scientist who gabbles the gobbledegook. Written by Geoff Meed (*I Am Omega*); directed by Nick Lyon (*Grendel*).

BLACK WATER (2007)

Of a blip of 2007 croc movies (*Rogue*, *Primeval*), this is the smallest-scale, taking the 'in a pickle' approach of the influential *Open Water*. Believable, reasonably suspenseful and the survivor isn't who you expect – but it's a bit ho-hum.

Just-pregnant Grace (Diana Glenn), husband Adam (Andy Rodoreda) and blonde best friend Lee (Maeve Dermody) take a road trip at the sweltering post-Christmas height of Australian summer. After touring a farm where it's established that crocodiles are nippy buggers, the trio unwisely take a boat tour of mangrove swamps with a guy (Ben Oxenbould) who isn't even the advertised guide, 'Backwater Barry'. Well away from civilisation, the boat is overturned by a crocodile, the guide chomped and the trio are literally stuck up a tree. As in *Open Water*, characters bicker (when someone recites an ominous nursery rhyme about 'Mr Crocodile', others mention it's not very helpful) and debate courses of action. They can't decide whether to await help, clamber from tree to tree and swim for the shore or get the capsized boat back in business.

The crocodile isn't onscreen much, but every ripple suggests it might come back. It presents sinister ridges above the waterline at crucial moments ('Just fuck off,' snarls Lee). Characters act credibly with a mix of stupidity, bravery, ingenuity and unhelpful mood swings, but aren't easy to put up with. The tagline, apt to all cleft-stick films, is 'what would you do?'; in all probability, most of us would whine and blubber like these folks, but that doesn't make them less irritating. 'Based on true events' – but aren't they all? Written and directed by Andrew Traucki (*The Reef*) and David Nerlich.

BLOOD SURF (KROCODYLUS) (2000)

'MAN, THIS IS GONNA BE BETTER THAN... WHAT WAS THE NAME OF THAT SHARK FLICK?'

This cluttered terror-by-beast epic needs to drop in extraneous shark and pirate attacks to stretch an elementary plot to feature length. In the remote waters of Lilo Cay, a team of documentary filmmakers work on a project about the dangerous sport of bloodsurfing (which involves surfers cutting their feet so they can barrel through waters full of hungry sharks). They come up against a 'saltie', a thirty-foot-long seafaring crocodile which eats sharks like whitebait and chomps its way through the supporting cast with monotonous regularity. Duncan Regehr takes the Robert Shaw role as the vengeance-seeking skipper who has become a drunk since the croc cut short his tour guide career by eating his customers, but has too little to do, while the young, bland cast run through the usual wisecracking, screwing-around and screaming. Written by Sam Bernard (*Warlock: The Armageddon*) and Robert L. Levy (*Smokey and the Bandit*). Directed by James D. R. Hickox (*Children of the Corn III: Urban Harvest*).

BLUE DEMON (2004)

'YOU'RE GOING TO TRY TO CONTROL SIX SHARKS WITH YOUR LAPTOP, A CELLPHONE AND A CAR RADIO?'

No relation to the well-known Mexican wrestler. Though light on jokes (the supporting villains are known as 'the Sharks Brothers') or indeed wit ('Dude, where's my shark?'), this Syfy mutant-shark movie seems to be an intentional comedy rather than a gore opus – as if it were trying for (and missing) the tone of Joe Dante's *Piranha*. Nearly-divorced marine biologists Marla (Dedee Pfeiffer) and Nathan Collins (Randall Batinkoff) work for midget boss Lawrence Van Allen (Danny Woodburn) on a project to genegeneer smart great whites for use in the war on terror. The sharks, bred to attack in the sea and freshwater, escape on the day cigar-chomping General Remora (Jeff Fahey) inspects the facility and the Collinses get back together while on the run from terrorism charges and trying to track down the killer fish. Remora sticks a Russian suitcase nuke into the jaws of prime shark Red Dog, intent on blowing up a chunk of the California coastline (including the Golden Gate Bridge) to justify higher defence spending (as if the US government has ever needed an excuse). The CGI sharks are substandard in a pathetic field, and the fill-in action/chase stuff is mild. A long end crawl includes snippets so you can identify the no-name supporting cast – which at least means spectacular bikini blonde bit-player Galina Chtyrva (who hasn't worked since) is identifiable. Written by Lisa Morton (*Glass Trap*), Ron Oliver (*Hello Mary Lou: Prom Night II*), Brett Thompson (*Britannic*) and director/producer Daniel Grodnik.

BOA (NEW ALCATRAZ) (2001)

Before the rise of The Asylum, the Unified Film Organisation (UFO) seemed to own the franchise on 21st century B rubbish. This crossbreeds *Fortress* with *Anaconda*. An experimental international prison deep under Antarctic ice holds only the worst offenders (in an unexplored twist, political dissidents rather than serial killers). A giant prehistoric snake emerges from icy suspended animation and picks off the guards, so the whiny warden (Craig Wasson) and married reptile experts (Dean Cain, Elizabeth Lackey) team up with the cons – a Chechnyan 'Minister of Defence' (Mark Sheppard), a super-hacker who 'brought down AOL' (Dana Ashbrook), an IRA terrorist with a fear of snakes (Amandah Reyne), etc. – to organise an escape before everyone gets constricted or swallowed. Like many similar movies (cf: *Octopus*, *King Cobra*, *Arachnid*), its long first act keeps switching settings and moods to set up monster stuff, which is then disappointingly conventional.

The snake is feeble CGI, as expected, and the cons a lot less entertaining than they ought to be. Busy producer/director Phillip J. Roth (*A.P.E.X.*, *Dragon Fighter*) co-wrote with Terri Neish.

BOA VS PYTHON (2004)

Though this comes from the outfit behind *Python* and *Boa*, its only narrative connection to earlier entries is a tangential reference to *Python II*. However, it might be the ultimate shot-in-Bulgaria-pretending-to-be-America CGI snake-hunt. Unethical cigar-chomper Broddick (Adam Kendrick) and a red-streaked cutie unsubtly named Eve (Angel Boris) import an 'eighty-to-a-hundred foot' python to be let loose on a hunting preserve and killed by rich nutcases. The damn thing escapes and takes refuge in and around a power plant, occasionally eating young lovers or obnoxious TV reporters. Broddick calls in his psycho buddies – none played by actors who can really fill one-note but colourful roles – to go after the reptile. G-Man Sharpe (Kirk B.R. Woller) teams dolphin-hugging bikini-babe boffin Monica (Jaime Bergman) with unshaven herpetologist Emmett (David Hewlett) to unleash Betty, a remote-controlled, genetically-engineered big boa. The idea that the good snake will track the bad one is daffy enough to be fun, though things get tacky as the python basically rapes Betty and further ticks her off by eating one of her new-laid eggs. Everyone winds up wandering about a familiar decommissioned Soviet-era industrial installation, preyed on by the bad snake, the good snake, the trigger-happy hunters or sudden floods. The CGI is inadequate, and the best snake moment is the sex scene, as the scientists and federal agent react differently to a video hook-up of a mating we crucially don't see. Nonsense, if whacky enough to be amusing. Written by Chase Parker (*Reign of the Gargoyles*) and Sam Wells (*Shark Hunter*); directed by David Flores (*Lake Placid 2*).

CREATURE (PETER BENCHLEY'S CREATURE) (1998)

There was barely enough plot in Peter Benchley's 1995 novel *White Shark* for a B movie; indeed, the book owes rather a debt to the 1977 movie *Shock Waves*. Because Benchley was in the King-Koontz bracket as an airport bestseller, the property – like his *The Beast*

– was turned into a two-part TV miniseries. The book's Nazi backstory is replaced with a *Piranha*-style Vietnam War mad science experiment, and the New England backdrop becomes the more colourful Caribbean. A sub-plot about voodoo-worshipping 'natives' is straight out of the 1940s, as an island police chief (Blu Mankuma) is upset because, after years of arguing for rationality, it has turned out that there are monsters after all.

Scriptwriter Rockne S. O'Bannon and director Stuart Gillard, reteamed after the *Outer Limits* pilot they made for the same Trilogy outfit, spin Benchley's sparse text into an okay two-part entertainment, with likable if not outstanding performances and a Stan Winston creature. Divorced marine biologists Dr Simon Chase (Craig T. Nelson) and Dr Amanda Mayson (Kim Cattrall) set up shop in the abandoned US Navy facility where the monster was made in 1972, with teenage son Max (Matthew Carey) in tow. The monster – a shark-dolphin-human hybrid – is loose again, though the script is fuzzy about why it hasn't made trouble for a couple of decades. At the end of Part One, it evolves legs so it can get about on land to forage for live human food. Sneering Admiral Richland (Colm Feore) shows up from Guantanamo Bay with a cadre of *Aliens*-ish bug-hunters, but they get creamed quickly, so it's down to civilian ingenuity to defeat the monster – which gets a nicely spectacular finish ('There's a reason it's called explosive decompression.').

Length really hurts, as *Creature* repeatedly cuts away from monster menace to other locations where fresh characters are apprised of what's going on and rush to the rescue only to get deeper in trouble. The monster itself is, contrary to the script, 'just a killing machine'. It looks embarrassingly like the *Street Sharks* cartoon, while little is made of its genetic link to loitering guilt-ridden loon 'Werewolf' (Giancarlo Esposito). The script works in some lectures on marine ecology: a major sub-plot has Chase arguing that white sharks should be protected, because Benchley – who cameos as Exec's Buddy – thought better of attitudes fostered by *Jaws*. Nelson and Cattrall are always welcome, and the slimy, toothy physical effects work is better than the depthless CGI that has supplanted the style in contemporary shark mutant cable trash – but it's still just TV fodder.

CROC (2007)

For a shot-in-Thailand TV movie about a giant crocodile, this is surprisingly solid. The *Jaws* plot offers few surprises, but the characters are likeable (or interestingly not), CGI is kept to a minimum, and its low-key amiability compares well with mean-spirited contemporaries. An Australian croc turns up on a Thai beach and takes a few human snacks – it looms towards a toddler but swims away and no one listens when the kid says a crocodile has come to visit, though it later snatches another child – before the authorities catch on. Nice guy Jack McQuade (Peter Tuinstra) runs a croc zoo, which unethical hustlers are trying to shut down so they can build a road across the site. They let Jack's crocs loose, which means they take the blame for the monster rampage. Jack teams with one-legged salt Hawkins (Michael Madsen), who is tracking the killer croc, and Evelyn (Sherry Phungprasert), an animal welfare officer, to go after the monster. The reptile eats the villainous entrepreneurs (one in his own swimming pool) before being tracked to the cave where it stashes kills to rot before eating them (as in *Rogue*). The film has nice patter – after it's over, Hawkins reveals he lost his leg fork-lift driving – and doesn't always kill the expected people, so major characters aren't automatically safe. Written by Ken Solarz (*Crime Story, Profiler*); directed by Stewart Raffill (*The Adventures of the Wilderness Family, The Ice Pirates*)

CROCODILE (2000)

It signals how much less ruthless Tobe Hooper's second killer crocodile movie is than his first (*Death Trap/Eaten Alive!*) that an annoying poodle – which is actually the cause of the trouble – does not get eaten as the little girl's pet did in the earlier film. An auteur touch of *Lemon Popsicle* producer Boaz Davidson, who devised the story, is the extensive beer-drinking-and-puking, getting-laid-and-breaking-up activities of a crowd of buffed models and hunks pretending to be college kids on spring break. Hooper has no interest in these people and the performers can't handle the romantic triangles and simmering jealousies of the soapy script, so these scenes are just dead wood until centuried and barnacled croc Flat Dog shows up and – after the poodle eats its clutch of eggs – starts chewing everyone in sight. Copping some *Blair Witch Project* licks, there's a bit of whiny bickering and torch-lit woodlands panic as whittled-down survivors hike from their run-aground boat through the swamps. A pair of supporting degenerates hint at the Hooper of old: a gator farmer with a grudge against the beast (it ate his grandfather) and a resentful sidekick who encourages the monster to kill his boss because 'I'm tired of all his buggering'. The part-CGI Flat Dog is more active than the stiff model of *Death Trap*, but never lives up to the legendary rep established in a campfire tale-telling session. Riding the scaly tail of *Lake Placid*, it is no better or worse than the similar *Blood Surf* or *Komodo*. Scripted by Michael D. Weiss, Adam Gierasch and Jace Anderson.

THE CURSE OF THE KOMODO (2004)

Directed by Jim Wynorski (credited as Jay Andrews), this cable TV time-waster has one tiny, silly new idea: General Foster (Jay Richardson) is inspired to fund Project Catalyst (growing big komodo dragons for combat use) by Wynorski's earlier *Dinosaur Island*. We know he's mad because he says it's a good movie.

On an island off Pearl Harbor, Professor Phipps (William Langlois) works to wipe out world hunger despite his backers' obvious military aims. The result is one big komodo dragon (it's supposedly eaten all the others) which lashes with its long tongue (the venom turns people into blotch-faced madmen, allowing for mild zombie action) and is represented by CGI so poor I miss the blown-up lizard footage from things like *King Dinosaur*. After a storm, the island is home to a dwindling band of survivors who hope for rescue even as Foster plans to send in two whole bombers to napalm the place (or at least run burning jungle stock footage). Evoking Charles Griffith's oft-used crooks-flee-into-danger plot (*Naked Paradise*, *Beast from Haunted Cave*), flask-chugging helicopter pilot Jack (Tim Abell) shows up with a trio of cash-toting crook casino robbers (buff hardman Paul Logan, vampy Melissa Brasselle, doomed Cam Newlin). The professor's crew includes his devoted assistant (Yorkshire-accented Gail Harris) and dim-bulb daughter (Glori-Anne Gilbert, who has a topless swimming and breast-washing scene). The compound is protected by an electric fence which depends on a failing generator, and the dragon shows up whenever things get quiet – then just stands there as everyone fires a million bullets without so much as rippling its CGI hide.

In the end, the Prof sacrifices himself by letting himself get eaten while holding a lump of plastic explosive he could as easily have thrown into the monster's mouth. Though it makes a fuss about the fact there's only one monster, the shock finish has Logan stranded on the island (because he can't even walk twenty yards to pick up a bag of money and get to the helicopter in time) and attacked by more of the things. Maybe, in the future, this will become a nostalgia item like, say, *The Giant Gila Monster* – but I doubt it: there's something annoying about its offhand willingness to be just a piece of crap.

DARK AGE (1987)

Seemingly the first Australian terror-by-croc movie, made well before *Blood Surf* (though it was re-released as *Blood Surf 2*), *Black Water* and *Rogue*. It includes elements of the *Jaws* template (including the crass local government who want the problem solved fast before business suffers), but veers off into unexpected territory (perhaps influencing *Lake Placid*) as the emphasis shifts from tracking and killing the giant reptile to protecting it from the ocker nature-violators responsible for sending it on a rampage. Steve Harris (John Jarratt in a pre-*Wolf Creek* nice-guy role), a nature warden in shorts, hates poacher Besser (Max Phipps, a nasty in *Thirst* and *Mad Max 2*), whose night-time killing spree leads to the first death and stirs up the vengeful 'Numunwari'. Steve respects aboriginal elder Oondabund (Burnham Burnham), who regards the perhaps-ancient crocodile as sacred and won't help kill it.

As in many Ozsploitation films, the likeliest victims throw beer cans into the swamp or generally act like dicks – one beach lout is eaten while beating up a tramp. The most shocking death is that of an aboriginal child swallowed whole, but Oondabund says the kid was sickly and the croc was just naturally thinning the herd – a genuinely alien point of view which even the liberal hero has a hard time getting behind. Besser loses an arm but still makes trouble, and the climax has his mob menacing Steve's girlfriend (Nikki Coghill) and murdering his penned crocs and trying to slaughter Numunwari before it's returned to its natural habitat. It has a sometimes-inappropriate score, occasionally stiff model effects and falls down in soap opera relationship stuff, but some oddly amateurish performances work in context. With David Gulpilil, a fixture in aboriginal-themed films (*Walkabout*, *The Last Wave*). Scripted by Sonia Borg, Stephen Cross and Tony Morphett from Grahame Webb's novel *Numunwari*; directed by Arch Nicholson (*Fortress*).

DARK WATERS (2003)

A cable TV 'original' from busy writer-director Phillip J. Roth (*A.P.E.X.*, *Boa/New Alcatraz*), this vest-pocket *Deep Blue Sea* is an (accidental?) precursor of *The Life Aquatic with Steve Zissou*. An undersea facility is attacked in formation by CGI sharks trained and operated by a sneaky Navy weapons project. Things get more interesting when we meet the 'hero', third-generation undersea explorer Dane Quatrell III (Lorenzo

Lamas) – a near-gigolo sleaze who spends his time fundraising (dogging a pair of trust-fund blonde twins) for non-existent expeditions in partnership with equally cynical sidekick Robin (Simmone Mackinnon). Dane and Robin are kidnapped then hired by a businessman (Bruce Gray) to investigate the shark attacks. After their crew are wiped out, the pair are imprisoned on a submarine where Quatrell's long-lost father (Ross Manarchy) chafes at the misuses of his shark project and a mad martinet captain (Stefan Lysenko) orders summary executions. The script is full of clichés, like the absurd 'ventilation shaft' which enables Robin to escape from a holding cell on a submarine, and the sharks do little except lap up to chomp minor villains late in the day. The most fun comes from Lamas and Mackinnon, seizing an opportunity to play reprehensible heroes. Co-written by Brett Orr (*Maximum Velocity*).

DINOCROC (2004)

This Roger Corman-produced Syfy Channel nothing-in-particular monster movie at least offers value-for-money ham acting alongside the usual piss-poor CGI beastie. An unethical genegeneering company fouls up the safety protocols and a lab-bred prehistoric crocodile – a species which might hold the key to extended lifespan, freedom from disease, etc. – gets loose in a small community. While corporate spokesbitch Paula Kennedy (Joanna Pacula) denies responsibility, it falls to the local animal officer (i.e. dog-catcher) Diane Harper (Jane Longenecker), her inventor ex-boyfriend Tom Banning (Matthew Borlenghi) and Crocodile Dundee parody Dick Sydney (Costas Mandylor) to put together a *Jaws* triumvirate and hunt the monster – though not before groan-inducing jokes like Tom's little brother (Jake Thomas) overhearing Diane admit, 'I like Dick.' In a surprisingly ruthless touch, the kid is decapitated by the monster – though his three-legged dog survives. With Charles Napier (heroine's sheriff dad), Bruce Weitz (doomed scientist) and Max Perlich (comedy deputy). Director Kevin O'Neill (who went on to *Dinoshark*) and writers Frances Doel, John Huckert and Dan Acre at least try for the quirky character/anti-corporate politics feel of Corman productions from *Piranha* to *Carnosaur*.

DINOCROC VS. SUPERGATOR (2010)

This follows Roger Corman-produced schlock *Dinocroc* and *Supergator*, and carries over a few names – Delia Sheppard replaces Kelly McGillis as Dr Kim Taft, though she doesn't really resemble the character from *Supergator* – but is pretty much a remake of director/co-writer Jim Wynorski/Rob Robertson/Jay Andrews' *Komodo vs. Cobra* with slightly different monsters. Unethical bioengineering tycoon Jason Drake (David Carradine) sponsors a program to raise giant mushrooms on Hawaii to solve world hunger, but is really interested in the military applications of giant reptiles. Notice how in the real world armies don't deploy, say, man-eating tigers or black mambas in war-zones? The reasons for that have never troubled the writers of Syfy schlock. A dinocroc (a big bipedal crocodile) and a supergator (a big alligator with added spines) get loose and eat folks. Drake sends in mercs who get wiped out swiftly, then hires hunter Bob Logan (Rib Hillis), known as 'The Cajun', and English-accented hatchet woman Victoria (Lisa Clapperton) to cope with the problem. Meanwhile Paul Beaumont (Corey Landis), a FBI snoop in a running-joke Hawaiian shirt, teams with short-shorted animal protection officer Cassidy Swanson (Amy Rasimas) to investigate the chompings. Dr Taft explains the setup in flashback, then gets killed in hospital by the nasty Victoria, leaving the trio – augmented by Cassidy's doomed sheriff dad (John Callahan) – to herd the monsters together for the title bout (dinocroc wins). There's a detour to a hotel wrecked by a hurricane, an interesting locale which more could have been made of – an Elvis fan tourist is eaten, but the guide is more interested in revealing that Corman's *She Gods of Shark Reef* was shot here. The CGI is shit, the performances amiable but lightweight and Wynorski has never really progressed beyond rudimentary.

DINOSHARK (2010)

'I WAS JUST TELLING HER ABOUT THE SIBERIAN STURGEON I WAS TRYING TO FREEZE THE DNA OF FOR FUTURE REGENERATION.'

A prehistoric shark freed from a chunk of Alaskan ice by global warming heads to Mexico to attack the usual tourist festival, unforgivably disrupting an all-girls' open-sea volleyball game and more genially leaping out of the water to chomp a parasailing idiot. The *Jaws* hero triumvirate are boat bum Trace McGraw (Eric Balfour), marine biologist/volleyball coach Carol Brubaker (Iva Hasperger) and cop Luis (Aarón Díaz). Producer Roger Corman takes a heftier acting role than is his wont as a marine biopaleontologist who explains the creature can only be killed by a shot to the eye. With the usual parade of incidental victims, misunderstandings among the good guys, poor CGI/creature design (this is no *Sharktopus*), lightly likeable leads trying hard, non-stop salsa to ramp up the thin excitement. Carol pleads that the monster be caught and studied, but personally kills it at the end. It feels like an update of Corman's first production, *Monster From the Ocean Floor*, and you can't help thinking it got made because he got a deal on waterbikes and speedboats. The regulation 'oh, but there's another monster' ending cheaply recycles effects footage from the opening. More entertaining than most, but fluff. Written by Frances Doel (*Big Bad Mama*) and Guy Prevost (the *Wasp Woman* remake); directed by Kevin O'Neill (*Dinocroc*).

47 METERS DOWN (IN THE DEEP) (2016)

This menaced-on-holiday movie pits a pair of luckless, perhaps foolish tourists against sharks and the sea. In *Open Water*, progenitor of the cycle, the doomed couple bob on the surface, unable to see what is coming for them; in this variation, the ordeal takes place almost entirely underwater. Co-writer/director Johannes Roberts ups the suspense by staying with the imperilled women, not including cutaways to would-be rescuers worrying up on the boat.

Lisa (Mandy Moore), depressed after a break-up, takes a Mexican holiday with her more impulsive sister Kate (Claire Holt). A couple of guys in a bar (Yani Gellman, Chris J. Johnson) convince them to take a cut-price shark-spotting trip in a small boat captained by competent-seeming Taylor (Matthew Modine). Lowered in a cage, the sisters are supposed to go no deeper than five meters, but the winch breaks and they plunge to the seabed – with a heavy chunk of equipment on the top hatch to keep them trapped, unless someone takes off her helmet to slip between the bars.

The film plays out in near-real time as Lisa and Kate deal with the minutiae of their quandary: having to swim up from the safety of the cage to shark-infested waters to get a signal to communicate with Taylor, a limited air supply and (when replacement tanks are supplied) the possibility they'll hallucinate from excess nitrogen, the threat of the bends if they panic and break for the surface, being pinned under the cage when an attempt to lift it fails and frequent swim-bys from gathering sharks as minor cuts bleed into the water. Moore and Holt play most of the film behind masks, and are engaging enough without overdoing the backstory. The all-CGI sharks are better realised than the fish in Syfy schlock like the *Sharknado* or *2-Headed Shark Attack* films. A tricksy last reel, which might or might not be a hallucination of the deep, evokes the wind-up of *The Descent*. Co-written by Roberts' frequent collaborator Ernest Riera.

FRANKENFISH (2004)

A pleasant, silly, sometimes-surprising little monster movie. When a swamp-dweller in a Louisiana bayou is gruesomely killed while fishing, medical examiner Sam Rivers (Tory Kittles) and ecologist Mary Callahan (China Chow) take a boat upstream to investigate and come upon a small community of river-dwellers besieged by giant genetically-engineered snakehead fish. The monsters have been bred to order for a lunatic hunter (Tomas Arana) and escaped after a hurricane wrecked the boat in which they were being transported; the low-rent Count Zaroff and his cronies show up late, mostly to provide new victims after the fish have chewed through the rest of the supporting cast.

The film is clever enough to break some of its rules, with theoretically safe characters (like wise old black woman Donna Biscoe) getting killed and the token white asshole lawyer (Matthew Rauch), who whines and complains and bitches throughout, surviving *almost* until the fade-out (he is consumed by the tiny offspring of the big monster).

Director Mark A.Z. Dippé, whose debut was the dud *Spawn*, handles conventional suspense well, and the sparely used CGI creatures are quite impressive. They bite hard and leap out of the water, but otherwise aren't especially invulnerable (the big one gets shredded in the big fan of a swamp boat). Written by Simon Barrett (later Adam Wingard's favoured scenarist) and Scott Clevenger.

FRESHWATER (2014)

'WAIT, BRITT IS TRAPPING HUMANS
TO FEED HIS GATOR?'
'HE SEEMS TO REALLY ENJOY IT.'

This dispiritingly lifeless *Lake Placid* knock-off wastes a seemingly surefire exploitation premise: action chick Zoë Bell (*Death Proof*) vs a serial killer who uses an albino alligator as a murder weapon. It offers bare minimum plotting, characterisation and gore and doesn't even manage a smidgen of suspense. The effects have a weirdly unfinished look, as if six more CGI passes were needed to add missing detail: the aftermath of one attack is conveyed by a hat floating in unbloodied waters and the 'monstergator' – whose pale colour, incidentally, spoils the whodunit aspect, since only one character loudly proclaims he's from New York where those flushed-away gator babies grow into albino sewer denizens – is a weightless, depthless digital cutout.

In a small lakeside community, the gator snacks on out-of-towners, but expert Brenda Gray (Bell) and a forensics guy (Tom O'Connell) think this is no ordinary hungry rogue reptile since the severed body parts have slivers of metal as well as teeth in chew-wounds. On an island, a bunch of obnoxious kids are picked off slasher movie-style while the sheriff (Joe Lando) and a dimwit deputy (Christopher Biewer) wander uselessly. A hilariously minimal flashback shows the first finger-nipping meeting between alienated madman and cute rubber baby gator, but the mechanics of using a free-ranging alligator as a murder weapon aren't even considered and we never see killer and pet working together.

The conventional ending would be to have the monster turn on its master (cf: *Death Trap*) and be spectacularly blown up, but this has the heroine just about realise what's going on before she's ordinarily shot in the chest and forgotten about as the villain gets on with his business. Sometimes, obvious comebacks are irresistible: sadly, *Freshwater* is foul. Written and directed by Brandeis Berry.

GHOST SHARK (2013)

A great white dies in a magic cave and resurrects as a translucent phantom to get revenge on its killers. The ghost shark can lurk in any body of water, so the monster leaps out of a swimming pool, a bikini carwash, a toilet bowl and even pouring rain. The leads are sisters Ava (Mackenzie Rosman) and Cicely (Sloane Coe) – who might have swapped roles, since the supposed kid sister looks older than the grownup one – and the nearest thing to a guest star is tall Richard Moll as the embittered lighthouse keeper who has a motive for not blowing up the cave and exorcising the shark spook. The crooked mayor (Lucky Johnson), a *Jaws* leftover, is the father of the guy (Jaren Mitchell) who doesn't call off his pool party after one of his friends is decapitated. Too meagre and cheapskate to be much fun. Repetitive CGI bisection-and-blood-spurt deaths pall, even if the film is ruthless enough to off obnoxious little kids. Written by Paul A. Birkett (*Arachnoquake*), from a story by Eric Forsberg (*Snakes on a Train*) and director Griff Furst (*Swamp Shark*) – and quite possibly a mean-spirited spoiler for *Ghost Shark 2* (see below).

GHOST SHARK 2: URBAN JAWS (2014)

This New Zealand comedy was made in dribs and drabs between 2010 and 2014. Like *Surf II*, it was a sham sequel – until the Syfy Channel squashed the joke by coincidentally or maliciously making an actual *Ghost Shark* – to which this isn't a sequel. Set in Auckland, New Zealand, it goes a lot further into the strange, as angry ghost sharks – of which there are many thanks to mass killing of sharks for their fins – manifest in any form of water, including steam, ice, lubricant, an ice lolly, a puddle and the ocean. Mayor Jack Broody (Campbell Cooley), who once nuked a ghost shark, wants to call off the water festival, putting out a cover story that there's a water-themed serial killer on the loose. Burnout Tony Palantine (Steve Austin) and embittered ghost-shark-hunter Tom Logan (Johnny Hall) track the spook, while Marco Guerra (Robert Nascimento) – who is running against Broody – nags away in an attempt to uncover the truth. Skits about folks killed by the ghost Great White while eating a lolly or masturbating are littered throughout, but it gets weirder when Logan sets off an EMP to dispel the ghost and ventures into a black and white afterlife where the monster impersonates his dead girlfriend (Kathleen Burns) and – on the principle that she's a shark so she'll die if she doesn't keep moving – he hugs her poignantly to death. Short enough not to wear out its welcome. Written and directed by Johnny Hall and Andrew Todd.

GYO (GYO: TOKYO FISH ATTACK!) (2012)

An interesting, apocalyptic anime. Three girls go on a post-graduation trip to Okinawa, though they don't seem to like each other much even before a crisis sets them against each other: the virtuous, faithful heroine Kaori thinks too much about the boyfriend she's left in Tokyo, conventionally sexy Erika is a slut who picks up guys for threesomes and 'third wheel' Aki is a dumpy, bespectacled tagalong. A bad smell betokens the arrival of an odd menace – zombie fish which invade dry land on mechanical insect-legs… first a single odiferous small specimen, then a deadly blundering shark, finally a swarming horde. Erika is infected and transforms into an obese green warty ogress who gets her own set of metal spider-legs; as in source manga creator Junji Ito's *Tomie*, there's an uncomfortable disgust with teenage female sexuality, including variations on the anime tentacle rape quirk. Various contradictory explanations involve World War II mad science, parallel universes and natural phenomena, but it's all an excuse for an escalation of weirdness: vast human-fish-insect colonies fuelled by their own noxious gases, a circus exploiting the mutations in post-transformation Tokyo. The tone is uncertain: the character interplay between the girls is frankly nasty, but the film wavers between transgression (in a flesh-twisting Clive Barker-Shinya Tsukamoto vein), low comedy (a *lot* of fart jokes) and surrealism. The monsters are imaginative, and there are great set pieces: a plane coming down perilously on a runway overrun with fish which slick up the landing gear, a subway crash caused by the monsters, a game of tag with the monster shark in the holiday home. Written and directed by Takayuki Hirao.

ICE SHARKS (2016)

> 'IT'S GONNA TAKE A HELL OF A LOT MORE THAN A SHARK TO KEEP ME AWAY FROM YOU.'

Another Syfy/Asylum novelty shark movie – with a modish global-warming theme. Due to changing weather conditions in the Arctic, local sharks ('greenies') can more easily get their favoured human snacks – pulling a whole dog team and a fed up Inuit off an ice shelf in the opening sequence. A team of scientists are attacked – with a shark-fin shredding through the ice in a key image – as their floe breaks up. Much of the film plays for suspense as an all-weather habitat sinks to the sea bed and the boffins improvise ways to fend off sharks, communicate with the surface and escape in scientifically implausible fashion. Writer-director Emile Edwin Smith (*Mega Shark versus Mecha Shark*) plots reasonably well, with attacks and crises at regular intervals, and the no-name cast emote intensely while gabbling techie dialogue. Trash, but with flickers of watchability.

JERSEY SHORE SHARK ATTACK (2012)

> 'FOLKS, YOU'RE NOT GOING TO BELIEVE THIS. JOEY FATONE, FORMERLY OF *NSYNC, HAS JUST BEEN EATEN BY A SHARK. EVERYONE WE'VE TALKED TO IS REALLY UPSET.'

A mash-up of the popular (i.e. unknown in Britain) reality show *Jersey Shore* and the faded *Jaws* xeroxes which still proliferate on Syfy. A load of albino sharks are loosed by undersea drilling and eat folk around a Jersey development, including desperate guest celeb Joey Fatone. Leftovers from *The Sopranos* and other NJ crime efforts (Jack Scalia, Tony Sirico, Paul Sorvino) show up, as does actual *Jersey Shore* veteran Vinny Guadagnino. Buffed/hairstyled guys and girls whine between generic shark attack shit.

TC (Jeremy Luke) – which stands for The Complication, not Top Cat – and Nooki (Melissa Molinaro) get past the tragic misunderstanding which keeps them apart when he saves her from being eaten after her high heel gets stuck in a hole in the deck. William Atherton is the developer who ignores the shark rumours. Sirico reminisces about a historical shark attack and provides the infobyte that sharks should be speared through the left eye, 'because it's the Devil's eye.' Too few folk get eaten. Story by Jeffrey Schenck, Peter Sullivan, Richard Gnolfo and Michael Ciminera (script by Gnolfo and Ciminera), though it's hard to see how four heads were needed. Directed by John Shepphird (*Chupacabra Terror*).

KING COBRA (1999)

Seth, a thirty-foot genetically-engineered snake with the head of a king cobra and the tail of a diamondback rattler, escapes during a laboratory fire and slithers towards the town of Fillmore. The mayor (Hoyt Axton) is reluctant to declare a state of emergency for fear of ruining the local beer festival. A young doctor ('Scott Brandon', actually co-director Scott Hillenbrand) and a deputy (Kasey Fallo) call for eccentric herpetologist Nick Hashimoto (Pat Morita) to save the day. Harking back to the 1970s' retro-'50s style of *Piranha*, this familiarly-plotted, ordinarily-filmed reptile-on-the-rampage movie offers a venom-spitting creature manufactured by the Chiodo Brothers which often creeps in subjective camera towards victims. Erik Estrada is cast against type in a tiny 'special appearance' as a flamboyant gay stereotype. Axton performs a brief song, 'Seth is the Devil'. Written and directed by David and Scott Hillenbrand.

KOMODO (1999)

> 'I THINK THEY'RE CONTESTING OUR PLACE IN THE FOOD CHAIN.'

A regulation trapped-with-monsters quickie. Visitors to an island supposedly off the shore of Carolina (actually somewhere in the Australias) are menaced by CGI creatures. Though the title gives the game away, ex-effects technician-turned-director

Michael Lantieri keeps the monsters offscreen and purportedly mysterious for half the running time. Teenage Patrick (Kevin Zegers, later of *TransAmerica*), traumatised by the deaths of his parents (and his dog), retreats into an amnesiac fugue, but his psychiatrist Victoria (Jill Hennessy) brings him back to the site of the tragedy to stir his memories. The local evil oil company knows a bunch of giant, flesh-eating lizards are on the loose, but keeps quiet for nebulously nefarious purposes. Oates (Billy Burke), a rebellious company minion, hooks up with Patrick and his shrink, and they have a last-reel confrontation with the monsters which allows for distant echoes of *Jurassic Park*. The monsters have too little personality and, despite their voracious appetites, all manner of contrivances are required to bring victims within snapping distance. Nice bit at the end with a flare popping off inside the last creature's throat, though. Written by Hans Bauer (*Anacondas*) and Craig Mitchell (*What's Up, Hideous Sun Demon*).

KOMODO VS. COBRA (2005)

'I DIDN'T KNOW A BEAUTIFUL LADY SCIENTIST WOULD COME EQUIPPED WITH A SENSE OF HUMOUR.'

This disappointing vs movie isn't really related to earlier movies featuring komodo dragons or cobras – though writer-director Jim Wynorski did make the lookalike *Curse of the Komodo*. A Greenpeace-type activist (Ryan McTavish), his starlet girlfriend (Renee Talbert), an edible blonde (Glori-Anne Gilbert) and other munchable space-fillers are ferried to an island by crusty he-man skipper Stoddard (Michael Paré) to expose the unethical Project Carnivore. Sole survivor Dr Susan Richardson (Michelle Borth) doles out the backstory about an honourable program to raise giant crops perverted by soldiers who wanted a serum to make enemies 'blow up like balloons'. The main effect is the unleashing of the title pair of giant reptiles, who set new lows in appalling CGI as they swallow folks, hiss at each other and lurch around – some big leeches show up, too, and speculation as to what the infection will do to exposed human beings sets up a capper where a bitten, forgotten victim doesn't grow into a giant but somehow has reptile eyes and a forked tongue. Paré, who also produced, plods through the *Gilligan's Monster Island* business.

LAKE PLACID 2 (2007)

> 'MAN, THIS LAKE IS REALLY STARTING TO FREAK ME OUT. DO YOU KNOW HOW MANY PEOPLE HAVE DISAPPEARED FROM AROUND HERE IN THE LAST FEW YEARS?'

Set in Maine/shot in Bulgaria, this returns to the well nearly a decade on from Steve Miner's *Lake Placid*. Though it misses the added bite lent the original by name players and David E. Kelley's witty script, it provides a template to turn a one-off into a franchise. Extra-large crocodiles are nurtured by a batty old lady (Cloris Leachman) who takes their side against the local humans (which doesn't stop her getting eaten). The monsters predate on a couple of eco-warriors and a gang of cloddish, superficial teens ('Seriously, Larry, I wouldn't let you rub my feet even if you were the CEO of Prada.'). The sheriff (John Schneider), a wildlife officer (Sarah Lafleur), an Oirish blowhard hunter (Sam McMurray) and a rebellious sidekick (Joe Holt) stalk and splat the character-free CGI reptiles. So cheap that even a seaplane is rendered by terrible computer graphics. Wry Schneider just about gets through with dignity, but everyone else has to act like some sort of idiot to keep the plot going. The refreshing avoidance of cliché in *Lake Placid* congeals into an enthusiastic embrace of the obvious. Scripted by Todd Hurvitz and Howie Miller; directed by David Flores (*Boa vs Python*).

LAKE PLACID 3 (2010)

This return to Maine/Bulgaria is another disposable Syfy schedule-filler with nudity and awful CGI. EPA-guy hero Nathan Bickerman (Colin Ferguson) inherits a lakeshore cabin from the insane croc-feeding aunt of the earlier films, and his really stupid kid (Jordan Grehs) tosses shoplifted meat to the crocodiles the sheriff (Michael Ironside) says aren't around any more. Guide-poacher lunatic Reba (Yancy Butler) is hired by the boyfriend (Mark Evans) of a missing hot girl (Kacey Barnfield) to deal with things. It has much screaming and blasting, but CGIdiles just slither across the image weightlessly and are especially fakey when interacting with people they are supposedly dragging and chewing. Ferguson and Butler almost give the impression they care enough to deliver performances – Butler's grouchy old reprobate characterisation is unusual and she wound up staying on with the franchise, down to *Lake Placid vs Anaconda* – but everyone else goes 'eek' and the girls find reasons to take their tops off before being eaten. Yes, it has an open ending. Written by David Reed (*Boogeyman*). Directed by G.E. Furst, who later made *Swamp Shark* – though it's a joke here when someone wonders if a body found in the woods was left by a shark attack.

LAKE PLACID: THE FINAL CHAPTER (2012)

> 'REBA, CAN YOU ENLIGHTEN US AS TO WHY WE HAVE TO PROTECT THESE CREATURES THAT HAVE KILLED DOZENS OF PEOPLE?'

Reba (Yancy Butler) from *Lake Placid 3* is back, now a poacher-turned-gamekeeper, and a new sheriff, Theresa Giove (Elisabeth Röhm), is in office in Marshfield, Maine, that croc-haunted spot which looks a lot (in the sequels) like Bulgaria. There's a lot of plotty stuff, considering the point is to feed as many folk to CGI reptiles as possible. The single mom sheriff and a single dad army engineer (Paul Nicholls) cosy up as he builds an electric fence around Black Lake (it's not even called Lake Placid) while her bookish daughter Chloe (Poppy Lee Friar) is on a swim-team outing imperilled thanks to the intervention of a shifty tree-hugger in league with croc poachers and a bus driver too busy looking at porn on his phone to notice he's driving down the wrong road, through an open gate in the electric fence and into a killing zone. The chief hunter, Jim Bickerman (Robert Englund, pulling on a hip-flask), is the embittered son of the croc-feeding lady from the first two *Lake Placids*. Butler and Röhm are game, though Englund has done this shtick way too often. Written by David and Marin Reed (David did *Lake Placid 3*); directed by three-first-names Don Michael Paul (*Tremors 5: Bloodlines*).

LAKE PLACID VS ANACONDA (2015)

Screenwriter Berkeley Anderson (*Robocroc*) is new to both the *Lake Placid* and *Anaconda* franchises, but deftly shuffles together ingredients from all *eight* previous entries for this Syfy time-waster and still manages to throw in a sorority rush week sub-plot to up the victim count.

Yancy Butler reprises her role as alcoholic hunter Reba from the *Lake Placid* sequels, now given the poison chalice job of sheriff in the Black Lake area. Robert Englund carries over from *Lake Placid: The Final Chapter*, down a couple of limbs and an eye as local rogue Jim Bickerman. Manic tycoon Sarah Murdoch (Annabel Wright) and mercenary Beach (Stephen Billington) represent the evil genetics corp. who've been tinkering with an orchid-and-reptile-derived immortality serum since *Anacondas: The Hunt for the Blood Orchid*. To further their ends, the science crew need to implant anaconda eggs into a crocodile, so the Murdoch Corporation hires Bickerman to get them into the Lake Placid croc enclave, where things go wrong as usual – unloosing CGI crocs and 'condas into the Bulgaria-passing-for-New England woods just as sorority bitch queen Tiffani (Laura Dale) drags pledges to the lakeshore for hazing. Quite a few of the supporting coeds do nude scenes before dying. After the first few maulings, Sheriff Reba calls in wildlife warden Tull (Corin Nemec), who is concerned that his daughter Bethany (Skye Lourie) is among the imperilled bikini babes. There are scenes in which anacondas constrict a car and a crocodile, but as usual with Syfy the execution falls far short of the concept.

In the end, one major villain is left unkilled and a batch of eggs in the woods hatch hybrid beasties – suggesting that *Crocaconda*, a further entwining of the franchises, is all but inevitable. Butler, Englund and Wright attack the script with gusto, and Ali Eagle is fun as the wry, cynical goth pledge. Directed by A.B. Stone (*Atomic Shark*).

MALIBU SHARK ATTACK (MEGA SHARK OF THE MALIBU) (2009)

'FATHER WILL WANT TO SUE THE CITY OF MALIBU FOR PUTTING ME AT RISK.' 'WITH A BIT OF LUCK, ALL THE LAWYERS WILL HAVE DROWNED.'

More flat cable-TV sharksploitation, passing off Australia as California. Peta Wilson (*La Femme Nikita*) is a gruff lifeguard and Chelan Simmons (a CGI monsterfest regular) fills a pink bikini top and short shorts as an annoying, whiny blonde. Some macho guys in orange *Baywatch* shirts say tough things like, 'We can't just sit here and let them pick us off one by one.' Warren Christie is the alpha hero who wins the arguments about being allowed to volunteer for dangerous swimming, while Remi Broadway (whose name might be more suitable for gay porn) is the younger sidekick palmed off with the second-billed woman. A ton of swim-on or paddle-by characters are killed by 'prehistoric' goblin sharks (with weird horn-bump foreheads) agitated by an underwater quake/tsunami the genre hadn't yet evolved to bill as a sharknami. A scientist (Sonya Salomaa) pleads to protect the fish because of the knowledge to be gained from their appearance in the modern world, but everyone else just doesn't want to be eaten – naturally, the boffin gets killed early. The sharks swim by in repeated CGI shots. The climax takes place in a half-flooded building site, with *Deep Blue Sea* waist-high waters and power tools – chainsaw, buzzsaw, nail gun – used as shark repellents. Written by Keith Shaw (*Deep Evil*); directed by David Lister (*The Meeksville Ghost*).

MEGALODON (SHARK-ZILLA) (2002)

'AN EIGHTY-FOOT-LONG PREHISTORIC FISH IS WORTH HANGING AROUND FOR.'

A news report name-checks Carl Denham and Robert Armstrong from *King Kong*, signalling a knowingly retro side of this SciFi Channel CGI monster movie. A mixed bunch of media folk, deep-sea explorers and oil-men on a rig which lowers like a big elevator to the seabed run into a prehistoric survival – a giant shark ancestor which bites minisubs. Robin Sachs is the industrialist with an image problem, Leighanne Littrell the reporter who passes out when diving deep and Al Sapienza the white-haired tough eco-warrior hero. Amiable, if a little light on big shark action – an early encounter with a smaller living fossil is more impressive than the standard swim-and-chew business with the main menace. A long, slow end credits crawl pads out the running time. Writers Gary J. Tunnicliffe (effects man) and Stanley Isaacs have bit-roles. Directed by Pat Corbitt.

MEGA PIRANHA (2010)

Mutant Venezuelan piranha get bigger, leaping out of the Orinoco to eat bikini babes and diplomats. Eventually, they adapt to salt water so they can quit terrorising a South American country the filmmakers don't care about and devastate the USA. Another slack, dull effort from the company who gave you *Mega Shark versus Giant Octopus*, this has barely enough entertainment to fill a trailer with bad special effects shots (the fish look like angry PacMen and have as much screen presence). '50s rubbish like *The Giant Claw* and '70s rubbish like *Empire of the Ants* have a watchable charm which the makers of these quickies will never manage. With songstress Tiffany, warming up for *Mega Python vs. Gatoroid*. Joke's over. Written and directed by Eric Forsberg (*Arachnoquake*).

MEGA PYTHON VS. GATOROID (2010)

'I MEAN, WHAT'S CRAZY ABOUT THIS? WE'RE JUST FEEDING STEROIDS TO GATORS. THERE'S NOTHING CRAZY ABOUT THIS. WHAT COULD GO WRONG?'

With a sharper script and less clumping direction this might have been an amusing parody of the sort of film it sounds like – but it's the Asylum drek as usual, with director Mary Lambert (remember *Pet Sematary?*) in has-it-really-come-to-this? mode.

The high concept isn't the title contest but a clash between '80s pop princesses Deborah Gibson and Tiffany, veterans respectively of *Mega Shark versus Giant Octopus* and *Mega Piranha*. In an imaginary Florida where the Everglades and Bronson Caverns are adjacent, eco activist Nikki Riley (thin blonde Deb) lets some big snakes go free to chomp wildlife in the swamps. Park ranger Terry O'Hara (ample redhead Tiff) feeds steroids to gators (via chickens), which ups their size but also embiggens the egg-eating snakes. The leading ladies indulge in a lengthy catfight with food smearing (in evening dress) during a formal fundraiser further inconvenienced when giant reptiles show up and eat special guest star Micky Dolenz (as himself).

The divas and the hero (A. Martinez) deploy dynamite and save the state, but both women are gruesomely and stupidly killed in the process. There are a few actual jokes, like the number of Floridans packing guns in formal wear, but the format is so devalued it would take a greater effort than anyone is willing to make to craft a pastiche which isn't just another shit film – frankly, anyone thinking of investing in one of these would be well advised to give the money to Larry Blamire instead. Scripted by Naomi Selfman (*Mega Shark versus Crocosaurus*). Both leading ladies contribute soundtrack songs (Tiffany's 'Serpentine', Gibson's 'Snake Charmer').

MEGA SHARK VERSUS GIANT OCTOPUS (2009)

'...WAIT, ARE YOU TRYING TO TELL ME THAT A PREHISTORIC EXTINCT SHARK ATE MY WHALE?'

Maverick marine biologist Emma MacNeil (Deborah Gibson) is in the Antarctic filming a whale pod when someone in a passing helicopter unethically tests a sonar device which maddens the cetaceans. They batter their heads against a crumbling ice shelf which releases a megalodon (giant prehistoric shark) and a giant octopus (made-up beast out of *It Came from Beneath the Sea*) flash-frozen in mid-combat by the last ice age.

The creatures go on separate rampages in the Pacific – the octopus strangling a Japanese oil rig, the shark leaping out of the ocean to bite an airliner. Emma, in trouble for getting her borrowed minisub damaged, is working in California when a chewed whale coincidentally washes up on her patch. A big shark tooth prompts her crusty Irish old hippie mentor Lamar (Sean Lawlor) to deduce that the megalodon is responsible, but it takes a reel or two for the authorities (sinister men in suits) to twig that two different killer beasts are at work. Emma pools resources with Japanese boffin Seiji (Vic Chao); a quickie between lab sessions inspires the notion of using pheromones to lure the creatures somewhere manageable – the shark gets San Francisco Bay and the octopus Tokyo Bay. Neither plan works out well, and the shark trashes Golden Gate Bridge in a brief effects shot. The tentacular devastation of Tokyo is all offscreen, though Seiji looks properly upset when he talks about it. Since the scheme to trap the monsters separately didn't work, the brain trust decide to bring them back together and let them finish their fight.

Some aspects suggest dry satire – Lorenzo Lamas fumes as a military commander ('… now if we don't find a viable means of stopping this fucker, sharkzilla's gonna own the seas!'), Chao tries for a dubbed labcoat/Godzilla vibe and pop pixie Gibson is a hoot as an eco-warrior ('It's not easy being brilliant under armed guard.') – but it's severely let down by awful CGI. Admittedly, the climax delivers on its title as monsters tussle while humans sit in a nearby submarine barking running commentary. Potentially spectacular scenes are rushed and shots of the underwater titans rushing at the camera are tediously repeated. Written and directed by Jack Perez (*Some Guy Who Kills People*), under the nom de film Ace Hannah (a reference to an anecdote in Robert Aldrich's *Vera Cruz*).

MEGA SHARK VERSUS CROCOSAURUS (2010)

'WAIT, WE CAN'T BE LOOKING FOR A MEGALODON AND A PREHISTORIC CROCODILE!'

A sequel to *Mega Shark versus Giant Octopus* – one of those rubbish films civilians tend to have heard of (mostly because the trailer scored a lot of YouTube hits) and a few have even watched all the way through. The megalodon (prehistoric giant shark) has survived its bout with the cephalopod and now gets into it with a giant prehistoric crocodile dug out of a blood diamond mine in the Democratic Republic of Congo (played by Bronson Caves, a location seen in everything from the original *Invasion of the Body Snatchers* to *The Searchers*). On the shark's case is Dr Terry McCormick (Jaleel White), a revenge-seeking expert in hydrosonics, hydrophonics or hydroponics (depending on White's line readings – hydroponics wouldn't be much use in monster fighting). His fiancée (Nicola Lambo) is killed when the shark jumps over a warship (through the miracle of reversed footage, it jumps back too). The croc is trailed by unethical hunter Nigel Putnam (Gary Stretch, resembling Pierce Brosnan after an extensive depussification course), who was smuggling the reptile and some of its many eggs across the Atlantic when the shark capsized his ship.

The monsters rampage in Miami – but the CGI is pitifully unable to match even the effect of low-budget 1950s movies where Bronson Caves hosted a gorilla in a space helmet (*Robot Monster*) or a snarling Venusian turnip (*It Came from Outer Space*). This trend of SciFi/Syfy Channel we-don't-take-it-seriously-so-why-should-you creature features sours thanks to an underlying contempt for the audience. Most of the film consists of people squabbling in small dark rooms, while special effects shots look like placeholders until the real sequences can be achieved. This has the most perfunctory city-smashing rampage ever filmed, and neither titular mess of pixels exhibits anything like a personality. Solidly written killer croc pictures with good effects and decent characters (*Rogue*, *Lake Placid*) risk being driven to extinction by a shitnado of contemptible tosh with minimal entertainment value. The last line, honestly, is 'What a crock!' Written by Naomi Selfman (*Evil Eyes*), from a story by Micho Rutare (*Meteor Apocalypse*); directed by Christopher Ray (*3-Headed Shark Attack*).

MEGA SHARK VERSUS MECHA SHARK (2014)

'ALL RIGHT, ROSIE, IF IT'S NOT A MESS UP THERE YOU CAN CRAWL OUT THROUGH THE CHUM CHUTE.'

Pity poor *Mega Shark*… In the days before anyone had seen the film, a YouTube clip of the airliner attack from *Mega Shark versus Giant Octopus* got a gazillion hits and folks who'd never endured a Syfy Original frothed to see what they assumed would be a camp classic. Then, as sequels trundled out, sunny-day shark-movie followers decamped to enthuse about the even shoddier *Sharknado* series. The Asylum, who produce both franchises, toss off *Mega Shark versus* sequels with a lack of care remarkable even by their low, low standards. Here, Debbie Gibson, returning from the first film after sitting out *Mega Shark versus Crocosaurus*, plays all her scenes alone in a laboratory, literally phoning in her role as megasharkologist Emma MacNeil. The drama is carried by Rosie (Elisabeth Röhm) and Jack (Christopher Judge), the husband-and-wife science team behind the Mecha Shark, a robot deployed to fight a new megalodon which escapes from an iceberg being dragged to Egypt to solve a water shortage. Yes, this lifts from Toho's *King Kong Escapes* and *MechaGodzilla* films, though the horrible CGI realisations of shark and widget compare badly to the baggiest suit ever worn by a sumo wrestler staggering through miniature Tokyo.

In a reference to the series' highlight, Mega Shark leaps out of the sea to attack a plane, but Mecha Shark leaps after it and knocks it off course. Late in the day, the mecha AI goes rogue thanks to an admiral (Matt Lagan) being an idiot and our heroes have to defeat their own creation while it rampages through Sydney before they even pay attention to the megalodon. Given that no one watches these things for the sensitive portrayal of the leads' interracial relationship, it's a drag that (yet again) so much of the film is people in offices talking to each other or chatting with their screens. All the rampages are truncated or stuck with repeated CGI shots, as if not enough effects footage were processed in time for air date. Written by H. Perry Horton (*2-Headed Shark Attack*) from a story by Jose Prendes (*The Haunting of Whaley House*); directed by Emile Edwin Smith (*Age of Ice*).

MEGA SHARK VERSUS KOLOSSUS (2015)

> 'YES – THE MEGALODON IS MY WHOLE LIFE. YOU SAY THAT AS IF IT'S A NEGATIVE.'

The serial-style *Mega Shark* franchise continues with this fourth entry, which pitches in borrowings from *Pacific Rim*, *Godzilla* and Marvel Comics, deploys acres of dull

American naval manoeuvre footage and skips around the globe while skimping on the 'bot-on-shark action promised by the title.

Yet another mega shark, a parthogenetic clone of one of the previous fish, ravages the world's oceans and puts two anti-shark submarines (whose all-female crews sport black leather cat-suits with plunging necklines) out of action. Oceanologist Dr Alison Gray (Illeana Douglas, surprisingly earnest – though when dramatic green lighting kicks in she looks like Kermit the Frog) clashes with a mercenary British boffin (Jeff Hatch) over what to do while an admiral whose character name keeps switching from Perry to Jackson and back (Ernest Thomas, doing a bad Samuel L. Jackson impersonation) works himself up into a shark-killing frenzy, losing a bunch of ships and collaterally damaging many offscreen civilians (extras are in comically short supply) in the process. Meanwhile, near Chernobyl, undercover CIA pixie Moira King (Amy Rider, channelling young Meg Tilly) is present when Cold War Soviet doomsday machine Kolossus, a stomping giant robot with explosive capabilities, is awoken. A ton of plot stuff happens, much involving a tech gazillionaire (Brody Hutzler) with big plans, to get the shark and the robot ('surf and turf') together to have a fight in the Black Sea, and then we don't see much of it since there's too much betraying and ranting to pay attention to. In a one-scene cameo as Kolossus's creator, Patrick Bauchau puts as much into a bitter mad science speech as Bela Lugosi did in *Bride of the Monster*. Screenwriter Edward DeRuiter (*2-Headed Shark Attack*) awards himself a role as the tagalong techie. Directed by Christopher Ray (*Mega Shark versus Crocasaurus*).

MEGA SNAKE (2007)

> 'YOUNG LADY, I SPENT SIX YEARS IN A VIETNAMESE PRISON CAMP. I THINK I CAN HANDLE A FEW ANIMALS!'

Yet another cable TV movie about a giant CGI reptile. Aptly named dolt Duff Daniels (John T. Woods) swipes the semi-legendary Nteka jar from wise Indian Screaming Hawk (Ben Cardinal). *Gremlins*-like terms and conditions are attached: 'There are three rules. First, never let Nteka out of the jar. Second, never let it eat anything living. And finally, *never fear the heart of the snake*.' Naturally, Duff drops the jar, letting

Nteka out. Once free, it gets big and eats living things, including goats and people. Whatever 'never fear the heart of the snake' means, Duff doubtless does that too. Duff's commitment-phobic, snake-fearing brother Les (Michael Shanks) and his ex-girlfriend Deputy Erin (Siri Baruc) track the critter. The mayor (Michael McCoy) refuses to cancel the county fair just so enough extras are around to be swallowed in the climax. Too much footage is spent on Les and Erin's post-breakup failed relationships with obnoxious Sheriff Bo (Todd Jensen) and the local goodtime girl (Laura Giosh) – though this does feed into the plot again when sulky, smug Bo won't take zoology-qualified Erin's word on the giant snake culprit seriously until she leaves a thirty-foot shed skin on his doorstep. In a bit of loose-end-tying, Feedback (Matthew Atherton), winner of the SciFi Channel's *Who Wants to Be a Superhero?* reality show, has a tiny guest appearance in costume. Scripted by Robby Robinson and Alexander Volz, from a story by producer Boaz Davidson; directed by Tibor Takács (*The Gate*).

OZARK SHARKS (SUMMER SHARK ATTACK) (2016)

Though the CGI fish attacks are weaker even than the average *Syfy* shark flick, the plot is utterly rote (as in *Shark Lake*, a pregnant bull shark spawns an inland killer brood), a few shots of underwater looming are repeated over and over and a severed arm prop is reused for a whole bunch of characters (including a black dude – though it's a white arm), this is a far more engaging and watchable effort than most comparable chum. All credit to screenwriter Marcy Holland (from a story by Greg Mitchell) and director Misty Talley (*Zombie Shark*) for realising that these films stand or fall on the characters – not the monsters.

There are a scattering of disposable bikini babes and speedo jocks, but we mostly spend time with a family who are believable and likeable, even when someone's using a homemade cannon to zap a leaping mama shark with an entire fireworks display. It's not weighed down by soap sub-plots, but neatly establishes who these folks are and how they relate to each other – and when an engaging grandma or a comic relief tagalong pal get killed, it's actually affecting. Rick (Michael Papajohn) and Diane (Laura Cayouette) head out to a mountain lake with Grandma (Sharon Garrison), son Harrison (Dave Davis) and sulky daughter Molly (Allisyn Ashley Arm). With her nose in a gloomy book all the time, Molly is unhappy because her boyfriend Curtis (Ross Britz) will be out of phone contact – but he shows up anyway.

Rick confides that he was happier when Curtis was Harrison's slacker idiot best friend than he is with him as a slacker idiot prospective son-in-law, and there's a nice vibe between the guys as Harrison is weirded out by his bro hooking up with Molly. A potential minefield of an irritating character, Curtis is well played, spacey and in the end a bit heroic as he is studded with bullet-like shark teeth after cleverly pulling a shark through a wood-chipper. The local survivalist loon (Thomas Francis Murphy) provides an arsenal of Rube Goldberg weaponry before being eaten, but the Sheriff (Terence Rosemore) spends the film shrugging off 'prank calls' about sharks. MVP is the appealing, plainly talented Arm, who goes beyond the call of duty as a shrugging emo who transforms into *Jaws*-era Robert Shaw over the course of a bloody day at the lake.

PIRANHA (1995)

> 'YOU ASSHOLE!'
> 'GREAT DIALOGUE. I LOVE
> IMPROVISATION. JUST LIKE
> IN AN ALTMAN FILM.'

Well before Alexandre Aja's *Piranha 3D*, Joe Dante's 1978 *Piranha* was remade as a 'Roger Corman Presents' cable-TV movie which recycles monster footage from the original (though isn't as reliant on old stuff as the redo of *Humanoids from the Deep*) and sticks close to John Sayles' script. It has a few fresh gore effects, but seems to use only one new toothy rubbery silly piranha. Even if scenes of camping kids or tourists being bitten are threadbare in regards to effects, stunts and even the number of extras involved, the suspense mechanics work. The cast is likeable (though not as distinctive as Dante's original choices): Alexandra Paul is the (mannish) PI seeking missing kids, William Katt the shack-dwelling writer (an ex-lawyer, who grew a conscience and deliberately lost an environmental case), Monte Markham the bad-guy tycoon and Darleen Carr the military-funded mad scientist. Also with early gigs for Mila Kunis (as a preteen afraid of the water) and Leland Orser (as a film school-grad commercials director) and cameos for James Karen and Kaz Garas, plus Soleil Moon Frye, Kehli O'Byrne and the seriously stacked Lorissa McComas as fishbait. Scripted by Alex Simon (*Bloodfist VIII*); directed by Scott P. Levy (*The Alien Within*).

PLANET OF THE SHARKS (2016)

'YOU WANT TO JUMP-START
THE ROCKET BY USING THE POWER
FROM A SHARK? COME ON!'

The Asylum's policy of greenlighting anything shark-related continues. A glimpse of the Statue of Liberty underwater suggests this wants to be a fishier *Planet of the Apes*, but the rising tides angle inevitably turns it into a tardy, ill-advised imitation *Waterworld*. The ice caps have melted and sharks learn dolphin-like leaping stunts to snack on humans who live on a few floating platforms and boats. An alpha shark with sparkles inset in her nose leads a school of killer fish, who prove a nuisance to an all-purpose motherly scientist (Lindsay Sullivan), a grizzled boat captain (Brandon Auret), a babe boffin (Stephanie Beran), the owner of the last bow tie on the planet, a whiny chubby guy who makes reasonable protests about stupid courses of action and still gets eaten, and a burnouse-wearing black girl who scores yearning close-ups but no one remembered to write lines for (the script also fails to establish the names of most of the characters, and the actors are difficult to identify from the credits). The gang work earnestly on sending up an atmosphere scrubber to save the planet, seemingly unaware of how funny lines like 'This launch window may be our only chance to use the scrubber' are in the UK. A kite-surfing babe delivers a gizmo into the middle of the shark-swarm, drawing them to an undersea volcano which is set off by an orbiting laser-zapper. The alpha's mutant bioelectricity is just what the good guys need to get their rocket off a launchpad. For a film set all at sea, a great deal of it takes place inside a large corrugated iron warehouse where folks type urgently and utter solemn dialogue while – as usual with The Asylum – an orchestral score works overtime to pretend that something exciting is happening. Scripted by director Mark Atkins (*Sand Sharks*) and Marc Gottlieb.

PRIMEVAL (2007)

'THAT CROCODILE IS LIKE OJ SIMPSON.
HE MESSED UP WHEN
HE KILLED THAT WHITE WOMAN.'

Unusually, this terror-by-crocodile picture is set in Africa rather than America or Australia – and extrapolates from real-life stories about 'Gustave', a river-dwelling croc in Burundi who has gained a dangerous rep.

A famous white lady forensic scientist who is examining corpses left by a genocidal civil war is killed by the crocodile, and disgraced journo Tim Manfrey (Dominic Purcell, the dreadful Dracula from *Blade: Trinity*) is sent to Africa to get the story by Murdoch-lite boss Roger Sharpe (Patrick Lyster). Also in the party are Aviva (Brooke Langton), the trophy girlfriend Roger uses to cover up his homosexuality; jive-talking cameraman Johnson (Orlando Jones), who makes one jaw-dropping political statement ('I'd never say this in front of a bunch of white people, but slavery was a good thing – anything you gotta do to get the fuck out of Africa is okay with me!'); Krieg (Jürgen Prochnow), a hard-bitten Robertshawlike hunter who nurtures a personal grudge against the croc who ate his wife; Collins (Gideon Emery), an eco-friendly zoologist who wants to take Gustave alive; and war orphan Jojo (Gabriel Malema), who dreams of going to America for a happier life. There's a lot of Africa-is-hell business with corrupt officials and massacre-happy warlords – the major human villain (Dumisani Mbebe) is both – and a steroided death squaddie even takes the time to try to rape the heroine before the monster gets him.

Long-time hack scripters John Brancato and Michael Ferris (*Watchers II*, *Catwoman*) drop in too many significant lines about how it's man's fault nature is so dangerous – corpses thrown into the river during the Hutu-Tutsi conflict have given Gustave his taste for man meat – and, gee, aren't we no better than crocodiles, really. The croc action is okayish, but not a patch on *Lake Placid* or *Rogue*. Directed by Michael Katleman.

RAGIN' CAJUN REDNECK GATORS (ALLIGATOR ALLEY) (2013)

This Syfy original gets bonus points for escalating absurdity. On the eve of hunting season, a Louisiana bayou township is terrorised by a new breed of 'redneck gators', who have been mutated by 'bad shine' poured into the swamp by the Robichaud family. The reptiles have red puffy patches around their necks to justify the title and spikes on their tails to impale the unwary. Heroine Avery Doucette (Jordan Hinson) comes home from college and ticks off her father (Ritchie Montgomery) more by telling him she's now a vegan liberal. Even worse, she gets back with her deputy sheriff ex Dathan Robichaud (John Chriss), though the Doucettes and the Robichauds have been feuding for a hundred years. The community form a trigger-happy posse, with a TV 'gator whisperer' (Victor Webster) getting in the way until he is chewed, but several Doucettes are bitten or eat the redneck gators at a celebratory cook-out. Thanks to unethical chemicals in the bad shine, they transform into – get this! – weregators. Nasty Wade Robichaud (Thomas Francis Murphy) sets out to hunt and kill them, incidentally ending the feud. Avery – whose boyfriend has also gone scaly – intervenes to bring about a bloodbath which leads to a happy ending. Scripters Keith Allan (*11/11/11*) and Delondra Williams (*Wuthering High/ The Wrong Boyfriend*), working from a story by Rafael Jordan (*Yeti Curse of the Snow Demon*), churn out all the cajun clichés, but only Amy Brassette (as a croaking matriarch upset when her husband throws her beloved dog to the gators as a diversion) plays full-out swampy degeneracy. An earnest emotional streak adds to the fun (the heroine recognises her transformed daddy by his gold tooth). The monsters are nippy CGI things. Directed by Griff Furst (*Arachnoquake*).

RAGING SHARKS (2005)

'HAVE YOU TRIED SATURATING WITH DEUTERIUM YET?... THEY'RE HYDROGEN ISOTOPES CHARGED WITH THERMAL NEUTRONS. THERE'S NOTHING LIKE IT ON EARTH!'

The pre-credits scene of this NuImage quickie will make you think the SciFi Channel have changed their schedule without telling anyone. Spaceships ram each other while bark-faced aliens grunt urgently as if this were a space opera called something like *Terminal Space* (ships and costumes are from NuImage's *Alien Lockdown*) rather than the expected *Jaws* knockoff. Things get on track when the losing ship jettisons a glowing orange pod into the seas of nearby Earth. After an expository title ('Impact Zone – Bermuda Triangle – 5 Years Later'), *Raging Sharks* plays to expectations. Alien particles are found near Oceana, an undersea base everyone pronounces as if it were an Irish name. *Abyss*-type soap-opera scientists alternate shouting at each other with heartfelt character dollops about children or hobbies which are supposed to make us upset when they die. Oceana is attacked by several shark species working in cahoots: we mostly see one regular shark – plus a few CGI fish and footage recycled from other shark films.

Dr Mike Olsen (Corin Nemec, *Mansquito*), Oceana's commander, is topside when the base is cut off and motivated to effect a rescue because his wife Linda (Vanessa Angel, *Puppet Master vs Demonic Toys*) is in temporary command, despite grumbling from wrench-wielding British handyman-cum-shop steward Harvey (Bernard van Bilderbeek, opting for a more sensible byline after being billed as Binky van Bilderbeek on a few films). Mike has to fend off nasty government inspector/lawyer Stiles (Todd Jensen, *Bats: Human Harvest*), while crusty Captain Riley (Corbin Bernsen, *Atomic Twister*) is gruffly good intentioned but not very helpful.

After a regulation attack on surfers and bathers in Bermuda – either tipped in from another film or matched surprisingly well by Bulgarian locations – an autopsy discloses that the raging, co-operating sharks are full of weird alien orange crystals. Mike and Stiles make their way into Oceana to supervise an evacuation, but extra crises require people to go outside and get killed. For a reel or so, the shark/alien stuff is put on hold, and the film is all about running around the base skirmishing with cackling maniacal villain Stiles as leaks spring and wires spark. After supporting Oceanans (Elise Muller, Simona Levin, Atanas Srebrev, Emil Markov) have died, a poignant moment has Mike and Linda staggering about the wrecked base as tragic choral music plays – but Stiles pops up (with an axe!) for another fight and gets a proper back-spearing. Opera excerpts play as a spaceship arrives and aliens retrieve or detonate their capsule, which seemingly dispels the sharks who have been guarding it from untrustworthy Earthers (attacking Bermuda was probably over-enthusiasm). Mike and Linda escape – apparently because a by-product of an alien encounter is the ability to breathe underwater. The persistent Stiles swims along evilly, but is finally eaten by a shark which hasn't departed like all the others. On board the rescue sub, nobody believes Mike's yarn about aliens.

Written by producer Les Weldon (who might conceivably get the joke, since much of the dialogue evokes *Airplane!*), directed by Danny Lerner (*Shark in Venice*).

RATTLERS (1976)

This is remembered mainly for its lurid poster: a naked screaming babe in a bathtub full of snakes. Of course, the scene onscreen is less impressive: as all of two sluggish serpents do their best to stay away from a flailing housewife (Celia Kaye).

A couple of boys venture into California desert in search of a 'real-live skeleton' and fall into a pit full of snakes. Handsome snake expert Dr Tom Parkinson (Sam Chew Jr), so underfunded he doesn't even own a pair of those long-handled tongs real-life herpetologists rely on (they would come in handy in several scenes), teams with photographer Ann Bradley (Elisabeth Chauvet), a women's-libber who rubs his chauvinist ass the wrong way – though they bond as they visit the sites of horrible deaths (sadly, the budget isn't there for makeup snakebites). Colonel Stroud (Dan Priest), head of a covert bioweapons program, has dumped a leaky canister of nerve gas in a mine. Designed to make enemy soldiers turn on each other in a frenzy, the gas makes reptiles aggressive, though the film has no real way of showing this. We see snakes coiled and hear rattles and hisses, but there's scant footage of actual attacks – so the climax has to involve mad renegade Stroud shooting people (including the Atlanta-born cop who has moved west because you never hear of policemen being shot in small desert towns) then blowing himself up with a dropped grenade (he doesn't even suffer the traditional hoist-by-his-own-petard fate of eco-villains and get bitten by the rattlers).

It has that sunny, casual look of the '70s (Chew models a natty safari jacket), but also that odd lack of urgency which distinguishes some exploitation movies from that laid-back decade. The sheriff (Tony Ballen) reacts to a rash of deaths by assigning a couple of civilians to poke around and leaving it at that. In the third act, hero and heroine take time out from the snake-hunt for an evening of balancing on fountains in Vegas. Written by Jerry Golding and director John McCauley (*Deadly Intruder*).

RED WATER (2003)

South Africa plays Louisiana in this mash-up of the menaced-by-thugs-in-the-backwoods plot (cf: *Key Largo*) and the ever-popular *Jaws* formula.

A bull shark, the only freshwater variety (as in several subsequent inland shark films), snacks on a pretty teenage swimmer and a nice old grampa, luring bounty hunters to the wrong stretch of river. Meanwhile, two sets of folks head for Black Cove, where the fish might be mystic guardian of two sunken treasures – an oil/natural gas deposit and a stash of drug-dealer's cash. Struggling charter-boat captain Sanders (Lou Diamond Phillips) is talked into an expedition by his scientist ex-wife Kelli (Kristy Swanson) and corporate idiot Bradley (Gideon Emery), though Cajun mate Emery (Rob Boltin) mutters warnings. Also poking around are the twitchy mob minion who dumped the cash (Jaimz Woolvett), the bullying thug sent to retrieve it (Coolio) and a crazy-brave criminal diver (Langley Kirkwood). The two groups bicker, the oil well blows, the money gets spread in the water, and the shark keeps coming back to snack again. As in *Dracula 3000*, Coolio gives the most obnoxious performance – but here, at least, he gets eaten.

Screenwriters J.D. Feigelson (*Horror High*) and Chris Mack (*Vampire Vermont*) dwell on so many sub-plots and B-picture cliché arguments (including a surprise betrayal among thieves) that the shark sometimes gets sidelined for too long – though good use is made of the oil drill in killing it in the finale. Despite minor mystical mutterings, the fish seems to be just a fish rather than a supernatural creature. Directed by Charles Robert Carner.

THE REEF (2010)

Having done *Open Water*-up-a-tree-with-a-crocodile in *Black Water*, Aussie director-writer Andrew Traucki here does *Open Water*-in-open-water-with-sharks. A small-scale, effective terror-by-the-elements-and-nature effort, it trades in the primal fear of dangling in the ocean with predators prowling beneath, ready to nip off the odd limb or decapitate a huge turtle to leave a gruesome floating lump.

Luke (Damian Walshe-Howling) has a dream job delivering boats all around the South Pacific. He invites good-looking, athletic, not-necessarily-sea-skilled friends (Adrienne Pickering, Zoe Naylor, Gyton Grantley, Kieran Darcy-Smith) along with him on his latest trip. The boat founders in mid-ocean, and the only way to survive is a long swim to land. After panic and recriminations, four of the young folks set off, only to run into a shark which seems to take an especial delight in persecuting them. In the end, a caption reveals the final girl (Naylor) was saved but the remains of the others were never found.

Like *Black Water*, it's familiar but done well.

ROBO CROC (2013)

> 'BESIDES THE FACT THAT MY ANKLE'S SPRAINED AND WE'RE BEING CHASED BY A GIANT CROCODILE, I'M FINE.'

When a space capsule crash-lands in a wildlife park, a cloud of experimental nanobots (a CGI tealeaf storm) transforms saltwater crocodile Stella into a metallic killing machine. Park keeper Duffy (Corin Nemec) and Colonel Montgomery (Steven Hartley) team up to catch the apex predator, but mad scientist Dr Riley (Dee Wallace, overdoing it enjoyably) uses the contrived crisis as a field test for a lunatic weapons system. As brass and boffins bicker, stranded kids – including Riley's son (Jackson Bews), his dork best friend (Quinlan Hill), a couple of bikini hotties (Iva Iankulova, Florence Brundell-Bruce) and expendable jock bullies (Dimitar Balabanov, Christian Hammerdorfer) – are hunted by the beast.

Lightly amiable, shot-in-Bulgaria Syfy nonsense, this compounds implausibilities with clichés, but at least offers a cool mutant (at one point, it does the mandatory takedown of a low-flying helicopter) and a couple of committed performances. Nemec often brings his A game to Z movies, elevating proceedings the way 1970s heroes like Sam Elliott, Bradford Dillman and Christopher George add value to *Frogs*, *Piranha* and *Grizzly*. Nemec balances sympathy for infected wildlife with human concern, banters nicely with his love interest and shows grit in action. In an instance of trash movies not keeping up with social issues, the sympathetic kids are bullied because they take creeper photos of the bikini girls on their phones, which is presented as likeable, amusing behaviour. Written by Berkeley Anderson (*Lake Placid vs Anaconda*); directed by Arthur Sinclair.

ROGUE (2007)

Writer-director Greg McLean's *Wolf Creek* follow-up again feeds tourists to an archetypal Australian menace – a lantern-jawed giant crocodile ('They're pretty much living dinosaurs who have been perfecting their hunting skills over two hundred million years.').

In a hot-as-hell outback town, a deftly characterised group embark on the proverbial three-hour tour with local guide Kate Ryan (Radha Mitchell) and chug up a tidal river to look at dangerous wildlife. Enmity between yokels and incomers is established as a crafty barman (Barry Otto) dumps a dead fly in the coffee after overhearing a comment about 'terrible service' (actually referring to mobile phone coverage). Then the tour boat is buzzed by a couple of those strine scuzzbos endemic to Ozsploitation (cf: *Mad Max*, *Razorback*, *Storm Warning*). Beery lout Neil (Sam Worthington) gives Kate a hard time, suggesting *Straw Dogs*-like history between them, spurring mild-mannered American journo Pete (Michael Vartan) to speak up. However, the real trouble starts when, despite grumbles from some who have buses to catch, Kate takes a detour to answer a distress flare. The crocodile – not strictly a rogue since it's defending territory against interlopers – wrecks the boat and strands the party on a small island, which shrinks every minute (as in *Attack of the Crab Monsters!*). One tourist is snatched by the monster when nobody is looking and Neil comes along to jeer at the castaways, then has to join the party when his boat is trashed too. Refreshingly, the lout doesn't become a whining traitor or entirely convert to take over as heroic leading man either.

All the characters make some sense and register as individuals: Russell (John Jarratt, the psycho from *Wolf Creek*, in a kinder, gentler role) has bought two tickets and quietly empties a loved one's ashes into the water (screenwriters, pay attention: the gesture makes us understand the character; an explanation would only trivialise him); terminally ill Elizabeth (Heather Mitchell), committed to her family's survival (Mia Wasikowska plays one of her daughters), neatly bonds with the grieving Russell; Gwen (Celia Ireland) is traumatised by the early loss of her matey husband and credibly freezes up while trying to span the water on a rope and panicky people are urging her to get on with it. Even the annoying camera buff (Stephen Curry) and the cheery fat girl (Caroline Brazier) aren't just comedy relief – and the film doesn't squander the impact of its casualties by inflicting too many of them.

After a mid-section in which the group try to rig up escape methods or signal for help and the reptile makes sorties to whittle them down, McLean changes gears: the monster grabs Kate and the survivors scatter, but Pete ventures into the creature's cavernous lair and battles with it to rescue the injured but undigested heroine. Here, we get solid monster movie stuff as a wimp from the city becomes a resourceful, determined wilderness man to save the girl from the seemingly malicious giant creature (the last act of *Wolf Creek* also has injured folks desperately struggling in a killer's lair). Using a combination of animatronics, CGI and real beasts, the film creates an entirely convincing monster, even when seen up close and personal. François Tétaz's soundtrack is especially effective, relying on weird atonal outback noises, but the good nasty humour of the enterprise is sealed by a vintage recording of 'Never Smile at a Crocodile' over the end credits.

SAND SHARKS (2012)

'I THINK WHAT JIMBO IS TRYING TO SAY IS THAT WE CAN'T JUST CANCEL THE PARTY BECAUSE A FEW PEOPLE GOT KILLED. THAT'S BAD BUSINESS.'

The parade of absurd shark horrors continues in this light-hearted, callous, deliberately dumb picture.

Sharkologist Sandy Powers (Brooke Hogan) suspects a prehistoric killer fish (cue a reference to *Dinoshark* and the line, 'Don't go all Roger Corman on me.'), but then discovers the menace is a new mutation, adapted to swim through sand (cf: *The Outer Limits* 'The Invisible Enemy') and chomp unwary beachcombers. Sleazy prodigal Jimmy Green (Corin Nemec) returns to White Sands, so intent on promoting his Sandman Festival he'll cover up carnage to stay in business ('Fifteen people died the last time you threw this island a party!'). Jimmy butts heads with Sheriff John Stone (Eric Scott Woods) – presumably named after the one in 'Sloop John B' – and an ex-girlfriend cruelly tagged 'Deputy Doughnuts' (Vanessa Lee Evigan) by his vicious current squeeze (Gina Holden). Even after his father, the mayor (Edgar Allan Poe IV!), is eaten, Jimmy presses on with a scheme to lure thousands (visibly, tens) of teens to the beach to spend money.

Director Mark Atkins (*Planet of the Sharks*) and writer Cameron Larson (*Xtinction: Predator X*) spend so much time with the weasely leading man that they don't make much of the silly but workable suspense mechanics of monsters under the sand (cf: *Blood Beach*). Cruder-looking (even) than the average Syfy quickie, it gets an edge from old-fashioned gore and wiseass attitude.

THE SEA FIEND (DEVIL MONSTER) (1936)

'THE MEN THINK HE'S INSANE...
AND THEY HAVE NO CONFIDENCE IN
HIM AS A FISHERMAN.'

Surviving prints of this slapdash exotic adventure have a caption halfway through asking for audience patience during a reel-change. *The Sea Fiend* was aimed at markets where a dual-projector system would seem a luxury… but a few shots of topless native girls swimming, grinding corn (maximising jiggle) or simply standing about would satisfy audiences willing to put up with acres of frolicking seal, aggressive octopus, leaping fish ('I never saw so many tuna.') and crashing wave footage.

White-haired Mrs Francisco (Mary Carr) begs sailor hero Robert Jackson (wooden Barry Norton, 'Juan Harker' in the 1931 Spanish-language *Drácula*) to search 'every inch' of the South Seas region for her long-lost son José (Jack Del Rio), whose ship was wrecked in the Galapagos years earlier. Robert nobly accepts the mission: he's in love with Louise (Blanche Mehaffey), the schoolteacher José is still notionally engaged to, and almost admits he hopes to prove the missing man dead so they can get together. The first half has little footage with the actors as narration is piled on clips from earlier films of an educational or exploitative nature. In a bizarre stretch, Robert explains an undersea battle as an 'evil' octopus is about to eat a 'good' fish when a moray eel dashes to the rescue and a school of smaller fish assail the octopus. Staged in a tank (sea creatures sometimes flatten against glass), this is peculiarly sadistic – the fish are plainly being encouraged to attack each other. After the 'money shots', which might appease grain-milling fetishists, the expedition locates the island where José has gone native (or is at least going after native girls). A Lugosi-accented Native Chief (Bill Lemuels) has made the castaway his heir, but Robert shanghais swarthy, shifty José by knocking him out, forcibly rescuing him from an apparently happy new life. In the most exciting footage staged for the film, José shows off tuna-fishing skills while plotting harm to his love rival.

The title creature is a giant manta ray who bothers tuna fishers – and is again treated horribly (the filmmakers shot its harpooning the old-fashioned non-special effects way). José turns heroic and loses an arm in battle with the fiend/fish, prompting Robert to wonder whether they did him a favour by rescuing him. When they reach home port, Louise gushes, 'Oh, Robert, how can I ever thank you?' but runs to José, who responds with a one-armed hug. The stricken Robert is thanked by José's mother, perhaps musing this isn't the ending he (or the audience) expected. It's almost a refreshing finish, if clumsily staged and acted. For a marginal effort, it exists in a variety of versions: a Spanish-language *El Diablo del Mar* (with bigger name stars – Carlos Villarias of that Spanish *Drácula* and Movita of *Mutiny on the Bounty*/Mrs Marlon Brando fame) and an abbreviated 1945 re-release (*Devil Monster*). Directed by S. Edwin Graham.

THE SHALLOWS (2016)

Lurking beneath the surface of this enjoyable hokum is an essay on the sort of man-against-the-sea existential survivalism which usually requires a grizzled Spencer Tracy (*The Old Man and the Sea*) or Robert Redford (*All Is Lost*) rather than a surfer chick in a bikini and wetsuit. While on a search-for-meaning vacation in Mexico (played by Australia), med school near-dropout Nancy (Blake Lively) gets stuck on a rocky outcrop in sight of a 'secret beach' she is visiting in tribute to her dead-from-cancer mother. Representing nature at its nastiest is a shark who hangs around the cove to chew bits off a dead whale, incidentally kill some locals and engage Nancy in a protracted duel which prompts her to find inner (and outer) strength.

It parallels sharksploitation suspensers (*Open Water*, *The Reef*, *47 Meters Down*), but plays a different game. Most of those feature implacable, unbeatable menace (and downbeat endings), but this plays more like a survival-against-the-odds-in-the-wild picture (*127 Hours*, *Cast Away*) as a competent, smart heroine uses what comes to hand to keep going. As is traditional, Nancy suffers a bad wound and has to patch herself up – using her earrings as sutures – then fight pain and delirium. In these stories, it's useful to have something for the lone protagonist to talk to; here, a watch which counts down to the high tide serves for a while before the heroine fixes on 'Steven Seagull' a blood-spattered bird who lasts longer than the 'there are no sharks here' surfers and the drunken opportunist thief who serve as bloody chum to keep the shocks coming. It prolongs the agony for a taut 86 minutes, with wicked twists – Nancy has a chance to move to a more secure perch on a buoy, but must swim through a shoal of stinging jellyfish to get there… she gets a flare gun from the buoy as a ship hoves into view, but drops the cartridges in the sea and fires off a dud…

To put it mildly, director Jaume Collet-Serra (*Orphan*) is not a subtle filmmaker, but he does tosh with conviction – and is abetted by Lively's star turn in a gruelling role. The photo-realistic shark is used sparingly, but puts the dodgier digital likes of *Mega Shark* and *Sharknado* to shame (an old harpoon in the creature's mouth evokes the British comic strip *Hookjaw*). Screenwriter Anthony Jaswinski (*Vanishing on 7th Street*) takes care to establish why the fish is swimming where it's not supposed to be (Nancy has strayed into its feeding ground) and that it has its own natural enemies in the jellyfish and scraping coral (which the heroine has to cope with too). As a movie monster, the shark scores one great leap-and-chomp stunt, a couple of excellent gore moments and exits in bloody, spectacular fashion.

SHARK ATTACK (1999)

A lackadaisical cable-TV cutdown of *Deep Blue Sea*. When his best friend Marc (Cordell McQueen) is eaten during a wave of attacks on an island off Africa, two-fisted grad student Steven McKray (Casper Van Dien) investigates. Noticing that an arm found inside the shark wears the victim's regular (as opposed to diving) watch, Steve realises that – as we saw in the prologue – Marc didn't get sharked while diving, but was bludgeoned bloody and tossed to the fish by human baddies. Steve and the dead man's sister (Jenny McShane) naturally suspect arrogant scientist Dr Miles Craven (Bentley Mitchum), who is using steroids to accelerate shark metabolisms so he can synthesise an experimental cancer cure. Predictably, Craven turns out to be only unethical – the real villain is local bigwig Rhodes (Ernie Hudson, with a clipped Brit-African accent), who foments panic so he can buy up waterfront property and benefit from a big offshore oil strike. It hasn't got the resources to make the sharks more than dangerous window dressing, tossing the odd attack (a bikini-girl tourist losing a dangling leg) among regular action scenes – a barroom brawl, many boat chases, fights, explosions. Dialogue and performances are straight from stock and could date back fifty years. Written by Scott Devine and William Hooke, who also did *Shark Attack 2* and *Shark Attack 3: Megalodon*; directed by Bob Misiorowski.

SHARK EXORCIST (2015)

> '**THAT'S THE THING ABOUT ALMOST DYING, EMILY. IT IS A REAL BUZZKILL.**'

Writer-director Donald Farmer has cranked out schlock since the 1980s (*Cannibal Hookers*, *Vampire Cop*) without improving; since the early 2000s, the quality (*Chainsaw Cheerleaders*, *Cannibal Cop*) has declined further. This mash-up is barely an hour long, with a ten-minute end credits crawl (featuring silent footage of a girl shopping for shark plushies), and doesn't deliver on the promise of its beyond-a-joke title. Bikini babe Ali (Angela Kerecz) is bitten by a CGI shark and miraculously heals, now possessed by a shark demon. Father Michael (Bobby Kerecz) wants to exorcise her and gets puked on. A nun (Alaine Huntington) prefers stabbing girls to saving them. A sorority initiation at shark-attack lake leads to a mean girl getting chewed up. Ali prowls around a carnival wearing plastic shark-fangs. A mangled female corpse is discovered by a guy who vomits but still admits he'd like to do her (charming). The camera is pointed at girls in swimming suits for quite a while. And the shark attacks again. Entry-level crap, without a trace of wit, charm or entertainment.

SHARK IN VENICE (2008)

Though less hyped than *Snakes on a Plane*, this has an equally appealing title hook – and falls even further short of its promise. Yes, a great white shark zooms around Venetian canals (and, in an obligatory scene, bites a gondola in half)… but, sadly, little comes of the daffily endearing premise.

Hirsute mafia guy Vito Clemenza (Giacomo Gonnella) is seeking a fabulous treasure hidden under the city – in a *Da Vinci Code*-on-a-dollar-a-day flashback – by Marco Polo on behalf of the Medici Brothers (who historically hung out in Florence, but never mind). To discourage divers who might find the fortune before he does, the baddie imports baby sharks and lets a big one loose in the waterways – though, as it turns out, 75% of its diet consists of Vito's own minions, scuppering his own plan. While searching for his missing-presumed-eaten father, diving hero David

Franks (Stephen Baldwin, looking back on the role of young Barney Rubble as a career highlight) finds the treasure. Clemenza kidnaps David's girlfriend (Vanessa Johansson, pitching fair to be the Tisa Farrow, Dedee Pfeiffer or Tracy Tweed of her generation) to force him to lead the villains to the loot.

Even for a film which sets out to be stupid, this is full of 'oh come on now' moments – like the swords and shields lying around the treasure cave which can be picked up and used in a fight scene, and the Venetian cops' seeming success in keeping a lid on shark panic after several daylight attacks. Director Danny Lerner is clearly an auteur – his credits include *Shark Zone* and the classic *Raging Sharks* (not to mention producing two *Shark Attack* sequels) – but this is a lesser work. A fight in the water, which naturally ends up with the baddie eaten, goes on for tedious minutes of splashing. Aside from token location shots, it was made in Bulgaria.

SHARK KILLER (2015)

Director-writer Sheldon Wilson began with modestly effective horror (*Shallow Ground*, *Kaw*), before slipping to TV disaster (*Snowmageddon*, *Mega Cyclone*). His South African-shot sharksploitationer tries for a slightly fresh tone, but leaden comedy banter and noxious ideas of what might constitute endearing character business make it tougher going even than the average '*nado* or '*topus* effort.

Lifeguard Chase Walker (Derek Theler, who combines the bod/looks of Chris Pratt and Channing Tatum with the acting ability of a sandbag) professes to hate the ocean, but specialises in killing sharks by swimming up to them with a knife and repeatedly stabbing their CGI heads. In Capetown, his estranged foster brother Jake (Paul du Toit) wants Chase to kill a shark that has eaten a huge diamond which turns out to belong to maniacal gangster Nix (Arnold Vosloo). Supposedly likeable rogue Jake is a weasel who'd happily stab a woman in the leg and toss her into the sea as sharkbait. Chase keeps introducing himself as if he were the much-loved lead of a long series of *Chase Walker – Shark Killer* adventures, rather than a smug, smarmily lecherous creep we hope never to see again. The shark element is minor, with Nix – who gets the flambé treatment and shows up covered in burn scars in the climax – as the major menace.

Co-written by Richard Beattie (*Prom Night IV*, *High Plains Invaders*).

SHARK LAKE (2015)

> '*I DON'T BELIEVE THAT SHARK WILL RESPOND TO A RESTRAINING ORDER.*'

The USP here is 'Dolph Lundgren vs a shark', so it's disappointing that the star spends way more time brooding about or bonding with his estranged pre-teen daughter than thumping fish. Clint Gray (Lundgren), who smuggles rare animals for dodgy clients, accidentally lets a freshwater-tolerant pregnant shark loose in Lake Tahoe. While Clint serves a prison term, Meredith Hernandez (Sara Lane, of *Sun Choke* and *Beyond the Gates*) – the cop who caught (and shot) him – adopts his moppet Carly (Lily Brooks O'Briant). The shark spawns a brood of co-operating killer fish, who are snacking on tourists by the time Clint gets out. Meredith teams with an expendable ichthyologist (Michael Aaron Milligan), while the Sheriff hires a showoff British shark hunter (Miles Doleac) who's supposed to have a show on the BBC. In a narrative feint, Clint is pressured by the mobster who bought the shark in the first place to get hold of the big fish – but the plot is all contrivance to get Clint, Meredith and the kid in the same boat surrounded by poorly CGId sharks. Lundgren and Lane actually do good work, but are ill served by Gabe Burnstein and David Anderson's soap-infested script. Directed by Jerry Dugan.

SHARKNADO (2013)

> '*THESE FISH SURE HAVE A HANKERING FOR ME. SEEMS LIKE ONE TASTE OF BAZ JUST ISN'T ENOUGH.*'

Anyone who grew up loving *Attack of the Crab Monsters*, *Piranha* and *Alligator* (or even *Anaconda* and *The Relic*) is entitled to feel rooked that The Asylum and Syfy Channel have drowned the monster movie genre in disposable shit. It's hard to imagine anyone in the future being nostalgic about a *'nado* movie.

The foundation of a beyond-a-joke franchise, *Sharknado* offers an attention-getting title (NB: *Arachnoquake* got there first), '80s/'90s nostalgia or just-out-of-rehab players (is John Heard *really* not getting better offers than this?) and just enough footage of terrible CGI sharks in a terrible CGI tornado to fill a trailer. Otherwise, it's cynically thrown-together rubbish... not funny when it tries for snark, padded with family arguments and weather footage, and unexciting in its action/peril scenes (compare the better-made, not-entirely-dissimilar *Bait*). Yes, a tornado off the California coast sucks up sharks and tosses them at victims. Bar owner/ex-surfer Fin Shepard (Ian Ziering), his Aussie sidekick Baz (Jaason Simmons) and waitress girlfriend Nova (Cassie Scerbo) rescue his nagging ex-wife April (Tara Reid) and trek inland, stopping off to save folks (an interminable school bus rescue scene features much rappelling off a bridge) or watch them get bitten. The moment of glory comes after Nova has fallen out of a helicopter into the maw of a flying shark – Fin lets himself (and a chainsaw) be swallowed, then saws his way out of the fish, rescuing the girl. In a slightly creepy subtext, Fin gets back with his family, and Nova is passed on as a potential girlfriend for his chopper pilot son (Alex Arleo).

Weather conditions or use of rain/wind machines vary from shot to shot and that shaky-cam attempt to suggest an ongoing hurricane gets wearisome quickly. Hard to see why it got more attention than *Jersey Shore Shark Attack* or *Ozark Sharks*. Written by Thunder Levin (*Atlantic Rim/From the Sea*); directed by Anthony C. Ferrante (*Boo*).

SHARKNADO 2: THE SECOND ONE (2014)

Every so often, a random exploitation film gets a smidgen of mainstream notice – usually because of a snappy title (*Snakes on a Plane*) or outrageous premise (*The Human Centipede*) – though that doesn't mean that many more people actually watch it. The Asylum's *Sharknado* built on their *Mega Shark* versus formula, casting gossip column has-beens and deploying loads of terrible CGI, and displaced enough cultural water to earn annual sequels.

In a sharks-on-a-plane opening, April (Tara Reid) gets her hand chomped off and a pilot (Robert Hays, joking about *Airplane!*'s meal choices) is killed so hero Fin Shepard (Ian Ziering) can land the plane himself. The new sharknado attacks New York City, as three fish-infested twisters converge on the Empire State Building. The new setting allows for an albino alligator in the sewer which chews a city worker and enables a shark flood on the subway, a trip to the ball park where an old-time slugger (Richard Kind) bats a shark into the homerun board, and the spiked severed head of the Statue of Liberty bowling down a road killing people. A new feature is the number of crammed-in celebrity walk-ons: a terrible scene-hogging extra turns out to be blogger Perez Hilton (strangely, later rather good in the po-mo slasher *Most Likely to Die*), Billy Ray Cyrus and Andy Dick play Dr Quint and Officer Doyle, Judd Hirsch is a cab driver, real TV weather folk send themselves up, and tiny cameos highlight Jared Fogle (later disgraced in a paedophilia scandal), Downtown Julie Brown, Pepa (but not Salt), Wil Wheaton, Tiffany Shepis, Kelly Osbourne and Judah Friedlander.

The actual plot has Fin looking out for the estranged best friend (Mark McGrath) who married his sister (Kari Wuhrer) and not getting together with the woman who has been crushing on him since school (a matronly Vivica A. Fox) because he wants to reconcile with April. Reid gets her hand replaced by a buzzsaw. Lots of sharks fall and things are blown up… but with CGI that looks like placeholder effects, performances (the enthusiastic Ziering excepted) that pretty much involve just turning up and too many blah jokes. Written (again) by Thunder Levin; directed by Anthony C. Ferrante.

SHARKNADO 3: OH HELL NO! (2015)

The third instalment attacks the whole East Coast, specifically targeting Washington DC, the Orlando Universal Studios Tour (cuing half-decent *Jaws* jokes) and Cape Canaveral… then takes a trip into orbit to climax with Sharknado in Space.

Fin Shepard (Ian Ziering) has earned a Presidential medal and a (functional) golden chainsaw award, and reconciled with ex-wife April (Tara Reid), who is pregnant – which leads to her giving birth inside a space shark during re-entry. Nova (Cassie Scerbo), Fin's ex-girlfriend from the first film, returns as a leather-clad, sharknado-chasing vigilante vixen. A personal story requires Fin reconcile with his astronaut father Gil (David Hasselhoff, playing straighter than in *Piranha* 3DD) and board a secret military space shuttle in a desperate attempt to zap the storm from orbit. The series is surprisingly right-wing – offering a gung-ho shark-killing President (Mark Cuban) and cameos for manic conservative pundit Ann Coulter (playing the Veep) and lunatic Republican Michele Bachmann (as herself), plus a climax which depends on Ronald Reagan's Strategic Defence Initiative being operative (in homage to the space weapons get-out of Meteor?) and a ton of family values homilising between random characters getting splatted by CGI sharks.

With Bo Derek (Orca) as April's mom, Michael Winslow from the *Police Academy* films, Jackie Collins (as herself, with dialogue), George R.R. Martin (presumably not as himself, with death scene), Tim Russ, Penn and Teller, Jerry Springer, Al Roker, Kathie Lee Gifford, Lou Ferrigno (doing a 'you won't like me when I'm angry' gag) and Jedward (not dying – and managing to give the most irritating performances with least allotted screen time in history). It has slightly more laughs than the average *Scary Movie* sequel, which is saying very little, but the weightless carnage effects got tired in the first film. A final blackout gag leaves the survival of a major character in doubt – The Asylum claimed they would do a *Mr. Sardonicus* online poll to see if April would be alive in part four (spoiler: she is). Scripted by Thunder Levin; directed by Anthony C. Ferrante.

SHARKNADO: THE 4TH AWAKENS (2016)

Syfy/The Asylum and the writing-directing team of Anthony C. Ferrante and Thunder Levin are evidently committed to keeping *Sharknado* sequels coming, though are equally evidently willing to put in only a bare minimum of effort with them. This is the low-budget equivalent of the *Transformers* franchise – loud, annoying, self-congratulatory tosh taking screenspace which could be more usefully employed by almost anything else.

At the end of *Sharknado 3*, a viewer poll was announced to decide whether shark-bitten April (Tara Reid) lived or died; no word on the results, but Reid returns here as a flying cyborg with laser-hands. It's been five years since the last sharknado, and shrill bighead tycoon Aston Reynolds (Tommy Davidson) has constructed a device to prevent them... even as he's unwisely filled a new hotel in Las Vegas with sharks. Inevitably, a twister (a sandstorm, for a change) strikes and the sharks fly again, with a trip to Kansas for *Wizard of Oz* gags (none actually funny) and a final face-off between the extended Shepherd family and a nukenado full of irradiated sharks.

David Hasselhoff is back (cue pointless cameo from *Baywatch* stars Gena Lee Nolin and Alexandra Paul) and Gary Busey joins up as a mad scientist. It has extended injokes about Christine (the Stephen King titular car), *Grease 2* (an Adrian Zmed cameo) and a crossover with the parallel *Lavalantula* series (a Steve Guttenberg cameo paying back

Sharknado star Ian Ziering's cameo in *Lavalantula*), plus Stacey Dash (continuing the series' fondness for showbiz/political figures) as a mean mayor, Gilbert Gottfried, the Chippendales, Lloyd Kaufman (a sure sign that Roger Corman won't return your calls is casting Lloyd Kaufman in a cameo), series regular/weatherman Al Roker (who adds 'nado' to anything), Cheryl Tiegs and Susan Anton (look them up), and more feeble CGI than the mind can take. Even the game Ziering, who has heroically shouldered the whole series, is looking distinctly fed up with these annual damp squibs.

SHARK SWARM (2008)

Another xerox of a xerox of *Jaws*. Screenwriters Matthew Chernov and David Rosiak obviously know genre history – one of their attack sites is Spivey Point (from *The Fog*) and the expert played by F. Murray Abraham (©Oscar® winner!) is named after *Grizzly* director Bill Girdler. For a B-level effort, the cast is quality: John Schneider, Daryl Hannah and Armand Assante may have walking, talking cliché parts (heroic fisherman, blonde wife, wormy businessman), but at least have presence – though Roark Critchlow is stiff as the fisherman's marine biologist brother, who hits on the environmentalist heroine (Heather McComb) even when she's covered with shark guts.

Developer Hamilton Lux (Assante) poisons the waters of Full Moon Bay to wreck the fishing industry so he can buy property cheap. The goop, dumped by minion baddie Markus (John Enos III), maddens sharks and a swarm of mostly-CGI fish attack the community. It spends too much time on its above-water plot and neglects the gore – Markus does try to feed the goodies to sharks, but a promised set-piece attack on a mass sea baptism doesn't come off. Originally a two-part 167-minute saga – mostly seen in an abbreviated version. Directed by James A. Contner.

SHARKTOPUS (2010)

'EXCUSE ME, THERE'S A KILLER SHARK-OCTOPUS HYBRID HEADED THIS WAY. WOULD YOU PLEASE LEAVE THE MARINA IN AN ORDERLY FASHION?'

Shady government contractor Nathan Sands (Eric Roberts) gene-splices octopus and shark to create the S-11 (why not the S-8?), a giant mutant which can be steered by a brain-controlling collar and deployed in dangerous waters against, say, pirates or drug-smugglers. The opening cheekily riffs on the shark attack genre: a swimming bikini babe is stalked by a floating fin (resembling the inflatable one used as a gag in *Jaws*), only for the tentacled, maw-tastic hybrid to show up and rip the regular killer fish to bits. Nicole (Sara Malakul Lane), Sands' hot librarian-look daughter (i.e. babe with glasses), resists an unethical Navy man (Brent Huff) who wants further gory field tests, but domineering dad orders her to keep going. The control collar is knocked off, whereupon sharktopus heads for the *Queen Mary* to kill a couple of painters who are talking about the worst way to die, then swims south to terrorise the coast of Mexico.

Screenwriter Mike MacLean (*Dinocroc vs. Supergator*) makes a stab at the knowing genre fare producer Roger Corman pioneered from the 1950s to the 1970s, though that 'worst way to die' shtick isn't exactly John Sayles. Corman gets an amusing beachcomber cameo poking fun at his penny pinching as he salvages a gold doubloon and walks on after another bikini girl has been shredded in front of him. Then, monotony sets in. Hoping to get the monster back, Sands hires adventurer-marine biologist maverick Flynn (Kerem Bursin) and sends Nicole along for bickering banter. Bursin has impressive muscle tone, but plays smug wiseass rather than crusty hero. After paying for Roberts, the film clearly had no budget for even halfway decent names (say, Lance Henriksen or Dean Cain) and is thus populated by hot-body stiffs who can't even play cliché without falling over.

All the characters, plus some hitmen, take to the seas while the CGI monster offs a great many extras with bursts of painted-in-pixels gore. The monster has that curiously not-there feel which makes you miss even the plastic-bag-over-the-head jellyfishman of *Sting of Death*, let alone the Paul Blaisdell or Rob Bottin rubber critters of yore. The sharktopus comes ashore to rampage at a dance festival for a busy, meaningless climax. Roberts is mean all the way up to his heroic death, but doesn't even provide the limited gravitas he lent to Corman's *Raptor*. Directed by Declan O'Brien (*Wrong Turn 3*).

SHARKTOPUS VS PTERACUDA (2014)

> 'HOW CAN A BUSINESS INNOVATE WITHOUT KILLING A COUPLE OF CIVILIANS?'

Roger Corman's New Horizons outfit rides the mutant shark wave with this daffy sequel, which has the usual terrible CGI effects but fairly engaging characters and an air of eager-to-please pulpiness.

Lorena (Katie Savoy) finds an egg sac left around at the end of *Sharktopus* and raises a hybrid in a struggling marine attraction run by her crass, moneygrubbing uncle (Hensy Pichardo). Meanwhile, biotech innovator Symes (Robert Carradine) genegineers the pteracuda as a substitute for drone warfare – only to have it go rogue after six and a half minutes when an industrial spy walks off with the control codes. With both monsters terrorising tourists, Symes and his security guy Hamilton (Rib Hillis) get together with Lorena to set the sharktopus to catch the pteracuda – whose weakness turns out to be a magpie eye easily distracted by trailing a disco ball behind the boat.

Various obnoxious comic characters – including Conan O'Brien as himself – get gored (sharktopus tentacles have deadly barbs), bitten in half or generally killed. Savoy keeps things grounded with a surprisingly deeply-felt performance, while Carradine channels mid-period Ron Silver as the all-round unethical mad science businessman who is inevitably torn apart when both mutants get hold of him. Next up: *Sharktopus vs Whalewolf.* Scripted by Matt Yamashita (*Death Race 2050*); directed by Kevin O'Neill (*Dracano*).

SHARKTOPUS VS WHALEWOLF (2015)

In this third entry, the sharktopus keeps busy snacking on folks – interrupting a funeral at sea by eating the deceased and his widow – but attention shifts to the debuting co-star monster.

In the Dominican Republic, Dr Reinhardt (Catherine Oxenberg, whose comedy German accent would shame Harvey Korman or John Astin) uses animal extracts in unethical rejuvenation treatments. Disgraced baseball player Felix Rosa (Mario Arturo

Hernández), her latest customer, is infused with wolf and orca DNA and becomes the whalewolf, whose transformation has something to do with the full moon since it affects regular werewolves and also the tides whales are sensitive to(!). The good guys are competent local foxy cop Nita Morales (Akari Endo), drunken yacht skipper Ray Brady (Casper Van Dien) and Ray's sidekick Pablo (Jorge Eduardo De Los Santos), who squabble as the creatures off various victims while squaring up for their title bout. A complication is that a local voodoo priest (Tony Almont) is coercing Ray and Pablo into bringing him the heart of the whalewolf for use in some dire ceremony.

Director Kevin O'Neill and screenwriter Matt Yamashita, held over from *Sharktopus vs Pteracuda*, are light on continuity (though there's a good gag as Reinhardt has photos of the villains of both early *Sharktopi* in her lab) but strong on non sequitur gags about dating shows, overage starlets, stupid Yanquis, monster bathroom habits, etc. The CGI is dreadful, of course – the monsters look more like a poorly realised version of the live-action/animated mix found in the *Scooby-Doo* theatrical features and do not remotely seem to exist in real space. The cartoonish, minimal look hurts the film, especially because the ridiculous whalewolf almost shows personality – and Hernández is funny as the creature's human form. Van Dien and Oxenberg, worthy inheritors of the Christopher and Lynda Day George B-feature power-couple mantle, go all out for ridiculous charm. Oxenberg, after a career-long blonde ingénue run, has plainly been waiting all along to play a Disney villainess on Syfy.

SILENT PREDATORS (1999)

> 'WHY WERE OUR KIDS ALLOWED TO PLAY HERE IF THIS TOWN IS INFESTED WITH RATTLESNAKES?'

Why would anyone brushing off an unproduced John Carpenter script from the 1970s (once known as *Prey*) pick the title *Silent Predators* for a movie about a type of snake named for the noise it makes? Not only do the 'mutant rattlesnakes' – offspring of a vicious tropical snake which escapes in a 'twenty years ago' prologue and a Southern California diamondback – rattle offscreen while red-filtered snake-eye lenses peer at victims... but these supposed predatory reptiles manage a lot of hissing and spitting too.

In a small town, new fire chief Vic Rondelli (Harry Hamlin) butts heads with property developer Max Farrington (Jack Scalia) when he wants to 'overreact' to a first-reel death by spreading panic about the mutant strain snakes. Feisty p.a. Mandy (Shannon Sturges) is torn between loyalty to her boss and attraction to the new guy in town, but Vic gets on her nerves by blithely assuring her women tend to exaggerate the size of snakes they have encounters with. Bad decisions: the mayor (David Spielberg) thinking it's not worth cancelling the little league game because all the snakes are on the other side of town (yes, there are snakes under the stands), Farrington taking dynamite into the abandoned mineshaft 'where the snakes are breeding' and his exterminator sidekick being bitten just as he's lighting a fuse. When the mine collapses, Mandy is trapped in her car *Dante's Peak*-style as the non-silent hissing gets nearer. Patty McCormack plays a covert snake-lover – her friendly snake gets one false scare, as does a rubber reptile put on the baseball field by the visiting team. One tiny nice gag: the hero has the wrong phobia ('I hate spiders.'). Directed by Noel Nosseck (*NightScream*).

SILENT VENOM (2009)

> 'WOMEN ON A SUBMARINE. IT JUST ISN'T NATURAL.'

Presumably, director Fred Olen Ray and writer Mark Sanderson were thinking of *Snakes on a Plane* – a phenomenon which never quite happened – when they threw this cheapie together, but the snakes-on-a-sub premise was done before (and better) in the 1974 TV-movie *Fer-de-Lance*. Hot scientist Dr Andrea Swanson (ex-Emmanuelle Krista Allen) and weasely assistant Jake (Louis Mandylor) are evacced from an island research centre on a submarine commanded by macho sailor guy O'Neill (Luke Perry). Jake brings along a bag full of twenty venomous (mostly real) reptiles on orders from Major Drake (Robert Catrini), who crops up in dull expository office scenes with Admiral Wallace (Tom Berenger), and also a couple of much bigger (CGI and rubber) specimens. Yes, they get loose. Jake also does all-purpose rottenness, purloining the only antivenom on the sub, while the commander ('Snakes, I hate 'em!') fires off his pistol at stray snakes and some inessential personnel get bitten. Running into the Chinese navy in waters where the US shouldn't be sailing doesn't help. Not very entertaining, even as schlock.

SNAKEHEAD TERROR (2004)

Though it opens with a montage of newspaper headlines about a prior 'frankenfish' outbreak, this is not a sequel to the lively *Frankenfish*. A small town's economy has been ruined since the local lake was poisoned to get rid of a plague of snakehead fish. The local coroner (William B. Davis) and his dimwit brother (Gary Jones) try to boost the tourist trade by dumping human growth hormone in the waters – which, of course, makes the surviving poison-resistant snakehead grow to monstrous size. The greying macho sheriff (Bruce Boxleitner) and a foxy ichthyologist (Carol Alt) poke at gruesomely bitten corpses while the sheriff's daughter (Chelan Simmons) and her inept teenage friends are besieged in a cottage on an island by fin-walking voracious monsters. Electric shock does for the critters. There are a few plot wrinkles and the cast are appealing (even if the lines they get stuck with aren't), but the fish are home computer-level CGI wrigglers. Scripted by Anthony L. Greene (*Gargoyle*) and Patrick J. Vitale; directed by Paul Ziller (*Stonehenge Apocalypse*).

SNAKES ON A TRAIN (2006)

Unwise advertising lines department: 'this is one train you definitely (sic) should have missed.' An instant *Snakes on a Plane* knock-off, rushed into production before anyone involved could have seen the higher-profile exploitation item – which in any case turned out to be a fizzle rather than a franchise-founder.

Wilder in its premise than the 'original', this is threadbare in execution: the audacious finale has a giant snake swallow an entire train, but the meagre budget is laughably unable to deliver the effect. Alma (Julia Ruiz), a Mexican girl under a Mayan curse, is smuggled across the border and onto a Los Angeles-bound train. Brujo (Alby Castro), her magician boyfriend, hopes his uncle can cure her of vomiting green goo containing deadly snakes (played by harmless grass snakes with dubbed in rattles and hisses) which slither around the speeding train, infecting a few other passengers. It takes an hour for the crisis to boil over, with time wasted on a sub-plot about a dim-bulb girl heroin smuggler (Amelia Jackson-Gray) and a bogus cowboy cop (Philo Beddoe).

When snake action starts, it's gruesome – a cute little girl (Lola Forsberg) is swallowed whole by a python – but unimpressive. Alma eventually surrenders to her curse, sporting giant vampire fangs and green skin, and becomes the train-swallowing giant, before a magic necklace whips up a tornado which sucks her into the sky. Scripted by Eric Forsberg (*Arachnoquake*); directed by Peter Mervis (oddly billed as 'the Mallachi Brothers').

STANLEY (1972)

'OUR TRIBE NOW CALLS YOU THE LOVER OF SNAKES, THE SNAKE MAN.' 'YOU THINK I CARE?'

Even the DVD sleeve admits *Stanley* is a rip-off, using Leonard Maltin's quote '*Willard* with snakes' (if not his generous two-star rating). This lackadaisical snakesploitation picture from Florida-based director William Grefé (*Death Curse of Tartu*) is among the poorest of a crowd of similar '70s quickies (*Frogs*, *Rattlers*, *Kiss of the Tarantula*, *Jennifer*). It copies the turning worm plot of *Willard*: a put-upon central character spends the first act being abused, betrayed, exploited and kicked around by hateful folks; the second act (i.e. the money material excerpted in the trailer) has him get his own back with the help of his pet vermin, before a finale in which he discovers he probably should have learned to forgive and forget. As the antihero burns to death in his shack, he whines, 'Maybe in Hell I'll find out what I am.'

Seminole Indian Vietnam veteran Tim Ochopee (Chris Robinson) lives in the swamp with his pets Stanley and Hazel ('People just don't understand friendly rattlesnakes.'). The baddies are headed by crass local entrepreneur Thomkins (Alex Rocco), who had Tim's dad shot in the backstory. He tries to persuade Tim to hunt snakes for belts ('Some fag fashion designer in Paris publically said animal skins is "in" this year.') until he gets a swimming pool full of water moccasins. A subplot has sleazy strip club proprietor (are there any non-sleazy strip club proprietors in the movies?) Sidney Calvin (Rey Baumel) persuade his over-the-hill danseuse wife (Marcia Knight) to do a strip-geek act, climaxing with her biting the head off one of Tim's beloved pets (she works out that, including matinees, she'll be 'biting the heads off nine snakes a week'). After his enemies are dead, Tim takes Thomkins' pouting blonde daughter Susie (Susan Carroll) to his shack to be the Eve in his Eden – but she gives him a hard time for using snakes the way the Man used him in 'Nam ('Two years of whites telling reds to kill the yellow.').

In trying to get some of that *Billy Jack* 'avenging Indian veteran' drive-in action, the film sabotages its own premise: Willard was a wimp momma's boy who could *only* fight back through his rats, but Tim is a combat-hardened outdoor guy who ought to be able to take care of himself without relying on reptiles. Screenwriter Gary Crutcher (*The Name of the Game is Kill!*) throws in the odd strained bit of poetic or cynical dialogue (talking about the Garden of Eden, Sidney refers to 'Adam's homosexual friend, the Forbidden Fruit') which still doesn't give the characters any depth. A funny, pompous, folk-protest, pro-animal theme song labels the human race 'an infectious disease'.

SUPERCROC (JURASSIC CROC) (2007)

'PEREZ, I DIDN'T MEAN TO BELITTLE YOUR CONTRIBUTION TO KEEPING US ALIVE. I'M GRATEFUL FOR YOUR KNOWLEDGE OF CROCODILES.'

A prehistoric crocodile rampages across California, searching for stolen eggs which scientists are using to develop next generation impenetrable armour. After enormous firepower, chemical weapons and attack helicopters fail, Perez (Cynthia Rose Hall) – a bereaved private soldier raised in Florida – realises the creature's weakness is its soft underbelly, so a quickly rigged up roadside bomb slipped under the beast does the trick. In The Asylum house style, director Scott Harper (*AVH: Alien vs. Hunter*) cuts between a crowded control room, where a general (David Novak), a forensic palaeontologist (Kim Little) and various state and military button-pushers earnestly talk about what's going on in the field, and that same field (indeed, just the one), where a rescue grunt (Matthew Blashaw) tags along with Perez as she spiels handy croc facts and the action always seems to be taking place round the corner from where the camera is. The CGI beastie is wretched, especially in the mandatory chewing-out-a-helicopter scene. Scripted by Steve Bevilacqua (*Hillside Cannibals*).

SUPERGATOR (2007)

> '**YOU'RE RIGHT – TOURISTS CAN'T DEMAND THEIR MONEY BACK WHEN THEY'RE DEAD, BUT THEIR FAMILIES CAN STILL SUE YOU FOR WILFUL NEGLIGENCE.**'

With *Primeval* in the pipeline, Roger Corman's New Horizons put imitative giant croc quickie *Primevil* into production – when *Primeval* tanked, the ripoff emerged under a new title. Grizzled scientist Kim Taft (Kelly McGillis) genegeneers a prehistoric giant alligator ('a man-eating turbogator from hell') which gets loose in Hawaii, a territory proud of its lack of dangerous animals. She teams with high-priced hunter Jake Kilpatrick (John Colton) to track the beast. After killing a courting couple, some bikini models and a photographer, stoners looking for a high, and other short-lived passersby, the monster sets its sights on eating a party of young vulcanologists led by earnest Dr Kinney (Brad Johnson). The growling CGI creature (which has its own choral theme) scores a high body count, but the film never works up anything like urgency – even though monster attacks are compounded by a volcano on the point of erupting (more bad CGI).

As is often the case, the model is obvious: Kinney and Kilpatrick develop a Dreyfuss-and-Shaw macho relationship, an official ignores warnings before the monster invades a luau and the ending (involving a bitten-in-half hunter and a shotgunned propane gas tank) is a landbound rewrite of *Jaws*. However, the film also echoes vintage Corman pictures like *Piranha* or *Humanoids from the Deep*. Written by longtime Corman associate Frances Doel (*Dinocroc*) and director Brian Clyde (*Operation Rogue*).

SUPERSHARK (2011)

Syfy Channel listings try to sell this as a comedy, though it isn't notably wittier than *Dinoshark*, the *Mega Shark* films or any of a dozen other prehistoric shark quickies. Writer-director Fred Olen Ray had a heavy touch even when trying for cult comedy (*Hollywood Chainsaw Hookers*) and his product blanded out to paste after his '80s heyday. Doing an amusing Corman-like low budget monster movie really needs sharp scripting, decent acting and a degree of smarts this doesn't have. A supershark is released from hibernation in an incident inspired by the Deepwater Horizon spill: an oil drilling platform uses a chemical to dissolve undersea rock and causes eco-disaster. Exec Roger Wade (top-billed John Schneider) tries to sound sincere, rogue marine biologist Kat Carmichael (Sarah Lieving) and crusty for-hire Skipper Chuck (Tim Abell) investigate, *Baywatchy* subplots fail to take fire, and the fin-walking CGI beast eats folk (including a couple of swimwear contest winners). The heroine works out that radio waves annoy the shark, so the army hires annoying DJ Dynamite Stevens (Jimmie JJ Walker) to play rock music at the thing – a potentially witty idea scuppered by the inability to license anything appropriate (or listenable) as an ultimate weapon.

SWAMP SHARK (2011)

Ever feel that the one thing sorely lacking in sharkbait pictures is the swampland stereotypes found in killer gator/croc movies? In this Syfy snooze, a prehistoric shark is let loose in a bayou and crashes the local gator festival. A plot involves restaurateur Rachel Broussard (Kristy Swanson) warding off the advances of slimy Sheriff Watson (Robert Davi) while weedy Fed Tommy (D.B. Sweeney) tries to expose Watson's involvement in an animal-smuggling racket which has (of course) not turned out well. Rachel's younger sister Krystal (Sophie Sinise) unwisely boards a party boat with townie dolts who get her imperilled. The result is as expected: feuding sub-plots, idiot characters who show up only to die, a Cajun shark-hunting expedition, wikipedia nature trivia and near-miss stars fading out. Scripted by Charles Bolon (*Monsterwolf*), Jennifer Iwen and Eric Miller (*Ice Spiders*); directed by Griff Furst (*Lake Placid 3*).

TENTACLES (TENTACOLI) (1977)

A widescreen *Jaws* cash-in from Italian hack Ovidio G. Assonitis (*Piranha II: Flying Killers*). Ocean Beach, California is terrorised by a prehistoric giant octopus set free when Trojan Construction, an unethical company run by Mr Whitehead (a miscast Henry Fonda), drills an underwater tunnel. In the opening sequence, a baby is pulled from its pram while a bus passes – setting a tone of ruthlessness upheld by the inexplicit deaths of both possible heroines (Delia Boccardo, who would work with Andrei Tarkovsky and Luigi Cozzi, and Sherry Buchanan, of *Zombi Holocaust*) and an entire flotilla of teen yacht-race competitors.

The monster is attracted by radio waves, setting up silly suspense as a sailor-suited mother (Shelley Winters) chats with her doomed offspring over a walkie-talkie. Assonitis gets clever-clever with fast edits and still-frame montages, intercutting an Uncle Sam-suited clown telling jokes, the Coast Guard helicopter trying to warn the sailboat kids and an endless shot of the rubber octopus head ploughing through water showing its unblinking malevolent single eye. Reporter Ned Turner (John Huston), brother of the bereaved mother, digs into the story, turning up at autopsies to irritate the Sheriff (Claude Akins) and the authorities, but stays out of the climax in which oceanographer Will Gleason (Bo Hopkins) sics his matched pair of trained killer whales on the octo-baddie. Sadly lacking in urgency, it holds back on the gore needed to establish how nasty this beast actually is. None of the distinguished cast get anything worth saying. Scripted by Jerome Max (*Ryan's Hope*), Tito Carpi (*The New Barbarians/ Warriors of the Wasteland*) and Steve Carabatsos (*El Condor*).

THIS AIN'T JAWS XXX (2011)

Unlike most XXX-rated 'parodies', this Hustler production makes more-than-contractual attempts to poke fun at its subject. After Quint (Evan Stone) has said he'll defeat the shark with his penis, Hooper (Alexis Ford) takes a look at a looming CGI fish and says, 'We're going to need a bigger dick.' The comparison-of-scars routine ends with Hooper showing a horseshoe-shaped mark she says she got in Tijuana when 'the damn donkey kicked at the end of the act'. Otherwise, it's a ten-minute Sweded *Jaws* padded with hours of rote sex. Sheriff Brody (Dale DaBone) and his wife (Jayden Cole) get it on in a scene with notably poor sound recording – a phone goes off unanswered and traffic audibly passes their supposed beach house. Produced and directed by Stuart Canterbury (*The Whores Have Eyes*).

¡TINTORERA! (1977)

'THESE STONES HAVE BEEN DEFYING THE FURY OF THE ELEMENTS FOR CENTURIES.' 'I WISH HUMAN RELATIONSHIPS WERE STRONG LIKE THAT, BUT YOU KNOW THEY USUALLY END UP DESTROYING THEMSELVES.'

One of the tsunami of *Jaws* imitations which flooded the international market in the wake of the 1975 megablockbuster, this Mexican epic is *una película de* René Cardona Jr (*Guyana: Cult of the Damned*). The script is based on a novel (I'd hazard a guess semi-autobiographical) by Ramón Bravo, who also supervised the underwater photography. In its mercilessly extended international cut (127 minutes), *¡Tintorera!* is a bizarre, excruciating mix of mondo, exploitation and something approaching pretentious art movie.

Playboy Esteban aka Steve (Hugo Stiglitz, with a weird red beard) recovers from a nervous breakdown (i.e. he looks dead glum) on a yacht moored off a coastal resort and has a romantic adventure with tourist Patricia (Fiona Lewis, robbed of her distinctive voice in the dubbing). She admits she's falling in love, but doesn't want to be emotionally involved and dumps Esteban for Miguel aka Mikey (Andrés García), a grinning diving tutor-cum-gigolo. Patricia gets up early one morning and takes a dip which ends with her getting eaten by a passing *tintorera* shark. No one notices and she's never mentioned again. After the bruising experience of being dumped – yes, Cardona worries more about self-pitying Hugo Stiglitz than Fiona Lewis being killed and eaten! – Steve and Mikey make up their squabble and become a tag-team, bedding hippie-chick sisters Kelly (Jennifer Ashley) and Cynthia (Laura Lyons). These sisters are introduced in a slap-and-tickle comedy rape scene with middle-aged truck drivers, where the victims really do 'lie back and enjoy it', suggesting the writer-director is as much of a sexist pig as his lead characters. Now blood brothers, the guys hunt sharks together (cuing real-life shark snuff footage, with the repeated image of thick red blood flowing out of gills) and have a ménage à trois with Gabriella (top-billed Susan George, unflatteringly shot) in a long montage of three-way fun every place but the bedroom (or bedcabin) accompanied by a horrible song ('We'll Be Together Until Goodbye').

This idyll ends when Miguel is eaten by the *tintorera*, who evidently holds a grudge. In a gruesome bit, a real shark swims with Miguel's fake head in its mouth and pilot fish nibble at the ragged flesh. Gabriella, upset, goes home (also never to be mentioned again) and a numbed Steve throws himself into hedonism again, getting back with the hippie sisters. The last straw comes during a midnight swim (horrid electro thrumm underwater music accompanies the fish) when the shark eats Cynthia. Steve's final *liebestod* is with the shark(!); he hunts it in revenge for its eating his best pal and seems to die killing it. Cardona has a weird conviction that the beach-bum lifestyle is interesting – maybe he'd seen that excellent Sam Elliott movie *Lifeguard?* – but the lead guys are assholes and the bikini girls seem idiots for putting up with them. Presumably, the gayish vibe between often naked leading men Stiglitz and García – hunk Mikey displaces Esteban's camp sidekick/servant Colonado (Roberto Guzman) on his yacht – is intentional. With moose-jawed Miguel Angel Fuentes (*Pumaman*) as a bodyguard.

2-HEADED SHARK ATTACK (2012)

'WAIT, HAVE YOU EVER WELDED UNDERWATER BEFORE?'

The Asylum again take a surefire goofy low-budget monster movie premise and bungle it by bringing nothing else to the table.

Top-billed Carmen Electra, prominent in the box-cover art, spends most of the film sunbathing on the deck as far away from the young cast as possible, then gets eaten along with the other token grownup (Charlie O'Connell). How can the death of the supposed lead be such a throwaway? Professor Babish (O'Connell, cast in the hope of reminding you his brother was in *Piranha 3D*) takes a boatload of kids on a study semester. A two-headed mutant shark (conjoined shark twins?) attacks in the vicinity of an atoll which is sinking (like the one in *Attack of the Crab Monsters*) thanks to seismic activity unrelated to the shark mutant or indeed anything else. The actual lead is Kate (Brooke Hogan, *Sand Sharks*), a competent blonde who has to overcome a fear of the water, and the regulation dickhead is Cole (Geoff Ward), a steroided bully who keeps making things worse by panicking and trying to save himself, leaving others to die.

It's a problem that sharks are so singleminded that this one having two heads makes no difference at all to the plot: it can gulp two victims at a time (and does so regularly) or tear single victims apart between its heads… Given that two headedness is all that distinguishes this crap CGI toon from any other mutant shark in the overcrowded pond, it's not really enough. In a crowded field, O'Connell gives the worst performance (his exaggerated response to a minor wound is especially ineffectual), though you have to admire Electra's ability to suggest she's barely even in a film supposedly built around her. Scripted by H. Perry Horton (*A Haunting in Salem*); directed by Christopher Douglas-Olen Ray (*Mega Shark versus Crocosaurus*).

3-HEADED SHARK ATTACK (2015)

The sequel to *2-Headed Shark Attack*; I hope the third film in the trilogy is a prequel called *1-Headed Shark Attack*. Director Christopher Olen Ray (aka Christopher Douglas-Olen Ray aka Christopher Ray; son of Fred Olen Ray, the maker of *Supershark*) returns with another shark-themed throwaway.

After the three-headed shark crunches up a hideously botoxed and siliconed bikini babe on an atoll, the plot simmers at a science station where Professor Thomas (Jena Sims) and Dr Nelson (Jaason Simmons) study mutations. Once most of the scientists are killed – with the ever-favourite guy-gets-bitten-while-sitting-on-a-toilet gag used again – the young intern survivors run into a party boat to meet a bunch of other characters who are only here to get killed. Danny Trejo cameos as hard guy Max Burns, who machetes off the middle head. However, the monster sprouts three smaller deformed heads in its place – becoming a *five*-headed shark – and bites Max to death. So it's down to tiny heroine Maggie (Karrueche Tran), boring hero Greg (Brad Mills) and longest-surviving tagalong Stanley (Rob Van Dam) to face the monster and blow it up.

Not remotely serious, but not remotely amusing either – and busier than it is exciting, with many scenes of people swimming or sailing into danger while other people jump up and down anxiously. Written by Bill Hanstock and Jacob Cooney (*Apocalypse Pompeii*).

L'ULTIMO SQUALO (GREAT WHITE) (1981)

'ONE THING'S FOR SURE – IT WASN'T A FLOATING CHAINSAW.'

This was sued off American screens by Universal as a blatant imitation of *Jaws* (which it is); at some point the studio must have given up, or else their lawyers would be besieging the Syfy Channel every week.

The Vincenzo Mannino (*Murder-Rock*) script, from a story by Ugo Tucci and Marc Princi, mixes elements from *Jaws* and *Jaws 2*, even throwing in a pinch of *Orca*. A great white shark terrorises windsurfers in Port Harbor, an American town played by Maltese locations, and writer Peter Benton (James Franciscus – name misspelled in the credits) teams with Scots-accented shark hunter Ron Hamer (Vic Morrow) to destroy the beast. Some idiot kids try to get there first and Benton's daughter (Stefania Girolami, daughter of director Enzo G. Castellari) has her leg bitten off. Mayor Wells (Joshua Sinclair), the glad-handing porn-moustache politician who insisted the windsurfing contest go on despite the first attack, goes after the fish with a helicopter and contrives to get eaten – primarily because he omits to bring along any weapons and secondarily because he's a clumsy idiot. Finally, Benton – presumably based on *Jaws* author Peter Benchley – detonates the explosive belt Hamer was wearing when he got swallowed and ends the reign of terror.

A cynical subplot features a ruthless TV reporter happy to let people get eaten so long as he gets good footage that can facilitate his move to a network. The shark is a ridiculous but impressive big prop intercut with *Blue Water White Death* mondo footage. The MOR pop music is excruciating.

UP FROM THE DEPTHS (1979)

'MR SUKI, THAT'S A BEAUTIFUL DEAD FISH YOU HAVE THERE.'

Sometime after the epic shoot of *Apocalypse Now*, Sam Bottoms returned to the Philippines to star in a Roger Corman-backed mutant shark quickie, though that says more about the ups and downs of his career than his love for the place. In the wake of *Piranha*, itself a *Jaws* cash-in, it's a standard marine monster movie, without even much character eccentricity to recommend it. It seems to have been a disastrous production, post-dubbed because the original dialogue track (and script!) was lost and beefed up with cheap monster effects (from Chris Walas and Robert Short) that barely afford a glimpse of the stiff, undefinable creature amid endless frothing bloody waters.

Ecological changes drive deep-sea creatures to the shallows around a Hawaiian resort (played by the Philippines, with grass skirts, pineapples, luaus, tikis and other yes-this-is-Hawaii set dressing) and one large specimen kills a lot of folk. A snippy manager (Kedric Wolfe) fulfils the mayor-in-*Jaws* hush-it-up-for-the-sake-of-tourism role, and oddly doesn't get killed... though he acts like a crass jerk throughout. The traditional coalition of heroes consists of a beach bum (Bottoms), his con-man uncle (Virgil Frye), an assistant manager (Susanne Reed) and a marine biologist (Charles Howerton). Some scenes intended as raucous comedy – as when mention of a sea monster panics everyone at a party though they are safely on dry land or a dimwit model (Iris Lee, doing or dubbed with a silly Brit-Aussie accent) tosses off idiocies, like 'Actually, I'm more attunuated to music... especially trombone players,' to fill in time before she gets eaten – aren't terribly amusing. The only real funny-perverse touch comes when the scientist's corpse is strung along behind the boat as bait to lure the monster into eating a bomb.

Scripted by Alfred M. Sweeney and an uncredited Anne Dyer, Corman associates with few to no other writing credits. Directed by Charles B. Griffith, Corman's go-to screenwriter for witty horror (*A Bucket of Blood*), but never much of a megaphone man.

USS INDIANAPOLIS: MEN OF COURAGE (2016)

'AS A COMMANDER IN THE IMPERIAL JAPANESE NAVY IT WAS MY DUTY TO KILL YOU, BUT AS A MAN I HAVE REGRETS.'

This resolutely old-fashioned film is essentially *Quint's Speech from Jaws: The Movie*. An inflated botch of the true story already dramatised in the 1991 TV-movie *Mission of the Shark: The Saga of the U.S.S. Indianapolis*, this chronicles the grim fate of the ship which delivered the A-bombs to the Pacific theatre of war in 1945. A disaster-movie clutch of setup storylines (pals at odds over a gal, racial friction which lands black and white brawlers in the brig, a missing engagement ring that's fallen into the hands of a compulsive gambler with heavy debts, a martinet officer who loses the respect of the men) are paid off after a torpedo strike as over a thousand crewmen are pitched into the water to bob about as easy prey for a circling pack of sharks. Director Mario Van Peebles plays down the horrors – so shark attacks are perfunctory and there's more irksome chat between the suffering survivors than blood-in-the-water scariness. Among the faintly camp aspects are earnest but hackneyed performances from Nicolas Cage as Captain McVay, who seethes through a long third-act court martial for 'failure to zigzag', and Tom Sizemore as a swab who spends a lot of time playing with his severed foot.

VENOM (1981)

With an eclectic cast of international names and amazingly contrived setup, this troubled production (director Piers Haggard took over from Tobe Hooper) is less entertaining than it ought to be. Based on a novel by Alan Scholefield, the exposition-heavy Robert Carrington (*Wait Until Dark*) script fritters away potentially solid suspense situations.

The high concept is that a gang of kidnappers and some innocent victims are besieged in a London mansion by the police, as a black mamba – 'Probably the most deadly snake in the world,' toxicologist Dr Stowe (Sarah Miles) repeatedly tells people – crawls through spacious heating ducts and leaps out periodically to scare good people and kill bad ones. An African snake wouldn't last minutes in draughty London, so the house is kept at greenhouse temperature because imperilled kid Philip (Lance Holcomb) has asthma – as well as enough pocket money to assemble a private zoo and a famous wildlife explorer grandfather (Sterling Hayden, aptly grizzled). The villains are icy kraut Jacmel (Klaus Kinski), unreliable chauffeur Dave (Oliver Reed) – who shotguns copper John Forbes-Robertson (unrecognisable from *Legend of the 7 Golden Vampires*) at the worst possible time – and saucy maid Louise (Susan George), who snogs both male baddies and takes an early bath after being bitten. Also with Nicol Williamson as a hardy Scots copper commanding the siege, Edward Hardwicke as an establishment figure leaving the situation to stew and Michael Gough as the reptile man from London Zoo (a perhaps-bogus end credit claims his character helped handle the deadly reptile – though it looks to be a puppet more often than it's real). Cabbie Hugh Lloyd and pet shop owner Rita Webb – who caresses a gila monster as she gets the snakes mixed up – do working class comedy, and Cornelia Sharpe gives the film's worst performance as Philip's distraught mother. The pros do the best they can under the circumstances, which in Reed's case includes having the mamba slide into his trousers and bite his balls.

The mamba, brownish-grey rather than black (it gets the name from the colour of the inside of its mouth), is forgotten for long stretches and rarely lives up to its fearsome reputation – indeed it only hurts the bad people. The film keeps missing tricks: Stowe has anti-venom on hand, but no one sympathetic is bitten then saved with a risky injection; Jacmel cuts a finger off Louise's corpse and pretends he's torturing Stowe, but he's such a baddie we wonder why he bothers with fakery; grandpa has a bad heart and Philip is asthmatic, but neither have life-threatening health crises during the siege. The punch line, of course, is the hatching of a mamba egg deep in the heating system.

VIPERS (2008)

'FIRST COMES THE SLITHER, THEN COMES THE SLAUGHTER!'

Another orgy of poorly CGId snakes. Corporate suit Burton (Corbin Bernsen) lets loose genetically engineered vipers on an island just to see what happens. After a setup introduces a cross-section of locals with intricate backstories which feel like a précis of five seasons of soap opera, the snakes start biting and chewing (not a common reptile tactic, in reality) and the characters get whittled down. Evil enforcer Brownie (Stephen E. Miller) makes things worse and token sensitive scientist Dr Collins (Jessica Steen) tries to help. The leads are market gardener Nicky (Tara Reid), who has a sideline in medical marijuana, and Gulf War veteran doctor Taylor (Jonathan Scarfe), having trouble replacing a respected pillar of the community (Don S. Davis). A tangle involves a whiny teenage girl (Genevieve Buechner) whose separated parents (Aaron Pearl, Claire Rankin) hook up with a blonde sexpot (Mercedes McNab), who gets snaked early, and the sheriff (Mark Humphrey), who doesn't last much longer. The snakes never look remotely real or threatening. Written by Brian Katkin (*Scarecrow Gone Wild*); directed by Bill Corcoran (*Atomic Twister*).

XTINCTION: PREDATOR X (ALLIGATOR X) (2010)

> 'KATRINA DUG UP A LOT OF CRAP, INCLUDING THOSE TWO BAYOU METH-HEAD INBREDS.'

Typical Syfy schlock. Not only is a giant prehistoric alligator, recreated by mad scientist Dr Leblanc (Mark Sheppard), roaming in the bayou, but a couple of meth-brewing goon brothers (Scott L. Schwartz, Ricky Wayne credited as Rick Robinson Jr) menace and murder folks without the need for even cheap pixel manipulation. Heroine Laura (Elena Lyons, very terrible), ex-wife of the villain, returns to the swamp to ask after Pappy (Phillip Beard), who has been fed to the gatorsaur(™) by the inbreds as part of a cracked scheme to get hold of his land, which happens to have the right seawater/saltwater mix for the monster to spawn. The sheriff (Lochlyn Munro) is in love with Laura. The regulation number of people get killed, and limbs float about. Screenplay and story by George M. Kostuch, Cameron Larson, Caleb Michaelson and Claire Sanchez (four people!); directed by Amir Valinia (*Lockjaw: Rise of the Kulev Serpent*).

ZOMBIE SHARK (2015)

> 'WHY DO THOSE PEOPLE KEEP COMING TO THE WATER? THEY'RE SETTING UP A ZOMBIE SHARK BUFFET.'

A great moment in exploitation cinema is the zombie vs shark fight in Lucio Fulci's *Zombi 2* (*Zombie Flesh Eaters*)… which involves a stuntman in zombie makeup visibly underwater (holding his breath?) tussling with a real-live shark and, in a gruesome effect, biting a chunk out of the fish. The scene established that at the tail end of the 1970s, the zombie superseded *Jaws* as a movie monster. It took thirty-six years for the dynamite exploitation combo to be repeated – and, in 2015, sharks *and* zombies were busier than ever, making it all the more disappointing that this bluntly titled time-waster is so disposably useless.

'Bruce' – patient zero of the zombie shark outbreak, recognisable by a harpoon sticking out of him – is talked up as fearsome, but is just another mass of sub-1990s computer game pixels. A rubbery severed shark head puppet has more personality – and even that isn't well used. A few desultory zombies stumble around, but the film can't muster the enthusiasm to combine its threats properly. For instance, there's no sense that fleeing the sea to escape the sharks will take characters to places where they are in peril from zombies. Overprotective Amber (Cassie Steele) and her younger sister Sophie (Sloane Coe) go to Red Plum Island for a weekend with Amber's soon-killed boyfriend Jenner Branton (Ross Britz) and catty, bosomy Bridgette (Becky Andrews). Jenner is swallowed whole with boat keys in his pocket, trapping the girls on the island as sharks terrorise random characters, the zombie infection spreads and a storm cuts them off from mainland help. Bad weather doesn't hit because it would be too expensive to stage, even though the rules of movie suspense dictate that fighting zombies, sharks and zombie sharks during a tropical storm would be more exciting than traipsing from one mild attack to another as folk repeatedly fall over, trip into the water, linger in dangerous places or generally position themselves so CGI monsters can get them.

A guilt-ridden scientist (Laura Cayouette) – who zombified sharks as part of a program to improve battlefield surgery because her brother died in action – and ultra-tough but not especially effective security guy Max Cage (Jason London) rattle off dialogue as time-wasting cutaways show the girls' parents not being able to do anything. Writer Greg Mitchell's odd ending might have been effective if better managed. Throughout, it's stressed that the parents don't trust Amber to look after her sister, so she is determined to protect the kid. When Sophie gets swallowed, Amber takes out Bruce's harpoon and goes full-on Ahab to destroy the monster. Predictably, if ridiculously, Sophie is alive inside the fish and Amber cuts her out, only for it to turn out that she's now a zombie and Amber has to stick a knife in her head. This tortuous, cruel plotting renders the sister act build-up pointless and director Misty Talley (*Ozark Sharks*) throws it away with a shrug anyway.

Acknowledgements

It was Mark Dinning at *Empire* magazine who suggested the original 'Video Dungeon' column, back in the era of VHS… the feature has evolved over the years, expanding or diminishing at the whim of every redesign. Besides Mark, thanks are due to a host of former or serving *Empire* staffers who have been involved in one way or another – Liz Beardsworth, Jo Berry, Kat Brown, Katharine Busby, Nick de Semlyen, Phil de Semlyen, James Dyer, Angie Errigo, Ian Freer, Chris Hewitt, David Hughes, Dan Jolin, Colin Kennedy, Barry McIlhenny, Ian Nathan, Helen O'Hara, Jonathan Pile, Lucy Quick, Olly Richards, John Royle, Fola Salako, Mark Salisbury, Stephanie Seelan-George, Adam Smith, Phil Thomas, Caroline Westbrook, Terri White, Ally Whybrew and Damon Wise. Also to the many, many publicists, distributors and filmmakers who have supplied tapes, discs, downloads and links – and, of course, all those *Empire* readers who first turn to the column when each new issue shows up. Thanks also to Virginie Sélavy (*Electric Sheep*), Steve Thrower (*Eyeball*), Mark Adams and Finn Halligan (*Screen Daily*), Alan Jones and David Miller (*Shivers*), Steve Puchalski (*Shock Cinema*), Stefan Jaworzyn, Stephen Jones and Dave Reeder (*Shock Xpress*), Nick James, Kieron Corless and James Bell (*Sight & Sound*) and Tim Lucas (*Video Watchdog*) – who have all commissioned reviews of outré films from me. And nods of gratitude for those who've been through successive FrightFests (and similar events) with me, even when things looked really bleak – Prano Bailey-Bond, David Barraclough, Anton Bitel, Randy Broecker, Hayley Campbell, Billy Chainsaw, Simret Cheema-Innis, Sarah Cleary, David Cox, David Cross, Ian and Laura Cruikshank, Meg Davis, Greg Day, Jennifer Eiss, Harvey Fenton, Dick Fiddy, Nigel Floyd, Lisa Gaye, Jennifer Handorf, Sean Hogan, David Hyman, Kier-la Janisse, Mark Kermode, Dan Martin, Maura McHugh, Kat McLaughlin, Marc Morris, Helen Mullane, Charlie Oughton, Jonathan Rigby, Josh Saco, Dean Skilton, Jake West, Laura Westcott and many other friendly faces. The seeds of this book were planted in an era of *House of Hammer* and *Fangoria*, major release double bills like *The Funhouse/My Bloody Valentine* or *The Toolbox Murders/Zombie Flesh Eaters*, Hammer and Universal horrors on BBC2 late on Saturday nights, Scala All-Nighters and swiftly-banned VHS nasties… but it emerges in an age of Cigarette Burns, the Duke Mitchell Film Club, Shudder, Arrow Video, Science+Fiction Trieste, the Criterion Collection, Eureka, the IMDb and YouTube. I'm just glad we can still see the films.

At Titan, this project was enthusiastically supported by Simon Ward, who commissioned it, and brought to term by Jo Boylett. This volume represents a tiny selection of the material I have gathered – many, many other categories remain to be explored, from Aliens to Zombies.

APPENDIX

CONFINEMENTS AND DANGEROUS GAMES

AfterDeath (2015)
Already Dead (2007)
Aquarium (2004)
As Good as Dead (2010)
ATM (2012)
Awaiting (2014)
Bane (2009)
Basement (2010)
Bereavement (2010)
Blackout (2008)
Blooded (2011)
Bloodlust! (1961)
Blood Trails (2006)
Bone Dry (2007)
Breathing Room (2008)
The Breeder (2011)
Broken (2006)
Burning Bright (2010)
Captifs (Caged) (2010)
Captured (1959)
The Cellar Door (2007)
Cheap Thrills (2013)
5150, rue des Ormes (5150 Elms Way) (2009)
Claustrofobia (2011)
The Clinic (2011)
Coffin (2011)
The Condemned (2007)
Cord (Hide and Seek) (2000)
Curve (2015)
Death Race (2008)
Desyat Negrityat (Ten Little Niggers) (1987)
Dolan's Cadillac (2009)
Dread (2009)
Elevator (2011)
The Elevator (1974)
The Entrance (2006)
Exam (2009)
The Experiment (2010)

The Facility (Guinea Pigs) (2012)
Faults (2014)
Femina Ridens (The Frightened Woman) (1969)
Final Girl (2013)
Gakkô ura saito (Tokyo Gore School) (2009)
A Game of Death (1946)
Gusha No Bindume (Hellevator) (2004)
La Habitación de Fermat (Fermat's Room) (2007)
Hoffman (1970)
Homecoming (2009)
Hostel Part III (2011)
House of 9 (2005)
The Human Race (2013)
Hunger (2009)
The Hunters (2011)
i-Lived (2015)
The Incident (1967)
Inshite miru: 7-kakan no desu gêmu (Death Game; The Incite Mill) (2010)
Iron Doors (2010)
Jue ming pai dui (Invitation Only) (2009)
The Keeper (2004)
The Killing Room (2009)
Live Feed (2006)
The Loved Ones (2009)
The Maze Runner (2014)
Nerve (2016)
Night Drive (2010)
Nothing (2003)
October Moth (1960)
100 Feet (2008)
Open House (2010)
Otis (2008)
Paintball (2009)
Perfect Strangers (2003)
Pet (2016)
Preservation (2014)
Raze (2013)
Redd Inc. (Inhuman Resources) (2012)
El Rey de la Montaña (King of the Hill) (2007)
Riaru onigokko (Tag) (2015)

Room (2015)
Rovdyr (Manhunt) (2008)
RPG (Real Playing Game) (2013)
Satsujin Douga Site (Death Tube; Murder Site)
　(2010)
Season of the Hunted (2003)
Senseless (2008)
The 7th Hunt (2009)
Shuttle (2008)
Sil Jong (Missing) (2009)
Steel Trap (2007)
The Strange Vengeance of Rosalie (1972)
Territories (Checkpoint) (2010)
Terror Trap (2010)
That Cold Day in the Park (1969)
13 Game Sayawng (13: Game of Death) (2006)
13 Sins (2014)
31 (2016)
Tokyo 10+01 (2003)
247°F (2011)
Trapped (1973)
13 Tzameti (2005)
UKM: The Ultimate Killing Machine (2006)
Unknown (2006)
Vile (2011)
War Games: At the End of the Day (2011)
Winter's End (2005)
You Belong to Me (2007)

CRYPTIDS AND CRITTERS

Abominable (2006)
Absentia (2011)
Backwoods Bloodbath: Curse of the Black Hodag
　(2007)
Banshee!!! (2008)
Bigfoot (1970)
Bigfoot Holler Creek Canyon (2006)
The Blackout (2009)
The Boogens (1982)
The Burrowers (2008)
Creature (2011)
Creature from Black Lake (1976)
Curse of Bigfoot (1975)
Deadly Descent: The Abominable Snowman (2013)
Las Garras de Lorelei (The Loreley's Grasp; When the
　Screaming Stops) (1974)
Hybrid (Super Hybrid) (2010)
Hypothermia (2010)
Ice Queen (2005)
Indigenous (Prey) (2014)
It Waits (2005)
The Lonely Ones (2006)
Mammoth (2006)

Man-Thing (2005)
Mexican Werewolf in Texas (2005)
The Monster (2015)
Nymph (Mamula; Killer Mermaid) (2014)
Red Clover (Leprechaun's Revenge) (2012)
The Sand (2015)
Sasquatch Mountain (2006)
Sasquatch: The Legend of Bigfoot (1976)
Siren (2010)
Skullduggery (1970)
The Snow Creature (1954)
Swamp Devil (2008)
Thale (2012)
13th Child (2002)
Throwback (2013)
Troll 2 (Trolli) (1990)
The Unknown (Clawed: The Legend of Sasquatch)
　(2005)
Yeti (Yeti: Curse of the Snow Demon) (2008)

FAMOUS MONSTERS

Alucard (2005)
Alvin and the Chipmunks Meet Frankenstein (1999)
Army of Frankensteins (2013)
Bandh Darwaza (1990)
Batman/Dracula (1964)
The Batman vs Dracula (2005)
Boltneck (Big Monster on Campus; Teen Monster)
　(2000)
Bonnie and Clyde vs Dracula (2008)
El Castillo de los Monstruos (1957)
Deafula (1975)
Dear Dracula (2012)
Die Hard Dracula (1998)
La Dinastía di Dracula (Dynasty of Dracula) (1978)
Doctor Dracula (Lucifer's Women) (1975/1981)
Dracula (2006)
Dracula (2009)
Dracula (2012)
Dracula Exotica (Love at First Gulp) (1980)
Dracula: Lord of the Damned (2011)
Dracula Reborn (2012)
Dracula's Curse (Bram Stoker's Dracula's Curse)
　(2006)
Dracula's Guest (2008)
Dracula Sucks/Lust at First Bite (1979)
Dracula: The Dark Prince (2013)
Dracula: The Impaler (The Impaler) (2013)
Dracula 2012 (2013)
Dracula II: Ascension (2003)
Dracula III: Legacy (2005)
Dracula 3000: Infinite Darkness (2004)
Drakula Istanbul'da (Dracula in Istanbul) (1953)
Emmanuelle vs. Dracula (2003)

Fracchia contro Dracula (1985)
Frankenstein (1910)
Frankenstein (1973)
Frankenstein (1994)
Frankenstein (2004)
Frankenstein (2004)
Frankenstein (2007)
Frankenstein (National Theatre Live: Frankenstein) (2011)
Frankenstein (2015)
Frankenstein '80 (Mosaico) (1972)
Frankenstein Reborn (2005)
Frankenstein's Army (2013)
Frankenstein's Great Aunt Tillie (1984)
Frankenstein's Wedding… Live in Leeds (2011)
The Frankenstein Syndrome (The Prometheus Project) (2010)
The Frankenstein Theory (2011)
Frankenstein vs. the Creature From Blood Cove (2005)
Frankenstein vs. the Mummy (2015)
Frankestein, El Vampiro y Compañía (1962)
Furankenshutain no kaijû: Sanda tai Gaira (The War of the Gargantuas) (1966)
Furankenshutain tai chitei kaijû Baragon (Frankenstein Conquers the World) (1965)
Graf Dracula in Oberbayern (Dracula Blows His Cool) (1979)
Halâl 'alaik (Shame on You) (1953)
… Hanno Cambiato Faccia (1971)
Heisse Nächte auf Schloss Dracula (Hot Nights at Castle Dracula) (1978)
Història de la meva mort (Story of My Death) (2013)
House of Frankenstein (1997)
Hrabe Drakula (1970)
Jonathan (1970)
Lady Dracula (1977)
League of Frankenstein (2015)
Leena Meets Frankenstein (1993)
The Librarian: Curse of the Judas Chalice (2008)
Lust for Dracula (2004)
Mina Murray's Journal (2016)
Monster Brawl (2011)
Mystery and Imagination: Dracula (1968)
Mystery and Imagination: Frankenstein (1968)
Nocturna (1979)
Orlak, el Infierno de Frankenstein (1960)
The Passion of Dracula (1979)
Pehavý Max a strasidlá (Frankenstein's Aunt; Freckled Max and the Spooks) (1987)
Revenant (Modern Vampires) (1998)
Riti, Magie Nere e Segrete Orge Nel Trecento… (The Reincarnation of Isabel; The Ghastly Orgies of Count Dracula) (1973)
Saint Dracula (Dracula The Dark Lord) (2012)

Santo en El Tesoro de Dracula (Santo in the Treasure of Dracula) (1968)
Sevimli Frankenstayn (My Friend Frankenstein; Turkish Young Frankenstein) (1975)
Sharkenstein (2016)
Shisha no Teikoku (The Empire of Corpses) (2015)
The Sins of Dracula (2014)
Stan Helsing (2009)
Subject Two (2006)
Tales of Dracula (2015)
This Ain't Dracula XXX (2011)
Transylmania (2009)
Las Vampiras (1969)
Vlad (2003)
Way of the Vampire (Bram Stoker's Way of the Vampire) (2005)
Yami no teiô kyuketsuki Dracula (Dracula Sovereign of the Damned) (1980)
Zinda Laash (The Living Corpse) (1967)

FOUND FOOTAGE

Afflicted (2013)
Alone With Her (2006)
Alternative 3 (1977)
The Amityville Haunting (2011)
Are You Scared? (2006)
Are You Scared 2 (Tracked) (2009)
The Bay (2012)
Be My Cat: A Film for Anne (2016)
Blackout (2013)
Black Water Vampire (2013)
The Borderlands (Final Prayer) (2013)
The Buried Secret of M. Night Shyamalan (2004)
The Burningmoore Incident (Reality Kills) (2010)
Camp Dread (2014)
Classroom 6 (2015)
The Darkest Dawn (2016)
Daylight (2013)
Day of the Mummy (2014)
Demonic (2015)
The Den (2013)
The Devil's Music (2008)
Digging Up the Marrow (2014)
The Dinosaur Project (2012)
Director's Cut (2016)
The Dyatlov Pass Incident (Devil's Pass) (2013)
Emergo (Apartment 143) (2011)
La Entidad (The Entity) (2015)
Episode 50 (2011)
Europa Report (2013)
Evidence (2012)
Evidence (2013)
Evil Things (2009)
EVP (2012)

The Execution of Gary Glitter (2009)
Exists (2014)
Exorcism (2014)
Extinction (The Expedition) (2014)
Found Footage 3D (2016)
The Gallows (2015)
Gerber: Istoria di Melissa (The Gerber Syndrome)
  (2010)
Grave Encounters (2011)
Grave Encounters 2 (2012)
Heidi Slater (2015)
Hollow (2011)
The Houses October Built (The Houses of
  Halloween) (2014)
Hungerford (2014)
Hunting the Legend (2013)
Inner Demons (2014)
JeruZalem (2015)
Lake Mungo (2008)
The Lost Coast Tapes (2012)
The Mirror (2014)
Mr Jones (2013)
Mockingbird (2014)
Muirhouse (2012)
Open Windows (2014)
Outpost 37 (Mankind's Last Stand) (2013)
The Paranormal Incident (2011)
Population Zero (2016)
Resurrecting "The Street Walker" (2009)
Rough Cut (2013)
Shoping-Tur (Shopping Tour) (2012)
The Sigil (2012)
Skinwalker Ranch (Skinwalkers) (2013)
Somebody's There (The Pigman Murders) (2015)
The Taking (The Taking of Deborah Logan) (2014)
Tape 407 (2012)
The Tapes (2011)
388 Arletta Avenue (2011)
The Unfolding (2015)
Unfriended (2015)
Unidentified (2013)
Vampire Diary (2006)
Vampires (2009)
The Visit (2015)
Willow Creek (2013)
Without Warning (1994)
The Woods (Bigfoot Trail) (2013)

HARD CASE CRIME

The Ace of Hearts (1921)
AKP: Job 27 (2013)
The Big Night (1951)
Il Boss (The Boss) (1973)
Caged (1950)

The Capture (1950)
The Chase (1946)
Crown v. Stevens (1936)
Dangerous Voyage (Terror Ship) (1954)
Death is a Woman (1965)
Decoy (1946)
Dillinger and Capone (1995)
Drive a Crooked Road (1954)
Enragés (Rabid Dogs) (2014)
Eyewitness (Sudden Terror) (1970)
Five Star Final (1931)
Gangsters (Play for Today: Gangsters) (1975)
The Girl Hunters (1963)
The Hoodlum (1951)
Hot Boyz (Gang Law) (2000)
The Killer Within Me (2003)
Kill Me Tomorrow (1957)
Lights of New York (1928)
Machinegunner (1976)
Moonrise (1948)
Il Mostro dell'isola (The Island Monster) (1954)
The Neighbor (The Neighbour) (2016)
Nid de Guêpes (The Nest; The Wasps' Nest) (2002)
Offbeat (1961)
The Penalty (1920)
Piccadilly Third Stop (1960)
Piggy Banks (2005)
Pochi no Kohuhaku (Confessions of a Dog) (2006)
The Pot Carriers (1962)
The Riddle (2007)
The Riverside Murder (1935)
The Scotland Yard Mystery (The Living Dead) (1934)
The Silent Partner (1978)
Strip Tease Murder (1961)
Les Vampires (1915)
Villain (1971)

HIGH ADVENTURE

Alabama Jones and the Busty Crusade (2005)
Antinea, l'Amante della Città Sepolta (Journey
  Beneath the Desert) (1961)
L'Atlantide (1921)
L'Atlantide (1932)
L'Atlantide (1972)
Aventura al centro de la tierra (Adventure at the
  Centre of the Earth (1966)
Le Avventure Straordinarissime di Saturnino
  Farandola (1915)
Chitty Chitty Bang Bang (1968)
Cobra Woman (1944)
Confessions of an Opium Eater (Souls for Sale; Evils
  of Chinatown) (1962)
Curucu, Beast of the Amazon (1956)
Dark Streets of Cairo (1940)

The Forbidden Territory (1934)
Green Mansions (1959)
The Island at the Top of the World (1974)
Legend of the Lost (1957)
Mysterious Island (Jules Verne's Mysterious Island) (2005)
Nabonga (1944)
She (1925)
Siren of Atlantis (1949)
Terry and the Pirates (1940)
Das Tiger von Eschnapur (The Tiger of Eschnapur) (1959)/Das Indische Grabmal (The Indian Tomb) (1959)
Ukradená Vzducholod (The Stolen Airship; Le Dirigible Volé) (1967)

SECRET AGENT MEN (AND WOMEN)

After Tonight (1933)
Agente S 03 Operazione Atlantide (Operation Atlantis) (1965)
Big Jim McLain (1952)
The Broken Horseshoe (1953)/Operation Diplomat (1953)
D.E.B.S. (2004)
The Delta Factor (1970)
Escape in the Fog (1945)
The Fearmakers (1958)
The Gay Diplomat (1931)
Hammerhead (1968)
International Gorillay (International Guerillas) (1990)
The Kremlin Letter (1970)
Madame Sin (1972)
Missione speciale Lady Chaplin/Operazione Lady Chaplin (Special Mission Lady Chaplin) (1966)
Mister Jerico (1970)
Le Monocle Rit Jaune (The Monocle) (1964)
O.K. Connery (Operation Kid Brother) (1967)
Operation C.I.A. (1965)
Operation: Endgame (Rogues Gallery) (2010)
The Return of Mr Moto (1965)
Spione (Spies) (1928)
The Spook Who Sat By the Door (1973)

SERIAL KILLERS AND COPS
Anamorph (2007)
The Calling (2014)
Christopher Roth (2010)
Chugyeogja (The Chaser) (2008)
Cimarron Strip: Knife in the Darkness (1968)
Cover Girl Killer (1959)
11th Victim (1979)
Ellery Queen: Don't Look Behind You (1971)

Le foto di Gioia (Delirium) (1987)
Francesca (2015)
Giallo (2009)
Horsemen (Horsemen of the Apocalypse) (2009)
Indagine su un Cittadino al di Sopra di Ogni Sospetto (Investigation of a Citizen Above Suspicion) (1970)
The Lodger (The Phantom Fiend) (1932)
The Lodger (2009)
The Lost Angel (2005)
M (1951)
Murder! (1930)
Murder Rock (Murderock – uccide a passo di danza; Murder Rock – Dancing Death) (1984)
Mýrin (Jar City) (2006)
Niet voor de Poesen (Because of the Cats; The Rape) (1973)
The Playbirds (1978)
The Pledge (2001)
Resurrection (1999)
The Ripper (1985)
The Ripper (1997)
The River Murders (2011)
The Sport Killer (Killer's Delight; The Dark Ride) (1977)
Suspect Zero (2004)
Thr3e (2006)
Urge to Kill (1960)
You Can't Stop the Murders (2003)

WEIRD HIPPIE SHIT

Alba Pagana (May Morning) (1970)
Alex in Wonderland (1970)
Angel Unchained (1970)
. . . Artemis . . 8 . . 1 . . (1981)
Barn of the Naked Dead (Terror Circus) (1974)
Between Time and Timbuktu: A Space Fantasy (1971)
The Big Cube (1969)
Black Moon (1975)
Blood and Lace (The Blood Secret) (1971)
Blood Freak (1972)
Bread (1971)
Candy (1968)
Curse of the Headless Horseman (1972)
Day the Fish Came Out (1967)
Dionysus in '69 (1970)
Drive, He Said (1971)
Eggshells (1969)
Fata Morgana (1971)
Forbidden Zone (1980)
Gas! - Or - It Became Necessary to Destroy the World in Order to Save It (1970)
Get to Know Your Rabbit (1972)

Godmonster of Indian Flats (1973)
Gonks Go Beat (1965)
Goodbye Gemini (Twinsanity) (1970)
Good Times (1967)
Groupie Girl (1970)
Happy Birthday, Wanda June (1971)
Hex (1973)
Hi, Mom! (1970)
Identikit (The Driver's Seat) (1974)
The Insomniac (1971)
Joanna (1968)
The Love Witch (2016)
More (1969)
Murder a la Mod (1967)
Permissive (1970)
Un Posto ideale per uccider (Oasis of Fear) (1971)
Pufnstuf (1970)
Pussycat, Pussycat, I Love You (1970)
Reflections of Evil (2002)
O Ritual dos Sádicos (O Despertar da Bestia; Awakening of the Beast) (1970)
Roma Drogata… La polizia non può intervenire (Hallucination Strip) (1975)
A Safe Place (1971)
Secret Ceremony (1968)
Separation (1968)
Straight on Till Morning (1972)
Sunburst (Slashed Dreams) (1975)
Tam Lin (The Devil's Widow) (1971)
There's Always Vanilla (The Affair) (1971)
Toomorrow (1970)
The Touchables (1968)
The Toy Box (1971)
Wonderwall (1968)
Work is a 4-Letter Word (1968)
Zachariah (1970)

WILDLIFE

Aatank (1996)
Anacondas: The Hunt for the Blood Orchid (2004)
Anaconda 3: Offspring (2008)
Anacondas: Trail of Blood (Anaconda 4: Trail of Blood) (2009)
Avalanche Sharks (2013)
Bait (2012)
Beneath (2013)
Bering Sea Beast (Damn Sea Vampires!) (2013)
Bermuda Tentacles (2014)
Black Water (2007)
Blood Surf (Krocodylus) (2000)
Blue Demon (2004)
Boa (New Alcatraz) (2001)
Boa vs Python (2004)
Creature (Peter Benchley's Creature) (1998)

Croc (2007)
Crocodile (2000)
The Curse of the Komodo (2004)
Dark Age (1987)
Dark Waters (2003)
Dinocroc (2004)
Dinocroc vs. Supergator (2010)
Dinoshark (2010)
47 Meters Down (In the Deep) (2016)
Frankenfish (2004)
Freshwater (2014)
Ghost Shark (2013)
Ghost Shark 2: Urban Jaws (2014)
Gyo (Gyo: Tokyo Fish Attack!) (2012)
Ice Sharks (2016)
Jersey Shore Shark Attack (2012)
King Cobra (1999)
Komodo (1999)
Komodo vs. Cobra (2005)
Lake Placid 2 (2007)
Lake Placid 3 (2010)
Lake Placid: The Final Chapter (2012)
Lake Placid vs Anaconda (2015)
Malibu Shark Attack (Mega Shark of the Malibu) (2009)
Megalodon (Shark-Zilla) (2002)
Mega Piranha (2010)
Mega Python vs. Gatoroid (2010)
Mega Shark versus Giant Octopus (2009)
Mega Shark versus Crocosaurus (2010)
Mega Shark versus Mecha Shark (2014)
Mega Shark versus Kolossus (2015)
Mega Snake (2007)
Ozark Sharks (Summer Shark Attack) (2016)
Piranha (1995)
Planet of the Sharks (2016)
Primeval (2007)
Ragin' Cajun Redneck Gators (Alligator Alley) (2013)
Raging Sharks (2005)
Rattlers (1976)
Red Water (2003)
The Reef (2010)
Robo Croc (2013)
Rogue (2007)
Sand Sharks (2012)
The Sea Fiend (Devil Monster) (1936)
The Shallows (2016)
Shark Attack (1999)
Shark Exorcist (2015)
Shark in Venice (2008)
Shark Killer (2015)
Shark Lake (2015)
Sharknado (2013)
Sharknado 2 The Second One (2014)
Sharknado 3: Oh Hell No! (2015)

Sharknado: The 4th Awakens (2016)
Shark Swarm (2008)
Sharktopus (2010)
Sharktopus vs Pteracuda (2014)
Sharktopus vs Whalewolf (2015)
Silent Predators (1999)
Silent Venom (2009)
Snakehead Terror (2004)
Snakes on a Train (2006)
Stanley (1972)
Supercroc (Jurassic Croc) (2007)
Supergator (2007)
Supershark (2011)

Swamp Shark (2011)
Tentacles (Tentacoli) (1977)
This Ain't Jaws XXX (2011)
¡Tintorera! (1977)
2-Headed Shark Attack (2012)
3-Headed Shark Attack (2015)
L'Ultimo Squalo (Great White) (1981)
Up from the Depths (1979)
USS Indianapolis: Men of Courage (2016)
Venom (1981)
Vipers (2008)
Xtinction: Predator X (Alligator X) (2010)
Zombie Shark (2015)